Broadband Telecommunications Technology

Byeong Gi Lee
Minho Kang
Jonghee Lee

Artech House
Boston • London

Library of Congress Cataloging-in-Publication Data

Lee, Byeong Gi
Broadband Telecommunications Technology/Byeong Gi Lee, Minho Kang,
Jonghee Lee
Includes bibliographical references and index.
ISBN 0-89006-653-X
1. Broadband communication systems. 2. Integrated services digital networks.
I. Kang, Minho. II. Lee, Jonghee. III. Title.
TK5103.7.L43   1993   93-12352
621.382—dc20   CIP

British Library Cataloguing in Publication Data

Lee, Byeong Gi
Broadband Telecommunications Technology
I. Title. II. Kang, Minho. III. Lee, Jonghee.
621.382

ISBN 0-89006-653-X

© 1993 ARTECH HOUSE, INC.
685 Canton Street
Norwood, MA 02062

International Standard Book Number: 0-89006-653-X
Library of Congress Catalog Card Number: 93-12352

D
621-38
LEE

10 9 8 7 6 5 4 3 2

Broadband Telecommunications Technology

For a complete listing of the *Artech House Telecommunciations Library*,
turn to the back of this book

Contents

Preface

The ideal form of telecommunications would be one that enables the exchange of people's thoughts and feelings *whenever* and *wherever* they desire without users being constrained by time and place. In reality, the field of telecommunications has steadily progressed in such a direction, allowing information transfer to occur in a more *direct* and *natural* manner, thus enabling people to communicate with one another as if they are conversing in the same room, however far apart they might actually be.

The telephone, invented about a hundred years ago, was a momentous step towards the realization of such an ideal in telecommunications by connecting the ears and mouths of people who lived in different places of the world through electronic means. However, the need and desire for more direct and natural communications have inevitably opened the door in recent times to visual telecommunications as well, propelling significant advances in broadband telecommunications, and the ensuing impact is predicted to be even more extensive and far-reaching than that of the telephone. Furthermore, computer technology, which has progressed in the past forty years independently of communication technology, has finally been combined with the latter, making it possible to exploit the powerful data processing and storing capabilities of computers in addition to the information transfer capability of telecommunications.

Therefore, the emergence of such broadband telecommunications will have a tremendous influence on every aspect of human society and will bring about fundamental changes in our political, economic, social, and cultural lives in the 1990s.

The rapid advances in telecommunication technologies today are well attested by the profusion of specialized terminologies. Introduction of such a large number of technical terms is unprecedented in the history of telecommunications. With the term ISDN already being perceived as if it were a relic of the past, we saw in the mid-1980s the introduction of the acronyms ATM and BISDN, preceded by Metrobus, SONET, and SDH, and associated terms such as STS-m, STM-n, AAL, and ATM cell also came into circulation. On the other hand, PON and FTTH became widespread in relation to optical media; FDDI, DQDB, SMDS, and FR in relation to high-speed data services; and optical CATV, HDTV, MPEG, and others in relation to broadband video services. Terms such as *synchronous, integrated, broadband, high- speed, fast-packet, connection-oriented, video, optical*, and *multimedia*, which characterize various different aspects of future telecommunications, have almost become common adjectives. Amidst the flood of such novel terms and concepts, it is an especially important task to define their respective meanings, delineate their interrelationships, and draw light on their role in the future of broadband communications, and this was one of the main motivations for this book.

This book represents an attempt by those of us in the telecommunications fields to capture such technological trends and to enhance the reader's general understanding of broadband telecommunication technologies. It is based on the lecture notes for a series of short courses conducted at Seoul National University every summer since 1987, whose audiences were the engineers working in the telecommunications industry. The Korean version of the book was published in May 1992, and the positive response it received encouraged us to bring forth this English version. The book contains practical details regarding broadband telecommunications and also features theoretical treatment of various new concepts that have been introduced in association with broadband telecommunications. We therefore hope that this book will prove to be a useful reference for anyone interested in the broadband telecommunications field, including research and development engineers in the field, the managers and administrators in the telecommunications industry, and the professors and students who desire a better grasp of future telecommunication systems.

This books treats the general aspects of technologies associated with future broadband telecommunications. Chapter 1 establishes the foundation for understanding broadband telecommunication systems by presenting a brief history of telecommunication technologies and introducing the base technologies for broadband information telecommunications. Chapter 2 discusses optical communication technology (especially optical subscriber technology), which is the major transport medium that plays a key role in making broadband telecommunications possible. Chapter 3 concentrates on synchronous digital transmission (SDH/SONET), which is the major transmission technology in the broadband telecommunications era. Chapter 4 describes BISDN, which is the eventual goal of broadband telecommunications, and the associated ATM, which is the means of realizing BISDN. Lastly, Chapters 5 and Chapter 6, respectively, treat high-speed data communication networks and broadband video services, which are the most representative applications of broadband telecommunications.

Acknowledgments

We would like to express our gratitude to a number of people who helped in publishing this book.

We first thank the graduate students at the Telecommunication and Signal Processing Laboratories of Seoul National University (SNU), namely Seok Chang Kim, Kyung Soo Kim, Jun Won Lee, Dae Young Kim, Jung Gyu Lee, Han Seok Kim, Sung Ryong Park, Woo Jun Kim, Moo Ryong Chung, Jae Hwan Chang, Young Mi Joo, and others. We also thank Sang Hoon Lee, DooWhan Choi, Young Whan Kim, Sanggyun Han, Chang Jun Chae, Youngtak Kim, Soon-Hwa Jang, Woon Ha Kim, Suncheol Gweon, Hyun Rho Yoon, and Suk Won Yoon of Korea Telecom; Man Seop Lee of Electronics and Telecommunications Research Institute; Jongho Lee and Youn Goo Kim of MODACOM Company, who helped in collecting and organizing information, reviewing the manuscripts, and drawing figures and tables.

We are grateful to S. J. Chen, G. W. Cyboron, and J. Anderson of AT&T; G. R. Ritchie, G. Estes and Y. C. Ching of Bellcore; P. H. K. Wery of BNR; J. P. Coudreuse of CNET; B. G. Kim of the University of Lowell; and K. R. Rao of the University of Texas, Arlington, who provided helpful information and documents.

We especially appreciate the help of Tae Sub Yoon of UCLA and Dae Young Kim of Stanford University who toiled tirelessly to bring about the publication of this English version. We could not possibly have published the book without their help.

We thank the Electronics Engineering Department of SNU, the Electrical Engineering Department of UCLA, and Korea Telecom for offering comfortable environments and facilities important for the completion of the manuscript.

Finally, we would like to thank Chul Woo Yang of Kyohaksa Publisher, who published the Korean version and approved the publication of this English version, Mark Walsh of Artech House, who recommended the publication of this book, and Pamela Ahl, who provided excellent coordination.

October 1992
Byeong Gi Lee
Minho Kang
Jonghee Lee

Chapter 1
Introduction to Broadband Telecommunications

The developmental process of modern communications can be said to be an evolution to a more direct and natural form of communication. To illustrate: delivering messages via a third person was soon replaced by the mail service, which was subsequently supplemented by the telephone, allowing direct, delay-free conversation between two remote parties. From this perspective, it can easily be predicted that the next evolutionary step following the telephone will be the video phone, which enables a more natural and realistic mode of conversing. Such an evolutionary scenario can also be applied to the field of broadcasting. A purely listening form of broadcasting was inevitably followed by television, with the added visual dimension, and black-and-white televisions became obsolete with the advent of color televisions. In the same context, ordinary color televisions of today will soon be transformed into *high-definition television* (HDTV), which can display even more realistic and natural-looking pictures.

As can be inferred from the examples of video phone and HDTV, the evolution of future communications will be via *broadband communication* centered around video signals. The associated services make up a diverse set of high-speed and broadband services ranging from video services such as video phone, video conferencing, video surveillance, *cable television* (CATV) distribution, and HDTV distribution to the high-speed data services such as high-resolution image transmission, high-speed data transmission, and color facsimile. The means of standardizing these various broadband communication services so that they can be provided in an integrated manner is no other than the *broadband integrated services digital network* (BISDN). Simply put, therefore, the future communications network can be said to be a broadband telecommunication system based on the BISDN.

For realization of the BISDN, the role of several broadband communication technologies is crucial. Fortunately, the remarkable advances in the field of electronics and fiber optics have led to the maturation of broadband communication technologies. As the BISDN becomes possible on the optical communication foundation, the relevant manufacturing technologies for light-source and passive devices and for optical fiber have advanced to considerable levels. Advances in high-speed device and integrated-circuit technologies for broadband signal processing are also worthy of close attention. There has also been notable progress in software, signal processing, and video equipment technologies. Hence, from the technological standpoint, the BISDN has finally reached a realizable state.

On the other hand, standardization activities associated with broadband communication have been progressing. The *Synchronous Optical Network* (SONET) standardization centered around the T1 Committee eventually bore fruit in the form of the *Synchronous Digital Hierarchy* (SDH) standards of the *International Consultative Committee in Telegraphy and Telephony* (CCITT), paving the way for synchronous digital transmission based on optical communication. The standardization activities of the *integrated services digital network* (ISDN), which commenced in the early 1980s with the objective of integrating narrowband services, expanded in scope with the inclusion of broadband services, leading to the standardization of the BISDN in the late 1980s and establishing the concept of *asynchronous transfer mode* (ATM) communication in the process. In addition, standardization of various video signals is becoming finalized through the cooperation among such organizations as CCITT, the *International Radiocommunications Consultative Committee* (CCIR), and the *International Standards Organization* (ISO), and reference protocols for high-speed packet communication are being standardized through ISO, CCITT, and the *Institute of Electrical and Electronics Engineers* (IEEE).

Various factors such as these have made broadband communication realizable. Therefore, the 1990s is the decade in which matured broadband communication technologies will be used in conjunction with broadband standards to realize broadband communication networks. In the broadband telecommunication network, the fiber-optic network will represent the physical medium for implementing broadband communication, while synchronous transmission will make possible the transmission of broadband service signals over the optical medium. Also, the BISDN will be essential as the broadband telecommunication network established on the basis of optical medium and synchronous transmission, and ATM is the communication means that enables the realization of the BISDN. The most important of the broadband services to be provided through the BISDN are high-speed data communication services and video communication services.

The goal of this book is to provide a broad but detailed description of the technologies fundamental to constructing broadband telecommunication systems. Therefore, the five essential components described in Figure 1.1—fiber-optic communication technology, synchronous digital transmission, BISDN and ATM, high-speed data communication, and broadband video communication services—will form the core contents of the book. These five topics are treated in order in Chapters 2 through 6. In this introductory chapter, the background of broadband telecommunications will be reviewed briefly.

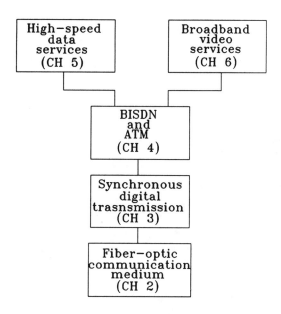

Figure 1.1 Technologies for broadband telecommunication systems.

The organization of this chapter is as follows. The basic technologies underlying the communication network will be reviewed first, and then the progress of the telecommunication technologies will be examined in terms of transmission, switching, signaling, packet communication, ISDN, and BISDN. Finally, the key technologies essential for the implementation of broadband telecommunication systems will be discussed in reference to optical communication medium, broadband transmission, ATM communication, high-speed data network, and broadband video technologies.

1.1 TECHNOLOGIES IN TELECOMMUNICATION NETWORKS

The broadband telecommunication system takes the form of a communication network in which broadband services are provided in conjunction with existing narrowband services. The future broadband telecommunication system will thus be built on the foundation of the existing communication networks. In this context, it is desirable to examine the basic technologies underlying the existing communication networks, along with their developmental processes, in preparation for a full-fledged discussion on broadband telecommunication technologies. In this opening section, therefore, we will review such telecommunication technologies, and their respective developmental processes will be reviewed in the next section.

In this section, we will first survey the communication networks in general, and then review the communication functions involved in the circuit-mode communication networks in terms of transmission, switching, and signaling. Afterwards, we will look at the packet-mode network counterpart, which is comparatively young. Finally, we will review the technologies involved in the ISDN, in which the circuit-mode communication services meet the packet services.

1.1.1 Communication Networks

Defined in broad terms, a communication network can be said to be a system composed of the interconnection of basic communication components. Hence, a communication network can be represented in terms of nodes and links to interconnect the nodes. A communication network is required in providing communication services to a multiple number of users dispersed in a wide area. Communication services are represented in the form of traffic within the communication network. Here, traffic designates a flow of information or messages through the communication network. Consequently, within the context of the traffic concept, a communication network can be described as a system in which equipment is interconnected to transport traffic originating from various communication services.

When the communication network is depicted as a combination of nodes and links, the nodes represent communication equipment in the subscriber premises, as well as intraoffice and interoffice transmission equipment, while links represent the transmission facilities. So, if examined from the system standpoint, the basic components of a communication system can be divided into subscriber equipment, switching systems, and transmission facilities. Subscriber equipment is generally located within the subscriber premises and has the role of transmitting and receiving information, as well as controlling signals between subscribers and communication networks. Transmission facilities provide communication pathways for transporting information between subscribers. In general, transmission facilities consist of transmission media such as copper wire, waveguide, atmosphere, and optical fiber, and various electronic devices deployed along the transmission media. Here, electronic devices perform the function of amplifying, regenerating, and transforming transmitted signals. Also, transmission equipment in the central offices carry out the function of connecting transmission facilities to the switching systems. The switching system has the function of interconnecting transmission facilities at various locations and adjusting traffic pathways within the communication network. So the communication information generated from the subscriber equipment is transmitted to the switching systems via transmission facilities and interlinked via switching systems, thus accomplishing communication.

For the communication traffic systems of the network to be comprehensible to one another, the transmission facilities and switching systems must be able to provide signaling functions in addition to the functions described above. *Signaling* refers to the process of transferring a variety of information for the purpose of controlling the setup of communication links within the network, as well as the related operations. For example, making a call involves the transmission of three types of signals: for indicating the beginning, the address, and the end of a call. The information capacity required for signaling is small compared to the general information transfer capacity; hence, signaling information has up to now been transmitted as a part of the general communication channel, and signaling functions have been performed by transmission apparatuses inside the network and by switching systems.

The basic components of a communication system are as follows. The portion that links telephone offices is called the *interoffice transit network* or *trunk network*, and the portion that links telephone office and the subscriber is called the *subscriber network*. The transmission line that composes the interoffice network is called the *trunk*, and the transmission line inside the subscriber network is called the *subscriber loop* or *customer loop*. Also, the type of exchange that accommodates subscriber loops is called the *local exchange* (LE), and the exchange that links only the trunks is called the *inter-exchange* (IE) or *transit exchange* (TE). The corresponding signaling scheme is also divided into subscriber loop signaling and trunk signaling. If communication networks are classified in terms of traffic, they can be divided into *public switched telephone network* (PSTN), *packet-switched public data network* (PSPDN), private data network, and telex network. Among them, PSTN is the largest and employs a circuit switching scheme, while PSPDN and private data network are data communication networks that are based on a packet-switching scheme.

In the following sections, we will investigate the development and the future evolutionary direction of communication technologies. We will first study the developmental process of transmission, switching, and signaling for public communication networks, then examine packet communication networks. Lastly, the ISDN will be examined, which appeared in the process of integrating circuit-mode public communication networks with packet-mode communications, as well as the BISDN, which can be said to be the final product of this integration process.

1.1.2 Transmission Technology

Transmission refers to the function of transferring subscriber information and control signals from one point inside the communication network to another. Transmission is classified with subscriber transmission, which joins subscribers to the central office, and with interoffice transmission, which joins central offices. The transmitted

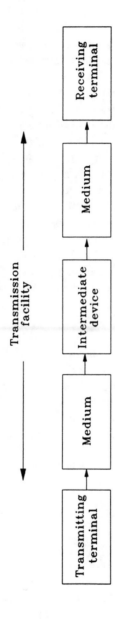

Figure 1.2 Block diagram of transmission systems (unidirectional).

information signals are in either the analog or digital form, and transmission is differentiated into analog transmission or digital transmission according to the transmission format. Also, depending on the transmission medium, transmission is divided into wired transmission via copper wire or coaxial cable, wireless transmission via terrestrial microwave links, satellite transmission via satellite links, and optical transmission via optical fibers.

A transmission system consists of transmission facilities and transmission terminal equipment. In the transmission system block diagram of Figure 1.2, the transmission medium and the repeater correspond to the transmission facilities, and transmitter terminal equipment and the receiver terminal equipment correspond to the transmission terminal equipment. The transmitter transmits a given information signal by converting it into a format suitable for the transmission medium. The information signal is delivered to the receiver after several stages of repeaters, and is subsequently recovered.

The transmission facility is composed of the transmission medium and the corresponding repeater. The transmission medium is the link for conveying transmitted signals, and the repeater equipment assumes the role of recovering, compensating, converting, and regenerating the transmitted signals. The transmission terminal equipment converts the transmitted information signal into a format appropriate for the transmission medium, and subsequently recovers the original signal. For this purpose, it performs such functions as information-to-electrical signal conversion, analog-to-digital conversion, modulation, multiplexing, transmission coding, and electrical-to-optical/electromagnetic wave conversion, while the receiver terminal equipment performs the reverse set of functions.

1.1.3 Switching Technology

Switching refers to the function of establishing communication links by interconnecting a multiple number of subscriber service equipment. Achieving such interconnection in a cost-effective way is the rationale for switching. This is due to the fact that $n(n-1)/2$ transmission lines are required for interconnecting n nodes without switches, while only n transmission lines will do if switches are used. While the connection function is the main duty of switches, it also performs functions related to the operation of communication network and subscriber services. Switching is categorized into manual, mechanical, and electronic types, depending on the switching scheme.

As shown in Figure 1.3, a switching system is composed of a switching network, subscriber loop interfaces, trunk interfaces, switch control, *operation and maintenance* (OAM), and control network interface. The actual switching of signals is executed within the switching network, and the subscriber loop and trunk interface converts signals arriving from subscriber loops and trunks into a format suitable for

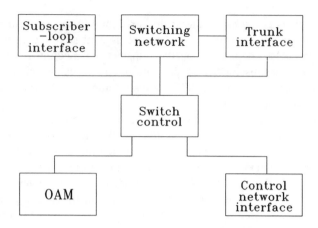

Figure 1.3 Block diagram of switching systems.

switching networks. OAM performs operation and maintenance functions of the switching system along with interfacing with operation support systems, while the control network enables accessing of the signaling network and the databases in the communication networks. The switch control is responsible for the control of all of these operations.

Switches are divided into space-division switches and time-division switches depending on the form of the switching circuit network, into wired-logic control and *stored program control* (SPC) depending on the control scheme used, and into concentrated control scheme and distributed control scheme depending on the degree of distribution of the control functions. The electronic switches currently in use all use SPC. Among them, those that employ the space-division scheme are sometimes called *semielectronic* switches, and those that employ time-division multiplexing are called *digital switches* or *all-electronic switches*. Most of the current digital switches adopt the distributed control scheme.

1.1.4 Signaling Technology

Signaling refers to the process of transferring information for the control of the communication connection setup within the communication network as well as related operations. Signaling can be classified, depending on the given function, into surveillance, addressing, and information. Surveillance implies control functions related to circuit connection, such as service request, response, alarm, and release. Address means the phone number of the destination. Information refers to the information on the progress of communication connections, such as dial tone and ringing tone.

Signaling can be divided into subscriber network signaling and trunk signaling, depending on the applicable range. Subscriber network signaling designates the signals transferred between subscribers and the central office, while trunk signaling refers to the exchange of signal processing-related information between central offices. In addition, there is special signaling for foreign exchange loops or *private branch exchange* (PBX)-interoffice loops. Depending on whether signaling information is transferred via the same transmission line as that of the user information, trunk signaling is categorized into channel-associated signaling scheme and channel separation signaling, or *common-channel signaling* (CCS) scheme. These two signaling schemes are compared in Figure 1.4.

Common-channel signaling scheme is a channel-separated signaling scheme in which a collection of signals are transmitted through a separate channel which is independent of the line through which information is transferred. Here, signals are conveyed to the central office of the receiving side via *signal transfer points* (STP), and the STPs form a signaling network. Signals are transmitted through a path different from the transmission information channel; hence, the employment of CCS shortens call setup time, allowing efficient utilization of the communication network and provision of various subscriber services in an expanded manner. On the other

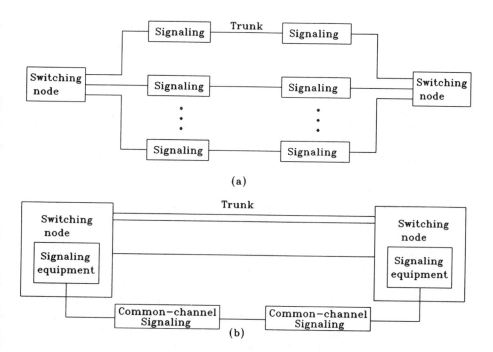

Figure 1.4 Signaling methods: (a) channel-associated signaling; (b) common-channel signaling.

hand, CCS has a drawback in that a signal format cannot guarantee the quality of the information transmission channel, and partial damage of the signaling network can incur paralysis of the entire communication network.

Subscriber network signaling functions include addressing, dial tone, busy tone, ringing tone, and on-hook/off-hook indications, while interoffice-transit signaling functions include addressing, wink, and on-hook/off-hook indications.

Among the large number of signaling functions recently provided, there are many OAM-related ones. An example is the communication maintenance signaling used in adjusting the traffic load distributed in interoffice networks. Also, a database installed in the communication network is consulted to determine the validity of a connection in alternate-billing telephone or credit-card-calling services, and this process requires associated signaling functions. Also, for the central offices that are remotely monitored via OAM systems, related signaling functions are provided separately. Development of such signaling functions can bring about the establishment of intelligent networks.

1.1.5 Packet Communication Technology

So far, the transmission, switching, and signaling technologies have been examined for the circuit switched public communication networks. In this section, the counterpart packet switched communication networks will be examined.

Packet communication is a mode of communication in which digital data information is transmitted and switched in the packet format. Therefore, in contrast to the circuit switched networks, information in packet communication networks is not transmitted in a consecutive flow of bit units, but in intermittent packet units. If digital circuit-mode transmission is compared with packet-mode transmission from this standpoint, circuit-mode transmission is manifested as a consecutive and regulated flow of digital bits, whereas in packet communication, packets consisting of digital bits flow in an irregular and intermittent manner. Here, occupation of consecutive channels is not required for packet delivery, and this represents the key difference between circuit switched networks and packet switched networks.

Packet communication was introduced and developed for data communication between computers and computer terminals. Consequently, packet communication has a close link with data communication, as well as with computer communication.

In order to realize packet communication, transmission, switching, and network operation schemes must be systematized appropriately. That is, schemes on packet format, packet delivery, and transmission path must be defined in a clear manner. Communication procedures regulated in this way for packet communication are called *protocols*. In general, packet communication is applied in a complex setting composed of numerous systems and communication networks; hence, the associated communication handling procedures are quite complicated. Therefore, if all

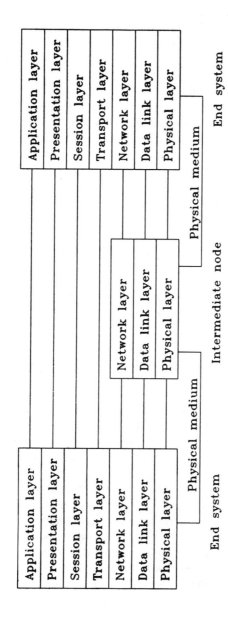

Figure 1.5 Layered architecture.

of these communication handling functions are regulated through a single protocol, then protocol becomes extremely complex. If, instead, information transfer procedures are appropriately separated into layers, then the development and implementation of communication handling functions become systematized and thus reduced in complexity. The reference model that was standardized in this spirit was the *Open Systems Interconnection* (OSI), and here communication functions are divided into seven-layer architectures as shown in Figure 1.5.

Examples of packet communication network include PSPDN, local-area communication network, and packet wireless communication network. In PSPDN, packet transmission is accomplished through packet switching at each node via a combination of interconnected nodes. Local communication networks are small-scale communication networks constructed to serve local areas, and in most cases have the character of wired data broadcast networks. That is, packets can be delivered directly to each receiver without going through intermediate nodes for switching. Local communication networks are used as small-scale private communication networks for local areas, and the representative examples are the *local-area network* (LAN) and the *metropolitan-area network* (MAN). LAN is a packet communication network that provides transmission speeds up to 10 Mbps for areas within a few kilometers, while MAN can provide speeds up to 150 Mbps within the range of 50 kilometers. The characteristics of regional communication networks are defined according to the transmission medium, network topology, and *medium access control* (MAC) protocol. On the other hand, the wireless version of the regional communication networks can be called *packet wireless communication networks*.

1.1.6 ISDN

ISDN is a digital communication network that provides various types of services in an integrated fashion. In other words, the ISDN is an integrated service digital communication network that not only encompasses basic voice communication, but also allows integrated provision of low-quality video and data services. Its targeted services are mainly narrowband services such as telephone, facsimile, teletex, telemetry, telewriting, and data terminals. The main feature of the ISDN is that the subscriber is interfaced with the communication network through a single access so that several services can be provided in unison, and that connection between the subscribers is accomplished digitally. That is, the subscriber network becomes digital, and various services become integrated upon that foundation.

ISDN allows handling of various voice as well as nonvoice services in an integrated manner. This is possible because various information handling procedures are carried out digitally. Therefore, circuit switching and packet switching can be provided simultaneously, and transmission is done in the digital domain. The ISDN also provides a common access point for the existing circuit switching network and

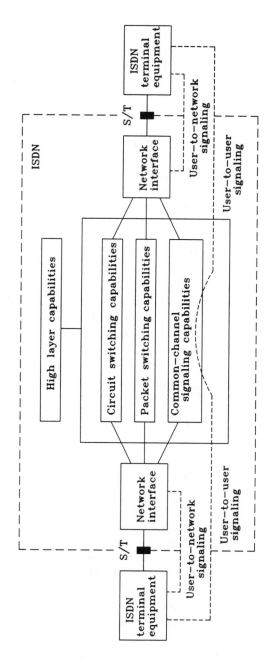

Figure 1.6 Basic architectural model of an ISDN.

the packet switching network, and allows sharing of various information resources within the communication network. In other words, various databases are maintained inside the communication network that can be used in common by all the subscribers and service providers. In addition, the ISDN can provide various kinds of communication processing and information handling functions and simplifies operation and administration of the communication network.

The basic structure of the ISDN is as shown in Figure 1.6. In the figure, it can be seen that the ISDN user terminal equipment is connected to the ISDN through the S/T reference access point. Here, signaling information between the user and the network is transferred through the D channel. Network access distributes user communication information to the appropriate destinations of the circuit switching network and the packet switching network, and various signals for call handling are transmitted through common-channel signaling. In the figure, *high-layer capabilities* represent auxiliary functions such as protocol conversion and rate conversion.

1.2 EVOLUTION OF TELECOMMUNICATION TECHNOLOGIES

Now that we have reviewed the technologies supporting the communication networks, we can examine their respective developmental processes. We will first see how the transmission, switching, and signaling technologies progressed in the past to establish today's circuit-switched public network.

We will then review how the packet-mode communication network became equipped with today's systematic layered protocol structures. Following this, we will examine how the existing circuit-mode and packet-mode networks evolved into the ISDN, and eventually into the BISDN. Based on this overview of the developmental processes of the telecommunication technologies, we will summarize the general trends of telecommunication technology developments.

1.2.1 Developmental Process of Transmission Technology

The developmental process of transmission can be summarized as an evolution from analog mode to digital mode. In the early days of the telephone after its invention in 1876, a single channel was assigned per line for analog transmission; but with the development of the vacuum tube and with the advances in filter theory, an analog system employing *frequency-division multiplexing* (FDM) was introduced in 1925 and a coaxial cable system was installed in 1936. Analog wireless transmission was developed simultaneously, leading to the trans-Atlantic wireless telephone system in 1927, and the microwave wireless broadcast system was proposed in 1941. Analog transmission system made great advances from the 1950s to 1970s. With the maturation of vacuum tube technology, the microwave transmission system extended into the 4-, 6-, and 11-GHz frequency regions, and the development of digital wireless transmission systems was initiated in 1969. The invention of transistors helped coaxial cable systems grow substantially in the 1960s, leading to the establishment of the L4 system consisting of 3600 channels per coaxial cable and the L5 system of 10,800 channels.

The concept of *pulse code modulation* (PCM), which is fundamental to digital transmission, was issued a patent as early as 1926. But commercial application of PCM did not materialize until the introduction of the 24-channel T1 carrier system in 1962. With the maturation of device technology, the digital channel bank that featured toll quality was developed by the year 1972, and the 96-channel T2 carrier system was introduced as well. It was followed by testing of high bit rate digital systems employing *time-division multiplexing* (TDM), but they were not put to practical use because of their high costs relative to the equivalent analog carrier systems. Their economic viability began to be demonstrated when optical transmission finally became realizable. The first DS-3 optical transmission system was commercialized in 1979, and it was installed for long-distance transmission in 1983.

Satellite transmission began with the launching of the communication satellite INTELSAT I in 1965. The number of transponders used at that time was two, the frequency band was 50 MHz, and the communication capacity amounted to 480 channels. The numbers grew with succeeding launches, reaching 34 transponders, a frequency band of 2,482 MHz, and communication capacity of 36,000 channels by the INTELSAT VB. Carrier frequency used was in the 4/6- and 12/14-GHz bands, and a 20/30-GHz band is also being tested. The multiple-access technique is required, as several earth stations must communicate with one another by sharing a single communication satellite, and *frequency-division multiple access* (FDMA) and *time-division multiple access* (TDMA) are employed for this purpose. Since the transmission medium of satellite transmission is atmosphere, it employs an analog form of transmission as in the case of microwave transmission.

In the early stages of optical transmission, a method of propagating light through the atmosphere as in the case of wireless transmission was attempted, but waveguide transmission using optical fiber was ultimately chosen as the transmission medium. Optical transmission began to be practical when its attenuation characteristics were lowered to 20 dB/km in the early 1970s. Optical transmission is accomplished by modulating transmitted information by a laser diode or a light-emitting diode, passing the information signal over optical fiber, and reconstructing the information by the *pin* diode or the *avalanche photo diode* (APD) device. Digital transmission based on PCM and TDM became more practical only after being supplemented by optical transmission. The 45-Mbps optical communication system was put to use in the early 1980s, followed by the development of 90-, 145-, 180-, 410-, and 560-Mbps large-capacity systems, and currently 1.2-, 1.7-, 2.4-Gbps systems are also being developed. These systems will eventually converge in a synchronous digital transmission founded on SONET.

1.2.2 Developmental Process of Switching Technology

The developmental process of switching technology can be examined in the light of advances in switching networks and control schemes. Switching networks evolved from the electromechanical space-division types to the electronic space-division types, and subsequently into those employing the SPC scheme. The initial control schemes evolved from the concentrated control to the wired logic control and then into the SPC. Therefore, the step-by-step switches of the electromechanical direct control widely used up to the 1920s has finally evolved into today's digital switches of the electronic SPC.

The concept of automatic switching, first introduced in 1879, was not put to practical use until the advent of step-by-step switches. In step-by-step switching, a single rotation of the dial causes the point of contact to move linearly or circularly by a proportional amount, making connection in proper sequence. Step-by-step switches were in wide circulation up until the introduction of crossbar switches in the 1930s. In crossbar switching, the distributed common control scheme is used independently of the switching networks, while switching networks use coordinate crossbar switches in which horizontal and vertical lines are cross-connected. The patent application for the crossbar switching concept was first filed in 1913, and the first commercial crossbar system was installed in 1938. The No. 4 Crossbar system was installed in 1943, and the No. 5 Crossbar system in 1948. The No. 5 Crossbar system is still widely used.

Propelled by advances in vacuum tubes and transistors, electronic switching technology accelerated in the 1950s. Implementations of various electronic devices for the logic circuit of the interface and the switching contact of the circuit-switching network were attempted, and a wired-logic control was also proposed during this period. However, the commercial electronic switch No. 1 *electronic switching system* (ESS) was not actually installed until 1965. No. 1 ESS is a switch that employs space-division and SPC–based schemes. The time-division digital electronic switch began to be developed in the 1970s, and No. 4 ESS and No. 5 ESS were installed in 1976 and 1982, respectively. Other large-capacity digital electronic switches such as AXE-10, DMS-100, EWSD, S1240, GTD-5, and TDX-10 were developed around the same period. However, widespread installation of such digital switching systems in communication networks was not possible until recently.

As was stated earlier, time-division digital switches are more economical than the space-division analog switches. That is, switching of digital information is possible without extra conversion or multiplexing processes. Transmission systems are becoming digital due to the various advantages inherent in digital transmission, and the corresponding digitalization of switching systems can be considered a natural outcome. A digital switch that possesses both circuit switching and packet switching capabilities will be needed consequently, and it will be succeeded by a packet-based ATM switch.

1.2.3 Developmental Process of Signaling Technology

It is desirable that signaling schemes be simple and universal, and thus be efficiently used in the communication network. Consequently, subscriber network signaling has been providing a simple way of connecting subscribers to the telephone office, while trunk signaling, which is ultimately a signaling between machines, has evolved in the direction of raising the efficiency and flexibility of the communication network, even at the cost of added complexity. As a result, trunk signaling has advanced in parallel with trunk transmission facilities, influencing in turn the development of switching systems.

The early signaling schemes were based on direct current until the introduction of the in-band/out-of-band signaling scheme, which accompanied the appearance of analog transmission carrier systems. As digital transmission equipment such as the T1 carrier system began to be installed after 1962, digital bit signaling based on robbed bit or out-slot bit began to be employed as well. The channel-separated signaling scheme was tried out after the establishment of SPC switching system No. 1 ESS in 1965, to be superseded by the *common-channel interoffice signaling* (CCIS) scheme, which began to be provided with the commercialization of No. 4 ESS digital switch in 1976. It subsequently became widespread, and was systematized into international reference protocols such as CCITT CCS systems No. 6 and No. 7. When the CCS scheme was first used, it was based on 2.4-kbps packet transmission, but it is currently based on 64-kbps packet transmission.

In summary, the developmental process of signaling schemes can be said to be an evolution of interoffice transit network signaling from channel-associated signaling to common channel signaling. Channel-associated signaling renders relatively simple surveillance and addressing functions for communication call setup. But it has difficulty with transferring network OAM signals, in detecting calls, or collectively transmitting various different types of traffic. Furthermore, channel-associated signaling has almost nothing to contribute to flexible operation of the communication network or intelligent provision of communication services. Therefore, the evolution of channel-associated signaling to common channel signaling can be said to be propelled by the objective of raising communication network flexibility and intelligence. Further development and specialization of signaling can lead to the formation of intelligent networks.

1.2.4 Developmental Process of Packet Communication Technology

The development of packet communication has a close relationship with that of computers. The concept of packet communication first appeared on the scene with the development of large-scale computers in the 1960s. Packet communication was required in order to link a great number of computer terminals to the large central computers. The primary example of a packet communication network that was constructed to meet this very objective was the TYMNET by Tymshare Co.

Afterwards, computer manufacturing companies contributed in numerous ways to the further advancement of the packet communication network. Communication processors for use in packet communication among computers were developed, along with the corresponding software. Such a drive ultimately led to the establishment of the concept of layered communication architecture. *Systems Network Architecture* (SNA), introduced by IBM in 1974, can be said to be its most representative product.

Afterwards, each computer company created its own proprietary communication topologies, and interconnection consequently became difficult. The responsibility of studying possible standard communication topologies for open systems connection was entrusted to ISO, and the outcome was the OSI Reference Model.

ARPANET, developed by the United States Department of Defense, contributed greatly to the progress of packet communication technology. This project was initiated in the late 1960s and continued through the 1970s, and its basic objective was to interconnect large computers. The process of implementing this project propelled associated research in communication processors, routing, and flow control algorithms, and led to advancements in several packet communication technologies. Also, the development of ARPANET contributed in the formation of packet switching public data networks throughout the world, such as Telenet of GTE (1974), Datapac of Canada (1976), and Transpac of France (1978). It also influenced the standardization of packet switching network interface protocol X.25 by CCITT.

Although the origin of regional packet networks was in data transport, research activities are also underway to integrate isochronous information such as voice. For the LAN, this is manifested by the *Integrated Services Local Network* (ISLN) and, for the MAN, by the *Fiber Distributed Data Interface* (FDDI) II and the *Distributed Queue Dual Bus* (DQDB). Furthermore, gigabit networks are also under development as high-speed packet communication networks to succeed LAN and MAN.

Today, various types of computers are in wide distribution, and these computers in turn support and control various forms of communication. Furthermore, demand for novel data information systems is increasing rapidly, greatly outpacing the demand for voice services. Therefore, packet communication is predicted to assume a more important role in the future. However, voice will continue to maintain a superior role as telephone networks gradually become digital and optical, and it is necessary to conceive a developmental scenario in which packet switched and circuit switched networks can coexist simultaneously. Such changes will be manifested in circuit mode-oriented integrated access in the ISDN, and a packet mode integrated network based on ATM cells in the BISDN.

1.2.5 Evolution of ISDN

In examining the evolutionary process of the ISDN, it is necessary to note the development of the communication network that preceded it. As was observed previously, communication network has evolved from the analog mode into the digital mode. First, transmission became digital with the appearance of the T1 carrier system, and digital transmission laid down a solid foundation when the optical transmission systems were developed in the 1980s. The switching mode began to become digital when switches E-10 and No. 4 ESS were installed. Digital switching systems attracted attention by being highly cost-effective when used in conjunction with readily established digital transmission, and the 1980s saw the development and installation of a great number of digital switches. As a result, considerable progress was made in the digitalization of today's communication networks, especially in the case of interoffice networks. However, subscriber networks have on the whole remained analog. As transmission and switching became digital, signaling schemes also went through many changes, as discussed earlier, finally reaching today's common-channel signaling scheme via the in-band/out-of-band analog signaling and the robbed-bit/out-slot bit digital signaling schemes.

Packet communication networks began to appear independently in the 1960s with the objective of providing a link between computers and data terminals, and they advanced rapidly with the developments in the associated software and hardware, and began to be employed as packet switched public data networks when the OSI reference was established in the 1980s. Packet communication networks are constructed and operated independently of circuit switched networks, and their size is relatively small. But demand for packet communication networks has grown rapidly as data information capacity becomes larger, and study on processing real-time signals such as voice in packets has also been underway.

On the other hand, in the light of great changes on the industrial front, we are entering into a society in which the information industry plays an increasingly dominant role. In other words, the number of people whose professions involve collecting, processing, and handling of information resources will soon greatly outnumber people working in other industries, such as agriculture or manufacturing. The information industry has grown considerably, spurred by the accompanying advances in computer, communication, and electronics industries, and this in turn has transformed our world into one global information society. Information capacity became greatly enlarged as a result, and demand for a more diverse set of services has also increased.

In order to absorb such data information needs, circuit switching networks have been providing data services through modems, *digital data services* (DDS), and *circuit-switched data capability* (CSDC). This can be said to be an integration of voice and nonvoice services achieved via public telephone networks. On the other hand, study has been underway also in the packet communication field for local communication networks in order to accommodate voice services through such means as ISLN and FDDI II. However, while these approaches can provide partial solutions, they are not able to do so worldwide. As a means of providing a more fundamental and comprehensive solution, international standardization activities with the ISDN have been in progress since the late 1970s under the supervision of CCITT. The standardization study carried out around CCITT's Study Group 18 bore fruit by producing the ISDN's basic frames by 1984, and even specifics were standardized by 1988. Such a groundwork paved the way for the construction of ISDN systems and the provision of commercial services throughout the world in the mid-1980s.

The basic philosophy of the ISDN is first to digitalize subscriber networks and provide various types of communication services in an integrated manner. This is guided by the possibility of dealing with various services in a generalized manner if the communication network is digitalized in bit units. Transmission and switching in trunk networks are already being performed in digital mode, and complete digitalization of the communication network is possible if subscriber networks become digital as well. As far as signaling schemes are concerned, common-channel signaling is already possible in trunk networks; hence, the only required step is to provide a signaling scheme that is suitable for the digitalization of subscriber loops in subscriber networks. Here, voice and data information passes through the subscriber loops after being integrated in a digital mode; hence, the central office needs to possess the capability of differentiating each type of signals and applying circuit switching and packet switching, respectively, or separating each and delivering it respectively to the public switched telephone network and packet-switched public data network. Signaling information is also transmitted after being integrated with voice and data information, and hence the central office also needs to maintain functions for separating and handling signaling information and transferring them to common-channel signaling networks. Therefore, the ISDN has a structure in which various services are first integrated in digital mode at the communication network terminations inside the subscriber premises, and then passed through subscriber loops and divided and delivered appropriately to the circuit switched network, packet switched network, and signaling network via the central office.

1.2.6 Evolution Toward BISDN

In the midst of the evolutionary process of integrating services and forming the ISDN, the demand for high-speed packet communication and video communication services has increased continuously, and the capability for their provision has steadily improved as well. High-speed packet communication has come to be established in the form of FDDI LAN and DQDB MAN, and further development into gigabit communication networks is being planned. In the video communication service field, the main enterprises involve opticalizing existing CATV networks, providing new HDTV services, and transforming ordinary telephone services into video phone and video conferencing services. Also, a great deal of research has been carried out to provide multimedia communication services associated with high-speed packet communication and video communication services.

Such high-speed packet and video communication services by nature require high-speed and broadband communication channels. Such a requirement cannot be accommodated by 64-kbps based ISDN, and this brought about a necessity for the broadband ISDN (BISDN), which is able to provide such broadband services in an integrated fashion. Consequently, CCITT began to proceed with BISDN standardization activities near the latter half of 1980s, and basic frameworks for the BISDN were completed near the end of the decade. With the emergence of the BISDN, the existing ISDN began to be called *narrowband ISDN* (NISDN).

Conceptually, the BISDN is no more than an extension of the ISDN to accommodate broadband services. In other words, the BISDN will function as a communication network that can provide integrated broadband services such as high-speed data services, video phone, video conferencing, high-resolution graphics transmission, and CATV services, along with such NISDN services as telephone, data, telemetry, and facsimile. Therefore, if the basic structure of the ISDN shown in Figure 1.6 is supplemented with broadband service functions, the result becomes the basic structure of the BISDN. In implementation, however, the BISDN uses a mode of transmission that is completely different from the NISDN because of the sheer diversity of services. That is, as a means of accommodating various characteristics and distribution properties of broadband service data, ATM is employed. It achieves packet-oriented integration of broadband services, and hence evinces a fundamental difference from the NISDN, whose service integration is circuit-oriented.

The BISDN is based on transmission speeds and capacities at the 155-Mbps, 622-Mbps, and 2.4-Gbps levels. The associated standards include CCITT G Series Recommendations for SDH, SONET standards of the T1 Committee, and the CCITT I Series Recommendations, which support the concept of ATM-based BISDN. Here, SDH is a novel system whose goal is integrated accommodation of the existing *Plesiochronous Digital Hierarchy* (PDH), while ATM is an attempt to accommodate packet-mode transmission inside existing circuit-mode communication networks. Consequently, the BISDN can be said to be a highly innovative communication network in many respects compared to existing communication networks.

Figure 1.7 shows the conceptual composition of the BISDN. It can be observed that SDH/SONET and ATM are used as transmission and switching modes, respectively, and that BISDN *network terminations* (NT) are used for broadband access. It can also be inferred from the figure that, in the BISDN, existing NISDN services and various new broadband services are accommodated collectively and that PBXs and LAN/MAN can be interconnected.

However, actual implementation of the BISDN has a great number of associated fundamental difficulties. An example is the difficulty of broadband signal switching, and this is due not only to the high speed of broadband switching, but also to the diversity of signal speeds and service times. That is, signal switching in the BISDN is no easy task because broadband signals possess a diverse set of speeds that range from tens of bits per second to hundreds of megabits per second, and service time distribution that ranges from a few seconds to several hours. On the

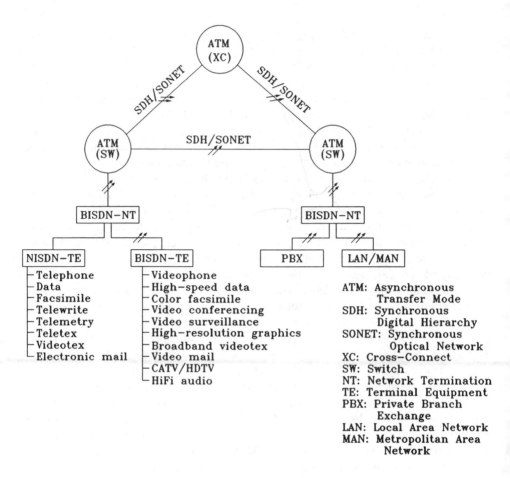

Figure 1.7 Conceptual structure of the BISDN.

other hand, traffic control in the BISDN emerges as an especially crucial task. In the BISDN, all information exists inside public networks in the form of packets, and hence critical damage of the given service is contingent upon the success or failure of proper resource management.

In spite of the difficulties, detailed preparations for realizing the BISDN are underway, and various studies are in progress to overcome the obstacles facing the implementation of the BISDN. For this purpose, various means of economical implementations are being suggested, and an immense amount of investments are being planned. Hence, it is anticipated that the 1990s will see the development and operation of trial systems of the BISDN throughout the world, as well as actual provision of commercial services.

1.2.7 Trends of Communication Network Development

According to the development processes of communication network examined so far, the following general trends can be discerned.

First, communication networks have steadily developed in the direction of further digitalization. Digitalization in transmission technology was initiated in conjunction with PCM, followed by digitalization of switching technology, and signaling schemes also changed accordingly. Digital transmission has the inherent drawback of consuming more bandwidth per channel compared to analog transmission. For instance, whereas a 4-kHz band might suffice for analog transmission, a 64-kbps bit rate is required for transmission in the digital mode. Nonetheless, digital transmission has continued to progress in spite of these unfavorable conditions, due to the following advantages of digital transmission.

To begin with, digital transmission is free from transmission-induced noise. Consequently, no deterioration in transmission quality occurs, even in long-distance transmission involving multiple stages of multiplexing and demultiplexing procedures. The main source of noise in digital transmission is quantization, but this can be reduced to imperceptible levels by increasing the number of bits. In digital mode, information is handled in terms of time slots (that is, in terms of bits), which renders assembling and separation of several types of information simple, and this is achieved by the insertion or extraction of corresponding time slots. Consequently, it becomes possible to treat information with various different characteristics such as voice, video, and data information in an integrated manner. Signaling is also easy to perform in digital mode, surveillance and OAM of the network is easy, and the quality and stability of transmission can be raised through the employment of error detection and correction coding.

The digital mode is also simpler than the analog mode in design and manufacturing of integrated circuits, and it is also superior with respect to information storage. Especially after the introduction of digital switches, the digital mode became more cost-effective than the analog mode in interoffice transmission. Consequently, interoffice transmission links are continuing to become digital, and subscriber transmission links will also become digital in step with the advances in optical transmission technology.

The second trend is the expansion of data services and the corresponding advancement of data communication networks. Public communication networks were originally voice-oriented, and as computers became more widespread, the necessity for data communication emerged more clearly. However, initially only a simple form of packet communication was required to connect large computers and terminal equipment, but as large numbers of computers came into use and the personal computers became universal, data communication services grew dramatically. Furthermore, in step with such trends as *office automation* (OA) and *factory automation* (FA), various sorts of manufacturing and handling tasks became more reliant with computers, which aided in universalizing data communication. Such a drastic increase in demand for data services helped regional communication networks grow rapidly, and it subsequently brought about a need for the ISDN.

The third trend is the integration of communication networks in order to cope with the diversity of the services provided. As communication network services which were generally voice-oriented expand in scope into various data and video services, communication networks are becoming integrated to accommodate this change. If these diversifying services must be accommodated separately, as was the case in the communication networks of the past where telephone networks, data networks, and telex networks existed independently, then disorder or complexity is unavoidable, which is undesirable from the standpoint of economical viability and communication efficiency. Therefore, a solution has been sought in the direction of allowing each service to access existing communication networks in an integrated manner regardless of its type, and ultimately lead the communication network itself to become integrated as well. The ISDN was conceived as the initial solution. Conceptually, the BISDN is no more than an expansion of the ISDN, so even packet communication, video phone, video conference, and CATV video services can be integrated and provided jointly.

The fourth trend is that communication networks are becoming more intelligent. This has been made possible by the introduction of common-channel signaling, which allows the transfer of information needed in communication connection through a separate network unrelated to the communication information itself. That is, intelligent communication networks are materialized by first constructing an independent signaling network based on common-channel signaling, and upon that foundation, providing several types of intelligent connection services. This permits the provision of diverse types of *intelligent network* (IN) services to the user, such as alternate billing services and virtual private network services.

Further trends can be found in the individualization and personalization of communication networks. As users desire the mobility and reliability of wireless communication that can transcend the geographical and time restrictions of wired communication, we see the emergence of *personal communication networks* (PCN), which can overcome the limitations of wireless or mobile phones. The motivation behind the personal communication network is to employ small-scale personal portable phones and the concept of signaling networks to allow the user access to the network with a personal number and also to use the network in an interworking relationship with existing public communication networks. Multimedia communication, which can also handle data and video, is sought for the future, but bandwidth restrictions inherent in wireless communication emerge as a fundamental problem.

Such trends of communication network development are also compatible with the subsequent evolutionary trends outlined in Figure 1.8. The figure illustrates the role of the public communication network, which acts as the parent that integrates data networks and video communications networks, which in turn evolve into the

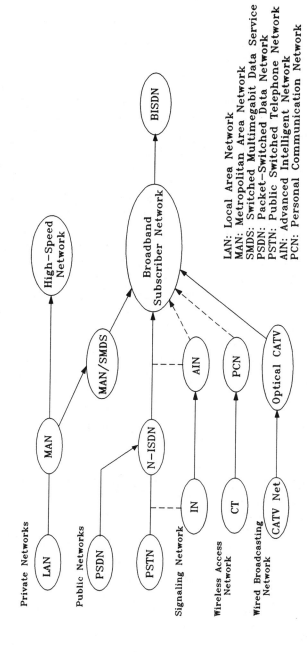

Figure 1.8 Evolution of telecommunication networks.

BISDN. The development of signaling networks from IN to *advanced IN* (AIN) and that of the wireless access network from CT 2/3 to the PCN are also depicted.

1.3 KEY TECHNOLOGIES OF BROADBAND TELECOMMUNICATION SYSTEMS

As was stated earlier, the broadband telecommunication system is in essence a communication system that provides various high-speed and broadband services in an integrated manner via the BISDN. For it to be realized in practice, maturation of several technologies is essential. First, optical transmission technology is indispensable for enabling broadband transmission, and it can be divided into the optical medium technology for efficiently using the optical physical medium and the broadband transmission technology for constructing interoffice and subscriber network transmission systems over the optical medium. High-speed switching technology is required to enable broadband switching. Since the BISDN is founded on ATM, the required high-speed switching technology is no other than the ATM switching technology. Also, since the BISDN is an ATM-based public network, traffic control technology within the network is extremely critical. On the other hand, high-speed data communication technology that can effectively handle high-speed packet services, broadband video communication technology for efficient compression, transmission, and recovery of broadband video services, and the multimedia technology for combining various services and provide them as multimedia services are also important. This section reviews such key technologies required to realize broadband communication systems.[1]

1.3.1 Base Technologies for Broadband Telecommunications

Before reviewing the key technologies for the construction of broadband communication systems, we examine the developmental status of various base technologies that are required for realization of broadband telecommunication systems.

Base technologies for broadband telecommunications have matured in step with the increasing demand for broadband services. Maturation of optical communications is crucial for the realization of broadband communication. Accordingly, optical fiber loss has been reduced to below 0.5 dB/km, dispersion has also been lowered to negligible levels, and the emergence of the erbium-doped fiber amplifier has made

---

[1]The contents of Sections 1.3.2 to 1.3.6 are treated in detail in Chapters 2 through 6 of this book. These chapters can therefore be used as references for more detailed explanation of the new terms and concepts in these sections.

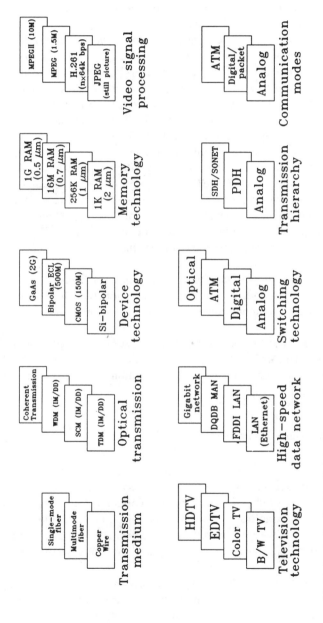

Figure 1.9 Technologies for broadband telecommunications.

unrepeatered, long-distance transmission possible. In the case of light-emitting devices, the performance of laser diodes has been drastically improved, and edge-emitting LED has advanced to the point where it can be satisfactorily connected with optical fiber for use in subscriber networks.

Advances in integrated circuit and transistor technologies are also worthy of close attention, with bipolar *emitter-coupled logic* (ECL) or *gallium arsenide* (GaAs) transistors currently possessing high-speed processing capability from hundreds of megabits per second up to a few gigabits per second, while *complementary metal oxide semiconductor* (CMOS) technology permits processing up to the 150-Mbps level. Memory devices crucial for the storage of high-speed data and image/video signals have been evolving to an unprecedented degree.

The recent advances in signal processing have made compression, conversion, and recovery of video signals simple, and if the above advances are complemented by *very-large-scale integration* (VLSI) technology, efficient terminal equipment at the user's side can be constructed. Also, developments in high-quality monitors and high-sensitivity cameras have advanced to the point that BISDN terminal equipment associated with various video services can now be made. Related TV technology has improved significantly as well, encompassing *extended-definition television* (EDTV) and HDTV.

Recent advances in software and microprocessor technologies have made high-speed control a possibility, which in conjunction with fast operating devices enables high-speed data communication, high-speed switching, and synchronous transmission.

Therefore, the base broadband technologies are now ready for realization of broadband telecommunication systems, whose specific embodiment is the ATM-based BISDN. Figure 1.9 provides a pictorial representation of the above-mentioned technological environments.

1.3.2 Optical Medium Technology

As high-speed data services and video communication services are emerging in step with today's rapidly developing information society, a need is created for the construction of broadband trunk and subscriber networks that can integrate such broadband services with the traditional voice services. In order to achieve integration of these communication networks, as well as the realization of the broadband telecommunication networks, the construction of optical subscriber networks is of fundamental importance.

In order to implement optical subscriber networks into the existing telecommunications networks, additional components and technologies are required. They are optical subscriber cables, connectors, splicing, *optoelectronic integrated circuits* (OEIC) for the simple maintenance and the economic viability, and narrow spectrum laser diodes and optical filters for wavelength division multiplexing. In addition, optical amplification is required in order to cope with the limiting of repeater spacings or power splitting due to losses and dispersion of optical fibers. Also, coherent optical communication technology, which can fully and minutely utilize the wide frequency bandwidth of lightwave and increase the sensitivity of optical receivers, might eventually be employed as the ultimate optical communication technology.

It is anticipated that single-mode optical fibers will be widely used as the main transmission medium of interoffice and subscriber networks. While initially the method of using existing telephone lines or coaxial cables for the final sections of the subscriber network will be considered, in the long run, single-mode optical fibers will become universal. This is because, compared to multimode optical cables, single-mode optical cables have a greater information transmission capacity, superior performance, and the virtue of being compatible with novel technologies such as concentrated *wavelength division multiplexing* (WDM) and coherent optical communication.

The required information transfer capability in broadband communication systems would be around a thousand times that of the existing communication networks, and throughput at the terabits per second class would be needed as well. Some of the ways in which transmission capacities can be so drastically increased are WDM and coherent communication. Between the two, the method that is ready for use in the current interoffice or subscriber networks is WDM. WDM is a scheme in which mutually different pieces of communication information are modulated onto several lightwaves with slightly different wavelengths and transmitted through a single optical fiber. The application of WDM in a communication network can result in higher transmission capacity and simpler routing and switching. Also, employment of WDM in optical subscriber network allows the terminal equipment inside the network to be constructed from simple passive optical devices.

In the future, high-speed, time-division multiplexing and WDM will be employed to achieve higher capacities, to be joined by the coherent communication in the long run. Also, repeater spacings will be widened with the development of the optical fiber amplifier and soliton. At this juncture, such a high level of performance becomes an important specification in designing long-distance sections beyond 1000 km, while low price is more important in short-distance sections within the range of 50 km.

In the case of single-mode optical cables, bandwidth of around 15 THz is usable in principle near 1300 nm, and bandwidth around 20 THz is usable near 1550 nm. Such bandwidths, in conjunction with the development of frequency-adjustable lasers, make optical switches possible and can be used as the base technology for next-generation optical switches. Wavelength control will gradually become more sophisticated, and frequency-tunable lasers are anticipated in the near future.

1.3.3 Broadband Transmission Technology

The broadband transmission technology that will have a critical role in broadband telecommunication networks is no other than synchronous digital transmission. Synchronous digital transmission technology is a novel transmission mode based on SDH or SONET. It systematically accommodates existing North American and European digital tributaries, and makes possible ATM transmission of the BISDN.

SDH offers numerous innovations compared to the existing PDH. SDH employs 125-μs frame structure, and can thus easily access DS-0 level signals and collectively accommodate all the existing digital tributaries inside the 155-Mbps STM-1 signal (STS-3c in the case of SONET). Transmission handling procedures are systematized in accordance with the layering concept, and this is reflected in the formats of overheads. A novel point technique is used in achieving synchronization, and on that basis it makes the establishment of a global communication network possible. Furthermore, it applies the concept of single-step multiplexing in the synchronous multiplexing procedures of forming the STM-1 signal, and thus can manage repetitive *add-drop multiplexing* (ADM) and *digital cross-connect* (DXC) efficiently.

The name *synchronous digital hierarchy* arises from the fact that SDH adopts a synchronous multiplexing structure in multiplexing tributaries into the STM-1 signal. The use of synchronous multiplexing renders multiplexing/demultiplexing simple, makes it easy to approach low-speed tributaries, can enhance efficiency of OAM functions, and facilitates expansion into higher bit rates of the future. Here, overheads contained inside the STM-1 effectively form the OAM network, and higher-speed signals can be obtained by further multiplexing the base STM-1 signal (for instance, multiplexing 4 and 16 of STM-1's results in STM-4 (or STS-12c) at 622.080 Mbps and STM-16 (or STS-48c) at 2,488.320 Mbps, respectively.

In broadband telecommunication systems, therefore, it is important to construct a communication network that can fully utilize the inherent benefits of SDH. ADM and DXC, especially, are constituent elements that can apply the special features of SDH to make possible the formation of point-to-multipoint network configuration through the employment of hub, and hence assume the most important role in synchronous digital transmission. They also allow the constituent elements of the network to be connected in various ways, such as star and ring configurations, and thus allow flexible reconfigurations of the network structure. Considering that the existing public networks and subscriber networks are solely based on the star topology, we can expect that the introduction of SDH along with ring topology would add various new features to future networks.

1.3.4 ATM Communication Technology

The ultimate goal of broadband telecommunication can be said to be the BISDN, and the unique feature of the BISDN is the use of ATM. ATM was devised as a way of collectively accommodating all of the diverse characteristics possessed by broadband services. In other words, it is a means of accommodating services with opposing characteristics, such as circuit-mode and packet-mode services, low-speed and high-speed services, and *continuous bit rate* (CBR) and *variable bit rate* (VBR) services. This is made possible by first segmenting all service signals into packets of fixed size, called *ATM cells*, so that communication networks may only take part in the proper transfer of them. Here, ATM cells are multiplexed through *asynchronous time division multiplexing* (ATDM), which is the source of the term "asynchronous" in ATM.

ATM communication technique can be said to be a communication mode that integrates the existing circuit-mode digital communication method with the packet-mode communication method. First of all, ATM has a close connection with the packet-mode communication in that it uses ATM cells as its basic means of transport; but there is a difference in that the packet mode was created for VBR non-real-time data signals, whereas ATM can manage equally as well with real-time, CBR signals. Also, packet mode is generally used for LANs, whereas ATM can be used for vast public networks and is hence accompanied by various problems inherent in any large network, such as address assignment, access and flow control, switching, and transmission. On the other hand, the fundamental difference between ATM and the circuit-mode communication is that, whereas the circuit mode functions by allocating a separate service channel and transferring information signals in a continuous bit stream through it, ATM operates by segmenting the information signal so as to fit it onto the ATM cells, then it transfers them through a *virtual channel* (VC) in a *virtual path* (VP). Thus, the accompanying ATM procedures such as establishing connections, signaling, transmission, and switching present various new problems.

ATM is a novel communication technique which is introduced together with the BISDN and includes several complex new technologies. Among the most difficult are ATM traffic control technology and ATM switching technology. ATM traffic control is a critical factor which dictates the success of communication services through the ATM network, and hence can be regarded as a fundamental problem of ATM communication. Traffic control encompasses *connection admission control* (CAC) for allowing user's call setup, *usage parameter control* (UPC) for monitoring the observance of the traffic characteristics agreed on at call setup, *congestion control* (CC) for monitoring traffic and the occurrence of congestion within the ATM network, as well as the application of appropriate measures to alleviate the congestion, and *priority control* (PC) for ensuring the priority of each service. Of course, similar traffic control methods have been studied for existing packet communication networks, but they differ considerably in terms of network scale, transmission distance, transmission speeds, and traffic volume.

ATM switching also emerges as a fundamental problem to resolve. ATM switching is high-speed packet switching employing a 155.52-Mbps bit rate as the base unit. Consequently, its main associated difficulty is in the high speed, and concepts such as parallel processing, self-routing, and optical switching are being considered as possible solutions. Also, ATM switching requires short time delay, low cell-loss rate, and high throughput, in addition to point-to-multipoint switching capability. Large-capacity ATM switches are required, especially for use in the BISDN, and must be easily implementable in VLSI. It is a challenging task indeed to realize an ATM switch that can satisfy all these various requirements.

On the other hand, signaling technology for broadband communication is also important. Signaling schemes based on existing common channels must continue to be supported and at the same time allow smooth transition into the ATM-based signaling scheme founded on ATM. In the BISDN especially, signaling schemes must be equipped with a capability for providing multimedia services, as well as multiparty call services.

1.3.5 High-Speed Data Communication Network Technology

With increasing speed and distributed processing, the communication capacity of such a LAN environment is going beyond local areas and into wide areas, and the need for high-speed, wide-area networking, with internetworking of LANs as its main objective, is being recognized. Thus, a means of constructing a cost-effective high-speed network in a gradual manner is highly desirable.

The related technologies whose research and development are in progress around the world include *frame relay* (FR), MAN, *switched multimegabit data service* (SMDS), and ATM.

The FR technology, based on frame multiplexing at the data link layer, enables high-speed transmission by minimizing network functions for error control and flow control in order to meet high-speed traffic access requirements for interconnection between LANs. The main feature of a network based on FR is the provision of multiple data links up to the DS-1 rate through bandwidth allocation on demand and single access lines.

MAN is referred to as a high-speed information network for metropolitan areas, and has its conceptual origin in the advanced form of LAN from the computer network field, a MAN based on BISDN technology, and a MAN that unifies CATV and telecommunication. In MAN systems, DQDB is widely employed, which is a MAN protocol specified in IEEE 802.6.

The SMDS, which is a cell relay technique, is a high-speed, connectionless packet switched service, and DQDB is used as a subscriber network access protocol. Consequently, the SMDS will be one of the first services to provide switched broadband services, and is anticipated to be provided through the BISDN from then on.

ATM is being developed as the switching and transmission technology for high-speed data services, and the IEEE 802.6 MAN protocol is being used as one of the ATM-based BISDN local loop implementation technologies. Construction of such an ATM network requires an enormous amount of investment and time, and hence the application area is expanding through the MAN and SMDS, which satisfy current user needs and act as the foundation for the BISDN.

Aside from the above-mentioned high-speed data networks, the gigabit network is another evolving technology. The gigabit network refers to a data network whose physical layer supports the bit rates of 1 Gbps and above. It can be used as a backbone network for LANs and MANs and is in high demand in the high-performance computing and distributed computing environments.

1.3.6 Broadband Video Communication Technology

Usually, a broad bandwidth is required for the transmission of video signals; hence, the video signal compression and restoration technologies are essential for the effective use of the transmission line. So broadband video technology usually consists of the coding technology for compressing tremendous amounts of video information, the transmission technology for the efficient transmission of compressed video information, and the terminal technology integrating the first two.

Video compression technology adopts various video/image coding techniques to eliminate redundant information from an image signal within the range that its characteristics do not change perceptibly. Image coding techniques can be categorized into prediction coding, transform coding, vector quantization, subband coding, and entropy coding. Today, all of these coding techniques can be realized with the current VLSI technology. CCITT and ISO have adopted a coding technique that integrates prediction coding, transform coding, and entropy coding as the international standard.

For the economical provision of various information communication services with different characteristics, a communication network is required that can accommodate diverse forms of information media and at the same time maintain a unified access structure and transmission mode. From this viewpoint, it is difficult to provide a broad spectrum of video information communication services with the existing PSTN or NISDN. An alternative approach is the BISDN based on ATM, which relies on packetized video transmission. The ATM transmission technique offers many advantages from several standpoints, since it can achieve an efficient integration of complex information such as video, voice, data, image, and text through a single network, and it can adapt easily to ever-changing consumer demands and service environments. However, packet-based transmission raises a new set of problems to be solved, including packet jitter and packet loss, which were not a problem in circuit switching networks.

Terminal technology has a close relationship with the attributes of the services to be provided. For example, in services with large-scale broadcasting characteristics, the video information compression stage is more complex than the video information reconstruction stage, but in conversational services the compressor and the reconstructor must coexist inside the same device; hence, for an economical implementation, the two parts should have the same degree of complexity. The worldwide development trend in terminals is to adopt a common coding device rather than using different decoders for different services.

Among the typical broadband video services are the video phone and the video conferencing services, which are to be provided through the public broadband communication networks in an interactive manner. Another set of popular broadband services can be found in CATV and HDTV services that are distributive in nature. Existing CATV systems are anticipated to be upgraded to optical CATV systems en route to their participation in the BISDN. Optical CATV could be further advanced to carry HDTV service signals as HDTV technology evolves in the future.

SELECT BIBLIOGRAPHY

Ambrosch, W. D., A. Maher, and B. Sasscer, *The Intelligent Network*, Berlin, Heidelberg, New York, London, Paris, Tokyo: Springer-Verlag, 1989.

Andrews, F. T., "The Evolution of Digital Loop Carrier," *IEEE Commun. Mag.*, March 1991, pp. 31–35.

Bell Telephone Laboratories, *Transmission Systems for Communications*, 5th ed., Bell Telephone Laboratories, 1982.

Bellamy, J., *Digital Telephony*, 2nd ed., John Wiley and Sons, 1991.

Bellcore, *Telecommunications Transmission Engineering*, Vols. 1–3, 3rd ed., 1990.

Benedetto, S., E. Biglieri, and V. Castellani, *Digital Transmission Theory*, Prentice-Hall, 1987.

Berman, R. K., and J. H. Brewster, "Perspectives on the AIN Architecture," *IEEE Commun. Mag.*, Vol. 30, No. 2, Feb. 1992, pp. 27–33.

Bhargava, A., *Integrated Broadband Networks*, Artech House, 1991.

Bocker, P., *ISDN*, Berlin, Heidelberg, New York, London, Paris, Tokyo: Springer-Verlag, 1988.

Bylanski, P., and D. G. W., Ingram, *Digital Transmission Systems*, Peter Peregrinus, 1980.

Calhoun, G., *Wireless Access and the Local Telephone Network*, Artech House, 1992.

Cheong, V. E., and R. A. Hirschheim, *Local Area Networks*, John Wiley and Sons, 1985.

Dicenet, G., *Design and Prospects for the ISDN*, Artech House, 1987.

Elbert, B. R., *Primitive Telecommunication Networks*, Artech House, 1988.

Freeman, R. E., *Telecommunication Transmission Handbook*, 2nd ed., John Wiley and Sons, 1981.

Handel, R., "Evolution of ISDN Towards Broadband ISDN," *IEEE Network Mag.*, Vol. 3, No. 1, Jan. 1989, pp. 7–13.

Hawley, G. T., "Historical Perspectives on the U.S. Telephone Loop," *IEEE Commun. Mag.*, March 1991, pp. 24–28.

Kreager, P. S., *Practical Aspects of Data Communications*, McGraw-Hill, 1983.

Libois, L. J. (CNET), *Electronic Switching*, North-Holland, 1983.

McDonald, J. C., *Fundamentals of Digital Switching*, Plenum Press, 1983.

Millman, S., *A History of Engineering and Science in the Bell System: Communication Science (1925–1980)*, AT&T Bell Lab., 1984.

Minoli, D., *Telecommunications Technology Handbook*, Artech House, 1991.

Murano, K., et al., "Technologies Towards Broadband ISDN," *IEEE Commun. Mag.*, Apr. 1990, p. 66.

Noll, A. M., *Introduction to Telephone and Telephone Systems*, Artech House, 1986.

O'Neil, E. F., *A History of Engineering and Science in the Bell System: Transmission Technology (1925–1975)*, AT&T Bell Lab., 1985.

Owen, F. F. E., *PCM and Digital Transmission Systems*, McGraw-Hill, 1982.

Proakis, J. G., *Digital Communications*, McGraw-Hill, 1983.

Schindller, Jr., G. E., *A History of Engineering and Science in the Bell System: Switching Technology (1925–1980)*, AT&T Bell Lab., 1984.

Schwartz, M., *Telecommunication Networks*, Addison Wesley, 1987.

Sklar, B., *Digital Communications*, Prentice-Hall International, 1988.

Spragins, J. D., J. L. Hammond, and K. Paulikowski, *Telecommunications: Protocols and Design*, Addison Wesley, 1991.

Stallings, W., *Advances in ISDN and Broadband ISDN*, IEEE Computer Society Press, 1992.

Stallings, W., *Data and Computer Communications*, Macmillan, 1985.

Stallings, W., *Tutorial: Computer Communications: Architectures, Protocols, and Standards*, 2nd ed., Computer Society Press of the IEEE, 1987.

Stallings, W., *Tutorial: Integrated Services Digital Networks (ISDN)*, 2nd ed., The Computer Society Press of the IEEE, 1988.

Stallings, W., *Tutorial: Local Network Technology*, 3rd ed., Computer Society Press of the IEEE, 1988.

Toda, I., "Migrations to Broadband ISDN," *IEEE Commun. Mag.*, Vol. 28, No. 4, Apr. 1990, pp. 55–58.

Weinstein, S., "Telecommunications in the Coming Decades," *IEEE Spectrum*, Nov. 1987, p. 64.

Chapter 2
Optical Subscriber Network

Fiber-optic cables and their associated wide-bandwidth (channel) capacity are finally reaching into homes and small businesses in lieu of copper twisted pairs. This will result in an expanded market for television and computer networks, and may dramatically change future lifestyle. For example, by working away from the office via a computer terminal, people can enjoy more flexible work schedules and more pleasant environments. Physicians can send X-ray and other medical data instantly to distant specialists for evaluations, and patients can send cardiac information to their physicians without leaving home. Shopping, banking, education, and even the printed media can be accessed solely through so-called videotex services as nationwide information networks become accessible to home terminals. One can imagine that freeways and air traffic could be less jammed as more people's travel needs are met by advanced telecommunication network services. Computers with speech recognition capability may interact with other home electronics or even robotic systems. HDTV alone will have a huge impact on the broadcast and telecommunication industries. All of these social changes would take advantage of the expanded capacity of fiber links tying homes and businesses together. The present cost of installing fiber in the individual home for *Plain Old Telephone Service* (POTS) is estimated to be more than double that of conventional copper wire. However, from the standpoint of the broadband services mentioned above, installing fiber provides more economic solutions.

The major new issue in the migration strategies toward the BISDN is the cost-effective installation of the optical subscriber network. Essentially, the goal of any migration strategy to an optical subscriber network should be from one or all of the following viewpoints: market-driven strategy, new service-oriented strategy, and advance-investment strategy.

The first strategy is to replace existing metallic subscriber loops with optical fibers wherever possible, even if only narrowband services are required. This is done with the expectation that these subscribers will eventually use broadband services. This is the market-driven strategy. For some time to come, the market-driven strategy will focus on business users. In the case of large buildings, the cost of installing

---

optical subscriber loops for narrowband services is already less than that for metallic loops. The market-driven strategy of installing optical loops only where they are needed will not be sufficient to promote the use of optical systems. This is far too passive an approach and will not allow a satisfactory response to user demand for new services. To hasten the start of broadband services by establishing common platforms for network service providers, a new, more aggressive service-oriented strategy is called for. At this time, it is difficult to predict exactly how the demand for new services for the home will develop. Nevertheless, cable TV can be expected to provide the impetus for the transition to broadband services. In order to stimulate the offering of new services, it is necessary to provide a network that is capable of more than just cable TV program distribution. A flexible and multipurpose platform that would also allow HDTV distribution and bidirectional communications must first be put into place. Early installation of such a platform would allow for the early announcement of broadband services, which would in turn stimulate demand.

The third strategy is to press ahead with the introduction of optical subscriber loops to accelerate technological innovation, even if the cost is somewhat high. This is called *advance-investment strategy*. When we look at the pace of previous technological developments, it is clear that the pace has been accelerated in proportion to the total initial investment. A larger initial investment eventually results in lower overall development costs. In addition, there is a good possibility that the early establishment of platforms will create a new demand for new services. If this demand is fed back into technology development, the crossover point for metallic and optical loops can be brought forward. There are thus two major benefits to the advance investment strategy: acceleration of technological innovation and accelerated introduction of new services. The advance investment strategy will provide a lower overall investment cost for total system development than that which would be necessary when hurrying to introduce optical subscriber loops once demand for broadband services has appeared.

The purpose of this chapter is to offer a comprehensive examination of the particulars of the broadband technologies required to construct an optical subscriber network. We will examine the growing need and the basic structures of the subscriber network and its present deployment status in some selected countries. Afterwards, we will investigate the operating principles and properties of the network-related constituent elements whose emergence has made the realization of the subscriber network possible, and we will go on to explore possible paths for future development of the optical subscriber network toward the BISDN.

2.1 INTRODUCTION

Existing subscriber networks assume the role of linking subscriber terminals established on the subscriber's premises to the communications network. Two-wire or four-wire copper cables are usually used, providing analog voice frequency services to general residential subscribers. But high-speed data services and video communication services are emerging in step with today's rapidly developing information society, creating a need for the construction of a broadband subscriber network that can integrate such broadband services with the traditional voice services. In other words, the goal of the ISDN or BISDN is to evolve into a broadband integrated communications network so that broadband information such as high-speed data and video images can be transported through a single digital network. Along with such efforts to integrate the separately existing communications networks, the networks supporting communication between computers have simultaneously developed into the LANs and MANs. To achieve integration of these communications networks, as well as the realization of the computer communications networks, the construction of optical subscriber networks is of utmost importance.

In the United States and Japan, the construction of optical subscriber networks began as early as the late 1970s, and the feeder portion of the subscriber loop, a line that runs from the central office to a remote terminal within a kilometer of the homes, has become fiber. But the connections between the remote terminals and subscriber's homes have remained twisted pair. Now several countries are developing technologies to replace the final kilometers of the copper wire with the optical fiber.

The basic subscriber network topologies can be in star, bus, or ring configurations, depending on the network evolution strategy, operation and maintenance, and economic viability. Subscribers can be general residential subscribers who demand basic services like telephone and low-speed data or distributive services such as TV and music broadcast. They can also be business subscribers who request such services as video telephone, video conferencing, high-resolution documents, and high-speed data. The star/star configuration or the bus/star configuration, which allows the construction of an economical network employing passive optical devices such as the star coupler and wavelength division multiplexer are generally more appropriate for residential subscribers, while business subscribers who require high-speed data services are best served by integrating existing LANs and MANs into the high-speed broadband public networks.

In order to implement optical subscriber networks in the existing telecommunications network, additional components and technologies are required. They are optical subscriber cables, connectors, splicing, optoelectronic ICs for maintenance simplicity and economic viability, and narrow-spectrum laser diodes and filters for wavelength division multiplexing. In addition, optical amplification is required in order to cope with the limiting of repeater spacings due to losses and dispersion of optical fibers. Also, coherent optical communication technology, which can fully and minutely utilize the wide frequency bandwidth of lightwave and increase the sensitivity of optical receivers, is needed as the eventual optical communication technology employed.

The most likely evolution scenario from the existing networks toward the BISDN should be considered from the viewpoint of transport capability enhancements in accordance with future service provision.

A network's direction of development, which follows the installation of optical cable at the service area, will first evolve into the form of *fiber to the office* (FTTO), which introduces optical cable to large-volume business subscribers, then *fiber to the curb* (FTTC), which extends optical cable to business areas or newly developing residential areas, and ultimately *fiber to the home* (FTTH), which introduces optical cable as far as the individual subscriber premises.

2.2 OPTICAL SUBSCRIBER NETWORK DEVELOPMENT

The basic elements of a communications network are the switching system, the interoffice trunk network, and the subscriber loop network. The subscriber loop network links the subscriber terminal to the central office switch, which traditionally has been two-line copper wire. But the *digital loop carrier* (DLC) system was introduced in the 1970s to increase line efficiency, and the *fiber loop carrier* (FLC) system was introduced in the late 1980s to further increase the line efficiency and to prepare for future services. Optical fiber can accommodate not only the presently existing POTS, but also the future broadband services such as CATV, *video response system* (VRS), high-speed data, and BISDN services, due to its technological flexibility based on broadband and integrating characteristics. When the BISDN becomes applied throughout the entire telecommunications network, broadband subscribers can flexibly access broadband services whose bandwidths range from 64 kbps to 600 Mbps. For that to happen, the introduction of the optical network to subscriber premises is essential. Also, it is anticipated that with the development of optical techniques such as coherent optical transmission, *dense wavelength division multiplexing* (DWDM), and *subcarrier multiplexing* (SCM) can be introduced to subscriber distribution networks.

In this section, we will examine the growing need for an optical subscriber network from the viewpoint of broadband services, then go on to describe and compare basic topologies of optical subscriber networks. Next, the present deployment status of optical subscriber networks will be examined for some selected countries.

2.2.1 Growing Needs for Optical Subscriber Networks

Existing electrical communication services have mainly aimed for voice services alone, but nowadays there is an increasing demand for various broadband services such as video telephone, video conferencing, high-speed data communications, CATV, HDTV, hi-fi stereo, and others. Therefore, it is anticipated that comunication networks will eventually be developed into the BISDN, which economically integrates existing telephone networks, privately established data networks (LAN, MAN, SMDS), and the cable TV networks. In order to provide broadband services other than POTS, optical subscriber networks need to be deployed through the provisioning of optical fibers to each subscriber, which so far have been used mainly for high-speed trunk and long-distance communication.

Current telephone networks with copper wires suffer from low transmission speeds and high loss and are not appropriate for broadband services in the available bandwidth.[1] In contrast, optical fiber can provide broadband services such as high-speed data and video with its almost unlimited bandwidth, low transmission loss, and freedom from electromagnetic interference effects. Congestion in the underground cable ducts can be relieved through optical cables. Therefore, in order to provide broadband services to each subscriber, the introduction of optical subscriber network is a logical solution for the introduction of new services.

Furthermore, the fast-developing optical technology has dropped the prices of optical devices and optoelectronic ICs drastically, and therefore the construction of optical subscriber networks is becoming comparable in cost and performance to copper-wire subscriber networks.

2.2.2 Subscriber Network Topologies

A network-topology design in optical subscriber networks should consider the following: economic feasibility, expandability, powering, reliability, simplicity of communication maintenance, subscriber distribution, and the attributes of the furnished services. Powering is a key concern for a growing group of telephone companies and vendors considering FTTH systems. Two solutions for *optical network unit* (ONU) powering have emerged: central powering from shared network sources and local powering from nearby sources. Local powering can be categorized by ac-metered service and customer-fed backpowering. Comparisons among these alternatives are summarized in Table 2.1. A network topology can be categorized into star, bus, or ring structures, depending on the way service information is distributed to the subscriber. These aspects of network structures will be examined in detail here.

The transmission line in optical subscriber networks can be divided broadly into feeder networks, distribution networks, and service networks. Figure 2.1 represents a local-access network model which assigns the connection between the telephone office and the subscriber network in a layered manner. The feeder cable connects the telephone office and the remote node, the remote node is connected to

---

[1] The bandwidth of coaxial cables used for CATV systems is around 500 MHz for transmission distances up to 1 km. But bandwidth is reduced abruptly with further distances, and, because of their branching structure, they are not suitable for bidirectional communication.

Table 2.1
Comparison of Powering

	AC Utility Powering	*DC Local Powering*	*Central Powering*
Equipment first costs	Lowest	1.25 × ac	Highest, 1.5 × ac
Power system operating efficiency	Highest, 82%	64%	Lowest, 62%
Battery maintenance & replacement	Hundreds of points per CSA	Hundreds of points per CSA	One or two points per CSA
System survivability	Catastrophic ac outages are a problem	Catastrophic ac outages are a problem	Immune to outages
		Customer could impact operation	Aerial feed subject to environment
Utility/customer interface	Utility and/or licensed electricians	Customer and licensed electricians	None All internal to LEC

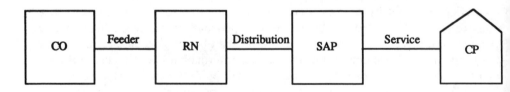

CO : Central Office
RN : Remote Node
SAP: Service Access Point
CP : Customer Premise

Figure 2.1 Local-access network model.

the *service access point* (SAP) via distribution cables and, lastly, the SAP is connected to the individual subscribers through the use of service line cables. Ultimately, the entire feeder, distribution, and service line cables will be replaced by optical fibers. However, until the introduction of broadband services, the optical fiber will first be used only down to the remote node, then to the SAP. The service line cable is the last one to be replaced by optical cable, since the existing copper wire is sufficient for simple voice rate services. In a local-access network, the feeder, distribution, and service networks can have different forms of network topologies. Figure 2.2 is an illustration of the star, bus, and ring network topologies.

The star structure is the configuration in which each node is connected to the central node via optical fiber. In the bus structure, all the nodes are connected to the central node via a single bus, and internode bidirectional communication can be accommodated by using an independent bus structure between two nodes. In the ring structure, each node is connected to the central office through the optical fiber in a closed-loop configuration. In contrast to the star or bus structure, ring structure provides information transfer between the nodes without additional equipment.

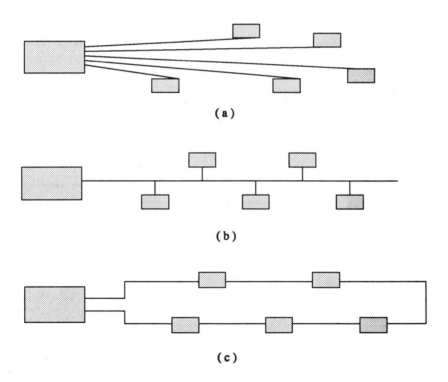

Figure 2.2 Network topology: (a) star; (b) bus; (c) ring.

Whereas the network's physical structure indicates its physical layout, the network's logical structure indicates how information transfer is logically accomplished in the network. For instance, if each communication node is assigned its own frequency, wavelength, time slot, and cell, then the network can have a logical structure different from its physical structure. Hence, as shown in Figure 2.3, the network's physical and logical structures may not be the same.

When a network structure is selected for the applicable parts of the subscriber network, several important factors should be considered, including initial and maintenance costs, future network evolution, reliability, technological evolution, flexibility with regards to future service provision, and information security for secure communication needs.

The physical star/logical star structure can provide the widest possible bandwidth to each subscriber and is most flexible in terms of future service potential. In this structure, bandwidth management is simple, fault diagnosis and maintenance can be accomplished systematically, and the maintenance cost is low. Services based on this structure enjoy a high degree of security, but this structure requires a high initial installation cost. Therefore, this structure is most appropriate in highly populated areas. Large numbers of subscribers in concentrated areas often justify the high initial cost of installation.

In the physical star/logical ring structure, signals coming into the central node from several adjacent nodes are transmitted to the target node after bypassing all the optical fiber links between the source node and the target node, thus effectively forming a logical ring structure. The main drawback of the structure is that the information is transmitted through all the nodes in the logical ring, which makes bandwidth management difficult. It also requires a high-speed interface and does not allow systematic error detection; thus, the structure is usually applied in situations where a logical ring structure suffices initially, but has the capability to convert eventually to the star structure with increasing bandwidth.

In the physical ring/logical star structure, all the nodes are physically interconnected in a ring configuration, and each node is assigned its own characteristic frequency band, wavelength, and time slot. Since the optical fibers are shared, its initial setup cost is low compared to the physical star structure, but the adoption of high-speed electronic devices increases cost. It is a logical star structure, and thus has improved information security.

The physical ring/logical ring structure is appropriate where a high level of security is not a priority and the overall traffic is comparatively low. Consequently, in order to provide bidirectional broadband services such as the point-to-point video switching service in this structure, another overlay network is necessary.

Table 2.2 lists the attributes of physical/logical topologies. The topology currently being considered the most in the distribution network structure is the physical star structure since it offers the highest degree of security and bandwidth extension capability. For the feeder network, the star or the ring structure is used frequently

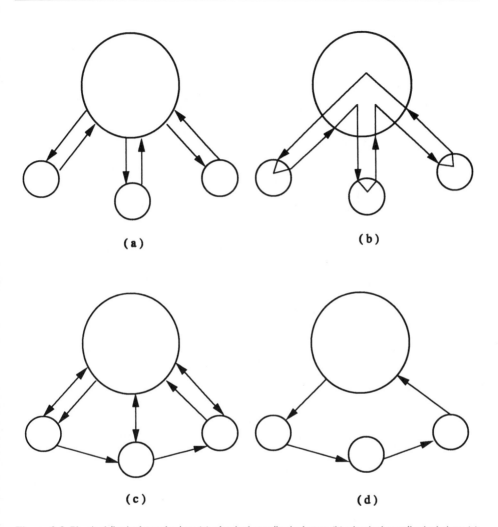

Figure 2.3 Physical/logical topologies: (a) physical star/logical star; (b) physical star/logical ring; (c) physical ring/logical star; (d) physical ring/logical ring.

for voice or data services, and the bus structure is widely used for video distribution services. Figure 2.4 represents topologies of these double optical subscriber networks, with the star/star structure of Figure 2.4(a) being the most flexible structure for providing voice, data, and image communication, and the bus/star and bus/bus structure in Figure 2.4(b) the most suitable for providing distributed video services. In the ring/star structure shown in Figure 2.4(c), the feeder network is composed of two rings that rotate in opposite directions. This structure is popular for data services.

Table 2.2
Attributes of Star/Ring Topologies

Characteristics	Physical Star		Physical Ring	
	Logical Star	Logical Ring	Logical Star	Logical Ring
O&M	Easy bandwidth administration	Difficult bandwidth administration	Moderate bandwidth administration	Difficult bandwidth administration
Evolution (POTS → ISDN)	Excellent	May require overlay	Depends on implementation	May require overlay circuit
Security	Excellent	Low	Depends on implementation	Low
Future	Good	Bad	Good	Good
Example	SLC-5, PPL	NA	Fujitsu optical shuttle bus	NA
Initial Cost	More fiber Lower O/E cost More O/E	More fiber Higher O/E cost Fewer O/E	Less fiber O/E cost depends on implementation	Less fiber Higher O/E cost Fewer O/E
Reliability	Good	Good	Excellent	Excellent

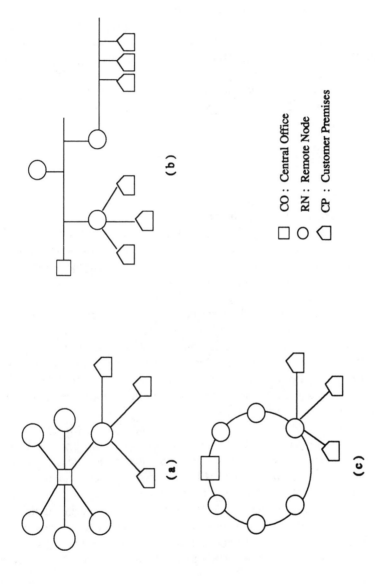

Figure 2.4 Topologies of optical subscriber network: (a) star/star; (b) bus/star and bus/bus; (c) ring/star.

CO : Central Office
RN : Remote Node
CP : Customer Premises

2.2.3 Present Deployment Status

A need to establish optical subscriber networks began to be recognized in some countries as early as the late 1970s. Various forms of optical subscriber network constructions took place in the 1980s according to the geographical situation, the level of technology, the population density, and the service provision of each country. As we enter into the 1990s, high-speed data and broadband video services are beginning to be provided not only to large business buildings, but also to residential subscribers. In this section, we will survey optical subscriber networks' present deployment status in the U.S., Japan, England, France, Germany, Netherlands, and some typical examples of optical subscriber systems will be introduced.

United States

In the United States, most telecommunication technologies and services are being developed not by a national body, but by such private companies as AT&T, which provides long-distance as well as international telecommunication services, and seven *regional Bell operating companies* (RBOC), which are assuming a leading role in regional telecommunication network services. Hence, the optical subscriber networks in the U.S. are being developed by private telecommunication service providers.

The first experimental optical subscriber network system was installed in November 1986 by Southern Bell at Hunter's Creek in Orlando, Florida, and it provided video services to each household. From then on, various experimental and commercial models have been developed and tested on site by numerous service providers.

AT&T Bell Laboratories, Bell Communications Research (Bellcore), and other advanced research organizations are testing model systems and developing key technologies for future subscriber networks.

Bell Laboratories developed the *Subscriber Loop Carrier* (SLC) Series-5 systems, which they have established and installed in many regions in the U.S. since 1988. Designed to provide broadband services for subscribers, the SLC-5 system is an optical fiber-based *fiber in the loop* (FITL) network system and can be viewed as an enhanced version of the DLC system (see Figure 2.5).[2]

The SLC-5 system uses the double star network as shown in Figure 2.6, and in order to achieve bidirectional transmission between the subscriber and the central office through just a single optical fiber, a fused fiber coupler is employed to separate optical signals transmitted in the opposite direction. Lasers with 1.3 μm wavelength

---

[2]DLC transmits a T1 carrier signal (created by multiplexing a large number of subscriber signals) to the *remote node* (RN) or the SAP through the feeder or distribution networks.

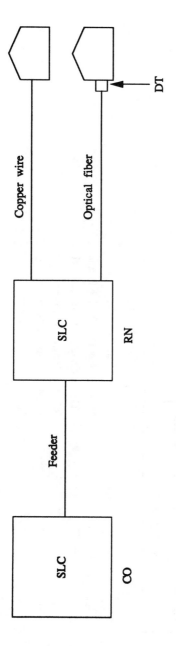

SLC : Subscriber Loop Carrier
CO : Central Office
RN : Remote Node
DT : Distant Terminal

Figure 2.5 SLC system architecture.

50

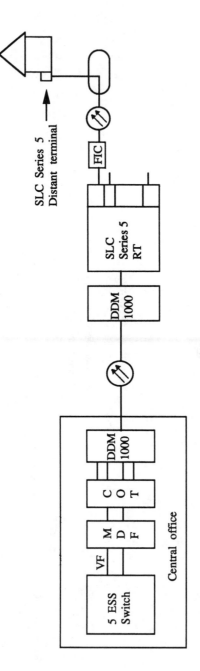

Figure 2.6 AT&T's SLC-5 FTTH feature.

SLC Series 5
Distant terminal

VF : Voice Frequency
MDF : Main Distributing Frame
COT : Central Office Terminal
RT : Remote Terminal
DDM : Digital Multiplexer
FIC : Fiber Interconnect

and *pin* diodes are used for the transmitter/receiver modules. AT&T Bell Laboratories has also been testing more advanced SLC-2000 systems in commercial environments. The SLC-2000 system was designed to flexibly accommodate the introduction of new services or changes in existing services.

Bellcore proposed an optical subscriber network named *LambdaNet* (see Figure 2.7). LambdaNet uses distributed-feedback lasers with a very narrow linewidth. Wavelength is assigned to transmit voice, data, and video signals through an $N \times N$ star coupler. Transmission speeds and packet switching up to 2 Gbps are possible. The star coupler multiplexes several optical wavelengths to be transmitted. When transmitted to the receiving nodes, each node can select the assigned optical wavelength using the wavelength demultiplexing procedure.

Bellcore proposed another system, called *passive photonic loop* (PPL), shown in Figure 2.8, whose concept is similar to that of LambdaNet. This double star network assigns a characteristic wavelength to each subscriber and employs high-density WDM, which uses diffraction grating to enable the central office to sort the subscriber signals according to the wavelength.[3] Although the upstream signal from a given subscriber is multiplexed with other subscriber signals using WDM at a remote node or at a SAP and then sent to the central office, the central office identifies each subscriber by inspecting the optical wavelength of the channel. The high-density WDM system requires a very narrow laser linewidth; thus, the use of a DFB laser diode with a stable wavelength is essential.

Raynet, which is a transmission system manufacturing company, has developed an optical fiber bus system commercially used in several RBOCs in the U.S. and in Canada. As shown in Figure 2.9, its distribution network uses a physical bus/logical star passive optical network structure. The *office interface unit* (OIU) at the central office or remote node provides various types of services to the *subscriber interface network* (SIU) through the optical bus. Up to eight subscribers are connected to each SIU. In this system, the number of optical fibers needed at the feeder network or the distribution network has been reduced by imposing greater functional responsibility on the complex electronic circuitry.

Japan

In 1978, the Visda Co., under the supervision of the Japanese government, completed an onsite experimental version of the *Highly Optical Visual Information System* (Hi-OVIS) optical subscriber network in Icoma Newtown, located between Osaka

---

[3]WDM devices are widely used between a central office and a remote node or between a remote node and SAPs as a means of sharing a single-mode optical interface feeder network. An individual information channel modulates a laser with a specific wavelength at the central office and the modulated optical signal is transmitted to the proper subscriber through the optical fiber feeder cable. Then the correct information signal is selected at the remote equipment site. Consequently, only the preassigned subscriber can receive or transmit information on a preassigned wavelength; thus, the level of security is high.

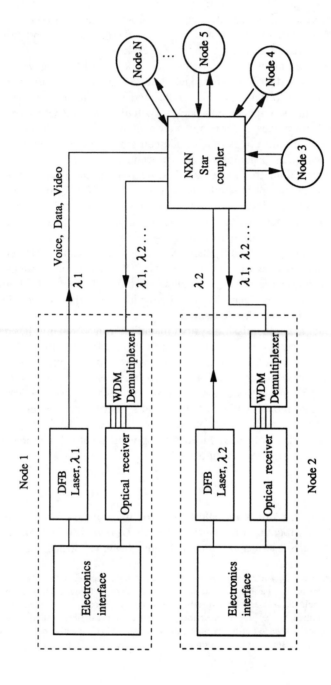

Figure 2.7 Block diagram of a LambdaNet star network.

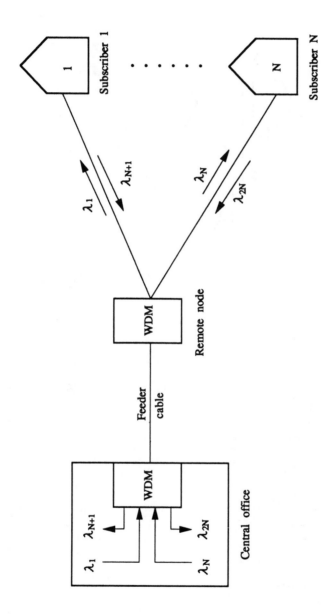

Figure 2.8 PPL architecture.

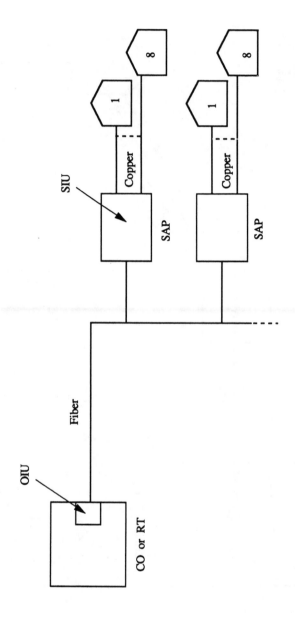

OIU : Office Interface Unit
SIU : Subscriber Interface Unit
SAP : Service Access Point

Figure 2.9 Raynet fiber bus system architecture.

and Nara. Hi-OVIS, which is the world's first bidirectional CATV service trial system, was planned for a period of four years beginning in 1973 and used for demonstration purposes since 1978. In order to provide completely bidirectional services, each home was equipped with home terminals such as a TV, keyboard, TV camera, and microphone. Optical fiber connected the information center to 158 common households, the city hall, fire station, school, and college, and the services are still being provided today. Figure 2.10 shows the Hi-OVIS system configuration, and it can be seen that the information center transmits programs from the TV broadcast station or programs stored at the information center to the view-requesting homes by way of a subcenter. Also, TV camera images from the homes can be sent to the information center, and can thus be used for crime prevention. The subcenter performs video switching for both downstream and upstream transmission.

Then, in 1986, the NTT Corp. in conjunction with the Interactive Basic Information Systems (IBIS) Development Corp., installed the so-called Advanced Hi-OVIS optical subscriber network in the central part of Osaka, making it possible for the subscriber to access a variety of information using just a single terminal. The customer premises services system shown in Figure 2.11 included 1.3-Gbps HDTV, multimedia services, National Television System Committee (NTSC) video, and data services. The configuration of this system is almost identical to Hi-OVIS, except that the advanced Hi-OVIS provides a more diverse set of services and the video switching is accomplished inside the information center.

As a part of the *Information Network System* (INS), which was developed by NTT as its main enterprise, an optical subscriber network providing video conferencing and 64-kbps ISDN services was installed in the Musasino region on the outskirts of Tokyo in 1984. Using this onsite test system as a basis, NTT performed an onsite test of a bidirectional video distribution system that could accommodate 2B+D ISDN services from 1986 through the following year. The associated upstream and downstream signals were composed of broadband video, low-speed data/optional video, video control signals, and 2B+D channels. This system could also provide home-shopping and videotex services.

With such onsite tests and technologies established in the previous model as a foundation, NTT introduced a new fiber-optic subscriber-loop transmission system—the new *central terminal* (CT)/*remote terminal* (RT) system—to provide analog telephone and ISDN basic rate interface services in 1991.

The new systems can utilize underground facilities in metropolitan areas and replace old analog switches cost-effectively in rural areas. Consequently, rural customers can be accommodated by digital local switches, and thus they can receive various kinds of new analog telephone services that could not be offered using the old analog switches. This system is also aimed at promoting the centralization of network facilities and simplification of operation and maintenance work.

The system configuration of the CT/RT system is as shown in Figure 2.12. We observe that CTs are located in telephone offices with a digital local switch

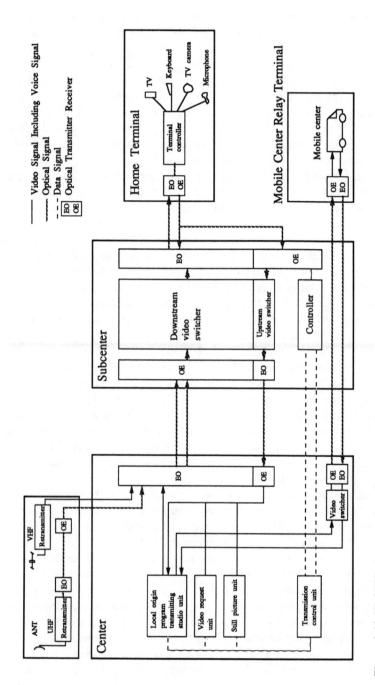

Figure 2.10 Hi-OVIS system configuration.

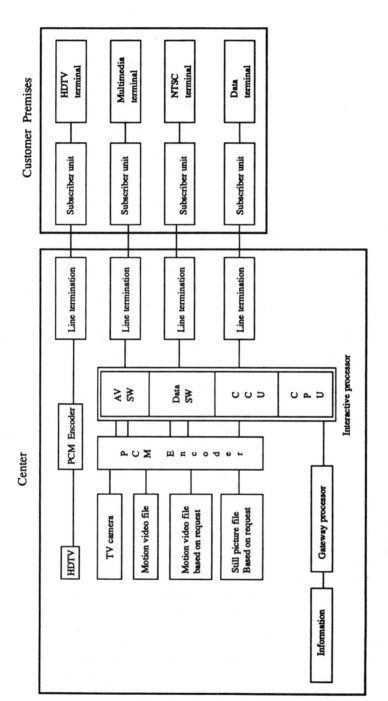

Figure 2.11 Advanced Hi-OVIS configuration.

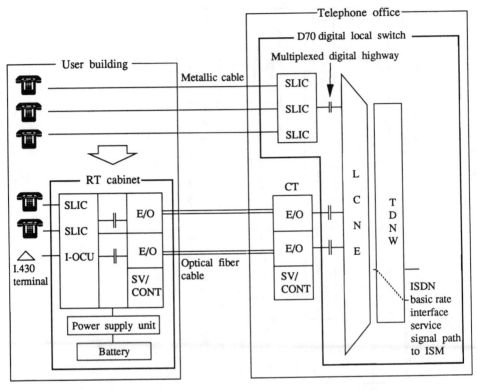

I-OCU   : ISDN Office Channel Unit
LCNE   : Line Concentration Network Equipment
SV/CONT : Supervision and Controller
ISM   : ISDN Module
SLIC   : Subscriber Line Interface Circuit

Figure 2.12 NTT's new CT/RT system configuration.

(D70). RTs are installed in user premises in metropolitan areas, or in enclosures and telephone offices in rural areas. In this system, analog telephone signals and ISDN basic rate interface service signals are mixed in the RT's interface block and transmitted to a D70 digital local switch in CT through an optical fiber. The digital switch separates the ISDN basic rate interface service signal from the analog telephone signal and processes the analog signal. The ISDN basic rate signal is sent to an *I-interface subscriber module* (ISM), where it is processed.

Two CT/RT models are available, with transmission capacities to handle either 100 or 400 subscribers, respectively. The 100-subscriber CT/RT can support a practical maximum of 112 subscribers or 24 ISDN basic rate interface services, while the 400-subscriber CT/RT can support four times that number. The transmission rate of the 100-subscriber CT/RT is set to 8.192 Mbps, and that for the 400-subscriber CT/RT is set to 32.768 Mbps.

England

Two of the most widely used optical subscriber networks in England are the *flexible access system* (FAS) and the *passive optical network* (PON). FAS is a system that multiplexes 2-Mbps unit signals up to a 140-Mbps bit rate at the subscriber's side and then transmits the multiplexed signals to the central office, where they are processed to yield the 2-Mbps signals which are then divided among the leased lines and the telephone network. The main objective of FAS is to use optical fibers to construct a network that can cope with large-scale accommodations for large-scale subscribers and to construct a reliable network while curtailing operating costs.

The PON encompasses small-scale subscribers as well. It originated as the *telephony over passive optical network* (TPON), used for telephone or data networks, and is being developed into a broadband network called *broadband passive optical network* (BPON).

TPON, first developed by British Telecom Research Laboratories (BTRL), uses a physical star/logical bus structure for the feeder or distribution network, as shown in Figure 2.13, and uses a passive splitter to distribute service signals from the central office to a multiple number of subscribers.

In the downstream direction, it transmits the subscriber's TDM signals to the remote node or the SAP using a single-mode optical fiber. There, a passive splitter is used to divide and distribute the optical signal to the corresponding subscriber. Thus, a great number of subscribers can share the same feeder or distribution network, thus reducing the quantity of optical fibers used and the number of optical transmitter/receiver modules, resulting in an economical system. The optical interface at the subscriber's side receives the signal and separates the TDM signal belonging to each subscriber.

In the upstream direction, the TDMA technique is used at the feeder and the distribution network. The information from the subscriber terminal is loaded onto the time slot preassigned to the corresponding subscriber and is then delivered to the central office. Here the synchronization signal required to perform TDMA is remotely controlled from the central office by employing a distance adjustment control. Since the signal in the downstream direction is broadcasted to every subscriber, a TPON system requires an apparatus to maintain security, and a possible solution is to employ an optical interface that allows each subscriber to access only the specified time slots.

In 1989, British Telecom (BT) performed a TPON experiment near London, as shown in Figure 2.14. It tested the possibility of the optical fiber pipeline, which

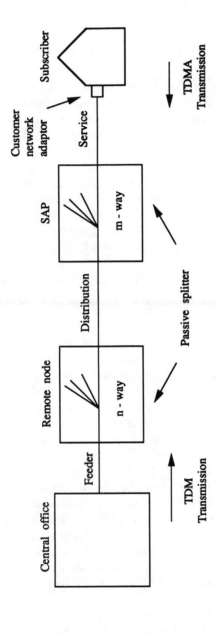

Figure 2.13 TPON architecture.

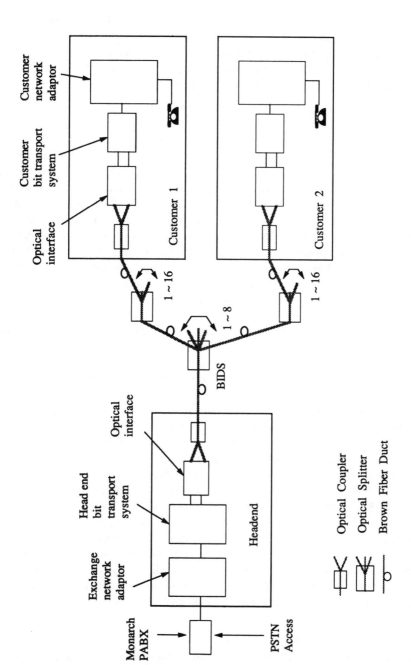

Figure 2.14 TPON demonstrator layout.

can initially provide telephone as well as low-speed data and broadband services such as TV and hi-fi stereo. The key technology employed in this system is the *broadband integrated distributed star* (BIDS) system, developed at BTRL, which allows the user to select the desired service through remote adjustment and whose structure is the star structure with switching capability.

France

France possesses Europe's most ambitious plan for an optical fiber-based integrated video communications network, which is attested by the well-known example of the Biarritz project. As the POTS systems reached saturation level (in installation numbers), a new investment opportunity was sought in the telecommunications industry, and thus the Biarritz project was instigated as an attempt to regain superiority in the new optical communication technology area. By directly linking the earth station of the broadcast satellites and the video communications network, the project attempted harmonious operation between broadcasting and telecommunication industries. Under this spirit, French *Post, Telephone, and Telegraph* (PTT) started an experiment in 1979 to test advanced optical device technologies and new broadband services under actual working environments, and a video communications network including CATV was implemented in the French resort city of Biarritz (see Figure 2.15). In this 2-Mbps network, the operating center, the distribution center, central office, and subscribers are connected in a multiple star network topology, with services for CATV and hi-fi music broadcasts provided in one direction only, and commercial voice services in both directions. Bidirectional broadband services using dedicated links is also possible.

According to the French video communications network construction plan devised in 1982, the goal was to install video communication terminals in 1.4 million households by 1985, and in 15 million households by the end of the present century. Hence, the French planned to provide cable TV, satellite broadcast, video conferencing, facsimile, videotex, telephone, and other such services by covering the entire nation in the star-configuration multipurpose optical fiber network exemplified in Figure 2.15. The implementation and technical operation of the video communications network have been entrusted to the French Telecommunications Corp. under the design guidance of the *Centre National d'Etudes des Telecommunications* (CNET).

The star configuration with bidirectional communication was used for the network topologies, and initially both the feeder network and the distribution network were to be installed with optical fiber, but cost considerations led to the replacement of the distribution network portion with coaxial cable.

Germany

The Deutsch Bundes Post (DBP) of West Germany commenced an experiment on the broadband integrated optical fiber city network, *Breitbandiges Integriertes Glasfoser Fernmelde Orts-Netz* (BIGFON) in ten regions outside of Berlin (see Figure 2.16).

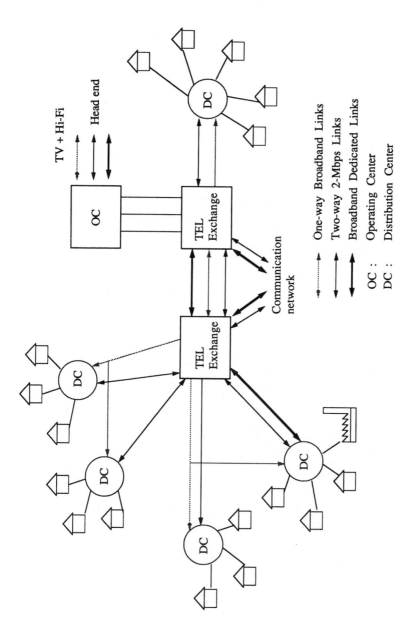

Figure 2.15 Multistar topology of the video communications network in France.

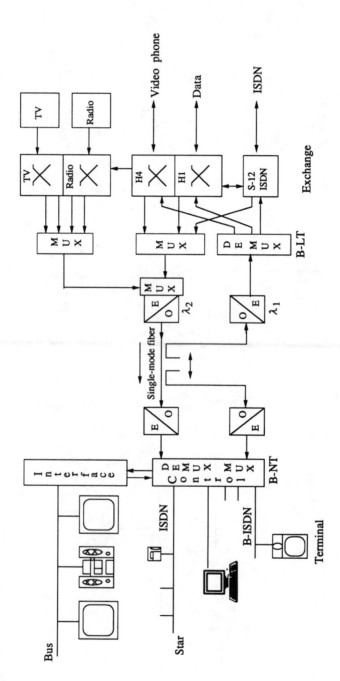

Figure 2.16 BISDN/CATV configuration in Germany.

The BIGFON project was DBP's broadband subscriber system installation plan, conceived as a part of the ISDN trial project, and it provides such distributed services as CATV and hi-fi music broadcasts, in addition to the commercial telephone, video telephone, data, and other various communication services. The motivation behind this project was to accelerate the development of optical communication systems, to support the popularization of the ISDN within West Germany, to give impetus to the development of optical devices, and to accelerate the standardization process of the integrated services of the broadband systems.

The experiment on the broadband trunk network followed under the name BIG-FERN in order to examine cost and technology performance. The high-speed broadband public network employed a mixture of optical cables and broadband switches mainly aiming for the large-scale subscribers. Coaxial cable was used for the CATV service, and existing copper cable was used for the telephone service. Such a concept began to be implemented in 1986, and a two-line optical communications network connecting 29 cities was completed by 1990. This network adopted two hierarchical topologies employing single-mode optical fiber, mesh network between trunk networks, and star configuration between trunk network and the central office. The broadband switch consists of a 2-Mbps time-division switch and a 140-Mbps space-division switch.

The Netherlands

The *totally transparent optical subscriber system* (TTOSS) shown in Figure 2.17 was proposed by Philips Research Laboratories of The Netherlands. TTOSS employs

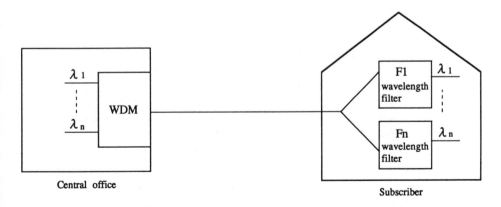

Figure 2.17 TTOSS network configuration.

the star configuration to connect the central office and the subscribers with single optical fibers.

Currently, a pair of optical fibers in each direction of transmission is used for every subscriber. But henceforth WDM will be adopted to transmit signals in both directions through just a single optical fiber by using a different wavelength in each direction of transmission. Additional services can be provided in the future without modifying the existing system simply by adding signals with a new set of wavelengths.

2.3 KEY TECHNOLOGIES FOR OPTICAL SUBSCRIBER LOOP

Optical communication technology has been significantly improved in many aspects since the early 1970s, and the application of optical fibers to almost the entire transmission spectrum is commonplace nowadays. Optical communication systems using optical fiber has numerous advantages over copper-wire communication systems. Low-loss and broadband characteristics of optical fiber can increase repeater spacing to hundreds of kilometers with channel capacity of tens of gigabits per second. Most repeater stations required under a copper-wire-based communications system can be eliminated with optical fiber systems. In addition to the inherent broadband property of optical fiber, lightwaves of different wavelengths can be simultaneously multiplexed and transmitted on a single optical fiber; thus, the number of channels or channel capacity can be increased with optical fiber installation without also increasing transmission speed. In addition, due to the thinness and the light weight of optical fiber, cable space in the cable duct can be significantly spared, which can contribute to economical construction and maintenance of the cable network. Also, optical fiber's noninductive property allows the proximity of electrical cables generating electrical inductions and offers additional advantages, such as the enhanced operator safety and quality assurance of the telecommunication services. The active progress in the development of these key technologies will facilitate the realization of the optical subscriber network's FTTH stage, rendering introduction of new services easier.

In this section, optical fiber's transmission characteristics will be examined first, then optical subscriber cables and the passive optical devices such as directional and star couplers and WDM will be introduced. They will be followed by a description of the optoelectronic ICs, which can integrate semiconductor lasers and photodiodes into electronic ICs on a single chip. Finally, principles of the optical fiber amplifier and coherent optical communications will be reviewed.

2.3.1 Optical Fiber

The optical fiber used in interoffice trunk transmission can also be used in optical subscriber network. As an aid to a more thorough understanding of the characteristics of optical communication, we will first investigate optical fiber's waveguide operation, as well as its transmission characteristics.

Propagation Principles in Optical Fiber

Optical fiber, which is a slender strand of silica, is designed so that the refractive index in the center portion is slightly greater than that of the outer portion. The center portion is called the *core*, and the outer portion is called the *cladding*.

As shown in Figure 2.18, an optical fiber can be broadly categorized into three types according to its refractive index profile and the lightwave propagation characteristics. In the *step-index multimode fiber* of Figure 2.18(a), when the light reaches a boundary between two materials such as core and cladding, each possessing a different refractive index, a part of the light is transmitted through while the rest is reflected. But when the angle that the incident light from a dense medium, such as the core, forms with the surface of the less dense medium becomes less than the critical angle, then light is totally reflected internally. This phenomenon is called *total internal reflection*, and by applying this principle, a beam of light entering the

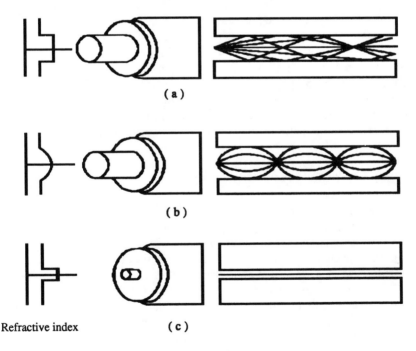

Refractive index

Figure 2.18 Light transfer types of fibers: (a) step-index multimode; (b) graded-index multimode; (c) single mode.

core portion of the optical fiber at less than the critical angle experiences total reflection at the core-cladding boundary. If optical fiber is bent abruptly, the angle that the optical path forms with the boundary may become greater than the critical angle causing light to stray to the cladding portion, resulting in increased loss.

In these step-index multimode optical fibers, the optical path difference between a straight beam of light and one that is totally reflected with the maximum reflection angle results in a proportional amount of time offset at the optical receivers; thus, transmission capacity greater than tens of megahertz-kilometers is difficult. Such a phenomenon, called *mode dispersion*, is explained in the next section.

An optical fiber designed to reduce this time offset is the graded-index multimode optical fiber, shown in Figure 2.18(b). Inside this optical fiber, the index at the core is the greatest and reduces monotonically toward the cladding, resulting in a *graded-index* (GRIN) distribution. In this arrangement, the speed of the light bent along a far path increases with decreasing index value; thus, the reflected beam of light can arrive at almost the same time as the straight beam, which increases transmission capacity by as much as a few GHz-km. CCITT has standardized the core diameter of the multimode optical fiber to 50 μm and the cladding diameter to 125 μm.

Inside the step-index or GRIN multimode fibers, hundreds of light modes with different angles of reflection can propagate along the fiber; thus, these types of fibers are called *multimode fibers*. But, as depicted in Figure 2.18(c), if the diameter of the core is reduced even further and the index disparity between the core and the cladding is also reduced, then it can be arranged in such a way that only one mode of light is supported to propagate. Such an optical fiber is called *single-mode fiber*, and in this case no time offset is generated, since there is only one mode; thus, bandwidth greater than 100 GHz-km can be obtained. CCITT has standardized the diameter of the core diameter of the single-mode fiber to around 10 μm.

Transmission Characteristics of Optical Fiber

The transmission performance of the optical fiber is characterized by transmission loss, which limits repeater spacing and transmission bandwidth, which limits maximum channel capacity. Figure 2.19 shows transmission characteristics as a function of the optical wavelength, and it can be seen that the minimum loss wavelength occurs approximately at 1.55 μm and the minimum chromatic dispersion occurs at around 1.3 μm. Let us examine transmission loss and dispersion more closely.

The light loss, which is the main source of transmission loss, can be divided into scattering loss, absorption loss, loss due to structural instability, and loss due to microbending. Scattering loss occurs when the light comes in contact with an object whose size is not much greater than the wavelength, which causes scattering of the light in all directions. This is an unavoidable loss due to a phenomenon called

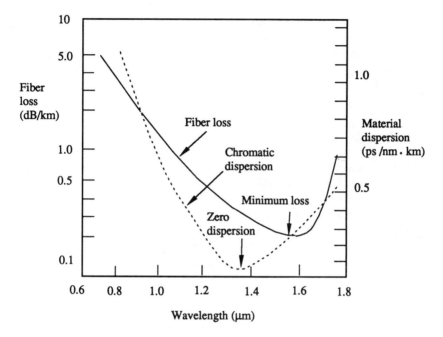

Figure 2.19 Transfer characteristics of fiber.

thermal agitation, which causes an alteration in the density and components of the optical fiber whose alteration period is less than the wavelength of light when the optical fiber solidifies during the manufacturing process.

Absorption loss is due to the phenomenon in which incident light is absorbed by the impurities and then converted to heat inside the fiber.

Also, there is loss due to instabilities in the fiber structure, such as minute fluctuations in the boundary plane between the core and the cladding, and the irregularities in the optical fiber's inner structure influence the propagation of light. Such structural instabilities can cause the optical fiber to excite mode conversion, allowing a part of the electromagnetic wave to escape outside the core, resulting in increased light loss.

Lastly, microbending loss is due to minute, periodic bending of the optical fiber's axis when irregular pressure is applied on the optical fiber's surface after the optical fiber manufacturing process. Microbending not only can cause overlap in different propagation modes of the optical fiber, but can also induce the propagation modes to disperse or radiate outside the core; thus, it must be heeded at the time of manufacture.[4]

---

[4]Considering that the transmission loss of standard coaxial cable with the lowest propagation attenuation is around the 3.5-dB/km level at 2.5 MHz, optical fiber's loss down to 0.2 dB/km at 1.0 GHz is truly remarkable.

Next, we examine optical fiber's dispersion property, which limits the transmission bandwidths of the signal. The light pulses transported as a chain of signals along the optical fiber can be distorted in shape, with their pulse width widened, and as they propagate over a long distance, this can cause adjacent pulses to overlap. This phenomenon, called *dispersion*, limits optical fiber's transmission capacity. Dispersion can be categorized into mode dispersion, chromatic dispersion, and structural dispersion, depending on the instigator.

As depicted in Figure 2.20, mode dispersion is a phenomenon arising from the different propagation times for each propagation mode. Mode dispersion occurs in multimode optical fibers, and the GRIN multimode optical fiber is an instance of the minimization of mode dispersion through the control of the core index profile.

Chromatic dispersion, which is also called material dispersion, refers to the phenomenon in which the fluctuation in the refractive index of silica (base material of optical fiber) according to the wavelengths of the propagating light enlarges the pulse width. Figure 2.21 is a depiction of the basic principle of chromatic dispersion, whose occurrence is attributable to the fact that the light emanating from the optical source has a finite linewidth spectrum rather than being a truly monochromatic wavelength.

Structural dispersion is a phenomenon in which the angle that a light ray corresponding to a given mode forms with the optical fiber's axis alters with wavelengths constituting the light due to an alteration in the structure of the optical fiber. This causes the actual length of the transmission path to change, resulting in variation in the arrival time of the light ray. Structural dispersion is not critical in multimode optical fibers, while in single-mode fibers, which are free of mode dispersions, the cross-sectional refractive index composition can be designed so that the structural dispersion cancels out the chromatic dispersion. Single-mode optical fibers manifest 3.5 ps/nm-km of chromatic dispersion at a wavelength of 1300 nm, but a new type of single-mode optical fiber has been developed whose structure manifests zero dispersion wavelength at certain wavelengths. Figures 2.22 and 2.23 represent the index distribution and dispersion characteristics of the dispersion-shifted and dispersion-flattened single-mode optical fibers, respectively, both of which show zero dispersion characteristics in the vicinity of the 1.55-μm wavelength. Since the single-mode optical fiber displays numerous desirable properties, including wider bandwidths than those of multimode fibers, it is used exclusively in long-distance transmission and broadband subscriber transmission, and it is considered to be an appropriate medium for coherent optical communication.

2.3.2 Optical Subscriber Cable

As discussed in Section 2.2, many countries around the world are adopting optical cable as new subscriber feeder cable or distribution cable to prepare for the broadband services. The design constraints of the optical subscriber cable structure are

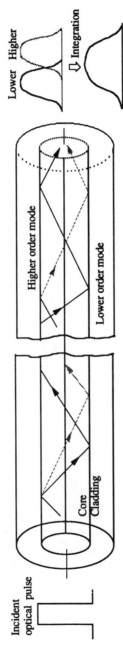

Figure 2.20 Principles of mode dispersion.

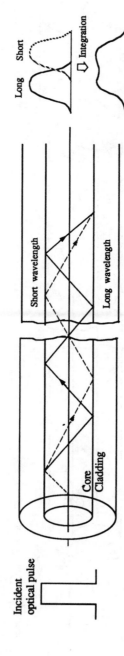

Figure 2.21 Principles of chromatic dispersion.

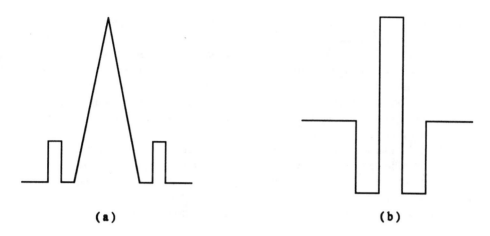

Figure 2.22 Relative index profiles of dispersion-shifted and dispersion-flattened fiber cross sections: (a) dispersion-shifted fiber; (b) dispersion-flattened fiber.

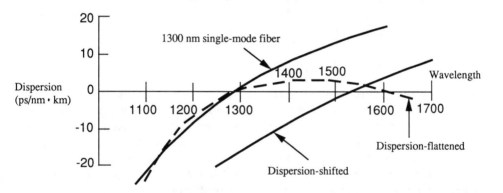

Figure 2.23 Dispersion characteristics of dispersion-shifted and dispersion-flattened single-mode fibers.

ease of connection, installation location, diversity of applications, simplicity of maintenance, and economic viability. Each of the above items must be carefully studied and examined before full-scale application. We will now examine optical cable's characteristics, structures, splicing, and connection.

Characteristics of Optical Cables

The optical fibers can be divided into single-mode optical fiber cable and multimode optical fiber cable, as discussed in Section 2.3.1. In the early field trials for the optical subscriber network, multimode optical fibers were widely used, but currently single-mode fibers are predominantly used in field tests or commercial applications. Since most subscribers are distributed within a few kilometers of the central office, multimode cables have sufficient channel capacity if just the initial services are considered. However, the almost unlimited bandwidth of single-mode cable is attractive in preparation for future expansion, since the unit price is not so different from that of the multimode cable. However, since connection or splicing is more difficult and time-consuming compared to that of multimode cables, preassembled pigtails or connectors are frequently used.

Optical cable at 1300-nm wavelength shows good cost-performance compromise in subscriber networks as well as in trunk networks, and the present technology level is considered mature. Wavelengths up to 1550 nm are considered useful for information services and WDM applications of the future. Within an optical subscriber network, if a central office needs to accommodate over one thousand subscribers, multistrand optical cables composed of more than a hundred strands of optical fibers are required. In addition, it is convenient to place remote nodes and SAPs in between the central office and the subscriber for convenient splicing and branching of subscriber cables. Also, while two-strand optical fibers should basically be provided to every subscriber, it is worthwhile to examine the possibility of the WDM accommodation for remote subscribers.

Structures of Optical Cables

Feeder cable is applied between central offices and remote nodes. It is mainly used as duct-type cable, but can be also used as aerial-type cable when required. Distribution cable, applied between the remote node and SAP, is used as duct-type and aerial-type. There is also service line cable, which is composed of one to two optical fibers. Service line cable is used to transmit signals from the SAP to the subscriber. It is connected to the transmitter/receiver module and test equipment inside the subscriber premises. In contrast to multi-fiber-optical cable, it is composed of one or two strands of doubly coated optical fibers, and it must be designed so that long-term reliability is ensured under various working conditions inside a building.

Most optical cables possess unit configuration; hence, splicing and branching are easily accomplished. The feeder cable from the central office, especially, is usually composed of more than 100 fibers, and it is anticipated to increase to more than thousand fibers in certain cases. Distribution cables and service line cables contain tens or hundreds of fibers or one to two fibers. Figure 2.24 shows typical structures of optical cables grouped with the number of fibers.

In contrast to the existing interoffice types, optical subscriber cables must be easy to handle, separable in units, and easy to manufacture in high fiber density, since they require diverse structures depending on the usage and location.

Optical cables used in optical subscriber networks are categorized into feeder-type and distribution-type cables according to their functionality and depending on

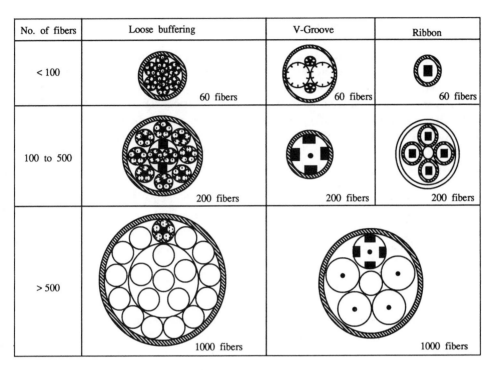

No. of fibers	Loose buffering	V-Groove	Ribbon
< 100	60 fibers	60 fibers	60 fibers
100 to 500	200 fibers	200 fibers	200 fibers
> 500	1000 fibers	1000 fibers	

Figure 2.24 Examples of subscriber loop cables with different basic elements.

the location of usage, and can be subcategorized into duct-type, aerial-type, service line-type, and indoor-type cables.

Splicing and Connection

Difficulties of single-mode subscriber cable splicing are apparent in two aspects: they use single-mode fibers instead of multimode fibers and the number of fibers in the subscriber cable is much higher than that in the trunk cable. But the difficulties associated with single-mode subscriber cable splicing appears to have been solved through such means as multifusion splicing or mechanical splicing techniques. Currently, many telephone companies use *biconic* connectors and single-fiber fusion splicing for interoffice trunk networks. Since high-density is one of the optical subscriber network's special features, quick and precise splicing are especially demanded for multiple fibers. As a way of resolving the multifiber problem, multifusion splicing and multimechanical splicing have been developed. On the other hand, it is especially desirable to use preassembled optical connectors for *optical distribution frame* (ODF) and optical transmitter/receiver modules.

2.3.3 Passive Optical Devices

Passive optical devices are being used not only in optical subscriber networks, but also in instruments, signal processing, sensors, and other optical engineering fields, and even more diverse applications are foreseen for the near future. In passive optical devices, the light signal is not converted into an electrical signal, but the light signal itself changes propagation direction depending on the wavelength, and incident light beams of different wavelengths in the same direction can be separated into different directions, or vice versa, according to the wavelengths. The passive optical devices applicable in the optical subscriber network include the optical directional coupler, star coupler, and WDM device.

The optical directional coupler and the WDM device are used between the central office and the remote office to transmit signals in both directions using just a single fiber, and the star coupler is widely used in central offices for distributing broadband signals such as video to multiple subscribers.

Optical Directional Coupler

As discussed in Section 2.2.3, optical directional couplers are widely applied for the bidirectional optical communication systems with single fiber. Directional couplers are also used for transmission line monitoring, instrument applications, and optoelectronic parts. The optical directional coupler can be divided into the half-mirror type and the distributed-mirror type, depending on the principle employed. The half-mirror type uses a semireflecting mirror to cause light to separate and diverge in two directions, while the distributed-mirror type geometrically couples the optical fiber. The latter type is widely employed in communication and instrumentation systems, as indicated in Figure 2.25. Figure 2.25(a) is a representation of the basic configuration of bidirectional communication at the same wavelength, and here the optical directional coupler's isolation capability is important.

In Figure 2.25(b), a safety device has been added to raise the reliability of the system so that if either side malfunctions communication is still possible, and in Figure 2.25(c), a directional coupler has been applied in the *optical time domain reflectometer* (OTDR). It indicates the time offset between the original light beam and that reflected at the break point, and thus can be used as a position identifier.

Star Coupler

The star coupler splits a single optical signal into several uniform signals. Figure 2.26 represents the different structures of star couplers. The mixing element

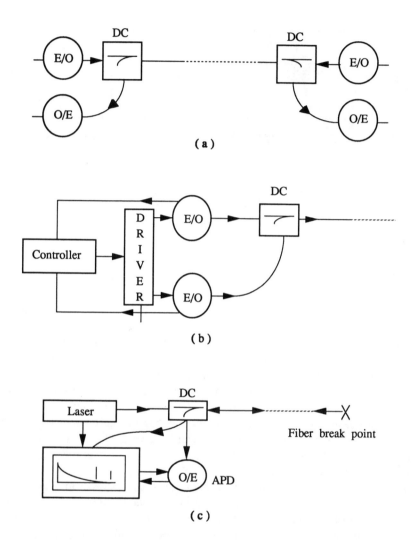

(a)

(b)

Fiber break point

(c)

DC : Directional Coupler

Figure 2.25 Applications of directional coupler: (a) one-wavelength bidirectional transmission; (b) optical sources protection circuit; (c) optical fiber break equipment.

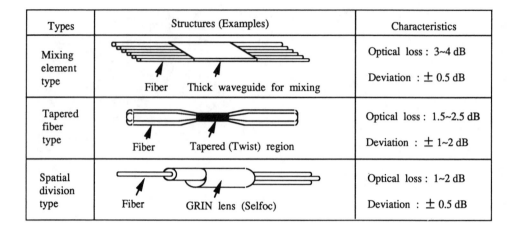

Types	Structures (Examples)	Characteristics
Mixing element type	Fiber Thick waveguide for mixing	Optical loss : 3~4 dB Deviation : ± 0.5 dB
Tapered fiber type	Fiber Tapered (Twist) region	Optical loss : 1.5~2.5 dB Deviation : ± 1~2 dB
Spatial division type	Fiber GRIN lens (Selfoc)	Optical loss : 1~2 dB Deviation : ± 0.5 dB

Figure 2.26 Structures and characteristics of star couplers.

type relies on internal optical multiple reflection to equalize the divided optical output.

In the tapered fiber type, a bundle of optical fibers is stretched thin under heat so that a lightwave propagating inside the core becomes radiated and split into the cladding, and resumes its course inside the adjacent fiber's core. In the spatial-division type, the GRIN lens splits the light into spatially separated optical fibers. This technique has optical splitting loss, and the maximum possible number of split outputs is limited to about four. In contrast, the number for the tapered type is around ten, and that for the mixing element type can be greater than ten. The respective optical losses are as listed in Figure 2.26, and it can be seen that the spatial-division type is superior in this respect.

A typical application is the optical database system shown in Figure 2.27, in which a star coupler is employed to enable simultaneous communication among a multiple number of terminals. The star coupler is suitable in any system that requires a division of the optical signal among an unspecified number of terminals.

Optical Wavelength Division Multiplexer

Silica optical fiber manifests extremely low loss in the wide-wavelength range from 0.8 to 1.6 μm, and this low-loss wavelength band can be used to simultaneously transmit a multiple number of optical signals on different wavelengths through a single optical fiber. Two indispensable components of WDM transmission are the wavelength division multiplexer, which multiplexes several signals with different

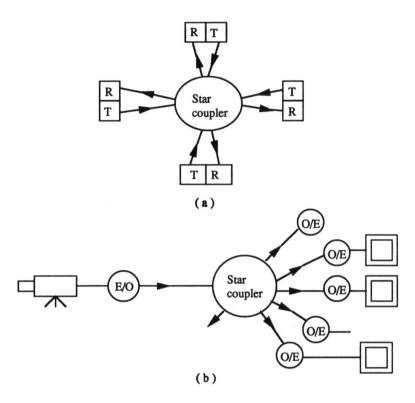

Figure 2.27 Applications of star coupler: (a) optical database system; (b) TV signal distribution system.

wavelengths onto a single optical fiber, and the wavelength division demultiplexer, which performs the reverse function.

Figure 2.28 shows three examples of possible WDM implementations. In Figure 2.28(a), a high-pass (short-wavelength) filter and a low-pass (long-wavelength) filter are used to separate a light into its respective wavelength components. In Figure 2.28(b), parallel beams of light are passed through a diffraction grating, and different directions of diffracted light corresponding to each wavelength are used to separate beams. As shown in Figure 2.28(c), with a prism, the light's angle of refraction varies according to wavelength, which allows multiplexing or demultiplexing.

2.3.4 Semiconductor Laser

Ever since the continuous oscillation of a GaAlAs semiconductor laser at room temperature was first reported in 1970, the semiconductor laser has been the most widely

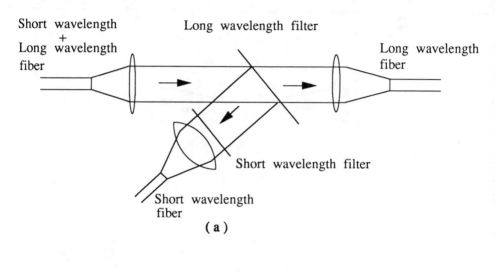

Short wavelength
+
Long wavelength
fiber

Long wavelength filter

Long wavelength
fiber

Short wavelength filter

Short wavelength
fiber

(a)

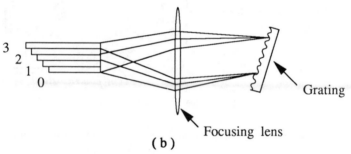

3
2
1
0

Grating

Focusing lens

(b)

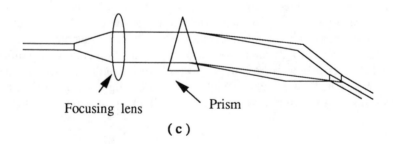

Focusing lens

Prism

(c)

Figure 2.28 WDM device structure: (a) filter type; (b) grating type; (c) prism type.

used light source for optical communications and optical information processing applications.

Without the invention of the semiconductor laser, the present optical fiber communication would not have been possible. Since the low-loss wavelength band of optical fiber is at the wavelength region of 1.1 to 1.6 μm, shown in Figure 5.25, the development of the InGaAsP lasers at these wavelengths has replaced the GaAlAs laser diode whose wavelength is around 0.8 μm.

Compared to other types of lasers, semiconductor lasers have high electrical-to-optical power conversion efficiency, can be modulated easily to higher speeds, and are extremely convenient due to their very small size. Also, depending on the material and design, the light-emitting wavelength can be chosen anywhere from visible to far infrared regions, and more than ten years of lifetime can be attained.

In this section, operating principles and structures of the semiconductor laser will be described, followed by a summary of the recent advances.

Operating Principles

GaAs and InP possess a direct transition energy band structure that is suitable for emitting light. Electrical current flows when a voltage is applied in the forward direction across the *pn* junction of these semiconductors. The electrons from the *n*-region and the holes from the *p*-region, respectively, migrate to opposite sides, and light is emitted as they recombine in the neighborhood of the *pn* junction.

In case the electrical current is lower than the threshold, the recombination of electrons and holes occurs in a random manner. Hence, there is no correlation in phase, wavelength, or direction among the radiations, and thus the stimulated emission prerequisite for laser action cannot be accomplished. But, if the pumping current is increased to a certain level called the *threshold level*, then population inversion is accomplished in the neighborhood of the *pn* junction as shown in Figure 2.29. Population inversion is a state where more electrons exist at the high energy level than at the low energy level. In this state, light is released in a controlled manner proportional to the rate of recombination. Here, the region at which the controlled release of light due to recombination occurs is called the *active* or *gain region*. Laser light is emitted if the gain obtained from the stimulated emission is greater than the loss of the resonator. The threshold current is an important parameter for the evaluation of the performance and operating conditions of lasers.

Let us try to think of an efficient semiconductor laser structure that will result in a low associated threshold current. In case the recombination of carriers (where carrier implies electrons and holes) occurs at a region where no population inversion has been formed (thus, outside the gain region), light emitted in this manner does not contribute to the stimulated emission of light. Consequently, if an energy level barrier is used to trap the carriers inside the gain region, then recombination for

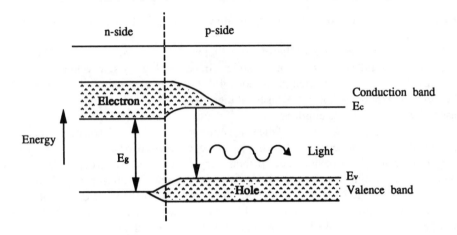

Figure 2.29 Principles of light emission in semiconductor lasers.

emission only occurs within the gain region, resulting in high efficiency or low threshold current. Furthermore, due to the amplification phenomenon based on light's stimulated interaction in the laser, more effective emission can be expected if the stimulated light is optically confined in the amplification region.

Figure 2.30 is a representation of a *double heterostructure* (DH) for a GaAlAs/ GaAs laser or InGaAsP/InP laser in which carriers are concentrated inside a specific intrinsic region. As shown in the figure, the GaAs active region at which emission occurs is located between the *n*-type InP, the *p*-type InP, and the *p*-type GaAlAs, with the 0.1-μm-thick active region and the 2- to 3-μm-thick cladding region. In order to induce a flow of current, a metal electrode is coated onto the laser's uppermost part and the lower part of the crystal substrate, and an insulating oxidation layer is grown between the metal electrode and the semiconductor region so that the flow of current is confined inside a portion shaped as a narrow stripe.

Generally, a junction between two different types of crystals is called a *heterojunction*. In a DH, active-region InGaAsP, which has a low energy gap, is wrapped with the cladding region InP, which has a high energy gap. In a laser with a DH, one of the heterojunctions is electrically a simple diode. If a forward current flows through the diodes, the carriers at the cladding regions are injected into the active region. Since the band gap of the active region is low, as shown in Figure 2.30, energy barriers form at both boundaries between the active region and the cladding regions, which has the effect of trapping the injected carriers. Consequently, the carrier concentration inside the thin active region becomes greatly increased, and the majority of the emission recombination now occurs inside the active region. Also, the refractive index of the GaAs that forms the active region is greater than that of the GaAlAs that forms the cladding region, and since light has the property of being

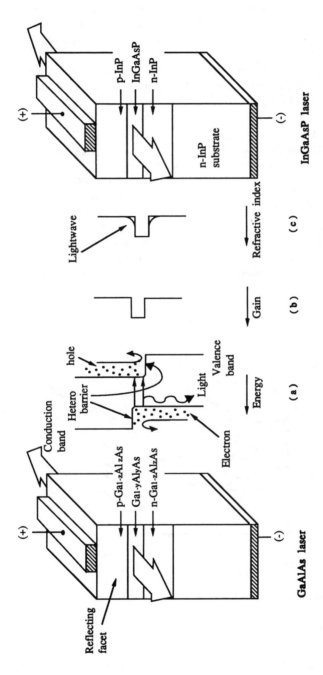

Figure 2.30 Structure of a double heterostructure semiconductor laser: (a) energy band; (b) gain distribution; (c) refractive index distribution.

drawn to a region with a high refractive index, light in the DH tends to be confined in the direction of the active region. Consequently, the concentrations of both the carriers and the lightwaves are increased substantially; thus, threshold current can be lowered accordingly.

Furthermore, if the carriers and lightwaves are bound inside the narrow width of the active region in a direction perpendicular to the growth region, then the threshold current can be reduced even more. This can be achieved by creating the metal electrode in the shape of a narrow stripe, as shown in Figure 2.30, in order to spatially control the flow of current. Such a structure is called the *striped heterostructure*. Since the light is guided to the gain region with a high carrier concentration, it is also called the *gain-guided heterostructure*.

Another way to confine the lightwaves in the direction parallel to the growth region is the buried DH illustrated in Figure 2.31. In the buried DH, the GaAs is surrounded in all directions by the GaAlAs, which has low refractive index, as was mentioned above, and it effectively forms a waveguide. Such a structure is called index-guided *buried heterostructure* (BH), which has the advantage of even lower associated threshold current. Compared to the gain-guided type, BH's characteristics are more stable; thus, it is used most effectively for telecommunications and information processing applications.

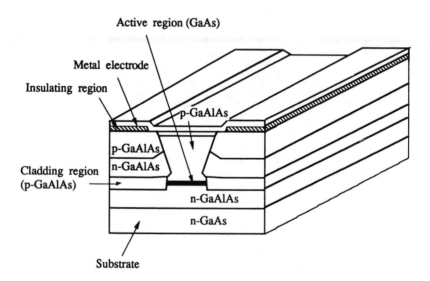

Figure 2.31 Semiconductor laser with buried DH.

Operation Characteristics

Figure 2.32 is a representation of the current-optical power characteristics of a semiconductor laser, and such a curve is called the *I-L characteristics curve*, where *I*

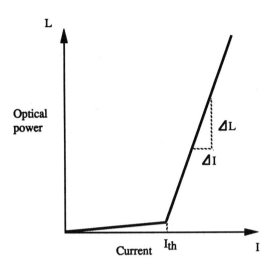

Figure 2.32 *I-L* characteristics of semiconductor lasers.

denotes current, and *L* the optical power. The optical power increases abruptly when the current is just beyond the threshold (I_{th}) level, and the region beyond I_{th} is the laser light emission region. The threshold current for the GaAlAs laser at 0.8 μm wavelength or the InGaAsP laser at the wavelength band of 1.1 to 1.6 μm is about 20 to 100 mA at room temperature. The bias voltage applied is usually around 1V to 2V.

As shown in the figure, optical power increases with increasing input current; hence, optical power greater than 10 mW can easily be obtained. But to ensure extended lifetime and stability of the transverse mode, the optical power around 5 mW is typically used.

The slope of the *I-L* characteristic curve in Figure 2.32 is called the *external differential quantum efficiency*, which is defined as

$$\eta_d = \frac{\text{increase in the externally emitted photon number}}{\text{increase in the input current}}$$

$$= A\lambda \frac{\Delta L \ (mW)}{\Delta I(mA)} \tag{2.1}$$

where

$$A\lambda = e/h\nu$$
$$= \begin{matrix} 0.69, \text{ when } \lambda = 0.85 \ \mu\text{m (GaAlAs laser)} \\ 1.05, \text{ when } \lambda = 1.3 \ \mu\text{m (InGaAsP laser)} \end{matrix} \tag{2.2}$$

with η_d = 30% to 50% at room temperature.

Between the threshold current of the laser diode and the temperature T_j of the emission region, the following relationship is established:

$$I_{th}(T_j) = T_0 \exp(T_j/T_0) \tag{2.3}$$

where T_0 is the characteristic temperature. If T_0 is high, the threshold current's dependence on temperature is low and laser emission at high temperatures is possible. In GaAlAs lasers, T_0 ranges from 100K to 150K, but in InGaAsP lasers, T_0 is only around 70K. Because of this, it is difficult to operate InGaAsP lasers at high temperatures, in contrast to the GaAlAs lasers.

Recent Advances

The early semiconductor lasers were of the GaAlAs/GaAs family, operated at 0.85 μm wavelength. However, silica fibers have shown dramatically lower loss and higher bandwidth at 1.2 μm to 1.6 μm wavelengths, and, accordingly, current semiconductor (such as InGaAsP/InP) lasers are operated at 1.2 μm to 1.6 μm. Besides the changes in the material used, variations in the structures of the growth layer and the electrode have led to the improvements in the laser diode characteristics for optical communication applications. An example is the *distributed feedback-laser diode* (DFB-LD) with longitudinal single-mode operation. Its narrow spectrum light can reduce the chromatic dispersion of the optical fiber; hence, the single-mode laser diode will be widely used in upcoming broadband optical communication systems. As shown in Figure 2.33, the cladding region of the DFB-LD is structured as a diffraction grating functioning as a distributed filter that screens only single-mode light with a narrow spectrum width. Also, the wavelength of the output light can be precisely adjusted by varying the periodic spacing of the diffraction grating at the time of manufacture. This control over the wavelength makes the DFB-LD extremely suitable for high-density WDM and coherent optical communications.

2.3.5 Optoelectronic Integrated Circuit

Since optical transmission speeds of tens of gigahertz are demanded along the optical fiber, efforts have been made recently to improve the performance of the optical devices and electrical circuits at such speeds. As a means of increasing the device speeds by reducing the size of the devices and the influence of external conditions on its performance, as well as to reduce costs and enhance reliability, *optoelectronic integrated circuit* (OEIC) technology, which integrates both optical devices and electrical circuits onto a single chip, has emerged. OEIC can reduce parasitic reactances

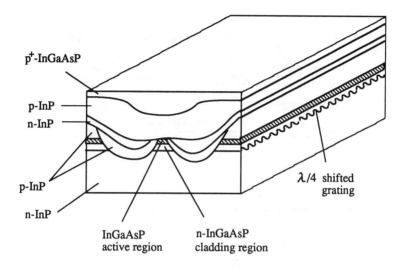

p⁺-InGaAsP

p-InP

n-InP

p-InP

n-InP

λ/4 shifted grating

InGaAsP active region

n-InGaAsP cladding region

Figure 2.33 Structure of DFB-LD.

and has low operation noise, and is thus useful for optical fiber submarine communication systems, which require high-speed laser diode modulation and high receiver sensitivity at the modulation speeds, and for the optical subscriber systems, which require low cost and enhanced reliability.

The OEIC employed for optical communication systems can be divided into GaAs-based and InP-based OEICs, depending on the substrate used. The GaAs-based OEIC uses GaAs to produce the substrate and is used in short-wavelength (0.8 μm to 0.9 μm) systems, and the InP-based OEIC, which uses an InP substrate, is used in long-wavelength (1.2 μm to 1.6 μm) systems.

Currently, the GaAs-based OEIC technology has sufficiently matured by adapting existing *field-effect transistors* (FET) or *metal semiconductor FETs* (MESFET), so that, as shown in Figure 2.34, its integration density is higher than that of the InP OEIC. Consequently, it is employed for short-distance high-speed transmission applications such as subscriber loop, CATV network, and optical LAN, as well as computer networks requiring low associated cost and able to fully realize the benefits of high integration density. InP-based OEICs, shown in Figure 2.35, are more appropriate as high-speed transmission devices because the long wavelength matches the fiber characteristics. The optical device technology using InP has already reached a stable stage, and electrical devices such as the *junction FET* (JFET), *metal-insulator semiconductor FET* (MISFET), and *heterojunction bipolar transistor* (HBT) using InP have been successfully fabricated. But the performance of OEIC is still inferior to the combined one of separate optical and electrical devices.

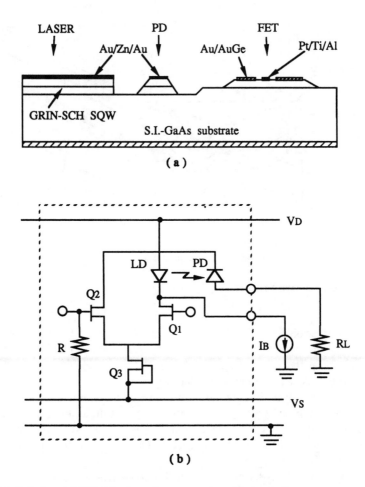

Figure 2.34 GaAs-based OEIC: (a) schematic cross section; (b) circuit diagram.

2.3.6 Optical Amplifier

As a means of coping with the limitation of repeater spacings due to losses and dispersion of optical fibers, and with the restrictions in the number of WDM channels or optical couplers, it is desirable to have purely optical amplifiers, which amplify the optical signal without an electrical conversion.

Depending on how the amplification is achieved, optical amplifiers can be divided into semiconductor laser amplifier and optical fiber amplifier. The semiconductor laser amplifier is produced by applying a nonreflective coating with a quarter-wavelength thickness to both facets of a common laser diode using such materials

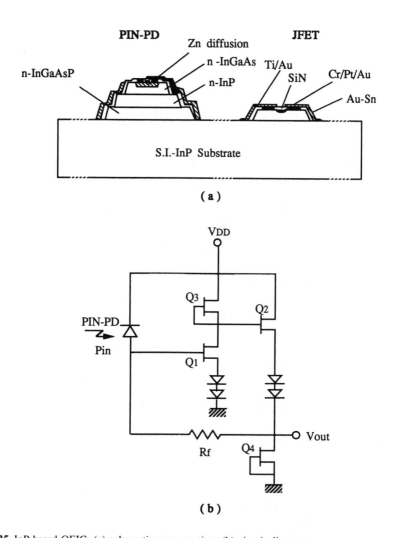

Figure 2.35 InP-based OEIC: (a) schematic cross section; (b) circuit diagram.

as SiO_2, ZrO_2, and Eu_2O_3. This coating causes the threshold current of the laser diode to increase by 1.5 to 1.6 times. If a pumping current slightly lower than the threshold current is supplied to the laser diode amplifier, then light incident only upon the coated facet of the laser diode amplifier is amplified without lasing. Such semiconductor laser amplifiers are used in optical switching systems.

Optical fibers can also achieve direct amplification without converting a light signal into its electrical equivalent by doping with a special material called *erbium*. Erbium-doped fiber can amplify a weak light signal if pumped with a laser. Since these optical fiber amplifiers can amplify light signals without any complicated equipment, they are useful for nonrepeater long-distance communication such as transoceanic undersea optical cables and for the multicasting of general optical subscriber systems or optical CATV systems. While optical fiber amplifiers have greater gain and can also amplify independently of polarized states of light as compared to the semiconductor laser amplifiers, they are difficult to integrate on a single chip, and the pumping light is hard to separate.

2.3.7 Coherent Optical Communication

In existing optical communications, the high frequency (around 200 THz) of lightwave is used as a carrier, but the wide frequency bandwidth is not fully utilized for information transfer. That is, existing optical communication is an intensity modulation/direct detection method that simply turns the source on and off according to the input signal, so the phase portion of the lightwave cannot be used for carrying effective information (see Figure 2.36(a)). In contrast, coherent optical communication fully exploits wave characteristics of the lightwave for information transfer and has the advantage of having high receiving sensitivity and frequency selectivity. Accordingly, it further increases repeater spacing and makes high-density WDM possible, and it has a tremendous transmission capacity at the terabit-per-second class, and hence, is considered the future optical communication technology.

Coherent optical systems can find potential application in unrepeated long-haul transmission as well as in multichannel subscriber loop systems for video distribution and broadband LAN. Figure 2.37 shows the application area of coherent optical communication. In this section, the basic principle and recent progresses are reviewed.

The basic principle of coherent optical communication is as depicted in Figure 2.38(b). The transmitter modulates input signals using *amplitude shift keying* (ASK), *frequency shift keying* (FSK), or *phase shift keying* (PSK) (see Figure 2.39) to a carrier lightwave with a very narrow frequency linewidth. The optical signal transferred along the optical fiber is heterodyne-mixed with light received from a separate local oscillation light source and is then converted into an electrical signal by way of an optical detector.

Therefore, electrical output from the optical detector is manifested as an *intermediate frequency* (IF) band signal, which is the frequency difference component of the carrier lightwave and local lightwave. In mathematical expressions, the received signal field E_S and the local oscillator field E_{LO} are, respectively,

$$E_s = P_s \exp[j(\omega_s t + \phi(t))] \tag{2.4}$$

and

$$E_{LO} = P_{LO} \exp[j\omega_{LO}t] \tag{2.5}$$

where P_S and P_{LO}, respectively, denote the received and local oscillated signal power.

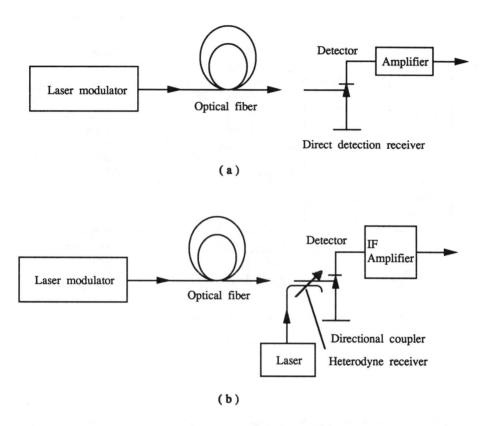

Figure 2.36 Intensity modulation/direct detection and coherent detection methods: (a) intensity modulation/direct method; (b) coherent detection method.

Since the optical detector detects only the intensity of the input electromagnetic wave, the detector output current $i(t)$ has the expression

$$i(t) = R_0(E_S + E_{LO})(E_S + E_{LO})^*$$
$$= R_0\{P_S + P_{LO} + 2P_S P_{LO} \cos[(\omega_S - \omega_{LO})t + \phi(t)]\} \quad (2.7)$$

where R_0 is the responsivity of a detector.

Therefore, the signal current i_S is

$$i_S = 2R_0 P_S P_{LO} \cos[\omega_{IF} + \phi(t)] \quad (2.8)$$

where $\omega_{IF} = \omega_s - \omega_{LO}$.

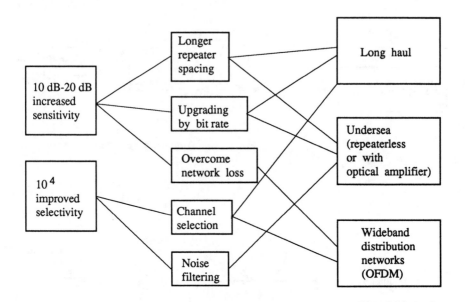

Figure 2.37 Application area of coherent optical communication.

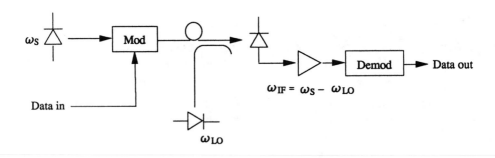

$$\omega_{IF} = \omega_S - \omega_{LO}$$

o Optical Modulation

- ASK
- FSK
- PSK

o Optical Demodulation

- Heterodyne ($\omega_S \neq \omega_{LO}$)
- Homodyne ($\omega_S = \omega_{LO}$)

Figure 2.38 Basic principle of coherent optical communication.

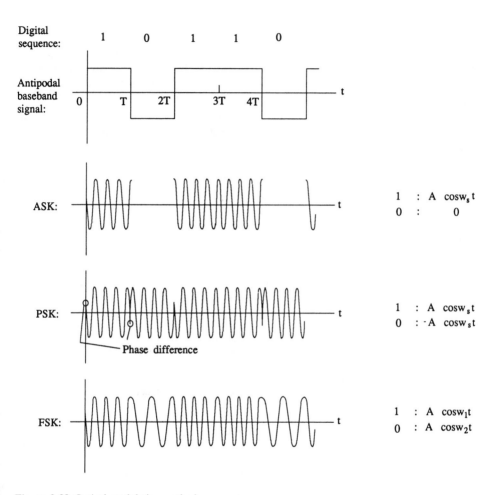

Figure 2.39 Optical modulation methods.

In such coherent optical communication, the primary factor influencing communication quality is the phase noise of the light source. Phase noise is related to frequency linewidth, and in order to minimize it, the linewidth of the laser diode used for the light source should be as small as 0.1 to 0.0001 times the bit rate. This coherent method can increase receiving sensitivity by more than 10 to 15 dB over that of the existing intensity modulation/direct detection, and since it can accommodate the information of many channels by changing the frequency of the local oscillator, optical FDM becomes possible. Employment of optical FDM enables high-volume distribution of video, as well as high-bit-rate data that can supply about 100 channels simultaneously to 1000 subscribers per system, and facilitates channel expansion. From the subscriber's point of view, channels can be easily selected via an optical tuner, as in the case of a radio broadcast system. Bidirectional services such as video telephone are also possible. For multichannel transmission technology employing coherent optical communication, there has been a test of 400 Mbps × 16 channels by FSK modulation, and the increase in the number of channels is not a big problem in principle.

In relation to this, various field tests (see Table 2.3) are in progress in the United States and Japan, and such coherent multichannel transmission technology is moving up from the basic research stage to the commercial feasibility test stage.

Table 2.3
Optical FDM Transmission Field Test (Examples)

Country	Company	Contents	Features
U.S.	AT&T	4 wavelengths, 6.8 Gbps, noncoherent FSK method, 70-km transmission	Uses two fiber amplifiers
	AT&T	Field test 1.7 ~ 2.5 GbPs, FSK method 419-km transmission Field test	Uses fiber amplifiers Roaring Creek Station-Sunbury Hub, Pennsylvania Operation test for one month
England	BTRL	2 wavelengths, 622 Mbps, DPSK, FSK method, 200-km transmission Field test	Uses two fiber amplifiers Edinburgh-Newcastle
Japan	NTT	2 channels, 2.5 Gbps, 450-km transmission Field test	Uses fiber amplifier Undersea transmission between Hiroshima and Oita
	NTT	100 channels optical FDM, 50-km transmission FSK modulation/direct detection method	Uses Mach-Zehnder filter Uses wideband channel space controller
	NEC	4 channels, 2.5 Gbps, 150-km transmission, CPFSK modulation	

2.4 Evolution Toward BISDN

As with any major infrastructures, development of a communications network necessarily extends over a very long time frame. Network evolution is a never-ending process, always characterized by mutual coexistence of older systems and new systems. Migration to the BISDN is no exception; development scenarios that give careful consideration to how the BISDN will interwork with existing systems are absolutely essential. As we will see from the three respective migration scenarios of NTT, Alcatel, and Korea Telecom in subsequent sections, the common aspects can be described as follows.

Through the first half of the 1990s, the main emphasis will be on business customers and on deploying fiber to reach these customers, and this stage is called FTTO. This will serve as a platform to begin providing cost-effective, anticipated high-speed ATM services by means of statistical multiplexing, albeit on a limited basis.

In this century, ATM technology will be introduced into the public network to transport high-speed data and video, thus signaling the onset of full BISDN availability. Meanwhile, advanced connection services to support personal communications will have been developed, so ATM will be applied to interoffice signaling within the network to realize a substantial increase in throughput between network databases and central offices. This will be operated through incorporation in the user information transport network. It is likely that the existing narrowband transmission portion of the network will be converted over to large-capacity ATM transmission at this stage.

By about 2015, fiber will begin to be extensively deployed into residential subscriber loops to at last realize FTTH. By this time, ATM will be firmly established as the basis of the BISDN. It is readily conceivable that advances in coherent lightwave-based integrated photonic technologies may result in an even more sophisticated network at this time.

2.4.1 NTT's Evolution Scenario

NTT's policy of establishing the fiber-optic infrastructure stands on NTT's service vision for the BISDN: *visual, intelligent, and personal* (VI&P) services. NTT was seeking what it termed "development partners" for a far-reaching broadband ISDN project integrating voice, data, and video over the Japanese telephone network. Northern Telecom, along with Fujitsu, Hitachi, NEC, Oki, and Toshiba, was selected to develop an ATM node system for ATM call switching. AT&T and Siemens, along with Fujitsu, Hitachi, Mitsubishi, and NEC, will develop an ATM link system that will allow cell-multiplexed transmission over loop and trunk lines using ATM technology. In this section, an overview of NTT's scenario for the evolution of conventional subscriber networks to optical subscriber networks is presented.

FTTO—The First Stage

FTTO is now being expanded to large office buildings in the business centers of large cities. The principal targets for deploying FTTO are newly constructed buildings. But the deployment of FTTO even to existing buildings is important because of its cost effectiveness when considering the congestion of ducts and the renovation of old metallic cables. The RT system, which can offer even low-speed services efficiently, is being employed. The RT system already has more cost advantages than the metallic system in coastal redevelopment business areas and newly developed resort areas. Similarly, optical fibers are being deployed to office buildings and apartment houses with the cost decrease. Thus, the gradual expansion of FTTO to medium- and small-sized buildings is needed as a next step. In the immediate future, FTTO will be developed mainly for low-speed services because of the clear demand for such services.

FTTZ—The Second Stage

In nonbusiness areas, ordinary homes are the main users. However, at present, there is neither a concrete image of nor an actual need for new services, which would require the extension of optical fibers to homes (FTTH). In addition, optical transmission systems for FTTH are currently more expensive than conventional metallic systems for POTS or the NISDN. This is the reason why NTT plans to promote *fiber to the zone* (FTTZ). Here "zone" means the area covered by the RT system. It ranges from an area of about 1000 subscriber lines to an area of a few dozen lines. Under FTTZ, users and the end of the RT system are connected by metallic cables, as shown in Figure 2.40. If an RT system with small capacity can be economically implemented, optical fiber can be extended in close vicinity to users.

FTTH—The Last Stage

In the previous stage, FTTZ, the network facilities between the RT system and users are metallic. The question is how these metallic networks are converted to optical fibers (FTTH). The shift from FTTZ to FTTH is dependent on the demand for high-speed/broadband services (especially the need for conversational bidirectional services), not just unidirectional services such as CATV. Since this demand will be sporadic, it will be difficult to meet it individually from the standpoint of infrastructure availability and speed. Therefore, the most desirable approach is to promote FTTZ and extend optical fibers to users who demand high-speed/broadband services.

2.4.2 Alcatel's Evolution Approach

The Alcatel's fiber-in-the-loop approach for small businesses and residential subscribers is based on a PON architecture as shown in Figure 2.41. Since a single fiber is optically split into several directions to serve several subscribers or groups of subscribers, the PON leads to a significant cost advantage over a full star architecture

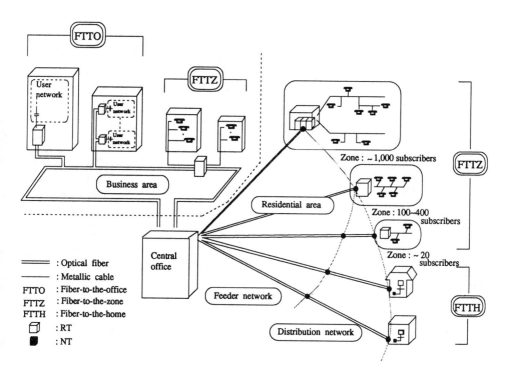

Figure 2.40 Optical fiber subscriber network configuration.

and allows future upgrade to a full star architecture by adding optical cables in existing ducts, with no civil work investment.

With the PON architecture, FTTO and *fiber-to-the-building* (FTTB) configuration are available for small business subscribers. Here the *optical network termination* (ONT) is installed on the subscriber premises or in the basement of the building. Up to 32 ONTs connected to a single fiber tree share the payload available in the tree. Network capacity may be upgraded in a second phase, either by expanding the system capacity with no change to the cable plant or eventually by upgrading the network to a star architecture if demand justifies it.

FTTB or FTTC configurations are available for residential subscribers through the same approach. In these configurations, the ONT is shared by all subscribers of a building (in the case of multifamily housing) or by all subscribers located near the curb (in the case of single-family housing). Subscribers and ONT are connected by passive copper drops. Although the long-term goal is FTTH in which an ONT is dedicated to a single subscriber, such an approach is considered uneconomical for residential subscribers before the second half of the decade, and FTTB or FTTC will be the only cost-effective solution for the short/medium term, allowing sharing of the system and the associated optoelectronic components by several subscribers.

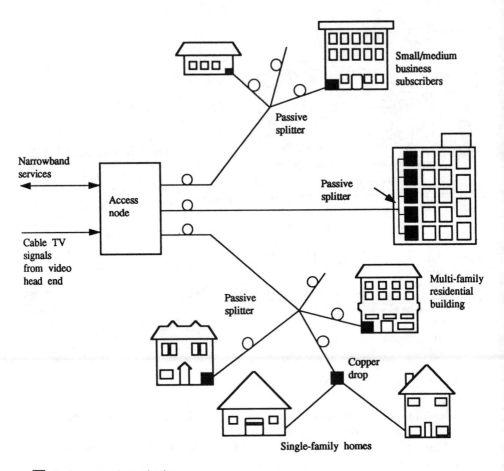

Optical network termination

Figure 2.41 Alcatel's fiber-in-the-loop approach.

FTTB or FTTC configurations will be upgraded to FTTH in the long term as the demand for high-speed and broadband services justifies it. This can be implemented by adding optical cables to existing ducts and installing drop fibers on the subscriber premises.

2.4.3 Korea Telecom's Evolution Strategy

Considering the disparities in communication environments in different countries, Korea Telecom is planning an economically viable strategy for the development of an optical subscriber network to meet the respective subscriber demands and requirements in Korea. Korea Telecom intends to expand an optical subscriber network through the following outlined steps.

Initial Deployment

In the initial stage, a priority is given to the large-volume business subscribers, who are expected to be major customers for high-speed broadband communication, and to the residential subscribers of new apartments who will potentially require multi-channel communication circuits. In the case of large-volume subscribers, such a platform allows easy accommodation of new demands for high-speed services and any upgrades, resolves serious duct saturation problems, and facilitates the provision of integrated connections, thus fully executing the role of an infrastructure for business subscribers. In the case of new apartments, since deployment of optical subscriber lines is sufficiently cost-effective relative to the copper subscriber lines, a future expansion of high-speed large-capacity services can be anticipated, thus eventually carrying out the role of an infrastructure required for the BISDN. Future CATV services will also be provided through such optical subscriber links, paving the path also for the integration of communication and broadcasting. For the optical subscriber network structure, the FTTO configuration will be constructed, resulting in the installation of RTs in large buildings and new apartments, the establishment of a *central office terminal* (COT) inside the central office, and the accommodation of large-scale demands through the optical cables deployed in between. A system implementing the FTTO is planned to be in operation by the year 1992, and, initially, services such as POTS, NISDN, leased line, and CATV will be provided.

Second Stage

The second stage is scheduled to commence in 1997. By this time, the associated broadband communication technologies would have sufficiently matured, and numerous demands for various broadband services are anticipated from the heavily populated residential areas and small-volume business subscribers. Therefore, when the existing copper wires are replaced by optical fibers, in order to replace the final subscriber links with optical fibers, the ONU will be installed as far as the vicinity of buildings and homes, accommodating an appropriate number of subscribers and traffic. Consequently, the optical cables that connect the COT inside the central office with the RT and the ONU, from which either the copper wires or coaxial cables accommodate subscribers, thus constructing the FTTC. In the FTTC configuration, the splitter can be installed on an optional basis between the RT and the ONU, and various configurations are possible depending on the position of the splitter. Figure 2.42 is an example of a FTTC that is configured without a splitter. Services to be

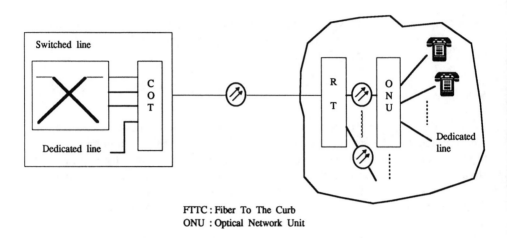

FTTC : Fiber To The Curb
ONU : Optical Network Unit

Figure 2.42 Korea Telecom's FTTC.

provided in the second stage include voice, data, G4 facsimile, image communication, and CATV.

Further Evolution

In the last stage, there will be a rapid increase in the number of high-speed large-capacity services for general residential subscribers, in step with the raised demand for the provision of such services as POTS, hi-fi music broadcasting, bidirectional video, video communication, and multimedia communication. By this time, the entire subscriber loop will have been replaced with optical fibers, deploying a single optical cable in each home. In addition, optical subscriber access equipment (ONU) will be installed on every subscriber premises, connecting optical cable from the COT inside the central office to the ONU within each household, thus constructing the FTTH suitable for ultra-high-speed large-capacity information transmission.

The final FTTH is predicted to become universal beginning with the year 2015. FTTH can secure sufficient bandwidth for each subscriber, and with its purely optical fiber composition has the advantage of simplifying OAM functions. Korea Telecom plans to connect the COT and the RTs installed in the central office in a ring structure, which has the advantage of being self-healing if a double ring structure is used to perform the path protection function. The RT, SAP, and ONU inside the subscriber premises are connected by optical cables and adopt a double star structure. This configuration is to be used as the PON structure. Transmission between the central office and the subscriber access point will be achieved through the ATM-based cells inside the STM envelope, which will gradually convert into purer forms of ATM transmission, until ATM is finally adopted in the full-scale BISDN.

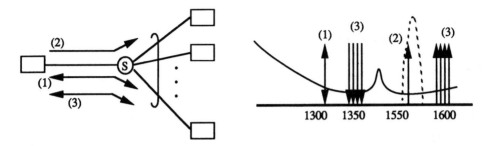

Figure 2.43 Wavelength spectrum for BISDN.

In addition, the use of a 1300-nm wavelength band (see (1) in Figure 2.43) TDM for bidirectional communication and a 1550-nm wavelength band (2) FDM for CATV, both inside a single optical fiber, is currently being reviewed for the BISDN. Dense WDM is expected to be used in the 1350-nm and 1600-nm wavelength bands (3) as demand for new services increases.

SELECT BIBLIOGRAPHY

Andrews, F. T., "The Evolution of Digital Loop Carrier," *IEEE Commun. Mag.*, March 1991, pp. 31–35.

Asatani, K., "Lightwave Subscriber Loop Systems Toward Broadband ISDN," *IEEE J. of Lightwave Tech.*, Vol. 7, No. 11, 1989.

Balmes, M., et al., "Fiber to the Home: The Technology Behind Hearthrow," *IEEE LCS*, Aug. 1990, pp. 25–29.

Bellcore TA-NWT-001209, "Generic Requirements for Fiber Optic Branching Components," 1991.

Bellcore TR-NWT-000909, "Generic Requirements and Objectives for Fiber-In-The-Loop Systems," 1991.

Bellcore TR-TSY-000303, "Integrated Digital Loop Carrier System Generic Requirements, Objectives, and Interface," 1990.

Bernard, C. W., et al., "Bidirectional Fiber Amplifiers," *IEEE J. of Photonics Tech. Lett.*, Vol. 4, No. 8, 1992, pp. 911–913.

Boinet, J. P., de Vecchis, M., and C. Verez, "Fiber in the Loop," *Elec. Commun.*, Vol. 65, No. 1, 1992, pp. 44–51.

Caroll, R. L., "Optical Architecture and Interface Lightguide Unit for Fiber-to-the-Home Feature of the AT&T SLC Series 5 Carrier System," *IEEE J. of Lightwave Tech.*, Vol. 7, No. 11, 1989.

CCITT Rec. G.651, "Characteristics of a 50/125-μm Multimode Graded Index Optical Fiber Cable," 1992 (Rev).

CCITT Rec. G.652, "Characteristics of a Single-Mode Optical Fiber Cable," 1992 (Rev).

CCITT Rec. G.653, "Characteristics of a Dispersion-Shifted Singlemode Optical Fiber Cable," 1992 (Rev).

CCITT Rec. G.654, "Characteristics of a 1550-nm Wavelength Loss-Minimized Single-Mode Optical Fiber Cable," 1992 (Rev).

Counts, B., "New Opportunities for the Fiber-in-the-Loop," 9 Dec. 1991, pp. 32–38.

Davis, J., and C. L. Jander, "FITL Spawns Power Concerns," *Telephony*, April 1991, pp. 24–28.47.

Eames, T. R., and G.T. Hawley, "The Synchronous Optical Network and Fiber in the Loop," *IEEE LTS Mag.*, Nov. 1991, p. 24.

Faukner, D. W., "Passive Optical Telephony Network and Broadband Evolution," *Proc. GLOBECOM '88*, Vol. 13, 1988, pp. 1579–1583.

Fukui, T., "Optical Subscriber Network Architecture for Broadband ISDN," *Proc. ICC'88*, pp. 883–889.

Gross, R. W., "Coherent Subcarrier Multiplexed System Sharing Transmitter and Lasers for Video Distribution in Subcarrier Loop," *IEEE J. of Lightwave Tech.*, Vol. 9, No. 4, 1991, pp. 524–530.

Hausken, T., and V. Brates, "Fiber-to-the-Home: U.S. Policy Issues," *IEEE Technology and Society Mag.*, Summer 1991, p. 22.

Hawley, G. T., "Historical Perspectives on the U.S. Telephone Loop," *IEEE Commun. Mag.*, March 1991, pp. 24–28.

Iguchi, Y., and S. Hashiba, "Development of a New CT/RT System," *NTT Review*, Vol. 3, No. 6, Nov. 1991, pp. 27–33.

Kaiser, P., "Status and Future Trends in Terrestrial Optical Fiber Systems in North America," *IEEE Commun. Mag.*, Vol. 25, No. 10, 1987, pp. 8–13.

Lattner, P. D., R. L. Fike, and G. A. Nelson, "Business and Residential Services for the Evolving Subscriber Loop," *IEEE Commun. Mag.*, March 1991, pp. 109–114.

Lidoyne, O., et al., "Optical Homodyne Receiver Using Injection-Locked Semiconductor Laser as Local Oscillator; Analysis," *IEEE J. of Lightwave Tech.*, Vol. 9, No. 5, 1991, pp. 659–665.

Lin, Y. K. M., "Fiber-Based Local Access Network Architectures," *IEEE Commun. Mag.*, 1989, pp. 64–73.

Midwinter, J., "Status and Future Trends in Terrestrial Optical Fiber in Europe," *IEEE Commun. Mag.*, Vol. 25, No. 10, 1987, pp. 14–17.

Miki, T., and R. Komiya, "Japanese Subscriber Loop Network and Fiber Optic Loop Development," *IEEE Commun. Mag.*, March 1991, pp. 60–67.

Morgen, D. H., "Fiber-to-the-Curb Power," *Telephony*, 8 July 1991, pp. 20–24.

Ohtsuka, T., "Digital Optical CATV System Using Hubbed Distribution Architecture," *IEEE J. of Lightwave Tech.*, Vol. 6, No. 11, 1988, pp. 1728–2735.

Reed, D. P., *Residential Fiber Optic Networks*, Artech House, 1992.

Rowbotham, T. R., "Local Loop Developments in the U.K.," *IEEE Commun. Mag.*, March 1991, pp. 50–57.

Saito, S., et al., "2223-km Coherent Transmission Experiment at 2.5 Gbps Using Erbium-Doped-Fiber In-Line Amplifiers and Dispersion-Shifted Single Mode Fibers," *IEEE J. of Lightwave Tech.*, Vol. 9, No. 2, 1991, pp. 161–169.

Sakaguchi, M., "Optical Switching Device Technology," *IEEE Commun. Mag.*, Vol. 25, No. 5, 1987, pp. 27–32.

Sakakibara, I., and F. Higushiyama, "Future Development of Optical Subscriber Networks," *NTT Review*, Vol. 3, No. 6, Nov. 1991, pp. 21–26.

Schaffer, B., "Synchronous and Asynchronous Transfer Modes in the Future Broadband ISDN," *Proc. ICC'88*, pp. 1552–1558.

Schumate, P. W., and R. K. Snelling, "Evolution of Fiber in the Residential Loop Plant," *IEEE Commun. Mag.*, March 1991, pp. 68–74.

Shimada, S., "Status and Trends in Fiber Optic Transmission Systems," *Proc. NTT International Symposium '90*, Nov. 1990, p. 16.

Shimada, S., "Status and Future Trends in Terrestrial Optical Fiber Systems in Japan," *IEEE Commun. Mag.*, Vol. 25, No. 5, 1987, pp. 18–21.

Shutmate, P. W., Jr., "Optical Fibers Reach Into Homes," *IEEE Spectrum*, Feb. 1989. pp. 43–47.

Snelling, R. K., J. Chernak, and K. W. Kaplan, "Future Fiber Access Needs and Systems," *IEEE Commun. Mag.*, Apr. 1990, p. 63.

Spencer, J. L., and D. S. Kobayashi, "Establishing Reliability and Availability Criteria for Fiber-in-the-Loop Systems," *IEEE Commun. Mag.*, March 1991, pp. 84–90.

Taylor, T. M., "Power and Energy in the Local Loop," *IEEE Commun. Mag.*, March 1991, pp. 76–82.

Tenzer, G., "The Introduction of Optical Fiber in the Subscriber Loop in the Telecommunication Networks of DBP TELEKOM," *IEEE Commun. Mag.*, March 1991, pp. 36–49.

Terada, Y., "Evolution of ISDN Towards BISDN," *NTT Review*, Vol. 3, No. 3, May 1991, p. 25.

Toda, I., "Migration to Broadband ISDN," *IEEE Commun. Mag.*, Apr. 1990, p. 55.

Tsuyuki, S., K. Asano, and H. Kadoya, "CT/RT for POTS and ISDN Basic Services," *NTT Review*, Vol. 3, No. 6, Nov. 1991, p. 27.

Yates, R. K., N. Mahe, and J. Masson, *Fiber Optics and CATV Business Strategy*, Artech House, 1990.

Yukimatsu, K., and T. Aoki, "Advanced Switching Technologies Toward Terabit Communication Networks," *Proc. Int. Con. Comm. Syst. (ICCS) '90*, Nov. 1990, p. 937.

Chapter 3
Synchronous Digital Transmission

As point-to-point optical communication evolves into point-to-multipoint optical communication, the concept of synchronous digital transmission appeared to be an efficient means of transmission for the optical networks. The fundamental concept of synchronous digital transmission was first introduced in the early 1980s, and it matured through the decade, along with the standardization of SONET interfaces and synchronous digital hierarchy. Synchronous digital transmission finds its solid foundation in SDH and, it also retains compatibility with the *network node interface* (NNI) and the *user-network interface* (UNI) standards of the BISDN.

SDH is a digital transport structure that operates by appropriately managing the payloads and transporting them through (synchronous) transmission networks. Before the advent of SDH, the most common digital hierarchy in use was plesiochronous digital hierarchy, which is still widely used in the form of European and North American DS-1, DS-2, DS-3, and DS-4 signals.[1] These PDH signals are multiplexed into the *synchronous transport module* (STM) signals in SDH, n of which merge into an STM-n signal. Compared to PDH, SDH appears extremely simple in operation. However, the process of synchronous multiplexing that maps PDH tributaries into STM-n signals is no trivial matter.

The term *synchronous* in SDH comes from the fact that the process of multiplexing plesiochronous tributaries into STM-n adopts a synchronous multiplexing structure. Some of the advantages of using a synchronous multiplexing structure are:

- Simplified multiplexing/demultiplexing techniques;
- Direct access to low-rate tributaries without the need to demultiplex/multiplex all of the intermediate signals;
- Enhanced operations OAM capabilities;

---

[1] Strictly speaking, the existing digital hierarchies should be described as asynchronous. However, since the variance of each asynchronous tributary nominal bit rate is within the specified error tolerance, it is called *plesiochronous*. Hence, in this text, the term plesiochronous will generally be used in the place of the term *asynchronous*.

- Easy transition to higher bit rates of the future in step with the evolution of the transmission technology.

Hence, one can conclude that the synchronous multiplexing structure is the very essence of SDH.

The type of communication that transmits plesiochronous digital tributaries through the baseband is called *digital transmission*, and, in the same manner, the new mode of communication that transmits synchronous digital tributaries is called *synchronous digital transmission*, or *synchronous transmission*. Accordingly, the process that multiplexes the existing DS-1 through DS-4 tributaries into an STM-*n* signal through synchronous multiplexing, reconstructs the signals via synchronous add/drop or cross-connect apparatus, and finally transmits and regenerates it through a synchronous optical network, in totality, can be called synchronous digital transmission. From a synchronous transmission standpoint, the current digital transmission can be classified as asynchronous digital transmission.

The objective of this chapter is to provide an in-depth description of synchronous digital transmission. To this end, the discussions in the chapter are organized in the following manner. Following an extensive introduction, the frame structure of the STM-*n* signal and associated topics will be discussed. First, a detailed description of the STM-*n* frame structure will be given, followed by an examination of the synchronous multiplexing process and the associated mapping of asynchronous tributaries into respective containers. Description of the frame, payloads, overheads, and pointers, will follow. In the latter half of the chapter, the link, network, and system structures will be examined. The synchronous multiplexing structure and the associated jitter problems will be studied, and the chapter will close with a discussion of synchronous transmission network structures.

3.1 OVERVIEW OF SYNCHRONOUS TRANSMISSION

In this section, a general overview of synchronous transmission will be given as an introduction to the more detailed analysis in ensuing sections. First, SDH will be compared to the existing PDH. Then, the layered approach to overhead assignment, which forms the basis for synchronous transmission, will be discussed, the synchronous multiplexing structure of the STM-*n* frame will be examined, and the novel pointer technique, which allows easy mapping of tributaries to higher-rate signals, will be described. After this brief but requisite review of pertinent terms, there will be a discussion of the unique features of synchronous digital transmission, followed by a summary of its standardization process. Finally, a brief comparison will be made of the synchronous transmission standards by CCITT and the T1 Committee.

3.1.1 PDH Versus SDH

The existing digital hierarchies were originally prescribed by the Bell System of North America and CCITT. North American DS signals were reaffirmed as the North

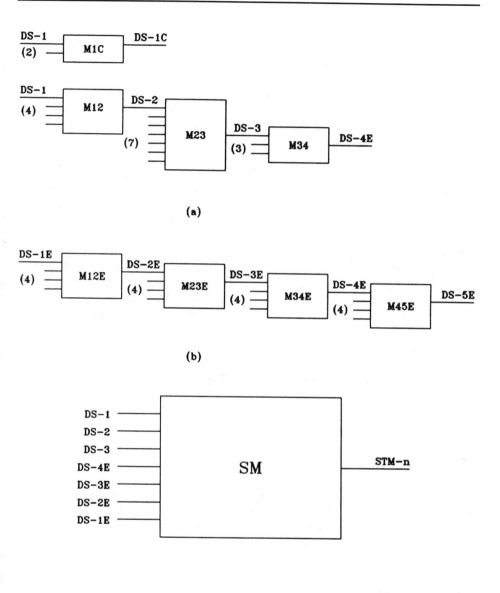

(a)

(b)

(c)

Figure 3.1 Digital hierarchy: (a) plesiochronous (North American); (b) plesiochronous (European); (c) synchronous.

American standard by the T1 Committee, which emerged after the breakup of the Bell System. These existing digital hierarchies are called the PDH to differentiate them from the nascent SDH.

PDH is currently the standard digital hierarchy and can be divided into North American and European designations, as shown in Figure 3.1(a,b). North American PDH consists of DS-1 (1.544 Mbps), DS-1C (3.152 Mbps), DS-2 (6.312 Mbps), DS-3 (44.736 Mbps), and DS-4E (139.264 Mbps); and the European PDH accommodates DS-1E (2.048 Mbps), DS-2E (8.448 Mbps), DS-3E (34.368 Mbps), DS-4E (139.264 Mbps), and DS-5E (564.992 Mbps).[2] Each multiplexing step is plesiochronous, and synchronization is achieved with the use of bit stuffing and positive justification.

SDH is composed of STM-n signals, as shown in Figure 3.1(c). Here, n is a fixed number, mainly 1,4,16, and indicates the number of multiples of the base STM-1 with the corresponding bit rates of 155.520, 622.080, 2,488.320 Mbps, respectively. The STM-n signal is formed by synchronously multiplexing DS-1, DS-2, DS-3, DS-4E, DS-3E, DS-2E, and DS-1E tributaries. The DS-1C and DS-5E signals are excluded from the synchronous multiplexing. The STM-n signal is formed by *byte-interleaved-multiplexing* (BIM) n of STM-1 signals. In this process, the overhead composition of each STM-1 signal becomes reorganized.

Comparing Figures 3.1(a,b) and 3.1(c), it is apparent that SDH has a much simpler structure than PDH. In SDH, North American and European tributaries go through only a single stage of multiplexing. In PDH, asynchronous multiplexing is used when a tributary is multiplexed into a tributary of higher bit rate. In SDH, synchronous multiplexing is used instead. Also, in PDH, DS-m is a higher tributary of the DS-$(m-1)$ signal, but in SDH, all the DS signals are equal in status.

3.1.2 Layering Concept and Overheads

Generally, a digital signal is transmitted hierarchically, via path, multiplexer, regenerator sections, and a physical medium, as illustrated in Figure 3.2. Each section of the transmission procedure can be viewed as forming a *layer*, and hence we can divide the entire digital transmission procedure into path layer, multiplexer section layer, regenerator section layer, and physical medium layer (or optical layer).[3]

The synchronous multiplexing structure allocates the requisite bit space systematically, in accordance with the layer concept. Figure 3.3 gives an example of

---

[2]There was also the DS-4 (274.176 Mbps) signal among the Bell System tributaries. The T1 Committee recommended the accommodation of DS-4E in its place and additionally prescribed a multiplexing path from DS-3 to DS-4E. In indicating the digital tributaries, E denotes the European designation, (i.e., *Conference of European Post and Telecommunications Administrations* (CEPT)).

[3]Here, the multiplexer section layer, together with the regenerator section layer, is called the *section layer*, and the section layer, together with the physical medium layer, is called the *transmission medium layer*. Refer to Section 3.10.

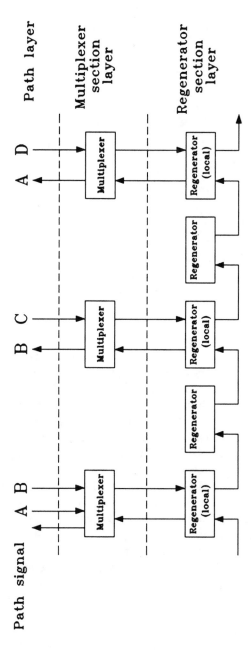

Figure 3.2 Illustration of the layering concept for digital transmission (unidirection).

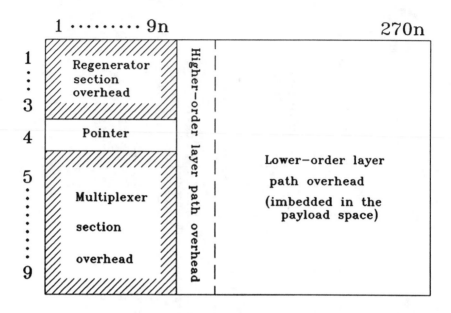

Figure 3.3 Layering concept embedded in the frame structure.

the application of the layer concept to organize an STM-n frame. In this figure, the STM-n frame is partitioned into five regions, four of which are providing an overhead function for different layers. The regenerator section overhead and multiplexer section overhead correspond to the regenerator section layer and multiplexer section layer, respectively, and the path overhead corresponds to the path layer. Path overheads for lower-order paths are included in the STM payload space.

The overheads used in synchronous multiplexing can be divided into *path overhead* (POH) and *section overhead* (SOH) in the spirit of the layering concept. Section overheads can further be categorized into *regenerator section overheads* (RSOH) and *multiplexer section overheads* (MSOH). The insertion of SOH is the last step in the construction of STM-n, and POH is inserted every time a *virtual container* (VC) signal is constructed (see Section 3.1.4 for a description of VC).

SOH is the overhead added or extracted at the regenerator or multiplexer section for maintenance, performance indication, and other operational functions. As shown in Figure 3.3, the SOHs, located above and below the *pointer* (PTR), are for the regenerator and multiplexer sections, respectively. For example, B1, which is the overhead located in the upper part of the PTR for *bit-interleaved parity* (BIP)-8, is checked and recalculated at every regenerator. But the 3-byte B2, which is the overhead located in the lower part of PTR for BIP-24, is checked only at the line termination. The POH can be categorized into higher-order POH and lower-order

POH, and in both cases POH is used for end-to-end communication between the point of assembly of a VC and the point of its disassembly.

The section and path overheads of the STM-1 frame are shown in Figure 3.4(a,b). The SOH has the size of 72 (= 8 x 9) bytes in the case of STM-1, while POH has the size of 9 bytes. Note that the 9 bytes in the fourth row are PTR bytes. In the figure, A1 and A2 are channels for framing; B1, B2, and B3 are for parity check; C1 and C2 are for signal labeling; D1 through D12 are for data communication; E1 and E2 are for path order wires; F1 and F2 are for network-user channels; G1 is for path status check; H4 is for position indication; J1 is for path trace; K1 and K2 are for *automatic protection switching* (APS); and Z3 to Z5 are assigned for use by path user and network operator. Z1 and Z2 are reserved for future growth, and the X bytes are for national use. The SOH bytes in the first row are excluded from scrambling when transmitting.

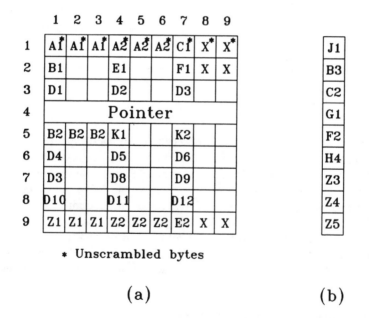

* Unscrambled bytes

(a)   (b)

Figure 3.4 The overhead structure for STM-1: (a) section overhead; (b) path overhead.

3.1.3 STM-n Frame Structure

The STM-n frame, the end product of the synchronous multiplexing procedure in the SDH that reflects the layering concept, has a typical structure, like the one shown in Figure 3.5. This structure occupies 9B x *n* x 270 bit space over 125 μs, and thus acquires *n* x 155.520-Mbps bit rate. The 9B x *n* x 9 partition of it is used for SOH and *administrative unit* (AU) PTR, and the remaining 9B x *n* x 261 is used for the payload. An instance of this structure would be an STM-1 signal.

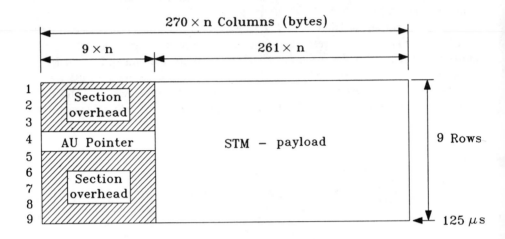

Figure 3.5 STM-1 frame structure.

If the STM-1 frame structure is observed more carefully, it can be seen that SOH is composed of 3 x 9B and 5 x 9B partitions of space. AU PTR is composed of 1 x 9B, whose internal contents are shown in Figure 3.4(a). The remaining 9B x 261 is reserved for the STM-1 payload, where one VC-4 signal or three VC-3 signals together with a *fixed overhead* (FOH) can be mapped into the STM-1 payload space. VC-4 and VC-3 consist of the corresponding payloads and 9 x 1B of POH, whose contents are as shown in Figure 3.4(b). VC-4 or VC-3, together with a corresponding AU PTR, results in AU-4 or AU-3. Therefore, an STM-1 payload, together with an AU PTR, is equivalent to AU-4. Attaching an SOH to AU-4 gives STM-1.

3.1.4 Synchronous Multiplexing Structure

As illustrated in Figure 3.1, the synchronous multiplexing structure works by treating every digital tributary on an equal basis to construct an STM-*n* signal. Figure 3.6 shows a typical synchronous multiplexing procedure. The numbers in the parentheses indicate the number of signals required to create the signal of the next higher bit rate. The asynchronous multiplexing (AM) process is shown in the smaller of two boxes, and synchronous multiplexing (SM) is shown to the right.

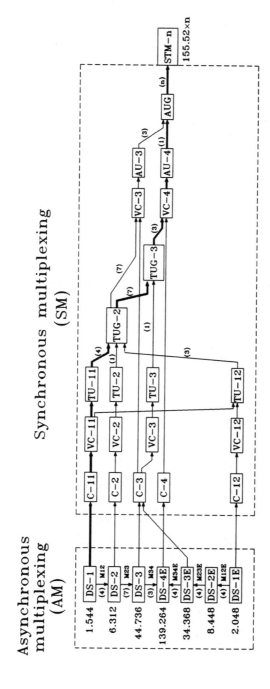

Figure 3.6 Synchronous multiplexing structure (rates in Mbps).

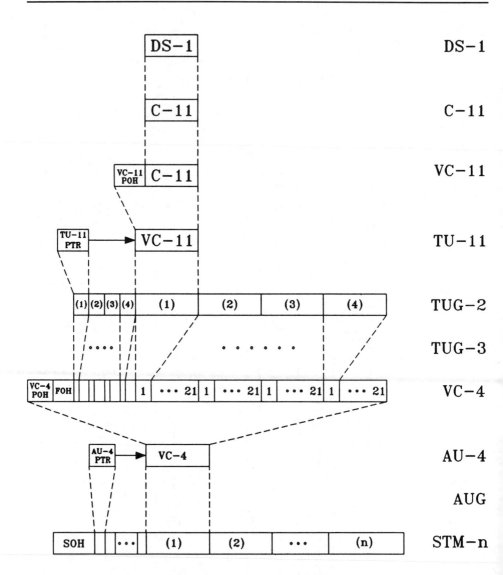

Figure 3.7 Example of multiplexing procedure for the multiplexing path
DS-1\C-11\VC-11\TU-11\TUG-2\TUG-3\VC-4\AU-4\AUG\STM-*n*.

In the first stage of synchronous multiplexing, each tributary is mapped to a corresponding *container* (C). Bit stuffing with *positive/zero/negative* (P/Z/N) justification is used for synchronization. If a POH is attached to the container, it becomes a VC, and if a pointer is added as well, it becomes a *tributary unit* (TU). When a VC is mapped into an STM-1 without going through other VCs, then the corresponding TU becomes an AU.

Assembling four TU-1 or three TU-12 creates a *tributary unit group* (TUG), and TUG can then be multiplexed into VC-3 or VC-4. TU-2 is equivalent to TUG-2 (they have equivalent bit rates), and TU-3 can be considered equivalent to TUG-3. VC-3 can be multiplexed into VC-4 via TU-3, or into AU directly through AU-3. An *administrative unit group* (AUG) has the same bit rate as AU-4, and thus their frame sizes are the same. Finally, multiplexing n AUG together with an SOH results in STM-n. The number $m = 1, 2, 3, 4$ attached to all signal units other than STM-m indicates that the corresponding signal unit is equivalent to the DS-m tributary in terms of rates. When $m = 1$, an additional number is attached to differentiate the North American (11) and European (12) DS-1 tributaries.

Figure 3.7 shows an instance of a synchronous multiplexing process; that is, the DS-1\C-11\VC-11\TU-11\TUG-2\TUG-3\VC-4\AU-4\AUG\STM-n path marked in bold lines in Figure 3.6. The DS-1 signal is first mapped into C11, then C11 becomes VC-11 with the addition of a VC-11 pointer. Attaching a TU-11 PTR to VC-11 and multiplexing four of them results in a TUG-2.

From the TUG-2 signal of the figure, we can see that TU-11, together with TU-11 PTR, can be easily extracted. Multiplexing seven TUG-2s and attaching FOH results in TUG-3, and multiplexing three TUG-3s and attaching FOH and VC-4 POH produces VC-4. Therefore, the VC-4 signal is equivalent to the signal constructed by multiplexing 21 TUG-2s and attaching VC-4 POH and FOH to the head of its frame.

As a result of this well-coordinated multiplexing procedure, we can see that 84 TU-11 signals can be accessed separately on a VC-4. In this case, the FOH is just an overhead to match the size of a VC-4 frame to that of VC-3. VC-4 together with AU-4 PTR produces AU-4, which is equivalent to AUG. Multiplexing n AUGs and adding an SOH produces STM-n.

3.1.5 Pointer and Synchronization

In the SDH, the pointer scheme is employed for the synchronization process. The pointer designates the location of the first byte of a VC within a TU or AU frame; the pointer is a variable in the sense that its value changes with the alteration of the VC's location. Examining Figures 3.6 and 3.7, we see that pointers in SDH include AU-4 PTR, AU-3 PTR, TU-3 PTR, TU-11 PTR, TU-2 PTR, and TU-12 PTR. Among them, AU-4 PTR and AU-3 PTR appear at the AU PTR slot of Figure 3.5, and TU-3 PTR occupies the upper part of the first column of the TU-3 frame. These three

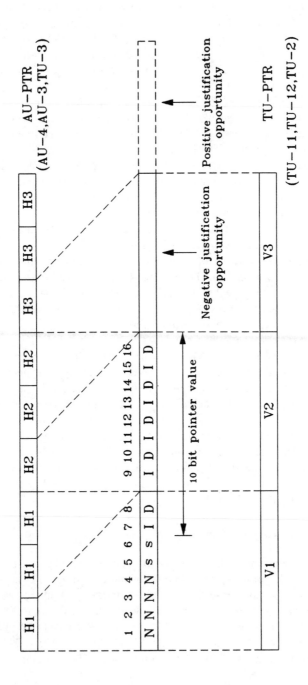

Figure 3.8 The pointer structure and function.

higher-order pointers are designated as H1, H2, and H3, and the lower-order pointers like TU-11 PTR, TU-2 PTR, and TU-12 PTR are designated as V1, V2, and V3. The low-order pointers are formed by partitioning a signal such as TU-11 into four sections of 125 μs each, and then taking the first bytes of each. The first three out of the first four bytes are called V1, V2, and V3, and the fourth of the bytes, namely V4, is reserved for future use. The payload of each TU follows immediately after the V2 byte and acquires the respective offset in the order, 0, 1, 2, ...

H1, H2, H3 and V1, V2, V3, although their designations are different, have the same basic functions as shown in Figure 3.8. Four *new data flag* (NDF) bits (N bits) indicate whether new data is being carried or not, and two ss-bits indicate the type of TU or AU. The ten bits that follow indicate the address of the corresponding VC, and consist of five *increment* (I) bits and five *decrement* (D) bits interleaved alternatingly. Either the I-bits or the D-bits are inverted when the address of the VC is increased or decreased. An H3 (or V3) byte is used to carry a payload byte in case of negative justification. In the case of positive justification, the byte that appears right after H3 is used to carry one dummy byte (three bytes for VC-4).

If there is a frequency offset between the frame rate of AUG and the payload data rate of VC, then the pointer bytes are used to cancel the offset through the use of P/Z/N justification. If the data rate of a VC is higher than that of TU/AU, the total amount of payload being carried increases proportionally. In this case, when the accumulated offset becomes one byte long (three bytes for VC-4), the D-bits are inverted and H3 or V3 carries one byte of data. In the resulting modified frame, the pointer value is decremented by one to account for the shifted address of the VC. What has been achieved is *negative justification*. When the payload data rate is higher than the frame rate, I-bits are inverted, H3 or V3 carries a dummy byte, and the address bit is incremented by one. This is called *positive justification*.

3.1.6 Characteristics of Synchronous Digital Transmission

As can be inferred from previous sections, synchronous transmission has some distinct characteristics, which will be discussed in detail in this subsection.

125-μs Frame

The first distinct feature of synchronous digital transmission is the fact that its frame structure consists of 125-μs time intervals. This is a special feature that cannot be found in the existing plesiochronous digital hierarchies. Its advantage is that low-level signals, especially DS-0, can be accessed directly from high-level signals, and that all data manipulations can be carried on at the byte-unit level. But it has a drawback in that it introduces a new problem, namely, waiting time jitter. This is an unavoidable result of P/Z/N justification, which is an inherent feature of synchronous multiplexing, and a viable solution is yet to be found.

Unification of Digital Hierarchy

The synchronous multiplexing structure accommodates both North American and European signals. That is, given any signal among North American DS-1, 2, 3 and European DS-1E, 2E, 3E, 4E, a generic STM-n signal can be constructed through the synchronous multiplexing procedure. Moreover, North American signals can be combined with European signals during this procedure and vice versa. This type of cross-continental unification has never been attempted previously. Of course, not all the proposed multiplexing paths are practical, but imposing the possibility paves the way toward future global network integration.

Layered Structure

One of the unique features of synchronous digital transmission is the fact that the frame structure is organized according to the layering concept. The division of overhead into SOH and POH is an instance of the application of this concept. Under this layered arrangement, SOH can perform its function independently of POH. SOH can be further divided into sublayers; for example, SOH located in the upper part of PTR can be devoted to regenerator section, and the one in the lower part to multiplexer section. The advantage of the layer concept is the "division of labor" of the transmission process, so that each required step can be performed independently of others.

Systematic Use of Overheads

As can be seen from the STM-1 frame, 9 x 9B of space is allocated for SOH and PTR. If the POH and PTR accumulated from multiple multiplexing steps are taken into account, the size of actual overhead increases significantly. For example, when a DS-4E with a bit rate of 139.264 Mbps is mapped to STM-1, the overhead can take more than 10% of the frame space. This was a luxury in existing plesiochronous digital hierarchies, but it can be accommodated without adding additional difficulties in the optical networks. Overhead, which is systematically divided into POH and SOH, can be fully utilized to enhance the communication operation and maintenance capability of the transmission network. By reserving some of the overhead space for future use, a means of future transition and growth is also provided.

Synchronization via Pointers

The synchronization of the overall transmission network is achieved by the repeated insertion of pointers during the synchronous multiplexing process. That is, the frequency offset between the system clock and the received signal is effectively nullified by the use of pointers and P/Z/N justifications. Such pointer-based synchronization method enables coping with plesiochronous environment with a small elastic store and thus global synchronization is possible. Synchronization through the use of the pointers corresponds to a P/Z/N bit stuffing if viewed from the standpoint of existing asynchronous multiplexing. Hence, pointer synchronization generates similar low-frequency, high-amplitude jitters. A solution to the problem is a topic of ongoing research.

One-Step Multiplexing

In the synchronous multiplexing process, a direct mapping from TUG-2 to VC-4 or from AU-3 to STM-1 is possible. This is one-step multiplexing which eliminates the need for intermediate steps. It is a novel scheme that is not found in existing asynchronous multiplexing systems. For communication networks that transmit high-rate signals through numerous multiplexing stages, it renders add/drop and cross-connect simple and economical. It should also be mentioned that one-step multiplexing is possible because of the container concept.

Network Concept

Another trait of synchronous digital transmission is that it is based on the network concept. The existing transmission system is inefficient because its structure is point-to-point in configuration; hence, add/drop and cross-connect at intermediate nodes are a cumbersome, multistep process. But since optical communication is becoming an increasingly common and popular means of digital transmission, a standardized transmission system based on the network concept is within the realm of possibility. In making it a reality, one-step multiplexing plays an important role. Efficient OAM through the use of the aforementioned layer concept should also help.

Global Transmission Network

Synchronous transmission can be said to encompass global communication. Global synchronization through the repeated use of pointers is what makes such a notion possible. Unification of the North American and European hierarchies is a significant step towards global unification. On that basis, and propelled by such preparatory measures as overhead allocation and multiplexing structure based on network concept, a future global communication network should become a reality in the near future.

3.1.7 Standardization Process of Synchronous Digital Transmission

For synchronous transmission to attain its unique features, Metrobus and SONET played an important role. Metrobus is an internally synchronous optical communication system developed by AT&T Bell Laboratories, and SONET is a North American optical communication interface standard subsequently proposed by Bellcore and approved by the T1 Committee. Metrobus challenged the classical optical communication concepts of existing systems and founded the concept of an internally synchronous optical communication system by exploiting such innovative ideas as one-step multiplexing, use of containers, versatile utilization of overheads, and the use of a 150-Mbps signal as the internal standard. SONET followed and contributed the layer concept with 50-Mbps signal as the base, the synchronization method via the use of pointers, and the systematization of overhead assignment. The present SDH inherited the best of Metrobus and SONET, and, makes standardized global communication a reality by employing 150 Mbps as the base signal and encompassing European digital hierarchy as well as the North American.

Metrobus

Metrobus is an optical communication system first proposed by J. D. Spalink of AT&T Bell Laboratories in 1982. It was developed on a full scale from early 1984 and entered the *first office application* (FOA) stage by early 1987. The prime objective of Metrobus was to develop an optimal communication system that takes full advantages of optical communication and that is most appropriate with respect to communication network evolution, device technology, and service growth. The name "Metrobus" arose from the fact that it was originally developed to accommodate all services in metropolitan areas. During the research and development stage of Metrobus, many new concepts were introduced. Among the most representative were point-to-multipoint optical network, internally synchronous system, visibility of DS-0, one-step multiplexing, simultaneous accommodation of tributaries by controlling the number of containers, establishment of 150 Mbps as the internal signal standard, and maximum utilization of overhead.

The idea of a point-to-multipoint network was considered revolutionary when it was first introduced because, at that time, all existing optical systems employed point-to-point communication. The concepts listed above played an indispensable role in making it a reality. Given the seemingly infinite bandwidth of optical communications, sufficient space could be allocated for overhead such that a devoted overhead channel could be constructed to employ applications that involve the whole optical network. The bit rate assigned for overhead, however, was over 4.5% of the total transmission capacity, an innovative concept difficult to accept at the time.

Choosing 150 Mbps (146.432 Mbps, to be precise) as the internal signal standard of the communication network was the key notion. First, 150 Mbps is the signal rate that can accommodate all signals from DS-1 (1.544 Mbps) to DS-4E (139.264 Mbps). From the service application standpoint, the existing voice, data, and video signals (including the compressed HDTV signals) can all be accommodated in 150 Mbps, and it is expected that CMOS technology can be easily used up to this rate. From the subscriber loop viewpoint, *light-emitting diode* (LED) and *pin* diodes can be used instead of laserdiode and *avalanche photodiode* (APD), and optical fiber coupling efficiency can be increased by employing graded-index multimode fibers instead of single-mode fibers.

One-step multiplexing was also a revolutionary concept at the time. Direct multiplexing of the DS-1 signal to the 150-Mbps internal standard signal without the involvement of intermediate DS-2 and DS-3 could not be found in the existing asynchronous multiplexers, and it acts as a cornerstone for efficient add/drop and cross-connect, which occur frequently in optical communication networks. One of the tools that makes one-step multiplexing possible is the idea of accommodating multiplexed tributaries by controlling the number of containers. In other words, by defining the size of a container, DS-1, DS-1C, DS-2, and DS-3 can be simultaneously loaded onto 1, 2, 4, and 28 containers, respectively. Since all the signals are manipulated on a container unit basis, add/drop and cross-connect can be executed efficiently.[4]

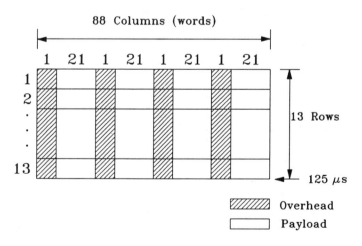

Figure 3.9 Metrobus frame structure.

The internal standard signal, composed of 13W (words) x 88, is shown in Figure 3.9, and has the bit rate of 146.432 Mbps. During the 125-μs/13 time in-

---

[4]The term "container" was first used when CCITT prescribed the STM-*n* signal.

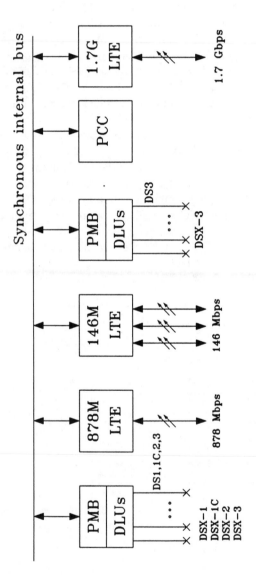

Figure 3.10 Metrobus system architecture.

terval, 88 words get loaded onto 88 containers; four of these are used as overheads, and each DS-*n* signal occupies a corresponding number of containers.

The introduction of the internal synchronization concept has signaled the beginning of the synchronous communication network. The internally standardized communication network is designed to serve a specific metropolitan area, and is therefore adequately equipped to establish communication with plesiochronous neighbors within the area. Here, the clock signal can be chosen from among the *basic synchronization reference frequency* (BSRF), the local oscillator frequency, and the frequency derived from the received signal.

The visibility of the DS-0 can be said to be a direct consequence of constructing a 125-μs-based frame structure. In other words, if the construction of the frame structure and the mapping of the tributaries into respective containers are all performed upon a 125-μs unit basis, the DS-0 signals obtained from the 8-kbps sampling rate are transparent or can be directly accessed from higher-order signals. Hence, a DS-0 signal from the 150-Mbps internal standard signal can be extracted efficiently.

The organization of the Metrobus system is shown in Figure 3.10. The line labeled "synchronous internal bus" corresponds to the 146.432-Mbps internal standard signal. This signal is produced from DS-1 through DS-3 signals after they go through the *programmable multiplex bank* (PMB). As is shown in the figure, the direct optical communication at 146Mbps, 878Mbps, or 1.7Gbps is possible either by passing the signal straight through *lightwave transmission equipment* (LTE) or by *word interleaved multiplexing* (WIM) 6 or 12 of the signals first, then transmitting the group through LTE. Also, at *programmable cross-connect* (PCC), the containers built out of 146Mbps signals to take the DS-1 bit rate are used to perform the cross-connect function.

SONET

SONET is an abbreviation for Synchronous Optical Network, and was first conceived by R. J. Boehm and Y. C. Ching of Bellcore. It was proposed as an optical communication interface standard to the T1 Committee (which functions as the North American standardization organization) at the end of 1984. As indicated in Figure 3.11(a), the frame proposed at that time had a 3 x 8 x 33B format, with a bit rate of 50.688 Mbps (= 3 x 8 x 33 x 8 x 8 kbps). This base signal was named *synchronous transport signal* (STS)-1, and it was determined that DS-3 or SYNTRAN DS-3, which carry basic tributaries, were to be byte-interleaved-multiplexed to higher-order signals through STS-1.[5]

---

[5]SYNTRAN (Synchronous Transmission) is a synchronous DS-3 signal and has the same rate and frame structure as the DS-3, but its effective payload is restructured to be transparent to DS-0. SYNTRAN DS-3 was first proposed in 1983 by G. R. Ritchie of Bellcore, and after two years of discussion was established as the North American signal standard by the T1 Committee.

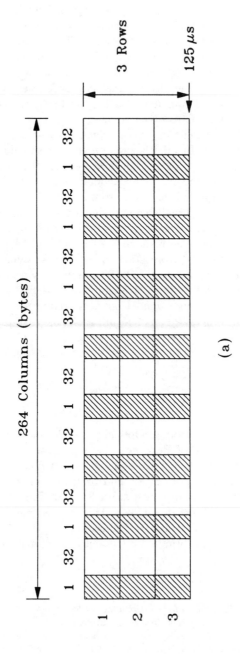

(a)

Figure 3.11 SONET frame structure (shaded region for overhead, blank space for payload): (a) initial stage structure; (b) midstage structure; (c) final stage structure.

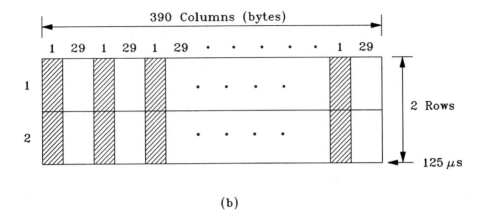

(b)

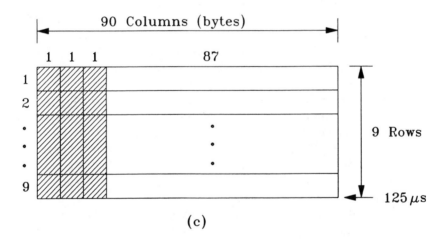

(c)

Figure 3.11 continued.

The initial SONET was proposed for the purpose of "midspan meet;" hence, there was skepticism as to its realizability and little advancement achieved toward its standardization during the first year after its inception. But the standardization process was rejuvenated by the announcement of Metrobus in September of 1985, and innovative ideas such as the concepts of layered system structure and pointer-based synchronization were proposed by T1 Committee participants to provide added momentum.[6] The original developers of SONET proposed the systematic refinement of the original frame structure according to the formula $(28 + L)(24 + M)(8 + N)$. What this formula signifies is the allocation of overhead spaces at the DS-3, DS-1, and DS-0 levels, which are, respectively, L of DS-1 size, M of DS-0 size, and N of bit size. A frame structure reorganization based on this formula, with $L = 2$, $M = 2$, $N = 0$, is the midstage SONET frame shown in Figure 3.11(b), which is a 26B x 30 structure with a 49.92-Mbps rate. AT&T Bell Laboratories then proposed that the Metrobus internal standard signal with a 26B x 88 frame structure and a 146.432-Mbps rate be adopted as a provisional SONET standard signal. This signal can be represented by a modified Bellcore formula, $\{J + K(28 + L)\}(24 + M)(8 + N)$, with $J = 1$, $K = 3$, $L = 1$, $M = 2$, and $N = 0$. Here, L, M, and N are the same as before, K indicates the number of DS-3-level signals, and J indicates the size of the overhead in terms of the equivalent number of DS-1 level signals.

A heated debate followed in the T1 Committee between the two alternate signal standard candidates. Even detailed functional comparisons could not clearly evince the superiority of 50 Mbps over 150 Mbps, or vice versa. Ultimately, the T1 Committee selected 49.92 Mbps as the STS-1 standard in the early part of 1986. At the time, CCITT was engaged in broadband optical channel standardization, and T1 proposed that 149.976 Mbps, which is three times the rate of the adopted SONET standard, be used as the North American standard. This signified that the T1 Committee, who selected 50 Mbps over 150 Mbps, ironically admitted the adequacy of 150 Mbps from the technical standpoint.

Afterwards, the SONET standardization process, steered by the T1X1 Working Group, sailed smoothly on, and by early 1987 even the specific standards were approved. But a full-scale mediation with CCITT ensued regarding the BISDN NNI interface standard. The 13B x 60 frame structure and 49.92 Mbps (or 149.976 Mbps in groups of three) were designed for North American digital signals, and thus were limited in their ability to accommodate European digital signals. Hence, the SONET frame structure was once again altered, as shown in Figure 3.11(c), to 9B x 90 with a new bit rate of 51.84 Mbps (or 155.52 Mbps in groups of three). This modification was approved at a Phoenix meeting in February 1988, and after a vote in April 1988 the SONET interface standardization was completed. The final SONET interface

---

[6]The concept of pointer was introduced to the T1 Committee by J. Ellson of Bell Northern Research in 1986.

standard reflects various contributions from Metrobus, such as the mapping of tributaries. SDH, as established by CCITT Recommendations G.707 to 709, is based on a signal that is three times the SONET standard, and thus has a 9B x 270 structure and a 155.520-Mbps bit rate.

Synchronous Digital Hierarchy

One of the results of the ISDN standardization by CCITT in the early part of 1980 was the selection of H1, H2, H3, and H4 as the user high-speed channels. Among the four, the H1 channel was standardized in two different forms: as the H11 channel of 1.536-Mbps rate based on the North American DS-1 signal, and the H12 channel of 1.920-Mbps rate based on the European DS-1 signal. The H2, H3, and H4 channels had a general outline appropriate to the existing digital hierarchy; but from 1985 on, they formed the basis for the ensuing broadband channel standardization. At first, 30- to 40-, 45-, or 60- to 70-Mbps bit rates were considered for the standardization, as well as the SONET standard 149.976 Mbps, which was proposed by the T1 Committee.

In July 1986, CCITT, with SG XVIII playing the central role, began the process of standardizing SDH, to be used for NNI independently of UNI. This was the instigating step towards full-scale SDH standardization, and for that purpose the T1 Committee and CCITT maintained a close relationship. For the standardization of the STM-1 signal, which is the essence of the BISDN's NNI, North America, at a meeting in Brasilia in February 1987, formally proposed the use of 50 Mbps based on STS-1 of SONET, while CEPT (see footnote 2) insisted on the necessity of using the 150-Mbps standard, which can accommodate both North American and European digital hierarchies. In the Hamburg meeting in July of the same year, the U.S. put forth a modified signal that was based on STS-3, with a 149.976-Mbps bit rate and a frame structure of 13B x 180, while CEPT responded by proposing a 9B x 270, 155.520-Mbps signal. The two organizations debated these alternatives heatedly for a while, with the problem of accommodating 8.448-Mbps DS-2E and 34.368-Mbps signals being the crucial point. The 9B x 270 structure won out and was finally chosen as the standard at the Seoul meeting in February 1988. This NNI standard was made official in CCITT Recommendations G.707 through 709 in June of that year, and the SDH based on the STM-1 signal with the 9B x 270 frame structure and 155.520 Mbps came into being.

Even after the 1988 CCITT recommendations were finalized, active study and research on SDH continued. When the initial SDH standard was determined in 1988, the synchronous multiplexing system already had a fixed structure like the one shown in Figure 3.12. But during the two years of study that followed, in which additional SDH standardizations were established through CCITT Recommendations G.781–784 and G.957–958, the synchronous multiplexing system was simplified, resulting

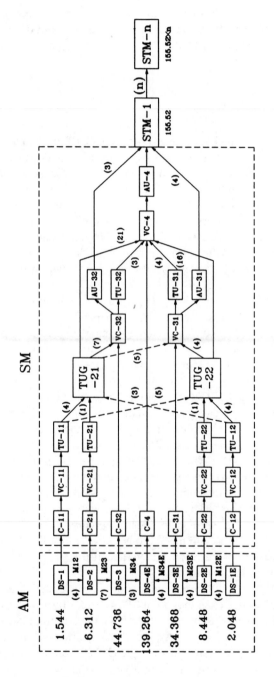

Figure 3.12 Early form of synchronous multiplexing structure (rates in Mbps).

in the one shown in Figure 3.6. We can see from the figure that the multiplexing paths of European tributaries converge across the board with those of the North American tributaries, and that the concepts of AUG and TUG-3 have been applied.

As can be inferred from the preceding discussion, the contributions of Metrobus on SONET, and SONET on the standardization of SDH, cannot be overemphasized. The unique features of SDH, such as the concepts of an optical communication network, an internally synchronous system, the visibility of DS-0 through a 125-µs time unit, one-step multiplexing, the accommodation of multirate signals by controlling the number of containers, the establishment of 150 Mbps as the internal signal standard, and the enhancement of adaptability and reliability through versatile use of overheads, are all derived from Metrobus. Also, the layered system structure, systematic overhead organization, synchronization via pointers, and the possibility of establishing a global network are the byproducts of SONET interface standardization. Upon such a foundation, SDH standardization, by accommodating both the North American and European hierarchies, makes the realization of a global communications network possible.

On the other hand, SDH, whose initial goal was the standardization of the NNI of the BISDN, also had a decisive influence on the BISDN UNI standard. First of all, prescribing the bit rate of BISDN UNI as 155.520 Mbps, and further prescribing the bit rate of the associated payload to be under 149.760 Mbps, is a direct result of the BISDN NNI standard. Also, the mapping of the ATM cells into VC-4 payloads for the purposes of SDH-based transmission at the BISDN UNI is another of the consequences. As described, SDH played a crucial role in introducing a new mode of transmission and finalizing the format of the BISDN.

3.1.8 SDH versus SONET

As discussed earlier, in relation to the standardization process of synchronous digital transmission, SDH and SONET maintain an extremely close relationship. SONET standardization activities were what made SDH standards possible, while SDH was instrumental in expanding the scope of SONET so as to make it applicable for a global communications network. Therefore, a description of SDH inevitably includes a treatment of SONET.

However, minute differences do exist between SDH and SONET. For example, the base rate of SDH is around 150 Mbps, while that of SONET is around 50 Mbps. (Refer to Figures 3.5 and 3.11c.) This implies that SDH employs DS-4E as the highest-level tributary to accommodate lower-order signals, whereas SONET employs DS-3 as the highest-level tributary. Of course, this is not a crucial difference, due to the concept of concatenation. In other words, concatenating three of SONET's base transmission signal 51.840-Mbps STS-1 is equivalent to the 155.520-Mbps STM-1 of SDH.

SDH and SONET also differ slightly in the respective diversity of transmission rates. SDH is based on STM-1 (155.520 Mbps), with STM-4 (622.082 Mbps) and STM-16 (2,488.320 Mbps) being the signals of primary interest. In contrast, STS-1 (51.840 Mbps) is used as the base signal unit in the case of SONET, with STS-3 (155.520 Mbps), STS-9, STS-12 (622.080 Mbps), STS-18, STS-24, STS-36, STS-48 (2,488.320 Mbps) being of primary interest. Here, the STM-n signal generally has the same transmission rate as STS-$3n$. To be more precise, STM-n is the equivalent of the concatenated signal STS-$3nc$. The optical counterpart of STS-m is called the *optical carrier level m* (OC-m).

With respect to the frame format, SONET is equivalent to the reduction of SDH by a factor of one-third. SDH has the 9 x 270B frame structure in the case of STM-1, while STS-1 of SONET has the 9 x 90B structure. Similar to the SOH of STM-1, which is located at the head of the STM-1 frame with the 9 x 9B format, the SOH of STS-1 is located at the head of the STS-1 frame with the 9 x 3B format. In both cases, the fourth row is allocated to the pointer. Examined in more detail, if the first, fourth, and seventh columns of the STM-1 SOHs are taken, then what results is the same as the SOH of STS-1. The functions of the components of the respective overheads are identical.

As was alluded to earlier, SDH and STM-1 employ different base signal units, namely, the 150-Mbps rate STM-1 and the 50-Mbps rate STS-1. This means that in the case of SDH the construction of STM-1 requires a systematic multiplexing of all the tributaries from DS-1 to DS-4, while STS-1 needs to multiplex just five of the tributaries, which are DS-1, DS-1E, DS-1C (3.152 Mbps), DS-2, and DS-3. Consequently, the creation of STM-1 necessitates the establishment of such intermediate signal units as C, VC, TU, TUG, AU, AUG, as was explained in Section 3.1.4, and also the systematic multiplexing procedures depicted in Figure 3.6. In contrast, STS-1 requires only one type of intermediate signal, called *virtual tributary* (VT). The VT is equivalent to the VC of SDH, and the VTs that correspond to VC-11, VC-12, and VC-2 are VT1.5, VT2, and VT6, respectively. Also, VT3 is the VT for the DS-1C signal.

SDH and SONET have different sets of intermediate signal units, and consequently the multiplexing structure of one is different from that of the other. SDH requires a systematic multiplexing structure that can link C, VC, TU, TUG, AU, AUG, and STM-n as shown in Figure 3.6, while the multiplexing structure of SONET only has to link DS-m, VT, and STS-1, and is therefore much simpler. Here, the method of mapping tributaries into VT1.5, VT2, and VT6 is equivalent to mapping into VC-11, VC-12, and VC-2, and the mapping of DS-1C into VT-3 is similarly based on P/Z/N justification. The mapping of these VTs into the payload space of STS-1 (i.e., the *synchronous payload envelope* (SPE)) is analogous to the mapping of related VCs into VC-3 via TUG-2. Lastly, the mapping of DS-3 into SPE is the same as the mapping of DS-3 into VC-3. However, the mapping of SYNTRAN DS-3 is additionally provided in SONET.

If the interrelationship between SONET and SDH is examined from the terminology point of view, VT1.5, VT2, and VT6, respectively, correspond to VC-11, VC-12, and V-2; STS-1 SPE corresponds to VC-3; and STS-3c to STM-1. Also, with respect to the terms related to layering, physical medium, regenerator section, multiplexer section, and path layer of SDH are respectively called photonic, section, line, and path layer in SONET. The respective terms relating to mapping, multiplexing, overhead, and synchronization are almost identical.

Like SDH, SONET is based on the layering concept and hence uses the 125-μs frame, systematically utilizes overheads, and has the same base transmission rate. Also, it collectively accommodates all of the North American digital tributaries as well as the European DS-1E, features one-step multiplexing, and employs the same synchronization technique based on pointers as the SDH and consequently can encompass all of North America under a single synchronous digital network.

3.2 ORGANIZATION OF STM-*n* FRAME STRUCTURE

The STM-*n* frame structure is the essence of SDH and synchronous digital transmission because all the distinct characteristics of SDH, such as the transmission rate, the visibility of DS-0, the layer concept, and synchronization via pointers, are incorporated in the STM-*n* frame. This section describes the organization of the STM-*n* frame structure and the function of each constituent frame space.

3.2.1 Structure of STM-*n* Frame

The STM-*n* frame structure occupies 9B x 270 x *n* space over 125 μs, as shown in Figure 3.5. This means that the 9 x 270 x *n* chunks of bytes are repeated 8000 times per second, which translates into the bit rate of 155.52 x *n* Mbps (9 x 270 x *n* x 8 x 8 kbps). The 9B x 261 x *n* partition of the frame is used for carrying the payload, the 3B x 9 x *n* and 5B x 9 x *n* partitions are devoted to the overhead, and the remaining 1B x 9 x *n* is used for the AU PTR. Typically, *n* of VC-4 or 3*n* of VC-3 can be mapped into the payload. Since an AU-4 (or AU-3) signal is produced by adding an AU-4 (or AU-3) PTR to the VC-4 (or VC-3) signal, the STM-*n* payload together with the AU PTR make up the composition of *n* AUGs.

The AUG is equivalent to AU-4. On the other hand, BIM of three AU-3s results in the AUG, as is shown in Figure 3.13. Additional BIM of *n* AUGs, together with an SOH, produces the STM-*n* signal, as shown in Figure 3.14. Hence, to study the STM-*n* frame, it is enough to examine the AUG signal, and to study SOH as well, it is sufficient to investigate the STM-1 signal. Therefore, unless a special need arises, the discussion will center around STM-1.

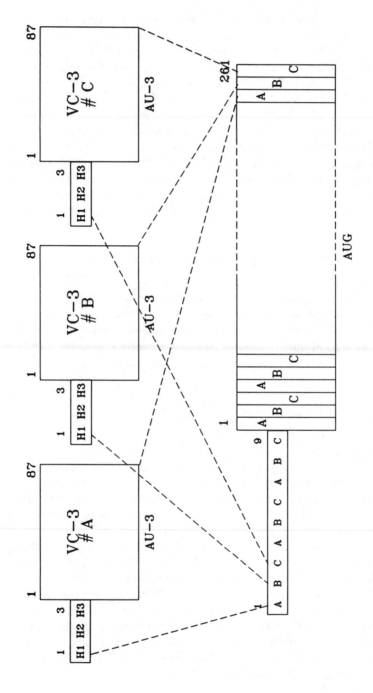

Figure 3.13 Organization of AUG.

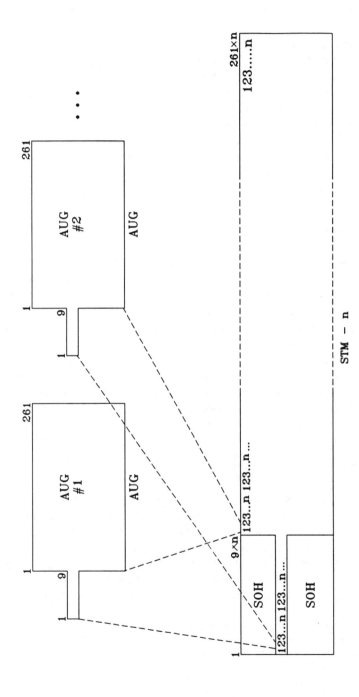

Figure 3.14 Organization of STM-*n*.

3.2.2 Structure of STM-1 Frame

The STM-1 frame is equivalent to an STM-n frame reduced by the factor of n, and has the 9B x 270 structure and 155.520-Mbps bit rate. The payload of STM-1 consists of 261 9B-sized columns. This corresponds to the space of one VC-4, or three VC-3s plus an FOH. On the other hand, the VC-4 signal consists of a single column of POH and 260 columns of VC-4 payload. Hence, it can be observed that the maximum payload that can be transmitted via STM-1 is 149.760 Mbps (= 9 x 260 x 8 x 8 kbps, or 155.52 Mbps x 260/270). Similar to the STM-n frame structure, the overhead portion of the STM-1 frame consists of a pair of SOHs and the AU PTR. The upper three rows are used for the regenerator section layer, the lower five rows are for the multiplexer section layer, and the fourth row is assigned to the AU PTR.

3.2.3 STM-1 Payload

The payload of STM-1 is used to carry the VC-4 or VC-3 signal. The loading of the VC-4 (or the VC-3) onto the STM-1 payload is done in a floating mode, with the pointer indicating the address of its first byte. Since the STM-1 payload consists of 2349B (= 9B x 261), if an address is assigned to each of 3B units of the payload, 783 total number of addresses are required. The address assignment in the row direction from 0 to 782 immediately after the AU PTR is shown in Figure 3.15. Such an addressing scheme is useful not only for the AU-4, but also for the AU-3. In the case of AU-3, three sets of 3 x 783 addresses are required to assign a unique address to three sets of the AU-3. Therefore, at least 10 bits are required for addressing the STM-1 payload. The address thus assigned also indicates the degree of offset of each address location from the pointer location.[7]

3.2.4 AU PTR

The nine bytes of AU PTR from the fourth row of the STM-1 overhead consist of three triplets of H1, H2, and H3, as shown in Figure 3.8. They are employed to keep track of the shifting address of the first bytes of the VC-4 or VC-3. If the STM-1's payload is carrying a VC-4 (i.e., in the case of AU-4), only the first triplet of H1, H2, and H3 is used. On the other hand, in the case of AU-3, each of the H1, H2, H3 triplets independently keeps track of the address of each AU-3. From the 24 bits that correspond to the three bytes of H1, H2, and H3, only 10 bits are needed

---

[7]This implies that the addresses to be indicated by the AU-4 PTR or AU-3 PTR total 783 in number. The number of addresses to be represented by the TU-3 PTR, TU-2 PTR, TU-12 PTR, and TU-11, are 765, 428, 140, and 104, respectively. Hence, 10 bits are sufficient for all these purposes. See Section 3.7.2.

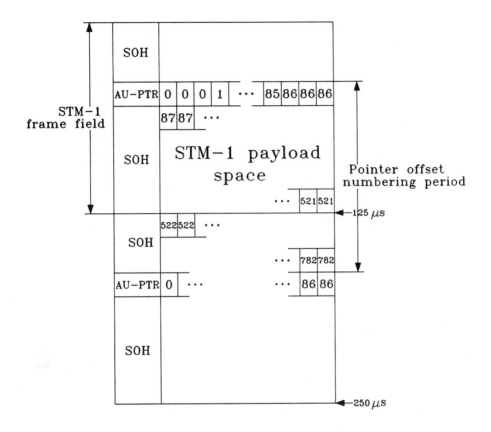

Figure 3.15 Addressing (or pointer-offset numbering) of the STM-1 payload.

to indicate the addresses from 0 to 783, and hence the remaining 14 bits are used for other purposes, as illustrated in Figure 3.8. A more detailed discussion of this matter will be given in Section 3.7.

3.2.5 Section Overhead

The SOH is split into the upper and lower parts by the AU PTR, which is located in between. The upper part is the RSOH and is used to raise the transmission reliability between regenerators. Each regenerator looks at only this part of the overhead and ignores the information carried in the rest of the frame. The lower part corresponds to the MSOH and is used to carry the information necessary to perform multiplexing and demultiplexing. When an STM-1 signal flows into the multiplexer through the local exchange regenerator, the multiplexer checks and examines only this part of the overhead. More details will be given in Section 3.6.

3.2.6 Transmission of STM-*n*

The transmission of STM-*n* in its natural form may result in long sequences of 0s and 1s. To prevent this, a scrambling scheme is used. The *frame synchronous scrambler* (FSS), whose generating polynomial is $1 + x^6 + x^7$, is used. This scrambler operates at the transmission rate and applies to all of the STM-*n* frame except for the first row of SOH, which is left unscrambled because it contains frame alignment words A1, A2 (see Section 3.6.2). The scrambler is reset to 1111111 following the last byte of the first row of the SOH, and then commences its frame scrambling function.

3.3 SYNCHRONOUS MULTIPLEXING STRUCTURE

Synchronous multiplexing refers to the procedure of multiplexing various tributaries into the STM-*n* signal. It involves the mapping of the tributaries into respective containers or virtual containers, aligning them on a tributary unit basis, multiplexing them in groups of tributary units, further aligning on an AU basis, multiplexing in groups of AUs, pointer processing, concatenation, and so on.

In this section, a general description of synchronous multiplexing will be given, with Figure 3.6 as the reference. A more detailed multiplexing structure will be described in the following section.

3.3.1 Formation of Tributaries

The tributaries that form the SM structure can be either North American or European. In Figure 3.6, the right rectangle represents the SM structure, and the left rectangle represents the existing AM structure. Hence, it can be seen that all of the tributaries are mapped into the STM-*n* either by going through both the AM and the SM, or directly through the SM.

To elaborate, we take American tributaries as an example. As can be seen from the figure, each of the DS-1, DS-2, and DS-3 signals can be directly mapped into the corresponding container in the SM, or can be asynchronously (or plesiochronously) multiplexed into a higher tributary, and then mapped to a larger container in the SM. Hence, the DS-1 can be either loaded directly onto the C-1 or multiplexed to the DS-2 first, and then get mapped into the C-2. The same scenario applies to DS-2 and DS-3.

The European SM structure is somewhat less complete than its North American equivalent.[8] The original SDH multiplexing structure (as shown in Figure 3.12) could accommodate direct mapping of all North American and European plesiochronous tributaries to the SM structure by supplying a suitable container to each tributary. However, for practical reasons, the structure was simplified, resulting in the one shown in Figure 3.6. As can be inferred by comparing the two figures, the direct mapping of DS-2E into the SM structure is not possible in the simplified version. DS-2E has to be multiplexed to the higher tributary DS-3E first and then mapped into C-3 before it can enter the SM structure.

3.3.2 Signal Elements of SM Structure

The signal elements that form the SM structure include the container, the VC, the TU, the TUG, the AU, the AUG, and the STM.

Container

The container is the most elemental unit of the SM structure in the sense that all of the North American and European PDH tributaries have to be mapped into the respective containers before they can proceed with the SM process and emerge as a part of the STM-n.

Containers of the SM structure are categorized into classes C-1, C-2, C-3, and C-4, with the number denoting the corresponding digital hierarchical levels. C-1 can further be categorized into C-11 and C-12, with C-11 accommodating the North American DS-1, and C-12 accommodating the European DS-1E. C-4 can carry either a DS-4E from the PDH, or the ATM cells of the BISDN. Particulars of the respective tributary mappings will be described in Section 3.5.

Virtual Containers

The VC's function is to support the connections between the path section layers in synchronous transmission. The VC consists of the payload, which carries the information data, and the POH. The payload portion corresponds to a container, and the whole VC frame is repeated every 125 or 500 μs. The four classes of VC, namely, VC-1, VC-2, VC-3, and VC-4, correspond to C-1, C-2, C-3, and C-4, respectively. Similar to C-1, VC-1 can be further categorized into VC-11 and VC-12. VC-1 and VC-2 are called the *lower-order VCs* and VC-3 and VC-4 are called the *higher-order*

---

[8]Although the initial SDH multiplexing structure was a complete one like the one in Figure 3.12, practical considerations and the desire for systematic multiplexing procedures led to a simplification to the structure in Figure 3.6.

VCs. The POH for the lower-order VCs is called *V5* and the POH for the higher-order VCs is called *VC-3 POH* or *VC-4 POH*.

Tributary Unit

The TU was designed to provide an adaptability between higher-order and lower-order path layers. For instance, lower-order VCs can be mapped into higher-order VCs through a TU or a TUG. A TU is created by attaching a TU PTR to a lower-order VC, and here the pointer is used to indicate the degree of offset of the lower-order VC relative to the starting position of the higher-order VC's frame. The TU is categorized into TU-1, TU-2, and TU-3. TU-1 is further categorized into TU-11 and TU-12, depending on the type of VC it contains.[9]

Tributary Unit Group

The role of the TUG is to collect one or more TUs and load them onto a fixed location on the payload of a higher-order VC. No overhead is added when a TUG is formed from the TUs. There are two classes of TUG: TUG-2 and TUG-3. TUG-2 is formed by assembling a homogeneous group of TU-1s or by a direct mapping of a single TU-2. Similarly, TUG-3 could be an assembly of TU-2s or a single TU-3.

Administrative Unit

AU functions as an adaptor between the higher-order path layer and the multiplexer section layer. As before, AU consists of the payload and the AU PTR. The payload carries a higher-order VC, and the AU PTR indicates the relative offset between the starting positions of the AU payload and the frame of the multiplexer section layer. In other words, the two types of AU, namely, AU-3 and AU-4, carry VC-3 and VC-4, respectively, and the AU PTR indicates the degree of offset of VC-3 or VC-4 with respect to the STM-*n* frame.

Administrative Unit Group

One or more AUs occupying a fixed location on an STM payload is called an AUG. An AUG can consist of three AU-3s or a single AU-4.

---

[9]The *lower-order* VCs refer to VC-1 and VC-2 and *higher-order* VCs refer to VC-3 and VC-4. In contrast, the lower VC and upper VC are relative concepts that indicate the relative relation between VCs; for example, VC-3 is a lower VC of VC-4.

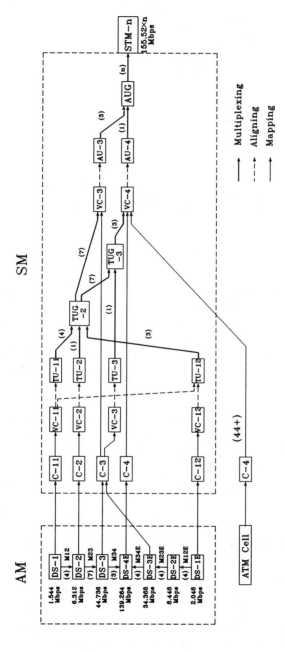

Figure 3.16 Classification of synchronous multiplexing procedure (including the path for ATM cell).

Synchronous Transport Module

The STM is the final product of the SM structure and is the signal that is actually transmitted over the synchronous transmission networks. STM-*n* is formed by byte-interleaving *n* AUGs and the addition of SOH to the beginning of its frame. Here, *n* of the numbers 1, 4, and 16 are of primary interest.

3.3.3 Procedures of Synchronous Multiplexing

Figure 3.6 depicts the synchronous multiplexing process in terms of the signal elements. If the figure is modified to reflect the various required procedures of SM, namely, mapping, aligning, pointer processing, and so on, then Figure 3.16 is the result.[10] In the figure, the solid arrow represents mapping, the dotted arrow represents aligning, and the boldfaced arrow represents multiplexing.

Mapping

Mapping is the appropriate transformation of tributaries into the corresponding containers or VCs across the SDH network border.[11] Since the tributaries are sent from an asynchronous environment, P/Z/N justification is required before they can be mapped into the synchronous containers or VCs.

Aligning

Aligning refers to the process of loading a VC onto a TU or an AU, along with the "frame offset" information. Here, the frame offset is due to the clock discrepancy between the VC and the corresponding TU or AU. The VC is aligned on 1B or 3B unit basis, and the alignment status is indicated by the TU or AU PTR.

Pointer Processing

Pointer processing is employed when the frame offset occurs due to the differences in the clock frequencies between a VC and the corresponding TU or AU. Pointer

---

[10]The bottom part of the figure shows the mapping of ATM cells into the VC-4. Detailed discussion of the procedure will be given in Section 3.5.7.

[11]A VC is nothing more than a container with a POH attached to it, and thus carries the identical payload as the container. Hence, when it is said a tributary is mapped into a container, there can also be the implication of a mapping into a VC because the two mapping procedures are equivalent.

processing involves the indication of the starting position (and its alteration information) of the VC on the payload space of the TU or AU, and the associated P/Z/N justification information.

Multiplexing

The process by which multiple lower-order path layer signals are adapted into a higher-order path layer signal, or the appropriate transformation of multiple higher-order path layer signals into a signal element of SM or AM, is called *multiplexing*.[12] Figure 3.16 shows characteristic multiplexing processes, such as the adaptation of TUs through a TUG so that they can be fitted onto a higher-order VC, or the adaptation of AUs through an AUG so they can be loaded onto the STM-*n*. Here, when the TU or the AU is multiplexed to the TUG or the AUG, no additional overhead is employed, while when the TUG is multiplexed to a higher-order VC, a POH is added, as was the case when a container was mapped into a VC. The SOH is added when AUG is multiplexed to the STM-*n*.

Concatenation

Concatenating multiple VCs, then reducing the total load to the capacity of a single VC while maintaining the integrity of the bit sequences is called *concatenation*. For example, if there exists a payload that needs an x number of containers for mapping, since it is difficult to preserve the correct bit sequence when they are divided into x number of VCs and then transmitted, the x VCs are concatenated to form a new virtual container VC-2-*xc* and are then transmitted. This is equivalent to the formation of a VC-4-*xc* by concatenating x VC-4s. Here, x denotes the number of concatenated VCs, and the letter c stands for concatenation. TU-2-*xc* and AU-4-*xc* are formed in a similar way.

3.3.4 Synchronous Multiplexing Structure

If Figure 3.6 or 3.16 is studied, it can be seen that the synchronous multiplexing structure can be broadly categorized into the lower-order structure, which involves C-1 and C-2, and the higher-order structure, which involves C-3 and C-4. In Figure 3.17, these two structures are drawn separately.

Lower-order multiplexing entails the transformation of the low-level tributaries DS-1, DS-1E, and DS-2 into TUG-2 after they go through multiple stages of mapping and multiplexing via corresponding containers, VCs, and TUs. Here, the peculiarity is that the tributary DS-2E is not a part of lower-order multiplexing because

---

[12]This is multiplexing in the narrow sense of the word. Multiplexing in the wide sense encompasses mapping, aligning, pointer processing, and concatenation.

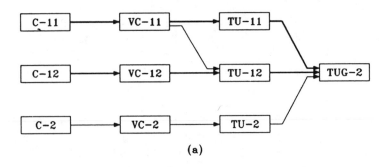

(a)

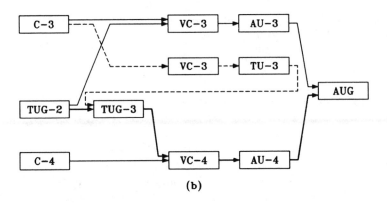

(b)

Figure 3.17 Synchronous multiplexing structures: (a) lower-order multiplexing; (b) higher-order multiplexing.

it has to be multiplexed to DS-3E and then get loaded onto the C-3. Also, it is worthwhile noting that the DS-1 can be mapped into C-11 and VC-11, and then multiplexed to TUG-2 via TU-11 or TU-12. Creation of TUG-2 marks the end of the lower-order multiplexing stage, and from then on TUG-2 is on an equal level with C-3 and C-4 and is hence a part of the higher-order multiplexing.

High-order multiplexing involves the multiplexing of high-level tributaries into the AUG and the STM-*n* via VC-3 or VC-4, and subsequently via AU-3 or AU-4. The associated signals include the tributaries DS-3, DS-3E, DS-4E, and TUG-2. Here, both DS-3 and DS-3E are mapped into C-3 and then VC-3. VC-3 can be aligned directly within AU-3 or multiplexed to VC-4 via TU-3, and then be aligned within AU-4.

Therefore, every multiplexing path is bound to go through the higher-order multiplexing stage, and the low-level tributaries must, in addition, go through lower-order multiplexing. As shown in Figure 3.17, there are four different multiplexing paths from the lower-order tributaries to TUG-2. Also, two independent multiplexing paths exist from TUG-2 to AUG, and, hence, a lower-order tributary can be multiplexed to AUG in eight different ways. On the other hand, higher-order multiplexing paths are three in number. Hence, in sum, 11 independent multiplexing paths exist within the SM structure.

Among the 11 different paths, the path that emerges as the most economical is the C-1\VC-1\TU-1\TUG-2\TUG-3\VC-4\AU-4\AUG path, which is highlighted in Figure 3.6. Since, from the point of view of a DS-1/DS-1E signal or the 64-kbps DS-0 signal, TUG-2 or TUG-3 is simply an assembly of TU-1s, DS-1/DS-1E is multiplexed directly to VC-4 via VC-1. Since this path evades the need for extra asynchronous multiplexing stages, it is the shortest path from DS-1/DS-1E to STM-n (this multiplexing path is described in detail in Section 3.1.4).

On the other hand, the path that is considered to be the most inefficient is the C-3\VC-3\TU-3\TUG-3\VC-4\AU-4\AUG path, which is indicated by a dotted line in Figure 3.17(b). Of course, in this path AUG-3 has no significance. However, the DS-3\VC-3\TU-3\VC-4\AU-4\AUG path is less efficient than the DS-3\VC-3\AU-3\AUG path. In addition, from the point of view of a DS-1/DS-1E, two stages of synchronous multiplexing are required for the signal to reach DS-3. Therefore, the path with the dotted line is the longest and is, hence, the least efficient of the 11 STM-n paths.

3.4 SYNCHRONOUS MULTIPLEXING PROCEDURES: A DETAILED DESCRIPTION

In the preceding section, an overview of synchronous multiplexing was given in terms of its signal elements, the various procedures it entails, and some characteristic multiplexing paths. With that section as the foundation, the present section will focus on a detailed description of synchronous multiplexing procedures. First, the multiplexing of lower-order VCs to TUG-2 will be studied, then the multiplexing of higher-order VCs or TUG-2s to the AUG. The respective mapping of each tributary to a corresponding container or a VC will be examined in the section that follows.

3.4.1 Multiplexing of Lower-Order VCs to TUG-2

As shown in Figure 3.18, the lower-order virtual containers VC-11, VC-12, and VC-2 are composed of 104B, 140B, and 428B, respectively. The first of the bytes, designated as V5, functions as the POH for each VC, and the remainder of the bytes are allotted for carrying the containers C-11, C-12, and C-2. The frame content of

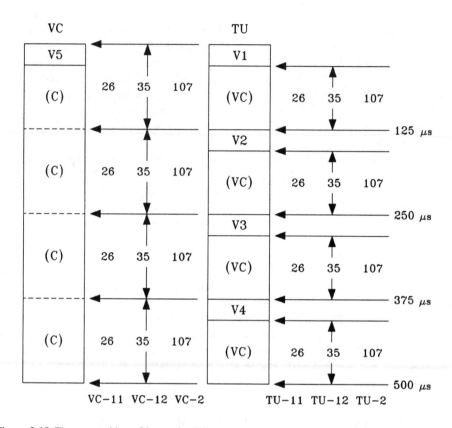

Figure 3.18 The composition of low-order VCs and TUs.

each lower-order VC is a concatenation of four container frames, each 26B, 35B, or 107B over 125 μs long, resulting in a 500-μs multiframe.

As can be seen in Figure 3.12, if four pointer bytes designated V1, V2, V3, and V4 are attached to the beginning of each of the frames of a VC, a TU is created. Hence, the multiframe of a TU occupies 27B x 4, 36B x 4, or 108B x 4 over 500 μs, with the 26B x 4, 35B x 4, or 107B x 4 portion corresponding to the four sets of payloads, and four bytes of pointers reflecting the relative positions of the payloads within the TU multiframe.

In terms of the base 125-μs frame unit, the sizes of TU-11, TU-12, and TU-2 are 9B x 3, 9B x 4, and 9B x 12, respectively, consisting of 3, 4, and 12 9B columns. Hence, if four TU-11s or three TU-12s are joined together through BIM, 12 columns result, equivalent to a single TU-2.[13] These 12 columns can be used to create a single

---

[13]The fact that TU-2 and TUG-2, created by multiplexing four TU-11s, have an identical size, has the same significance as obtaining tributary DS-2 by multiplexing four DS-1s.

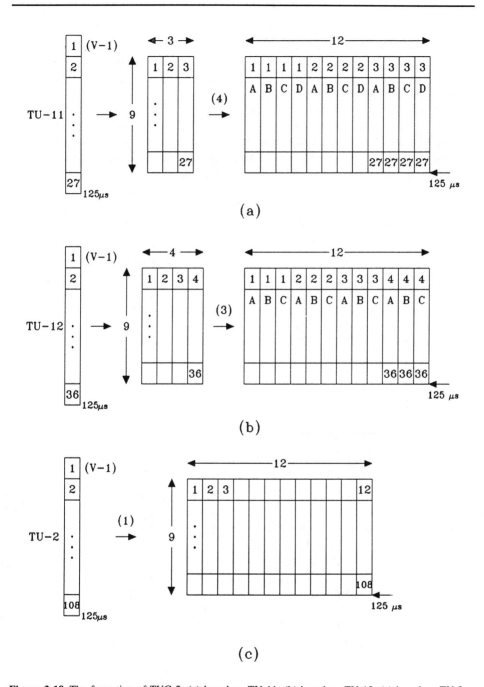

Figure 3.19 The formation of TUG-2: (a) based on TU-11; (b) based on TU-12; (c) based on TU-2.

TUG-2, and such a formation is depicted in Figure 3.19. When TUG-2 is formed, the TUs are made to have the same phase; that is, the starting points of each multiframe are identical, and the phase status is indicated by the H4 byte in the POH of the higher-order VC.

As can be seen in Figure 3.17(a), VC-11 can be aligned within TU-12 and then multiplexed to TUG-2. This is made possible by transforming the shape of VC-11 to resemble VC-12 first, and subsequently performing the alignment. Since VC-11 occupies 26B over 125 μs and VC-12 takes up 35B per 125 μs, 9B of fixed stuff bytes are needed to pad the VC-11. Figure 3.20 depicts such a transformation of

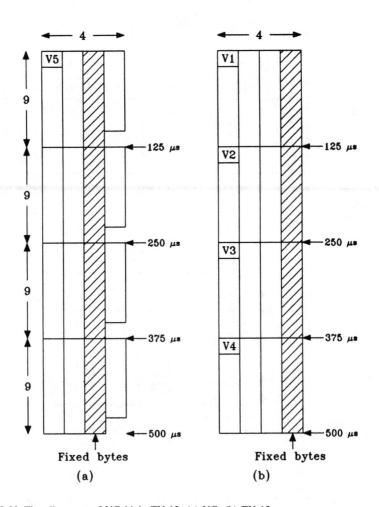

Figure 3.20 The alignment of VC-11 in TU-12: (a) VC; (b) TU-12.

VC-11 to VC-12. The figure displays a multiframe consisting of four 125-μs frames. The portion with dashed lines corresponds to the fixed stuff bytes. The dummy bytes are selected to have even parity. The resulting TU-12 is displayed to the right.

3.4.2 Mapping to VC-3

The VC-3 consists of 85 9B columns. The first column is used for the POH, and the remaining 84 columns correspond to the payload, which can carry a C-3 or a TUG-2. The C-3 is mapped into the VC-3 as shown in Figure 3.21(a). A description of its internal structure is given in Section 3.5. As for TUG-2, seven can be mapped to the VC payload, as shown in Figure 3.21(b). Since each TUG-2 contains 12 9B columns, 84 columns of the VC payload can be filled to its maximum capacity. Here, all the TUGs have the same phase within the VC-3, and the phase information is conveyed by the H4 byte in the POH of the VC-3.

3.4.3 Multiplexing to TUG-3

TUG-3 consists of 86 9B columns, allowing the mapping of one VC-3 or TU-3, or seven TUG-2s into its payload. As shown in Figure 3.22(a), the addition of three pointer bytes H1, H2, and H3 to the VC-3 results in the TU-3, and the further addition of six fixed stuff bytes in the same column results in the TUG-3. Here, the starting position of the VC within the TU-3 (hence, within the TUG-3) can vary, and this information is indicated accordingly by the pointer bytes. One thing that should be mentioned about the mapping of VC-3s into TUG-3 is that only the VCs mapped from the C-3s are allowed, not those mapped from the TUG-2s.

The TUG-2 is mapped into the TUG-3 in a similar fashion, but in this case a POH is not needed. This is because TUG-3s are multiplexed to the VC-4 as a single unit, and the POH can be added at that instant. Figure 3.22(b) depicts the multiplexing of TUG-2s to the TUG-3, and here pointer bytes such as the H1, H2, and H3 from Figure 3.22(a) are lacking. The absence of a pointer is indicated by the *null pointer indication* (NPI), and this is achieved by filling the two bytes that correspond to H1H2 with the value 1001ss111110000 (see Section 3.7.2 for a description of pointer functions).

3.4.4 Mapping Into VC-4

The VC-4 is composed of 261 columns, with each column being 9B in size. The first column is used for the POH, and the remaining 260 columns are employed to carry the payload, to which can be mapped a C-4 or TUG-3. The multiplexing of

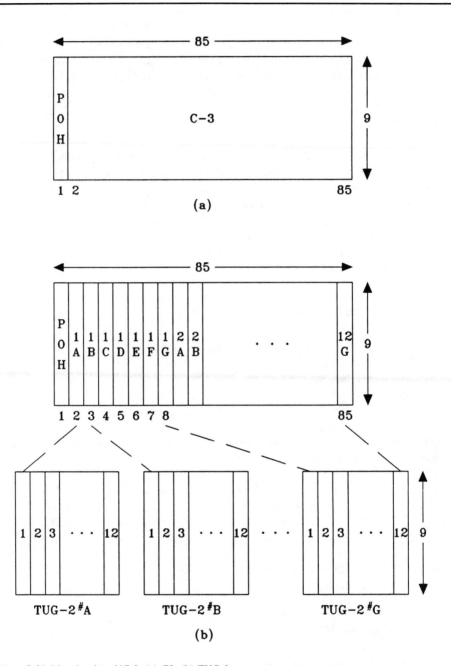

Figure 3.21 Mapping into VC-3: (a) C3; (b) TUG-2.

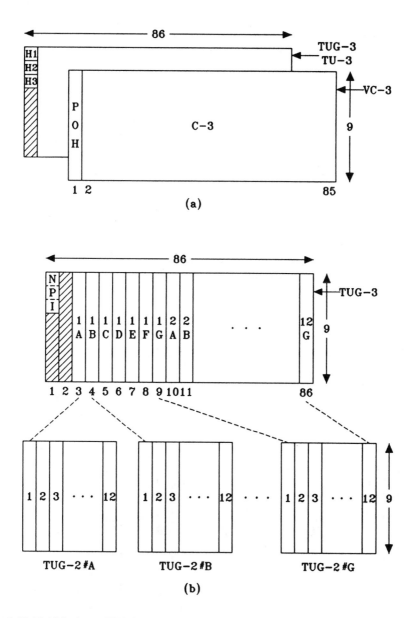

Figure 3.22 Multiplexing to TUG-3: (a) VC-3/TU-3; (b) TUG-2.

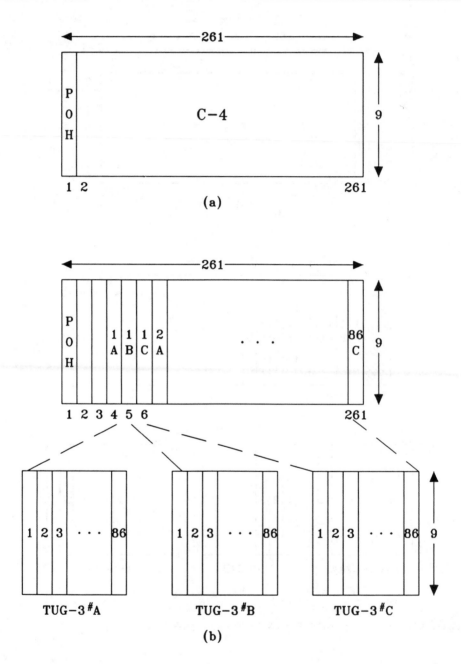

Figure 3.23 Mapping into VC-4: (a) C4; (b) TUG-3.

the C-4 to the VC-4 is shown in Figure 3.23(a). The internal structure of C-4 is discussed in detail in Section 3.5.

Three TUG-3s can be byte-interleaved together and mapped into the payload of VC-4, as shown in Figure 3.23(b). Since each TUG-3 is 9B x 86 in size, loading three of them to the VC-4 leaves it with two spare columns, which can be filled with fixed stuff bytes. All the TUGs are arranged to have the same phase within the VC-4, and the phase information is carried by the H4 byte, which is a part of the VC-4's POH.

3.4.5 Multiplexing to AUG

An AUG is composed of 261 9B column plus 9 1B columns, which are placed at the beginning of the fourth row, as shown in Figure 3.13. The addition of an SOH 3B x 9 and 5B x 9 in size transforms the AUG into the STM-1. Also, byte-interleaving n AUGs and the addition of a corresponding SOH results in the STM-n, as shown in Figure 3.14. AUG can be formed either from three AU-3s or from a single AU-4.

An AU-4 is produced by attaching a 9B pointer to the VC-4. The pointer bytes are H1, Y, Y, H2, 1*, 1*, H3, H3, H3, with Y and 1 representing 1001ss11 and 11111111, respectively.[14] Three H3s are due to the fact that, in the case of VC-4, P/Z/N justification is done on a three-byte basis. A single AU-4 is directly mapped into the AUG.

An AU-3 is formed by adding two 9B columns of fixed stuff bytes to the VC-3 so that it acquires 87 columns in all, and then adding a 3B pointer. VC-3 can float within the AU-3, and its starting point is indicated by the AU-3 pointer. The fixed stuff bytes are placed in the thirtieth and fifty-ninth columns, and the three associated pointer bytes are H1, H2, and H3. The AUG is produced by byte-interleaving three AU-3s, and the process is depicted in Figure 3.24.

3.4.6 Concatenation of AU-4

If the payload to be transmitted is greater than the transmission capacity of a single VC-4, AU-4-xc, which is a concatenation of x AU-4s, can be used instead. Since externally AU-4-xc looks identical to the AUG-x, a pointer is used to indicate the concatenation status. The concatenation pointer's format is equivalent to x byte-interleaved AU-4 PTRs. Here, the first of the set maintains its normal pointer function,

---

[14]Asterisks are used in this chapter to denote a byte consisting of identical bits. For example, 1* denotes 11111111, and likewise, R* denotes RRRRRRRR.

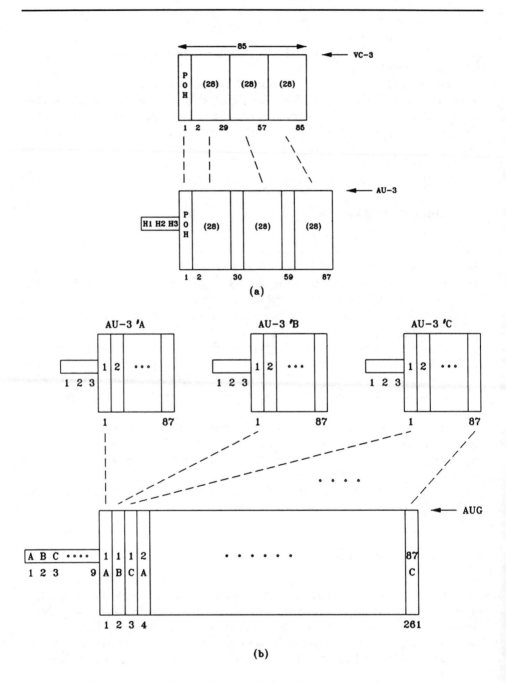

Figure 3.24 Multiplexing to AUG: (a) alignment of VC-3; (b) multiplexing of AU-3.

and the remaining $x - 1$ pointer elements denote the concatenation status, which is achieved by setting H1 and H2 bytes to 1001ss1111111111.[15]

The concatenated administrative unit's payload consists of $261x$ columns. When $x = 1$ (e.g., in the case of AU-4), the payload is partitioned into 1 column devoted to the POH and 260 columns for carrying the C-4, which translates into a payload capacity of 149.76 Mbps (= 260 x 9 x 64 kbps). When $x > 1$, only one of the x first columns is used for SOH, and the remaining $x - 1$ columns are stuffed with fixed overheads. Hence, the payload capacity becomes $149.736x$ Mbps, and consequently, in the case of $x = 4$, the capacity becomes 599.04 Mbps.

3.5 MAPPING OF TRIBUTARIES

In the preceding two sections, the synchronous multiplexing structure and the multiplexing procedures within it were examined. Hence, the multiplexing of a container or a virtual container to the STM-n via AUG and other intermediate signal elements was studied. In this section, the attention will shift to the mapping process of tributaries into the respective containers and virtual containers. This is a highly significant step that can be said to be the crucial link between the asynchronous multiplexing structure of the existing digital hierarchy and the nascent synchronous multiplexing structure. First, asynchronous and synchronous mappings will be examined, then floating mode and locked mode will be studied, and finally the mapping method for each respective tributary will be discussed.

3.5.1 Asynchronous and Synchronous Mapping

The mapping of a tributary into a virtual container can be classified as asynchronous, bit-synchronous, or byte-synchronous. Since a tributary is generally formed by using a clock that is independent of the clock used to make the corresponding virtual container, asynchronous mapping can be said to be the most common. However, those tributaries that are created as links to the synchronous multiplexers can be manipulated to use the same clock as the synchronous multiplexers, and in this case it is much simpler to use synchronous mapping. Such synchronous mapping is useful in permitting the direct entrance of DS-0 into the SM structure via DS-1 or DS-1E. Depending on whether the boundary of the DS-0 byte is exposed or not, synchronous mapping can be subdivided into bit-synchronous and byte-synchronous modes.

---

[15]Note that the union of Y and 1* can also function as a concatenation indicator. Here, *ss* does not signify anything. See Section 3.7.2.

Asynchronous Mapping

Asynchronous mapping is applicable when the tributary clock is independent of the container clock or the virtual container clock. In practice, the respective clocks have a plesiochronous relationship. Asynchronous mapping can be applied to all the tributaries (i.e., DS-1, DS-1E, DS-2, DS-3, DS-3E, and DS-4E).

The most basic procedure in asychronous mapping is the synchronizing and resolving the respective clock offsets. In the case of DS-1, DS-1E, DS-2, and DS-3E, $P/Z/N$ justification via bit-stuffing is used, and in the case of DS-3 and DS-4E, only the positive justification with bit stuffing is used.

$P/Z/N$ justification is used when the nominal transmission capacity of the signal after the synchronization procedure is identical to its nominal bit rate before the procedure; in other words, when, as in the case of mapping of tributaries, the bit rate of a VC payload is the same as the nominal bit rate of the corresponding tributary. In this case, *zero justification* is maintained in normal situations, but when the tributary bit rate becomes lower than the bit rate of the VC payload, when the accumulated offset becomes one bit long, a null bit (or a garbage bit) is sent in place of effective information data (*positive justification*). Conversely, if the tributary's bit rate becomes high with respect to the VC bit rate, a spare bit in the payload is used to absorb the offset (*negative justification*).

The $P/Z/N$ justification function is performed through the justification opportunity bits J_1, J_2, and the execution status is indicated through the use of the justification control bits C_1 and C_2. J_1 is used as an overhead bit in normal operation, but acts as a spare bit to carry the extra data in the case of negative justification; similarly, J_2 is normally a part of the effective payload, but is used to carry the null bit in the case of positive justification.

DS-1, DS-1E, and DS-2 each have three sets of C_1 and C_2 control bits, and DS-3E has five. If C_1s are all 0, this signifies that J_1 is a regular information bit, and if C_1s are all 1, it implies that J_1 is carrying a spare bit. Similarly, C_2 indicates whether or not J_2 is carrying a null bit. If, due to an error in the transmission process, there appears to be a lack of unanimity among the C_1 and C_2 bits, the receiver extracts the correct justification status according to the majority vote rule.

Positive justification is the synchronization procedure that is applied when the nominal transmission capacity of the signal after the synchronization becomes higher than its original nominal bit rate. In this case, since no negative justification occurs, only the opportunity bit and control bit for positive justification are needed. These bits are denoted by J and C, respectively. For every DS-3 or DS-4E, five C-bits are assigned to every J-bit. If the Cs are all 0, this signifies that J is an information bit, and if Cs are all 1, this means that J is a justification bit, and the majority vote rule applies in case of bit errors.

Bit-Synchronous mapping

Bit-synchronous mapping is a mapping procedure that is used when the tributary's clock is synchronized with the container clock or the virtual container clock. Hence, synchronous mapping does not require synchronization and consequently no justification occurs. Bit-synchronous mapping is the general case of synchronous mapping and is performed on a bit basis regardless of the internal composition of the tributary involved. In other words, with the exception that no synchronization procedure is required, bit-synchronous mapping is equivalent to asynchronous mapping. Bit-synchronous mapping applies to tributaries DS-1, DS-1E, and DS-2.

Byte-Synchronous Mapping

Byte-synchronous mapping is a special case of synchronous mapping, which is used when DS-0 is mapped into the VC such that its boundary is exposed. Byte-synchronous mapping can be applied to DS-1 and DS-1E. When one of these tributaries is to be byte-synchronously mapped into a VC, its frame identity must be confirmed first, and then each DS-0 byte must be mapped into an assigned location. At this point in the operation, the frame bits and signaling bits of the tributary must be mapped also.

In the case of DS-1, the frame bits and the signaling bits are byte-synchronously mapped directly to preassigned locations. There are four signaling bits for each frame, and, hence, to represent signaling bits for 24 DS-0s, six frames in all are required. Consequently, 24 frames are required to represent the ABCD signal, which would occupy 3 ms ($= 125$ μs x 24) of time. To be able to distinguish between these frames, overheads P_0, P_1 are used, and, especially for operation in the locked mode[16], H4's (from the higher-order VC POH) 3-ms mode is used.[17]

In the case of DS-1E, 30 DS-0 channels are visibly mapped into the VC-12. If DS-1E is operating in *channel-associated signaling* (CAS) mode, multiframe bits as well as signaling bits are mapped into one DS-0-sized channel in the VC-12. If it is operating in the *common channel signaling* (CCS) mode, one additional DS-0 channel is added instead, for 31 DS-0 channels in all (see Table 3.2 in the following subsection). In both cases, it is not essential to map the frame bits, but sufficient space is reserved for them just in case. For indicating the multiframe and CAS for 30 channels, 16 frames (2 ms) are required, and to be able to identify each of the frames, overheads P_0 and P_1 are used. In the locked mode, H4's 2-ms mode is used.

---

[16]When the lower-order VC is allowed to float within the corresponding TU, this is called the *floating mode* of operation, and, inversely, if the VC is locked within TU, this is called the *locked mode*. See Section 3.5.2.

[17]H4 is used to indicate the multiframe status and can give 500-μs, 2-ms, and 3-ms indications. See Section 3.6.4.

3.5.2 Floating and Locked Modes of Operation

In general, after the lower-order tributaries are mapped into VC-n (n = 11, 12, 2), VC-n floats freely in the payload of corresponding TU-n, and its address is indicated by the TU-n PTR. This is called the *floating mode* of operation. However, when VC-n is synchronized with VC-m(m = 3, 4), VC-n maintains a fixed location within the TU-n. Consequently, the starting position of the VC is fixed to the starting position of the TU-n payload, and, hence, is called the *locked mode* of operation.

In locked mode, the TU-n PTR is not separately needed. Also, the fact that VC-n and VC-m are synchronized implies that they were created at the same place, which in turn implies that they will follow the same transmission paths. Hence, in this case, POH V5 for VC-n is not separately needed. In other words, in locked mode, V1, V2, V3, V4, and V5 bytes are not required, and, consequently, there is no need to construct a 500-μs multiframe.

Therefore, the mapping technique for the floating mode of operation is defined separately on a 125-μs frame unit basis. In the case of VC-11 and VC-12, a type of mapping that combines byte-synchronous and locked modes can be defined. Here, as a mark for the CAS phase, the H4 byte in the POH of higher-order VC-m is used. To be more specific, a 3-ms mode using five bits from H4, namely, P_1, P_0, SI_1, SI_0, and T, is employed for VC-11, and a 2-ms mode using CI_3, CI_2, CI_1, and T-bits is used for VC-12 (see Section 3.6.4 for a detailed description of the H4 byte).

3.5.3 Mapping of DS-1 and DS-1E

DS-1 and DS-1E are mapped into VC-11 and VC-12 in the floating mode, and the mapping format is depicted in Figure 3.25. Such a format is common to both asynchronous and synchronous modes. In the figure, I* represents the tributary information byte (hence, I* = IIIIIIII), R* is a byte that is composed of fixed R-bits (or R* = RRRRRRRR), and the bytes W_1 to W_4 and Y_1 to Y_4 can vary depending on whether or not the mapping is performed in asynchronous mode.

In asynchronous mode, W_1 = RRRRRRIR, W_2 = W_3 = C_1C_2OOOOIR, W_4 = C_1C_2RRRJ$_1$J$_2$R, and Y_1 = R*, Y_2 = Y_3 = C_1C_2OOOORR, Y_4 = C_1C_2RRRRRJ$_1$. Here I represents the effective information bit, O represents the overhead bit, and three C_1 bits and three C_2 bits are the justification control bits corresponding to the justification opportunity bits J_1 and J_2, respectively. In the case of VC-12, the J_2 bit is the first of the bits in 32I* space, which immediately follows Y_4.

In bit-synchronous mode, W_1 = W_4 = 10RRRRIR, W_2 = W_3 = 10OOOOIR, and Y_1 = Y_4 = 10RRRRRR, Y_2 = Y_3 = 10OOOORR. Since there is no justification required in bit-synchronous mode, J_1 and J_2 have been altered to R and I, respec-

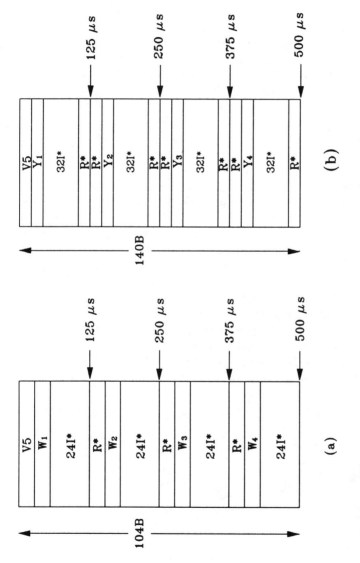

Figure 3.25 Mapping of DS-1 and DS-1E (floating mode): (a) DS-1; (b) DS-1E (see Table 3.1 for W_1 to W_4 and Y_1 to Y_4).

tively. Also, to reflect this change, the values of C_1 and C_2 have been fixed to all 1s and 0s, respectively.

In the byte-synchronous case, $W_1 = W_2 = W_3 = W_4 = P_1P_0S_1S_2S_3S_4FR$, and $Y_1 = Y_2 = Y_3 = Y_4 = P_1P_0RRRRRR$. Here F represents the DS-1's frame bit, and S_1 to S_4 represent the signaling bits. Also, P_1P_0 are used to adjust the phase of the signal frame, with the initial frame acquiring $P_1P_0 = 00$. In the case of DS-1E, the first byte from the 32I* space is filled with the R* or the first byte from DS-1E, the seventeenth byte is used for a multiframe indication or to contain signaling bits, and the remaining 30I* are used as information channels. If CCS is employed, the seventeenth byte is used to carry an additional channel of information, since signaling bits are unnecessary within VC-12 in this case.

In locked mode, POH V5 is not separately needed, and V5 equals R* at all times. In bit-synchronous mapping, in addition, $W_1 = W_2 = W_3 = W_4 = W = 10RRRRIR$ and $Y_1 = Y_2 = Y_3 = Y_4 = Y = 10RRRRRR$. Also, for byte-synchronous mapping, $W_1 = W_2 = W_3 = W_4 = W = RRS_1S_2S_3S_4FR$, and $Y_1 = Y_2 = Y_3 = Y_4 = R*$. If this is the case, the mapping can be performed on a 125-μs unit basis, and the mapping format of Figure 3.25 simplifies to that of Figure 3.26. The format of other information bytes is identical to that of the floating mode case.

Table 3.1 gives a summary of the contents of W_1 to W_4 and Y_1 to Y_4 bytes for the locked-mode and floating-mode operations.

When the locked mode is employed, the phase relationship between the signal bits is indicated by the POH H4 in the higher-order VC. In the case of DS-1, since the ABCD signal marks for 24 DS-0 channels require 24 frames, this relationship is represented by H4's 3-ms mode bits $P_1P_2SI_2SI_1T$. In the case of DS-1E, each frame can convey two signaling channels, which means that for 30 signaling channels and an additional multiframe indication, 16 frames are required, and this relationship is indicated by the H4's 2-ms mode bits $CI_1CI_2CI_1T$. Table 3.2 shows a comparison of the locked mode and the floating mode in terms of the signaling phase alignment

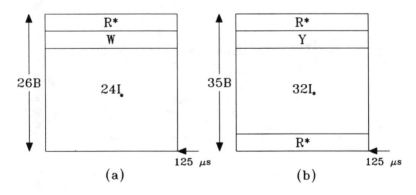

Figure 3.26 Mapping of DS-1 and DS-1E (locked mode): (a) DS-1; (b) DS-1E.

relationship. In the table, the subscripts 1 to 24 or 1 to 30 on the ABCD signaling marks indicate the corresponding signal's channel numbers.

3.5.4 Mapping of DS-2

The procedure for mapping the DS-2 into the VC-2 is depicted in Figure 3.27. The picture displays only a single 125-μs frame, and the 500-μs multiframe is just four replications of such a frame structure, with the exception that the first byte, denoted by V5/R*, becomes V5 in the first frame and R* in the remaining three frames.

In asynchronous mapping, the byte contents of W_1 to W_4 become $W_1 = IIIIIIIR$, $W_2 = W_3 = C_1C_2OOOIR$, $W_4 = C_1C_2IIIJ_1J_2R$, and for the synchronous case, $W_1 = IIIIIIIR$, $W_2 = W_3 = 1OOOOOIR$, $W_4 = 10IIIRIR$. It should be noted, about the

Table 3.1
The Contents of W_1 to W_4 and Y_1 to Y_4
(a) Floating Mode

		Asynchronous	*Bit Synchronous*	*Byte Synchronous*
DS-1 to VC-11 mapping	W_1	RRRRRRIR	10RRRRIR	$P_1P_2S_1S_2S_3S_4FR$
	W_2	$C_1C_2OOOOIR$	10OOOOIR	$P_1P_2S_1S_2S_3S_4FR$
	W_3	$C_1C_2OOOOIR$	10OOOOIR	$P_1P_2S_1S_2S_3S_4FR$
	W_4	$C_1C_2RRRJ_1J_2R$	10RRRRIR	$P_1P_2S_1S_2S_3S_4FR$
DS-1E to VC-12 mapping	Y_1	RRRRRRRR	10RRRRRR	$P_1P_0RRRRRR$
	Y_2	$C_1C_2OOOOIR$	10OOOORR	$P_1P_0RRRRRR$
	Y_3	$C_1C_2OOOOIR$	10OOOORR	$P_1P_0RRRRRR$
	Y_4	$C_1C_2RRRRJ_1*$	10RRRRRR	$P_1P_0RRRRRR$

*+J_2 is the bit right behind J_1

(b) Locked Mode

		Bit Synchronous	*Byte Synchronous*
DS-1 to VC-11 mapping	W_1	10RRRRIR	$RRS_1S_2S_3S_4FR$
	W_2	10RRRRIR	$RRS_1S_2S_3S_4FR$
	W_3	10RRRRIR	$RRS_1S_2S_3S_4FR$
	W_4	10RRRRIR	$RRS_1S_2S_3S_4FR$
DS-1E to VC-12 mapping	Y_1	10RRRRRR	RRRRRRRR
	Y_2	10RRRRRR	RRRRRRRR
	Y_3	10RRRRRR	RRRRRRRR
	Y_4	10RRRRRR	RRRRRRRR

Table 3.2
Signaling and Phase Indication
(a) DS-1

Signaling				Floating Mode		Locked Mode				
S_1	S_2	S_3	S_4	P_1	P_0 (VC-11)	P_1	P_0	SI_2	SI_1	$T(H4)$
A_1	A_2	A_3	A_4	0	0	0	0	0	0	0
A_5	A_6	A_7	A_8	0	0	0	0	0	0	1
A_9	A_{10}	A_{11}	A_{12}	0	0	0	0	0	1	0
A_{13}	A_{14}	A_{15}	A_{16}	0	0	0	0	0	1	1
A_{17}	A_{18}	A_{19}	A_{20}	0	0	0	0	1	0	0
A_{21}	A_{22}	A_{23}	A_{24}	0	0	0	0	1	0	1
B_1	B_2	B_3	B_4	0	1	0	1	0	0	0
B_5	B_6	B_7	B_8	0	1	0	1	0	0	1
B_9	B_{10}	B_{11}	B_{12}	0	1	0	1	0	1	0
B_{13}	B_{14}	B_{15}	B_{16}	0	1	0	1	0	1	1
B_{17}	B_{18}	B_{19}	B_{20}	0	1	0	1	1	0	0
B_{21}	B_{22}	B_{23}	B_{24}	0	1	0	1	1	0	1
C_1	C_2	C_3	C_4	1	0	1	0	0	0	0
C_5	C_6	C_7	C_8	1	0	1	0	0	0	1
C_9	C_{10}	C_{11}	C_{12}	1	0	1	0	0	1	0
C_{13}	C_{14}	C_{15}	C_{16}	1	0	1	0	0	1	1
C_{17}	C_{18}	C_{19}	C_{20}	1	0	1	0	1	0	0
C_{21}	C_{22}	C_{23}	C_{24}	1	0	1	0	1	0	1
D_1	D_2	D_3	D_4	1	1	1	1	0	0	0
D_5	D_6	D_7	D_8	1	1	1	1	0	0	1
D_9	D_{10}	D_{11}	D_{12}	1	1	1	1	0	1	0
D_{13}	D_{14}	D_{15}	D_{16}	1	1	1	1	0	1	1
D_{17}	D_{18}	D_{19}	D_{20}	1	1	1	1	1	0	0
D_{21}	D_{22}	D_{23}	D_{24}	1	1	1	1	1	0	1

Table 3.2 (cont'd)

(b) DS-1E

		Signaling						Floating Mode		Locked Mode			
S_1	S_2	S_3	S_4	S_1	S_2	S_3	S_4	P_1	P_0 (VC-12)	CI_3	CI_2	CI_1	T(H4)
0	0	0	0	x	y	x	x	0	0	0	0	0	0
A_1	B_1	C_1	D_1	A_{16}	B_{16}	C_{16}	D_{16}	0	0	0	0	0	1
A_2	B_2	C_2	D_2	A_{17}	B_{17}	C_{17}	D_{17}	0	0	0	0	1	0
A_3	B_3	C_3	D_3	A_{18}	B_{18}	C_{18}	D_{18}	0	0	0	0	1	1
A_4	B_4	C_4	D_4	A_{19}	B_{19}	C_{19}	D_{19}	0	1	0	1	0	0
A_5	B_5	C_5	D_5	A_{20}	B_{20}	C_{20}	D_{20}	0	1	0	1	0	1
A_6	B_6	C_6	D_6	A_{21}	B_{21}	C_{21}	D_{21}	0	1	0	1	1	0
A_7	B_7	C_7	D_7	A_{22}	B_{22}	C_{22}	D_{22}	0	1	0	1	1	1
A_8	B_8	C_8	D_8	A_{23}	B_{23}	C_{23}	D_{23}	1	0	1	0	0	0
A_9	B_9	C_9	D_9	A_{24}	B_{24}	C_{24}	D_{24}	1	0	1	0	0	1
A_{10}	B_{10}	C_{10}	D_{10}	A_{25}	B_{25}	C_{25}	D_{25}	1	0	1	0	1	0
A_{11}	B_{11}	C_{11}	D_{11}	A_{26}	B_{26}	C_{26}	D_{26}	1	0	1	0	1	1
A_{12}	B_{12}	C_{12}	D_{12}	A_{27}	B_{27}	C_{27}	D_{27}	1	1	1	1	0	0
A_{13}	B_{13}	C_{13}	D_{13}	A_{28}	B_{28}	C_{28}	D_{28}	1	1	1	1	0	1
A_{14}	B_{14}	C_{14}	D_{14}	A_{29}	B_{29}	C_{29}	D_{29}	1	1	1	1	1	0
A_{15}	B_{15}	C_{15}	D_{15}	A_{30}	B_{30}	C_{30}	D_{30}	1	1	1	1	1	1

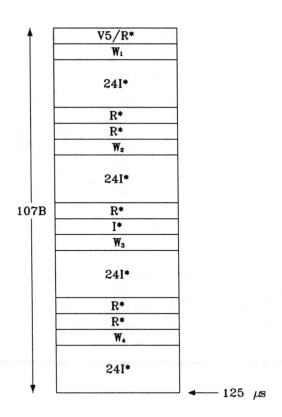

$$W_1 = IIIIIIIR \quad W_2 = W_3 = C_1C_2\,000IR \quad W_4 = C_1C_2IIIJ_1\,J_2R \text{ (asynchronous)}$$
$$W_1 = IIIIIIIR \quad W_2 = W_3 = 100000\,IR \quad W_4 = 10IIIRIR \text{ (synchronous)}$$

Figure 3.27 Mapping of DS-2.

operation of the justification bits C_1, C_2, J_1, and J_2 that, for the DS-1 or the DS-1E, justification occurs every 500 μs, but it occurs every 125 μs for the DS-2 signal.

3.5.5 Mapping of DS-3 or DS-3E

The mapping procedure of the tributary DS-3 into the VC-3 is shown in Figure 3.28(a). Inside the 125-μs frame, the $(3Q + 25I^*) \times 3$ format subframe in the slanted line is repeated nine times. The subframe's organization is shown in detail in Figure 3.28(b). In the picture, $W_1 = RRCIIIII$, $W_2 = CCRRRRRR$, and $W_3 = CCRROORJ$,

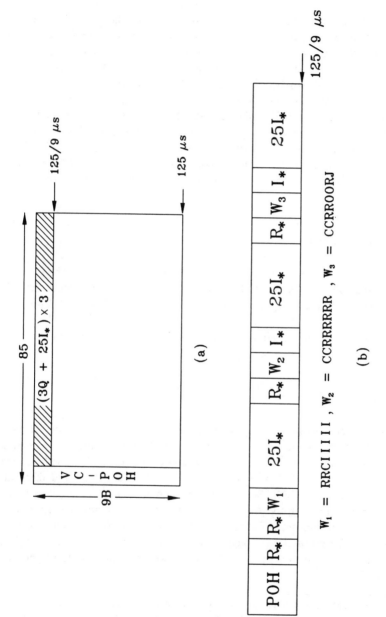

$W_1 = \text{RRCIIIII}$, $W_2 = \text{CCRRRRRR}$, $W_3 = \text{CCRROORJ}$

(b)

Figure 3.28 Mapping of DS-3 into VC-3: (a) 125 μs; (b) 125/9-μs subframe.

respectively. Hence, for the synchronization of DS-3, positive justification is used every 125/9 μs, and 5 C-bits are used for the justification control.

The tributary DS-3E is mapped into the VC-3 as shown in Figure 3.29(a). Within the 125-μs frame, the 125/3-μs subframe is repeated three times, and the subframe is divided into three smaller subframes of 125/9 μs each. The 125/9-μs subframes all have a format like the one shown in Figure 3.29(b), except for the Q1 to Q4 bytes. These Q-bytes become Y_1, Y_1, I^*, and I^* in the first two 125/9-μs subframes, and Y_1, R^*, Y_2, and Y_3 in the third of the 125/9-μs subframes, where $Y_1 = RRRRRRC_1C_2$, $Y_2 = RRRRRRRJ_1$, and $Y_3 = J_2IIIIIII$. This relationship is displayed in Table 3.3. Consequently, it can be inferred that for synchronization of DS-3E, P/Z/N justification is employed every 125/3 μs, and for justification control, five pairs of C_1 and C_2 bits are used. Also, since one fixed stuff byte is inserted for every three effective information bytes, it can be seen that about a quarter of the VC-3 payload is wasted.

3.5.6 Mapping of DS-4E

The mapping of DS-4E into the VC-4 is depicted in Figure 3.30(a). The $(Q + 12I^*)$ x 20 format subframe in the slanted line is repeated nine times within the 125-μs frame, and the subframe's organization is as displayed in Figure 3.30(b). In the figure, $Y_1 = Y_2 = Y_3 = Y_4 = Y_5 = CRRRRROO$, and $Y_6 = IIIIIIJR$. For the synchronization of DS-4E, positive justification is employed, and for justification control, five C-bits are used.

3.5.7 Mapping of ATM Cell

The ATM cell is composed of 5 bytes of header and 48 bytes of information data. The fifth of the ATM header bytes corresponds to the *header error control* (HEC) byte and is produced by applying *cyclic redundancy checking* (CRC) with generating polynomial $g(x) = x^8 + x^2 + x + 1$ to the preceding four bytes and then adding 01010101 to the resulting CRC. Such a tracking scheme enables the detection of the boundary of an ATM cell in the ATM cell bit stream. Before any mapping or transmission, the 48 bytes from the ATM information space go through a *self-synchronous scrambling* (SSS) based on the characteristic polynomial $x^{43} + 1$. So a treated ATM cell can be mapped into the VC-n or VC-n-xc and then go through synchronous multiplexing.[18]

---

[18]In case an ATM cell stream is mapped into the VC-4-xc, it is mapped into the container space of 260x columns, and $x - 1$ columns out of the x columns for POH are filled with fixed stuff bytes. The composition of ATM cells is described in detail in Chapter 4. When an ATM cell is mapped into the VC-4, VC-4's POH C2 byte is recorded as 00010011 to indicate this status (see 3.6.4.).

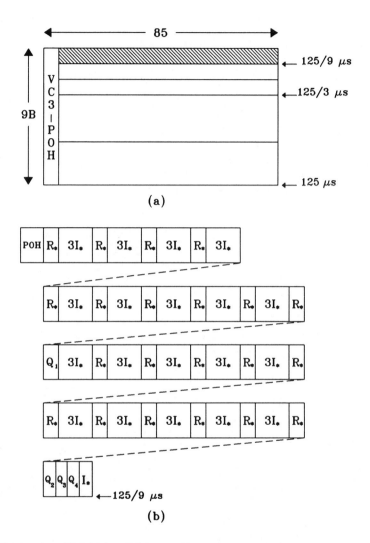

Figure 3.29 Mapping of DS-3E into VC-3: (a) 125-μs frame; (b) 125/9-μs subframe (see Table 3.3 for Q_1 to Q_4).

Table 3.3
The Structure of Q_1 to Q_4 Bytes

Location	Q_1	Q_2	Q_3	Q_4
First 125/9 µs subframe	Y_1	Y_2	I*	I*
Second 125/9 µs subframe	Y_1	Y_2	I*	I*
Third 125/9 µs subframe	Y_1	R*	Y_2	Y_3

$Y_1 = RRRRRRC_1C_2$, $Y_2 = RRRRRRRJ_1$, $Y_3 = J_2$ IIIIII

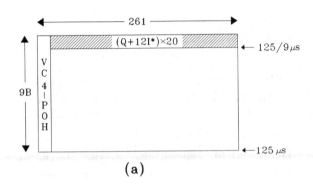

(a)

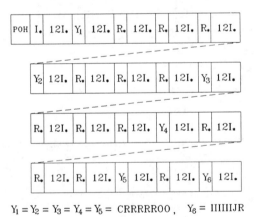

$Y_1 = Y_2 = Y_3 = Y_4 = Y_5 = $ CRRRRROO, $Y_6 = $ IIIIIIJR

(b)

Figure 3.30 Mapping of DS-4E into VC-4: (a) 125-µs frame; (b) 125/9-µs subframe.

We now examine the mapping of an ATM cell into the VC-4. The size of an ATM cell is 53B, and the payload of VC-4 can accommodate 2340B, which is not an even multiple of 53B. Consequently, ATM crosses the VC boundary, and the starting location of an ATM cell varies from one VC-4 to another. In this case, the VC's POH H4 byte can be used for easy detection of the ATM cell boundary.[19]

That is, the distance from the H4 byte to the initial location of the ATM cell is counted, and this information is stored in the H4 byte. Since the distance can vary from 0 to 52, 6 bits of H4 are allotted for this purpose. The mapping of an ATM cell into the VC-4 and the associated H4 indicator are shown in Figure 3.31.

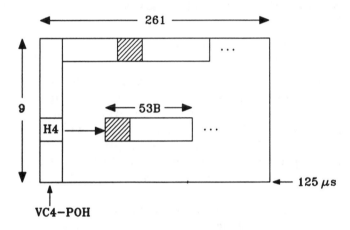

Figure 3.31 Mapping of ATM cells.

The receiver can detect the ATM cell boundary in two possible ways. First, after searching through the STM-n frame, it locates the VC-4 starting location through the AU-4 PTR, and then it can find the ATM cell boundary by reading the H4. The second method is by first ascertaining the starting position of AU-4, then picking out the ATM cells, and subsequently searching for the ATM cell boundary using the HEC byte (see Section 4.7 for a more detailed description of HEC).

3.6 OVERHEAD

Synchronous transmission is founded on the layer concept, which divides the digital transmission process into the path layer, the multiplexer section layer (sometimes called the *digital section*), the regenerator section layer, and the physical medium layer, as illustrated in Figure 3.2. Such an organization is reflected in the various

---

[19]H4 is usually employed to furnish the multiframe phase information when the lower-order tributaries are mapped into the VC. However, in the case of ATM cell mapping, such a function is not required and H4 is free to be used for other purposes.

types of overhead. Overhead consists of the SOH, which is applicable to the multiplexer section and the regenerator section, and the POH, which applies to the transmission paths for various virtual containers. Hence, the SOH can further be divided into the RSOH and the MSOH. Similarly, the POH can also be divided into the higher-order POH associated with the HO VCs and the lower-order POH, which is used for the lower-order VCs. Such relationships are illustrated in Figure 3.3.

In this section, the functions and compositions of various types of overheads will be studied in detail. First, the overall organization of the SOH will be examined, followed by a study of the RSOH and the MSOH. Afterwards, POH will be discussed in terms of the lower-order POH and the higher-order POH.

3.6.1 Composition of Section Overhead

The SOH applies to the regenerator and multiplexer sections, and it was designed for the reliable transmission of STM-n. After n ($n = 1, 4, 16$) AUGs are byte-interleaved together, an SOH is added to form the STM-n signal. Consequently, for STM-n, the format of the SOH is well-regulated, and the SOH for $n = 1, 4, 16$ are shown in Figure 3.32. In the figure, the portion above the AU PTR corresponds to the RSOH, and the portion below it corresponds to the MSOH for all three cases.

As can be deduced from Figure 3.32, the SOHs for STM-1, STM-4, and STM-16 have a well-organized relationship with respect to each other. Inside the overhead, the size of A1, A2, B2, C1, Z1, Z2, and X can be increased by a factor of n, and the remaining parts are fixed at one byte each. This is because:

- To maintain a short frame-alignment time as n increases, the A1 and A2 bytes have to be lengthened accordingly;
- To preserve the accuracy of the bit error confirmation function, more B2 bytes are required as the signal unit becomes bigger;
- As the size of STM increases, the STM identifier byte C1 has to be lengthened as well; and
- With increasing n, it is natural to have longer Z1 and Z2 bytes for future growth and the longer X-bytes for different national uses.

On the other hand, as STM-16 is reduced to STM-4 and to STM-1, the corresponding restructuring of the overhead is even more regulated. When STM-16 is reduced to STM-4, if the $4m + 1$th ($m = 0, 1, \ldots, 35$) columns are taken from the 144 columns of the STM-16's SOH, the end product is identical to the 9B x 36 SOH of the STM-4. Similarly, if $4m + 1$th ($m = 0, 1, \ldots, 8$) columns of the STM-4 SOH are taken, the 9B x 9 STM-1 SOH can be obtained.[20]

---

[20]North American SONET's STS-1 is one-third the size of STM-1, with 90 9B columns. Its section overhead has a 9B x 3 structure and is equivalent to the STM-1's SOH with its $3m + 1$ ($m = 0, 1, 2$) columns taken.

(a) STM-1

	1	2	3	4	5	6	7	8	9
1	A1	A1	A1	A2	A2	A2	C1	X*	X*
2	B1			E1			F1	X	X
3	D1			D2			D3		
4	AU pointer								
5	B2	B2	B2	K1			K2		
6	D4			D5			D6		
7	D7			D8			D9		
8	D10			D11			D12		
9	Z1	Z1	Z1	Z2	Z2	Z2	E2	X	X

(b) STM-4

	1	12	13	24	25	28	29	36
1	A1 A1 ········· A1		A2 A2 ········· A2		C1	C1 C1 C1	X* ····	X*
2	B1		E1		F1	X X X	X ····	X
3	D1		D2		D3			
4	AU pointer							
5	B2 B2 ········· B2		K1		K2			
6	D4		D5		D6			
7	D7		D8		D9			
8	D10		D11		D12			
9	Z1 Z1 ········· Z1		Z2 Z2 ········· Z2		E2	X ·········		X

(c) STM-16

	1	48	49	96	97	112	113	144
1	A1 A1 ········· A1		A2 A2 ········· A2		C1	C1 ··· C1	X* ····	X*
2	B1		E1		F1	X ·········		X
3	D1		D2		D3			
4	AU pointer							
5	B2 B2 ········· B2		K1		K2			
6	D4		D5		D6			
7	D7		D8		D9			
8	D10		D11		D12			
9	Z1 Z1 ········· Z1		Z2 Z2 ········· Z2		E2	X ·········		X

*Unscrambled X bytes

Figure 3.32 Comparison of section overheads: (a) STM-1; (b) STM-4; (c) STM-16.

3.6.2 Regenerator Section Overhead

RSOH is the overhead that is looked at only by the regenerators. It is located right above the pointer bytes within the STM-n frame and consists of the bytes A1, A2, B1, C1, D1, D2, D3, E1, and F1, as shown in Figure 3.32.[21] A1 and A2 function as alignment marks for differentiating the STM-n boundaries and are fixed at A1 = 11110110, and A2 = 00101000. B1 is a BIP byte of period 8 used for the error monitoring function. B1's ith (i = 1, 2, ..., 8) bit performs even parity check on only the ith bits of the STM-n bytes. BIP-8 is calculated after the entire STM-n frame gets scrambled, and is recorded onto B1 of the following STM-n frame before scrambling. C1 functions as an STM identification number. That is, within the STM-n, each STM-1 is granted its unique identification number, and this number is used for aligning the STM-n frame or for extracting a single STM-1 frame. D1, D2, and D3 are *data communication channels* (DCC) used by the regenerator sections. Since the capacity of each channel is 64 kbps, DCC's total capacity becomes 192 kbps. E1 is an order wire channel used by the regenerator section for voice communication. F1 is a user channel reserved for communication network operators. The X-byte is assigned for national uses.[22]

3.6.3 Multiplexer Section Overhead

The MSOH is checked by the multiplexers only and is passed transparently through the regenerators. Here, the multiplexer is an apparatus used to assemble or disassemble an AUG. The MSOH is located below the pointer in the SOH portion of the STM-n frame and consists of the bytes B2, D4 to D12, E2, K1, K2, Z1, and Z2.

B2s are BIP check bytes used for the multiplexer section's error-monitoring function. The STM-n's B2 consists of $3n$ bytes; hence, the parity check is achieved via the BIP-$24n$ format. That is, the ith (i = 1, 2, ..., 24n) bit of B2 performs a parity check on every 24nth data bit, starting with the ith bit, and modifies itself to 1 or 0 so that the total number of 1s is even. Here, BIP-$24n$ is performed on the entire STM-n frame except for the RSOH, and is recorded onto B2 before scrambling.

D4 to D12 are the MSOH's DCCs with the total capacity of 576 kbps. E2 is the MSOH's order wire which can be used for voice communication. K1 and K2 are the APS channels reserved for the APS signal. K1 is the section repair and maintenance indicator used as the *alarm indication signal* (AIS) or the *far end receive failure* (FERF) signal. If 6th, 7th, and 8th bits of K2 are 111, it means that K2 is

---

[21]The parts of the overhead that have been left blank in Figure 3.32 currently have no designated functions.

[22]In Figure 3.32, the X-bytes with asterisks (*) are the bytes that are left unscrambled. This is due to the fact that the first row of the SOH does not go through the scrambling treatment.

representing the AIS, and if the bits are 110, K2 is representing the FERF status. Z1 and Z2 have been reserved for future usage.

3.6.4 High-Order Path Overhead

The high-order path overhead is the POH that is attached to the high-order virtual containers such as VC-3 and VC-4. The higher-order POH inhabits VC-3/VC-4's first column and executes various functions required for the reliable transport of the VC's payload. High-order POH is made up of J1, B3, C2, F2, G1, H4, and Z3 to Z5 bytes, as shown in Figure 3.33(a).

B3 is a BIP check byte used for the path error-monitoring function. B3 executes the parity check through the BIP-8 format, which is calculated before scrambling on the corresponding B3 and VC-3/VC-4.

C2 is a signal label byte for indicating the composition of the VC-3/VC-4. Of its 256 possible binary values, 00000000 indicates "VC-3/VC-4 unequipped—nonspecific payloads." Other label contents are as listed in Table 3.4.

The F2 byte is allocated for path user communication purposes between path equipment.

G1 is a channel used by the receiver to convey back to a VC-3/VC-4 transmitter the path condition and performance. As illustrated in Figure 3.33(b), the first four bits of G1 give the number of *far-end block errors* (FEBE). In other words, after the B3 byte's BIP code is examined, the count of errors that have been detected is written on the FEBE bit space. G1's fifth bit designates FERF status; its value is 1 in the receive failure condition. The FERF bit operates in path AIS, signal failure, or path trace mismatch conditions. G1's remaining three bits are not used.

The H4 byte functions as a position indicator for specific payloads. The use of H4 is obligatory for locked-mode TUs; H4 is optional for floating-mode TUs.

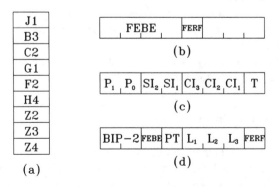

Figure 3.33 Path overheads: (a) higher-order path overhead; (b) G1; (c) H4; (d) lower-order path overhead V5.

Table 3.4
C2(Path Signal Label) Code

Code Binary	Hex	Mapping Code
00000000	00	VC-3/4 path unequipped
00000001	01	Equipped nonspecific
00000010	02	TUG structure
00000011	03	Locked TU
00000100	04	Asynchronous mapping of DS-3 or DS-3E into C-3
00010010	12	Asynchronous mapping of DS-4E into C-4
00010011	13	ATM
00010100	14	MAN (DQDB)
00010101	15	FDDI

H4's eight bits are named P_1, P_0, SI_2, SI_1, C_3, C_2, C_1, and T, respectively. Among them, P (or P_1, P_0) is used for counting up to four, SI (or SI_2, SI_1) for counting up to three, CI (or CI_3, CI_2, CI_1) for counting up to eight, and T for binary count. Since a single STM frame is 125 μs in duration, to indicate the 500-μs mode, CI_1 and T can be used; for 2-ms mode, C and T; and for 3-ms mode, P, SI, and T can be used (see Table 3.2 for an illustration). Here, the 500-μs mode is employed in indicating the multiframe status of the lower-order TUs that have been multiplexed to VC-3/VC-4. The 2-ms and 3-ms modes indicate the signaling phases of DS-1E and DS-1, respectively. On the other hand, a VC-4 that carries an ATM-cell does not require a multiframe indicator; hence, in this case, H4 is used to denote the starting position of the ATM cell (see Section 3.5.7).

J1 is a path trace channel; it operates by repetitively transmitting a 64-byte fixed length pattern so that a receiving terminal can verify its continued connection to the correct transmitter.

Z3 and Z5 are respectively assigned to path user and network operator for their appropriate use, and Z4 is a spare byte for future use.

3.6.5 Lower-Order Overhead

Lower-order overhead is attached to a lower-order VC and, therefore, to a VC-1 or a VC-2. It is designated as V5 and is the first byte of a VC-11, VC-12, or VC-2. V5 can be said to be an abridged version of the higher-order path overhead, and it executes various functions necessary for the reliable transport of the lower-order VC's payload.

Table 3.5
Functions of Section and Path Overheads
(a) Section Overheads

Overhead	Function	Note
A1, A2	Frame alignment	11110110, 00101000
B1	. Regenerator section error monitoring	BIP-8
B2	Multiplexer section	BIP-24
C1	STM-1 identifier	
D1–D3	Regenerator section data communication	
D4–D12	Multiplexer section data communication	
E1, E2	Order wire	
F1	User channel	Network manager
H1, H2	AU-4 PTR/path AIS	
H3	Pointer action	Negative justification
K1, K2	Automatic protection switching	
K2 (bits 6–8)	Section AIS/section FERF	111/110
Z1, Z2	Reserved byte	
Z2 (bit 18–24)	Section error reporting (FEBE)	B2 error count

(b) Path Overheads

Overhead	Function	Note
B3	Path error monitoring	BIP-8
C2	Path signal label	ATM cell mapping indication
F2	User channel	Path equipment user
G1 (bits 1–4)	Path error reporting (FEBE)	B3 error count
G1 (bit 5)	Path FERF	1
H4	Multiframe indication	ATM cell offset (bits 3–8)
J1	Path trace	
Z3–Z5	Reserved byte	
V5	Lower-order POH	B3, G1, J1, C2 functions

As illustrated in Figure 3.33(d), some of the functions of V5 are BIP check (BIP-2), FEBE indication, *path trace* (PT), signaling representation (L_1, L_2, L_3), and FERF indication. L_1, L_2, and L_3 can denote whether the associated tributary is mapped into the corresponding VC in asynchronous mode, bit-synchronous mode, or byte-synchronous mode. The various functions of the SOH are summarized in Table 3.5.

3.7 POINTERS

In synchronous transmission, the synchronization required in the synchronous multiplexing process is achieved through the use of pointers. Such a synchronization process is needed because, in general, a VC is created using a different clock from the one associated with the AU or the TU. When a VC is aligned within an AU or TU, a pointer conveys the information regarding its starting location; when the address changes, the pointer is also altered to keep track of the shifted location.

In this section, pointers in general and synchronization through the use of pointan examinationers will be discussed. First, the composition and various functions of pointers will be examined, and the synchronization process via pointers will be described.

3.7.1 Composition of Pointers

Pointers can be grouped into higher-order pointers, such as AU-4 PTR, and TU-3 PTR and lower-order pointers, such as TU-11 PTR, TU-12 PTR, and TU-2 PTR.

The higher-order pointer is contained in the bytes H1, H2, and H3. In the case of AU-4/AU-3, the higher-order pointer is located in the left part of the fourth row of the AU-4/AU-3 frame, as shown in Figure 3.13 and Figure 3.24. As for TU-3, its pointer is positioned in the top portion of the frame's first column, as shown in Figure 3.22(a). Among the three bytes, H1 and H2 function as the address indicator for the starting location (or its variance) of the corresponding VC, and H3 is used for the execution of negative justification. One byte each of H1 and H2 is assigned for every 125-μs frame; but three H3 bytes are assigned to AU-4 and only a single H3 byte is used in the case of AU-3 or TU-3.

The lower-order pointer is contained in the bytes V1, V2, and V3. As illustrated in Figure 3.18, these bytes correspond to the first bytes of the four 125-μs partitions of a 500-μs TU frame. Hence, V1, V2, and V3 each appear once in every 500-μs frame. If the lower-order TU is restructured in 9B x n (n = 3, 4, 12) format, as shown in Figure 3.19, V1, V2, and V3 are always positioned in the first row and first column. The functions of V1, V2, and V3 are identical to those of H1, H2, and H3; this relationship is depicted in Figure 3.8.

3.7.2 Functions of Pointers

The 16 bits of H1 (or V1) and H2 (or V2) can be divided into three sections, as shown in Figure 3.8, with each serving an independent function. The first 4 bits carry the NDF; the next 2 ss bits indicate the signal type of the frame; and the last 10 bits contain 5 increment bits and 5 decrement bits in an interleaved format.

The NDF is fixed to 0110 in the regular employment of the pointer. However, in case a need arises for an alteration of the pointer value or the exclusive use of the pointer for a specific purpose, the NDF is inverted to 1001.

The signal type indicator bits ss are assigned the value 10 for every higher-order pointer; but in the case of lower-order pointers, ss become 00 for TU-2, 10 for TU-12, and 11 for TU-11 (the ss bit values are not defined in the case of specialized indications such as concatenation or null pointer). This is listed in Table 3.6.

The address bits indicate the starting location of the VC in the regular mode of operation; however, when the need arises for an alteration of the pointer value, the change is reflected through the inversion of I- or D-bits. If the VC has been shifted up (farther from the beginning of the host frame), only the I-bits are inverted; in the reverse situation, only the D-bits are inverted.

As shown in Figures 3.15 and 3.34(a), the address for the AU-4/AU-3 PTR indication begins immediately after the H3 byte. The same situation applies for TU-3. However, in the case of TU-2, TU-12, and TU-11, the address assignment begins right after the last bit of the V2 byte, which is illustrated in Figure 3.34(c–e). Therefore, each address indicator denotes the degree of offset from the pointer H3, as in the case of higher-order pointers, or from the V2, as in the case of lower-order pointers.

The range of addresses to be indicated by the pointer address bits is different for each signal element. For instance, the address ranges from 0 to 782 in the case

Table 3.6
The Range of Pointer Address

Pointer	Signal Type (ss)	Range of Address
AU-4	10	0–782
AU-3	10	0–782
TU-3	10	0–764
TU-2	00	0–427
TU-12	10	0–139
TU-11	11	0–103

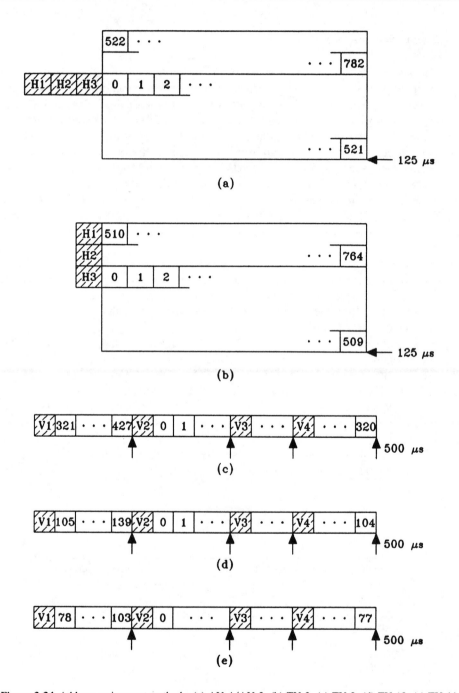

Figure 3.34 Address assignment methods: (a) AU-4/AU-3; (b) TU-3; (c) TU-2; (d) TU-12; (e) TU-11.

of AU-4 or AU-3[23]; the range is 0 to 764 for TU-3. Table 3.6 gives a summary of different address ranges for various signal elements.

H1 (or V1) and H2 (or V2) bytes are also used as a concatenation indicator. If AU-4-xc is taken as an example, the AU-4 PTR for the first of x AU-4s operates in the regular pointer mode, while the remaining $x - 1$ AU-4 PTRs designate the concatenation status. Here, the concatenation indication code is 1001ss1111111111.

When a lower-order TU is multiplexed to TUG-3 via TUG-2, a separate pointer for TUG-3 is not necessary. On the other hand, a TU-3 that has VC-3s aligned within it requires the TU-3 PTR. However, TU-3 and TUG-3 have an identical 9B x 86 structure, as illustrated in Figure 3.22. Therefore, in the case of TUG-3, the site that corresponds to the TU-3 PTR is occupied by the NPI code 1001ss1111100000.

3.7.3 Synchronization via Pointers

In general, the VCs that are aligned within the AU or TU are created from a different source, which has a different clock from the one that produced the AU/TU. Of course these two clocks have a plesiochronous relationship, and the degree of discrepancy between the two is small and within the specified tolerance. However, since they are not perfectly synchronized either, a synchronization procedure is always needed, which can be achieved through the use of pointers.

The general principle of the synchronization procedure via pointers is as follows. First of all, VC does not get "locked" into the AU/TU, but is allowed to "float" within the frame's payload, and the address of the VC's first byte is recorded in the pointer. If the bit rate of the VC is lower compared to that of the AU/TU, then when the accumulated data offset becomes one byte long (three null bytes if AU-4), one null byte (three null bytes for AU-4)[24] is inserted into the payload, the starting address of the VC is shifted up by one, and the altered status is again recorded in the pointer. Hence, the clock discrepancy between the VC and AU/TU has been effectively resolved. Such a process is called *positive justification*. If the VC's bit rate is too high with respect to that of the AU/TU, an opposite treatment called *negative justification* is used to resolve the clock offset. To elaborate, when the data offset becomes one byte long (three bytes for AU-4), one spare byte is used to convey the extra byte of data and the address of the VC is shifted down by one, and, as before, the pointer value is altered to reflect the change. Here, H3 (or V3) is the spare byte that conveys the extra data.

---

[23]Even though the same address assignment method is used for AU-3 and AU-4, the number of bytes denoted by each respective address is different, with one byte of AU-3 corresponding to three bytes of AU-4. This relationship also holds for the size of H3 bytes for each respective signal.

[24]To be more accurate, it should be written, "when the accumulated offset data becomes one address location long." This length is equivalent to the size of H3, which is three bytes in the case of AU-4, and 1 byte for the others.

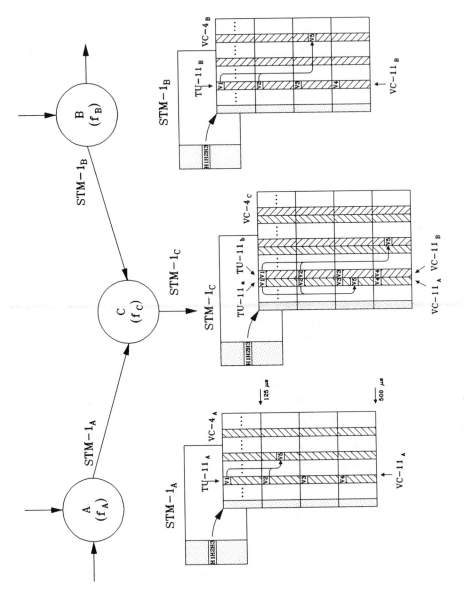

Figure 3.35 Illustration of synchronization by pointers.

Figure 3.35 illustrates the pointer-based synchronization techniques. In the picture, STM-1$_A$, STM-1$_B$, and STM-1$_C$ are the synchronous transport modules that have been produced at three different network nodes, A, B, and C, using three different system clocks, f_a, f_b, and f_c. Inside STM-1$_A$, VC-4$_A$ floats freely, with its starting location indicated by the pointer bytes H1 and H2. If the multiplexing path VC-11\TU-11\TUG-2\TUG-3\VC-4 is considered, the inside of the VC-4 is occupied by 84 TU-11s. If a designated TU-11 is picked out and is named TU-11$_A$, it consists of three columns, as shown in the picture. It also consists of four 125-μs frames, which together form a 500-μs multiframe. Within the first bytes from the first rows of each 125-μs frame reside the bytes V1, V2, V3, and V4. TU-11$_A$ and VC-4$_A$ are generated using the same clock, and VC-11$_A$ is allowed to float inside the TU-11$_A$ frame. VC-11$_A$'s first byte is designated V5, and its address is indicated by the pointer bytes V1 and V2. Such an internal organization also applies to STM-1$_B$, VC-4$_B$, TU-11$_B$, and VC-11$_B$.

Suppose that VC-11$_A$ from STM-1$_A$ and VC-11$_B$ from STM-1$_B$ are transported to network node C and multiplexed together to form STM-1$_C$ after an add/drop procedure. This implies that VC-11$_A$ and VC-11$_B$ each get realigned by the VC-4's clock, which is the same clock that was used to produce the TU-11$_a$ and TU-11$_b$, the TUs newly generated within STM-1$_C$ to accommodate VC-11$_A$ and VC-11$_B$. The VC-11's realignment relationship is indicated by the pointer's V1 and V2. If there is an accumulated offset due to any discrepancy between the VC-11's clock and the TU-11's clock, then the TU-11 PTR is employed to remedy the situation. If the add/drop operates at the VC-4 level and a similar problem arises, then the AU-4 PTR is employed to resolve it.

3.7.4 Execution of Justification

Now we investigate, using an illustration, the execution of the justification process, which is an inseparable part of the pointer-based synchronization procedures. For this purpose, AU and TU from Figure 3.34 have been conceptually integrated together and restructured as shown in Figure 3.36. The pointer portion in the slanted line corresponds to the H1, H2, and H3 (or V1, V2, and V3) from Figure 3.34. In Figure 3.36, the address ranges from 0 to $N - 1$, with $N - 1$ being 782, 764, 427, 139, and 103, corresponding to the signals AU-4/AU-3, TU-3, TU-2, TU-12, and TU-11, respectively.

In the figure, the address location 0 is positioned in the middle of the frame, and, in the case of AU-4/AU-3, this corresponds to the location right after the H3 byte or after the V2 byte, as in the case of TU-2, TU-12, and TU-11. NJ and PJ represent the negative and positive justification opportunity bytes, respectively. PJ's actual position is that which immediately follows H3 (or V3). N, s, and I/D are for NDF, signal type, and increment/decrement indications, as was explained in Section

Pointer space

H1   H2   H3
(V1) (V2) (V3)   VC alignment space (floating)

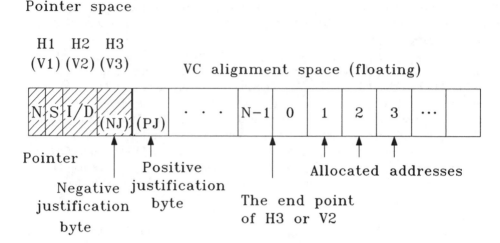

Figure 3.36 Conceptually integrated AU/TU structure.

3.7.2. During the justification execution process, N is always fixed to 0110, and *s* acquires one of the values listed in Table 3.6 depending upon whether the associated signal is an AU or a TU.

First, we study the execution procedure of positive justification with Figure 3.37 as a reference. In the figure, the number $N - 1$ from Figure 3.36 is specified to be 8; *t* denotes the *t*th frame, and $t + 1$ represents the next frame. Just before the positive justification procedure is initiated, the VC's starting address is recorded as 2 by the I/D-bits, and the entire VC alignment space is filled with the VC data (a). Once the positive justification starts, all five I-bits from I/D are inverted, the PJ execution byte is loaded with one null byte (or left as a blank space), and the VC data get loaded only onto the remaining VC alignment space. In that case, the VC's starting address gets incremented by one (b). After the termination of the PJ procedure, the VC's new starting location 3 is recorded onto the I/D-bits, and the space for VC gets filled with the effective VC data (c).

The negative justification procedure's basic technique is equivalent to that of positive justification except for the direction of execution. We examine its operation using Figure 3.38, with the condition before the execution being identical to the positive justification case(a). When the negative justification is executed, the five D-bits are inverted, the NJ byte acquires effective VC data, and the entire VC space also gets filled with the VC data. In that case, the VC starting point address gets decreased by one (b). Immediately following the termination of negative justification, the new VC starting point address 1 is recorded onto I/D, and the entire VC is now filled with the effective VC data (c).

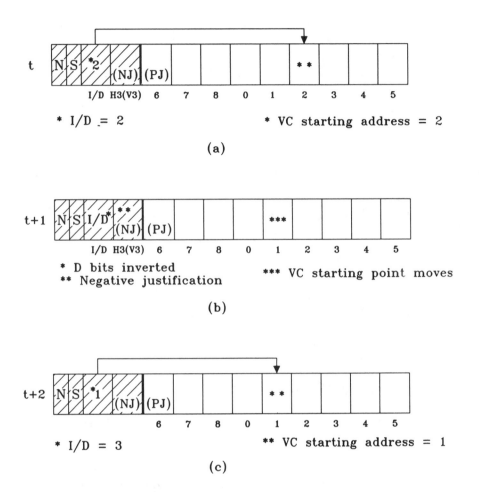

Figure 3.37 Illustration of positive justification: (a) before justification; (b) during justification; (c) after justification.

The pointer I/D address or the AU/TU size indicator can be altered without going through the normal justification procedure. The new pointer address or the new signal type indicator can be sent while the NDF is in the inverted condition 1001. (Here, the NDF can be said to be acting as an "interrupt" command.)

In case an error in transmission causes damage to the I, D, or N- (data flag) bits, the majority vote rule applies. That is, if three or more of the five ID bits are inverted, this is interpreted as denoting justification execution, and if three or more of the four N-bits are inverted, this is considered an NDF.

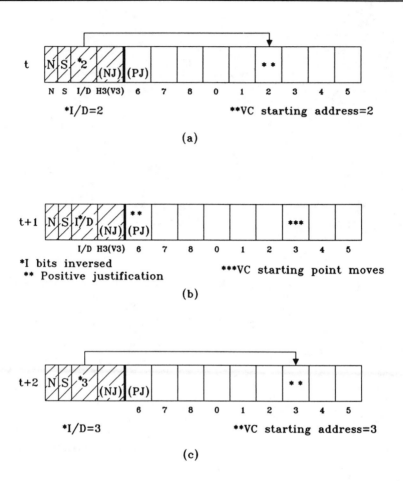

Figure 3.38 Illustration of negative justification: (a) before justification; (b) during justification; (c) after justification.

3.8 STRUCTURE OF SYNCHRONOUS MULTIPLEXER

In Section 3.3, the synchronous multiplexing structure was examined, followed by an overview of the synchronous multiplexing procedure in Section 3.4. Hence, the synchronous multiplexing procedure was studied in terms of the lower-order paths, higher-order paths, and the synchronous transport module. It was also observed that the processes associated with the lower-order and higher-order paths include mapping, the insertion of POH, aligning, multiplexing, and so on. With these two sections as a basis, the present section will give a systematic and detailed examination of the synchronous multiplexer's structure.

3.8.1 Synchronous Multiplexer's Functional Structure

The synchronous multiplexer's functional structure in its normal mode of operation is as shown in Figure 3.39. In the picture, G.703 represents an existing plesiochronous tributary,[25] and STM-m and STM-n represent synchronous transport modules. The top path that starts from STM-m takes the STM-m and demultiplexes it to extract a higher-order VC, which is subsequently multiplexed again to form the STM-n. Also, the middle path involves the multiplexing of a lower-order tributary G.703 into the STM-n via both the lower-order procedure and higher-order procedure. Finally the lower path represents the multiplexing procedure of a higher-order tributary G.703. Hence, this diagram can be said to encompass all the basic multiplexing functions that the synchronous multiplexing structure supports, including the multiplexer for the existing tributaries, synchronous multiplexers for synchronous tributaries, add/drop multiplexers, and interworking multiplexers.

Comparing Figure 3.39 with Figure 3.16, we examine the function of each block. In Figure 3.39, the *physical interface* (PI) represents the function for interfacing with the tributary G.703; the *lower-order path adaptation* (LPA) represents the function for mapping the tributary DS-n ($n = 11, 12, 2, 3, 4$) into the container C-n; *lower-order path termination* (LPT) is the function for creating and adding the VC-1/2 POH to the container C-1/2.[25] Lower-order path connection (LPC) is a type of cross-connect function for the elastic storage of lower-order VCs inside the higher order VCs. It is used on an optional basis depending on the type of multiplexer.

Higher-order path adaptation (HPA) is the function for mapping TU-1/2 into VC-3/4 via a pointer, and *higher-order path termination* (HPT) is the function for creating and attaching a higher-order POH to TU-1/2. Also, *higher-order path connection* (HPC) is a cross-connect function for the flexible storage of VC-3/4 inside the STM-n.

Section adaptation (SA) is the function for multiplexing AU-3/4 to the STM-n payload through the use of a pointer, *multiplexer section protection* (MSP) is the function for switching signals to another line for protection purposes, *multiplexer section termination* (MST) is the function for the creation and insertion of the MSOH (SOH rows 5 to 9), and *regenerator section termination* (RST) is the function for the creation and insertion of the RSOH (SOH rows 1 to 3). Finally, the *SDH physical interface* (SPI) represents the function for interfacing an STM-n signal to a physical medium.

Other functions include the *message communication function* (MCF), which is the function for utilizing the DCC, the *synchronous equipment management function* (SEMF), the *multiplexer management function* (MMF), the *multiplexer timing source* (MTS) for network synchronization, and the *multiplexer timing physical interface* (MTPI).

---

[25]It should be noted that sometimes it is called G.702. See, for example, Chapter 4.

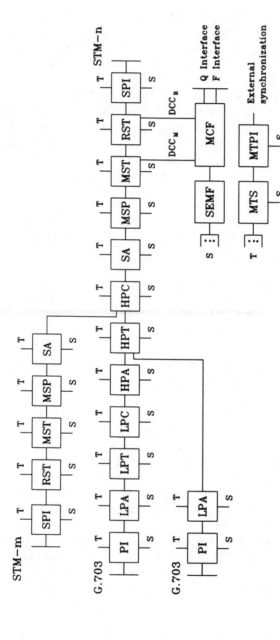

Figure 3.39 Generalized multiplexer functional block diagram.

In the picture, T represents the timing signal, S represents the supervisory (monitor, alarm, control) signal, and Q and F are the message interfaces to MCF, with especially Q being the MCF access point to the *telecommunication management network* (TMN). Among the functions, only the PI and the LPT vary with each payload, and the remaining functions are payload-independent.

3.8.2 Function of Each Constituent Block

As shown in Figure 3.39, the synchronous multiplexer's constituent functions can be categorized into lower-order path function, higher-order path function, and transport termination function. The lower-order path function consists of G.703 PI, LPA, LPT, and LPC, while the higher-order path termination function is composed of HPA, HPT, and HPC. The transport termination function is composed of SA, MSP, MST, RST, and SPI.

Lower-Order Path Function

G.703 interface functions as the interface between the multiplexer and the physical medium. In the G.703 receiving direction, it extracts data and timing information from the G.703 signal and sends them off to an LPA block, and in the transmission direction it creates a tributary from the data and timing signals. When the incoming G.703 signal is in the *loss of signal* (LOS) state, the PI generates an "all 1" signal and transmits it instead of the data.

LPA signifies the capacity to receive data and clock signals from the PI and create a container C-n (n = 11, 12, 2, 3, 4) out of the input information. Hence, the specific LPA function varies from tributary to tributary, and, as a way of differentiation, the nomination scheme LPA-n (n = 11, 12, 2, 3, 4) is used.

Referring to Section 3.5, it can be inferred that LPA-11, LPA-12, or LPA-2 has asynchronous and synchronous adaptation capability, while LPA-3 or LPA-4 only has the asynchronous adaptation capability.

LPT represents the capability for producing the VC-n by creating and attaching a POH to a C-n or, inversely, the ability to separate the POH from VC-n and process it. Here, POH is categorized into V5, which is used for the lower-order paths, and VC-3 POH, which is used for the higher-order paths. The associated functions of POH are path trace, signaling, path status and performance indication, path error monitoring, and so on.

The function of LPC is the flexible connection of VC-n (n = 11, 12, 2, 3) to the VC-n slots in the higher-order paths. This is a function that was not elucidated in the multiplexing structure illustrated in Figure 3.16. LPC is not equipped in the multiplexer types I, II, IIa, and IV, and, in this case, VC-n is maintained in a fixed connection state in the higher-order path.[26] The type III multiplexer with the add/drop and cross-connect capabilities is also equipped with LPC. A connection matrix is employed to record the lower-order path's connection status.

Higher-Order Path Functions

The HPA function represents the TU-n (n = 11, 12, 2, 3, 4) pointer management capability. The associated functions include pointer generation, pointer translation, and justification. The ability to assemble VC-n (n = 11, 12, 2) and adapt them to the VC-4 payload or, conversely, to dismantle VC-4 into the VC-n is called HPA-$n/4$, and the ability to process VC-3 in the same manner is called HPA-$n/3$.

The HPT function represents the capacity to generate and insert the higher-order VC-n POHs or to separate them from the VC-n. Here, the information regarding path trace, signal identification, path status and performance, and path error monitoring is directed to SEMF. If multiframe alignment is required, the POH's H4 byte manipulation is also connected to SEMF.

HPC's function is the flexible connection of VC-n (n = 3, 4) to the VC-n slots inside the multiplexer section. The multiplexer types I, II, and IV are not equipped with HPC. As with LPC, a connection matrix is used to record the higher-order path's connection status.

Transport Termination Function

SA's function is to adapt the higher-order path to AU, to assemble or disassemble the AUG, to perform BIM or demultiplexing, and to generate and translate pointers.

The MSP's function is to protect the STM-n signal from the breakdown of the multiplexer section (or RSP and SPI functions and the physical medium). The MSP function at both ends involves the continuous monitoring of the STM-n signal and the exchange of relevant information through channels K1 and K2. The protection switching is conducted on the entire multiplexer section, and the protection structure is $1 + 1$ or $1{:}n$.

The MST's function is the production and disposal of the MSOH. The associated overheads include B2, K1, K2, D4 to D12, Z1 to Z2, and E2. Among these, B2 is used for error monitoring inside the multiplexer section, K1 and K2 are used for section protection purposes, and D4 to D12 are data communication channels for the multiplexer section (DCC_M), which are used in conjunction with the MCF.

The function of the RST is the generation and disposal of the RSOH. The corresponding RSOH comprises the A1, A2, B1, C1, D1 to D3, E1, and F1 channels. A1 and A2 are used for frame alignment, B1 for the regenerator section's error

---

[26]A multiplexer can be categorized into types I, Ia, II, IIa, IIIa, IIIb, and IV depending on its capability (see Section 3.8.3).

monitoring, and C1 for STM-1 identification. D1 to D3 are DCCs for the regenerator section (DCC_R) used in connection with the MCF. E1 is an order wire channel, and F1 is a user channel. Among the RSOH channels, A1, A2, and C1 can be transparently rebroadcasted instead of being generated anew or terminated in regenerators.

The SPI functions as an interface between the regenerator termination and the SDH physical medium. Here, the SDH physical medium is usually electrical or optical. In the SDH receive direction, the STM-n data and the clock information are extracted, and, in the transmission mode, a reverse function is executed.

3.8.3 Classification of Multiplexers

The multiplexer can be categorized into types I, II, III, and IV according to its execution capabilities and utilization purpose. It can be further categorized into a and b subtypes, depending on whether it is equipped with the LPC and HPC functions or not. Hence, the four types can be subclassified into I, Ia, II, IIa, IIIa, IIIb, and IV. Figure 3.40 is an illustration of these types from the viewpoint of interfacing signals. The specialized role of each type can be deduced from the picture, with type I/Ia being a basic multiplexer, II/IIa being a synchronous multiplexer, IIIa being a basic add/drop multiplexer, IIIb being a synchronous add/drop multiplexer, and IV being an interworking multiplexer.

Basic Multiplexer (types I, Ia)

The basic multiplexer takes G.703 tributaries and multiplexes them together to create the STM-n. Hence, if the left upper branch from Figure 3.39 (i.e., the demultiplexing portion for the STM-n interface signals) is eliminated, then the resulting structure is equivalent to the type I multiplexer. The basic multiplexer equipped with LPC and HPC functions is classified as type Ia, and the one without is classified as type I. Therefore, type Ia differs from type I in that it can support the flexible connection of VC-1/2s or VC-3/4s.

Synchronous Multiplexer (Types II, IIa)

The synchronous multiplexer's special function is to assemble multiple STM-m signals to form the STM-n signal ($n > m$). To illustrate, if the middle and lower branches are removed from Figure 3.39 and replaced with the paths interfaced with the STM-m, then the synchronous multiplexer results. The synchronous multiplexer, as described, is classified as type IIa; if the HPC function is lacking, then it is classified as type II. As before, type IIa differs from type II in its capacity to provide a flexible

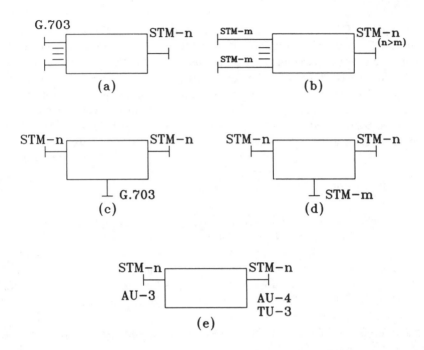

Figure 3.40 Classification of multiplexers: (a) types I and Ia (basic); (b) types II and IIa (synchronous multiplex); (c) types IIIa (basic add/drop); (d) types IIIb (synchronous add/drop); (e) type IV (interworking).

connection of the VC-3/4 signals. Without the HPC function, the type IIa multiplexer is directly connected to the SA function, and therefore two SAs can be combined together to form a single SA.

Add/Drop Multiplexers (Types IIIa, IIIb)

The add/drop multiplexer takes the G.703 tributary or the STM-*n*, performs an add/drop procedure on the signal, and transmits it as a part of another STM-*n* signal. The type that operates on the G.703 tributary is classified as the basic add/drop multiplexer (IIIa), while the kind that operates on the STM-*m* is the synchronization multiplexer (IIIb). These two add/drop multiplexers are illustrated in Figure 3.41(a,b). Comparing Figures 3.39 and 3.41, it can be inferred that the type IIIa multiplexer is equivalent to the structure that results if the two branches connected to the HPT (which has the G.703 signal interface) in Figure 3.39 are displaced to the bottom of the HPC. Here, the HPC enables the add/drop of VC-1/2 within the VC-3/4. The type IIIb multiplexer has basically the identical function as the type IIIa multiplexer,

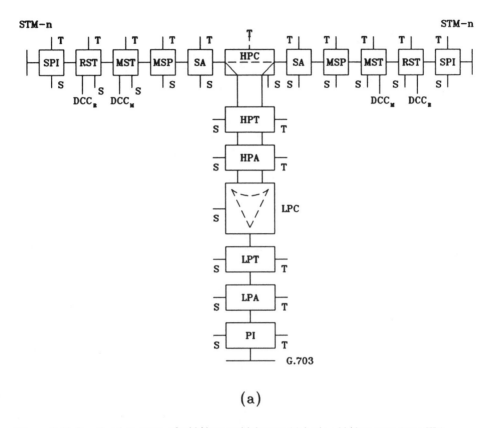

Figure 3.41 Functional structure of add/drop multiplexers: (a) basic add/drop type (type IIIa)

except that its add/drop signal is STM-*m* rather than G.703. Hence, type IIIb is equivalent to type IIIa if the LPC's lower path (LPT\LPA\PI\G.703), which is a part of type IIIa's function, is replaced by the LPC's upper path (HPA\HPT\SA\MSP\RST\SPI\STM-*m*). Here, since a separate HPC function is not required for the add/drop procedure on STM-*n*, it is not a part of type III's function.

Interworking Multiplexer (Type IV)

The interworking multiplexer's function is to integrate inside the STM-*n* those payloads that conform to the AUG-3 structure with the payloads that are organized according to the AU-4/TU-3 structure. Hence, type IV's function comprises the STM-*n*\SPI\RST\MST\MSP\SA\HPT path, which disassembles the AU-3, and the HPT\SA\MSP\MST\RST\SPI\STM-*n*, which assembles the payloads in the

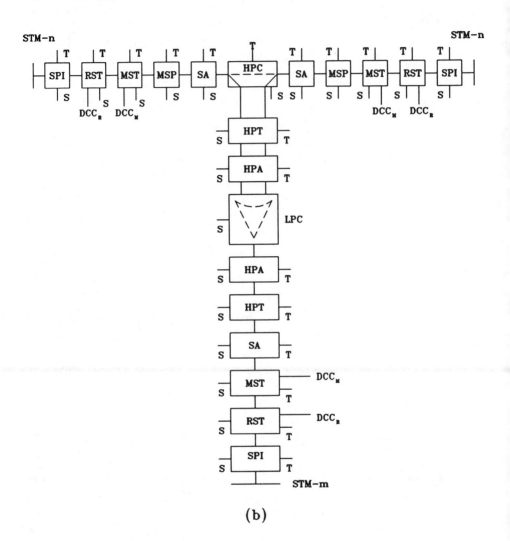

(b)

Figure 3.41 continued (b) synchronous add/drop type (type IIIb).

AU-4/VC-4 format, and vice versa. Since performing interworking is type IV's sole objective, HPC and LPC functions are not required.

3.8.4 Operation and Management Functions

The OAM channels for synchronous transmission exist inside the STM's POH and SOH. Inside the POH reside the channels for indicating path AIS, *loss of pointer* (LOP), FERF, FEBE, and error checking. Inside the SOH there are also channels for indicating the section AIS, LOS, *loss of frame* (LOF), FERF, FEBE, and error checking. In addition, SOH supports the *network operator maintenance channel* (NOMC), which includes order wire (E1, E2), user channel(F1), and data channels D1 to D12. Also, for OAM purposes, an additional TMN can be employed.

SEMF represents the function for accepting the OAM-related signals through the regenerators or multiplexers to be sent to the MCF, or its reverse. MCF receives the message and transmits it through the SOH's DCC, or delivers it to the TMN, and it can also function in the reverse direction. Figure 3.42 depicts this relationship in terms of multiplexers and regenerators. In the picture, regenerator-related DCCs represent the D1 to D3 channels within the SOH (DCC_R), and the multiplexer-related DCCs represent the D4 to D12 channels within the POH (DCC_M).

The generation of administration-related signals and the corresponding countermeasures are as shown in Figure 3.43. In the figure, relevant actions are categorized into section, higher-order path, and lower-order path layers, with the generation and the detection of the signals indicated by the filled circles and the countermeasures by the blank circles. In the section layer, in the event of the detection of LOF, LOS, or section AIS in the received signal, or if a serious bit error (B2) is detected, the far end is notified of the condition (FERF), and a VC-3/4 path AIS is sent to the higher-order path. In the higher-order path, if higher-order path AIS or higher-order path LOP is detected, it is reported to the far end (higher-order path FERF), and lower-order path AIS is sent to the lower-order path. Also, if any bit error (B3) is detected, it is confirmed and notified to the far end (FEBE). In the lower-order path layer, the far end is notified if the lower-order path AIS or the lower-order path LOS is detected, and AIS is sent to the associated containers. Also, any bit error is confirmed and reported to the far end (FEBE/V5).

The Roman numerals II, III, and I, which are displayed in the right half of Figure 3.43, represent the three classes of multiplexers and the range of OAM signals each can deal with. That is, the class II multiplexer can detect the OAM-related signals and apply relevant countermeasures for the SOH, the class III multiplexer can do the same for the SOH and higher-order path overhead, and the class I for the overheads of all three layers.

If a major failure is detected in the line system (line system is a part of the network's operation and maintenance function), protection switching is practiced.

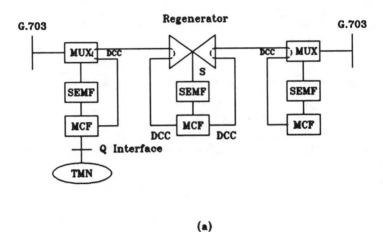

(a)

(b)

Figure 3.42 OAM-related functions and channels: (a) regenerator section; (b) multiplexer section.

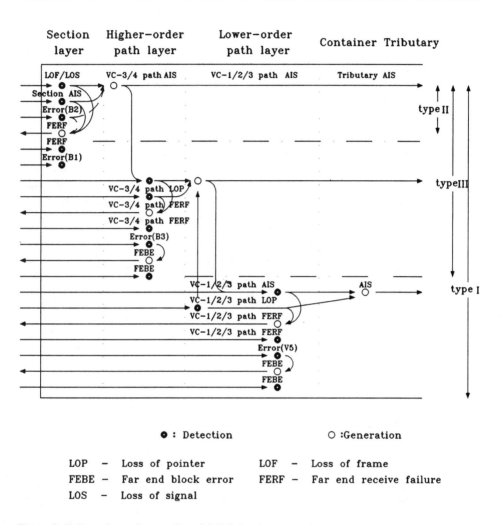

Figure 3.43 Detection and generation of OAM signals.

Here, the line system designates the path that starts at the multiplexer termination, goes through the regenerator, and ends at the starting point of the far-end multiplexer.[27] Protection switching is executed to protect all functions and equipment between a pair of MSPs, and thus inside the section that includes MST, RST, SPI, and so on. Protection and switching can be performed in the 1 + 1 or 1:n (n = 1

---

[27]To be more accurate, the line system starts from RST, goes through SPI and regenerator, and terminates at the far-end SPI and RST. Here, SPI and RST functions should be considered to be a part of the regenerator function.

to 14) format; the employment of the protection action can be unidirectional or bi-directional, and can also be revertive or nonrevertive. In the 1:n format, a single protection line has to support n lines; thus, revertive employment that returns the protection line to its original form after the repair is desirable. The protection switching architectures for 1 + 1 and 1:n cases are illustrated in Figure 3.44. Automatic protection switching is a means to enhance the transmission reliability of the network. In the synchronous transmission network, further enhanced reliability is achievable, since ring-type architecture is also available in place of the conventional star-type architecture. That is, the flexible add-dropping and dynamic cross-connecting capability of the synchronous transmission network effectively renders a ring-type architecture with the add/drop multiplexers and digital cross-connects forming its constituent network node elements. In the ring network, it is possible to reconfigure

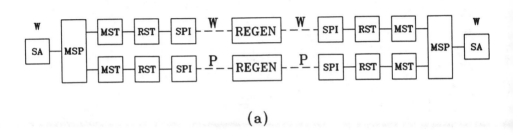

(a)

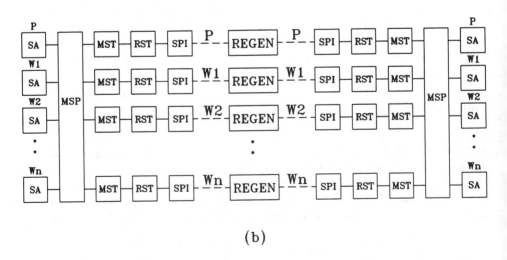

(b)

Figure 3.44 Protection switching architectures: (a) 1 + 1; (b) 1:n.

the network connection whenever link failure occurs such that the connection can detour the failed links, thus further improving the transmission reliability.

3.8.5 Timing and Synchronization Function

In the functional structuring of the multiplexer from Figure 3.39, the functional block associated with time and synchronization is the MTPI. The MTPI provides the function for physically interfacing the external synchronization signal to the internal timing source. The role of the MTS is that of providing a timing standard to each functional element of the multiplexer.

The external synchronization signal that can provide reference timing to the synchronous transmission network time comes from three different sources. The first is the G.703 external synchronization interface, the second is the G.703 tributary interface, and the third is the STM-n interface. The 2.048-kHz synchronization signal is furnished by the G.703 synchronization interface; and timing signals can also be regenerated and used as the reference using the signals received through the G.703 interface and the STM-n interface. If the reference timing signal is lost, then the multiplexer has to switch to a different synchronization signal.

Even though the synchronous digital transmission was originally conceived to be operated within a synchronized communication network, it can be accommodated in plesiochronous networks through pointer manipulations. Consequently, the synchronous transmission network's jitter and wander performance is determined by the internal and external clock performances of the synchronous transmission network, the output wander at synchronous network interface, and the jitter and wander of the synchronous line system. Also, the jitter and wander of the G.703 tributary output, which is dependent on the performance of pointer manipulation, is determined by the jitter and wander performance of the synchronous transmission network and the jitter and wander handling capability of the synchronous multiplexer/demultiplexer at the boundary of the synchronous network.

Consequently, jitter and wander is an important performance indicator for the synchronization of the synchronous digital network. The tolerance range of jitter and wander in the synchronous digital network is regulated for the G.703 interface and the STM-n signal, and is categorized into multiplexer-related jitter and line system-related jitter. If light transmission is employed, the jitter related to the transmission line system is of no concern. However, in the synchronous transmission network, because the pointer technique is used as a means of achieving synchronization, waiting time jitter especially emerges as an important problem to resolve. A detailed description of the jitter and wander requirement of the synchronous transmission network, along with the related waiting time jitter performance analysis, is given in Section 3.9.

3.9 JITTER PROBLEM IN SYNCHRONOUS TRANSPORT SYSTEM

The pointer technique is one of the most distinct features of synchronous digital transmission. It can be regarded as an influence of computer and software technologies on communication technology. The pointer-based synchronization method can achieve synchronization without repetitive frame search procedures, and it can also cope with a plesiochronous environment with small elastic store, making synchronization possible over a wide area.

However, because the pointer technique is linked with the 125-μs duration frame, it generates low-frequency and high-amplitude jitters. This is because the justification ratio corresponds to 0.5 and the justification is performed on byte sizes of one or three. The justification ratio of 0.5, from the standpoint of waiting time jitter, is quite an undesirable value, and has therefore been avoided by exisiting plesiochronous transmission systems.

Besides the multiplexer-related jitter, which includes waiting time jitter, there is also transmission line-related regenerator jitter. However, because the synchronous digital transmission system employs lightwave for transmission, there should be no concern that the regenerator jitter becomes greater than that contributed by the current digital transmission. Consequently, the main focus of this section will be waiting time jitter, which emerges as a peculiar problem of synchronous transmission.

In the present section, the requisite jitter and wander accommodation for synchronous transmission and the associated jitter generation, transfer, and tolerance requirement details will be discussed first. Afterwards, the relationship between pointer-based P/Z/N justification and the existing bit-stuffing P/Z/N justification method will be examined, and on that basis waiting time jitter will be analyzed. The waiting time jitter caused by the m-bit P/Z/N justification will be analyzed first, and this will be applied to an actual synchronous multiplexing path of the synchronous digital transmission system.[28]

3.9.1 Jitter and Wander Requirements

In synchronous transmission, the specification details for jitter and wander are determined in terms of the STM-n and G.703 interfaces. The characteristics of the jitter and wander associated with these interfaces have a close connection to the input timing extraction circuitry.

---

[28]Sections 3.9.4 to 3.9.5 contain a detailed analysis of the jitter problem, and can be omitted without detracting from the reader's understanding of the entire section.

STM-n Interface

Jitter from the STM-*n* interface should be accommodated by the SPI. The STM-*n* signal can be used for synchronizing the MTS; here, MTS should be able to accommodate STM-*n*'s maximum absolute jitter and wander. If the input STM-*n* is devoid of jitter, the jitter generated in SPI's output STM-*n* signal should not exceed 0.01 UI_{rms}.[29]

The output jitter and wander have to meet the short-term stability requirements, as shown in Figure 3.45. Here, the clock's degree of stability is indicated by the average *time interval error* (TIE). If the MTS is used, the output jitter and wander are controlled by the characteristic attributes of the MTS and the input synchronization source. Also, in case the synchronization signal derived from the received signal is used (that is, if loop timing is used), the jitter and wander transfer characteristic is dependent on the jitter and wander of the input signal. The output jitter, measuring it after passing it through a 12-kHz highpass filter, should be below 0.01 UI_{rms}.

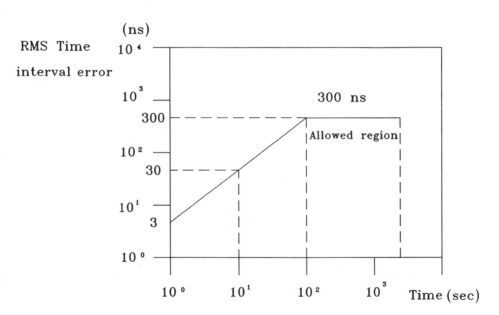

Figure 3.45 Short-term clock stability requirements.

---

[29]UI stands for unit interval, and UI_{rms} and UI_{p-p} stand for the root-mean square and the peak-to-peak value of UI, respectively. The length of 1 UI varies with each signal, and for various tributaries it has the following relationship—1.544 Mbps: 647 ns, 2.048 Mbps: 488 ns, 6.312 Mbps: 158 ns, 8.448 Mbps: 118 ns, 34.368 Mbps: 29.1 ns, 44.736 Mbps: 22.4 ns, 139.264: 7.18 ns, 155.52: 6.43 ns.

The transfer characteristic of jitter and wander can vary depending on whether or not the corresponding equipment performs synchronization, and if so, on the particular synchronization technique used. If no synchronization is performed, then jitter and wander are determined by the internal oscillator, and hence transfer characteristic does not have any meaning. But if synchronization is employed, then the transfer characteristic is determined by the filter characteristic of the *multiplexer timing generator* (MTG). The filter characteristic is dependent on whether loop-timing or MTS is used. The jitter transfer parameters for regenerators are shown in Figure 3.46 and Table 3.7. In the table, the regenerator that meets the type A parameters is called the *type A regenerator*, and the one that meets the type B parameters is called the *type B regenerator*.

The wander transfer characteristic due to AU/TU PTR adjustment can be controlled by the respective AU/TU PTR processor. Wander is influenced by the phase

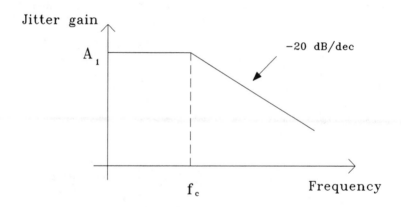

Figure 3.46 SDH jitter transfer characteristic (see Table 3.7).

Table 3.7
SDH Jitter Transfer Parameters (Refer to Fig. 3.46)

STM Level (type)	A_1 (dB)	f_c (kHz)
STM-1 (A)	0.1	130
STM-1 (B)	0.1	30
STM-4 (A)	0.1	500
STM-4 (B)	0.1	30
STM-16 (A)	0.1	2000
STM-16 (B)	0.1	30

differences among the input signals and the buffer states of the pointer processor. As the buffer size increases, the opportunity for pointer adjustment becomes limited. The buffer size allocated to the pointer processor varies with each AU/TU signal (e.g., a minimum of 12 bytes for AU-4, 4 bytes for AU-3 and TU-3, and 2 bytes for TU-1/TU-2).

The SDH equipment should be able to accommodate the range of input jitter which is displayed in Figure 3.47 and Table 3.8. If the type A regenerator is used, the corresponding SDH generator and equipment have to satisfy the type A tolerance requirement; and similarly, the type B regenerator has to meet the type B requirement.

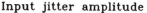

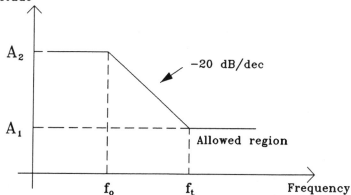

Figure 3.47 SDH jitter tolerance mask (see Table 3.8).

Table 3.8
SDH Jitter Tolerance Parameters (Refer to Fig. 3.47)

STM Level (type)	A_1 (UI_{p-p})	A_2 (UI_{p-p})	f_0 (kHz)	f_t (kHz)
STM-1 (A)	0.15	1.5	6.5	65
STM-1 (B)	0.15	1.5	1.2	12
STM-4 (A)	0.15	1.5	25	250
STM-4 (B)	0.15	1.5	1.2	12
STM-16 (A)	0.15	1.5	100	1000
STM-16 (B)	0.15	1.5	1.2	12

G.703 Interface

The jitter and wander tolerance for G.703 interface has to satisfy the reference requirements of the existing North American and European digital hierarchies.[30] The jitter tolerance specification for the G.703 interface is shown in Figure 3.48 and Table 3.9.

The jitter transfer characteristic also has to satisfy the reference specification of the existing G.703 digital hierarchy. The transfer characteristic of the North American multiplexer has to satisfy the specification indicated in Figure 3.49 and Table 3.10, and the European multiplexer has to satisfy the specification given in Figure 3.50 and Table 3.11

The multiplexer's output jitter for the North American 6.312-Mbps or 44.736-Mbps signal must not exceed 0.01 UI_{rms}, and if input jitter is absent, the respective demultiplexers' jitter must not exceed $1/3$ UI_{p-p} and $1/5$ UI_{p-p}, respectively. Also, the output jitter for European signals at 8.448 Mbps, 34.368 Mbps, 139.264 Mbps must not exceed 0.25 UI_{p-p}, $0.25UI_{p-p}$, and $0.3UI_{p-p}$, respectively. The output jitter for each signal after the requisite bandpass filtering must not exceed 0.05 UI_{p-p}.

The G.703 signal's total jitter and wander generation from both tributary mapping and pointer adjustment must not exceed the values prescribed in Table 3.12. In the table, columns for f_1 to f_4 and f_3 to f_4 display jitters of the cases when bandpass filtering is done with these specific passbands.

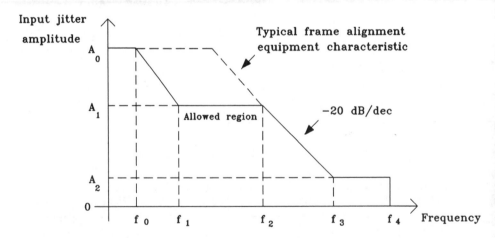

Figure 3.48 6.703 jitter tolerance mask (see Table 3.9).

---

[30]The North American digital hierarchy's jitter and wander tolerance requirements are regulated according to CCITT Recommendations G.824, G.743, and G.752, and the European's are regulated according to G.823. On the other hand, SDH's jitter-related requirements are specified in G.783 and G.958.

Table 3.9
G.703 Jitter Tolerance Parameters (Refer to Fig. 3.48)

G.703 Interface (Mbps)	Peak-to-Peak Jitter (UI_{p-p})			Frequency				
	A_1	A_2	A_3	f_0 (Hz)	f_1 (Hz)	f_2 (Hz)	f_3 (kHz)	f_4 (kHz)
1.544		2.0	0.05	—*	10	200	8	40
2.048	36.9	1.5	0.2	—	20	2400	18	100
6.312		2.0	0.05	—	10	200	32	160
8.448	152	1.5	0.2	—	20	400	3	400
34.368		1.5	0.2	—	100	1000	10	800
44.736		14	0.05	—	10	3200	900	4500
139.264		1.5	0.075	—	200	500	10	3500

*$f_0 = 1.2 \times 10^5$

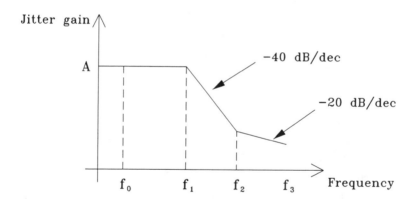

Figure 3.49 Jitter transfer characteristic for North American multiplexers (see Table 3.10).

Table 3.10
Jitter Transfer Parameters for North American Multiplexer
(Refer to Fig. 3.49)

G.703 Multiplexer	A (dB)	f_0 (Hz)	f_1 (Hz)	f_2 (kHz)	f_3 (kHz)
M12 (1.544 to 6.312)	0.5	10	350	2.5	15
M23 (6.312 to 44.736)	0.1	10	500	2.5	15

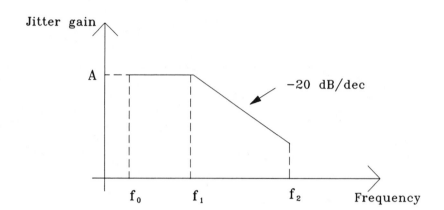

Figure 3.50 Jitter transfer characteristic for European multiplexers (see Table 3.11).

Table 3.11
Jitter Transfer Parameters for European Multiplexer
(Refer to Fig. 3.49)

g.703 Multiplexer	A	f_0 (Hz)	f_1 (Hz)	f_2 (kHz)
M12E (2.048 to 8.448)	0.5	—	100	10
M23E (8.448 to 34.368)	0.5	—	100	1
M34E (34.368 to 139.264)	0.5	—	300	3

3.9.2 Comparison of Stuffing-Based Justification and Pointer Techniques

Stuffing-based justification, which resolves clock offsets through the appropriate use of stuffing space is the current justification method in use for PDH tributaries. In case of P/Z/N justification via stuffing, a part of the frame format is allocated in advance for the positive justification bit, negative justification spare bit, and the control bit for indicating the justification status. In case the input signal rate becomes lower than the system's transmission rate, the positive justification bit gets filled with a null bit, and in the opposite case the negative justification bit gets filled with

Table 3.12

Combined Jitter Generation Specifications

G.703 Interface (Mbps)	Filter Characteristics			Maximum Peak-to-Peak Jitter (UI_{p-p})	
	f_1 (Hz) Highpass (20 dB/dec)	f_3 (kHz) Highpass (20 dB/dec	f_4 (kHz) Lowpass (−20 dB/dec)	f_1 to f_4 Bandpass Filtering	f_3 to f_4 Bandpass Filtering
1.544	10	—	40	1.5	—
				0.4*	0.075
2.048	20	18	100	0.75*	***
5.312	—	—	60	1.5	—
				0.4*	0.075
8.448	20	3	400	0.75**	***
				0.4*	0.075
34.368	100	10	800	0.75**	***
44.736	—	—	400	1.5	—
139.264	200	10	3500	—	—

*When the two adjacent pointer adjustments have the opposite polarity.
**When the two adjacent pointer adjustments have the same polarity.
***A double pointer adjustment of one polarity followed by another double pointer adjustment of the opposite polarity.

effective data. Also, if the rates are identical, neither positive nor negative justification occurs (zero justification).

Justification based on pointer technique, as was explained in Section 3.7, works by using the bits allocated in advance within the frame format to record the starting location of the VC. If VC signal rate deviates from the system transmission rate, the VC's starting point also changes; hence, the corresponding address also changes. That is, the address of the VC's starting point, or its deviation, is indicated by H1 and H2, and if the VC signal rate becomes lower relative to the system transmission rate, the byte following H3 acquires a null byte and the VC starting point address is shifted up by one. Also, if an identical rate is maintained by both sources, no change is made to H1, H2, and H3.

If the two justification methods are compared, it can be seen that the pointer technique-based justification and the corresponding stuffing-based P/Z/N justification produce the identical effect. That is, P/Z/N justification via pointer on a byte-unit basis has the same effect as the byte-stuffing-based P/Z/N justification. The main difference between the two methods is whether or not the information regarding the payload's starting point is exposed. In other words, in case of stuffed justification, the payload's starting point can only be found after the receiver extracts payloads and searches for the frame alignment word, whereas in the case of pointer-based justification, the starting point is identified at the same instant that the payload is extracted. However, as the payload starting point information does not have any bearing on the synchronization or jitter analysis itself, the pointer technique can be regarded as being equivalent to the corresponding stuffing-based P/Z/N justification.

3.9.3 P/Z/N Justification and Jitter

In synchronous transmission networks, each central office can be regarded as maintaining a system clock distributed from the central clock source, or an independent clock whose accuracy is within the tolerance limit. Here, the former case can be designated as synchronous, and the latter plesiochronous. At the central office, transmission signals go through add/drop and cross-connect procedures, accompanied by a synchronization process before or after. The network-node interface standard is what recommends the use of the pointer technique for this synchronization process. Here, as was noted in the preceding section, pointer synchronization can be considered equivalent to stuffing-based P/Z/N justification. However, since other synchronization methods such as the use of elastic store or the positive justification are also available, it is worthwhile to examine the advantages of the pointer technique over the other techniques.

First, we examine synchronization using elastic store only with the STM-1 signal as an example. STM-1's standard transmission rate is 155.520 Mbps, and if the maximum tolerance transmission error is set at 15 ppm, the STM-1 rate can range between 155.117667 Mbps and 155.522333 Mbps. If at some instant the incoming STM-1 rate is 155.522333 Mbps and the office system clock runs at 155.517667 Mbps, and discrepancy is maintained for one second, the two clocks' offset can amount to as much as 4666 bits. In order to accommodate this offset without loss of information, the size of elastic store must be at least 4666. Conversely, if the incoming rate is 155.517667 Mbps and the system clock 155.522333 Mbps, the error between the two clocks becomes -4666 bits (such a relationship is illustrated in Figure 3.51). Therefore, to cope with such a situation, the size of elastic store must be made to be greater than 9332 bits. It follows, then, that if only elastic store is used as a synchronization mechanism, its size must be quite large. To make the situation even worse, this example only applies to synchronous systems. In actual plesiochronous systems, bit slip is inevitable, and therefore synchronization via elastic store is impossible.

We now examine the case of synchronization using just positive justification. In synchronous digital transmission, the multiplexing/demultiplexing function fundamentally is achieved on a byte basis. Therefore, if positive justification is performed on a bit basis, the signal stream within the transmitted signal shifts in bit

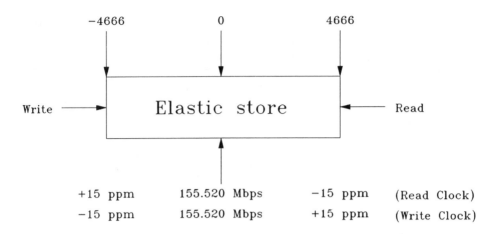

Figure 3.51 Illustration of synchronization using elastic store.

units, and thus the byte-level multiplexing/demultiplexing action becomes rather complicated.

To resolve the matter, positive justification must be performed on a byte basis. In this case, however, the corresponding amplitude becomes greater than that for bit-level positive justification, and since lower frequency jitter components also get included, the jitter power becomes even greater. Another problem for this case is that even if the input signal rate is the same as the system clock, positive justification-based synchronization can introduce waiting time jitter at all times.

If the STM-1 signal is synchronized via P/Z/N justification, whenever the input signal's transmission rate differs from the system clock by 24 bits, synchronization is performed using H3's three bytes and the three bytes that follow H3. In case the input signal rate is lower than the system clock's, when the accumulated phase difference becomes greater than three bytes, the synchronization is achieved by filling the three bytes that follow H3 with null bytes (positive justification); if the incoming clock is greater than the system clock, when the phase offset becomes more than three bytes long, H3 acquires three information bytes and synchronization is again achieved (negative justification). Also, if the two clocks have an identical rate, no justification is employed (zero justification). Consequently, three bytes for positive justification and three bytes for negative justification, and hence theoretically only six total bytes of memory data, are required for elastic store. Also, since all the processes are achieved on a byte basis, the byte boundary is always maintained.

Therefore, compared to the synchronization method using only elastic store, the required size of elastic store for P/Z/N justification is much smaller. In addition, P/Z/N justification can be used for synchronization in both the synchronous and plesiochronous systems. Compared to positive justification, P/Z/N justification can always maintain a 125-μs unit format and hence has the advantage that multiplexing and demultiplexing can be performed on a byte basis. Also, in case the input signal rate is the same as the system clock's, it has another advantage in that no waiting time jitter is involved. Furthermore, the use of the pointer technique exposes the payload's starting point, and hence it has the advantage that STM-1 can traverse several central offices and repeated add/drop or cross-connect processes in an efficient manner.

3.9.4 Jitter Analysis for P/Z/N Justification

Jitter in Bit-Based Justification

In order to analyze bit-based P/Z/N justification waiting time jitter, it is necessary to examine the waiting time jitter of the bit-level positive and negative justifications. If a synchronizer has the nominal input signal rate f_1, output signal rate f_0, and the frame rate f_m, and if one bit-based stuffing opportunity is allowed to every frame, the nominal *justification ratio* ρ_0 becomes:

$$\rho_0 = (f_0 - f_1)/f_m \qquad (3.1)$$

In the case of positive justification, since $f_0 > f_1$, ρ becomes a positive number, and for negative justification it becomes a negative number. An actual input signal rate conforms to CCITT Recommendation G.703 and has the maximum transmission rate error tolerance of Δf_1, and therefore the actual justification ratio ρ can be expressed as

$$\rho = \rho_0 + \Delta\rho \qquad (3.2)$$

where

$$\Delta\rho = \Delta f_1/f_m \qquad (3.3)$$

Once the justification rate is fixed, the corresponding waiting time jitter can be determined using Duttweiler's analysis technique.[31] That is, the waiting time jitter's power spectrum density $S_1(f)$ is

$$S_1(f) = \text{sinc}^2(\pi f)Q(f) + (\rho/2\,n)^2(\delta(f - \rho) + \delta(f + \rho)) \qquad (3.4)$$

---

[31]D. L. Duttweiler, "Waiting Time Jitter," *Bell System Technical Journal*, Vol. 51, Jan. 1972, pp. 165–208.

and the jitter power P_1 at the output of the demultiplexer's *phase-locked loop* (PLL) can be expressed as

$$P_1 = \int S_1(f)|H(f)|^2 df \qquad (3.5)$$

where

$$Q(f) = \sum_{n=1}^{\infty} (1/2\pi n)^2 \, (\text{rep}\delta(f - n\rho) + \text{rep}\delta\,(f + n\rho) \qquad (3.6)$$

$$\text{rep } \delta(f) = \sum_{k=-\infty}^{\infty} \delta(f - k) \qquad (3.7)$$

$\delta(f)$ denotes the delta function and the $H(f)$ is the transfer function determined by the PLL.

If (3.4) and (3.5) are examined, the jitter power P_1 emerges as an even function of the justification ratio ρ. Consequently, if the absolute value of the justification rate is the same for both positive justification and negative justification, waiting time jitter power of identical magnitude is generated for both cases. Therefore, the negative justification's waiting time jitter power can be represented by a curve symmetrical to that of the positive justification.

In the case of bit-level P/Z/N justification, the output signal rate is generally established to be the same as the nominal input signal rate. That is, $f_0 = f_1$. Also, one bit each is assigned for positive justification as well as negative justification for every frame. Consequently, if the frame rate is equal to f_m, (3.1) to (3.4) can be applied to both positive and negative justifications. Therefore, the waiting time jitter power generated due to bit-level P/Z/N justification is equivalent to the value calculated using (3.5) by varying ρ around 0 by $\pm \Delta\rho$.

If viewed from the P/Z/N justification standpoint, positive justification or negative justification can be said to be a special case of P/Z/N justification. This relation can be readily inferred from the frame format illustrated in Figure 3.52. If bits P and N are assigned for the positive and the negative justifications, respectively, then in the case of P/Z/N justification, both of the bits are used to perform justification. However, in the case of positive justification, the N-bit always gets filled with overhead or a garbage bit, and in the case of negative justification, the P-bit gets filled with payload. That is, although, as in the case of P/Z/N justification, both P- and N-bits are allocated, in the actual execution of justification, positive justification only uses the P-bit and the negative justification only uses the N-bit. If this relationship is examined from the standpoint of the justification ratio, the only

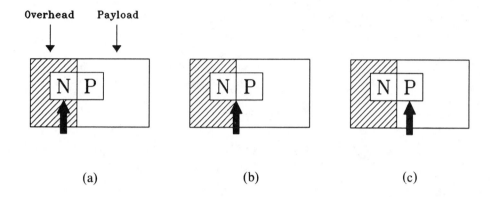

Overhead   Payload

(a)   (b)   (c)

Figure 3.52 Comparison of justification methods: (a) negative justification; (b) positive/zero/negative justification; (c) positive justification.

difference among the three justification types is the location of the nominal justification rate ρ_0. That is, in the case of positive justification, the justification ratio is located in the right half of the curve ($\rho_0 > 0$); in P/Z/N justification, ρ_0 is located at the origin ($\rho_0 = 0$); and in negative justification, ρ_0 is located in the left half ($\rho_0 < 0$).

Jitter in Multibit-Based Justification

If the waiting time jitter that is generated from using bit-level positive justification is pictorially represented, then, as can be seen from Figure 3.53(a), the justification occurs the first moment that the accumulated phase offset becomes greater than one bit. If this relationship is mathematically expressed, then

$$\phi(t) = (\lambda - 1) + \rho t - [\rho[t]] \tag{3.9}$$

In the equation, [ ] represents the Gaussian function, t denotes the time designated as the frame period, and ($\lambda - 1$) represents the initial phase offset. Also, ρ is determined through (3.1) to (3.3), and the nominal value for ρ is between 0 and 1. Further, ρt represents the phase offset that increases linearly with time due to the two signals' clock deviation, and $[\rho[t]]$ represents the justification execution function. If this function is analyzed, the value of $[t]$ only varies when the justification opportunity arises; hence, $\rho[t]$ only acquires the values ρ, 2ρ, 3ρ, . . ., and consequently $[\rho[t]]$ becomes an equation that is a staircase in shape, with the number of steps corresponding to an integral number of ρ. If this relation is used to calculate the jitter power, (3.5) is the result.

On the other hand, if this relationship is applied to the multibit (i.e., m-bit based) positive justification, the resultant waiting time jitter can be illustrated as shown in Figure 3.53(b). That is, the curve is a sawtooth that represents the justification that occurs the first moment the phase offset becomes greater than m bits.

In the figure, the slope ρ is the justification ratio as before, which is determined using (3.10) and (3.3), and the nominal value ρ_0 ranges from 0 to m, which is the number of bits used for justification. This is numerically expressed as

$$\phi_{\rho m}(t) = (\lambda - m) + \rho t - m[\rho[t]/m] \tag{3.10}$$

In this equation, the last term in the expression represents the execution of justification only when the phase offset is an integer multiple of m-bits, which happens when t becomes an integer; at that instant, the function changes abruptly by m-bits. If ρ is expressed in terms of multiple m-bits and denoted by ρ' (that is, $\rho' = \rho/m$), the nominal value ρ' ranges between 0 and 1 and (3.10) can be rewritten as

$$\phi_m(t) = (\lambda - 1) + m\rho't - m[\rho'[t]] \tag{3.11}$$

This equation can be said to be a generalized form of (3.9). That is, if m from (3.10) is set to 1, then $\rho' = \rho$, and thus (3.9) results.

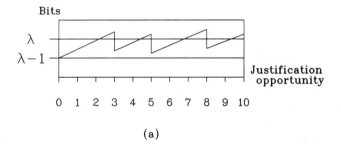

(a)

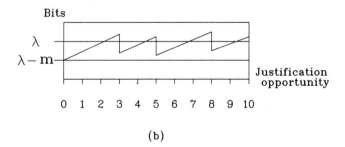

(b)

Figure 3.53 Waiting time jitter of positive justifications: (a) bit basis; (b) m-bit basis.

Therefore, the waiting time jitter formula for multibit-based positive justification can be derived directly from bit-based justification analysis. That is, if (3.11) is compared to (3.9), the only difference is that the time-varying portion is multiplied by the factor m. Since the essential results of the waiting time jitter analysis based on (3.9) are (3.4) and (3.5), the waiting time jitter analysis for the multibit positive justification similarly yields the spectrum density $S_m(f)$ and the jitter power P_m in the form

$$S_{m(f)} = m^2 S_1(f) \tag{3.12}$$

and

$$P_m = m^2 P_1 \tag{3.13}$$

The net result of the preceding derivation is that the power spectrum density and the jitter power for the m-bit case are m^2 times those for the single-bit case. Therefore, the waiting time jitter power for the m-bit case can be calculated simply by adding $20 \log m$ (dB) to the waiting time jitter power of the single-bit case.

This relationship can be extended and applied to jitter analysis for P/Z/N justification. That is, if $20 \log m$ (dB) is added to the single-bit P/Z/N justification's waiting time jitter power, then the waiting time jitter for the m-bit-level P/Z/N justification results.

3.9.5 Application to Synchronous Digital Transmission Systems

Now we apply jitter analysis to synchronous digital transmission systems, adopting the multiplexing path DS-1\C-11\VC-11\TU-11\TUG-2\TUG-3\VC-4\AU-4\AUG\ STM-n that is depicted in Figures 3.6 and 3.7. In this particular multiplexing path, three stages of synchronization processes occur, as shown in Figure 3.54. The first is the bit stuffing-type P/Z/N justification for the DS-1\C-11 mapping, the second is the one-byte-based pointer justification for the VC-11\TU-11 alignment, and the third is the three-byte-based pointer justification for the VC-4\AU-4 alignment.

Synchronization of DS-1

As depicted in Figure 3.54, bit-based P/Z/N justification occurs when the asynchronous DS-1 signal is mapped into the C-11. According to the recommendations, the C-11 frame occupies 500 μs of time, and hence the frame rate f_m becomes 2000/s.

Since the input signal's nominal rates are $f_1 = 1.544$ Mbps and $f_0 = f_1$, the nominal justification ρ_0 is equal to 0. Also, since the maximum tolerance of f_1 is

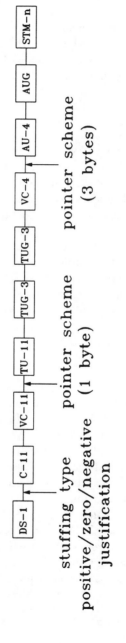

Figure 3.54 Synchronization processes involved in a synchronous multiplexing path.

equal to ± 50 ppm, Δf_1 is equal to 77.2 bps; thus, due to (3.3), $\Delta\rho = 0.0386$. If this value is plugged into (3.4) through (3.8) and if the transfer characteristic of the PLL's loop filter is defined as $(0.012/jf + 0.012)^2$, then jitter power corresponding to the darkened portion in Figure 3.55(a) is obtained. Here, when $\rho_0 = 0$, jitter power is at its maximum value, -10.923 dB, and when $\rho = \pm 0.0386$, it is at its minimum, -13.123 dB. This corresponds to an increase of about 10 dB compared to the case of positive justification used in M12 multiplexing.[32]

Synchronization of VC-11

When TU-11 is formed by synchronizing VC-11, the byte-based pointer technique is applied, as indicated in Figure 3.54. Consequently, the byte-based P/Z/N justification analysis of the preceding section can be used to calculate the waiting time jitter. According to the recommendations, VC-11's frame size is 125 μs per 26 bytes, and hence the input signal's nominal rate f_1 is 1.644 Mbps and the frame rate f_m is 2000/s, as before. Also, if VC-11's maximum tolerance error is assumed to be 50 ppm, $\Delta f_1 = 83.2$ bps and $\Delta\rho = 0.0416$. The nominal justification rate ρ_0 is equal to 0, and the number of bits m used for justification is 8; thus, modified justification rate ρ' equals $\pm\Delta\rho/m$; that is, its range is ± 0.0051. If these values are applied to (3.4) through (3.8) and (3.13), then jitter power corresponding to the darkened portion in Figure 3.55(b) is obtained. When $\rho' = 0$, the maximum jitter power is equal to 7.139 dB.

Synchronization of VC-4

When AU-4 is formed by synchronizing the VC-4 signal, the three byte-based pointer technique applies, as shown in Figure 3.54. Consequently, $m = 24$, and the m-bit-based P/Z/N justification jitter analysis can be applied. According to the recommendations, VC-4's frame size amounts to 261 x 9 bytes per 125 μs, the input signal's nominal rate $f_1 = 150.336$ Mbps, and the frame rate $f_m = 8000/s$. Also, if the maximum tolerance of VC-4 is assumed to be 15 ppm, the values $\Delta f_1 = 2255$ bps and $\Delta\rho = 0.28188$ can be obtained. The nominal justification rate ρ is equal to zero, and m is 24; thus, the modified ρ' is within ± 0.01175. Jitter power can be obtained in the same manner as before using these values, which is as plotted in Figure 3.55(c). When $\rho' = 0$, the maximum jitter power is equal to 16.681 dB.

If the jitter power curves from Figures 3.55(a,b,c) are compared with the ρ or ρ' set to zero, it can be ascertained that the jitter power curves of (b) and (c) are,

---

[32]The case of the M12 multiplexer was considered for the illustration of positive justification. This corresponds to the case in which $\rho_0 = 0.3353$ and $\Delta\rho = 0.0144$, and the accompanying jitter power is within the range of -22.417 to -20.624 dB.

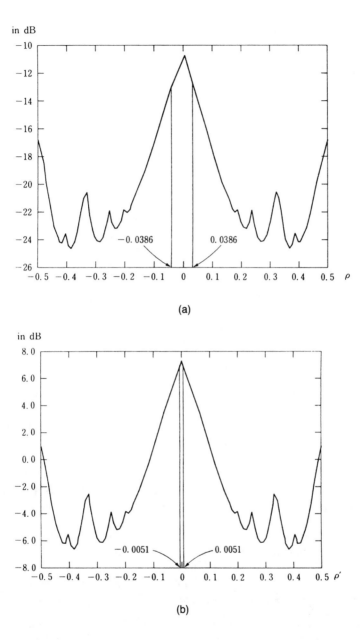

Figure 3.55 Waiting time jitter power of P/Z/N justification: (a) 1-bit based; (b) 1-byte based; (c) 3-byte based.

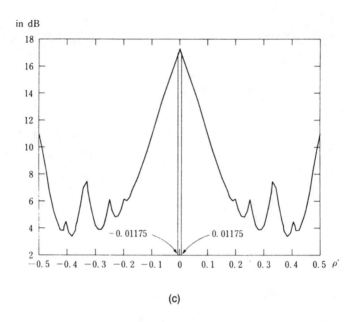

in dB

Figure 3.55 continued.

respectively, 18.06 (= 20 log 8) dB and 27.60 (= 20 log 24) dB greater than that of (a). These jitter values are associated with the case when multiplexing processes are applied as specified by the SDH, and thus can be said to represent the worst-case analysis. The actual synchronous system must restructure the multiplexer/de-multiplexer through such measures as distributed-bit processing so that the jitter is reduced to be within tolerable limits.

3.10 COMMUNICATION NETWORK FOR SYNCHRONOUS DIGITAL TRANSMISSION

The term *communication network* represents any generalized system that is composed of a variety of communication equipment as its key constituent elements, with the interconnection achieved through the link configuration. However, since the communication network is essentially used as a means of executing an information transport function, it can also be termed a *transport network* for convenience.[33] Of course,

---

[33]The term *transmission* denotes the actual physical process of transmitting an information signal over a physical medium, while *transport* applies at a more conceptual level, signifying the functional procedure of delivering information from one point to another. Therefore, in the present chapter, the conceptually systematized communication network is called *transport network*, while the physical network consisting of the actual equipment such as the multiplexer, the switching system, the cross-connect system, and so on, is termed the *transmission network*.

in a communication network the network control information for signaling, OAM, and so on are also transferred.

The communication network is a large, complex set with various components, and, therefore, for the design, operation, and management of a communication network, an accurate network model with well-defined functional entities is essential. In other words, it should be possible to approach a complex communication network by dividing its operation into specific functional blocks of interest. For this purpose, the concepts of vertical division (*layering*) and horizontal division (*partitioning*) are useful. The layering concept has been already examined in detail as being the very foundation of synchronous digital transmission. The partitioning concept can be viewed as being a naturally occurring phenomenon in step with the evolution of the communication network.

In this section, the layering and partitioning of the communication network will be examined from the transport network concept viewpoint, and a discussion of its actual organization and future evolution will follow.

3.10.1 Layering Concept and Layer Network

As was observed in Sections 3.1.2 and 3.6, the layering concept forms the basic foundation for synchronous digital transmission. The transmission process becomes layered, which means that it is divided into the path layer and the section layer. This is reflected in the STM-n structure in the form of POH and SOH. The path layer is further divided into the lower-order path layer associated with the VC-1/2 and the higher-order path layer associated with the VC-3/4.

Figure 3.56 is an illustration of the layering concept in its idealized form. In the figure, the circuit layer is placed on top of the path layer, with the physical medium layer put below the section layer. The circuit layer represents various kinds of services that are transported through a common path layer. The physical medium layer forms the lowest part of the transmission process and represents optical or radio media.[34] The physical medium layer and section layer can be combined and labeled the *transmission medium layer*.

If the layering concept is illustrated in conjunction with the synchronous transmission processes, then Figure 3.57 is the result. It can be seen from the figure that the circuit layer consists of the 64-kbps circuit-switched service, packet-switched service, leased-line circuit service, and so on. Also, the figure illustrates that inside

---

[34]The basic physical medium for synchronous transmission is optical fiber. However, transmission based on coaxial cable or radio should not be excluded from the discussion. In this case, a slight variation might result due to the special characteristic of each type of transmission medium.

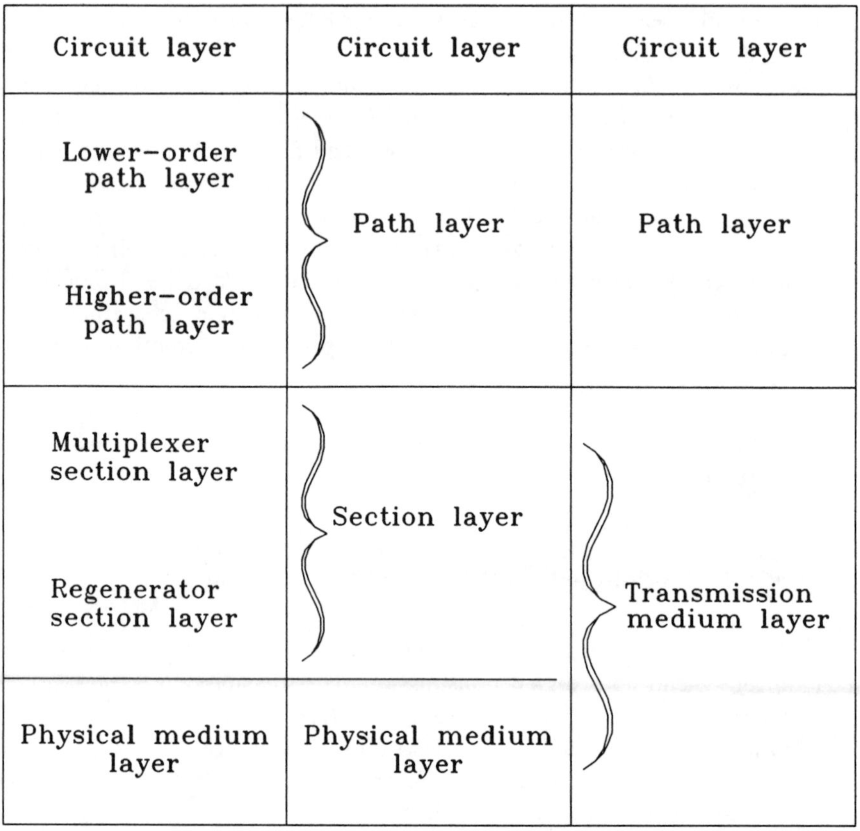

Circuit layer	Circuit layer	Circuit layer
Lower−order path layer / Higher−order path layer	Path layer	Path layer
Multiplexer section layer / Regenerator section layer	Section layer	Transmission medium layer
Physical medium layer	Physical medium layer	

Figure 3.56 Layering concept and layer naming.

the path layer the lower-order path layer consists of VC-11, VC-12, VC-2, and VC-3, while the higher-order path layer consists of VC-3 and VC-4.[35] AUG and MSOH are a part of the multiplexer section layer, and, finally, the RSOH is included in the regenerator section layer.

If the layering concept is applied as shown in Figure 3.56, the communication network can be divided into the circuit layer network, path layer network, transmission medium layer network, and so on. Here, the adjacent layer networks maintain a server/client relationship, and each layer network possesses its own OAM capability.

---

[35]For convenience, the layers associated with the VC-1/2 and VC-3/4 are called the *lower-order layer* and *higher-order layer*, respectively, while the *lower* and *upper layers* are used as relative concepts. If there is no conceptual ambiguity, they will be used interchangeably.

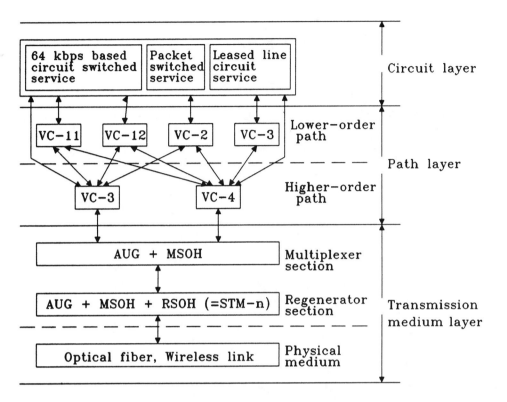

Figure 3.57 Illustration of layering concept.

The circuit layer network provides communication service to users through the circuit layer access points. Its target services include circuit-switched service, packet-switched service, and leased-line service. The configuration of the circuit layer network varies depending on the kinds of services a specific network can provide. The circuit layer network operates independently of the path layer network.

The path layer network delivers information to the path layer access points in support of the circuit layer network. The path layer network functions as a lower-order layer network that can be shared by different sets of services. The path layer network can be divided into the lower-order path layer and the higher-order path layer, and is independent of the transmission medium network.

The transmission medium layer network supports the path layer by transporting information from one path layer access point to another. The transmission medium layer network is dependent on the actual physical medium used, such as optical fiber and radio link. The transmission network's internal layers consist of the multiplexer section layer, the repeater section layer, and the physical medium layer.

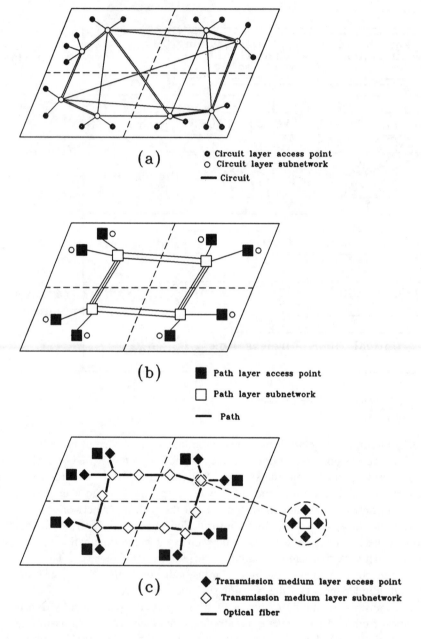

Figure 3.58 Illustration of layer network: (a) circuit layer network; (b) path layer network; (c) transmission medium layer network.

The circuit layer network, path layer network, and the transmission medium network are illustrated in terms of an actual physical network in Figure 3.58(a–c). In the figure, the circuit layer is the network connecting service transport termination points, while the path layer network can be seen as its sublayer which connects path layer access points. Here, the respective circuit from each circuit layer network follows one unique path in the path layer network. The transmission medium layer network becomes a physical layer that is established in accordance with the path layer network.

3.10.2 Partitioning Concept and Subnetwork

If the layering divides the transport network in the vertical direction, the partitioning corresponds to a division along the horizontal direction of the transport network. The partitioning applies to each layer network; hence, the transport network can be divided into three classes according to the layering concept, and each layer network can be subdivided into subnetworks according to the partitioning concept. Figure 3.59 is a graphical comparison of the layering concept with the partitioning concept.

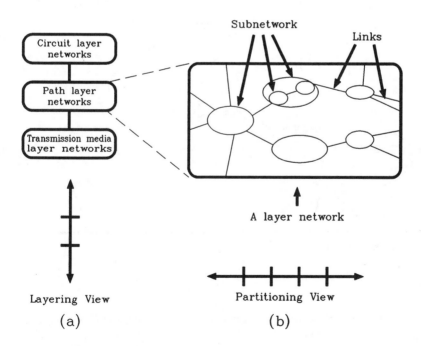

Figure 3.59 Comparison of the layering concept and the partitioning concept: (a) layering; (b) partitioning.

A partitioned layer network consists of subnetworks and the corresponding link connections. Subnetworks can further be partitioned into smaller subnetworks and link connections. Examples of subnetworks include the international network, national network, transit network, and access network.

Figure 3.60 illustrates the partitioning of a layer network into subnetworks and link connections. Figure 3.60(a) demonstrates the partitioning concept through an actual layer network, and Figure 3.60(b) is a conceptual demonstration of partitioning. Here, the second figure can be considered as illustrating a magnified version of the subnetwork in the first figure along the dotted line connecting trail termination points A and B.

In order to establish functional reference modeling of the transport network, it is necessary to examine the constituent elements, the transport entities, the transport handling functions, and the reference points. Among them, the network constituent

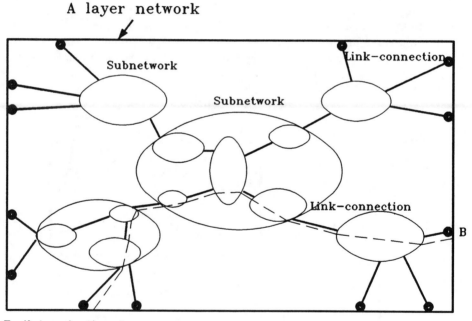

(a)

Figure 3.60 Illustration of partitioning: (a) physical configuration; (b) conceptual configuration.

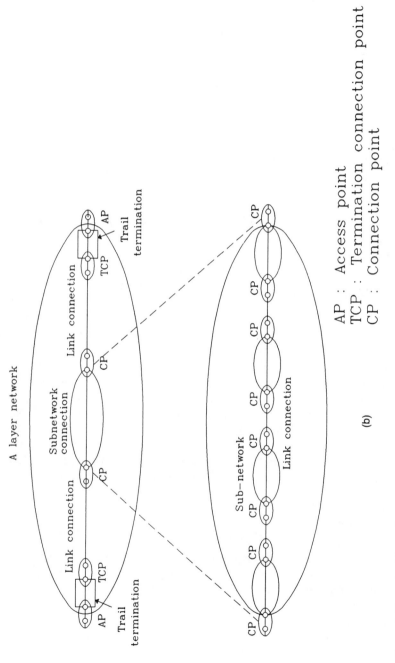

AP : Access point
TCP : Termination connection point
CP : Connection point

(b)

Figure 3.60 continued.

elements refer to the previously examined layer network, subnetwork, and link connections, which can be said to be a topological representation of the transport network. In the following section, the transport entities, transport handling function, and reference points will be examined with the illustration in Figure 3.61 as a basis.

Transport Entities

Transport entities refer to the connection that provides a transparent transport of information between the layer network's access points. In other words, between any pair of network access points linked by a transport entity, no change or degradation is made to the transported information. Transport entities include network connection, subnetwork connection, link connection, and trail.

Network connection provides transparent information transfer across a network at a given layer. It is a concatenation of subnetworks and link connections and is delimited by the network *connection points* (CP) located at the network boundary and hence by the *termination connection points* (TCP).

Subnetwork connection is a network connection across a subnetwork that is delimited by the connection point on the subnetwork boundary.

Link connection is the capability for the transparent transport of information between end points connecting two subnetworks. Link connection is bounded by the connection points on the boundary of link and subnetwork, and can be formed by concatenating smaller link connections.

Trail refers to the capability for transporting characteristic information between two *access points* (AP). Characteristic information is the information that is transferred within subnetworks. It is a signal of specified bit rates and format that goes through an adaptation process at the server network boundary. An instance of characteristic information would be the VC-n ($n = 11, 12, 2, 3, 4$). The trail is created by adding the trail termination function between an access point and a termination connection point. Examples of the trail include transport between terminal equipment, between multiplexers, and between line terminations.

Transport Handling Function

The transport handling function encompasses adaptation and trail termination. The *adaptation* function is the process of suitably adapting a characteristic information so that it can be transported from one layer to another. Examples of interlayer adaptation include multiplexing, channel coding, bit rate conversion, frame alignment, and justification.

The *trail termination* function appropriately handles information so as to ensure the integrity of information transfer within a trail. In general, the trail termination

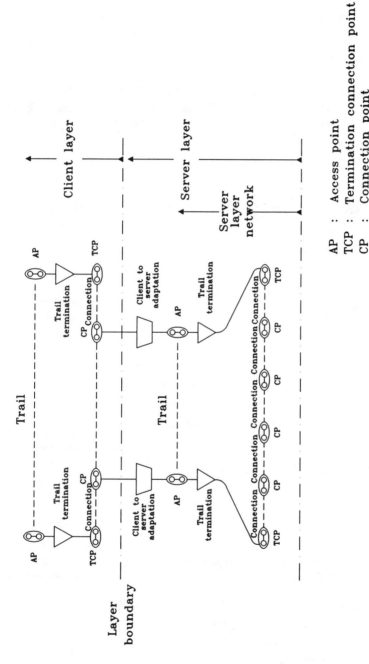

Figure 3.61 Illustration of network constituent elements.

function is embodied in the form of adding spare information at a trail termination source point and monitoring the information at the trail termination sink point.

Reference Points

The reference point is the point that forms the boundary for the handling function or transport entities, which include CP, TCP, and AP. The CP acts as the boundary for the network connection, subnetwork connection, and link connection. The TCP

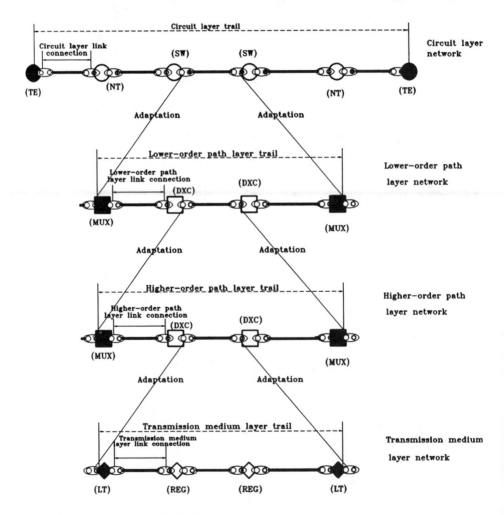

Figure 3.62 Interlayer association in the transport network.

is the connection point at which trail termination and the link connection meet, and is located at the network boundary. The AP forms the boundary between the adaptation function and the trail termination function and is the point of access between the server network and the client network.

Figure 3.62 illustrates interlayer association within a transport network, including the transport entities, transport handling functions, and access points. In the figure, the circle represents the terminations, access points, and subnetworks associated with the circuit layer; the square represents the termination function and subnetworks associated with the path layer; and the rhombus represents the function and subnetworks associated with the physical medium layer. The darkened objects correspond to the termination function, and the blank objects correspond to the subnetworks. The figure also illustrates various kinds of trails, such as circuit layer trail, lower-order path layer trail, higher-order path layer trail, and transmission medium layer trail. In the figure, TE, NT, SW, DXC, MUX, REG, and LT stand for terminal equipment, network terminations, switch, digital cross-connect, multiplexer, regenerator, and line termination, respectively.

3.10.3 Synchronous Transmission Network

Since the synchronous transmission network is not a newly built network, but a network built on the existing asynchronous transmission network, its constituent elements include not only those for synchronous transmission networks, but also access components to the existing networks.[36] Therefore, the main constituent elements of synchronous transmission network include synchronous multiplexers, add/drop multiplexers, digital cross-connect systems, existing circuit switching systems, *interface units* (IFU) to existing systems, *interworking unit* (IWU) among SDH signals, ATM switching systems for the BISDN, and the BISDN's network termination equipment.

The *synchronous multiplexer* acts as the synchronous transmission network's boundary and includes the basic multiplexer for synchronously multiplexing the existing plesiochronous tributaries to STM-n and the synchronous multiplexer that multiplexes the STM-m signal to a higher-level STM-n signal. As the plesiochronous networks evolve into synchronous networks, the function of the synchronous multiplexer will increasingly cover the direct multiplexing of lower-order tributaries. Also, in the network's future evolution into the BISDN, the linkage to ATM cells will be achieved through the synchronous multiplexers.

The *add/drop multiplexer* carries out the role of adding and dropping plesiochronous tributaries within STM-n signals or converting add/drop signals to STM-n. The add/drop multiplexer will assume an important role in the synchronous transmission network until a full-scale operation of the cross-connect system begins. The

---

[36]The synchronous transmission network represents the actual network consisting of the physical transmission equipment (see footnote in Section 3.10).

add/drop multiplexer enables the efficient handling of both the synchronous and plesiochronous signals while reducing the complexity of the network, and can therefore enhance the network's flexibility.

The *digital cross-connect system* is the network element that realizes the synchronous transmission network's inherent advantage by enabling the point-to-multipoint configuration through the use of a hub, and thus assumes the transmission network's most important function. The cross-connect system allows for the interconnection of transport entities in such diverse ways as star or ring topologies, and enhances the flexibility of the network structure.

The existing *circuit switch system* (C-SW) is also supposed to remain one of the synchronous transmission network's most important constituent elements. The STM-n IFU is the constituent element that enables the connection of the existing switching systems with the synchronous transmission network. The possibility of such a connection enables utilization of cross-connection within the exchange offices of the existing network, and thus enhances the network's functional efficiency. On the other hand, the establishment of the BISDN will necessitate the *ATM switching system* (A-SW) specifically for the BISDN's use. The ATM switch could completely replace the exisiting switch at some future time when the transport of all signals is achieved through the ATM cells.

Figure 3.63 is a brief example of the organization of the synchronous transmission network in terms of the constituent elements described above. In the figure, S-MUX represents the synchronous multiplexer, S-ADM the synchronous add/drop multiplexer, S-DXC the synchronous digital cross-connect system, S-IFU the STM-n interface unit for the existing switch, S-IWU the synchronous signal's interworking unit, and B-NT the broadband network termination. In the figure, the letter A denotes the ATM equipment, B the BISDN equipment, C the circuit-type equipment, and S the synchronous (SDH) equipment.

The synchronous transmission network of the future will be able to support three different signal formats. The first is the STM signal, obtained by synchronously multiplexing existing plesiochronous digital tributaries (STM/SDH). The second is a variant of STM, produced by mapping ATM cells into the VC-4 payload (ATM/SDH). The third is the ATM signal, consisting solely of ATM cells (ATM/cell). Among the three, the first is indicated by a bold line (STM/SDH) and the other two by a broken line in Figure 3.63.

All three signals have the identical 155.52-Mbps base bit rate. Among the three, the first and second signals are mutually interchangeable in terms of STM, and the second and the last also retain interchangeability in terms of ATM. However, the first and the third of the signals cannot efficiently coexist within a synchronous transmission network based on SDH. Therefore, to ensure an efficient construction of the network, it is desirable to limit the constituent signal to be interchangeable.

On the other hand, since it is possible to form the ATM/SDH signal by mapping the ATM cells to the STM signal, other types of packet formats can be mapped

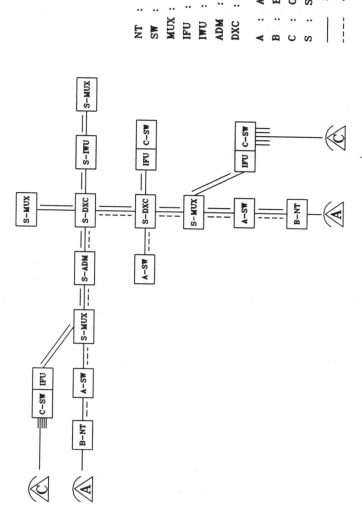

Figure 3.63 An example of synchronous transmission network.

NT : Network Termination
SW : Switch
MUX : Multiplexer
IFU : Interface Unit
IWU : Interworking Unit
ADM : Add-Drop Multiplexer
DXC : Digital Cross Connector

A : ATM
B : Broadband
C : Circuit
S : SDH

——— STM/SDH
- - - - ATM/SDH, ATM/cell

into the STM signal as well. This specific case of packet mapping can be denoted by "packet/SDH." Such signals have interchangeability with STM/SDH through the STM, and thus the two can coexist effectively within the same synchronous transmission network.

3.10.4 Evolution of Synchronous Transmission Network

The synchronous transmission network can potentially evolve in three separate directions. The first one is that of organizing the synchronous transmission network such that it overlays the existing plesiochronous networks. The second is that of establishing add/drop multiplexers and cross-connect systems first. The last is that of deploying the synchronous line system first. The direction that ultimately follows will naturally depend on the operating conditions of the existing communication networks and the development plan that is being conceived for the new synchronous network. But one thing that should be kept clear is that the particular evolutionary direction that is chosen should not hinder the establishment of a complete synchronous transmission network envisaged for the future.

The evolution of the actual synchronous transmission network will be realized with the current plesiochronous communication network as the foundation. Therefore, it is essential that the evolution proceeds so as to ensure compatibility with the existing network's facilities; and from this standpoint, the most desirable evolutionary path will be that of gradual conversion in which the parts of the existing network that require replacement, development, or expansion are upgraded with synchronous network equipment.

Since in the early stages of network evolution the structure of the synchronous transmission network will be slowly taking shape on top of the existing asynchronous network, the main interest is still focused on the existing network's constituent elements, to which will be added the elements that constitute the synchronous transmission network. Hence, as depicted in Figure 3.64(a), new equipment appears in the synchronous transmission network, such as the synchronous multiplexer, which multiplexes the exisiting plesiochronous tributaries in a synchronous manner, and the add/drop multiplexer, which adds or drops tributaries directly from the STM-n signal. At this stage of evolution, the synchronous transmission network's structure is functionally still inoperable as a whole; synchronous transmission network distribution will be synchronous line system-oriented. For practical utilization of synchronous line termination equipment, the role of the STM-n interface equipment that can achieve connection with the exisiting switches will be prominent.

In the early stages of the synchronous transmission network, the existing DS-1/1E, DS-2/2E, DS-3/3E, and DS-4E signals will still be used, but as the synchronous transmission network expands, the utilization of the existing asynchronous multiplexers will be diminished. That is, the DS-1/1E that has so far been multiplexed to higher-order signals such as DS-2/2E, DS-3/3E, and DS-4E, will then be

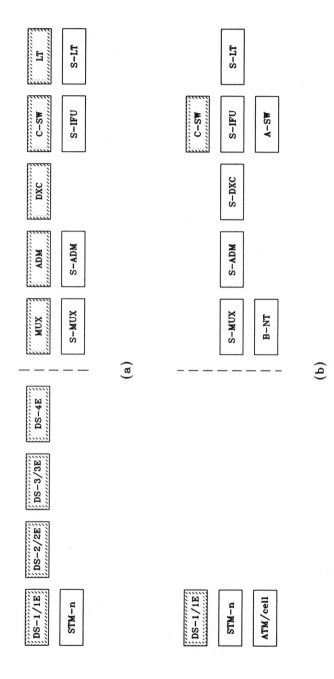

Figure 3.64 Signals and equipment according to the network evolution: (a) short-term; (b) long-term.

directly accommodated within the synchronous multiplexing process, and thus multiplexing will become greatly simplified. Therefore, one type of synchronous multiplexer can replace a number of different asynchronous multiplexers, enhancing the network's simplicity and economic viability.

As the relative importance of the plesiochronous system within the communication network is reduced and the scope of the synchronous system is broadened, formation of the synchronous transmission network will accelerate. Also, the synchronous transmission network will spread as the cross-connect system is introduced and achieves connection to the synchronous line system. The synchronous transmission network that evolves in such a manner will further expand to a point-to-multipoint format as the cross-connect system is used for exchange and interexchange. Also, the synchronous transmission network's evolution will be accompanied by the introduction of the BISDN, and the BISDN's base transport unit, the ATM cell, will conform to the concept of SDH and will be transmitted within the STM frame format. It follows then that, in the long run, the synchronous transmission network's constituent signals and apparatuses will be altered as shown in Figure 3.64(b).

SELECT BIBLIOGRAPHY

ANSI T1.105–1988, "American National Standard for Telecommunications—Digital Hierarchy—Optical Interface Rates and Formats Specification," 1988.

ANSI T1.106–1988, "American National Standard for Telecommunications—Digital Hierarchy—Optical Interface Specifications (single mode)," 1988.

ANSI T1.105–1991, "Digital Hierarchy—Optical Interface Rates and Formats Specifications (SONET)," 1991.

ANSI T1.105a-1991, "Supplement to T1.105," 1991.

Aprille, T. J., "Introducing SONET Into the Local Exchange Carrier Network," *IEEE Commun. Mag.*, Vol. 28, No. 8, Aug. 1990, pp. 34–38.

Asatani, K., K. R. Harrison, and R. Ballart, "CCITT Standardization of Network Node Interface of Synchronous Digital Hierarchy," *IEEE Commun. Mag.*, Vol. 28, No. 8, Aug. 1990, pp. 15–20.

Balcer, R., J. Eaves, J. Legras, R. McLintock, and T. Wright, "An Overview of Emerging CCITT Recommendations for the Synchronous Digital Hierarchy: Multiplexers, Line Systems, Management, and Network Aspects," *IEEE Commun. Mag.*, Vol. 28, No. 8, Aug. 1990, pp. 21–25.

Ballart, R., and Y. C. Ching, "SONET: Now It's the Standard Optical Network," *IEEE Commun. Mag.*, Vol. 27, No. 3, Mar. 1989, pp. 1–15.

Bars, G., J. Legras, and X. Maitre, "Introduction of New Technologies in the French Transmisison Networks," *IEEE Commun. Mag.*, Vol. 28, No. 8, Aug. 1990, pp. 39–43.

Bates, R. J., *Introduction to T1/T3 Networking*, Artech House, 1992.

Bellcore, SR-NWT-001756, "Automatic Protection Switching for SONET," Issue 1, 1990.

Bellcore, SR-NWT-002224, "SONET Synchronization Planning Guidelines," Issue 1, 1992.

Bellcore, TA-NWT-001042, "Generic Requirements for Operations Interfaces Using OSI Tools: SONET Path Switched Ring Information Model," Issue 3, 1992.

Bellcore, TA-NWT-001250, "Generic Requirements for Synchronous Optical Network (SONET) File Transfer," Issue 2, 1992.

Bellcore, TN-NWT-001042, "Generic Requirements for Operations Interfaces Using OSI Tools: Synchronous Optical Network (SONET) Transport Information Model," Issue 1, 1992.

Bellcore, TR-NWT-000253, "Synchronous Optical Network (SONET) Transport Systems: Common Generic," Issue 2, 1991.

Bellcore, TR-NWT-001230, "SONET Bidirectional Line Switched Ring Equipment Generic Criteria," Issue 2, 1992.

Bellcore, TR-TSP-000496, "SONET Add/Drop Multiplex Equipment (SONET ADM) Generic Criteria," Issue 3, 1992.

Bellcore, TR-TSY-00023, "Wideband and Broadband Digital Cross-Connect Generic Requirements and Objectives," Issue 2, 1989.

Bellcore, TR-TSY-000303, "Integrated Digital Loop Carrier System Generic Requirements, Objectives, and Interface," Issue 1, Revision 3, 1990.

Boehm, R. J., "Progress in Standardization of SONET," *IEEE LCS Mag.*, Vol. 1, No. 2, May 1990, pp. 8–16.

Boyer, G. R., "A Perspective on Fiber in the Loop Systems," *IEEE LCS Mag.*, Vol. 1, No. 3, Aug. 1990, pp. 6–11.

CCITT Rec. G.707, "Synchronous Digital Hierarchy Bit Rates," 1992 (Rev).

CCITT Rec. G.708, "Network Node Interface for the Synchronous Digital Hierarchy," 1992 (Rev).

CCITT Rec. G.709, "Synchronous Multiplexing Structure," 1992 (Rev).

CCITT Rec. G.781, "Multiplexing Equipment for the SDH," 1992.

CCITT Rec. G.782, "Types and General Characteristics of Synchronous Digital Hierarchy (SDH) Multiplexing Equipment," 1992.

CCITT Rec. G.783, "Characteristics of Synchronous Digital Hierarchy (SDH) Multiplexing Equipment Functional Blocks," 1992.

CCITT Rec. G.784, "Synchronous Digital Hierarchy (SDH) Management," 1992.

CCITT Rec. G.803, "Architecture of Transport Networks Based on the SDH," 1992 (Rev).

CCITT Rec. G.831, "Performance and Management Capabilities of Transport Networks Based on the SDH," 1992.

CCITT Rec. G.957, "Optical Interfaces for Equipments Relating to the Synchronous Digital Hierarchy," 1992.

CCITT Rec. G.958, "Digital Line Systems Based on the Synchronous Digital Hierarchy for Use on Optical Fiber Cables," 1992.

Ching, Y. C., and G. W. Cyboron, "Where Is SONET?" *IEEE LTS Mag.*, Vol. 3, No. 4, Nov. 1991, pp. 44–51.

Day, C. N., and C. H. Lin, "SONET and OSI: Making a Connection," *IEEE LTS Mag.*, Vol. 3, No. 4, Nov. 1991, pp. 52–59.

Eames, T. R., and G. T. Hawley, "The Synchronous Optical Network and Fiber-in-the-Loop," *IEEE LTS Mag.*, Vol. 3, No. 4, Nov. 1991, pp. 24–29.

Haque, I., W. Kremer, and K. Raychaudhuri, "Self-Healing Rings in a Synchronous Environment," *IEEE LTS Mag.*, Vol. 3, No. 4, Nov. 1991, pp. 30–37.

Hibino, M., and F. Kaplan, "User Interface Design for SONET Networks," *IEEE Commun. Mag.*, Vol. 30, No. 8, Aug. 1992.

Holter, R., "Managing SONET Equipment," *IEEE Network Mag.*, Vol. 5, No. 4, Jan. 1992, pp. 36–41.

Holter, R., "SONET: A Network Management Viewpoint," *IEEE LCS Mag.*, Vol. 1, No. 4, Nov. 1990, pp. 4–13.

Jakubson, J., "Managing SONET Network," *IEEE LTS Mag.*, Vol. 3, No. 4, Nov. 1991, pp. 5–13.

Kasai, H., T. Murase, and H. Ueda, "Synchronous Digital Transmission Systems Based on CCITT SDH Standard," *IEEE Commun. Mag.*, Vol. 28, No. 8, Aug. 1990, pp. 50–59.

Mazzei, U., A. Palamidessi, P. Passeri, and F. Balena, "Evolution of the Italian Telecommunication Network Towards SDH," *IEEE Commun. Mag.*, Vol. 28, No. 8, Aug. 1990, pp. 44–50.

Passeri, P., F. Balena, G. Bars, N. Vogt, and T. Wright, "Introducing SDH Systems in Europe," *IEEE LTS Mag.*, Vol. 3, No. 4, Nov. 1991, pp. 38–43.

Pelegrini, G. and P. H. K. Wery, "Synchronous Digital Hierarchy," *Telecom. J.*, Vol. 58, 1991, pp. 815–24.

Sandesara, N. B., G. R. Ritchie, and B. Engel-Smith, "Plans and Considerations for SONET Development," *IEEE Commun. Mag.*, Vol. 28, No. 8, Aug. 1990, pp. 26–33.

Sexton, M. J., and A. B. D. Reid, *Transmission Networking: SONET and the Synchronous Digital Hierarchy*, Artech House, 1992.

Sharifi, M., and B. Mortimer, "The Evolution of SDH: A View From Telecom New Zealand," *IEEE Commun. Mag.*, Vol. 28, No. 8, Aug. 1990, pp. 60–66.

Shirakawa, H., K. Maki, and H. Miura, "Japan's Network Evolution Relies on SDH-Based Systems," *IEEE LTS Mag.*, Vol. 3, No. 4, Nov. 1991, pp. 14–18.

Sosnosky, J., and T. H. Wu, "SONET Ring Applications for Survivable Fiber Loop Networks," *IEEE Commun. Mag.*, Vol. 29, No. 6, June 1991, pp. 51–58.

Spears, D. R., "Broadband ISDN Switching Capabilities From a Services Perspective," *IEEE J. of Select. Areas in Commun.*, Vol. SAC-5, No. 8, Oct. 1987.

To, M., and J. MacEachern, "Planning and Deploying a SONET-Based Metro Network," *IEEE LTS Mag.*, Vol. 3, No. 4, Nov. 1991, pp. 19–23.

Wu, T. H., *Fiber Network Service Survivability*, Artech House, 1992.

Wu, T. H., "SONET Ring Applications for Survivable Fiber Loop Networks," *IEEE Commun. Mag.*, Vol. 29, No. 6, June, pp. 51–58.

Wu, T. H., and M. E. Burrowes, "Feasibility Study of a High-Speed SONET Self-Healing Architecture in Future Inter-Office Networks," *IEEE Commun. Mag.*, Vol. 28, No. 11, Nov. 1991, pp. 33–51.

Chapter 4
BISDN and ATM

Conceived under the influence of the standardization process of the SDH, the BISDN is an expanded version of the ISDN which has the capability to accommodate various types of broadband signals while retaining the basic intent of ISDN. The BISDN's fundamental objective is to achieve complete integration of services ranging from low bit rate bursty signals up to broadband continuous real-time signals, including voiceband services such as telemetry, data terminal, telephone, facsimile, and broadband services such as video telephony, video conference, HDTV transmission, high-speed data transmission, and video signal transmission. Consequently, an efficient technique for dealing with such a diverse set of services in a generalized manner was desired, and ATM is the technique that was proposed as the solution.

In the background surrounding the emergence of the BISDN concept, there is an increasing demand for various types of broadband services, including video services. In order to accommodate all such broadband signals, the capability to integrate interactive services such as video telephone with distributive services like CATV is needed, as well as the capability to provide both the circuit-mode services and packet-mode services in a generalized manner. In addition, a technique that enables the joint accommodation of signals over a wide range of frequencies, including low-rate telemetry signals (few bits per second), midrange voice-speed signals (tens of kilobits per second), and high-rate video signals (hundreds of megabits per second) is also required. A possible solution for meeting these requirements is the scheme in which various service signals are first made to have a common external shape and then are piled up one by one and multiplexed together. Here, the ATM cell is the standardized external form, and the method for multiplexing a collection of ATM cells is ATDM. The communication mode based on ATM cells and the ATDM is ATM.

The ATM communication technique can be said to be a transfer mode that integrates the existing circuit-mode digital transfer method with the packet-mode transfer method. First of all, ATM has a close connection with the packet-mode transfer method in that it uses ATM cells as its basic means of transport; but there is a difference in that the packet-mode was created for variable-rate, non-real-time

---

data signals, whereas ATM can manage real-time fixed-rate signals as well. Also, the packet mode is generally used for LANs, whereas ATM can be used for a vast public network and is hence accompanied by various problems inherent in any large network, such as routing, access and flow control, switching, and transmission. On the other hand, the fundamental difference between ATM and the circuit-mode transfer method is that whereas the circuit mode functions by allocating a separate service channel and transferring through it information signals in a continuous bit stream, ATM operates by segmenting the information signal so as to fit it onto the ATM cell, then transferring it through a virtual channel. Thus, the accompanying ATM procedures such as connection setup, data processing, transmission, and switching raise various new problems.

The purpose of this chapter is to provide a detailed examination of the BISDN and ATM. Since the BISDN or ATM is a novel concept which was not introduced until the late 1980s, the particulars of its operation are still in the research stage. Therefore, this chapter will mainly concentrate on its fundamental principles, using CCITT's BISDN-related Recommendations as the reference.[1] Since ATM is a new transfer technique that was conceived as a means of realizing the BISDN, "BISDN" will at times be used interchangeably with "ATM network."

The structure of this chapter is as follows. First a comprehensive overview of the BISDN and ATM will be given. First, we will investigate various BISDN services and basic principles of ATM, as well as functional architecture and the user-network interface of the BISDN. Next, we will examine the protocol reference model of the BISDN, followed by a discussion of the physical layer, ATM layer, and the *ATM adaptation layer* (AAL) of the BISDN. Then, network aspects, signaling, and OAM of the BISDN will be investigated, along with an examination of the BISDN transmission and switching systems. Finally, ATM communication will be compared with high-speed packet communication and synchronous optical transmission.

4.1 OVERVIEW OF BISDN AND ATM TRANSMISSION

This section provides an overview of the chapter's overall content.[2] First, the BISDN's basic concept, service characteristics, technological background, standardization process, and basic principles will be examined, and the relationship between the ISDN and BISDN will be discussed as well. Next, the BISDN user-network interface will be examined.

---

[1]The current CCITT Recommendations that were approved in relation to the BISDN include I.113, I.121, I.150, I.211, I.311, I.321, I.327, I.361, I.362, I.363, I.364, I.371, I.413, I.432, and I.610. See Appendix A.

[2]This section gives an overall summary of the chapter. The reader may choose to read or skip over it.

4.1.1 Basic Concept of BISDN

As societal and business activities become more diversified, the demand for various multimedia and broadband services increases more rapidly. This is manifested in the sudden proliferation of data terminals and personal computers, the ubiquity of fax machines, the increased installations of video conferencing systems, and the success of the CATV industry and the increase in the number of its subscribers. The demand has also brought about a diverse set of broadband services such as video telephone, high-resolution picture transmission, high-speed data transmission, video surveillance, video retrieval services, and broadband videotex.

Since interactive services and distributive services are both present among the services in demand, there is a chance that each type sporadically forms its own communication network. Since the circuit-mode services and packet-mode services are also mixed together, each could develop a separate communication network of its own. However, the construction of an independent service-oriented network imposes a heavy financial burden and can bring about the obstruction of communication information transfer and disorder in the administration of the communication network. Therefore, it is desirable to integrate various networks into one universal communication network so that all the services can be provided in an integrated manner. The BISDN concept is just to achieve such an integrated service network by expanding the already standardized narrowband ISDN.

Therefore, the BISDN can be described as a digital communication network that utilizes broadband transmission and switching technologies to interconnnect concentrated or distributed subscribers and service providers, and to support integrated services with wide-bandwidth distribution that ranges from a few bits per second to hundreds of megabits per second.

From the service standpoint, the BISDN integrates narrowband services such as telephone, data terminal, telemetry, facsimile, and teletex with broadband services such as video telephone, video conference, high-resolution image transmission, high-speed data transmission, video surveillance, and CATV. Consequently, the BISDN can be said to be a communication network that takes the concept of the existing ISDN and extends it to enable the provision of various kinds of broadband services.

4.1.2 Characteristics of BISDN

The primary goal of the BISDN is the accommodation of all existing services along with those that will come into being in the communication networks of the future. Consequently, narrowband services such as telephone, data terminal, facsimile, telewriting, telemetry, teletex, videotex, and electronic mail are included as the basics, and broadband services such as video telephone, video conferencing, high-speed data, color facsimile, CATV, HDTV distribution, high-fidelity sound, video-mail,

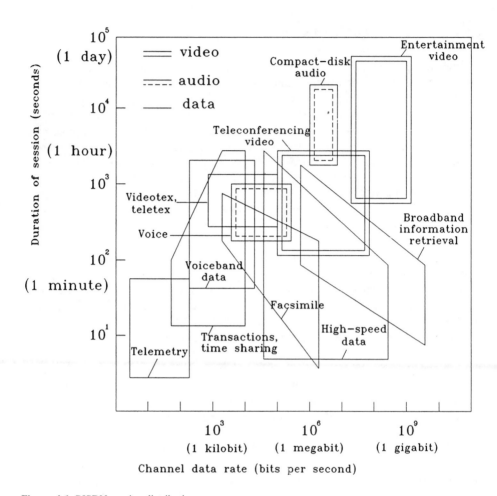

Figure 4.1 BISDN service distribution.

video monitoring, high-resolution picture transmission, and broadband videotex are additionally provided.

These BISDN services include services of all types and characteristics. Conversational services such as telephone or video telephone, message services such as electronic mail or video mail, and retrieval services for retrieving graphics or documents are all included. These are all bidirectional interactive services, but unidirectional distributive services such as CATV are included as well.

The most notable characteristic of BISDN services is that their bandwidth distribution is extremely wide. Whereas the service signals for narrowband ISDN are distributed around the 64-kbps voice signal, the signal distribution of the BISDN extends to very high bit rates to include digital tributaries and various video signals, as well as the high-speed data signals. Consequently, from the transmission rate standpoint, the service signals of the BISDN occupy an extremely wide range of bands, from the few bits per second used for the telemetry signals at the low end, to the hundreds of megabits per second for the video signals at the high end (see Figure 4.1). The service time also exhibits a wide-ranging distribution, from the few seconds required for low-speed data, to the minutes used in telephone conversations, and to the hours required for the video services. Therefore, the term *broad* in BISDN means, in its narrow sense, that the BISDN is capable of providing broadband services of hundreds of megabits per second, while in its wide sense it means that the BISDN's frequency (bit rate) distribution and service time distribution are both widely spread over the broad band.

Another distinct feature of the BISDN is that the continuous signals such as voice or video coexist with the signals that are bursty in character, such as terminal data. Whereas voice or video signals can acquire a constant fixed rate depending on how they were digitized, various data signals are variable rate signals whose rate can vary widely from moment to moment. On the other hand, whereas a voice or a video signal requires real-time processing, such a capability is not critical in the case of data signals.

Such disparities in the properties of BISDN signals make the switching and transmission in the BISDN a difficult task. This is because packet switching is more appropriate for low-rate or bursty signals, whereas circuit switching is more appropriate for voice or video signals. Also, for voice signals, time-division circuit switching is more efficient, while space-division circuit switching is more effective for high-speed video signals. Hence, it is a difficult problem indeed to find a way that will enable the switching and transmitting of various low-speed and high-speed signals along with the continuous and bursty signals.

4.1.3 Technological Background of BISDN

Since the services furnished by the BISDN have a diverse set of characteristics, as was examined in the preceding section, the maturation of several basic technologies is extremely crucial for the realization of the BISDN ideal. To begin with, since high-speed and broadband service signals will form the main axis of BISDN, high-speed processing and device technologies are indispensable, as well as broadband transmission and switching technologies. Also, since various video services will become the BISDN's primary services of interest, the maturation of image processing and implementation technologies is needed. As low-speed and high-speed services are intermingled, circuit-mode and packet-mode services coexist, and the corresponding communication network technology is essential.

These basic technologies have steadily grown into maturity, in step with the increasing demand for broadband services. To begin with, communication network technology has already matured; optical fiber attenuation has been reduced to below 0.5 dB/km, and the prices of light-emitting and light-detecting devices have fallen drastically. Advances in integrated circuit and transistor technologies are also worthy of close attention, with silicon bipolar or GaAs transistors currently possessing high-speed processing capability from hundreds of Mbps up to a few Gbps, while the CMOS technology can go up to the 150-Mbps range. Recent advances in software and microprocessor technologies have made high-speed control a possibility, which, along with fast operating devices, renders high-speed switching possible.

Due to the advances in signal processing techniques, the compression, conversion, and regeneration of various service signals have become an easy task, and the advances in computer technology have also made the collecting, handling, and processing of service signals a simple matter. In addition, if the above advances are complemented by VLSI technology, efficient terminal equipment at the user premises can be constructed. Also, developments in high-quality monitors and high-sensitivity cameras have advanced to the point that practical BISDN terminal devices associated with various video services can now be materialized.

On the other hand, the BISDN standardization process, which has been progressing on a grand scale since the mid-1980s with CCITT as its center of operation, inspired a great deal of research on the possible integration of various types of broadband service signals and the digitalization of communication networks, which also contributed significantly to advances in communication network technology. Such groundwork bore fruit in the form of ATM, which can enable the harmonious coexistence of various BISDN services possessing a disparate set of properties, and this signifies the maturation of the BISDN's service integration technology.

4.1.4 BISDN Standardization Background

During the ISDN standardization process in the early 1980s, CCITT established the H1, H2, H3, and H4 channels as the high-speed channels. Among them, the H1 channel became the ISDN's primary access in the form of the 1.536-Mbps H11 channel and the 1.920-Mbps H12 channel, and thus, together with the 2B + D basic access of 144 kbps, came to form the very foundation of the ISDN. For the remaining H2, H3, and H4 channels, only rough outlines were given that correspond to the broadband channels of the existing digital hierarchy.

As interest gradually shifted toward the broadband channels, starting around 1985, the bit rates 30 to 40 Mbps, 45 Mbps, and 60 to 70 Mbps were examined as the target standard for the H2, H3, and H4 channels. On the other hand, the T1 Committee once proposed the SONET-based 149.760-Mbps broadband channel as the candidate rate. Then, in July 1987, CCITT went ahead with the NNI standardization process separately from the UNI standardization.

The NNI standardization, which unfolded with the SG XVIII's working party (WP) 7 as the center of operations, went through numerous hardships and finally came to settle on the STM-1 signal with a 9B x 270 structure and 155.52-Mbps bit rate as the standard at the Seoul meeting in February 1988 (see Section 3.1.8). This is the very SDH standard that was subsequently confirmed in Recommendations G.707 to G.709. On the other hand, the BISDN's UNI standardization operation, which was propelled by the SG XVIII's *Broadband Task Group* (BBTG) completed Recommendation I.121 in 1988. This is the first document that established BISDN's basic outline, and it offered regulations on such issues as whether BISDN should be based on ATM, whether to divide the BISDN into interactive and distributive services, and whether the BISDN's functional configuration and basic structure should be the same as the ISDN's. Also, the protocol model for ATM was produced, and the size of the ATM cell was prescribed to be around 32 to 120 bytes. In addition, the broadband channels H21, H22, and H4 were assigned the unofficial bit rates of 32.768 Mbps, 43 to 45 Mbps, and 132 to 138.240 Mbps, respectively, and UNI was unofficially separated into the 150-Mbps class and the 600-Mbps class.

Afterwards, BBTG became WP8, and the UNI standardization operation suffered through another difficult time with questions regarding the ATM cell size, the bit rate at the interface, and the frame structure. Europe's proposal of 4 + 32 byte size (cell header + payload) for the ATM cell was in conflict with the U.S.'s proposal of 5 + 64 byte size, and ultimately the 5 + 48 byte size was agreed on as a compromise.[3] The bit rate to be used at the interface was selected as 155.520 Mbps under the strong influence of the previously completed SDH standardization as discussed in Chapter 3. Also, the physical medium's frame structure was decided either to have the STM-1 frame structure or to consist purely of a flow of ATM cells. The mapping of other G.702 signals was approved as well.[4] At the Matsuyama Conference in November 1990, WP8 finalized the matters that had been approved up to that point on 13 I Series Recommendations.[5] In this manner, various basic frameworks relating to the BISDN came to be completed.

4.1.5 Basic Principles of BISDN

As was mentioned earlier, the BISDN is a concept that was proposed as a means of satisfying the increasing demand for broadband services. The BISDN's basic purpose is to provide integrated interactive and distributive services, and to furnish narrowband services and broadband services simultaneously by employing mature high-speed transmission, switching, signal processing, computer, software, and device

---

[3]Some of the candidate ATM cell sizes included the 6 + 66 size proposed by Japan and the 5 + 60 size proposed by Korea.

[4]The G.702 signal refers to the existing plesiochronous digital hierarchy signals specified in Recommendation G.702.

[5]The I Series Recommendations that have been approved up to the end of 1990 are the same as the ones mentioned in footnote 1 except for I.364 and I.371.

technologies to construct a digital network that can integrate and furnish a diverse set of broadband services.

To meet these objectives, point-to-point/point-to-multipoint connections and on-demand/reserved/semipermanent connections must be supported. A BISDN must be intelligent enough to allow future growth and improvement in service characteristics, and it must be equipped with network operation, maintenance, control, and administration functions. The BISDN structure must be regulated in terms of functions so that it can ensure that the particular structure that is chosen does not hinder the advances in future technology or the evolution of the implementation method. Also, a BISDN must be flexible to accommodate new user demands or developments in the network itself. Furthermore, the evolution of a BISDN must occur in such a way that it can accommodate the existing networks and the ISDN naturally, and the establishment of access reference configuration or protocol must be grounded on the formerly established ISDN concept.

As a way to realize the BISDN's basic objective, an ATM is employed.[6] ATM is a transmission technique that segments various service signals, maps them onto ATM cells of a fixed size, and subsequently transports them using asynchronous time-division multiplexing. ATM is a connection-oriented method of communication that establishes virtual paths and virtual channels for the transfer of ATM cells. Thus, the use of ATM allows highly flexible network access and variable assignment of bandwidth. Also, since ATM is defined independently of the particular transport means of the physical layer, information transfer can be accomplished through diverse types of physical media and transport networks.

4.1.6 Comparison of BISDN With ISDN

The concept of BISDN started out as an extension of ISDN standardization. Consequently, the BISDN has many similarities with the ISDN at the conceptual level. However, from the practical implementation standpoint, the BISDN and ISDN share no common traits.

To begin with, from the viewpoint that the basic motivation is to achieve integration of services, the BISDN's role is the same as that of the ISDN; however, in the case of the BISDN, the services that are targeted for integration include broadband signals as well. Consequently, the BISDN's basic structural model is the same as the ISDN's, except that the ISDN's 64-kbps base narrowband capacity has been supplemented by the BISDN's broadband capability.

In terms of its functional structure or its basic configurations, the BISDN is identical to the ISDN. The fact that the functional groups consist of TE1, TE2, NT1, NT2, and TA and that the reference points are R, S, and T, is applicable to both networks.

---

[6]For a detailed explanation of ATM, see Section 4.3.

However, they are equivalent only in concept and are not compatible in practice. That is, a BISDN cannot be created simply by augmenting the ISDN with broadband service equipment; nor can the ISDN's TE be connected directly to the BISDN's NT. Consequently, the ISDN's functional groups or reference points and BISDN-related elements are equivalent only at the conceptual level and are entirely different in practice.[7,8] But it is possible to interface the ISDN's TE1 or TA through the BISDN's NT2.

From the practical implementation standpoint, the BISDN and ISDN are two fundamentally different types of networks. Whereas the ISDN's transmission method is equivalent to placing packet-mode transmission on top of the existing digital circuit mode transmission, the BISDN opts for ATM, which is an entirely different technique. In other words, if the ISDN can be said to be a circuit-mode-oriented network that accommodates packet-mode transmission, the BISDN is a packet-mode-oriented transmission network that can also accommodate circuit-mode. So, since each uses a different transmission technique, the BISDN differs from the ISDN in all aspects, including transmission, switching, signaling, and network administration. Therefore, it is reasonable to treat the BISDN and the ISDN as two entirely different entities except for the conceptual similarities.

4.1.7 Asynchronous Transfer Mode

ATM is the communication technique conceived as a way of materializing the BISDN and is a packet-mode transport technique with a peculiar form that employs ATDM. In a BISDN, information is transferred through a continuous flow of packets of fixed size called *ATM cells*. Consequently, service information is first curtailed to a fixed size, then mapped into the ATM cells, and subsequently goes through the ATDM procedure with other ATM cells, thus forming the BISDN's internal transmission signal. Here, ATDM is a type of statistical multiplexing technique that time-division multiplexes ATM cells from several different channels arriving in a mutually asynchronous manner.

When ATM is used, the capacity of a service channel is measured by the number of corresponding ATM cells. Consequently, the amount of information transfer capacity is reflected in the number of ATM cells. The transport capacity is allocated through a negotiation with the communication network at the time of call setup, according to the capacity required and the capacity available at the time.

---

[7]To denote this relationship, BISDN functional groups are appended with the prefix "B-" and the BISDN reference points with the subscript "B."

[8]From the signaling point of view, the long-term goals and objectives of BISDN signaling diverge from the ISDN. However, the current Q.93B and B-ISUP draft recommendations represent just minor changes to their ISDN counterparts. The ATM Forum is currently defining a modified version of Q.93B, which supports limited point-to-point connections.

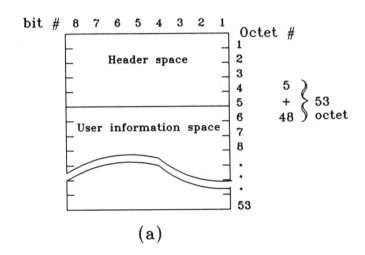

(a)

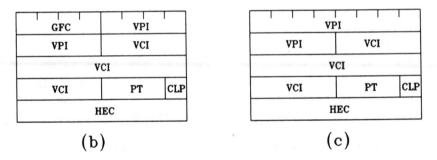

(b)   (c)

Figure 4.2 ATM cell structure: (a) cell structure; (b) header structure at UNI; (c) header structure at NNI.

ATM is a connection-oriented method that transfers service information by establishing a virtual channel. Whenever a virtual channel is setup, a connection identifier is assigned, and when the connection is removed, the identifier is removed as well. The sequence among ATM cells within a given virtual channel is preserved by an ATM layer function.

ATM prescribes a layered protocol reference model in order to achieve a systematic and flexible transport of information. The protocol model for this purpose is composed of the physical layer, ATM layer, AAL, and the higher-order layer. The AAL executes the function of mapping service signals into the ATM cells' payload space, while the ATM layer executes the ATM cell header-related functions for the transparent transfer of ATM cell payload space. The physical medium layer delivers ATM cells by converting them into a transmission bit stream.

An ATM cell consists of 53 bytes, which are divided into 5 bytes of header and 48 bytes of payload space (see Figure 4.2(a)). The main function of the cell header is to identify those that are a part of the same virtual channel among the ATM cells existing inside the ATDM information flow. This function is designated as *virtual path identification* (VPI) and *virtual channel identification* (VCI) in Figure 4.2(b,c). A virtual path implies a bundle of virtual channels that share a common path. Other cell header functions include identifying *payload types* (PT), indicating *cell loss priority* (CLP), and providing *header error control* (HEC). At the UNI, the cell header additionally provides the *generic flow control* (GFC) function.

4.1.8 BISDN's Functional Architecture

The BISDN is basically the same as the narrowband ISDN, in terms of the reference configuration, functional groups, and reference points. The BISDN's basic structural model is as depicted in Figure 4.3. The BISDN's structure includes higher-order capability and lower-order capability, with the higher-order capability being a TE-related function, and the lower-order capability encompassing broadband capability, 64-kbps-based narrowband ISDN capability, and interexchange signaling capability.

The BISDN's reference configuration is shown in Figure 4.4. Reference points are designated S_B and T_B, and B-TE1, B-TE2, B-TA, B-NT1, and B-NT2 represent the functional groups. In the figure, B-TE1, B-TE2, and B-TA are a part of the terminal equipment (B-TE), B-NT2 belongs to a private BISDN, and B-NT1 belongs to a public BISDN. The letter "B" stands for BISDN.

4.1.9 Protocol Reference Model

The BISDN's *protocol reference model* (PRM) is composed of the management plane, the control plane, and the user plane, as depicted in Figure 4.5. The management plane can be further divided into plane management and layer management. The plane management implies the management of the overall system, while layer management refers to the management of resources and user parameters as well as the OAM information.

The control plane takes charge of call control as well as connection information control, while the user plane is responsible for the transfer of user information. Protocols of the control plane and the user plane are categorized into higher-order layer, AAL, ATM cell layer, and physical layer, and the respective functions of each layer are as listed in Table 4.1.

The AAL is composed of the *convergence sublayer* (CS), which transforms user service information into a *protocol data unit* (PDU), and the *segmentation and*

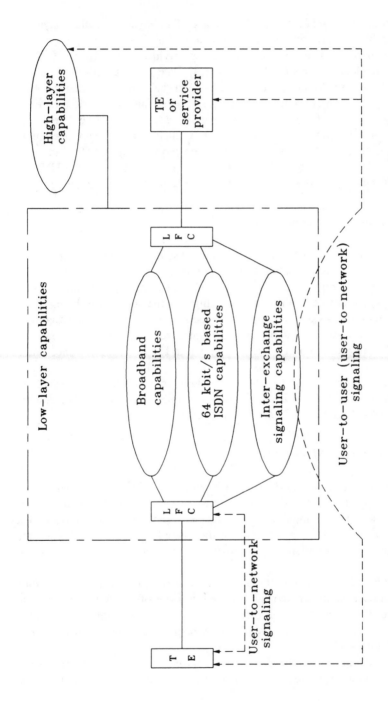

Figure 4.3 Basic architecture model of BISDN.

LFC – Local Function Capabilities

TE – Terminal Equipment

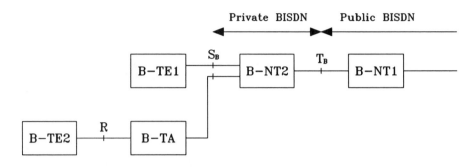

Figure 4.4 BISDN reference configuration.

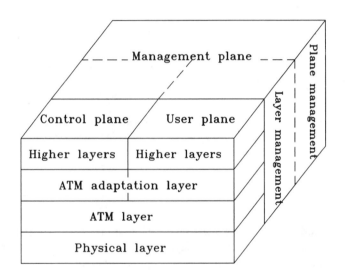

Figure 4.5 BISDN protocol reference model.

reassembly (SAR) sublayer, which segments the PDU to form the ATM cell's user information space.

The ATM layer applies the GFC section of the cell header to control access and information flow at the UNI. It also translates VPI/VCI and connects them to SAPs and multiplexes and demultiplexes ATM cells. The ATM layer can, in addition, process the PT and CLP bits and generate and extract ATM cell headers.

The physical layer is composed of the *transmission convergence* (TC) sublayer and the *physical medium* (PM) sublayer. Some of the TC functions include cell rate decoupling, generation and verification of the header error control byte, and the detection of cell boundary. Also, if the transmission is SDH-based, the function for

Table 4.1
Functions of Each Layer of BISDN PRM

Layer	Sublayer	Functions
ATM adaptation layer (AAL)	Convergence sublayer (CS)	Convergence functions
	Segmentation and reassembly (SAR)	Segmentation and reassembly functions
Asynchronous transfer mode (ATM) layer		Generic flow control
		Cell header generation/extraction
		Cell VPI/VCI translation
		Cell multiplex and demultiplex
Physical layer (PL)	Transmission convergence (TC)	Cell rate decoupling
		HEC header sequence generation/verification
		Cell delineation
		Transmission frame adaptation
		Transmission frame generation/recovery
	Physical medium (PM)	Bit timing
		Physical medium

the generation and extraction of the transmission frame is also a part of TC's responsibility. The physical medium sublayer signifies the final stage of the transmission process, and the medium can be either optical fiber or coaxial cable.

4.1.10 User-Network Interface of BISDN

Figure 4.6 is a depiction of the possible UNI configurations in terms of the reference points T_B, S_B, and R and functional groups B-NT1, B-NT2, B-TE1, B-TE2, and B-TA. In the figure, the configurations of (a–f,i,j) are the same as those of the ISDN, and (g,h) show that B-NT can accommodate reference points S and S_B simultaneously.

Figure 4.7 displays different physical configurations of UNI used for a multipoint connection. In the figure, (a) shows a centralized star configuration, and (b) shows a generic distributed configuration. Also, (c,d,e,f) represent the physical configurations for the distributed ring, starred bus, bus, and multiaccess structures, respectively. In the figure, MA signifies the *medium adaptor*, and W represents access points between MAs. Also, TE* indicates a TE with a bus configuration, and SS_B

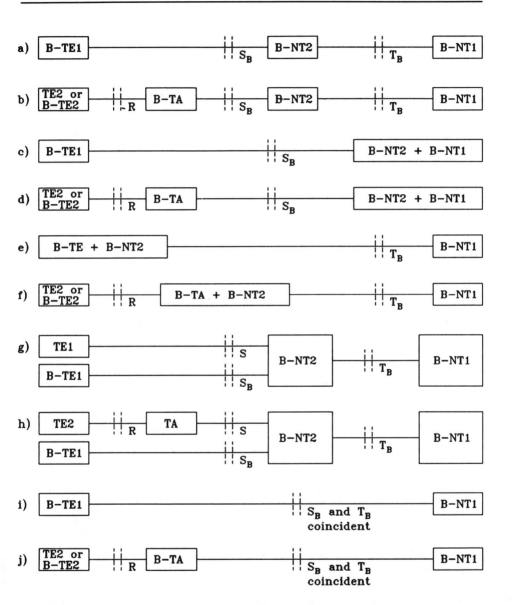

Figure 4.6 Physical configurations for UNI: (a,b) physical interfaces occur at S_B and T_B; (c,d) physical interfaces occur at S_B only; (e,f) physical interfaces occur at T_B only; (g,h) physical interfaces occur at S, S_B, and T_B; (i,j) physical interfaces occur at a location where S_B and T_B coincide.

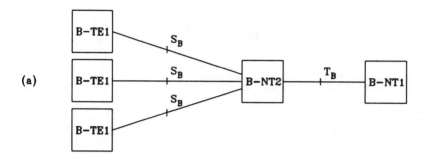

(a)

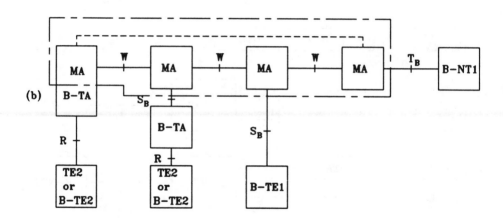

Figure 4.7 Physical configurations for multipoint applications: (a) centralized B-NT2 configuration (star configuration); (b) distributed B-NT2 generic configuration; (c) distributed ring configuration; (d) starred bus configuration; (e) bus configuration; (f) multiaccess configuration.

indicates access points between TE*s. MA and W are nonstandard equipment and a reference point, respectively, and TE* and SS_B are, respectively, equipment and a reference point that are equivalent to TE and S_B.

Reference point T_B provides point-to-point connection at the physical layer, accommodating both the cell-based and the SDH-based physical layers. Reference point S_B provides point-to-point connection at the physical layer, point-to-multipoint connection for the higher-order layer, and can jointly accommodate both cell-based and SDH-based physical layers.

B-NT1 performs various layer 1 functions, such as line transmission termination, transmission interface management, and OAM. B-NT2 executes layer 1 and

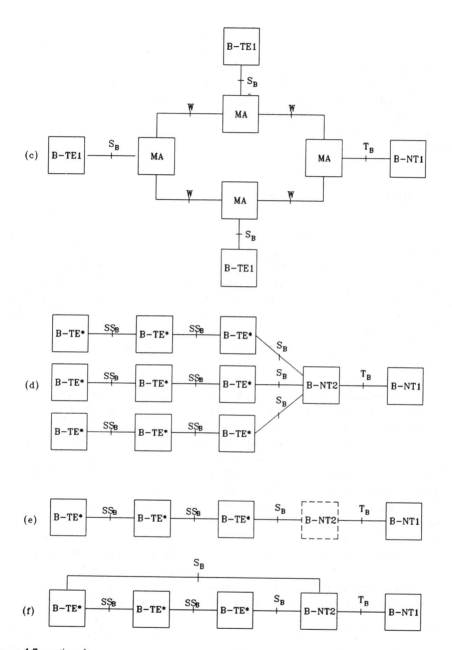

Figure 4.7 continued.

higher-order layer functions, and can be configured in concentrated mode or distributed mode. The associated functions include medium adaptation, cell-boundary search, concentration, buffering, multiplexing/demultiplexing, resource allocation, user parameter control, AAL functional interface management for signaling, signaling protocol management, switching of internal connections, and so on. B-TE performs other layer 1 and higher-order layer functions, including user-to-user and user-to-machine conversation, interface termination, signaling protocol management, and OAM.

4.1.11 BISDN Network Perspective

Since the BISDN is an ATM transport network, a concept of layered network similar to that of the synchronous transmission network also applies to it. In other words, the BISDN transport network can be layered into an ATM layer network and a physical layer network. An ATM layer network can further be divided into virtual channel level and virtual path level, and a physical layer network can also be divided into a transmission path level, digital section level, and regenerator section level.[9] The concept of a layered network is applicable for both the cell-based networks and SDH-based networks. The relationship between the two BISDN layer networks is illustrated in Figure 4.8.

At the VC level, a *virtual channel connection* (VCC) is provided for user-to-user, user-to-network, and network-to-network information transfer. As can be seen from Figure 4.8, the VCC is composed of a concatenation of VC links. User-to-user VCC is established between T_B or S_B reference points, and the cells associated with the same VCC are transported through the same path. At the VP level, the *virtual path connection* (VPC) capability is provided for the user-to-user, user-to-network, and network-to-network information transfers. As shown in Figure 4.8, VPC consists of a concatenation of VP links. User-user VPC is established between T_B or S_B reference points, and the cells associated with the same VPC are transported via the same path.

The physical layer network corresponds to a union of the transmission medium layer network and the path layer network of the synchronous transmission network. In other words, in SDH-based systems, the transmission path level is equivalent to the VC-4 transmission path, and the digital section level and regenerator section level are, respectively, equivalent to the multiplexer section and regenerator section.

---

[9]If this division is compared with the division in the synchronous digital transmission network, the ATM layer corresponds to the circuit layer network, and the physical layer corresponds to the transmission medium layer network. On the other hand, if the fact that routing is associated with ATM layer network is taken into account, then the ATM layer can be said to correspond to the path layer network. Also, the digital section is equivalent to the multiplexer section (see Section 3.10).

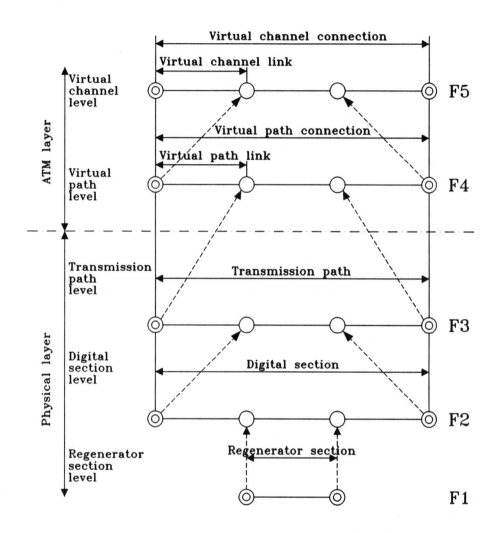

Figure 4.8 Hierarchical layer-to-layer relationship of BISDN.

4.1.12 General Principles of BISDN Signaling

The BISDN signaling scheme must possess the following capabilities: call setup when requested or on a permanent basis, provision of a multiconnection call, symmetric or asymmetric call setup, ATM VP and VC control for information transfer, support of broadband connections that have various different attributes, and support of interworking between different coding schemes. BISDN signaling must also have the capability to establish a call multiconnection and multiparty configurations, set up simultaneously multiple connections associated with one type of call, reconfigure connections via an intermediate processing entity, correlate the connection for the construction of a multiconnection call, and renegotiate connection-related traffic attributes during the duration of the call.

For establishing a VC for point-to-point or broadcast-type user-network signals, metasignaling is provided. Here, metasignaling implies the procedure for establishing signaling channels. The metasignaling procedure is a layer management function that is a part of the layer management plane and is associated only with the transfer of control information. Its functions include arbitrating when two or more pieces of terminal equipment are competing for the same VPI/VCI, administering capacity allocation for signaling channels, confirming whether a signaling channel is to be established or removed, and providing a reference for the signaling channel management procedures.

4.1.13 OAM Principles of BISDN

The OAM functions of the BISDN must include performance monitoring, fault detection, system protection, and fault-information transfer capabilities. To meet these requirements, a BISDN network is divided into five hierarchical levels. These five levels are equivalent to those mentioned in Section 4.1.11, which were classified in terms of layers. The VC level and VP level correspond to the VC level network and VP level network, respectively. The transmission path level is equivalent to the VC-4 path in an SDH-based network, the digital section applies between terminations of wired/wireless transmission system units, and the regenerator level is equivalent to sections between regenerator units.

The OAM information flows corresponding to these five levels are designated as F1 to F5 in Figure 4.8. Flow F1 represents the information flow between the regenerator and NT1, between LT and regenerator, or between regenerators; and F2 represents OAM information flow between NT1 and LT, between NT1 and NT2, or between LTs. F3 is the OAM information flow between NT and the *exchange termination* (ET), between NT2 and ATM *cross-connect* (XC), or between ATM XC and ET. F4 and F5 are OAM information flows between VP and AP, and between VC and AP, respectively. If ATM is cell-based, the OAM information flow F2 does not apply.

4.2 BISDN SERVICES

The target of the BISDN is to include services that can be provided by in the communication networks of the future. These include not only narrowband services such as telephone, data, facsimile, telewriting, telemetry, teletex, videotex, and electronic mail, but also broadband services such as video telephone, high-speed data, color facsimile, CATV, HDTV distribution, hi-fi sound, video mail, video surveillance, high-resolution picture, video conferencing, broadband videotex, and so on. The BISDN can also be classified according to the direction of information transfer, timing relations, and the channel connection type. The intent of the present section is to offer a comprehensive examination of various types of BISDN services.

4.2.1 Intrinsic Classification of Services

BISDN services can be categorized into interactive services and distributive services, depending on the direction of information transfer. Interactive services can be further categorized into conversational services, message services, and retrieval services. Distributive services can be subcategorized into controllable services and noncontrollable services (see Table 4.2).[10]

In general, a conversational service is the type of service that provides real-time, bidirectional communication between users at two ends. On the average, service information flows symmetrically in both directions, but it can occasionally be

Table 4.2
Classification of BISDN Services

Main Categories	Subcategories	Examples of Services
Interactive services	Conversational services	Video telephony, videoconference
	Messaging services	MHS, video mail service
	Retrieval services	Retrieval of film, document, etc.
Distributive services	Noncontrollable distributive services	Television, sound
	Controllable distributive services	Videography

[10]The corresponding CCITT technologies are, respectively, the distribution service with user individual presentation control and the distribution service without individual presentation control. Refer to CCITT Recommendation I.211.

asymmetric also. Examples of conversational services include video telephone, video conferencing, and high-speed data transmission.

A message service provides communication between users at two ends by way of storage devices. Here, the storage device can store, transfer, and process messages; that is, it possesses the capacity to compile, process, and transform information. Examples of message services include mailing service for film, high-resolution picture, voice information, and *message handling service* (MHS).

A retrieval service involves the retrieval of public-sector information stored in a central information center. On request, the desired information is transferred to the user on an individual basis. Here, the starting time of the information sequence can be controlled by the user. The targeted areas of retrieval service include film, high-resolution picture, voice information, and recorded information.

A noncontrollable distributive service refers to any general broadcasted service. Typically, a continuous stream of information is transmitted by a central service provider to an unlimited number of users within the network. Here, the users have access to the information flow, but have no control over the starting time or the program of the information flow. A typical example of noncontrollable service would be television and radio broadcasting.

Controllable distributive services are similar to noncontrollable services in the sense that a central service provider furnishes a continuous flow of information to a multiple number of users. But, unlike the noncontrollable distributive services, the information flow consists of information packets that are periodically repeated. Consequently, the user can selectively choose among the periodically distributed information packets, and thus can control starting time and program content of the packets. In other words, due to the periodic nature of the information content, the user can always receive the chosen information packets from their beginning. An example of a controllable service would be broadcast channel videography.

4.2.2 BISDN Services

Conversational Services

Conversational services include video services such as video telephone, video conferencing, video monitoring, and video and audio information transmission, and audio services such as multisound program signals. Conversational data services include high-speed data transmission, large-capacity file transfer, and high-speed remote monitoring, and text services include high-speed remote facsimile, high-resolution picture transmission, and document communication service (see Table 4.3).

Broadband video telephone is a means of transferring voice, motion video, still image, and text information from one user room to another. Video telephone service can be used for remote education, remote purchase, and remote advertising.

Table 4.3

Conversational Services

Type of Information	Examples of Broadband Services	Applications
Motion picture	Broadband video telephony	Tele-education, teleshopping
	Broadband videoconference	Tele-education, teleshopping, tele-advertising
	Video surveillance	Building security, traffic monitoring
	Video-audio information transmission service	TV signal transfer, video/audio dialogue contribution of information
Sound	Multiple sound-programmable signals	Multilingual commentary channels, multiple program transfers
Data	High-speed data transmission	Transfer of video and other high-speed data transfer (LAN or MAN interconnection, computer-computer interconnection), still image transfer, multistage interactive CAD/CAM
	Large-volume file transfer service	Data file transfer
	High-speed teleaction	Real-time control, telemetry, alarms
	High-speed telefax	User-to-user transfer of text, images, drawings, etc.
Document	High-resolution image communication service	Professional images, medical images, remote games
	Document communication service	User-to-user transfer of mixed documents

Video conferencing is a means of transferring voice, motion video, still image, and text from an individual to a group, or from a group to another group, at a minimum of two locations. Video conferencing can be employed for remote conferencing, remote education, teleshopping, and teleadvertising.

High-speed data transmission is a data transfer service used for establishing connection between LANs, MANs, and computers. In addition, video information transfer, still-image transfer, and multipoint interactive *computer-aided design* (CAD)/ *computer-aided manufacturing* (CAM) also require high-speed data service.

High-speed document transmission includes high-speed remote facsimile service for transferring text, video, and graphics between two users, and high-resolution video service for transferring professional-quality images such as medical images.

Message Service

Examples of message service include video-mail service, and document-mail service. Video-mail service is an electronic post-office box service that transfers moving images and sound, while document-mail service is an electronic mail box that can transfer mixed documents (see Table 4.4).

Table 4.4
Messaging Services

Type of Information	Examples of Broadband Services	Applications
Motion pictures (video) and sound	Video mail service	Video and sound, electronic mailbox
Document	Document mail service	Electronic mailbox service for mixed documents

Retrieval Service

Retrieval service is a data retrieval service for text, data, graphics, sound, still images, and moving images. Retrieval service includes broadband videotex, video retrieval, high-resolution image retrieval, document retrieval, and data retrieval (see Table 4.5).

Broadband videotex is videotex with moving images. It is used for remote education and training, remote software, teleshopping, and news retrieval.

Video retrieval service is mainly used for video entertainment, but it can also be used for remote education or training.

High-resolution image retrieval is also aimed at entertainment and can be used for remote education and training as well. It can also provide professional image communications service for medical image retrieval.

Distributive Service

Examples of noncontrollable distributive service include video service and services for text, graphics, still images, data, moving images, and sound. Video service is represented by the existing NTSC, *phase alteration by line* (PAL), and *sequential couleur avec memoire* (SECAM)-type television distributive services, as well as pay-TV service. Noncontrollable distributive service can also be employed for electronic newspaper, electronic publishing, unlimited data distribution, and audio/video signal distribution (see Table 4.6).

Controllable distributive service includes services for providing text, graphics, sound, and still images, with full-channel videography being the primary example. Videography can be used for remote education and training, remote advertising, news retrieval, and remote software services.

Table 4.5
Retrieval Services

Type of Information	Examples of Broadband Services	Applications
Text, data, graphics, sound, still images, motion pictures	Broadband videotex	Videotex including moving pictures, remote education and training, telesoftware tele-shopping, tele-advertising, news retrieval
	Video retrieval services	Entertainment purposes, remote education and training
	High-resolution image retrieval service	Entertainment purposes, remote education and training, professional image communications, medical image communications
	Document retrieval service	Mixed documents retrieval
	Data retrieval service	Telesoftware

Table 4.6
Distributive Services

Type of Information	Examples of Broadband Services	Applications
A. Noncontrollable services Video	NTSC, PAL, SECAM TV distribution	TV program distribution
	EDTV, HDTV distribution	TV program distribution
	Pay TV	TV program distribution
Text, graphics	Document distribution services	Electronic newspaper, electronic publishing
Data	High-speed information distribution	Distribution of unrestricted data
Motion pictures and sound	Video information distribution service	Distribution of video/audio signals
B. Controllable services Text, graphics, sound, still images	Full channel broadcast videography	Remote education and training, tele-advertising, news retrieval, telesoftware

4.2.3 Characteristics of BISDN Services

As was explained in the preceding section, the BISDN encompasses all of the services that may come into being in the communication network of the future. Consequently, various types of services with differing characteristics coexist within the BISDN. They include multimedia services that have wide or narrow bandwidth, those that are circuit-mode or packet-mode, and real-time or non-real-time. The manifestation of such a diverse set of characteristics is the most distinct feature of the BISDN services.

Provision of Multimedia Services

The first characteristic of BISDN services is that they are multimedia in character. For example, video telephone is a multimedia service that simultaneously involves three different media: audio, video, and data. Depending on the particular service provided, text or graphics can also be included. Also, terminal equipment that is dissimilar can be interconnected inside the BISDN. For instance, to set up a video conferencing service, mainly video terminals will be connected, but a user with just a telephone terminal can be connected as well.

Coexistence of Interactive Services and Distributive Services

As was studied in the previous section, the integrated provision of both the interactive services and the distributive services is one of the BISDN's unique features. In existing communications networks, a separate network has to be constructed for each type; consequently, it is impossible to provide interactive services such as telephone through a distributive services network such as CATV. Within the BISDN, however, CATV service and video telephone service can be provided simultaneously.

Widely Ranging Bandwidth and Service-Time Distributions

One of the notable characteristics of BISDN services is that the associated bandwidth and service-time distributions are extremely wide. In the case of narrowband ISDN, the basic component signals are distributed around the 64-kbps-rate signal. But the BISDN also encompasses all of the digital tributaries, various video signals, as well as high-speed data signals. Consequently, from the bit rate standpoint, BISDN signals evince a widely ranging distribution, from the few bits per second used for the telemetry signal to the hundreds of megabits per second required for video signals. Service time can also range from a few seconds of low-speed data to the hours required for video services.

Therefore, "broadband" in the narrow sense means that the BISDN has the ability to provide broadband services whose speeds go up to hundreds of megabits per second, but its meaning in the broad sense is that its bandwidth and service-time distributions are spread over the broadband.

Coexistence of Continuous-Type and Bursty-Type Services

Another feature of the BISDN is that continuous signals such as sound and images can coexist with bursty signals such as terminal data. Depending on how they are digitized, voice and video signals can be converted into a signal with a constant bit rate or into a signal whose bit rate varies slightly. But in the case of data signals, the bit rate always varies widely. Also, although voice or image services require real-time processing capability, data services do not. Consequently, in the BISDN, services with fixed bit rates can coexist with the services with variable bit rates, and similarly, real-time services can coexist with non-real-time services. On the other hand, in existing communications networks, voice services are provided by way of circuit switching, whereas data services are furnished by way of packet switching. Hence, circuit-mode services and packet-mode services coexist within the BISDN.

4.2.4 Classification According to Service Characteristics

The BISDN service classification given in Section 4.2.1 can be said to be a classification from the user's point of view. However, from the communications network's viewpoint, the services can be classified according to the bit rate (constant or variable), timing relations (real-time or non-real-time), and channel connection mode (connection-oriented or connectionless).

Constant Bit Rate Services and Variable Bit Rate Services

Examined from the bit rate point of view, BISDN services can be broadly categorized into those whose bit rates are maintained uniformly and those with variable bit rates. The former are CBR services, and the latter are VBR services.

The most representative example of a CBR service is the 64-kbps PCM voice signal. Video signals or data signals can also be provided in the CBR service format. But since data signals generally manifest VBR characteristics, it is more natural to provide them as a VBR service. On the other hand, both the voice and video signals can be furnished also as VBR services.

The CBR service's bit rate is determined through a negotiation between the user and the network, and as long as the service is continued, the same bit rate is maintained. In the case of VBR services, the bit rate can vary during the time the service is provided. Since excessive variation can obstruct the operation of the network, the network must be notified in advance of the VBR service's characteristic parameters at the time of call setup.[11]

Real-Time Services and Non-Real-Time Services

BISDN services can be categorized into real-time and non-real-time services, depending on whether the service provision is accomplished in real time or not. Real-time services can deteriorate in quality or become unintelligible if the associated information transfer becomes delayed; hence, they are sensitive to the time it takes for the unit-information-entities (ATM cells) to be transferred. On the other hand, the quality of non-real-time services is insensitive to delays in information transfer. Examples of real-time services include video telephone and video conferencing, and non-real-time services are represented by data transmission.[12]

Connection-Oriented Services and Connectionless Services

From the standpoint of the channels within the communications network, services in general can be divided into *connection-oriented* (CO) services and *connectionless* (CL) services. The existing circuit-mode services are all CO services. Among the packet-mode services, those that employ VCs are CO, and those that use the datagram scheme are CL.

Service Classification According to Characteristics

From the viewpoint of processing service information, it is convenient to classify services according to their characteristics. That is, rather than using such criteria as whether the service in question consists mainly of images or sound, it is more useful to consider such service attributes as the character of the bit rate, the timing relations, and the channel connection mode, as far as the information processing within the communications network is concerned. Accordingly, in the ATM communication network, service classification according to characteristics of the services is mainly applicable for the AAL.

According to service attributes, BISDN services are divided into class A, B, C, and D services. Class A services are real-time, CBR, and CO services, an instance

---

[11]Characteristic parameters include average bit rate, maximum bit rate, bit rate distribution, and burstiness of the bit rate. CCITT SG XVIII is currently studying the matter.

[12]Note, however, that, in many cases, end-user applications that treat data as a real-time service, albeit without any need for timing information. A prime example of this can be found in remote procedure calls for distributed computing applications, where the delay requirements from client-server-client are very stringent.

of which is the constant-rate video signals. The service attributes for other service classes and the respective examples are as listed in Table 4.7.

Table 4.7
Service Classification

Service Class	Timing Relation Between Source and Destination	Bit Rate	Connection Mode	Examples of Services
Class A	Required	Constant	Connection-oriented	Constant bit rate video
Class B	Required	Variable	Connection-oriented	Variable bit rate video
Class C	Not required	Variable	Connection-oriented	Connection-oriented data transfer
Class D	Not required	Variable	Connectionless	Connectionless data transfer

4.2.5 Summary of BISDN Services

It is worthwhile reiterating the point that due to its all-encompassing nature, the BISDN must be able to accommodate services of all types with various characteristics. In other words, the BISDN must be able to meet the real-time/non-real-time requirements, manage both CBR- and VBR-type services, and provide both CO and CL connections. Also, the communications network must be able to maintain the quality of the requested services and provide the requisite bit rate capacity.

The BISDN provides the services in the ATM cell format. Since ATM operates in the CO mode by sending ATM cells through the establishment of VCs, the provision of real-time services is possible. But as the continuous service signals must be converted into an intermittent ATM cell stream, difficulty arises in the transfer of synchronous signals. In that case, an adaptive clock, a synchronization pattern, or a time stamp can be used by the receiver to restore the timing information sent by the transmitter (see Section 4.12 for a detailed explanation of synchronization information transfer).

The BISDN can accommodate both CBR and VBR services. In the case of CBR services, just the bit rate at the time of call setup is needed to decide whether the connection should be granted or not. But in the case of VBR services, other parameters such as the average bit rate, maximum bit rate, bit rate distribution, and burstiness of the bit rate must be considered as well. Also, it must also be possible to renegotiate these parameters during the duration of the service.

The payload capacity that the BISDN can provide at the 155.520-Mbps user-network interface amounts to 149.76 Mbps. But if the five bytes used for the ATM cell header are excluded, the amount that gets loaded onto the ATM cell information space is reduced to 138.631 Mbps, and if the overhead inside the information space itself is considered as well, the payload's pure transfer capability becomes even smaller. In the case of the 622.080-Mbps UNI, the capacity increases about fourfold. Accordingly, the BISDN service capacity must be chosen after such transmission capabilities of the BISDN have been considered.

Two methods are possible for providing CL services within the BISDN: indirect and direct methods. The indirect method furnishes the CL services by converting them into the CO format. Since the BISDN's VCs are established at the AAL, the CL protocols that operate above the AAL are transferred transparently inside the BISDN. The direct method provides the CL services as they are, and, in this case, the CL service function terminates between CL protocols and is transferred to its destination by way of the routing information included within the ATM cell.

In the BISDN, it is important to maintain the required *quality of service* (QOS). The QOS is negotiated during the process of establishing the connection, and it can be renegotiated during the lifetime of the service. The corresponding QOS parameters can be elucidated inside the ATM cell or can be indicated indirectly in association with the service request. An instance of the former would be to record the QOS as a CLP in the header of ATM cell. The CLP indicates whether or not to lose the cell when the network is suffering from congestion.

The QOS can be classified according to such parameters as call setup delay, call removal delay, and call-interrupt probability. The classification can also be made in terms of information transfer parameters, which include *cell loss rate* (CLR), *cell insertion rate* (CIR), *errored cell rate* (ECR), and *bit error rate* (BER).

4.3 ASYNCHRONOUS TRANSFER MODE

ATM was conceived as a means to realize the basic principles of the BISDN. The BISDN's fundamental objective is the integrated provision of various types of services with a great number of disparate characteristics (see Section 4.2.4), and ATM is a means of accommodating this requirement of versatility. In the present section, the topics associated with the ATM communication mode itself (i.e., the asynchronous transfer mode, as well as asynchronous time-division multiplexing and the ATM cell) will be investigated.

4.3.1 Fundamental Principles of BISDN

The BISDN's basic objective is the construction of a digital network that can integrate various types of broadband services and offer them under a single unified scheme, applying advances in signal processing techniques and high-speed transmission, switching, computer, software, and semiconductor technologies. As was observed in the preceding section, the BISDN's target services are those that will soon emerge in future communications networks. These include all of the interactive and distributive services, wide- and narrow-bandwidth signals, and continuous and bursty signals.

Therefore, the BISDN must be able to integrate and provide both interactive and distributive services, provide broadband and narrowband services at the same time, and provide continuous-type services along with the bursty-type services. The BISDN must also have the capability of providing integrated real-time/non-real-time services, CBR/VBR services, and circuit-mode/packet-mode services.

The BISDN must be able to support switching and temporal/permanent connections, point-to-point and point-to-multipoint connections, as well as support on-demand, reserved, or permanent connections. It must be intelligent enough to accommodate the expansion and enhancement of service characteristics, and must also be powerful enough to manage OAM and the control of the network efficiently.

The establishment of the BISDN structure is to be regulated at the functional level so that it does not become an obstacle to future advances in technology or to improvements in the implementation method. Also, the BISDN structure must be equipped with the flexible network capability in order to accommodate new user requirements or growth in the network itself. On the one hand, the BISDN should evolve while the existing networks and the ISDN are continually supported, and, consequently, it is desirable to configure its interface reference or establish its protocol based on the ISDN concept.

4.3.2 Asynchronous Transfer Mode

ATM was devised as a way to realize all of the basic BISDN principles described above. It is a packet-mode transfer technique with a special format that employs ATDM. In the BISDN, service information is transferred by way of a continuous flow of packets of a fixed size, and these packets are called ATM cells. Accordingly, service information is first trimmed down to a fixed size and subsequently mapped into an ATM cell, and this cell is asynchronously time-division-multiplexed with other ATM cells to form the basic units of BISDN transmission. ATDM is a type of statistical multiplexing technique that time-division-multiplexes mutually asynchronous ATM cells from several different channels.

When ATM is employed, the capacity of a service channel is measured by the number of ATM cells. Consequently, the amount of transmitted information is reflected in the corresponding number of ATM cells, and the burstiness of the service information is indicated by the degree of ATM cell crowding. Here, the transmission capacity is assigned upon the user's request at the time of call setup, and this scheme endows a versatile transfer capability on all the services, including CL services.

ATM is a CO method that transfers service information through the establishment of virtual channels. A connection identifier is assigned whenever a VC is established, and when the connection is removed, the identifier is removed also. The order of ATM cells inside a given VC is maintained by way of an ATM layer function. Signaling information for setting up a call is delivered via specialized ATM cells.

Hence, it can be inferred that the use of ATM allows the integration of various BISDN services possessing many different characteristics. That is, broadband and narrowband services can coexist within the same communications network by using the ATM cells of the same format, differing only in the number of cells that each type requires. CBR services are made up of ATM cells with a uniform distribution, and while the VBR services are widely distributed, they are also made up of the same ATM cells as the CBR services. Also, the delay problem associated with real-time services is solved through the use of VCs, thus making their provision a possibility.

The ATM communications technique can be said to be an integration of the existing circuit-mode digital communications technique with the packet-mode communications technique. First, in the sense that the ATM communications system uses ATM cells as its basic unit of transmission, it has a close connection with packet-mode communication. But there is a significant difference in that the packet mode was developed to support non-real-time VBR data signals, while ATM can manage real-time, CBR signals as well. Also, packet-mode communication is generally used for regional LANs, whereas ATM is to be used for an enormous public network; thus, differences arise in terms of address assignment, access and flow control, switching, and transmission. On the other hand, the circuit mode has a fundamental difference from ATM in that, in the former, the information signal is transferred in continuous bit streams by allocating a separate channel for this purpose, while, in the latter, segmented service information is fitted onto ATM cells and transmitted through a VC. Consequently, a new set of problems is introduced in the accompanying connection setup, signal processing, transmission, and switching.

For a systematic and flexible information transfer, ATM prescribes a layered protocol reference model. The associated layers include the physical layer, ATM layer, AAL, and higher-order layer. The AAL performs the function of mapping service signals into the ATM cell's payload space, and the ATM layer executes the ATM cell header-related functions for the transparent delivery of the ATM payload space. The physical layer's function is to transfer ATM cells by converting them into transmission bit streams.

4.3.3 Asynchronous Time-Division Multiplexing

The TDM, which is widely used for multiplexing existing plesiochronous digital tributaries, is essentially a "synchronous" multiplexing technique as far as the system clock is concerned. This is because the TDM signals are constructed through the repetition of multiplexed frames created using the multiplexer system clock. This results in the appearance of low-speed signals at fixed locations inside the frames, as depicted in Figure 4.9(a). In other words, low-speed signals always exist at locations that are synchronized with the system clock.

ATDM is a type of multiplexing technique that stores each of the incoming low-speed signals inside a buffer, then retrieves and inserts the stored signals one by one into a multiplexing slot according to a priority-scheduling principle. The simplest example of the priority scheduling principle would be *first-in first-out* (FIFO), and here the input signals are ATM cells in the case of an ATM communications system. Therefore, as shown in Figure 4.9(b), the low-speed input signals do not occupy locations inside the ATDM signal in a well-regulated manner, and thus behave "asynchronously" compared to their TDM equivalent.

ATDM is superior to TDM in that it has a higher channel utilization factor. TDM assigns an exclusive channel to each of the incoming service signals; thus,

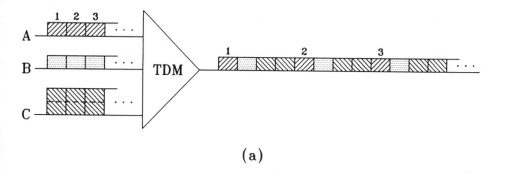

(a)

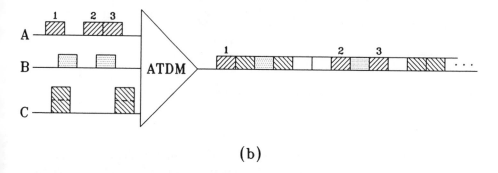

(b)

Figure 4.9 Comparison of TDM and ATDM: (a) TDM; (b) ATDM.

even when a given channel is in a vacant state containing no effective information, it is not possible to pass other service information through it. But since there is no exclusive channel allocation in ATDM, a blank channel can be taken by any incoming signal, resulting in a higher channel utilization factor.

Such channel utilization relationships are illustrated in Figure 4.10. In the figure, the length in the vertical direction denotes the channel capacity of the multiplexed signals, while the horizontal length corresponds to the time duration. Also, the parts in slanted lines or those that are darkened indicate the presence of effective information corresponding to the size of an ATM cell. In the case of TDM, since the multiplexed signal is no more than a combination of several independent channels, it can be seen that any vacant space in each channel is maintained as it is. But in ATDM the multiplexed signal consists of just a single channel; hence, any information vacancy can be collected together and used for providing a new service, consequently increasing the channel utilization factor.

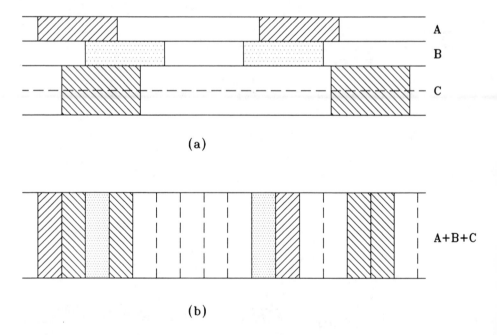

Figure 4.10 Comparison of channel use: (a) TDM (dedicated); (b) ATDM (shared).

4.3.4 ATM Cell

The ATM cell acts as basic unit of information transfer in the ATM communication. As shown in Figure 4.2(a), the ATM cell is composed of 53 bytes. Five of the bytes are for the cell-header field, and the remaining 48 bytes form the user information field. The cell-header field is divided into GFC, VPI, VCI, PT, CLP, and HEC fields. The associated bit sizes differ slightly at the NNI and the UNI. The bit sizes for the two interfaces are as shown in Table 4.8 and Figure 4.2(b,c).

Although the main function of the GFC header is the physical access control, it can also be used for reduction of cell jitters for CBR services, fair capacity assignment for VBR services, and traffic control for VBR flows. Such a function requires the power to control any UNI structure, whether it be a ring, a star, a bus configuration, or any combination of them.

The role of the VPI/VCI field is to indicate VC or VP identification numbers in order to distinguish cells belonging to the same connection[13] A separate, fixed VPI/VCI identifier is assigned in advance for indicating unassigned cells, physical layer OAM cells, metasignaling channel, and generic broadcast signaling channel (for a detailed discussion of VPs, VCs, and preassigned identifiers, see Section 4.8).

PT is used for indicating the presence of user information and for indicating whether the given ATM cell suffered from traffic congestion. CLP is a bit used for indicating whether the corresponding byte may be discarded during the time of network congestion. HEC is a CRC byte for the cell-header field and is used for sensing and correcting cell errors and delineating the cell header (see Section 4.7 for the detailed use of HEC).

As shown in Table 4.9, ATM cells can be classified according to the associated layers and functions (details regarding the ATM layer and the physical layer are given in Section 4.6). For instance, the *ATM layer cell* is a cell that is formed at the ATM layer, and the *physical layer cell* is similarly formed at the physical layer. The ATM cells are divided into assigned cells and unassigned cells, and physical

Table 4.8
Bit Allocation of Cell Header

Function	Bit Allocation	
	UNI	NNI
GFC	4	0
VPI	8	12
VCI	16	16
PT	3	3
CLP	1	1
HEC	8	8

[13]Assigning call, connection, and party-related indication functions, as well as QOS and priority indication capabilities, to the VPI/VCI field is currently being considered.

Table 4.9
Classification of ATM Cell

According to Layer	According to Function	Function
ATM Layer	Assigned cell	Services related to upper layer
	Unassigned cell	Services inherent to ATM layer
Physical Layer	Idle cell	Stuffing blank space
	Physical layer OAM cell	OAM cell

layer cells are divided into idle cells and physical layer OAM cells. *Assigned cells* refer to those cells that are allocated to ATM layer services, and the *unassigned cells* refer to the remaining types. *Idle cells* are created in order to fill the vacant space that results when there are no cells to be transmitted, and *OAM cells* are used for the transfer of OAM information of the physical layer. On the other hand, the ATM cells can also be divided into valid cells and invalid cells from the physical layer viewpoint. Here, *valid cells* designate those that have no errors or whose errors have been corrected, while *invalid cells* designate the other cells. The invalid cells are discarded at the physical layer.

4.4 FUNCTIONAL ARCHITECTURE OF BISDN

The BISDN's functional architecture is fundamentally equivalent to that of the ISDN. That is, in terms of such concepts as reference configuration, functional group, and reference point, the BISDN is nothing more than an extension of the ISDN, except that the internal functions of reference configuration, internal composition of the functional groups, and interface signal of the reference points are slightly different in each case.[14] The present section will focus on the BISDN's basic structural model, reference configuration, connection elements, functional groups, and reference points.

4.4.1 Basic Architectural Model of BISDN

As shown in Figure 4.3, the BISDN's basic architectural model is composed of lower-order layer capability and higher-order layer capability. Lower-order layer

---

[14]The functional architectural model of the ISDN is described in CCITT Recommendation I.324, and that of the BISDN is described in Recommendation I.327.

capability consists of broadband capability, narrowband ISDN capability, and inter-exchange signaling capability. Broadband capability refers to the ATM-based information transfer capability provided at the BISDN's UNI, as well as at the internal exchange entities of the communications network. Narrowband ISDN capability implies the circuit switching and packet switching capability based on the 64-kbps bit rate. Interexchange signaling capability is provided for performing signaling between offices, and here signaling information is also transferred by way of ATM. Lower-order layer capability also includes switching and transmission capability provided by the narrowband ISDN.

Higher-order layer capability in general is a function related to terminal equipment. However, depending on the type of service, the associated higher-order layer capability can be provided through a special node inside the BISDN. This node can be a part of a public communications network, or belong to some center operated by another system which is linked to the BISDN through the UNI or the NNI.

The *local function capability* (LFC) in Figure 4.3 corresponds to the switching and transmission function provided for local switching equipment, digital cross-connect equipment, and multiplexing equipment.

As can be seen in Figure 4.3, user-network signals apply between the BISDN's terminal equipment and LFC, and internetwork signals apply between the terminal equipment and the higher-order layer capability of the service provider.

4.4.2 Reference Configuration of BISDN

Fundamentally, the BISDN can be divided into user equipment and the public BISDN. User equipment includes terminal equipment and user networks, and here user networks are either the *broadband integrated services private branch exchange* (BISPBX) or private BISDNs. The reference point that links terminal equipment and user networks is called S_B, and the reference point that links user networks and public networks is called T_B. In case the user network has the same connection format as the public BISDN, the connection for the entire BISDN terminates at the S_B reference points, and S_B coincides with T_B if the user network is not present. Figure 4.11 is a pictorial representation of such a BISDN configuration.

4.4.3 Partitioning of BISDN Connection

The connection for the overall BISDN can be partitioned into *connection elements* (CE), *basic connection components* (BCC), and reference points. If the connection format for the overall BISDN is partitioned in terms of connection elements, a configuration such as the one in Figure 4.12 is obtained.

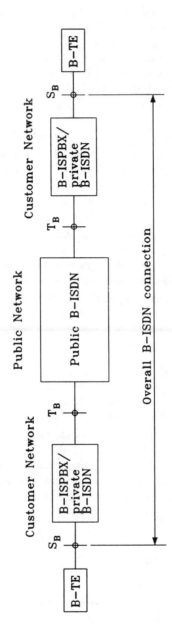

Figure 4.11 Overall BISDN configuration.

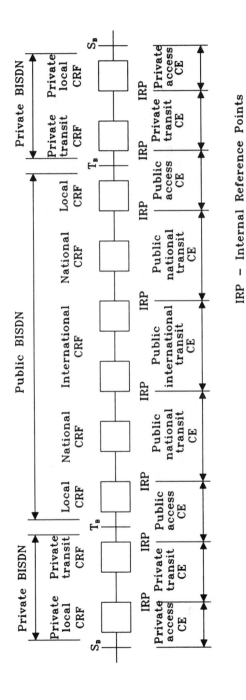

Figure 4.12 Connection elements within an overall BISDN connection.

Connection Element

As can be seen in Figure 4.12, the overall connection format, in which the private BISDN and the public BISDN are mixed, is composed of five connection elements, which are private access CE, private transit CE, public access CE, public national transit CE, and public international CE. These connection elements are partitioned with the *internal reference points* (IRP) between them as the boundary.

As shown in Figure 4.13, each connection element of BISDN is composed of five functional groups: VPI switching function (S_{VPI}), VPI control function (C_{VPI}), VCI switching function (S_{VCI}), VCI control function (C_{VCI}), and a mutual connection link. Among them, S_{VPI} and S_{VCI} provide switching-related functions, C_{VPI} and C_{VCI} provide control- and signaling-related functions, and the mutual connection link provides transmission-related function. Each connection element can consist of any combination of these functional groups.

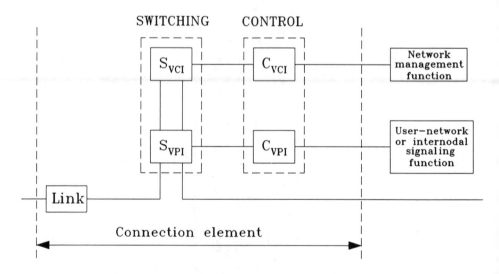

Figure 4.13 Connection element configuration.

Basic Connection Components

The basic connection component is composed of a *connection-related function* (CRF), access link, and transit link. Generally speaking, the CRF is a switching-related function, and access and transit links are transmission-related functions.

The CRF represents functions associated with call setup and control within each connection element, and includes the switch termination function, switching function, control function, network administration function, and OAM function.

The access link includes NT1, and, depending on the case, can also include multiplexer and other transmission equipment used for subscriber network access. The transit link includes the digital transmission and transit equipment used for general interoffice transmission.

Reference Point

As was mentioned earlier, the access reference point for the BISDN terminal equipment and user networks is designated with S_B, and the access reference point for user networks and public BISDN is called T_B. Given that the BISDN is an extension of the narrowband ISDN, other reference points such as K, M, N, and P can also be considered. In the existing ISDN, the reference point K is used for accessing existing telephone networks, M is for accessing special service providers, N is for accessing other ISDNs, and P is for accessing special network subscribers.

4.4.4 BISDN UNI Functional Group

In the BISDN, the functional groups are designated in the same manner as in the ISDN, and to indicate broadband, the prefix B is attached to each designation. That is, terminal equipment is called B-TE, and private or public BISDN network terminations are called B-NT. Among the B-TEs, BISDN terminal equipment is designated B-TE1, while the non-BISDN terminal equipment is designated B-TE2. Also, among the B-NTs, the private BISDN network terminations are indicated by B-NT2, and public BISDN network terminations are indicated by B-NT1. Accordingly, T_B becomes the reference point between B-NT1 and B-NT2, and S_B is the reference point between B-NT2 and B-TE1. On the other hand, B-TA acts as an adaptor for linking B-TE2 to BISDN, and R becomes the reference point between them. Figure 4.4 illustrates these relationships.

Network Termination 1 (B-NT1)

In general, B-NT1 encompasses functions that correspond to the first layer of the OSI protocol reference model. Functions of the B-NT1 include line transmission termination, transmission interface management, and OAM, and functions that relate to the transmission system itself can also be included. In case B-NT1 terminates a cell-based OAM information flow, a separate cell delineation function is required.[15]

---

[15]The powering problem of functional group B-NT1 is under study by CCITT.

Network Termination 2 (B-NT2)

B-NT2 encompasses functions corresponding to layer 1 and the upper layer, which include the following functions: medium adaptation (the function for adapting media and network structures which are different from one another), cell delineation, concentration, buffering, multiplexing/demultiplexing, resources allocation, usage parameter control, adaptation layer for signaling information about internal traffic, T_B and S_B interface management, OAM, signaling protocol management, and switching for internal connections. In special situations, B-NT2 can consist solely of physical layer functions. In case B-NT2 is absent, reference point S_B coincides with T_B (this coincidence is formed separately depending on whether the system in question is SDH-based or cell-based). B-NT2 can be implemented in concentrated or distributed mode (functional group B-NT2 uses the local powering method).

Terminal Equipment 1/2 (B-TE1/2)

Terminal equipment also includes functions that correspond to layer 1 and the upper layer. Functions of B-TE include user-to-user and user-to-machine interface and protocol functions, the interface termination function and other layer 1 functions, as well as the protocol management function for signaling information, the management function for connection with other equipment, and OAM functions. B-TE is divided into the B-TE1 type, which possesses the interface function that conforms to the BISDN's interface standard, and the B-TE2 type, which does not.[16]

Terminal Adaptor (B-TA)

The terminal adaptor includes the functions corresponding to layer 1 and the upper layer, and assumes the role of adapting B-TE2 or TE-2 to the BISDN interface.

4.5 PHYSICAL CONFIGURATIONS OF USER-NETWORK INTERFACE

UNI physical configurations of the BISDN differ greatly from those of the ISDN. In the BISDN, all the UNI physical configurations of the ISDN are accommodated, as well as the physical configurations for a shared medium such as those used for the LAN. This implies that the BISDN-based public network can achieve direct connection with the innermost parts of the subscriber networks. The present section will examine physical configurations of the BISDN UNI as an extension of the section on the functional architecture of the BISDN.

---

[16]CCITT is currently studying whether the functional group B-TE should be powered through the S_B interface.

4.5.1 Basic Physical Configurations at UNI

Figure 4.6 is an illustration of various forms of basic physical configurations at UNI in terms of the previously studied functional groups B-NT1, B-NT2, B-TE1, B-TE2, and B-TA, and the reference points R, S_B, and T_B.[17] Figure 4.6(a,b) represent the case in which the BISDN's physical interface occurs at the two reference points S_B and T_B; in (c,d) it occurs only at S_B, and in (e,f), it occurs at T_B only. Figures (g,h) represent the case in which the physical interface occurs simultaneously at the BISDN reference points S_B and T_B and at the ISDN's reference point S; and in (i,j), the reference points S_B and T_B coincide due to the absence of B-NT2. On the other hand, (b,d,f,h,j) can be viewed as representing instances in which the interface occurs only at reference point R. It can be inferred that these basic physical configurations of the BISDN are equivalent to those of the ISDN except for the instances in (g,h).

4.5.2 Physical Configurations for Multipoint Connection

The ability to accommodate various UNI physical configuration structures for multipoint connection is one of the BISDN's most notable features, allowing star, ring, bus, as well as starred-bus structures. In addition, the configuration of B-NT2s can be provided in both centralized or distributed type.

Figure 4.7 illustrates the instances of physical configurations employed for multipoint access. In the figure, (a) illustrates the centralized B-NT2 configuration, and (b) illustrates a generic distributed B-NT2 configuration. Also, (a) represents the star structure, (c) the distributed ring structure, (d) the starred-bus structure, (e) the bus structure, and (f) the multiaccess ring structure. MA is a medium adaptor for accommodating distributed B-NT2 with a special network structure, and W is the interface between MAs. W is a nonstandard interface, but can be made to be the same as the interface at the S_B reference point. B-TE* is a B-TE1 that provides shared-medium access capability, and SS_B is the interface between B-TE*s and is equivalent to the interface at the S_B reference point.

4.5.3 Basic Properties at the Reference Points S_B and T_B

The physical layer interface at the reference points S_B and T_B can be chosen to be either SDH-based or cell-based, and the ATM layer is common to both cases.[18] At the T_B reference point, just a single interface exists per B-NT1, and the physical medium is also a point-to-point connection with just a pair of transreceivers.

---

[17]The specifications on the ISDN UNI and the BISDN UNI physical configurations are given in CCITT Recommendations I.411 and I.413, respectively.

[18]The basic characteristics discussed in this section are those of the 155.520-Mbps UNI. Those belonging to the 622.080 Mbps are under study by CCITT.

More than one interface can exist per B-NT2 for the S_B reference point, and the interface at S_B can provide point-to-point connection for the physical layer and point-to-multipoint connection for the upper layers.

Since mutual compatibility exists between the interfaces at S_B and T_B, the two points coincide when the functional group B-NT2 is absent. Of course, here the cell-based S_B coincides with the cell-based T_B, and the SDH-based S_B with the SDH-based T_B (for a discussion of differences between cell-based and SDH-based systems, see Section 4.7).

4.5.4 Other Interface Functions

At the UNI, user information is transferred in the ATM cell format. Information regarding connection-related functions is also transferred by way of ATM cells. Physical layer-related OAM information is transferred via ATM cells in the case of cell-based transmission, and STM frame overhead in the case of SDH-based transmission. But ATM layer-related OAM information is always transferred by way of ATM cells.[19]

At the UNI, the timing information is delivered at the same instant as the ATM cell or the STM frame. The physical medium or the associated transmission system at the interface must be able to provide dependence on the bit sequence integrity.[20]

4.6 BISDN PROTOCOL REFERENCE MODEL

In the BISDN, a PRM is adopted in order to perform all of the various functions required by the network. The PRM involves separating the overall communications functions into several layers and defining the appropriate set of functions for each layer. Here, a lower-order layer has the role of providing a prescribed set of services to the adjacent higher-order layer, and transparent connection is achieved between two ends of the same layer. Conceptually, the PRM of the BISDN is an extension of the ISDN PRM, and is rooted in the OSI concept.[21] The BISDN protocol reference model is the focus of the present section.

---

[19]The UNI-related OAM information includes maintenance/administration signals, performance monitoring signals, and communications control provision signals. Details regarding OAM are given in Section 4.15.

[20]Problems in powering and activation/deactivation at UNI are under study by CCITT.

[21]The PRM for the ISDN is described in CCITT Recommendation I.326, and the one for the BISDN is described in Recommendation I.321. The OSI-based layered communications concept is described in Recommendation X.200.

4.6.1 Protocol Reference Model

The protocol reference model for the BISDN has a composition like the one shown in Figure 4.5, consisting of the user, control, and management planes. The management plane can be further separated into layer management and plane management. The user plane provides user-information-related functions; the control plane performs various control functions for service provision; and the management plane provides communications network management functions.

The user plane and the control plane each consist of the physical, ATM, AAL, and upper layers. The physical layer provides the physical medium and transmission functions, the ATM layer provides call transfer function for all of the BISDN services, and the AAL provides service-related functions for its upper layers. The upper layer of the user plane provides service information management functions, and the higher-order layer of the control plane provides functions associated with call control and connection control. Table 4.1 gives a detailed description of the respective functions of each layer.

4.6.2 Functions of Each Plane

The *user plane* provides functions for transferring user information flow, as well as associated control functions such as flow control and error correction. Here, the term *user information* implies various BISDN service information, such as voice, image, data, text, and graphics. User information can be passed transparently through the BISDN, or can be transferred after an appropriate processing procedure.

The *control plane* provides call connection and connection control functions. That is, the control plane provides the function associated with call establishment, call monitoring, and call release. It can also provide a control function for changing the characteristics of a readily established service.

The *management plane* provides the communications network monitoring function associated with user information and control information transfers. The management plane is divided into plane management function and layer management function. The plane management function performs management of the entire network through its role as an interplane arbitrator. Layer management function refers to the management function associated with the parameters and resources within each protocol entity (TE, network terminations, and so on) and manages the OAM information flows associated with each layer.[22]

---

[22]Refer to Section 4.15 for a discussion of OAM information flow. Details on management plane functions are given in CCITT Recommendation Q.940.

4.6.3 Physical Layer

The physical layer is divided into the physical medium sublayer and the transmission convergence sublayer. The functions of each sublayer are as listed in Table 4.1. The physical medium sublayer provides the physical medium and bit timing-related functions, and the TC sublayer provides functions for converting ATM cell flow into data bit/symbol streams and the reverse functions.

Physical Medium Function

The physical medium function is associated with the transmission medium itself. In the case of optical transmission, for example, it is a function related to optical fibers, light-emitting devices, light-detecting devices, and optical connectors.

Bit Timing Information Function

This function involves the conversion of data bit flow into a waveform adapted to a particular physical medium or the reverse conversion process, the insertion or the extraction of timing information, and line coding or decoding. Consequently, the information transferred from the physical medium sublayer to the transmission convergence sublayer consists mainly of data bit/symbol stream and the corresponding timing information.

Transmission Frame Generation and Extraction Function

This function involves the generation and extraction of the transmission frame. This function does not apply in cell-based transmission, since a separate transmission frame is not needed in this case. However, STM-*n* frames are required in SDH-based transmission, and DS-3 signal frames are required in G.702-based transmission (see Section 4.7).

Transmission Frame Adaptation Function

The transmission frame adaptation function involves the mapping of ATM cell flow into the payload of the transmission frame, or, conversely, the extraction of ATM cell flow from the transmission frame. This function is required in an SDH-based network or in a G.702-based network.

Cell Delineation Function

This is a function for identifying ATM cell boundaries in the ATM cell flow. In the transmitting direction, it performs the ATM cell scrambling function, and in the receiving direction performs cell delineation, confirmation, and descrambling functions (details regarding ATM cell delineation and scrambling are given in Section 4.7).

HEC Signal Generation and Confirmation Function

The associated duties include generating and confirming the HEC signal of the ATM cell header. In the transmitting direction, it generates the HEC signal for the first four bytes of the ATM cell header and inserts it into the fifth byte of the header. Conversely, it applies an identical procedure to the received signal to inspect whether the HEC signal is correct, and in the event an uncorrectable error is detected, the cell in question is discarded (see Section 4.7.4 for further discussion of HEC signal generation and errored-cell treatment).

Cell Rate Decoupling Function

The cell rate decoupling function augments the ATM cells that are carrying valid information using idle cells in order to match the overall cell rate to that of the corresponding payload capacity, or, conversely, extracts cells with effective information by removing idle cells.

4.6.4 ATM Layer

The ATM layer is independent of the physical layer, and its functions are as listed in Table 4.1.

Cell Multiplexing and Demultiplexing Function

This function provides the capability of multiplexing ATM cells from different VPs and VCs to form a composite cell flow, or the opposite demultiplexing capability. Here, the multiplexed cell flow does not have to be continuous.

Cell VPI/VCI Translation Function

This function is required at the ATM switch or the ATM cross-connect node, and its role is to map the values stored in the VPI/VCI field of each ATM cell header into a new set of values.

Cell Header Generation and Extraction Function

This function applies at the ATM layer's terminations, and involves the generation or extraction of the first four bytes in the ATM cell header. For the generation of the cell header, the associated information received from the upper layer is mapped into the corresponding field, and the opposite is executed for the cell header extraction process. This function also encompasses the translation of the *service access point identifier* (SAPI) into the VPI and the VCI.

Generic Flow Control Function

The GFC function is the function for controlling access and information flow at the UNI. Here, the information is transferred via assigned cells or unassigned cells.

4.6.5 ATM Adaptation Layer

The AAL is divided into the convergence and segmentation and reassembly sublayers. At the convergence sublayer, the function for converting the user service information coming from the upper layer into a protocol data unit, or the opposite process, is performed. At the SAR, the function for segmenting the PDU to form the user information field of the ATM cell, or the opposite process, is performed. The ATM adaptation function varies depending on the type of upper layer service. The AAL will be described in detail in Section 4.9.

4.6.6 Interlayer Information Transfer

For communication between two contiguous layers of the BISDN PRM, the information transfer in both directions must be specified in advance.

Between Physical Layer and ATM Layer

The ATM layer requests to the physical layer the transport of service data units, and the physical layer indicates that the SDUs sent by its counterpart physical layer entity are ready. The information transferred from the physical layer to the ATM layer includes valid cells (excluding idle cells and physical layer OAM cells) and the associated timing information. The information sent from the ATM layer to the physical layer consists of assigned cells and unassigned cells and the relevant timing information (timing information refers to the clock and the indication of the presence of the transferred data).

Between ATM Layer and AAL

The AAL requests to the ATM layer the transfer of ATM-SDUs, and the ATM layer indicates that the ATM SDUs from its counterpart AAL entity are ready. The information exchanged between the ATM layer and the AAL includes ATM cell payload, SAPI, and the relevant timing information.

Others

OAM-related information is exchanged between the physical layer and the management plane. The information transferred from the physical layer to the management plane can include indications of the loss of input signal, received errors, and degradation in error performance.[23] The information exchanged between the physical medium sublayer and the transmission convergence sublayer of the physical layer consists of logic symbol flow, or bit streams, and the associated timing information.

4.7 PHYSICAL LAYER OF BISDN

The main function of the BISDN's physical layer is to collect and organize ATM cells sent down from the ATM layer, transport them to the physical medium, and also perform the reverse of the process. The physical layer must also be able to deal with various obstacles that can occur during transmission. In order to accomplish the above objectives, the physical layer handles various procedures, which can be grouped into the transmission convergence sublayer and the physical medium sublayer, as shown in Table 4.1 (various functions of the physical layer are explained in detail in Section 4.6.3).

4.7.1 Interface Characteristics of the Physical Layer

The BISDN maintains a 155.520-Mbps or 622.080-Mbps transmission rate at the T_B reference point. Its structure is symmetric, but it can also be asymmetric in the case of 622.080 Mbps. The physical medium can be optical cable or coaxial cable, and the extension capability of 0 to 100m is required in the case of an electrical interface, and 0 to 800m in the case of an optical interface.[24]

---

[23]The information to be transferred from the management plane to the physical layer is under study by CCITT.

[24]If possible, extension capability of up to 200m is recommended in the case of electrical interface, and up to 2000m in the case of optical interface. Refer to CCITT Recommendation I.433.

Both cell-based and SDH-based signals are allowed at the T_B as well as at the S_B reference point (G.702-based case is allowed as well). The cell-based signal consists solely of ATM cell flows, and the SDH-based signal is formed by filling VC-4 payload space of an STM-frame with ATM cells. In the case of cell-based signals, OAM signals such as AIS, FERF, and FEBE are transported in the form of OAM cells. But in the case of SDH-based signals, the OAM signals are transported via STM's SOH or POH.

If the transmission speed of the physical medium is 155.520 Mbps inside the BISDN, the actual transmission capacity of the cells created at the ATM layer amounts to 149.760 Mbps. This capacity encompasses user information cells, signaling cells, as well as OAM cells, and corresponds to the capacity of the VC-4 payload space of the SDH-based signal. The remaining capacity of 5.760 Mbps gets filled with physical layer OAM cells and idle cells in the case of cell-based signals, and STM frame overheads (SOH, POH, pointer) in the case of SDH-based signals. As a method of identifying cell boundaries, the HEC technique is used for cell-based signals, and HEC or an SDH overhead can be used for SDH-based signals.

4.7.2 Cell-Based Physical Layer

In case the physical layer is cell-based, a flow of scrambled ATM cells is transmitted as is, without the use of an external frame. In other words, relevant HEC field is calculated and added to the ATM cells descended from the ATM layer, which are then transmitted directly after a scrambling process. Consequently, a function for generating transmission frames is not required. Here, a distributed sample scrambler with the characteristic polynomial $x^{31} + x^{28} + 1$ is used for scrambling (see Section 4.7.6 for a detailed explanation of distributed sample scrambling). ATM cell flow is a continuous flow of 155.520 Mbps, and the receiving end can extract timing information from it. Identification of ATM cell boundaries from a cell flow relies on the HEC technique (see Section 4.7.5 for a detailed explanation of HEC).

Of the cell flow capacity of 155.520 Mbps, 5.760 Mbps or more always gets filled with idle cells, physical layer OAM cells, and other physical layer reserved cells. This capacity corresponds to the section and path overheads of the SDH-based signal and is equivalent to 1/27 of a cell. Accordingly, the OAM cell portion provides various maintenance and performance monitoring functions which the section and path overheads provide. Here, representative examples of a maintenance signal are the AIS and the FERF (see Section 4.15 for more details on OAM functions).

Idle cells, physical layer OAM cells, and other reserved cells are identified by assigning a special bit pattern to the header of each type of cell. Various header bit patterns for the physical layer OAM cells are listed in Table 4.10. These physical layer cells are transported only as far as the physical layer of the receiving side and are not returned to the ATM layer; hence, it is meaningless to assign bit patterns in

Table 4.10
Header Bit Pattern of Physical OAM Cells

Application	Octet 1	Octet 2	Octet 3	Octet 4	Octet 5
Idle cell	00000000	00000000	00000000	00000001	HEC
Physical layer OAM cell (F1)	00000000	00000000	00000000	00000011	HEC
Physical layer OAM cell (F3)	00000000	00000000	00000000	00001001	HEC
Reserved cell for physical layer	PPPP0000	00000000	00000000	0000PPP1	HEC

terms of fields. In the table, P represents a bit that is usable at the physical layer, and Ps of the first octet become all 1s in the case of the NNI.

4.7.3 SDH-Based Physical Layer

If the physical layer is SDH-based, the ATM cells are transmitted by first mapping them into the STM-n frame of the SDH. First, the HEC field is calculated and inserted into the cells received from the ATM layer, and then idle cells are added to create a signal with the capacity of 149.760 Mbps; afterwards, self-synchronous scrambling with the characteristic polynomial $x^{43} + 1$ is applied to all the bits in the cell except the cell header, and then the cells are mapped into the VC-4 payload space (that is, the C-4 space) and transmitted in the form of an STM-n frame (a detailed explanation of the scrambling process is given in Section 4.7.7). The receiving side can extract and use clock information from the STM-n frame, and send the corresponding ATM cells up to the ATM layer after performing a reverse of the procedure just mentioned (for more information on the mapping of ATM cells into the STM frame, see Section 3.5.7).

When the ATM cells organized with the 149.760-Mbps cell rate are mapped into the VC-4 payload space, the starting point of the cells for every frame can be recorded in the path overhead's H4. The recorded information consists of the cell offset indication; that is, the interval from the endpoint of the H4 overhead to the starting point of the first ATM cell header that follows can be represented in byte units. The number of bits necessary for this is six, so bits 3–8 of H4 can be assigned for this. At the receiving side in this case, the ATM cell boundaries can be identified by first identifying the STM-*n* frame and subsequently reading its H4 byte.[25] Of course, the HEC procedure can be applied instead of this.

The section and path overheads of the STM frame provide various maintenance and performance monitoring functions associated with the SDH transmission process. These include STM frame alignment, STM-1 and path identification function, section and path error monitoring, section alarm indication, section and path far-end receive failure, section and path far-end error report, and path signaling indication (for a detailed discussion of the path and section overheads, see Section 3.6). The ATM cell mapping-related overhead also includes the C2 byte, which indicates that the frame in question is carrying ATM cells. The section overhead has a close connection with the OAM information flows F1 and F2, and the path overhead with F3 (the OAM information flow is treated in detail in Section 4.15).

4.7.4 G.702-Based Physical Layer

In the evolution toward BISDN, a capability is required for transmitting ATM cells in the form of existing plesiochronous digital hierarchy signals. Such a capability is called *G.702-based* or *PDH-based transmission*.

The physical layer for the G.702-based transmission is similar to that of the SDH-based transmission, except that the G.702 tributaries are used instead of the STM-*n* signal. Here, the cell transmission capacity can vary depending on the particular tributary used.

Among the G.702 tributaries employed for ATM cell transmission, those of primary interest are DS-1 (1.544 Mbps), DS-1E (2.048 Mbps), DS-3E (34.368 Mbps), DS-3 (44.736 Mbps), and DS-4E (139.264 Mbps).[26]

4.7.5 Header Error Control

The role of the HEC function is to correct any single-bit errors found in any part of the cell header and to detect any multibit errors. It operates by performing a cyclic redundancy check on the first four header bytes and then recording the result on the fifth byte; the process is repeated at the receiving end to extract relevant error information.

---

[25]Such an H4-based cell delineation scheme used to be a CCITT standard up until June 1992.

[26]In the case of DS-1, DS-1E, DS-3E, and DS-4E, it is simpler to leave the frame alignment marks for the tributary itself as they are and map ATM cells into the remaining payload space in a continuous manner. But in the case of the DS-3 tributary, the overhead bits are distributed into single bits which are 85 bits apart; hence, it is currently being examined whether it would be simpler to transmit the ATM cells by overlapping a separate frame on top of the DS-3 frame. Details regarding the G.702-based physical layer are under study by CCITT.

Typical errors that occur on optical fibers are a mixture of single-bit errors and bursty errors. In order to be able to cope with both forms of errors, the HEC establishes and employs two types of error checking modes, as shown in Figure 4.14, which are correction mode and detection mode. The correction mode is employed by default and it provides a single-bit error correction function.

Once an error is detected in the correction mode, it is corrected, and the receiver moves into the detection mode in the case of single-bit errors; if the error is multibit, the corresponding cell is discarded, and then the receiver moves into the detection mode. When an error is found in the detection mode, the cell is immediately discarded; if no error is detected, the receiver reverts to the correction mode.

Hence, the HEC employed in this manner provides the capability to correct any single-bit errors, along with the ability to detect bursty errors. The receiver moves from the correction mode into detection mode once a multibit error is found, which is due to the fact that the multibit error itself is an advance warning of a bursty error. That is, even though the error that appears after the multibit error might be diagnosed as a single-bit error, there is a greater probability that it is another multibit error.

Figure 4.15 is a flow graph of the possible error control and processing stages. After the HEC procedure, the ATM cell is identified either as a valid cell or an invalid cell. The valid cells can include actual valid cells and cells that carry errors. The valid cells with errors might be created due to an imperfection in the CRC, or because of a flaw in the error correction stage. The cells that are determined and discarded as invalid cells include those with uncorrectable multibit errors or those that are detected as bursty errors. They can also include correctable single-bit errors. The valid cells with errors and invalid (discarded) cells are the primary causes of degradation in the performance of the BISDN. Figure 4.16 is a plot of the probability of their occurrence as a function of the bit error rate (refer to CCITT Recommendation I.432).

The code that is used for HEC is a cyclic code with the generating polynomial $x^8 + x^2 + x + 1$. To elaborate, the first four bytes of a cell header are expressed

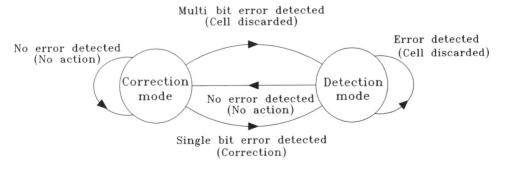

Figure 4.14 Modes of HEC operation.

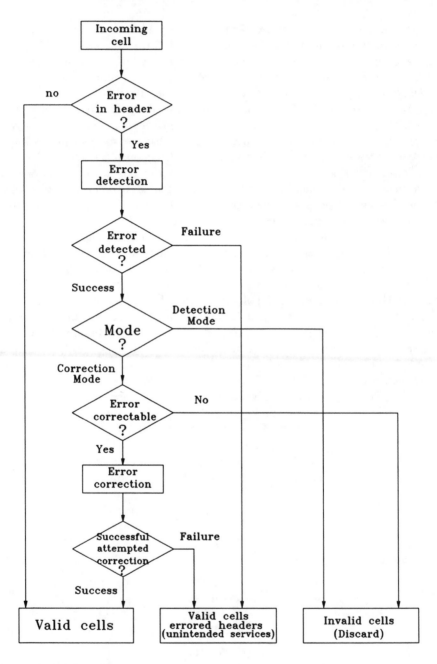

Figure 4.15 HEC flow chart.

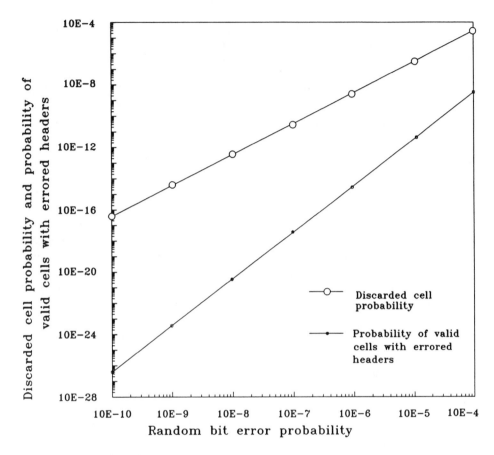

Figure 4.16 Probability of discarded cells and valid cells with errored headers.

as a thirty-first degree binary polynomial, which is then multiplied by x^8 and divided by the generating polynomial. The remainder is recorded in the HEC field, which is subsequently confirmed at the receiving side. Here, all of the arithmetic is performed in binary.

The confirmation device at the receiving side has to express five header bytes (including the HEC field) as a thirty-ninth degree binary polynomial, and check whether it is divisible by the generating polynomial. In case bit slips are present, the HEC performance can be enhanced if 01010101 is added to the fifth byte before transmission and subtracted at the receiving side before HEC processing.

4.7.6 Cell Delineation

Cell delineation is the function for locating cell boundaries of the incoming data flow. Basically, the method works by observing the degree of correlation between the ATM-cell's first four bytes and the fifth byte. That is, after five contiguous bytes are selected and expressed as a thirty-ninth order polynomial, if the polynomial is divisible by the real polynomial $x^8 + x^2 + x + 1$, then for the moment the result is regarded as a valid cell header. If the same holds true after the process is applied repeatedly in intervals of 53 bytes, then the result is confirmed as the ATM cell header. The cell delineation technique that uses the HEC has a state diagram shown in Figure 4.17. The three states of the cell delineation procedure are *hunt, presynch*, and *synch*, which are as follows.

1. In the hunt state, cyclic redundancy coding is performed on groups of five bytes (five bytes correspond to the length of one header) as they are moved over bit by bit. (It could be byte by byte in the SDH-based case.) If the correct HEC is found, it enters the presynch state.

2. In the presynch state, the cyclic coding is performed as bytes are moved over in groups of 53 (length of one cell). If the correct HEC is found δ consecutive times, the procedure moves into the synch state. However, if even a single incorrect HEC appears, the procedure reverts to the hunt state.

3. The synch state also performs cyclic coding on a cell-unit basis. The synch state is maintained even if occassionally incorrect HEC is discovered, but if incorrect HEC is discovered α consecutive times, then the loss of synchronization is assumed and the procedure moves back to the hunt state.

The consecutive header error indicator α, which is the criterion for determining deviation from synchronicity, and the consecutive header confirmation indicator δ,

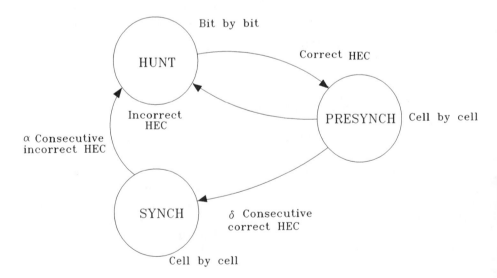

Figure 4.17 Cell delineation state diagram.

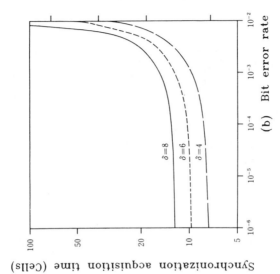

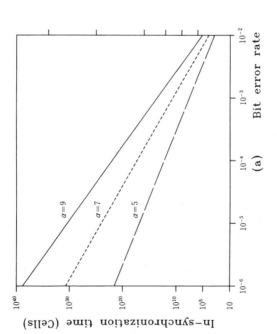

Figure 4.18 Performance of α and δ for 155.520-Mbps signal: (a) α and in-synchronization time; (b) δ and synchronization acquisition time.

which triggers the transition into the synch state, are two of the most important parameters for determining cell delineation performance. The performance evaluation for the 155.520-Mbps signal in terms of these parameters is shown in Figure 4.18 (refer to CCITT Recommendation I.432). It can be seen from the figure that $\alpha = 7$ and $\delta = 6$ give a satisfactory result.[27]

At an SDH-based physical layer, the STM frame is identified by searching out the bytes A1 and A2 of SOH from the received bit stream, then the AU-4 pointer bytes within the SOH are read in order to determine the VC-4 starting point, and finally the above HEC is applied to locate the ATM cell boundary. In the final step, the H4-based cell delineation can be applied instead of using the HEC. The performance comparison between H4 byte-based cell delineation and HEC-based cell delineation is displayed in Table 4.11. The former is the case in which the H4 byte is used for delineation and HEC for cell boundary loss confirmation, and the latter is the case in which HEC is used for both the delineation and loss confirmation. It can be inferred from the table that, at low bit error rates, the performances of each method are equivalently good, but as bit error increases, the use of HEC shows a better performance.

Table 4.11
Performance of Cell Delineating Algorithms (unit:byte)

Performance		*H4*	*HEC*
Maximum average synchronization time ($\delta = 6$)	Bit error rate 0.0001	380	
	Bit error rate 0.001	990	340
			380
Average time for detecting the loss of synchronization ($\alpha = 7$)		400	400

4.7.7 Scrambling

In the BISDN physical layer, scrambling is used as a complement and a means to improve the reliability of the cell delineation technique. At the same time, by altering the data of the information field to appear more random, scrambling brings about an enhancement in the transmission performance. The characteristics of the most representative scrambling techniques—*self-synchronous scrambling* (SSS), *frame*

---

[27]In the cell-based physical layer, only six of HEC's eight bits are used for cell delineation purposes; thus, a higher value of δ, which is 8, is used. See Section 4.8.

synchronous scrambling (FSS), and *distributed sample scrambling* (DSS)—are compared in Table 4.12.

For the SDH-based physical layer, SSS is used with the characteristic polynomial $x^{43} + 1$. The scrambling procedure applies to the entire information field of the 149.760-Mbps cell flow (including idle cells), excluding the header. During the cell delineation procedure at the receiving side, the descrambler does not operate in the hunt state, but does operate in the presynch and synch states.

In SSS, since each state of the *pseudo-random binary sequence* (PRBS) generator depends on the incoming signal, even if the scrambler and the descrambler are slightly out of synch, the synch state can be self-recovered. Therefore, a frame synchronization procedure is not separately required, thus simplifying the implementation of SSS. However, an error in the transmission affects the states of the descrambler's PRBS generator; hence, there is a possibility that one bit of input error magnifies to two bits of output error. A relatively simple characteristic polynomial $x^{43} + 1$ is adopted to limit the effective error multiplication rate to be two; its shortcoming is that its signal randomization performance is not optimal. However, it is complemented by the FSS process during the SDH frame generation, which scrambles the user information field as well as the header.

Such scrambling techniques are not appropriate for the cell-based physical layer, because the cell header is not scrambled again when it is transmitted.[28] Therefore,

Table 4.12
Comparison of Scrambling Techniques

Scrambling	*Characteristics*
Self synchronous scrambling (SSS)	No synchronization problem
	Randomizing effect good
	Error multiplication problem
	No synchronization sample transmission problem
Frame synchronous scrambling (FSS)	Synchronization by resetting at each frame
	Randomizing effect good for large-sized frames
	No error multiplication problem
	No synchronization sample transmission necessary
Distributed sample scrambling (DSS)	Synchronization by transmitted samples
	Randomizing effect is good even for small-sized frames
	No error multiplication problem
	Synchronization sample transmission necessary

---

[28]In SDH-based transmission, scrambling is again performed during the process of creating the STM frame; hence, such a problem does not arise.

DSS with the characteristic polynomial $x^{31} + x^{28} + 1$ is used to scramble and transmit both the header and the user information fields.[29]

The DSS method generates a sample of PRBS and performs binary addition (or XOR operation) on the bit streams of header and information fields. Here, the 8 bits of the HEC section are obtained by calculating a CRC-8 code for the 32 bits of the distributed sample scrambled header section.

To synchronize the PRBS generator of the transmitting side with that of the receiver, PRBS samples of the transmitter are added in binary to the bits of the HEC section before they are transmitted. The distributed sample scrambler of the transmitter generates and transmits two such sampled bits per cell. The receiving side searches for the cell boundary using the remaining six HEC bits until the scrambler and the descrambler are in sync. Once the cell boundary is found, the other two HEC bits are tracked; after they are found, their values are used to deduce the PRBS sample values. Since the distributed sample scrambler's characteristic polynomial has the order of 31, if cell delineation is performed correctly, then the synchronization between the respective scramblers of the transmitter and the receiver can be achieved after 16 cells.

Table 4.13 gives a comparison of the SSS used in SDH-based transmission and the DSS used in the cell-based transmission. Compared to the SSS, DSS is superior from the error multiplication standpoint, but is inferior in terms of synchronization time and the complexity of the descrambler. However, the chief difference between the two methods is whether or not the header is included as an object to be scrambled.

4.8 DISTRIBUTED SAMPLE SCRAMBLING

Scrambling is bit-level signal processing applied to transmission-rate signals just prior to transmission.[30] Its main function is to provide a high data-transition density, to reduce intersymbol interference, and to suppress static pattern-dependent jitter.

DSS is a scrambling technique recently adopted by CCITT for use in the cell-based physical layer of the BISDN. DSS is basically similar to FSS, which scrambles and descrambles the digital bit streams by adding *shift register generator* (SRG) sequences. But the DSS is different from the FSS in the method of synchronizing the state of the descrambler SRG to that of the scrambler SRG. In the FSS, the scrambler and the descrambler are synchronized by resetting the states of both SRGs to a prespecified state; while in the DSS the samples of the scrambler SRG are transmitted to the descrambler SRG for synchronization.

The following section concentrates on describing the operation of the DSS.

---

[29]Distributed sample scrambling, unlike the SSS, is a unique scrambling technique that only appears in ATM cell-based transmission. Its basic principles will be treated separately in Section 4.8.

[30]This section gives a detailed description of DSS, which is a unique scrambling method used in the cell-based physical layer of the BISDN, and so it may be skipped without detracting from the overall understanding of the chapter.

Table 4.13
Comparison of SSS and DSS

Scrambler	*SSS*	*DSS*
Characteristic polynomial	$x^{43} + 1$	$x^{31} + x^{28} + 1$
Error multiplication	2	1
Number of bits used in the header	0	2 (before synchronization) 0 (after synchronization)
Cell transmission possibility	Possible (using SDH based)	Possible
Malicious interference probability	$1/2^{43}$	$1/(2^{31} - 1)$
Synchronization time	43 bits	16 cells
Complexity of scrambler	43 SR* 1 XOR**	31 + 2 SR 2 XOR
Complexity of descrambler	43 SR 1 XOR	31 + 2 SR 19 XOR
Scrambling of header	Excluded from scrambling	Included in scrambling

*SR: Shift Register
**XOR: XOR Gate

4.8.1 Transmitter Operation

The transmitter SRG sequence is added (modulo-2) to the complete cell bit by bit except for the HEC field. The characteristic polynomial of the SRG in the DSS is $x^{31} + x^{28} + 1$.

The CRC byte for each cell is then modified by modulo-2 addition of the CRC calculated on the first 32 bits of the scrambled header. The first two bits of the HEC field are then modified again as follows by two samples from the SRG sequence. To the first HEC bit (HEC_8), the value of the SRG sequence that was used 211 bits earlier for scrambling (or s_{t-211}) is added in modulo-2. To the second bit of the HEC field (HEC_7), the current value (or s_t) of the SRG sequence is added. These samples are exactly half a cell apart so the first is delayed by 211 bits before being delivered. The SRG sequence and resultant transmitted data structures of the HEC field are as shown in Figure 4.19.

4.8.2 Receiver Operation

Receiver operation consists of three basic states: acquisition of scrambler synchronization, verification of scrambler synchronization, and steady-state operation. The

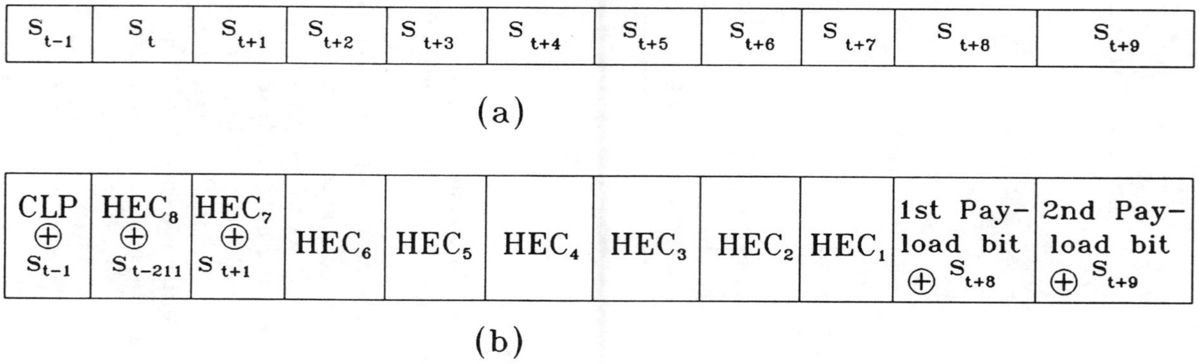

| S_{t-1} | S_t | S_{t+1} | S_{t+2} | S_{t+3} | S_{t+4} | S_{t+5} | S_{t+6} | S_{t+7} | S_{t+8} | S_{t+9} |

(a)

| CLP $\oplus$ S_{t-1} | HEC$_8$ $\oplus$ S_{t-211} | HEC$_7$ $\oplus$ S_{t+1} | HEC$_6$ | HEC$_5$ | HEC$_4$ | HEC$_3$ | HEC$_2$ | HEC$_1$ | 1st Payload bit $\oplus$ S_{t+8} | 2nd Payload bit $\oplus$ S_{t+9} |

(b)

Figure 4.19 Data structure at DSS: (a) SRG sequence; (b) resultant transmitted data element.

transition between these states may be determined by the value of the *confidence counter* (*C*). The state transition diagram for DSS is as shown in Figure 4.20.

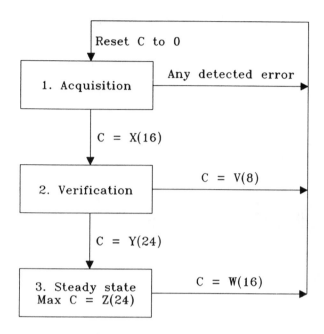

Figure 4.20 State transition of DSS.

Acquisition of Scrambler Synchronization

Cell delineation is determined using the last six bits of the HEC field only. The conveyed sample bits are extracted by modulo-2 addition of the predicted values for HEC_8 and HEC_7 from the received value. The descrambler generates its own samples of SRG state in the same manner and compares it to the delivered ones. Scrambler synchronization may, for example, be achieved by applying delivered samples at half-cell intervals to a recursive descrambler in the same interval they were extracted from the source PRBS. The second sample s_{t+1} (derived from HEC_7) is stored for 211 bits before it is used. The resultant descrambler configuration is shown in Figure 4.21. Synchronization principles of the scrambler and descrambler SRGs in relation to this figure will be given in Section 4.8.3.

The confidence counter, which initially is set to 0 is incremented by one for every cell received correctly, with no errors detected in the HEC bits 1 to 6. Any error detected in the cell header results in a return to the initial value. Transition to the verification state occurs when the counter reaches X (proposed value = 16).

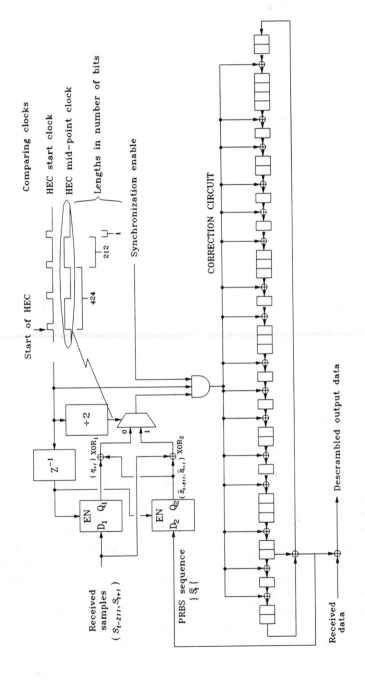

Figure 4.21 Descrambler of DSS.

Verification of Scrambler Synchronization

Verification is needed because undetectable errors in the conveyed bits may have occurred during the acquisition phase. The verification state differs from the acquisition in that the descrambler SRG is no longer modified with conveyed scrambler SRG sequence samples.

For every cell received without detected errors, the two conveyed samples are compared to their predicted values. For each cell with two correct predictions received, the confidence counter is incremented. If one or two incorrect predictions are made, then the counter is decremented. If the counter falls below V (proposed value = 8), the system returns to the acquisition initial state and the confidence counter is reset. The transition to the steady state occurs when the counter reaches Y (proposed value = 24).

Steady-State Operation (Synchronized Scrambler)

Steady state means that the scrambler and descrambler are completely synchronized. In this state, HEC_8 and HEC_7 bits can both be returned to normal use following their descrambling. Properties of error detection and correction are not affected by this process.

The rules for incrementing and decrementing the confidence counter are the same as for verification state. If the counter drops below W (proposed value = 16), it triggers an automatic return to the acquisition state. The confidence counter has an upper limit of Z (proposed value = 24).

4.8.3 Synchronization Principles of DSS

For a DSS scrambler and descrambler pair, we denote with $\mathbf{d_k}$ and $\mathbf{\hat{d}_k}$ the state vectors of the scrambler and descrambler SRGs, respectively. The DSS scrambler is synchronized to the scrambler if $\mathbf{d_k} = \mathbf{\hat{d}_k}$ for all k.

In order to synchronize the descrambler SRG whose SR size is L (=31) to the scrambler SRG state, L or more samples should be transmitted. So, in an efficient synchronization process, we need L times of sampling in the scrambler and L times of correction in the descrambler.

The expression $r + \alpha_i$, $i = 0, 1, \ldots, L - 1$, denotes the sampling time of the ith sample z_i (or $\hat{z}_i$), and $r + \beta_i$, $i = 0, 1, \ldots, L - 1$, denotes the correction time using the ith sample, where r indicates a reference time. This is depicted in Figure 4.22 (note that $\alpha_0 = 0$). Note that the ith correction is done after the ith sampling, but no later than the $i + 1$th sampling; that is,

$$r < r + \beta_0 \leqslant r + \alpha_1 < r + \beta_1 \leqslant \ldots \leqslant r + \alpha_{L-1} < r + \beta_{L-1}$$

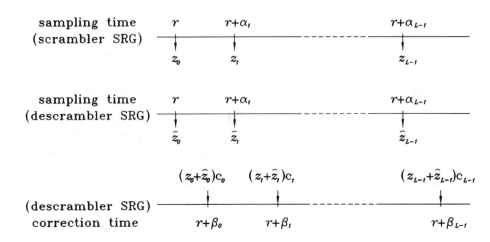

Figure 4.22 Timing diagram for sampling and correction times.

the synchronization of the descrambler, the state of the descrambler SRG is repeatedly corrected until the descrambler SRG sequence $\{\hat{s}_k\}$ becomes identical to the scrambler SRG sequence $\{s_k\}$. For each correction time, the transmitted sample $\hat{z}_i$ is compared to its descrambler counterpart $\hat{z}_i$, and a correction is made to the state of the descrambler SRG in case the two samples are not identical. This process is equivalent to correcting the state vector by adding a correction vector $\mathbf{c}_i$, $i = 0, 1, \ldots, L - 1$. Therefore, the correction process can be carried out in the following manner. First, add the two samples z_i and $\hat{z}_i$ (modulo-2 addition), then multiply $\mathbf{c}_i$ to the sum, and finally add the result at the time $r + \beta_i$ to the state vector $\mathbf{d}_{r+i}$. This is depicted in Figure 4.22 also.

We now state the conditions on sampling times, correction times, and correction vectors that provide appropriate guidelines on choosing the terms α_i, β_i, and $\mathbf{c}_i$ to synchronize the descrambler SRG with the scrambler SRG.[31]

First, the sampling times α_i's must be chosen such that the discrimination matrix

$$
\mathbf{D} = \begin{bmatrix} \mathbf{h}^t \\ \mathbf{h}^t \mathbf{T}^{\alpha_1} \\ \mathbf{h}^t \mathbf{T}^{\alpha_2} \\ \vdots \\ \mathbf{h}^t \mathbf{T}^{\alpha_{L-1}} \end{bmatrix} \tag{4.1}
$$

[31]See "Sampling and Correction Time Conditions in Distributed Sample Scrambling" in *Proceedings of IC³N '92* by S. C. Kim and B. G. Lee for a more detailed treatment.

becomes nonsingular, where $\mathbf{T}$ and $\mathbf{h}$ are, respectively, the state transition matrix and the generating vectors for the SRG.[32] Otherwise, the descrambler SRG states cannot be synchronized with the scrambler SRG states for any choice of correction times and vectors.

Second, if the sampling times α_i's are chosen such that the discrimination matrix $\mathbf{D}$ in (4.1) becomes nonsingular, then the descrambler SRG states can be synchronized with the scrambler SRG states for the correction vector $\mathbf{c}_i$, chosen such that

$$
\mathbf{c}_i = \begin{cases}
\mathbf{T}^{\beta_i}\Delta^{-1}\left(\mathbf{e_i} + \sum_{j=i+1}^{L-1} u_{i,j}\mathbf{e_j}\right), & i = 0, 1, \ldots, L - 2 \\
\mathbf{T}^{\beta_{L-1}}\Delta^{-1}, & i = L - 1
\end{cases}
\tag{4.2}
$$

for the arbitrarily chosen correction time β_i. In the equation, the $L - 1$ vector $\mathbf{e}_i$, $i = 0, 1, \ldots L - 1$, is the basis vector whose ith element is 1 and the others are 0; and $u_{i,j}$ is either 0 or 1 for $i = 0, 1, \ldots, L - 2$ and $j = i + 1, i + 2, \ldots, L - 1$. Therefore, the sampling times α_i should be chosen such that the resulting discrimination matrix $\mathbf{D}$ in (4.1) becomes nonsingular, and once this is done, we can arbitrarily select correction times β_i and select correction vectors $\mathbf{c}_i$ according to the expression in (4.2).

We apply the two conditions to the DSS for the cell-based ATM transmission in the BISDN. Then the sampling times are $\alpha_i = 212i$, $i = 0, 1, \ldots, 30$, and so the resulting discrimination matrix $\mathbf{D}$ in (4.1) becomes nonsingular. Therefore, if we choose the correction times $\beta_i = 212 + 212i$, we can obtain by (4.2) the common correction vector

$$
\mathbf{c} = [0110100110111001100111011000100]^t
\tag{4.3}
$$

This provides the descrambler circuit depicted in Figure 4.20.

4.9 ATM LAYER OF BISDN

The ATM layer possesses the processing capability associated with all of the fields of the ATM cell header except the HEC. That is, it performs GFC-related flow control, VPI/VCI-related ATM connection control, and other PT- and CLP-related

---

[32]The state transition matrix $\mathbf{T}$ is a matrix representing the relation between the state vectors $\mathbf{d}_k$ and $\mathbf{d}_{k+1}$, and the generating vector $\mathbf{h}$ is a vector representing the relation between the state vector $\mathbf{d}_k$ and the SRG sequence element s_k.

processing functions. In the transmitting direction, the ATM layer utilizes the information received from the higher layer and management plane to generate the header, and then appends the header to the user information field sent down from the AAL, and subsequently sends it down to the physical layer. In the receiving direction, the cells received from the physical layer are disassembled to extract and process the header, and the user information field is sent up to the AAL.

In the following sections, the BISDN ATM layer-related functions will be examined.

4.9.1 ATM Layer Connection

A transparent connection provided by the ATM layer to the higher layer is called the *ATM connection*; it is connected end to end through a concatenation of connection elements. The two kinds of ATM connections are VC and VP connections (see Figure 4.8). VC refers to a logical unidirectional connection between two end points for the transfer of ATM cells, and VP implies a logical combination of VCs.

Each VC is assigned a VCI and each VP is assigned a VPI. Inside a VPC, VC links that are different from one another can exist, and each is differentiated through the use of VCI. On the other hand, VCs belonging to different VPs may possess the same VCI. Hence, a VC can be completely identified solely on the basis of its corresponding VCI and VPI.

When switching occurs in a VCC, the value of the VCI is not identically maintained at both ends. Also, when the VP link terminates via a cross-connect equipment, a concentrator, or a switching equipment, the value of VPI can also change accordingly. But, VCI only changes when the VC link terminates, thus within the same VPC the same VCI value is maintained. These relationships are illustrated in Figure 4.23. In Figure 4.23(a), S_{VPI} and S_{VCI} represent VP switching and VC switching, respectively, and it can be seen that in VP switching the VCI is maintained as it is, and in VC switching both sides of VCI and VPI get altered. The corresponding ATM connection format for the VC and VP are as shown in Figure 4.23(b).

VC switching and VC/VP switching functions are illustrated in Figure 4.24(a,b). In the figure, VP switching corresponds to the add/drop or cross-connect, and VC/VP switching corresponds to normal switching function.

24 bits are allocated for VPI/VCI at the UNI, and 28 bits at the NNI. The actual number of bits for the VPI/VCI field used for routing at the UNI is determined through a negotiation between the user and the network. Here, the value chosen is the lowest of the values demanded by the user or the network. Only, the VPI values allocated must be consecutive, the values must be selected starting with the least significant bit, and the unused VPI bits should be left as 0. These relationship also apply to the VCI. For the indication of metasignaling VC and general broadcast

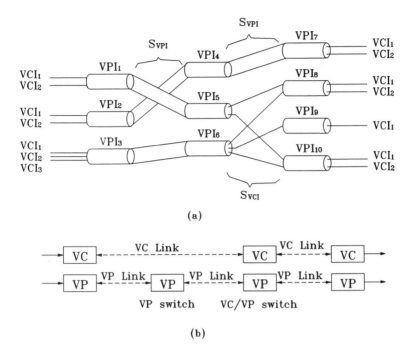

(a)

(b)

Figure 4.23 ATM layer connection: (a) VPI and VCI assignments; (b) VP and VC connections.

signaling VC, the fixed VP and VC identifiers are preassigned at the UNI as shown in Table 4.14.[33]

4.9.2 Virtual Channel Connection

VCC refers to a concatenation of VC links for achieving connection between ATM service access points (see Figure 4.23). Here, the term VC link implies the unidirectional virtual connection for enabling the transport of ATM cells between points where VCI is assigned and the points at which the VCI gets translated or removed. The VCC can be provided by the switching equipment, and can be permanent or semipermanent. The integrity of cell sequence is ensured within the same VCC. A VCC user is provided by the network with a set of QOS parameters such as cell loss rate and cell delay. At the time of VCC setup, user traffic parameters are prescribed through negotiation between the user and the network, and the network monitors the observance of these parameters.

---

[33]The preassignments at the NNI are being studied by CCITT. For more information on metasignaling, see Section 4.13.2.

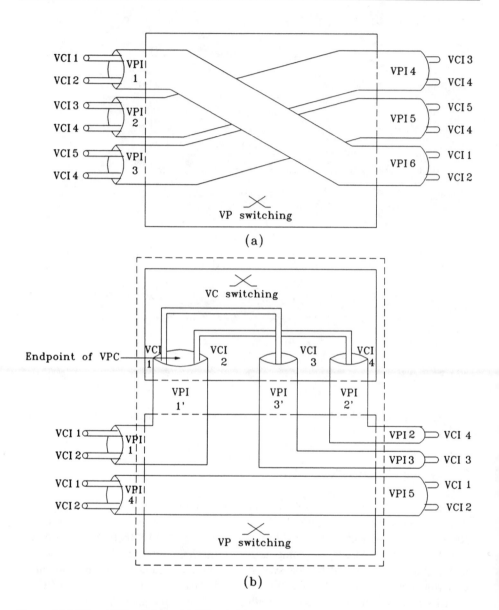

Figure 4.24 VP and VC switching: (a) VP switching; (b) VC/VP switching.

Table 4.14
Pre-assigned VPI/VCI Values (UNI)

Usage	VPI	VCI	
Metasignaling virtual channel	00000000 or XXXXXXXX	00000000	00000001
General broadcast signaling virtual channel	00000000 or XXXXXXXX	00000000	00000010
Segment OAM F4 flow	YYYYYYYY	00000000	00000011
End-to-end OAM F4 flow	YYYYYYYY	00000000	00000100

At the UNI, four different methods can be used for establishing or removing VCC. First, the signaling procedure can be bypassed if connection setup or release is achieved through a reservation. This method applies to permanent or semipermanent connections. The second is the use of a metasignaling procedure (signaling procedures are described in Section 4.13).

That is, a signaling VC is established or removed through the use of a meta-signaling VC. Third is the use of a user-to-network signaling procedure. This involves the use of a signaling VCC to establish or release a VCC for end-to-end communication. The fourth is the use of a user-to-user signaling procedure. This method employs a signaling VCC to establish or release a VCC internal to a VPC pre-established between two UNIs.

Four methods of assigning VCI values at the UNI are possible: assignment by the network, assignment by the user, assignment through a network-user negotiation, and the use of a standardized method. In general, the assigned VCI value itself is unrelated to the service provided through the corresponding VC. For such conveniences as terminal interchangeability or initialization, it is desirable to assign the same VCI value for some specific set of functions. For example, if a fixed meta-signaling VCI value is used at all UNIs, the initialization of the terminal equipment becomes simple. The preassigned VPI/VCI values are as shown in Table 4.14.[34]

Since cell header is processed at such network elements as the ATM switch, cross-connect equipment, and concentrator, the VCI or VCI/VPI translation process is performed at these sites also. Therefore, when a VCC is established or released inside an ATM network, the establishment or release of a VC link can occur at more than one NNI. Here, a VC link is established or released by way of internal signaling or an internetwork signaling procedure at ATM network elements.

---

[34]XXXXXXXX and YYYYYYYY in the table denote arbitrary VPI values. For the F4 OAM flow, see Section 4.15.

At NNI, VCI is preassigned in the following instances: unassigned cell indication, physical layer cell indication, metasignaling VC indication, and general broadcast signaling VC indication.[35] In the first two cases, the VCI (and VPI) is indicated as "all 0."[36]

4.9.3 Virtual Path Connection

Virtual path connection refers to a concatenation of VP links for connecting the points at which a VPI is assigned with those at which a VPI is translated or removed (see Figure 4.8).

Here VP link implies the VP link groups which join VPI assignment points and the setup/removal points. The VPC can be provided through switching equipment and can be permanent or semipermanent. Cell sequence is ensured for each VCC within the same VPC. QOS parameters such as cell loss rate and cell delay variation are provided for each VPC. Here, VPC QOS must be able to guarantee the best among the VCC service qualities maintained within the VPC. At the time of establishing VPC, the user traffic parameters are determined through a network-user negotiation, and the network monitors the observance of these parameters.

A VPC between VPC end points can be established or released in two possible ways. The first is to establish or release VPC without going through a signaling procedure. In that case, setup or release of the connection is achieved by way of a reservation. Secondly, the VPC is established or removed upon the need for such purposes as user control and network control.[37]

The cases in which VPI are assigned in advance are the same as the cases in which VCI is preassigned at NNI. That is, the VPI can be preassigned for unassigned cell indication, physical layer cell indication, metasignaling VC indication, and general broadcast signaling VC indication. In the case of unassigned cells and physical layer cells, the VPI (and VCI) are indicated as "all 0." In the case of metasignaling VC and general broadcast VC, the VPI at UNI are assigned as shown in Table 4.14.

4.9.4 Preassigned Cell Header

Cells reserved for physical layer use have pre-assigned values in the whole header. Here, the ATM cells used by the physical layer include idle cells and physical layer OAM cells.

At the UNI, the ATM cell headers for physical layer ATM cells and unassigned cells are preassigned in the form shown in Table 4.15.[38] In the table, P and A,

---

[35]Other cases are being studied by CCITT.

[36]The VCI and VPI values for the last two cases are being studied by CCITT.

[37]The requisite implementation details are being studied by CCITT.

[38]The metasignaling VP cells and the general broadcast signaling VP cells that were shown in Table 4.14 are the cells that have been assigned to the ATM layer.

respectively, represent bits that are usable at the physical layer and the ATM layer. Here, the *P*-bit can be used independently of how the header bits are to be utilized at the ATM layer. Similarly, bits corresponding to the CLP can be used independently of its application at the ATM layer, and as can be seen from the table it is set to 1 for the physical layer, and to 0 for the ATM layer.

Table 4.15
Pre-Assigned Cell Header Values at the UNI

Usage	Octet 1	Octet 2	Octet 3	Octet 4	Octet 5
For physical layer	PPPP0000	00000000	00000000	0000PPP1	HEC
For ATM layer unassigned cell	AAAA0000	00000000	00000000	0000AAA0	HEC

The header assignment for physical layer cells and the unassigned cells at the NNI is analogous to that at the UNI. That is, the preassigned cell header values at the NNI are as shown in Table 4.16, and it can be inferred that the result is equivalent to setting the bits which correspond to the GFC field to all 0s. The PPP1 portion of cell header for the physical layer are preassigned as 0001 in the case of idle cells, and 1001 in the case of physical layer OAM cells (see Table 4.10).

Table 4.16
Pre-assigned Cell Header at the NNI

Usage	Octet 1	Octet 2	Octet 3	Octet 4	Octet 5
For physical layer	00000000	00000000	00000000	0000PPP1	HEC
For ATM layer unassigned cell	00000000	00000000	00000000	0000AAA0	HEC

4.9.5 Other Header Field-Related Functions

Among the ATM layer's various functions, the most important can be said to be either the VPI- or VCI-related routing function, or the ATM connection function. Other ATM header field-related functions include the generic flow control function associated with GFC, service quality and cell loss priority indication function associated with CLP, and functions associated with PT (see Section 4.3.4).

Generic Flow Control Function[39]

The function of the GFC is to control traffic flows for various ATM connections of QOS associated with the ATM layer. The GFC controls medium access at the UNI and controls traffic in order to resolve short-term overload conditions. Other required functions include jitter reduction for CBR services and fair capacity allocation for VBR services.

GFC is applicable at the reference points S_B or T_B. At S_B or SS_B, GFC provides flow control capability for information generated at user premises. Here, traffic can occur in both directions at the S_B or SS_B interfaces. At T_B, GFC controls the traffic that is transported from the B-TE to the network. GFC is a special feature of the ATM layer and is provided independently of the physical layer. Also, it is applicable to any UNI configuration, whether it be star, bus, ring, or starred-bus. When the GFC function is not required, the GFC section is set to 0000.

Cell Loss Priority Function

Since the VBR services can widely vary in bit rates, at the moment when the various VBR services all manifest their maximum possible bit rates, the network can be severely congested. As a means of resolving such traffic congestion, the CLP function can be used. That is, priority level to be used for cell loss (or cell discard) is recorded in the CLP field of each ATM cell employed for VBR services, and when congestion occurs, the cells with lower priority are discarded first. If the CLP bit indicates 1, then it represents a cell with a lower priority that can be abandoned.

The cell loss priority function must be provided in conjunction with the QOSs determined at the time of establishing VPC/VCC. That is, it must be possible to provide the minimum guaranteed bit rate even after the cell loss processing, and the prescribed service quality must be maintained. Consequently, the network must determine the bit rate of the cells with the higher priority at the time of establishing the connection, and the rate must be negotiable even after the connection is completed.[40] The network must constantly monitor via usage parameter control whether the number of cells corresponding to a given connection exceeds the prearranged

---

[39] The GFC function is not used for equipment implementing the "uncontrolled transmission" set of parameters. For a more detailed description, refer to CCITT Recommendation I.361. The protocols of GFC are discussed in detail in Section 4.10.

[40] The renegotiation capability is required by CCITT Recommendation I.311, even though its implementation in the practical network may require challenging work with limited rewards.

value. When the cell traffic exceeds the negotiated level, even the cells that have been assigned higher priority can be ignored by the network.

Payload Type Indication Function

The payload type field indicates whether the contents of payload consist of user information or network information, and additionally provides indications of network congestion experience and ATM layer user-to-ATM layer user indication.[41] User information is composed of user information and service adaptation function information, and network information does not include any user information, but includes information on OAM F5 flows and resource management. While general ATM cells are created at a user terminal and enter the network through the UNI, the cells used for network information are created inside the network and cross over the UNI.

4.10 GENERIC FLOW CONTROL PROTOCOL

The GFC field is used to alleviate short-term overload conditions that may occur at the UNI by controlling the flow of traffic submitted to the network by users.[42] The GFC protocol must be able to ensure that the agreed minimum bandwidth capacity is available to each user, and any spare capacity is shared fairly among VBR services. Also, GFC protocol should be able to support all possible configurations such as star, bus, starred bus, and ring. The GFC protocol should also be insensitive to aggregate traffic, number of terminals, or distance between terminals.

In this section, we briefly introduce some GFC protocols satisfying those requirements, which are chosen from among the proposals submitted to CCITT.[43]

4.10.1 GFC Protocol Using Counter Reset Timing

This GFC protocol is based on the assumption that allocation of bandwidth in an ATM environment can be realized by allocating N number of transmittable cells in a time period T_p.[44]

---

[41]Among the three bits in the PT field, the first bit is used to indicate whether it is a user information (0) or network information (1); and the second bit, when it is used by the network, indicates whether the relevant information has experienced congestion (1) or not (0).

[42]This section concentrates specifically on GFC protocols, so the reader may skip it without losing the continuity of the chapter.

[43]The discussion in this section is based on the CCITT standard proposals that had been proposed upto 1992.

[44]This protocol was proposed to CCITT by England in 1990. Recently, Japan and England have merged their original proposals (respectively described in Sections 4.10.1 and 4.10.5) into a single protocol. This protocol supports *ATM ring* (ATMR) procedures which give excellent performance on slotted rings or buses with circumference less than 6 km. For larger rings or buses it is possible to operate with MSFC procedures, for which good control of CBR jitter has already been demonstrated. It also contains multiple priority characteristics which are a feature of DQDB-based protocols.

This counter-reset-timing-based protocol operates in the controlled mode or uncontrolled mode, depending on the actual bandwidth being used. In the uncontrolled mode, all the connected terminals are allowed free access to the network. But when the used capacity exceeds the agreed maximum, the terminals switch to the controlled mode, in which access is limited.

In the controlled mode, each terminal resets the counter with the initial value N, which is the number of cells that the terminal is allowed to transmit in a given period T_p. The counter is decremented for each cell transmitted until it reaches zero, after which the terminal may not transmit until the counter is reset. A specific controlling terminal generates a reset signal at every reset period T_p, which is determined by evaluating the actual bandwidth being used by all the terminals connected. Upon receiving the reset signal, other terminals can reset the counter to N and restart cell transmission. The remaining bandwidth can be allocated fairly among the VBR services by making the reset period T_p shorter if the used bandwidth decreases. The controlling terminal also drives other terminals into the uncontrolled mode if the used bandwidth goes below a certain prespecified level.

4.10.2 GFC Protocol Using Wait-for-Transmit Queues

In this protocol, the 4-bit GFC field protocol is split into two 2-bit subfields: GFC Transmit Control and GFC Priority. The GFC Transmit Control field is used to control transmission of cells between GFC protocol entities (that is, terminals and NT2s), and is equivalent to the REQ (Request) field of the DQDB protocol.[45] The priority field is used to minimize the delay and jitter of CBR services. CBR services are assigned higher flow control priority than VBR services, and among the CBR services higher bit rate services are given higher priority, since they are more sensitive to jitter.

If the GFC control field and Wait-for-Transmit queue are employed in a bus structure, the Wait-for-Transmit queues distributed around the terminals form a single virtual FIFO queue. This resolves the problem associated with the DQDB protocol where only single cells in the *distributed-queue state machine* (DQSM) of each terminal are grouped into a global virtual queue. This protocol therefore operates in the same manner as the g-DQ protocol. (For a more detailed description of DQDB, refer to Section 5.4.)

This protocol handles CBR services and VBR services in a slightly different manner due to their inherent differences. In a CBR service, cells are delivered to the Wait-for-Transmit queue at fixed intervals, and the terminals in the direction opposite to the transmission destination are notified upon each cell's arrival. A VBR service is assigned a bit rate, a peak rate, and a balancing parameter corresponding

---

[45]This protocol was proposed to CCITT by the United States in 1990.

to the bandwidth that was guaranteed during call setup. The balancing parameter is a priority used for allowing each VBR service to access the bus with a bandwidth greater than the guaranteed bandwidth. Its role is to distribute any surplus bandwidth in an equitable manner.

In a star configuration, if a cell arrives from an interface, the GFC notifies all other interfaces of its priority, thus forming a virtual FIFO queue. That is, if a cell priority N is received from an interface, a cell whose control field is filled with N is sent to all other interfaces.

4.10.3 Modified DQDB Protocol Using Empty Slot Counter

This protocol is a modification of the DQDB protocol and has several distinct features.[46] First, each TE maintains a counter that counts the number of idle cells it has sent out unused. Second, every time an idle cell is sent out, a "handshake" request is delivered to the opposite direction. Third, the length of the distributed queue is minimized through the use of the early request cancellation function. Fourth, the difference between the number of idle cells and the number of handshake requests sent to the opposite direction during the initialization phase can be used by each TE to predict its distance from the adjacent TEs. This resolves to some extent the inherent problem of unfairness in DQDB. Fifth, Each TE can have more than one outstanding request in the distributed queue. Sixth, it can be easily implemented, even in a ring structure.

To operate the distributed queues, each node maintains three types of counters for each bus direction: an idle cell counter, a request counter, and a countdown counter. The idle cell counter and the countdown counter are associated with the upstream (downstream) bus, while the request counter is associated with the downstream (upstream) bus. The basic difference between this protocol and that of the DQDB lies in the use of the idle cell counter.

The request counter is incremented whenever a request slot is received, and is decremented whenever an idle cell is forwarded. When a node receives data to transmit, it sends a request in the opposite direction and transfers its request counter value to its countdown counter. The countdown counter is decremented whenever an idle cell is forwarded and the data to be transmitted are loaded onto an idle cell when the counter value reaches zero. Except for decrementing the request counter as well as the countdown counter when an idle cell is forwarded, this part of the operation is equivalent to that of the DQDB. The main difference is that the idle cell counter is used to keep count of the number of idle cells forwarded in excess of requests from upstream nodes.

---

[46]This protocol was proposed to CCITT by Switzerland in 1991.

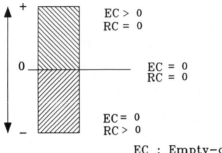

EC : Empty–cell counter
RC : Request counter

Figure 4.25 Request and empty cell counter illustrated by general counter.

The idle cell counter is incremented only when the request counter is zero and an idle cell is forwarded. It is decremented when the request cell is received by the opposite bus and the idle cell counter is positive. When the request counter is zero and the idle cell counter is positive,[47] it means that more idle cells have been forwarded to upstream nodes than needed. If the request counter is positive while the idle cell counter is zero, it means that the present node is a part of a distributed queue; that is, a virtual FIFO made up of cells to be transmitted in upstream nodes and downstream nodes. If a request cell arrives at a node where idle cell counter is positive and the request counter is zero, it is eliminated and not passed on to downstream nodes, since idle cells which can be used by the node that has sent the request have already been forwarded upstream by the present node (see above). This action results in minimizing the distributed queues being divided by the present node. There may be a problem in that the idle cell counter may keep count of idle cells sent upstream a long while ago. But this problem is eliminated by having nodes send a handshake request downstream for every cell forwarded upstream (downstream), so that the idle cell counter in a node is decremented if the idle cell forwarded is not needed in the node immediately following.

The four bits of the GFC field are used as follows: IDLE/FULL (bit 1), READ (bit 2), REQUEST/NONREQUEST (bit 3), and MONITOR (bit 4). Bit 2 and bit 4 are used in a ring configuration. Bit 2 is also used in conjunction with bit $1 = 1$ (i.e., full) to represent the fact that a node has read the contents of the cell, but was unable to convert it to an idle cell because it was part of a distributed queue. Since changing such a cell into an idle cell immediately may result in discrepancies in the counter values in the queue, the cell is given the status of READ. While in this state,

---

[47]The protocol definition results in allowing for only three possible combinations for the empty slot counter and request counter value, which represent the cases in which they are both zero and only one is zero and the other is positive. The case in which both counters are positive is impossible in normal operation, and therefore a single counter may be used for both counters (see Figure 4.25).

it cannot be used by another node with data to send. READ cells are converted to IDLE cells at the first node they encounter with a zero request counter.

4.10.4 Modified DQDB Protocol Using Priorities

This protocol is based on the DQDB, but with enhancements to ensure guaranteed bandwidth, fair bandwidth distribution, and greater capacity through destination release.[48]

In this protocol, there are three priorities available. Priority 1 or 2 is assigned to services such as the CBR services which are sensitive to jitter and delay, and priority 0 is assigned to other services.

The protocol basically differs from DQDB in the addition of a traffic shaping algorithm and in allowing more than one cell per connection in the distributed queue at any given time.

The goal of the traffic shaping algorithm is to allow a terminal to queue cells only up to the rate specified by the shaping parameters agreed upon at call setup. The protocol aims to define an appropriate distribution of shaping functions on all terminals so that all jitter in the network can be kept within acceptable bounds.[49]

This protocol differs from the DQDB in the following aspects. First, as the four bits of the GFC field are used for priority and request indication, the VPI/VCI is used to denote whether the corresponding cell is assigned or not. Also, connection-oriented services, which can suffer from jitter if the Wait-for-Transmit queue becomes too long, are allowed to place more than one cell in the global distributed queue instead of only one, as in the original DQDB. The connectionless services with the lowest priority may also place more than one cell in the distributed queue, but under the balancing principles. Third, the distributed queue at each TE must be capable of differentiating its own cells from the external cells, since there may be multiple cells from a single terminal in the global distributed queue at any given time. Lastly, destination release may be implemented in order to allow for reuse of capacity within the symmetric dual bus topology.

4.10.5 ATMR-Based GFC Protocol

The original ATMR protocol was developed for constructing a high-speed shared-medium network, but this protocol can be easily extended for use as a GFC protocol.[50]

---

[48]This was proposed to CCITT by Australia in 1991.

[49]There are two GFC field formats corresponding to the symmetric and asymmetric dual bus topologies, respectively. The GFC field for the symmetric bus contains a one-bit priority indication and three independent one-bit request fields. For the asymmetric dual bus, the GFC field has three priority indication bits in the direction towards the NT2.

[50]This was proposed to CCITT by Japan in 1990. See footnote in Section 4.10.1.

The ATMR is based on the slotted-ring architecture, with one slot corresponding to one ATM cell. The ATMR provides such basic functions as *access control* (AC) guarantee of the required bandwidth using CAC based on AC-Window, distributed monitoring of TE transmission state using busy address, fair distribution of remaining bandwidth using AC-Reset scheme, and the prevention of excessive use of cells using UPC-Window.

In order to guarantee the required bandwidth, the CAC procedure based on the AC-Window is applied. This procedure is based on the determination of the reference duration T_p for defining the bandwidth of a connection and the calculation of the AC-Window value corresponding to the required bandwidth based on this T_p. Each TE has an AC-Window counter (AC-CTR-W), the initial value of which is set equal to the AC-Window. This indicates the maximum number of cells allowed to be transmitted by the TE during a time interval equal to the T_p. The AC-CTR-W is decremented according to the number of cells transmitted from the TE. When AC-CTR-W becomes zero, the TE stops transmitting cells. The AC-CTR-W is reset to the initial value upon receiving the Access Control Reset (AC-Reset) cell. The AC-Reset cell is issued by the TE that has found that all other TEs have completed or stopped cell transmission for that T_p.

The issuing of the AC-Reset cell requires monitoring of the transmission status of other TEs by each and every TE. This is achieved by having every active, or busy, TE (it is active if it has cells to transmit and its AC-CTR-W is not equal to zero) overwrite its own *TE identifier* (TEID) onto the GFC field of each incoming cell. (Such a TE is called *specific address TE*, and specific address refers to the value written in the GFC field. Common address is written in the GFC field in the case of *nonspecific address TE*.) If a TE finds its own TEID in the GFC field, it means that all other TEs are inactive. If a different TEID is found, it means that another TE is still active (i.e., busy). Figure 4.26 illustrates this distributed monitoring scheme.

UPC-Window and UPC-flag are used to prevent the excessive use of cells by malicious users and to control cell-delay variation which different services may suffer from. The procedures concerning UPC-Window and UPC-flag are similar to AC-Window and AC-Reset. That is, both counters are initially set to some initial value and decremented as cells are transmitted, with the condition that the TE can transmit cells only if AC-Window and UPC-Window are not zero. Multiple UPC-flags may be used to control various long-term and short-term cell usage parameters. Figure 4.27 shows the use of short-term and long-term UPC-windows and flags. All the flags are issued at the *local exchange* (LEX) periodically. UPC-Window and UPC-flag, which were not considered for the original ATMR, are employed to alleviate the *cell delay variation* (CDV) problem.

4.11 ATM ADAPTATION LAYER OF BISDN

The AAL of the BISDN is a layer positioned between the ATM layer and the higher-order user service layer, and its main function is to resolve any disparity between

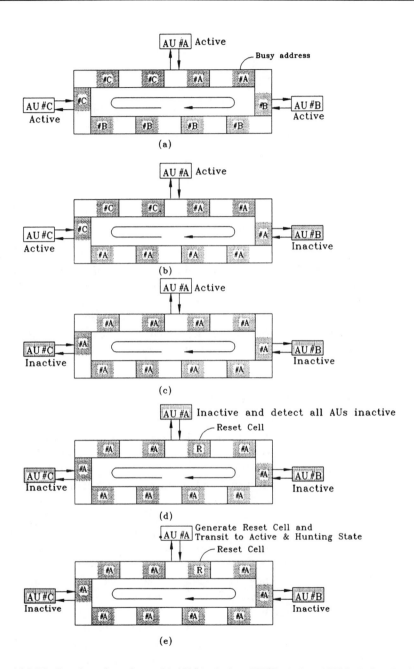

Figure 4.26 Distributed monitor scheme: (a) AU#A: Active, AU#B: Active, AU#C: Active; (b) AU#A: Active, AU#B: Inactive, AU#C: Active; (c) AU#A: Active, AU#B: Inactive, AU#C: Inactive; (d) AU#A: Inactive, AU#B: Inactive, AU#C: Inactive; (e) AU#A: (Generate Reset Cell) -> Active (and Hunting State), AU#B: Inactive, AU#C: Inactive.

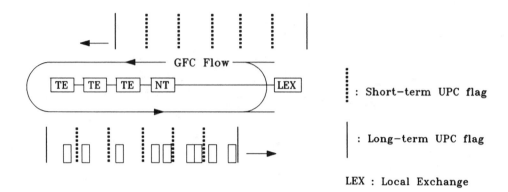

Figure 4.27 Example of UPC-flag usage.

the service provided by the ATM layer and the service demanded by the user. For that purpose, the AAL adapts user service information with the ATM cell format and performs handling of transmission errors, misinserted or lost cells, and errored cells. It also provides flow control function to meet the QOSs demanded by the user, and timing control function to restore the user signal. In the present section, various matters that relate to the AAL will be studied in detail.

4.11.1 Basic Issues to Consider in AAL

The user information field of the ATM cell is fixed at 48 bytes, while the user service information to be adapted to this space is extremely diverse in character. Under such a constraint, the AAL performs various functions, such as ATM cell adaptation, transmission error processing, lost cell and inserted cell processing, flow control, and timing information control. Consequently, it is necessary to consider the following factors.

First, it is necessary to restrict the number of possible protocol types to a minimum. Also, for efficient implementation of these protocols, it is desirable to simplify their structures (as a possible expedient, it is better to construct AAL PDUs or the overheads in byte units as much as possible). Also, it is a fundamental necessity that particular AAL *service data units* (SDU) used for packet-oriented services should have no influence on the design of the AAL.

A flow control function is needed for guaranteeing the user's QOS requirements. The user SDUs should be delivered in a specified time interval according to the user's needs. Also, supporting a multiplexing capability at the AAL should be a simple means of managing a diverse set of services. Furthermore, error detection and correction capability for processing transmission errors must exist, and a means of processing lost cells and inserted cells must be provided as well. The capability to deliver and recover timing information for real-time services must be provided also.

4.11.2 AAL Classification

Horizontal Classification

In order to group various user services in an effective manner with the above factors in mind, the AAL can be categorized into four types. This involves grouping BISDN services into four classes according to their attributes and dividing the AAL correspondingly. That is, as was examined in Section 4.2.4, the services can be categorized into four classes from A to D, depending on the nature of the bit rate, time-related characteristic, and connection mode, and the AAL can be divided accordingly into four types to match each service class. Here, the four types of the AAL are designated AAL-1 to AAL-4, respectively.[51]

To elaborate, AAL-1 provides AAL functions to services with CBR and real-time characteristics. That is, it provides the capability for delivering CBR SDUs using an identical bit rate, transferring timing information from the information source to its destination, and indicating recoverable and unrecoverable errors. Similarly, types AAL-2 to 4 each provide functions that are suitable for service classes B to D, whose attributes were described in Table 4.7. A summary of their most representative functions are given in Table 4.17

Vertical Classification

On the other hand, the AAL can also be divided vertically, into SAR sublayer and CS. That is, the process of converting *user-service data units* (U-SDU) into ATM cells executed by the AAL is divided into two sublayers. The SAR provides the functions associated with the segmentation and reassembly of U-SDUs, and the CS provides the capability for converging specified service-related functions to an upper service layer.

In the direction of transmission, the CS accepts U-SDUs from an upper user layer, to which it adds a header and trailer related to error handling and data priority preservation to create the SAR-PDUs, which are then sent to the ATM layer. In the direction of reception, the SAR sublayer analyzes the SAR-PDUs transported from

---

[51]AAL-5 is additionally being considered by the T1 Committee as a means to support a simple and fast transport of the existing transfer protocols.

Table 4.17
Major Functions of AAL-1 through AAL-4

AAL Type	Major Functions
AAL-1	Transfer of constant bit rate SDU with the same bit rate
	Transfer of timing information between source and destination
	Error recovery and indication of errored information which is not recovered by AAL-1
AAL-2	Transfer of SDU with variable bit rate
	Transfer of timing information between source and destination
	Error recovery and indication of errored information which is not recovered by AAL-2
AAL-3	Transfer of class C service SDU from AAL-SAP to AAL-SAP(s)
	Transfer by connection-oriented mode
AAL-4	Transfer of class D service SDU from AAL-SAP to AAL-SAP(s)
	Transfer of connectionless mode

the ATM layer, and the SAR-PDUs are collected and assembled together with the CS-PDUs and delivered to the CS. Then the CS analyzes the header and trailer of the transported CS-PDUs and extracts just the U-SDUs, finally delivering them to the upper user layer. Interentity protocols such as flow control are also handled at the CS. The handling procedures are conceptually illustrated in Figure 4.28. Such vertical classification applies equally to all four AAL types.

4.11.3 AAL-1 Functions

The delivery of constant-rate U-SDUs, along with the associated timing information using a common bit rate, and the indication of uncorrectable errors are some of the services that AAL-1 provides to the upper layers. AAL-1 provides a function for partitioning and reassembling user information. It also provides a function for handling cell delay variations and lost and inserted cells, and enables the receiver to extract timing information from the information source. As a provision against possible bit errors, AAL-1 monitors the *protocol control information* (PCI) and processes the AAL-PCI when the error does occur. Also, it monitors the user information field and corrects any bit errors found.

The AAL-1 reports to the management plane any error found during the transmission of user information. Lost cells, misinserted cells, and cells with errored AAL-PCIs are also reported, as well as the time synchronization status.

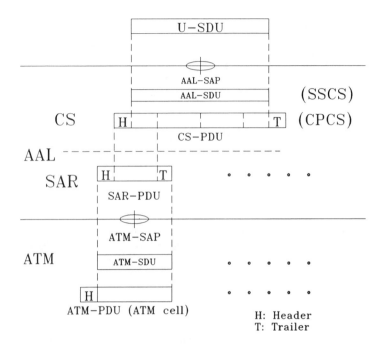

Figure 4.28 Processing of data at AAL sublayer.

SAR Sublayer

The function of AAL-1's SAR sublayer is to segment the CS-PDUs and then add a header to form the SAR-PDUs and send them to the ATM layer. Also, through a reverse process it reassembles the SAR-PDUs to recover the CS-PDU. An SAR-PDU formed at the SAR sublayer is as shown in Figure 4.29. The number of bits assigned to *sequence number* (SN) and *sequence number protection* (SNP) is four each, including one *convergence sublayer indication* (CSI) bit in the SN field; consequently, the size of SAR-PDU payload space becomes 47 bytes. SN is used for inspecting whether a cell loss or cell insertion has occurred, and the SNP is used for error correction in order to protect SN from errors. The CSI bit is used for special purposes such as indicating the presence of the CS function.

Convergence Sublayer

The AAL-1 CS provides bit error correction capability for high-quality video or audio signals, and, depending on the service, it can also provide clock recovery capability through such methods as monitoring the buffer fill. The services that require timing

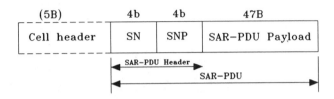

SN: Sequence number

SNP: Sequence number protection

Figure 4.29 SAR-PDU format for AAL-1.

elucidation can be satisfied by inserting timing information into the CS-PDU.[52] Other functions such as sequence number processing and treatment of lost/misinserted cells are also provided.

4.11.4 AAL-2 Functions

AAL-2 delivers real-time U-SDUs in variable bit rates along with the associated timing information, indicates unrecoverable errors, and provides other such services to the upper layers.

AAL-2, similar to AAL-1, provides a function for segmenting and reassembling user information. It also provides the capability for handling cell delay variations, treating lost or misinserted cells, and, at the receiving end, the capability for recovering the information source clock. As a measure against possible bit errors, AAL-2 monitors the AAL-PCI and treats any bit error that occurs. It also monitors the user information field and corrects any bit errors found.

AAL-2, similar to AAL-1, reports to the management plane any error generated during the transmission of user information. Lost cells, misinserted cells, and cells of AAL-PCI which have acquired errors are also indicated, as well as the timing synchronization loss status.

SAR Sublayer

The function of AAL-2's SAR sublayer is to segment variable CS-PDUs received from the CS, add a header and trailer to create the SAR-PDUs, send the SAR-PDUs

---

[52]The most fundamental problem that emerges when the real-time continuous signals are transferred in the ATM cell format is the delivery of the timing, or synchronization, information. This subject will be treated in detail in Section 4.12.

to the ATM layer, and, through a reverse process, reassemble SAR-PDUs and recover the CS-PDUs. Since AAL-2 treats real-time services as AAL-1 does, the SAR-PDU structure of AAL-2 is expected to be similar to the one in Figure 4.28.[53]

Convergence Sublayer

AAL-2 CS provides clock restoration capability for variable rate video and audio signals. For this purpose, a timing stamp or real-time synchronization word can be inserted into the CS-PDUs, and other methods can be used as well. The AAL-2 CS also processes sequence numbers in order to monitor whether any ATM-PDU has been lost or misinserted. If any lost or misinserted cell is found, it applies an appropriate measure. The AAL-2 CS also provides error correction for video and audio signals.

4.11.5 AAL-3 Functions

AAL-3's function is to establish an adaptation layer connection prior to the transmission, then transport class C service data with VBR characteristic. The services provided at AAL-3 can be divided into message-mode services and stream-mode services. In the message mode, an AAL-SDU passes across the AAL interface in exactly one AAL-IDU (interface data unit), while, in the streaming mode, it does so in one or more AAL-IDUs. Here, an internal pipelining function can be applied, and an AAL entity can initiate data transfer to the receiving AAL entity before it has the complete AAL-SDU available.

The above two service modes both provide assured operation and nonassured operation. The assured operation is the operation mode in which all the SDU's are accurately delivered in the order they are received from the ATM layer, lost or corrupted cells are retransmitted, and flow control is provided by necessity. The assured operation applies only to point-to-point ATM layer connections. In nonassured operation, lost or corrupted cells are not retransmitted. When need arises, damaged SDUs are transported to upper layers, and flow control capability is provided for point-to-point ATM connections, although not for point-to-multipoint connections.

SAR Sublayer

The AAL-3 SAR sublayer receives variable-length CS-PDUs from the CS, segments and appends a header and trailer to form the SAR-PDUs, which are then sent to the ATM layer. It can also reassemble SAR-PDUs through a reverse of the process and recover the CS-SDUs.

---

[53]Specifics on AAL-2 are under study by CCITT.

The structure of the SAR-PDU of AAL-3 is shown in Figure 4.30. In the figure, the *segment type* (ST) indicates whether the corresponding payload is BOM (Begin of Message), COM (Continuation of Message), EOM (End of Message), or SSM (Single Segment Message), and SN indicates the serial number of each message. The MID field is used when multiple CPCS (see the CS section) connections are multiplexed through one ATM layer connection, LI indicates the length of the SAR-PDU payload in octets, and CRC is the CRC code for the entire SAR-PDU including the header.

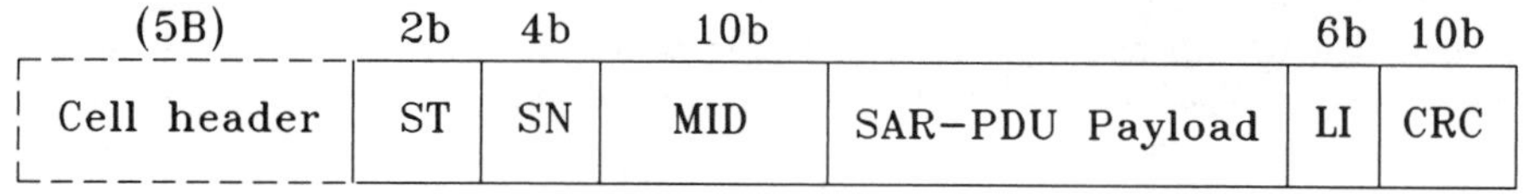

(5B)	2b	4b	10b		6b	10b
Cell header	ST	SN	MID	SAR–PDU Payload	LI	CRC

CRC : Cyclic Redundancy Check code

ST : Segment Type   MID : Multiplexing Identification

SN : Sequence Number   LI : Length Indicator

Figure 4.30 SAR-PDU format for AAL-3/4.

Convergence Sublayer

The AAL-3 CS provides various functions for AAL-3 service users, including transparent delivery of AAL-SDUs, mapping between AAL-SAP and ATM layer connections, error detection and treatment (CS-PDU damage detection and appropriate treatment procedure), message segmentation and reassembly, information identification, and buffer allocation. The AAL-3 CS also provides special functions specific to class C AAL-3 services.

Since both AAL-3 and AAL-4 handle non-real-time data services, they share various functions in common. Hence, the CS functions of AAL-3 and AAL-4 can be rearranged into the *common part CS* (CPCS) and the *service-specific CS* (SSCS) (see Figure 4.28). The CPCS is thus common to AAL-3 and AAL-4, but SSCS differs in each case.

The structure of the CPCS-PDU is as shown in Figure 4.31. In the figure, CPI indicates whether the corresponding PDU belongs to a common part, B/Etag is a tag attached to the header and trailer of a CPCS-PDU to be identical, BAsize indicates the size of buffer to be allocated in the receiver, PAD is a pad to create a

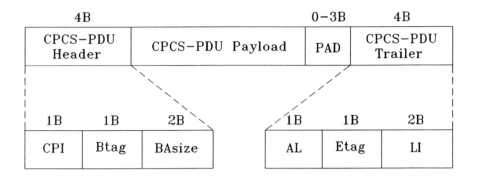

CPI : Common Part Indicator
Btag : Begin tag   AL : Alignment
BAsize : Buffer Allocation Size   Etag : End tag
PAD : Padding   LI : Length Indication

Figure 4.31 CPCS-PDU structure.

CPCS-PDU payload sized in multiples of 4 bytes, LI indicates the length of CPCS-PDU payload, and AL is a filler to make the CPCS-PDU trailer size 32 bits.

4.11.6 AAL-4 Functions

AAL-4 provides the capability for transporting variable rate class D service data at the adaptation layer without establishing a connection. Similar to AAL-3, AAL-4 provides both message-mode and streaming-mode services. Also, the services can be provided in assured or nonassured operation.

AAL-4 also provides the capability for delivering AAL-SDUs from a single AAL-SAP to a single AAL-SAP, or from a single AAL-SAP to multiple AAL-SAPs. Here, the former case is associated with the point-to-point AAL connections, and the latter corresponds to the point-to-multipoint connections. This relationship is depicted in Figure 4.32. In the transport of AAL-SDUs, AAL-4 users have an option to select those AAL-SAPs possessing the necessary QOS.

As shown in Figure 4.33, AAL-4 uses the services provided by the ATM layer. Multiple AAL connections are possible for a single ATM connection, and for this purpose the multiplexing capability is allowed at the AAL. As can be seen from the

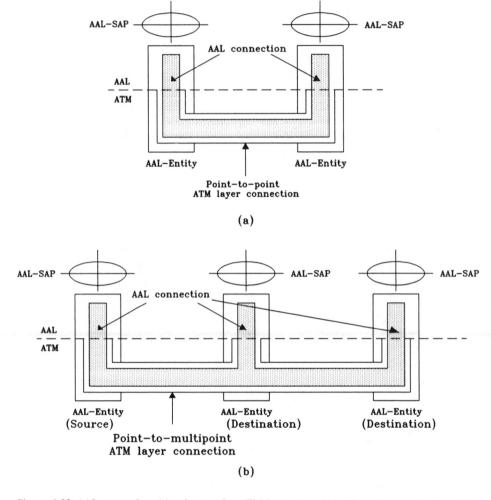

Figure 4.32 AAL connection: (a) point-to-point ATM layer connection; (b) point-to-multipoint ATM layer connection.

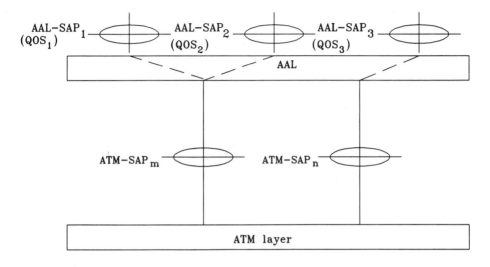

Figure 4.33 Relation between AAL-SAP and ATM-SAP.

figure, the user can choose AAL-SAP$_1$ at the time of data delivery, and thus has the power to choose the associated QOS$_1$.

Segmentation and Reassembly Sublayer

The functions of AAL-4's SAR sublayer are identical to those of AAL-3's sublayer, and the SAR-PDU structure of AAL-4 is as shown in Figure 4.30.

Convergence Sublayer

The AAL-4 CS provides various functions in support of AAL-4 service users. The particular function provided can vary depending on whether the service user operates in message mode or streaming mode. Associated functions include integrity of AAL-SDU (boundary detection of higher layer PDU and guarantee of its transparent delivery), mapping between AAL-SAPs and the ATM layer connections, error detection and treatment, message segmentation and reassembly, information identification, and buffer allocation. The AAL-4 CS, similar to the AAL-3 CS, can be divided into CPCS and SSCS, and the PDU structure of CPCS is as shown in Figure 4.31.

4.12 SOURCE CLOCK FREQUENCY RECOVERY

One of the important functions of the AAL for real-time services is the source clock frequency recovery at the receiver.[54] Due to the statistical nature of the ATM-based network, the ATM cells arriving at the destination will not be periodic, even in the case of CBR services. If the ATM-based network is asynchronous (i.e., different timing references for the nodes in the network), then the only information on the source clock frequency available at the receiver is the long-term average cell throughput. In this case, PLL can be used to regenerate the bit clock. However, if the ATM-based network is synchronous (i.e., the reference timings of the nodes are traceable to a single timing source), then it is possible to synchronize the transmission and service rate with the network timing. In this case, a synchronization pattern or time stamp can be used to solve the source clock frequency problem.

In this section, we examine the source clock frequency recovery methods in synchronous ATM-based networks. CBR timing recovery methods will be briefly discussed first, followed by a detailed description of the *synchronous residual time stamp* (SRTS) method. Lastly, source frequency clock recovery for the VBR services will be briefly considered.

4.12.1 CBR Timing Recovery Methods

For CBR timing recovery, two methods, the *synchronous frequency encoding technique* (SFET) and the *time stamp* (TS), have been introduced, which were later merged into the SRTS method.

The fundamental concept of SFET is that in a synchronous optical network, common clocks that are available at both the transmitter and receiver can be used as the timing reference. The source clock, which is asynchronous with respect to the network timing, is compared to the network clock, and the frequency difference information, together with the common network clock, is transmitted and then used to reconstruct the source clock at the receiver.

The TS method uses the common network clock and a 16-bit TS to convey source clock information. The TS is a 16-bit binary number representing the number of network clock cycles corresponding to a fixed number of service clock cycles. Since a common network clock is available at the receiver, the TS conveys necessary information for the reconstruction of the source clock. The TS was proposed to be carried in the CS overhead, which occurs once every 16 cells.

Each of the two methods has a mixture of advantages and disadvantages in terms of overhead efficiency and service adaptability. The advantage of SFET is that very little overhead is needed to convey the frequency difference information. The

---

[54]This section describes only the source clock frequency problems, so the reader may skip it without losing the overall continuity.

major concern in SFET, however, is that, for every new service, a new network-derived clock needs to be defined. The TS method can relax this constraint, but at the price of a larger overhead. These considerations have led to a solution based on a modified TS, referred to as the SRTS.

The SRTS method uses the *residual time stamp* (RTS) to measure and convey information on the frequency difference between a common reference clock derived from the network and a service clock. The same derived network clock is assumed to be available at both the transmitter and the receiver. The SRTS method is also capable of meeting the jitter requirements specified in CCITT Recommendations G.823 and G.824. This method will be described in detail in the following sections.

Aside from these three CBR timing recovery methods, there is an adaptive clock method. The adaptive clock method is a conventional method, widely used in existing terminals and the network. The receiver writes the received information into a buffer and then reads it with a local clock. The fill level of the buffer is used to control the frequency of the local network. The control is performed by continuously measuring the fill level around its medium position, and by using this information to drive the PLL, which provides the local clock. The fill level of the buffer may be maintained between two limits in order to prevent buffer overflow and underflow. Compared to the two previous methods, the adaptive clock method requires larger buffer size, but its response time is comparatively long.

4.12.2 Synchronous Residual Time Stamp Method

There are two clock frequencies involved in the SRTS method: the reference clock frequency, which is derived from the network frequency f_n, and the service frequency f_s, which depends on the service in question. The reference clock is required to be larger than or equal to the service clock, but smaller than or equal to twice the service clock or, equivalently, $f_s \leq f_r \leq 2f_s$. If the reference clock is derived from the network clock f_n such that

$$f_r = f_n/2^k \qquad (4.4)$$

for an integer k, then it is always possible to meet this requirement.

The fundamental idea of the SRTS method is to send to the receiver the information on the difference appearing between f_r and f_s. Since f_r is also available to the receiver, it is possible to determine f_s in the receiver based on the difference. As a time reference to measure the difference, we specify the period of RTS, which is T seconds long and which corresponds to N cycle time for the service clock f_s.

If M denotes the number of cycles the reference clock has during the RTS period, then

$$M = \frac{f_r}{f_s} N \tag{4.5}$$

So M is not an integer in most cases (see Figure 4.34). Let the integer part of M be M_q. Then M_q is actually made up of a nominal part and a residual part. The nominal part is obtained from the nominal value of f_r and is well known to the receiver also. The residual part conveys the frequency difference information and the quantization effect, which are unknown to the receiver. Therefore, the residual part is the information to be sent to the receiver for the delivery of the difference information.

The residual part of M_q is conveyed over the RTS, which is P bits long. The size P of RTS can be determined by considering the tolerance of the service clock f_s. If the tolerance of f_s is x, then the corresponding clock deviation y of the reference clock f_r has the expression

$$y = x \frac{f_r}{f_s} N \tag{4.6}$$

in view of (4.5) and Figure 4.34. Since the RTS should be capable of absorbing twice this deviation, it is necessary to choose the counter size P such that it meets

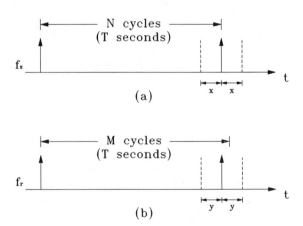

Figure 4.34 The principle of the SRTS method: (a) service clock; (b) reference clock.

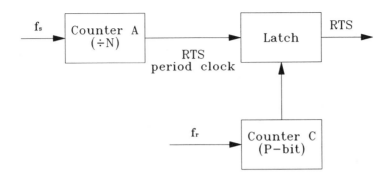

Figure 4.35 RTS generation process.

the relationship

$$2^{P-1} > 2\lceil y \rceil \tag{4.7}$$

where $\lceil y \rceil$ denotes the smallest integer larger than or equal to $\lceil y \rceil$.

The RTS can be generated using the process shown in Figure 4.35. In the figure, counter C is a P-bit counter which is continuously clocked by the reference clock f_r. The output of counter C is sampled every RTS period, and this period can be generated by counter A through the divide-by-N operation.

With a knowledge of the RTS and the nominal part of M_q, the value of M_q is completely determined at the receiver. This M_q can be used to produce the reference timing signal for a PLL to finally reconstruct the service clock.

For a practical application within the synchronous ATM network, we may choose f_n in (4.4) to be 155.52 MHz; N of 3,008, which corresponds to the number of bits in eight SAR-SDUs; tolerance x of 200 x 10^{-6}; and the size of RTS of four bits. The four RTS bits can be transmitted in the serial bit stream provided by four of the eight CSI bits in eight successive SAR-SDU headers (refer to CCITT Recommendation I.363 for a more detailed description of the CSI bit).

4.12.3 Source Clock Frequency Recovery for VBR Services

The aforementioned clock recovery methods, such as SFET, TS, SRTS, and adaptive clock methods are all for AAL type 1 CBR services. For AAL type 2 time-related VBR services, however, no fully reliable clock recovery methods are available yet. The CBR clock recovery methods can be modified for use in VBR environments, but the traffic characteristics of the VBR services are a critical factor for the modification. Since there is no fixed period or time reference in the cell stream of VBR services, the user must implant synchronization patterns within a layer above the

AAL to aid source clock frequency recovery. But the randomness of the VBR traffic characteristics again constrain the performance and applicability of this method. Figure 4.36 illustrates one possible arrangement to apply the SRTS method for VBR services, in which RTS carrying cells are accompanied by their indicating cells. The four indicating cells, starting with an even sequence number, indicate the location of the RTS carrying cells. It is important in this application to spread the traffic such that the minimum number of cells are guaranteed at all times.

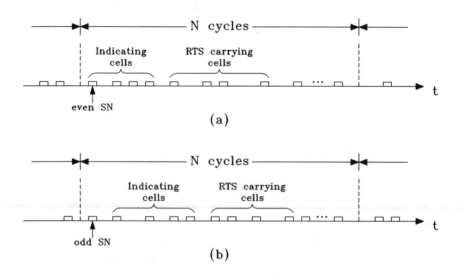

Figure 4.36 The illustration of SRTS for VBR services: (a) first cell with even SN; (b) first cell with odd SN.

4.13 NETWORK ASPECTS OF BISDN

In the present section, we will examine network configuration, signaling principles, traffic control, and resources management in BISDN.

4.13.1 Network Configuration

The BISDN is an ATM transport network, and can be layered into an ATM layer network, physical layer network, and higher layer network, as described in the preceding sections. The ATM layer network can be subdivided into the VC level and the VP level, and the physical layer network can be subdivided into the transmission path level, the digital section level, and the regenerator section level. Such layer and level divisions apply to both the SDH-based and cell-based networks. Layer relationships for the ATM transport network are indicated in Table 4.18 (see Section 4.9 for the discussion on VC and VP levels).

Table 4.18
Hierarchy of the ATM Transport Network

Layer	Level
ATM layer	Virtual channel level
	Virtual path level
Physical layer	Transmission path level
	Digital section level
	Regenerator section level

Virtual Channel Level

Virtual channel is a general term that signifies unidirectional communication capability to transport ATM cells. In ATM cells, the VC identifier is assigned visibly to each VC. VCI identifies a specific VC link contained in the VPC. A specific VC is assigned whenever VCs are switched within an ATM network. A VC link implies the unidirectional capability to transport ATM cells between two ATM entities at which VCI values get translated. A VC link is generated when the VCI values are assigned, and is terminated when the VCI values are removed. When a VCI value is assigned for a VC link at an interface, the same value is assigned for both directions of transmission.[55]

The routing function for the VC is performed at the VC switch. VC path mapping is accomplished by translating the VCI value of the incoming VC link into the VCI value of the output VC link. VC switching is depicted in Figure 4.24(a). The figure shows both VC and VP switching, and the upper portion corresponds to VC switching.

The VCC, as can be seen from Figure 4.8, is composed of a concatenation of VC links. The VCC is laid out between two VCC termination points, and in a point-to-multipoint configuration, more than two VCC termination points can exist. Here,

---

[55]Therefore, the routing field value (VCI + VPI) in one direction is also used for its opposite direction, and thus the VC links involved in the same communication can be easily identified. This is specified in CCITT Recommendation I.150 of June 1992.

VCC termination point implies a point at which a cell information field is switched between the ATM layer and the ATM layer service user.

At the VC level, the VCC is provided for user-to-user, user-to-network, and network-to-network information transfers. Here the sequence of the cells belonging to the same VCC are preserved by the ATM layer.

User-to-user VCCs are established between T_B or S_B reference points, and the ATM network elements transport all the cells associated with a given VCC through the same path. User-to-network VCCs are established between T_B or S_B reference points and the network nodes, and are used to link user equipment to network elements. Network-to-network VCCs are established between two network nodes and are employed for functions like network traffic management and routing.

Virtual Path Level

Virtual path implies a bundle of VC links, and here all the VC links in the bundle have the same termination point. In ATM cells, a VPI is assigned visibly for each VP. The VPI identifies a group of VC links sharing a common VPC. In an ATM network, a specified VPI value is assigned whenever VPs are switched. A VP link implies the capability for transporting ATM cells between a pair of ATM entities at which VPI values get translated. A VP link is generated when a VPI is assigned, and terminated when the VPI value is removed. When a VPI value is assigned for a VP link at an interface, the same value is assigned for both directions of transmission.

The routing function for VP is performed at the VP switch. VP routing is accomplished by translating the VCI value of the incoming VP link into the VPI value of the output VP link. VC switching is depicted in Figure 4.24(a,b).

As can be seen in Figure 4.8, the VPC is composed of a concatenation of VP links. The VPC is laid out between a pair of VPC termination points, and in the case of point-to-multipoint configuration, two or more VPC termination points can exist. Here, the VPC termination point is the point at which a VCI is generated, translated, or terminated.

At the VC level, the VPC is provided for user-to-user, user-to-network, and network-to-network information transfers. When a VC is switched, the VPC supported by the input VC link is first terminated, and the VPC supporting the output VC link is created anew. The cell sequence is preserved for VC links belonging to the same VPC.

The user-to-user VPC is set up between T_B or S_B reference points, and it provides VCC to users. ATM elements transport all of the associated cells through the same path. The corresponding VPI values are translated at the ATM network elements that provide the cross-connect or switching function. The user-to-network VPC is set up between T_B or S_B reference points and the network nodes, and it is used to link a group of user equipment to a network element. Network-to-network VPC is

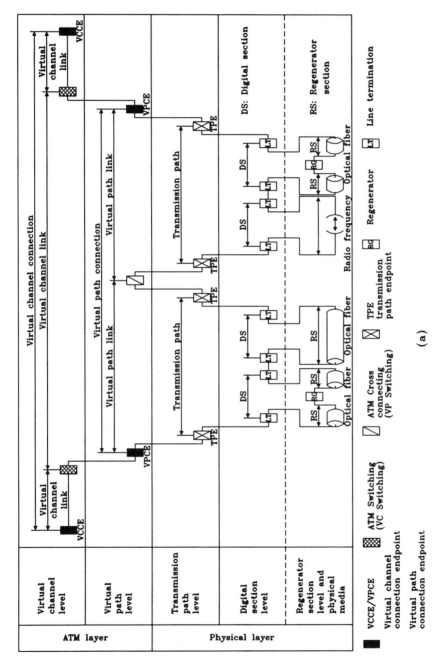

Figure 4.37 An example of various hierarchies in ATM transport networks: (a) cell-based transport network; (b) SDH-based transport network.

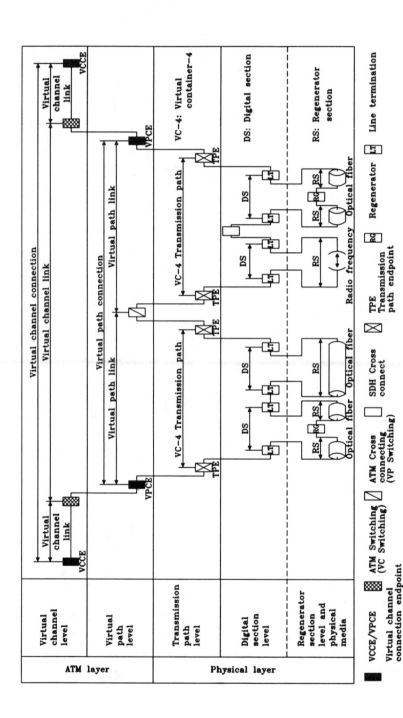

(b)

Figure 4.37 continued.

established between two network nodes, and its applications include network traffic management and routing. At the network node at which VPC is terminated, VCs inside one VP can be switched or cross-connected with VCs belonging to another VP (see Figure 4.24(a)).

Transmission Path Level

The transmission path is a path that joins together transmission path termination points at which the payloads of the transmission system are assembled or disassembled. The functions required at the transmission path termination points include functions for cell boundary identification and header error control. In SDH-based networks, transmission path implies the VC-4 transmission path, and in this case, the capability for mapping ATM cells into VC-4, or the opposite, is required as well.

Digital Section Level

The digital section is a section that joins line termination points at which continuous bit or byte streams are assembled or disassembled. In general, a single type of transmission medium is used inside a given digital section. In SDH-based networks, the digital section requires functions corresponding to the overheads located below the pointer in the STM frame structure (STM frame structure and overheads are discussed in Section 3.6). The SDH cross-connect for synchronous transmission corresponds to the switching function of the digital section level.

Regenerator Section Level

The regenerator section is a part of the digital section and joins together a line termination point and a regenerator, or two generators. In SDH-based systems, the regenerator section requires functions that correspond to the overheads located above the pointer in the STM frame structure.

In Figure 4.37, the concept of layer and level is illustrated in terms of an ATM transport network. In the figure, (a) illustrates the cell-based case, and (b) illustrates the SDH-based case. It can be inferred from the figure that the ATM switching (that is, VC switching) function belongs to the VC level, the ATM cross-connect (that is, VP switching) function to the VP level, and the SDH cross-connect function to the digital section level.

4.13.2 BISDN Signaling Principles

Diverse forms of services are provided in the BISDN; hence, in order to provide the associated call connections in an effective manner, signaling information is provided separately from the user information. That is, signaling information is transferred independently via signaling ATM cells. On the other hand, the metasignaling procedure can also be used for establishing VCs for signaling purposes.

Requirements for BISDN Signaling

First, the BISDN signaling scheme must be capable of controlling the ATM VCCs and VPCs for information transfer. This entails the capability for establishing, maintaining, and removing VCCs and VPCs, and providing semipermanent or permanent setup when required. Point-to-point, point-to-multipoint, and broadcast communication configurations must also be supported. It must also allow the negotiation of connection traffic parameters at the time of establishing connection, as well as renegotiation of the traffic parameters for the readily established connections.

Secondly, the BISDN signaling scheme must be capable of supporting simple multiparty and multiconnection calls. For this purpose, it must support symmetric or nonsymmetric simple calls and allow the possibility of establishing or removing multiconnections associated with a single call simultaneously. It should also allow the adding or removing of connections to or from a readily established call, or adding or removing groups. It should possess the ability to correlate connections making up a multiconnection call and to reconfigure a multiparty call or separate unspecified number of calls.

In addition, the capability to reconfigure readily established connections is required. Also, the accommodation of systems with different coding schemes must be supported, as well as the interworking with non-BISDN services.

Signaling Virtual Channel

For point-to-point signaling at the user-network interface, a single signaling VC in each direction is assigned at each signal termination point.[56] For selective broadcast signaling, a single signaling VCC is assigned for each service profile. (The service profile concept offers versatility in configuring broadcast signaling VC connections. The service profile is explained in CCITT Recommendation Q.932). In general broadcast signaling, a general broadcast signaling VCC is used irrespective of the service profile. For this purpose, fixed VPI and VCI values are assigned in advance (for VPI/VCI values used for general broadcast signaling VC, see Table 4.14).

---

[56]CCITT is studying whether the same VPI/VCI value should be assigned in both directions. It is also considering whether there should be one or multiple signal termination points per terminal.

Metasignaling

The metasignaling method can be used for setup, confirmation, and release of point-to-point and selective broadcast signaling VCC. Metasignaling implies the procedure of establishing a signaling VC. The metasignaling procedure is a layer management function that exists at the layer management plane, and is related only to the transfer of control information. Metasignaling is carried in a permanent VCC having fixed, preassigned VPI and VCI values.[57]

Metasignaling provides the capability for assigning signaling channel capacities, establishing and releasing signaling channels, and checking signaling status. It also provides a means to associate a call setup request with the corresponding service profile and to distinguish between any concurrent requests.

Signaling Configurations

Signaling can be configured in three possible ways, as illustrated in Figure 4.38. The first is the case in which a user utilizes a signaling procedure to establish a VCC with another user. Here, metasignaling is used to establish a signaling VC between the *customer equipment* (CEQ) and the CRF. The local CRF uses a VPI/VCI of the ATM cell header to provide an interconnection function.

The second is the case in which a user maintains a VPC connected to other nodes (local CRF, relay CRF, CEQ, etc.) via a local CRF. Here, VPC can be established without the signaling procedure by way of a reservation, or with the signaling procedure when required. When a VPC is established using a signaling procedure, metasignaling VC (used for establishing VPC) is used to establish signaling VC between CEQ and the local CRF. To establish VC links inside the VPC, the signaling procedure is applied between CEQ and the VPC termination node. The local CRF uses the VPI section of the ATM cell header to provide an interconnection function.

The third is the case in which the user maintains a VPC with other nodes through the local CRF, and maintains other VPCs for the purposes of providing a VC to other additional nodes. In this case, the CEQ uses metasignaling to establish the local CRF and signaling VC, which are used to establish a VPC or VCC with other nodes. The local CRF provides an interconnection function, using only the VPI of the ATM cell header section for the VPCs that do not terminate at the local CRF, and using both the VPIs and VCIs for the VPCs that terminate at the local CRF.

---

[57]CCITT is currently studying details that relate to metasignaling. For VPI/VCI values used for metasignaling VC, see Table 4.14.

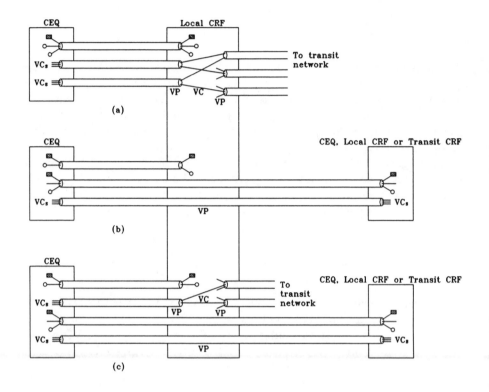

CRF : Connection Related Functions
CEQ : Customer Equipment

Figure 4.38 Signaling configurations and VPC/VCC establishment: (a) VCC establishment at local CRF; (b) VPC establishment at local CRF; (c) both VPC and VCC establishment at local CRF.

4.13.3 Traffic Control and Resources Management

The BISDN uses the ATM to accommodate various traffic types, thus satisfying various performance requirements demanded by the user and the network.[58] For this purpose, the ATM network provides several traffic control capabilities, such as CAC, UPC/*network parameter control* (NPC), PC, and CC.

---

[58]Details on traffic control are explained separately in Section 4.14.

Connection Admission Control

CAC is the measure adopted in order to determine at the call setup stage whether to grant or refuse the corresponding connection. As an outcome of CAC, if sufficient resources exist to accept the call request, and if it becomes clear that the call assignment does not affect the performance quality of the existing network services, then the call connection is granted. In a BISDN environment, it is sometimes necessary to establish more than one connection in order to set up a call, in which case CAC must deal with each VC and VPC separately.

At the time of call setup, the user requesting the call setup must use a signaling message to present the characteristics of the user traffic and the QOS required. In the case of reserved services or permanent connection services, this information can be indicated through an appropriate OAM procedure. CAC uses this information to decide whether to grant or to refuse the connection, determines the traffic characteristics for usage parameter control, and allocates network resources.

When the traffic characteristics are prescribed, such parameters as the service's average rate, peak rate, burstiness, and peak rate duration must be considered.[59] At the time of establishing the call, the user negotiates with the network to select the desired traffic characteristics. These characteristics are renewable upon the user's request during the duration of the call connection.

Usage Parameter Control/Network Parameter Control

With UPC/NPC, the network monitors and supervises the user traffic from the standpoint of the traffic volume and cell path validity, with the purpose of preventing damage of the network resources from malicious or unintended mistakes. That is, it helps monitor whether the user's traffic parameter exceeds the value negotiated at the time of call establishment and applies appropriate measures. Connection monitoring encompasses all connections crossing the UNI or internetwork interfaces. UPC and NPC apply to both user VCCs/VPCs and signaling virtual channels.

UPC/NPC checks whether the VCP/VCI values are valid. It also monitors the traffic volume associated with VP and VC and the access link's total traffic volume. Consequently, the UPC algorithm must be equipped with the capability to monitor illegal traffic conditions, discriminate between whether or not the confirmed parameter exceeds the specified range limits, and cope quickly with parameter usage violations, as well as be simple to implement. Here, the usage parameter can be a part or all of the traffic characteristic parameters used for CAC.

The UPC is executed at the access point's VP or VC and can occur at three different locations, as illustrated in Figure 4.39. First, in case the user is directly

---

[59]Details on traffic characteristic parameters are being studied by CCITT.

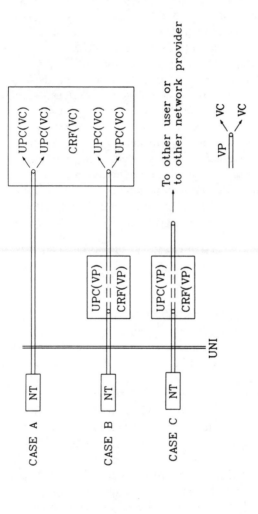

Figure 4.39 Location of the usage parameter control function.

NT : Network Termination
CRF: Connection Related Function

CRF(VC): Virtual Channel Connection Related Function
CRF(VP): Virtual Path Connection Related Function

connected to the CRF (VC), UPC is executed at the CRF (VC) (or VCCs) before the switching function. Second, in case the user is connected to the CRF (VC) via the CRF (VC), UPC is executed within the CRF (VC) on VCCs only and inside the CRF (VP) on VPCs only. Third, when the user is connected to other users or to another network provider via the CRF (VP), the UPC is executed at the CRF (VP) on VPCs only. VCC UPC will be done by another network provider when CRF (VC) is present.

NPC can be executed at three possible locations, as illustrated in Figure 4.40. First, in case the originating network is connected directly to the CRF (VC), NPC is executed at the CRF (VC) before the switching function. Second, in case the originating network is connected to the CRF (VC) via the CRF (VP), NPC is executed at the CRF (VP) on VPCs only before the VP switching function, and within the CRF (VC) on VCCs only before the switching function. Third, when the originating network is connected to the user or another network provider via CRF (VP), NPC is executed at the CRF (VP) on VPCs only. VCC NPC is performed by another network provider when CRF (VC) is present.

If a parameter usage violation is identified as a result of UPC, several measures can be applied. The simplest is to discard the cells in question. Other methods that can be considered include indicating the violator cells and removing the connection that contains the violator cells.

Priority Control

Users can employ the CLP bit to create traffic flows of many different priorities. On that basis, or using other methods, the ATM network can conduct traffic priority control.[60]

Congestion Control

Congestion refers to the situation in which the negotiated QOS can no longer be guaranteed by the network elements due to overloads in traffic or in control resources. Congestion can arise when the traffic flow changes unpredictably, or when defects appear in the network. The preventive measure applied to the network elements to alleviate the congestion effects and keep them from spreading to the rest of the network is called *congestion control*. Some of the possible congestion control methods are to reflect congestion conditions on CAC, to force the network to rearbitrate user parameters, and to allocate resources more expeditiously.[61]

---

[60]The related details are under study by CCITT.
[61]Specifics of congestion control are under study by CCITT.

340

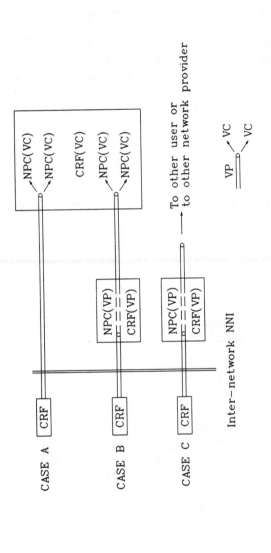

Figure 4.40 Location of the network parameter control function.

4.14 TRAFFIC CONTROL IN BISDN

The advantages of ATM lie in the efficient use of network resources and the flexibility to support various services.[62] But if these points are to be taken advantage of, the problems of traffic control and network resource management must be solved.

Traffic control has already been extensively studied in existing low-speed packet communication networks. But in these cases, the high QOS required by the anticipated BISDN services and the enormous size of the area over which services must be extended were not taken into account. Further, the transmission rate in the BISDN is high, but the speed of light for optical communication is a fixed constant. Therefore, the BISDN becomes latency-limited, while existing low-speed packet networks are bandwidth-limited. As a result, the window-based control mechanisms used in a large number of existing packet networks cannot be effectively used in controlling BISDN congestion. Another basic problem is that, in the BISDN, the traffic control problem will focus on preventing congestion rather than on dealing with it after it has occurred.[63]

In this section, we review the basic objectives of traffic control, resource management, and the reference model as defined by CCITT. Later, we examine the traffic parameters that specify a service's statistical properties, and then review various traffic control methods that have been proposed for the BISDN.

4.14.1 Basic Concepts of Traffic Control and Resource Management

The three main objectives of traffic control and resource management in the BISDN are to protect the network from congestion, to achieve network performance objectives, and to optimize the use of network resources.

To understand the structure of traffic control in the BISDN, the procedures of call setup and release need to be understood. In the following, a simple view of these procedures will be given, with an emphasis on traffic control.

When a user wants to set up a call, first the traffic parameters representing the statistical characteristics of the source are passed to the network. Next, the network CAC unit decides whether the call may be accepted without affecting the QOS of other calls in progress. If a new call is to be accepted, a traffic contract is set up with the source. The network then decides on the path to be used by the call in

---

[62]This section is devoted to traffic control and resource management mechanisms for the BISDN; hence, the reader may skip it without losing the overall continuity.

[63]In the 1992 CCITT Recommendations, ATM layer traffic control is defined as "the set of actions taken by the network to avoid congestion conditions," and ATM layer congestion control is defined as "the set of actions taken by the network to minimize the intensity, spread, and duration of congestion." In this section, however, both ATM layer traffic control and ATM layer congestion control will be regarded as part of the general problem of traffic control in the BISDN.

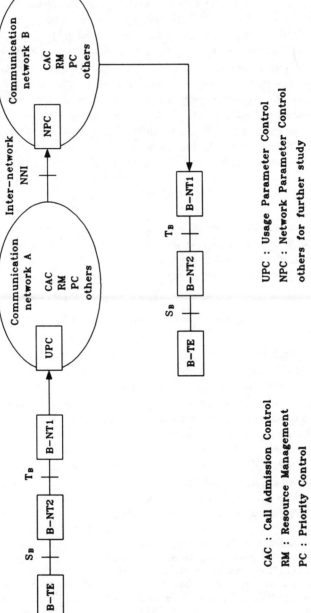

Figure 4.41 Reference configuration for traffic control and resource management.

sending its calls to their destination. (Depending on the actual call admitting procedure used, the path might be decided at call set-up time.) Once a call is connected, the source may send cells into the network at the rate specified in the traffic contract. The network monitors the traffic emitted from the source with a UPC algorithm at the UNI to make sure that the source is complying with its traffic contract. During this process, the network may allocate network resources in order to separate traffic flows according to service characteristics (resource management), or use feedback controls to control the traffic flow submitted to the network by the user. Also, the user may generate different priority traffic flows by using the CLP bit so that a congested network element may drop the cell if necessary (priority control).

Figure 4.41 shows the reference model for traffic control and resource management as defined by CCITT. CAC is performed over the entire network, while the UPC and NPC are located at the UNI and NNI, respectively.

4.14.2 Traffic Parameters

From a traffic control point of view, the only information needed when a call is set up in a synchronous network is the maximum cell rate of the source. Consequently, the call setup procedure is relatively simple, but there is a corresponding waste of bandwidth.

To increase bandwidth efficiency, the concept of statistical multiplexing is used in ATM. Statistical multiplexing aims to support services with less bandwidth than the sum of their peak rates (the amount of bandwidth used in synchronous networks). This can be achieved if a sufficient number of the statistical characteristics of the source traffic is known so that effective traffic control mechanisms can be implemented.

A traffic parameter as defined by CCITT is a specification of a particular traffic aspect of a source. An ATM descriptor is the generic list of traffic parameters which can be used to capture the intrinsic traffic characteristics of an ATM connection, while a source traffic descriptor is a set of traffic parameters used in the traffic contract negotiation between the user and the network to describe the traffic characteristics of the connection requested by the source. An example of a traffic descriptor would be {mean cell rate, maximum cell rate, average burst length}. These parameters individually describe some aspect of the source traffic, while the set describes the traffic characteristics of the source as a whole.

Traffic parameters must satisfy various conditions.[64] First, they must be understandable to the user or user terminal so that conformance should be possible. Second, the parameters should participate in resource allocation schemes for meeting network performance requirements. Third, these parameters should be enforceable by the UPC and NPC.

---

[64]In the 1992 CCITT recommendations, only the peak cell rate traffic parameter is defined. Other traffic parameters will be added in future recommendations.

If a number of sources are multiplexed, the individual characteristics get diluted; that is, characteristics measured in the network will be different from the original source traffic characteristics. So if the parameters are to be meaningful, the reference points for the definition of the parameters should be as close to the source as possible. Therefore, the traffic parameters should be defined at the ATM-SAP or somewhere in the ATM plane before multiplexing with other traffic takes place.

4.14.3 Traffic Control Methods

If congestion occurs anywhere in the network, the network QOS is degraded, resulting in poor service for the user. The main goal of traffic control is to prevent this from happening and to cure it once it has occurred.

Traffic control methods can be mainly divided into two types. The first type, called *reactive control*, reacts to congestion after it has started or when signs of impending congestion are found. The second type of control mechanism, called *preventive control*, aims to prevent congestion from occurring from the beginning.[65]

In existing packet networks, control mechanisms of the reactive type have been used. But in the BISDN, the large propagation delays and high data rate of the various services may render reactive control methods ineffective. Because of this factor, preventive control mechanisms are expected to be the main method used in ATM networks, rather than reactive control mechanisms.[66]

Another way of dividing traffic control mechanisms is by the level at which they are exercised, such as cell level and call level control mechanisms. Examples of cell level mechanisms include UPC/NPC and buffer management. Examples of call level mechanisms include CAC and VC path routing. Another possible level of traffic control could be exercised at the VP level, resulting in the simplification of CAC and routing.

4.14.4 Cell Level Traffic Control and Resource Management

Cell level traffic control and resource management are largely involved with two interrelated areas. One is the maintenance of the QOS for individual calls, and the second area is the UPC/NPC functions.

---

[65]In the 1992 CCITT recommendations, preventive control functions correspond to the ATM layer traffic control functions, while the reactive control functions correspond to the ATM layer congestion control functions.

[66]It has been shown in recent studies that if only preventive methods such as CAC-UPC are used, network performance will not be satisfactory. So the possibilities of using reactive mechanisms have also been actively studied. As a result, in CCITT Recommendation I.371 of June 1992, the use of *explicit forward congestion notification* (EFCN) was recommended. While the methods for realizing EFCN are well defined in the recommendation, it is also implicitly recognized that the network operator should not rely on this mechanism to effectively control congestion, since the use of this mechanism by CEQ is optional.

For the maintenance of QOS, priority mechanisms can be used. For example, the CLP bit in the cell header may be used to mark cells that may be lost when congestion occurs. Cell delay and cell loss rate are the main factors contributing to the QOS of individual calls. Both of these factors are affected by the type of buffer management scheme employed by the network. There are basically two approaches to buffer management. One approach, shown in Figure 4.42(a), is to use a different buffer for each priority level and to use a polling scheme to decide which cell should be transmitted. There are various possible polling schemes, among which the simplest is to always transmit the highest priority cell currently waiting in any buffer. Another type of buffer management scheme is to use a common buffer for all cells. All received cells are put into the buffer irrespective of priority. If the buffer is filled beyond a certain limit, the high-priority cells may suffer long delays or high cell loss rates, so an algorithm must be developed to control the delays and loss suffered by high-priority cells. One method, called the pushout scheme, is shown in Figure 4.42(b). When the buffer is full due to congestion, a newly received cell is dropped if it is of low priority. If the new cell is of high priority, then a lower priority cell already in the buffer is dropped to make space for the high-priority cell.

The UPC/NPC function is a mechanism for monitoring the traffic from a source to make sure that its parameters, such as the average cell rate, are within the limits set in the traffic contract. UPC is a function performed by the network that must be located as close to the user as possible. Consequently, UPC functions are located at the UNI, and by the same reasoning, NPC functions are located at the NNI.

Traffic parameters are defined as close to the user as possible, while the UPC/ NPC function occurs at the entrance to the network. But as the information cells of each traffic source are multiplexed by the GFC protocol in the CPN, and later on in the physical layer, the delay suffered by each individual cell in each case differs. This is called *cell delay variation* (CDV). Due to this, it can happen that even though a source is emitting traffic within the bounds set in the traffic contract, traffic flow of the source at the UPC may be declared to be noncomplying. This problem is yet to be solved.

A common example of the UPC/NPC algorithm is the "leaky bucket" method. The most basic form of it uses a token generator which generates tokens periodically. The tokens go into a token pool, and whenever a cell is transmitted a token is used from the pool. By controlling the size of the pool and token generation rate, various traffic parameters may be controlled. Leaky bucket is a simple algorithm which is easy to implement, and, by controlling the two parameters (pool size and token generation rate), an effective UPC function may be effected (see Figure 4.43).

Another example of the UPC/NPC algorithm is one which checks the number of cells transmitted during a constant interval called the *window*. At call setup, two numbers T and X are defined. X is the number of cells allowed to be transmitted during the interval T. This is also a simple method to implement, and by using different pairs of (T, X), various traffic parameters may be controlled.

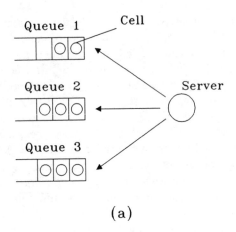

(a)

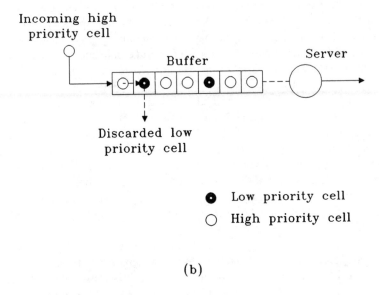

(b)

Figure 4.42 Example of cell-based control: (a) polling method; (b) push-out method.

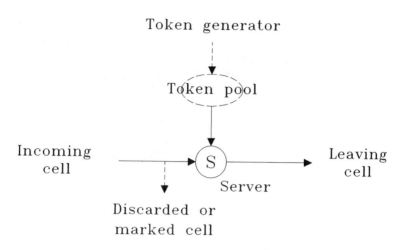

Figure 4.43 Example of UPC/NPC: "leaky bucket" method.

4.14.5 Call Level Traffic Control and Resource Management

The main examples of call level traffic control and resource management are CAC and VC routing. CAC is an algorithm which, following a call request, decides whether a call may be accepted while maintaining the QOS of existing calls. CAC is also involved with the call level QOS by way of the call blocking probability. By taking into account the current state of the network when a VC is routed, congestion may be prevented. Also, by rerouting calls passing through congested areas, congestion can be more quickly relieved and the spread of congestion may be blocked.

In all CAC algorithms a criterion is needed for deciding whether a cell should be accepted. One type of criterion could be based on the cell level QOS as follows.

The bandwidth of an ATM link is defined as W. It is assumed that for every service type i, n_i $(i = 1, \dots , k)$ calls are in service and that the cell level QOS is expressed as a function of the network state. An example of a QOS function would be the cell loss rate function. This is a function of the number of each type of call in progress and the ATM link bandwidth. Generally, it would be different for each type of service, and it would consequently have the following form: $f_i (W:n_1, n_2, \dots , n_k)$. If we assume that the call connection state is $(n_1, n_2, \dots , n_k)$, the following decision inequality must be true for each $i = 1, 2, \dots , k$.

$$f_i(W:n_1, n_2, \dots , n_k) < P_i(i = 1, 2, \dots , k) \tag{4.8}$$

In this expression, P_i is the cell loss rate demanded by the service i, and if this equation is true for each i, the cell loss rate of each service is within acceptable bounds. The set of possible call connection states $(n_1, n_2, \ldots, n_k)$ satisfying the above equation for each i may be called the *admissible call connection* set. In the end, all CAC algorithms are a way of deciding whether, if a new call is connected, the resulting new call connection state would be inside the admissible call connection set (Figure 4.44 illustrates the admissible set) for the case where there are only two types of services.

Based on the above method of evaluating the decision inequality, CAC algorithm may be divided into two types. The first type evaluates the decision inequality more or less directly for each new cell, while the second type of method decides indirectly whether (4.8) is satisfied.

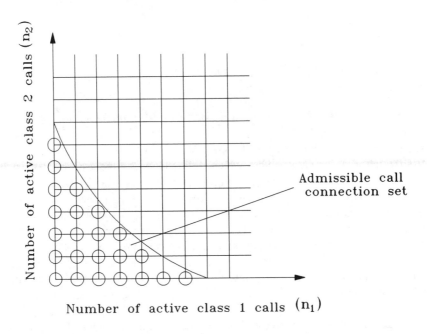

Figure 4.44 Example of admissible call connection set (2 classes of services).

Direct Method

In this method, every time a call request is received, the decision inequality is evaluated for the new call connection state. If this method is to be effective, fast and efficient methods for computing the QOS function are needed. Consequently, methods of this type invariably make assumptions to simplify the complexity involved in evaluating the decision inequality. For example, instead of evaluating the cell loss probability of a finite buffer queue, the probability of the queue length in an infinite-length queue growing larger than the size of the original finite buffer is calculated. Another example of simplification is the use of a simple traffic model, such as an on-off-type source model, instead of more accurate but probably more complex models.

Indirect Method

CAC methods of the indirect type usually use a look-up table, where the various parameter values needed in the CAC algorithm are stored. The execution time compared to the direct method is usually much shorter, and as the values stored in the look-up table are evaluated beforehand, these can usually be derived from much more accurate but complex models and methods. Indirect methods usually do not decide whether the QOS condition may be satisfied directly. Instead, another criterion is used.

Various criteria for the decision are possible, but here we only explain the method employing the concept of effective bandwidth. In this method, the criterion used for the decision is the amount of bandwidth needed by the new call connection state to satisfy QOS requirements. Since the real amount of bandwidth needed changes dynamically with time and will not be equal to any fixed value, we name this nominal bandwidth the *effective bandwidth*. Whenever a new call request arrives, the amount of effective bandwidth needed to satisfy QOS requirements may be defined as V. If the following inequality is satisfied, the call is established.

$$V(n_1, n_2, \ldots, n_k) < W \tag{4.9}$$

Here n_i denotes the number of calls of type i in progress, and W is the ATM link bandwidth. This equation means that the effective bandwidth needed to satisfy QOS requirements is less than the actual bandwidth of the ATM link.

The main problem is in calculating this effective bandwidth. The easiest method would be to designate the effective bandwidth as the peak rate, but this is the same as in the case of circuit-switched networks, and there would be no statistical multiplexing gain. Another method would be to calculate $V(n_i)$ separately for each n_i and approximate $V(n_1, n_2, \ldots, n_k)$ as follows:

$$V(n_1, n_2, \ldots, n_k) = V(n_1) + \ldots V(n_k) \tag{4.10}$$

Since this method does not take into account the statistical multiplexing effect among different types of sources, it cannot be said to be optimal.

If this method is used, various possibilities exist for approximating $V(n_i)$. One method would be to use a Gaussian model based on the mean and variance of the traffic source. Another method would be to calculate the minimum bandwidth needed for each source type i to satisfy the following inequality:

$$f_i(Z, n_i) < \min P_j (j = 1, 2, \ldots, k) \qquad (4.11)$$

In the expression, $f_i(Z, n_i)$ is the QOS function of service type i, P_j is the service type j's QOS requirement, and Z denotes the bandwidth needed for each source type.

The CAC algorithms explained above were mostly based on building and analyzing a mathematical model. But there are other methods for deciding whether a call should be admitted based on the continuous monitoring of the network state. An example would be a learning algorithm implemented with a neural network.

For some types of traffic sources, the CAC algorithms of the type mentioned above may be ineffective. For example, computer terminals engaged in file transfer are basically an on-off-type source, but at call setup time the average active time is not usually known. Consequently, various traffic parameters such as the mean cell rate may be basically unpredictable. These types of sources have more or less unpredictable distributions, so any fixed bandwidth allocated at call setup time would be meaningless unless it was the peak rate. For these services, a different CAC algorithm such as the *fast reservation protocol* (FRP) is needed which can allocate bandwidth dynamically as the call progresses. FRP initially allocates only a small amount of bandwidth to a source. When the source needs more bandwidth, it sends a request to the network for more bandwidth. When bandwidth is allocated, the source may transmit data at the higher rate; but until it is notified of the allocated bandwidth, the source must continue to transmit at the previous bandwidth. When the bandwidth is no longer needed, it may also be disallocated.

4.14.6 Virtual Path Level Traffic Control and Resource Management

Traffic control and resource management at the VP level have not been studied enough for them to be put into a fixed form, but the possibilities for the use of VPs are being actively studied. For example, instead of applying CAC to each link of a VC, CAC may be applied on the basis of VPCs setup beforehand. This would result in the simplification of CAC and VC routing operations. Priority control may also be applied on a VP basis. Another simplification would be in the case when congestion notification could be accomplished on a VP basis instead of for each VC individually.

4.15 BASIC PRINCIPLES OF OAM

The BISDN's OAM function must possess capability for performance monitoring, defect and failure detection, system protection, failure of performance information transfer, fault location inspection, and so on. As a systematic way to meet the above requirements, OAM information flow is assigned and monitored at every network level. In this section, we will examine the basic principles associated with the network OAM.

4.15.1 Principles of OAM

The BISDN OAM function is divided into five stages as follows.

The first is to monitor either continuously or periodically all the entities managed by the network in order to verify their normal operation. As a result of such a performance monitoring, maintenance event information can be generated. The second is to detect malfunction conditions through a continuous or a periodic inspection. As a result of defect detection, maintenance event information or various alarms can be generated. The third is to minimize the effect of the failure of the managed entity by blocking it or replacing it. As a result of such system protection measures, the failed entity is excluded from operation. The fourth is to deliver performance information or impairment information to other management entities. As a result, alarm indications can be delivered to other management planes, and a report on the ongoing status can be given. The fifth is to use an internal or an external test system to determine the impaired entity if the given impairment information proves insufficient. As a result of such impairment location determinations, the impaired entity can be isolated or replaced.

4.15.2 OAM Levels and OAM Information Flows

In order to perform the OAM function in a systematic manner, the OAM function itself can be divided into five OAM hierarchical levels. This is identical to the division which was made in terms of levels in Section 4.13.1. As a result, the OAM function is represented by five information flows: F1, F2, F3, F4, and F5, as shown in Figure 4.8. Because such a division is not always necessary, in case one of the levels is omitted, its respective OAM function can be performed by an upper level.

The OAM function associated with each level is independent of that of other levels. In order for a level to obtain information on performance quality and condition, it has to perform the necessary procedure itself. The result is delivered to the management plane, and also to the next higher level as the occasion arises. However, the higher-order layer function is not separately required to support the lower-order layer's OAM.

Physical Layer OAM Flows

The physical layer encompasses the regenerator section level, the digital section level, and the transmission path level, and the information flows can be defined as F1, F2, and F3, respectively. The method of providing the OAM function required to generate an OAM flow for each case depends on the particular physical layer transmission technique chosen.

In SDH-based transmission, F1 is conveyed via RSOH, F2 via MSOH, and F3 via POH. Parts of F3 are sometimes transported using physical layer OAM cells.

In the cell-based case, the multiplexer section is not applicable; consequently, OAM information flow F2 does not exist. Both F1 and F3 are conveyed via the physical layer's OAM cells, and the headers are assigned with the bit patterns indicated in Table 4.10. These physical layer OAM cells are not sent up to the ATM layer.[67]

The physical layer's OAM cells are inserted repeatedly into the ATM cell flow. Here, the insertion of physical layer cells must not hinder the transfer capability of the ATM layer. Consequently, the maximum frequency of physical layer OAM cells allowed is limited to 1 per 27 ATM cells. The minimum frequency possible is 1 physical layer OAM cell per 512 ATM cells.

In G.702's PDH-based transmission, the OAM flow is conveyed through the maintenance function possessed by the system (see Section 3.1.1 for more information on G.702 PDH). In this case, the capability to deliver OAM information other than bit messages is extremely limited.

ATM Layer OAM Flows

The ATM layer encompasses the information flows F4 and F5. Here, F4 and F5 are associated respectively with the VP level and the VC level. These information flows are delivered to the VPC and VCC using the cells that are responsible only for the ATM layer OAM function. These cells can also be used to achieve communication between peer layers residing in the same management plane.

The OAM information flow F4 provides, in support of the VPC OAM function, such capabilities as VPC alarm monitoring, VPC continuity check, and VPC performance monitoring. In case a VPC malfunction is detected at the VPC point, it sends VP-AIS in the direction of the downward termination point, and if a VP-AIS or a VPC malfunction is detected at the VP termination point, it sends VP-FERF in the upper direction. Also, in case no user information cells have been sent for a fixed duration of time, it creates and sends continuity check cells in order to verify the continuity of VPC. In addition, information relating to error blocking and cell loss/insertion is loaded onto the cells and delivered to the other party for the purpose of end-to-end monitoring.

In support of the VCC OAM function, the OAM information flow F5 provides such capabilities as VCC alarm monitoring, VCC continuity verification, and VCC performance monitoring. The details of their operation are analogous to those of F4.

---

[67]OAM cells are under study by CCITT.

4.15.3 OAM Functions

If the OAM flow of the BISDN user access is realized in terms of several physical configurations, then the result is as shown in Figure 4.45. As can be seen from the figure, F1 terminates at NT1 and the regenerator, F2 terminates at B-NT1, B-NT2, and L2, and F3 terminates at B-NT2, ET, and VP-XC. It can also be inferred that F4 terminates at B-NT2 and ET, and F5 at B-NT2 or B-TE.[68]

If physical layer OAM functions are divided according to each OAM flow type, then the result is as listed in Table 4.19 (refer to CCITT Recommendation I.610 for a more detailed explanation of Tables 4.19 and 4.20).In the table, the entries indicated with "S" and "C" represent SDH-based and cell-based transmissions, respectively, and "-" denotes the absence of any applicable data.[69] Also, PLOAM denotes the *physical layer OAM* and CN the *customer network* (for information on VC-4 and AU-4, which are mentioned in the table, see Chapter 3). The ATM layer's OAM functions are summarized in Table 4.20. In the table, AIS is the *alarm indication signal* which notifies the lower termination points that a failure has been perceived in the upward transmission flow. FERF is the *far-end receive failure*, which notifies the upward equipment that a malfunction has been perceived in the downward transmission flow.

Table 4.20
OAM Functions of the ATM Layer

Level	Function	Flow	Defect/Failure Detection	System Protection and Failure Information
Virtual path	Monitoring of path availability Performance monitoring	F4	Path not available Degraded performance	Under study
Virtual channel	Performance monitoring	F5	Degraded performance	Under study

4.16 ATM SWITCHING

The rapid pace of technological change has brought about fast switching system concepts.[70] These can be divided into two concepts: the *fast circuit switching* (FCS)

---

[68]The F5 OAM information flow that terminates at B-NT1 is currently under study by CCITT.

[69]The undetermined details which CCITT is currently studying are left as blanks in the table.

[70]This section concentrates on ATM switching only, so the reader may skip it without losing the overall continuity.

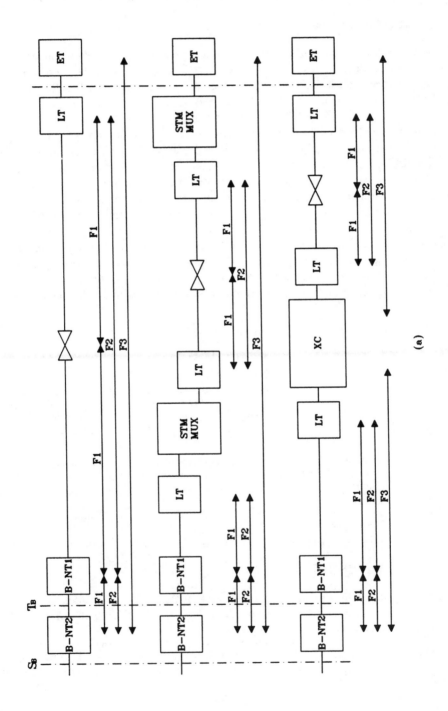

(a)

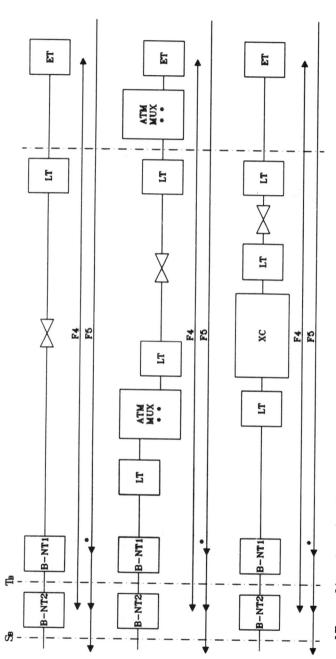

LT   : Line termination
ET   : Exchange termination
MUX : Multiplexer
XC   : Cross-connect
*   : Termination of the F5 flow at the B-NT1 (for further study)
**   : ATM MUX without VP termination

(b)

Figure 4.45 Examples of physical configurations and OAM information flows: (a) OAM flows F1, F2, F3; (b) OAM flows F4, F5.

Table 4.19
Physical Layer OAM Functions

Level	Function	Flow	Defect/Failure Detection	System Protection and Failure Information		
				B-NT2-B-NT1 Section	B-NT1-LT Section	B-NT2-Transmission Path Termination
Regenerator section	Frame alignment (S*)		Loss of frame	Section AIS/FERF		—
	Section error monitoring (S,C**)	F1	Degraded error performance	Section AIS/FERF		
	Section error reporting (C)		Degraded error performance	Section AIS/FERF		
	PLOAM cell recognition (C)		Loss of PLOAM cell recognition	Section AIS/FERF		—
	Cell delineation (C)		Loss of cell sync	Section AIS/FERF		
Digital section	Frame alignment (S)		Loss of frame	Section AIS/FERF	—	—
	Section error monitoring (S)	F2	Degraded error performance	Section AIS/FERF		
	Section error reporting (S)		Degraded errorperformance	Section AIS/FERF		—

		F3				
Transmission path	VC-4 offset (S)		Loss of AU PTR	—	—	Path AIS/FERF
	CN status monitoring (S,C)		CN-AIS			Path AIS
	Cell delineation (S,C)		Loss of cell sync			Path FERF
	Header error detection/ correction (S,C)		Uncorrectable header			(Path management message)
	Header error performance (S,C)	F3	Degraded header error			(Path management message)
	Cell rate decoupling (S,C)		Failure of insertion and suppression of idle cells			
	Path error monitoring (S,C)		Degraded error performance	—	—	Path AIS/FERF
	Path error reporting (S,C)		Degraded error performance	—	—	Path AIS/FERF
	PLOAM cell recognition (C)		Loss of PLOAM cell recognition	—	—	Path FERF

*S: SDH-based
**C: cell-based

concept and the *fast packet switching* (FPS) concept. The FCS relies on the fast setting up and taking down of connections so that the switching system does not allocate any circuit to a user during its idle state. The FPS concept is based on packet switching in the data communication network; but the FPS system employs a high degree of parallelism, distributed control, and the self-routing function to achieve high performance.

Our emphasis is placed on those switch fabrics that incorporate the FPS concept as their underlying switching technique. For simplicity of presentation, we assume that all lines have the same transmission capacity, all packets are of the same size, and that the arrival times of packets at the various input lines are time synchronized.

4.16.1 ATM Switching System Architecture

A packet switch is a box that routes the packets arriving at its inputs to their requested outputs. In this switch, there is no coordination among arriving packets as far as their destination requests are concerned, and thus more than one packet arriving in the same time slot may be destined to go to the same output port. This event raises packet conflict, and so buffering of packets within the switch must be provided. Thus, a packet switch is a box which provides switching and buffering.

From the functional point of view, an ATM switch is practically the same as a packet switch used in computer networks. The main difference between the ATM switch and the packet switch is the switching speed. Therefore, an ATM switch can be called a fast packet switch.

Figure 4.46 shows the structure of the ATM switch. The *line interface* (LI) performs optical-electrical signal conversion, cell synchronization, header translation, and insertion and extraction of routing information. The *call processor* (CP) and the *signaling processor* (SIG) are concerned with the ATM connection setup and release. The switch module routes cells using routing information of the cells.

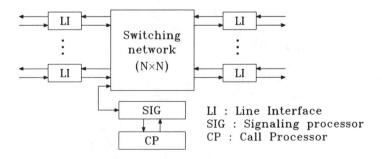

Figure 4.46 Overall structure of ATM switch.

The ATM switch should be designed to satisfy the following requirements for CBR and VBR services: (1) bounded delay (less than 1 ms/node), (2) arbitrary small packet loss probability (less than 10^{-9}/node for CBR services, and less than 10^{-7} for VBR services), (3) close to 100% throughput, (4) above 150 Mbps per port, (5) self-routing and distributed control, (6) modularity and scalability, and (7) multicast function.

In general, two types of conflicts can occur inside the ATM switch. First, when more than one packet destined for the same output port has arrived, a packet conflict occurs in the output port. We refer to this packet conflict as *output conflict*. This packet conflict can be solved by increasing the number of packets accepted simultaneously at output ports. Second, when packets with different destinations request the same internal link, an *internal packet conflict* occurs. Some solutions to this internal packet conflict may be considered. For example, operation speed can be increased for internal links rather than for the external lines; or the traffic at the input can be randomized so that the overall traffic may spread across the entire network.

4.16.2 Classification of ATM Switch Based on Switching Mechanisms

We can classify the ATM switch into the following classes according to switching mechanism: (1) shared-memory switch, (2) shared-medium switch, (3) crossbar switch, (4) multistage interconnection switch, and (5) switch with disjoint-path topology and output queuing.

Shared-Memory Switch

This switch consists of a single dual-port memory shared by all input and output lines (see Figure 4.47). Packets arriving on all input lines are multiplexed into a single stream which is fed to the common memory for storage. Internally to the memory, packets are organized into separate output queues. Simultaneously, an output stream of packets is performed by retrieving packets from the output queues

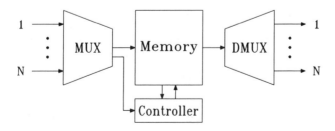

Figure 4.47 Basic structure of a shared-memory switch.

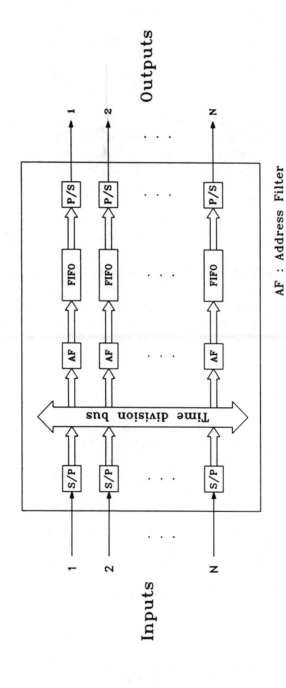

Figure 4.48 Basic structure of a shared-medium switch.

sequentially. This output stream is then demultiplexed, and packets are transmitted on the output lines.

For this type of switch, two main constraints must be satisfied. First, the processing time required for determining where to queue up the packets and for issuing the proper signals for that purpose should be sufficiently small to keep up with the flow of incoming packets. The second design constraint is the limitation on the memory access speed. Thus, the size of a switch is determined by the available memory speeds and achievable processing speeds. Examples of shared-memory fabrics are the Prelude switch of the CNET and the shared-memory switch of Hitachi.

Shared-Medium Switch

In the shared-medium switch, all packets arriving on the input lines are synchronously multiplexed onto a common high-speed medium of bandwidth equal to N (switch size) times the rate of a single input line. Each output line is connected to the bus via an interface consisting of an address filter and an output FIFO filter. The address filter determines whether or not the packet observed in the bus is to be written into the FIFO buffer. Functionally, this approach is similar to that of the shared-memory fabrics (see Figure 4.48).

As with the shared-memory architecture, an essential issue in realizing the shared-medium architecture is how to implement the high-speed bus and buffer memories. We can use parallel organization to solve this problem. An example of this switch fabric can be found in the ATOM switch proposed by NEC.

Crossbar Switch

Basically, a crossbar fabric consists of a square array of N^2 cross-point switches, one for each input-output pair (see Figure 4.49). A cross-point switch can assume two states: the cross state, which connects the horizontal input to the horizontal output and the vertical input to the vertical output, and the bar state, which connects the horizontal input to the vertical output and the vertical input to the horizontal output. For example, the input line i can be connected to the output line j by putting the (i, j) crosspoint in bar state and all others in cross state.

The crossbar fabric requires N^2 cross points, and therefore the size of realizable switches tends to be limited. In addition, the transit time is not constant over all input/output pairs unless artificial delays are introduced at the inputs and outputs of the switch. Examples of this fabric are the bus matrix switch of Fujitsu and the ATD switch of Siemens.

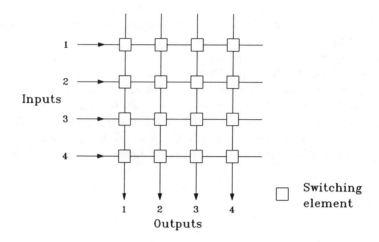

Figure 4.49 Basic structure of crossbar switch.

Multistage Interconnection Switch

The *multistage interconnection networks* (MIN) was studied extensively in the context of a circuit-switched telephone network. The goal was to design a nonblocking multistage switch with the number of cross points less than a single-stage crossbar matrix. Later on, several types of MINs, such as the Banyan network, have been proposed as a switching fabric for integrated telecommunication switching nodes.

In general, Banyan-switched networks belong to a class of multistage interconnection networks with the property that there is exactly one path from any input to any output. These networks include the Banyan network, baseline network, shuffle-exchange (or OMEGA) network, and flip network. Figure 4.50 shows the interconnection patterns of these networks.

Although these networks have different interconnection patterns, they have the same performance in a packet-switching environment. The principal characteristics of these networks are (1) they consist of $\log_2 N$ stages, (2) they have self-routing property for packet movements from any input to any output by using a routing header, (3) they can be constructed in a modular way from smaller subswitches, and (4) their regularity and interconnection patterns are very attractive for VLSI implementation.

While these networks have some attractive features, they are blocking networks in the sense that packets can collide with each other and get lost. The packet conflicts result in the reduction of the maximum throughput of the switch.

There are several ways to reduce the blocking or to increase throughput of Banyan-switched networks: (1) increasing the internal link speeds relative to the external speeds, (2) placing a buffer in every switching node, (3) using multiple

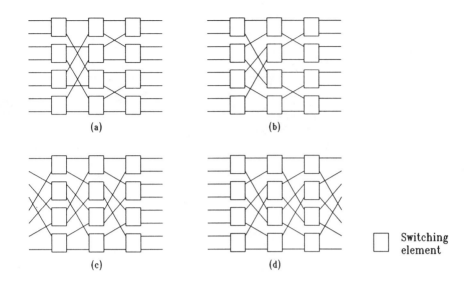

Figure 4.50 Interconnection patterns of Banyan-switched network: (a) Banyan network; (b) baseline network; (c) shuffle-exchange network; (d) flip network.

networks in parallel, (4) using multiple networks in series, (5) using a distribution network in front of the Banyan network to distribute the load evenly, and (6) using a Batcher sorting network in front of the Banyan network to sort the input packets based on the destination addresses.

Switch With Disjoint-Path Topology and Output Queuing

These switch fabrics are based on a fully interconnected topology in the sense that every input has a nonoverlapping direct path to every output so that no blocking may occur internally. They employ output queuing in order to resolve the output port conflict. Examples of this switch fabric are the knockout switch and integrated fabric.

The knockout switch uses one broadcast input bus from every input port to all output ports, as shown in Figure 4.51. That is, each output line has a bus interface connecting it to all input buses. Such an interface contains N address filters, one for each input line, which recognize packets addressed to the corresponding output line. The outputs of the filters are connected to an $N \times L$ concentrator, which selects up to L packets out of those accepted by the filters.

The advantages of this switch include low latency and no internal blocking. In addition, it is self-routing. However, each bus in this switch has a fan-out of more than the size of the switch. Therefore, as the network size grows larger, it becomes difficult to implement such a high fan-out bus.

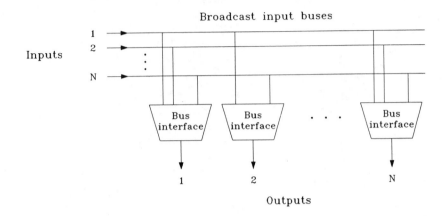

Figure 4.51 Basic structure of the knockout switch.

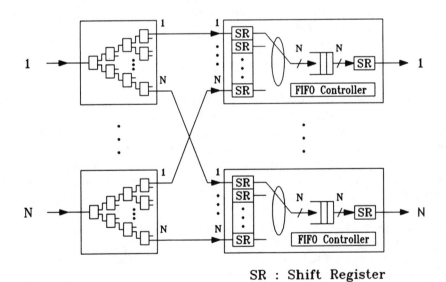

SR : Shift Register

Figure 4.52 Structure of the integrated switch.

The integrated switch is shown in Figure 4.52. Here a Banyan tree is used for each input line to route the packet at the input to the destination output port. Each output port has N registers of size equal to one packet. In every slot, the contents of all N registers corresponding to a given output line are emptied sequentially into a FIFO buffer.

4.16.3 Classification of ATM Switch Based on Buffer Arrangements

In an ATM network, since network resources are not deterministically assigned to each connection, packet contention is inevitable within the switch fabric. Therefore, in order to resolve the contention, buffers are necessary for routing each ATM cell to its destination output port. ATM switch fabrics can be classified into four categories, based on the arrangement of the buffers: (1) input buffer switch, (2) output buffer switch, (3) shared-buffer switch, and (4) cross-point buffer switch.

Input Buffer Switch

The input buffer switch has a dedicated buffer for each incoming port, as shown in Figure 4.53. The simplest form of input buffer switch (FIFO) suffers from their so-called *head-of-line* (HOL) effect, which causes throughput degradations. To prevent this phenomenon, some additional control functions such as the output contention algorithm are required.

There are three approaches for overcoming the HOL effect: doubling the operation speed, looking around not only the head but the succeeding cells in the buffer, and scheduling the output timing of each cell from the input buffer.

Output Buffer Switch

The basic configuration of the buffer switch is shown in Figure 4.54. The output buffer switch uses dedicated output buffers for each outgoing port. In this switch fabric, a broadcast-and-select mechanism is adopted. A broadcasting function is realized by using a parallel bus, a binary tree, or a high-speed transmission bus.

The output buffer switch requires a larger buffer than the input buffer switch; but the control logic is simpler and high throughput is maintained regardless of traffic conditions. Examples of this switch are the knockout switch, the integrated switch, and the ATOM switch.

Shared-Buffer Switch

The shared memory switch described in Section 4.16.2 can be considered a shared-buffer switch. Figure 4.55 shows the basic functional block diagram of shared-buffer switch.

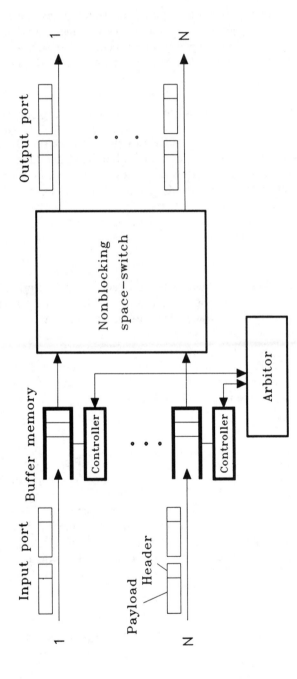

Figure 4.53 Structure of input queuing switch.

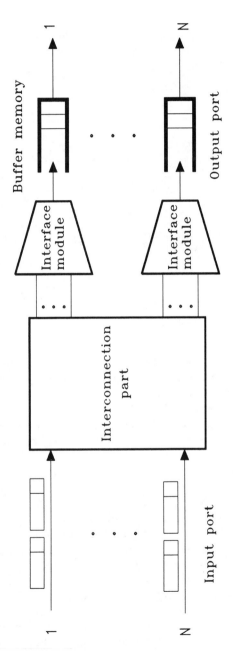

Figure 4.54 Structure of output queuing switch.

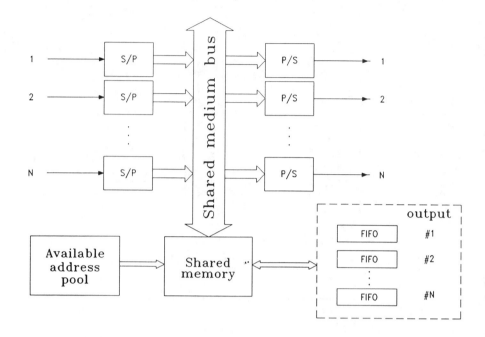

Figure 4.55 Structure of shared-buffer switch.

Incoming packets to the switch are first buffered temporarily so that they can be sequentially written onto a RAM. The WRITE address is provided by a circuit that keeps a pool of empty RAM locations. At the same time, the destination of each cell is recorded on a separate FIFO buffer pertaining to the output port (destination) of that particular cell. After the incoming cells are written onto the RAM, N cells are then read out from the RAM and distributed to the output pools.

Cross-Point Buffer Switch

The cross-point buffer switch has the most distributed control scheme among the four categories. In this switch, every cross-point element or switching element has a FIFO buffer, and the contention control algorithm determines from which buffer a cell will be selected. Though the control mechanism is relatively simple, the buffer size and control logic complexity are high.

4.16.4 Examples of Large-Scale Switching Systems

In practice, it is estimated that a central office of a broadband network would require switch fabrics with tens of thousands of high-speed ports and connections for hundreds of thousands of terminals.

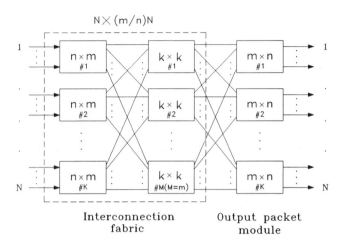

Figure 4.56 Example of two-stage architecture based on interconnection fabrics.

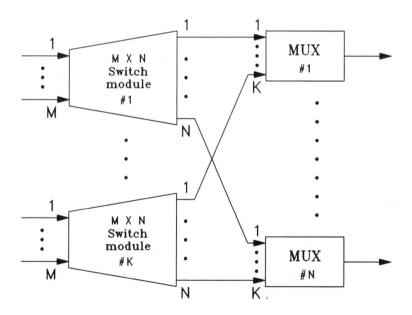

Figure 4.57 Example of two-stage architecture using multiplexers.

Most switch architectures discussed above cannot be easily scaled up to that size. For example, a Batcher-Banyan switch of ten thousand ports requires synchronization of up to ten thousand packets over a network of about 100 stages. The knockout switch also encounters significant difficulties for ten thousand ports also, since each bus in the architecture must have a fan-out of more than ten thousand. An approach to designing a very large switching system is to interconnect many independent small switch modules in a way that satisfies the overall switching requirements.

In the following section we review some architectures proposed for a very large packet switch.

Two-Stage Architecture Based on Interconnection Fabrics[71]

This switch architecture is depicted in Figure 4.56, where a partition is made between a front-end memoryless interconnection network and a column of output packet switch modules. The outputs are divided into groups of n lines each. All incoming cells are routed through the front-end interconnection network for instantaneous delivery based on their destination output group addresses. As such, the interconnection network can be memoryless and must perform its routing function for all the cells arriving in each time slot. For each output group, the corresponding output packet switch module has m ($m > n$) inputs, meaning that up to m cells can be accepted for that output group in each time slot. According to the generalized knockout principle, it is possible to pick $m << N$ to yield an arbitrarily small cell loss probability.

This switch offers several distinctive features. First, the parameter m in each $m \times n$ output packet module is independent of the switch size N. Consequently, the output section can grow indefinitely by using more and more fixed and identical $m \times n$ output packet modules. Second, elimination of memory in the interconnection network avoids multiple stages of queuing delay to input cells.

Two-Stage Architecture Using Multiplexers[72]

This architecture consists of a set of switch modules and multiplexers, as shown in Figure 4.57. Switch modules are independently operated packet switches and consist of a Batcher sorting network, a stack of binary trees, and a bundle of Banyan networks. This modular architecture is a combination of the Batcher-Banyan switch and the knockout switch.

[71]K. Y. Eng, M. J. Karol, and Y. S. Yeh, "A Growable Packet (ATM) Switch Architecture: Design Principles and Applications," *Globecom '89*, November 1989, pp. 32.2.2–32.2.7.

[72]T. T. Lee, "Modular Architecture for Very Large Packet Switches," *IEEE Trans. Comm.*, Vol. 38, No. 7, July 1990, pp. 1097–1106.

In this system, a set of switch modules is interconnected at the outputs by multiplexers. Thus, no interference occurs between switch modules. This architecture also allows for independent clocking of modules, which substantially simplifies timing and allows for simple fault tolerance by providing a spare module, not a duplication of the entire switch.

Three-Stage Interconnection Architecture[73]

This switch architecture, shown in Figure 4.58, consists of three stages of small switch modules, each of which can be realized by several switch fabrics. In this

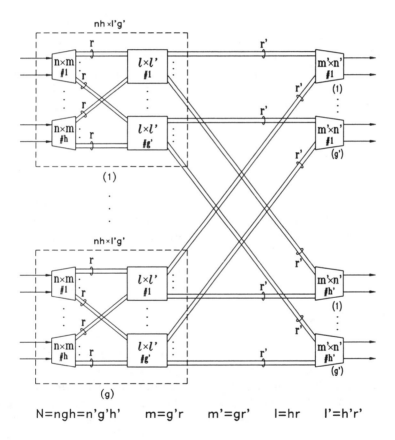

$$N=ngh=n'g'h' \quad m=g'r \quad m'=gr' \quad l=hr \quad l'=h'r'$$

Figure 4.58 Example of three-stage interconnection architecture.

[73]S. C. Liew and K. W. Lu, "A 3-Stage Interconnection Structure for Very Large Packet Switches," *ICC '90 Proc.*, pp. 316.7.1–316.7.7.

architecture, the technique of channel grouping (i.e., providing more than one phys-ical output port for each physical destination address) is used to improve the per-formance of the individual switch modules. There are multiple paths between any input and any output in this switch architecture, so packets arrive at the output out of sequence due to delay differences of the paths. However, the sequence integrity of packets can be maintained automatically by proper design of the individual switch modules.

4.17 INTEGRATED PRM FOR ATM, HSN, AND SDH

ATM communication, high-speed packet communications, and synchronous digital transmission have emerged independently of the others. ATM communication was born out of the BISDN UNI standardization process. The high-speed packet com-munication network appeared as an attempt to achieve faster and more universal data communication, which resulted in the *high speed network* (HSN). Synchro-nous digital transmission emerged out of the evolutionary process of optical communication systems.

However, in the BISDN-based communications networks of the future, they will evince an intimate, close-knit relationship, assuming mutually complementary roles. So, in this concluding section, we will briefly compare and contrast the three, and upon that foundation, illuminate their harmonious coexistence under a single universal scheme in the form of BISDN. First we will review ATM communications, high-speed packet communications, and synchronous transmission individually, and the section will conclude with an examination of the integrated protocol reference model.

4.17.1 ATM Communications

As examined previously, ATM was conceived during the standardization process of the BISDN in an attempt to create a new mode of information transfer which can accommodate both the existing circuit-mode services as well as the packet-mode services. In contrast to the existing digital transmission, which is a circuit-mode transmission technique that employs synchronous time-division multiplexing, ATM is a packet-mode transfer technique which employs asynchronous time-division mul-tiplexing, forming the basis for BISDN transmission. In the ATM transmission pro-cess, the basic unit of information transfer is the ATM cell, which consists of 53 bytes, and these cells are transmitted in the form of continuous flow or in a mapped state via the G.702 PDH or G.707 SDH signals.

If ATM communications is to be compared with high-speed packet communication or synchronous transmission, it is necessary to consider the protocol reference model, the physical layer, and the AAL among the extensive range of topics associated with the ATM communications technique. This is because the protocol reference model captures the overall interrelationship among the elements of ATM communication, while the physical layer and AAL each illustrates its relationship with the synchronous transmission and packet communication.

As was discussed in Section 4.6, the BISDN protocol model is composed of the user plane, the control plane, and the management plane. Among them, the respective protocols of the user plane and the control plane can be divided into the physical layer, ATM layer, AAL, and higher-order layer. The physical layer consists of the transmission convergence function and the physical medium functions directly allied with the physical layer, while the transmission convergence function can be divided into transmission frame-related functions and ATM cell-related functions. The ATM layer is responsible for various management functions related to the ATM cell header, such as GFC, and VPI/VCI translation. The AAL is responsible for management functions associated with the ATM cell payload, consisting of the convergence sublayer, which adapts user information into protocol data units, and the SAR sublayer, which segments the PDUs to form the ATM cell payload space. The various compositions and functions of each layer are elucidated in Figure 4.5 and Table 4.1.

ATM cell transmission can be accomplished through the means of existing G.702 tributaries or the new G.707 SDH signals, or through the flow of ATM cells themselves. SDH-based transmission is made possible by mapping ATM cells into the virtual container VC-4s carried inside the STM-n payload space. When the required capacity to be transmitted is too large, the concatenation mode can be employed to load the ATM-cells onto the VC-4–4c's. ATM cell transmission based on G.702 will continue to be a valid means of transport until the construction of SDH networks is completed. ATM cell-based transmission is based on the flow of ATM cells themselves, which saves the trouble of having to create a separate transmission frame, but it is not powerful enough to be used as the sole means of transport within a vast public network. Although both the SDH-based transmission and ATM cell-based transmission externally possess the same 155.52-Mbps bit rate, they are not mutually compatible.

In an ATM network, the principal function for accommodating packet data services is performed at AAL-3 and AAL-4. These layers have the capability to adapt connection-oriented and connectionless data packet services, respectively, and the associated functions are performed through the CS and SAR sublayers. Service provision via AAL-3 is achieved in an analogous manner to the provision of real-time VBR services via AAL-2. First, when the connection path is determined as a part of the call establishment process, the user data packets are transmitted along this path after being processed at the CS and the SAR sublayer. As a result, layer 1 to layer 4 functions for packet transmission can be accomplished through the ATM network. On the other hand, the provision of connectionless services that are dependent on AAL-4 is made possible by embedding a *connectionless services function* (CLSF) inside the ATM network. This is equivalent to overlaying a packet network composed of CLSF nodes on top of the ATM network. Therefore, if routing is done using the CLSF nodes, the effect achieved is equivalent to data transmission at a general packet network, and here the ATM network can provide layer 1 and layer 2 functions.

4.17.2 High-Speed Packet Communications

The rise in the processing speeds of computers and the increasingly all-encompassing character of information data produced the concept of high-speed packet communications, which became a reality with the maturation of optical communications technology. The existing 10-Mbps class packet communication is growing into the 100-Mbps class by way of the FDDI, and to 150-Mbps class via the DQDB, and the gigabit-per-second class is anticipated in the near future. Currently, high-speed packet communication systems are confined to regional communications networks such as the MAN and LAN. But in order to achieve interconnected communication, they will soon come to form a close-knit relationship with public communication networks, an example of which can be found in the SMDS.

FDDI is a LAN in a double-ring configuration that uses the IEEE 802.5 optical fiber as its transmission medium; it employs the token passing technique, which is analogous to the token-ring technique. FDDI II is an enhanced version of FDDI that provides synchronous-mode real-time services in addition to the packet-type services. DQDB is a 150-Mbps class IEEE 802.6 standard MAN that provides connection-oriented and connectionless services as well as the synchronous-mode services employing the DQDB structure. The main difference between DQDB and FDDI is not that the DQDB has a higher transmission rate, but that it has a simple protocol structure that can be easily interworked with the ATM network. (Refer to Chapter 5 on FDDI LAN, DQDB MAN, SMDS, and other topics related to high-speed packet communication.)

If the STM UNI structure is examined in relation to the required network structure for high-speed packet communications, the possible configurations that result are star, bus, and ring, as shown in Figure 4.7. Such UNI structures signify the possibility of extending the ATM to the *customer premises networks* (CPN), which in turn suggests the necessity for the ATM network to maintain a closely linked relationship with the LAN/MANs. As a matter of fact, the structure of Figure 4.7(c) is directly realizable using a DQDB MAN.

On the other hand, more fundamental solutions, other than the FDDI or the DQDB, are emerging to further advance high-speed packet communications in order to solve the speed problem of software, which is much lower than that of the corresponding hardware. Novel high-speed protocols are being proposed. Other means of raising the processing speed are also being sought in multiple processors or parallel processing VLSI designs. Also, there is active research and development of viable solutions to the delay problems caused by the store-and-forward type of data transfer, performance degradation problems due to the management overheads of each layer, or other problems inherent in the existing data communications, which make the current packet network protocol and implementation technology inadequate for high-speed communications and multimedia communications. When all of the fundamental problems have been worked out, then gigabit networks will become realizable, and efficient high-speed packet communication will become possible.

There are three different transmission paths available for high-speed packet communications. The first two are the transmission through AAL-3 and AAL-4, as was explained in the preceding section. That is, a high-speed packet service can be considered a class C connection-oriented BISDN service and be provided through AAL-3, or in the form of a class D connectionless BISDN service and provided through AAL-4. (AAL-5, which is an extension of AAL-3 and AAL-4, can also be considered.) The third is to employ a separate protocol processing procedure for high-speed packet communications purposes and then to map the packets onto the VC-4s of SDH. This can be a useful means of transmission if an improved protocol and expanded bandwidth are necessary for high-speed packet transfer.

4.17.3 Synchronous Digital Transmission

As was discussed in Chapter 3, synchronous digital transmission is a new form of circuit-mode transmission technique which appeared in the evolution process of optical communication systems. Synchronous digital transmission, with systematic multiplexing and synchronization schemes as its basis, makes the construction of an efficient communications network possible. It furnishes an effective, optical fiber-based means of transmission for public networks, as well as for the BISDN customer networks.

The original motivation behind synchronous digital transmission was to enable the multiplexing and transmission of existing G.702 tributaries in a systematic manner through the employment of synchronous multiplexing. Here, the tributaries are first mapped into one of the virtual containers VC-11, VC-12, VC-2, VC-3, and VC-4, then appended with POH and SOH, and finally transmitted in the form of $n \times 155.52$-Mbps STM-n. In addition, synchronous transmission can utilize many of the advantages of optical communications, and it possesses various special features, such as efficient add/drop and cross-connect of tributaries.

In the case of SDH-based ATM transmission, the ATM-cells get mapped into the VC-4 payload space as depicted in Figure 3.31; thus, the required capacity just for the cells of the ATM TC sublayer becomes 149.76 Mbps. Of course, if five bytes of the ATM cell header are excluded, the maximum payload that can be transmitted using ATM reduces to 135.63 Mbps. The POH and SOH belonging to the STM-n frame provide an OAM function to ensure that the ATM cells are reliably transported to their destination. Therefore, synchronous digital transmission assumes the role of a highly reliable physical layer for ATM communication.

As mentioned earlier, synchronous digital transmission can be used as a means of transmission, even for high-speed packet communication. To construct a high-speed packet network in order to connect the numerous LANs and MANs scattered about the vicinity of a public network, it is best to utilize the facilities of the existing public network. That is, if the synchronous digital transmission is used in the public network, then the services of a highly dependable physical layer are provided. In case the required transmission capacity is below 150 Mbps, the VC-4 can be used to map the packets, and if it is below 50 Mbps, they can be mapped to VC-3. On the other side, if the transmission capacity is at the 600-Mbps level, VC-4–4c can be used, and at the gigabit-per-second level, VC-4–16c can be used.

4.17.4 Integrated Protocol Reference Model

If the aspects examined in the preceding three sections are combined, then an *integrated protocol reference model* (IPRM) can be drawn, such as the one shown in Figure 4.59. In the figure, the portions in rising slanted line represent the parts essential to ATM communication, the portions in falling slanted lines represents the regions that can be occupied by high-speed packet communications, and the darkened portion represents the synchronous digital transmission's original region.

It can be seen from the figure that high-speed packet communications can be provided in the form of class C or class D services through AAL-3 or AAL-4. In case the packets are transported in the class C services format, only the layer 5 to layer 7 functions might be required at the higher-order layer, and layer 3 to layer 7 functions might be necessary in the case of class D services. This is because class C services, similar to those of class B, are connection-oriented services; thus, functions belonging to the physical layer, data link layer, network layer, and transport layer can all be provided by way of an ATM network.

On the other hand, as was examined in the previous section, high-speed packet communications can be furnished in the form of synchronous digital transmission with the SDH frame as the basis. This relationship is indicated in the figure, and here the layer 2 to layer 7 functions will be needed. If this is the case, then, unlike the case of class C or D services, an independent protocol can be formulated that does not rely on the ATM protocols. Consequently, it will be even more appropriate in configuring a high-speed packet communications network that is based on a novel structure.

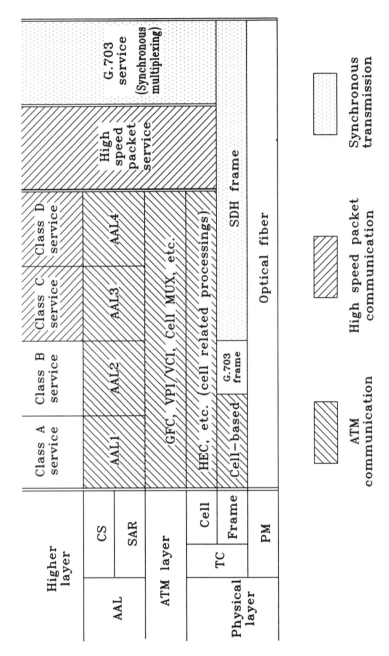

Figure 4.59 Integrated protocol reference model.

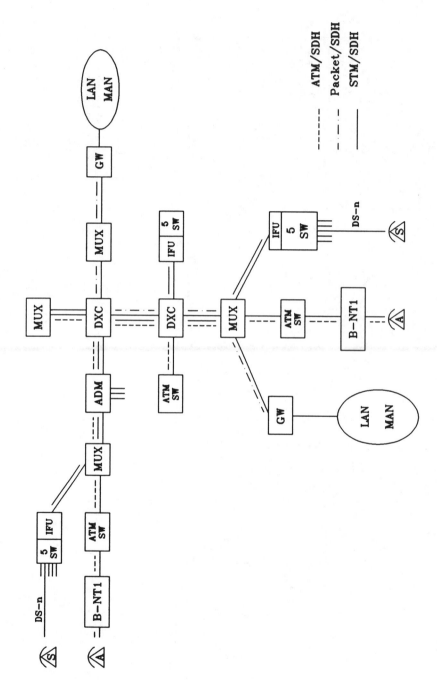

Figure 4.60 Signal composition of synchronous transmission network based on an integrated protocol reference model.

Such an integrated protocol reference model can be used to view a cross section of the future communications network. In case cell-based transmission is used for ATM communications, the communication network will consist of two types of signals that possess the same bit rate but without having any interrelationship. On the other hand, if SDH-based transmission is employed, then the STM-n signal will be the sole means of transport. Then, ATM communications, high-speed packet communications and synchronous digital transmission will all meet at the level of VC-4's to coexist inside the communication network. Therefore, these three types will pass through the synchronous ADM or the synchronous DXC together, thus enabling a generalization of the OAM of the communications network.

If such an IPRM is used to reconfigure the synchronous transmission network of Figure 3.63, then the structure shown in Figure 4.60 results. In the figure, dotted lines represent the mapping of ATM cells into VC-4/SDH to be transmitted inside an ATM communications network. Also, a broken line represents the case in which high-speed packets are mapped into the VC-4/SDH before being transmitted, and the solid line represents original synchronous digital transmission being employed to carry the PDH signals. Therefore, it can be inferred that in the broadband communications network of the future, these three different types of signals will be multiplexed together to pass through a common synchronous transmission network.

SELECT BIBLIOGRAPHY

Anderson, J., and M. D. Nguyen, "ATM-Layer OAM Implementation Issues," *IEEE Commun. Mag.*, Vol. 29, No. 9, Sept. 1991, pp. 79–81.

Armbruster, H., and G. Arndt, "Broadband communication and its realization with broadband ISDN, *IEEE Commun. Mag.*, Vol. 25, No. 11, Nov. 1987, pp. 8–19

ATM Forum, "ATM User-Network Interface Specification Version 2.0," 1992.

ATM Forum, "Network Compatible ATM for Local Network Applications," Phase 1, Version 1.0, 1992.

Basch, B. E., W. A. Bruwer, D. D. Casey, W. L. Smith, and D. R. Spears, "VISTAnet: A BISDN Field Trial," *IEEE LTS Mag.*, Vol. 2, No. 3, Aug. 1991, pp. 22–30.

Bauch, H., "Transmission Systems for the BISDN," *IEEE LTS Mag.*, Vol. 2, No. 3, Aug. 1991, pp. 31–36.

Boudec, J. Y. L., "The Asynchronous Transfer Mode: A Tutorial," *Computer Networks and ISDN Systems*, Vol. 24, 1992, pp. 279–309.

Breuer H. J., "ATM Layer OAM: Principles and Open Issues," *IEEE Commun. Mag.*, Vol. 29, No. 9, Sept. 1991, pp. 75–78.

Burgin, J., and D. Dorman, "BISDN Resource Management: The Role of Virtual Paths," *IEEE Commun. Mag.*, Vol. 29, No. 9, Sept. 1991, pp. 44–49.

Byrne, W. R., G. Clapp, H. J. Kafka, G. W. R. Luderer, and B. L. Nelson, "Evolution of Metropolitan Public Network and Switch Architecture," *IEEE Commun. Mag.*, Vol. 29, No. 1, Jan. 1991, pp. 69–82.

Byrne, W. R., B. L. Kilim, and M. D. Soneru, "Broadband ISDN Technology and Architecture," *IEEE Network Mag.*, Vol. 3, No. 1, Jan. 1989, pp. 7–13.

CCITT Rec. I.113, "Vocabulary Terms for Broadband Aspects of ISDN," 1992 (Rev).

CCITT Rec. I.120, "Integrated Services Digital Network," 1992 (Rev).

CCITT Rec. I.121, "Broadband Aspects of ISDN," 1990.

CCITT Rec. I.140, "Attribute Technique for the Characterization of the Telecommunication Services Supported by an ISDN and Network Capability of an ISDN," 1992 (Rev).

CCITT Rec. I.150, "BISDN ATM Functional Characteristics," 1992 (Rev).

CCITT Rec. I.211, "BISDN Service Aspects," 1992 (Rev).

CCITT Rec. I.311, "BISDN General Network Aspects," 1992 (Rev).

CCITT Rec. I.321, "BISDN Protocol Reference Model and Its Application," 1990.

CCITT Rec. I.327, "BISDN Functional Architecture Aspects," 1992.

CCITT Rec. I.35B, "BISDN ATM Cell Transfer Performance," 1992 (Draft).

CCITT Rec. I.361, "BISDN ATM Layer Specification," 1992 (Rev).

CCITT Rec. I.362, "BISDN ATM Adaption Layer (AAL) Functional Description," 1992 (Rev).

CCITT Rec. I.363, "BISDN ATM Adaptation Layer (AAL) Specification," 1992 (Rev).

CCITT Rec. I.364, "Support of Broadband Connectionless Data Service on BISDN," 1992.

CCITT Rec. I.371, "Traffic Control and Congestion Control in BISDN," 1992.

CCITT Draft Rec. I.374, "Network Capability for the Support of Multimedia Services," 1992.

CCITT Rec. I.413, "BISDN User-Network Interface," 1992 (Rev).

CCITT Rec. I.432, "BISDN User-Network Interface—Physical Layer Specification," 1992 (Rev).

CCITT Rec. I.610, "BISDN UNI Operations and Maintenance Principles," 1992 (Rev).

Cidon, I., I. Gopal, and R. Guerin, "Bandwidth Management and Congestion Control in Planet," *IEEE Commun. Mag.*, Vol. 30, No. 10, Oct. 1991, pp. 54–65.

Coudreuse, J. P., "Network Evolution Towards BISDN," *IEEE LTS Mag.*, Vol. 2, No. 3, Aug. 1991, pp. 66–70.

Daddsi, G. E., Jr., and H. C. Torng, "A Taxonomy of Broadband Integrated Switching Architectures," *IEEE Commun. Mag.*, Vol. 27, No. 1, May 1989, pp. 32–42.

Day, A., "International Standardization of BISDN," *IEEE LTS Mag.*, Vol. 2, No. 3, Aug. 1991, pp. 13–21.

Domann, G., "Two Years of Experience With Broadband ISDN Field Trial," *IEEE Commun. Mag.*, Vol. 29, No. 1, Jan. 1991, pp. 90–96.

Eckberg, A. E., B. T. Doshy, and R. Zoccolillo, "Controlling Congestion in BISDN/ATM: Issues and Strategies," *IEEE Commun. Mag.*, Vol. 29, No. 9, Sept. 1991, pp. 64–74.

Eigen, D. J., "Narrowband and Broadband ISDN CPE Directions," *IEEE Commun. Mag.*, Vol. 28, No. 4, April 1990, pp. 39–46.

Eng, K. Y., M. J. Karol, and Y. S. Yeh, "A Growable Packet (ATM) Switch Architecture: Design Principles and Applications," *IEEE Trans. Commun.*, Vol. 40, No. 2, Jan. 1992, pp. 423–439.

Filipiak, J., "M-Architecture: A Structural Model of Traffic Management and Control in Broadband ISDNs," *IEEE Commun. Mag.*, Vol. 27, No. 5, May 1989, pp. 25–31.

Frame, M., "Broadband Service Needs," IEEE Commun. Mag., Vol. 28, No. 4, April 1990, pp. 55–58.

Gechter, J. and P. O'Reilly, "Conceptual Issues for ATM," *IEEE Network Mag.*, Vol. 3, No. 1, Jan. 1989, pp. 14–16.

Gilbert, H., O. Aboul-Magd, and V. Phung, "Developing a Cohesive Traffic Management Strategy for ATM Networks," *IEEE Commun. Mag.*, Vol. 30, No. 10, Oct. 1991, pp. 36–45.

Goeldner, E. H., and M. N. Huber, "Multiple Access for BISDN," *IEEE LTS Mag.*, Vol. 2, No. 3, Aug. 1991, pp. 37–43.

Haas, Z., "A Protocol Structure for High-Speed Communication Over Broadband ISDN," *IEEE Network Mag.*, Vol. 5, No. 1, Jan. 1991, pp. 64–70.

Habib, I. W., T. N. Saadawi, "Controlling Flow and Avoiding Congestion in Broadband Networks," *IEEE Commun. Mag.*, Vol. 30, No. 10, Oct. 1991, pp. 46–53.

Handel, R., "Evolution of ISDN Towards Broadband ISDN," *IEEE Network Mag.*, Vol. 3, No. 1, Jan. 1989, pp. 7–13.

Handel, R., and M. N. Huber, *Integrated Broadband Networks: An Introduction to ATM-Based Networks*, Addison Wesley Publishing Co., 1991.

Hong, D., and T. Suda, "Congestion Control and Prevention in ATM Networks," *IEEE Network Mag.*, Vol. 5, No. 4, Jul. 1991, pp. 10–17.

Imai, K., T. Honda, H. Kasahara, and T. Ito, "ATMR: Ring Architecture for Broadband Networks," 1990.

Kishimoto, R., and I. Yamashita, "HDTV Communication Systems in Broadband Communication Networks," *IEEE Commun. Mag.*, Vol. 29, No. 8, Aug. 1991, pp. 28–35.

Kitawaki, N., H. Nagabuchi, M. Raka, and K. Takahashi, "Speech Coding Technology for ATM Networks," *IEEE Commun. Mag.*, Vol. 28, No. 1, Jan. 1990, pp. 21–27.

Lazar, A. A., and G. Pacifici, "Control of Resources in Broadband Networks With Quality of Service Guarantee," *IEEE Commun. Mag.*, Vol. 30, No. 10, Oct. 1991, pp. 66–73.

Lee, T. H., "Design and Analysis of a New Self-Routing Network," *IEEE Trans. Commun.*, Vol. 40, No. 1, Jan. 1992, pp. 171–177.

Li, S. Q., "Performance of a Nonblocking Space-Division Switch With Correlated Input Traffic," *IEEE Trans. Commun.*, Vol. 40. No. 1, Jan. 1992, pp. 97–108.

Lyles, J. B., and D. C. Swinehart, "The Emerging Gigabit Environment and the Role of Local ATM," *IEEE Commun. Mag.*, Vol. 30, No. 4, April 1992, pp. 52–59.

Mesiya, M. F., "Implementation of a Broadband Integrated Services Hybrid Network," *IEEE Commun. Mag.*, Vol. 26, No. 1, Jan. 1988, pp. 34–43.

Minzer, S. E., "Broadband ISDN and Asynchronous Transfer Mode (ATM)," *IEEE Commun. Mag.*, Vol. 27, No. 9, Sept. 1989, pp. 17–24.

Minzer, S. E., and D. R. Spears, "New Directions in Signalling for Broadband ISDN," *IEEE Commun. Mag.*, Vol. 27, No. 2, Feb. 1989, pp. 6–14.

Mitra, N., and S. D. Usikin, "Relationship of the Signalling System No. 7 Protocol Architecture to the OSI Reference Model," *IEEE Commun. Mag.*, Vol. 5, No. 1, Jan. 1991, pp. 26–37.

Murano, K., K. Murakami, E. Iwabuchi, T. Katsuki, and H. Ogasawara, "Technologies Towards Broadband ISDN," *IEEE Commun. Mag.*, Vol. 28, No. 4, April 1990, pp. 66–70.

Natarajan, N., and G. M. Slawsky, "A Framework Architecture for Multimedia Information Networks," *IEEE Commun. Mag.*, Vol. 30, No. 2, Feb. 1992, pp. 97–104.

Okada, T., H. Ohnish, and N. Morita, "Traffic Control in Asynchronous Transfer Mode," *IEEE Commun. Mag.*, Vol. 29, No. 9, Sept. 1991, pp. 58–63.

Olshanksy, R., "Subscriber Multiplexed Broadband Service Network: A Migration Path to BISDN," *IEEE LCS Mag.*, No. 3, Aug. 1990, pp. 30–34.

Prycker, M. D., "ATM Switching on Demand," *IEEE Network Mag.*, Vol. 6, No. 2, March 1992, pp. 25–29.

Rider, M. J., "Protocols for ATM Access Networks," *IEEE Network Mag.*, Vol. 3, No. 1, Jan. 1989, pp. 17–22.

Rigolio, G., and L. Verri, "Resource Management and Dimensioning in ATM Networks," *IEEE Network Mag.*, Vol. 4, No. 3, May 1990, pp. 8–17.

Roberts, J. W., "Variable Bit Rate Traffic Control in BISDN," *IEEE Commun. Mag.*, Vol. 29, No. 9, Sept. 1991, pp. 50–57.

Sato, K., H. Ueda, and N. Yoshikai, "The Role of Virtual Path Crossconnection," *IEEE LTS Mag.*, Vol. 2, No. 3, Aug. 1991, pp. 44–54.

Smouts, M., *Packet Switching Evolution From Narrowband to Broadband ISDN*, Artech House, 1992.

Special Issue, "Architecture and Protocols for Integrated Broadband Switching," *IEEE J. of Select. Areas on Commun.*, Vol. 9, No. 9, Dec. 1991.

Special Issue, "BISDN: High Performance Transport," *IEEE Commun. Mag.*, Vol. 29, No. 9, Sept. 1991.

Special Issue, "Congestion Control in High-Speed Networks," *IEEE Commun. Mag.*, Vol. 29, No. 10, Oct. 1991.

Special Issue, "Congestion Control in High-Speed Packet Switched Networks," *IEEE J. of Select. Areas on Commun.*, Vol. 9, No. 7, Sept. 1991.

Special Issue, "Gigabit Networks," *IEEE Commun. Mag.*, Vol. 30, No. 4, April 1992.

Special Issue, "Large Scale ATM Switching Systems for BISDN," *IEEE J. of Select. Areas on Commun.*, Vol. 9, No. 7, Sept. 1991.

Special Issue, "Teletraffic Analysis of ATM Systems," *IEEE J. of Select. Areas on Commun.*, Vol. 9, No. 3, April 1991.

Stallings, W., *Advances in ISDN and Broadband ISDN*, IEEE Computer Society Press, 1992.

Toda, I., "Migration to Broadband ISDN," *IEEE Commun. Mag.*, Vol. 28, No. 4, April 1990, pp. 55–58.

Vakil F., and H. Saito, "On Congestion Control in ATM Networks," *IEEE LTS Mag.*, Vol. 2, No. 3, Aug. 1991, pp. 55–65.

Walters, S. M., "A New Direction for Broadband ISDN," *IEEE Commun. Mag.*, Vol. 29, No. 9, Sept. 1991, pp. 39–43.

White, P. E., "The Role of the Broadband Integrated Services Digital Network," *IEEE Commun. Mag.*, Vol. 29, No. 3, March 1991, pp. 116–119.

Wolf, S., C. A. Dvorak, R. F. Kubichek, C. R. South, R. A. Shaphrst, and S. D. Voran, "How Will We Rate Telecommunications System Performance," *IEEE Commun. Mag.*, Vol. 29, No. 10, Oct. 1991, pp. 23–30.

Yoneda, S., "Broadband ISDN ATM Layer Management: Operations, Administration, and Maintenance Considerations," *IEEE Network Mag.*, Vol. 4, No. 3, May 1990, pp. 31–35.

Chapter 5
High-Speed Data Network

Spurred by rapid advances in semiconductor, transmission, switching, protocol, and computer technologies, information networks are becoming faster, more diverse, and more broadband-oriented, taking us ever closer to satisfying all the communication needs of human beings. The scope of communication needs is also diversifying from the transfer of simple voice sounds to the transfer of data, graphics, and images, and from the low transmission speeds of a few kilobits per second to the high transmission speeds of hundreds of megabits per second. Its area of coverage is globalizing, expanding from metropolitan to worldwide usage.

The LAN systems, which were installed to integrate a multiple number of computers and to share data and resources on the premises of universities, research institutions, and businesses, used to be mostly medium- to low-speed at around 10 Mbps, exemplified by Ethernet. But recently, the appearance of powerful, high-performance workstations, possessing network operating systems for LAN applications, has led to the emergence of the FDDI. The FDDI is a high-speed backbone LAN designed to accommodate distributed processing environments that integrate mainframes, and to link low-speed LANs scattered inside a building. With increasing speed and distributed processing, the communication capacity of such a LAN environment is going beyond local areas to wide areas, and the need for high-speed, wide-area networking, with the internetworking of LANs as its main objective, is being recognized. There are already networks that can interconnect LANs, such as the *packet-switched data network* (PSDN), *circuit-switched data network* (CSDN), and high-speed digital leased line. However, PSDN and CSDN, with transmission rates around 56 to 64 kbps, are too slow, and interconnection by leased lines in a mesh configuration imposes a heavy financial burden. Hence, a means of constructing a cost-effective high-speed network in a gradual manner is desired.

Standardization activities to realize the wide-area networking that meets the requirements of networking and multimedia communication are being carried forward at the associated standards bodies. The related technologies whose R&D and implementation are in progress around the world include frame relay, MAN, SMDS, and ATM.

The frame relay technology, based on frame multiplexing at the data link layer, enables high-speed transmission by minimizing network functions for error control and flow control in order to meet high-speed traffic access requirements for inter-connection between LANs. The main feature of a network based on frame relay is the provision of multiple data links up to the DS-1 rate through bandwidth allocation on demand as well as single access lines.

MAN is referred to as a high-speed information network for metropolitan areas, and has its conceptual origin in the advanced form of LAN from the computer net-work field, a MAN based on BISDN technology, and a MAN that unifies CATV and telecommunication. In MAN technologies, DQDB is widely employed, which is a MAN protocol specified in IEEE 802.6.

SMDS, which is a cell-relay technique, is a high-speed (DS-1 to DS-3), con-nectionless packet-switched service, in which DQDB is used as a subscriber-network access protocol. Consequently, SMDS will be one of the first services to provide switched broadband data services, and is anticipated to be provided through the BISDN from then on.

In the area of the plain old telephone network, the ISDN was conceived with the intent of achieving multimedia communication through a single network. How-ever, although the ISDN is an important technological advance which leads the way for the advent of the high-speed communication era, its rate at the UNI only amounts to 1.5 Mbps or 2 Mbps. Therefore, the BISDN has been proposed with the objective of realizing the high-speed communication required for computer networks, image information systems, and video communication systems. The transmission rate of the BISDN UNI, which is a CCITT standard, ranges from 155 Mbps to 622 Mbps. ATM is being developed as the switching and transmission technology for the BISDN. Construction of such an ATM network requires an enormous amount of investment and time; hence, the application area is expanding through the MAN and SMDS, which satisfy current user needs as well as act as the foundation for the BISDN. If the technologies mentioned above are classified in terms of application areas, the result is as shown in Figure 5.1.

In this chapter, we will first review open systems architecture, which is the basis for the computer communication networks, then describe in detail the high-speed data networks such as FDDI LAN, frame relay, DQDB MAN, and SMDS.

5.1 OPEN SYSTEMS ARCHITECTURE

For today's data communication, the concept of open systems interconnection as-sumes the role of a very fundamental discipline. It is the concept that enables com-patibility among data equipment from different vendors, thus allowing for intercon-nection among independently built data systems. In this section, we will consider

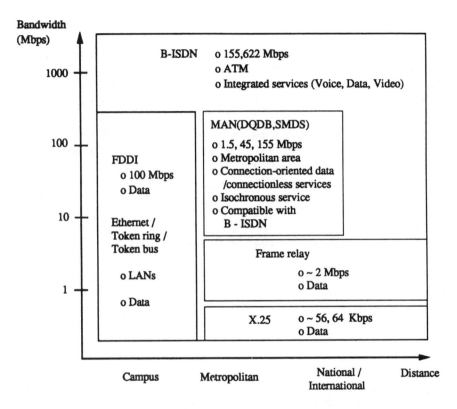

Figure 5.1 High-speed data networking areas.

the open systems interconnection and the related protocol reference model and open systems standards.

5.1.1 Background

Due to its indispensable role in everyday human life, today's computer has been introduced in almost every part of the home and the office, and is being used in various applications such as word processing, business, customer management, automation management, and point-of-sale management. Until recently, most computers were used as standalone devices. However, the unification of computer and data communication fields in the 1970s and the early 1980s brought about a large change in the technologies and products of computer/communication and related industries, leading to the conceptual separation of data and information. *Data* refers to a syntax that has been formatted in a way suitable for communication, processing, and analysis by computers or human beings, while *information* refers to the semantics assigned to data by human beings according to defined conventions.

If the unification of computers and communications is illustrated from the data and information point of view, then, as shown in Figure 5.2, computer communications can be categorized into the network service that provides bearer services (i.e., data transport service) and the end-to-end telematic service that provides information services.

For two entities to communicate with each other they must speak the same language and must define what, how, and when to communicate through a common convention acknowledged by both. The basic elements of protocol, which is a rule for the exchange of data between two entities, are syntax, semantics, and timing. *Syntax* includes such items as data format, coding, and signal levels; *semantics* includes control information for coordination and error handling; and *timing* includes speed matching and sequencing. In most cases, the task of communicating between two entities on different systems is too complicated to be handled by a single process or module. Figure 5.3 conceptually illustrates a structural set of protocols and represents the case in which two stations are connected through a multiswitched network. Between stations 1 and 2 of the figure, an application protocol is required that links the respective operations of two application processes and defines the appropriate syntax and semantics. Such an application protocol does not require information about the communication facilities existing in between, and it possesses an interentity process-to-process protocol corresponding to the network service entity. This protocol executes such tasks as flow control or error control. Also, a protocol is required between station 1 and network A, and between station 2 and network B, and the access protocol allows a device to access the network. Other protocols are required within the network itself, such as node-to-node protocol and entry-to-exit protocol. Finally, a protocol is required between networks, which is the internetwork protocol.

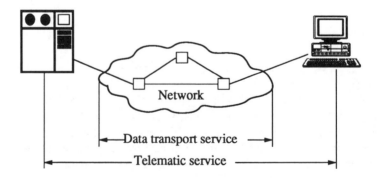

Figure 5.2 Concepts of computer communications.

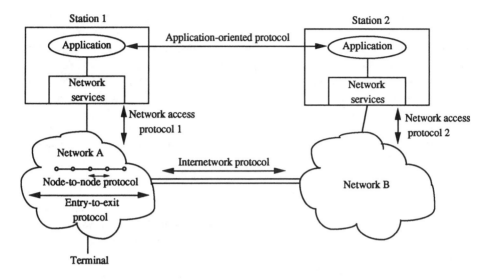

Figure 5.3 Relations of communication protocols.

Figure 5.3 is a general classification of protocols, and protocol architecture can be subdivided according to specific requirements. The structure of hardware and software required for defining functions of communications in this manner is called the *communication architecture*. In the following section, these concepts will be used as a focal point to describe the open systems architecture standards and the OSI Reference Model.

5.1.2 Open Systems Interconnection

The standards established by the international bodies for the computer industry of the past were mainly concerned with the internal operations of computers or connection with various types of peripheral devices. As a result, the hardware and software communications systems that were in circulation in the early days were plug-compatible systems that could only exchange information at the computers themselves. Such systems are called *closed systems*. Consequently, in order to exchange information with a computer from a different manufacturer, the respective standards of the other manufacturer must be followed.

In contrast, in the past few years several international standard bodies associated with common carriers have adopted standards that would allow interlinking of network devices. Recommendations adopted in this manner provided compatibility among equipment of different vendors, allowing a purchaser to select equipment most suitable to his needs among the diverse equipment categories.

Initially, the services provided by most common carriers were mainly associated with data transmission; hence, standards were only concerned with interfacing a device to the network. Recently, however, common carriers have begun providing extensive distributed information services, such as teletex and videotex. Accordingly, standard bodies associated with the telecommunications industry have enacted high-level standards related not only to network interfacing, but also to information exchanging control and data format between systems, enabling mutual information exchange among equipment of different manufacturers. Such a system is called an *open system*, and such an environment is called the *open systems interconnection environment* (OSIE).

In the mid-1970s, different forms of distributed systems rooted in public and private data networks became widespread, magnifying the necessity for an open system. From then on, various categories of standards have been developed, and the very first to be announced at ISO was the *OSI reference model*, which was concerned with the overall structure related to the complete communication system inside each computer.

The objective of the OSI reference model is to provide a framework for standards development, as well as support existing and evolving standards activities within the framework, and eventually enable communication between application processes of different computers supporting the same standards.

In conclusion, OSI is associated with information exchange between processes and allows an application process to carry out the distributed information processing task independently of the computer operation.

5.1.3 OSI Reference Model

In general, a communication system is composed of complex hardware and software parts, and in the early stages, the software of such systems was implemented in the form of single, complex, and unstructured programs. As a result, the software developed in this fashion was extremely difficult to test and modify. Also, communication protocols were too complicated to implement as single protocols and could not support different physical networks.

To overcome these problems, ISO adopted a layered approach for the reference model. According to the layered principle, a complete communication system was subdivided into several layers, each performing a well-defined task and implementing any new level of abstraction as a well-defined function. As indicated in Figure 5.4, such OSI specifications can be conceptually subdivided into three layers: protocol, services, and reference model.

Concepts of layered architecture cover layer entities, protocols, and services as a whole, as indicated in Figure 5.5. Every entity at a given layer communicates through the service access point within a system. Layer $(N + 1)$ communicates with

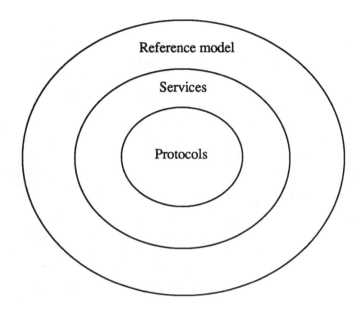

Figure 5.4 OSI specification.

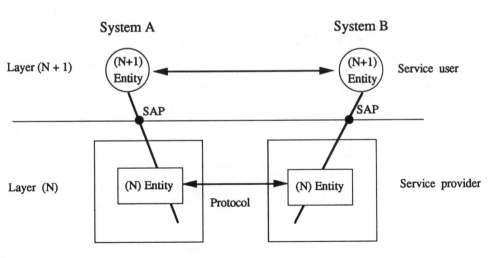

SAP : Service Access Point

Figure 5.5 Concepts of layered architecture.

another peer layer $(N + 1)$ by way of a service supported at layer (N), and layer (N) is called a service provider and layer $(N + 1)$ is called a service user.

Conceptually, the layers of a communication system perform one of two generic functions: network-dependent functions and application-oriented functions. As shown in Figure 5.6, the operational environment of a communication system can be divided into three distinct operational environments: (1) the *network environment*, which is concerned with the protocols and standards relating to the different types of underlying data communication networks; (2) the *OSI environment*, which embraces the network environment and adds additional application-oriented protocols and standards to allow end systems (computers) to communicate with one another in an open way; and (3) the *systems environment*, which is built on the OSI environment and is concerned with a manufacturer's own proprietary software and services to perform a particular distributed information processing task.

The selection of functions executed at each layer and at boundaries between the layers is based on the experience gained from the early standardization activities. Each layer performs a single well-defined function in an overall communication system interconnection, and achieves communication with the peer layer of a remote

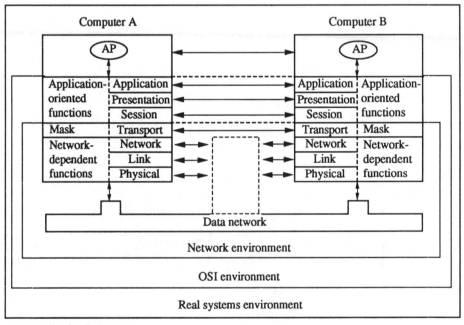

AP : Application Processor

Figure 5.6 Operational environments and OSI Reference Model.

system according to the protocol defined in exchanging message units composed of user data and additional control information. In this case, each layer possesses a single well-defined interface with the adjacent upper layer as well as with the adjacent lower layer. In conclusion, the implementation of the optional protocol layer is *independent* of the implementation of other layers.

As indicated in Figure 5.6, the logical structure of the OSI Reference Model is composed of seven protocol layers. The three lower layers (1 to 3) are *network-dependent* and represent the protocols associated with the data communication network that links a pair of communicating computers. On the other hand, the upper three layers (5 to 7) are *application-oriented* protocols that allow a pair of end-user application processes to interoperate through a service provided at the local operating system. The middle transport layer (4) assumes the role of a mask that conceals the detailed operations of lower network-dependent layers from the upper application-oriented layers. Basically, it is implemented above the service provided by the network-dependent layers in order to provide a network-independent message interchange service to the application-oriented layers.

As was stated above, the function of each layer is formalized into conventions used at that layer for communication with a peer layer of a remote system, and into protocols that define a set of rules. Consequently, each layer provides a defined set of services to the adjacent upper layer, as indicated in Figure 5.7, and uses the services provided by the adjacent lower layer in order to transmit protocol-related message units to a remote peer layer.

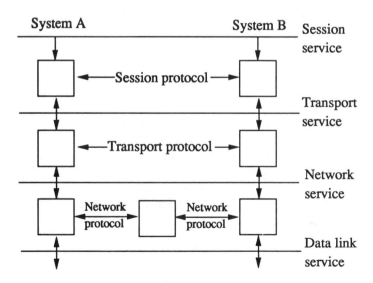

Figure 5.7 Services in OSI Reference Model.

The transport layer of Figure 5.7 provides network-independent message transport services to the session layer, which is the adjacent upper layer. In order to transmit a transport protocol-related set of message units to the peer transport layer of a remote system, it uses the services provided by the network layer, which is the adjacent lower layer. Therefore, although conceptually communication with the remote system's peer layer is achieved according to the protocol defined in each layer, in reality transmission is achieved through the services provided by the protocol message units of each layer and by the adjacent lower layer. Functions of each layer are summarized in Figure 5.8.

5.1.4 Open Systems Standards

While the OSI reference model standardizes the communication system structure as a template with the standards activities associated with each layer as the basis, it was not intended to standardize protocols associated with each layer. Rather, each layer is related to a set of standards, each of which provides different levels of functionality. Consequently, in a specific open systems environment, a set of standards is defined that can be used by all the systems included in that environment.

Currently, the main international bodies in carrying forward the standardizations on computer communications are ISO, IEEE, and CCITT. ISO and IEEE are working on standards to be used by computer manufacturers, and CCITT is defining standards required for linking different forms of national as well as international public network equipment. But as the degree of overlap in the standards of the computer and the telecommunications industries gradually increases, the degree of cooperation and commonality between the standards enacted at these organizations is increasing as well.

Before the OSI standards activity, the United States Department of Defense, through its own *Defense Advanced Research Projects Agency* (DARPA), carried out over several years of basic research on computer communications and networking. As a part of the research, computer networks associated with several universities and other research establishments were linked with the computer networks of DARPA, and this internetwork is called ARPANET. Recently, ARPANET expanded in scope through unification with the internet developed by government agencies, and such a combined internet is the *Internet* of today.

The protocol suite used at the Internet is known as *Transmission Control Protocol/Internet Protocol* (TCP/IP), and it includes both the network-oriented protocols and application support protocols. TCP/IP is broadly used in the existing internet, and hence a considerable portion of TCP/IP protocols was used as the basis for OSI standards. Furthermore, since TCP/IP does not require a license fee, all of the protocol specifications associated with it are in the public domain, and in order to create open systems networking environments, they are broadly used by commercial and public authorities as well. In practice, therefore, there are two major

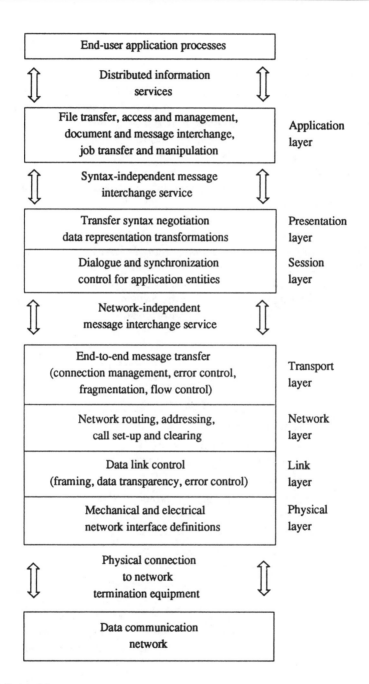

Figure 5.8 Protocol layer summary.

vendor-independent open systems standards: the TCP/IP protocol suite and those based on the OSI standards.

Figure 5.9 shows standards associated with the TCP/IP protocol suite. As was mentioned previously, the development of TCP/IP was completed in the early stages of OSI, and hence TCP/IP does not include all of the protocols related to the OSI layer. The specification methodology used in TCP/IP protocols is also different from that of the OSI standards. Still, a large portion of the functionality associated with the OSI layer is included in the TCP/IP suite.

As indicated in Figure 5.10, a range of standards is associated with each layer in the case of ISO/CCITT standards, and such standards allow an administrative authority to choose a set of standards most suitable for its application. The resulting protocol suite is known as the *open systems interconnection profile* (OSIP). A number of such profiles have now been defined, including *technical and office product system* (TOP), *manufacturing automation protocol* (MAP), and U.S. and U.K. GOSIP, for use in the U.S. and the U.K. government projects, respectively.

A suite that is similar to OSIP, known as *CEN Functional Standards*, is in use in Europe, and it is being defined through the *Standards Promotion and Application Group* (SPAG), which is composed of 12 European companies.

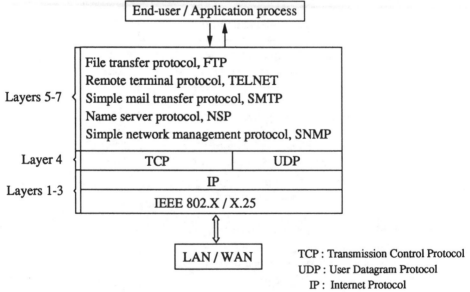

Figure 5.9 TCP/IP protocol suite.

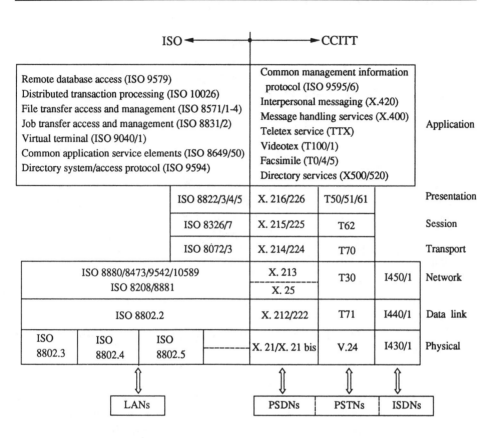

Figure 5.10 Standards summary.

5.2 FDDI LAN

Today, the high functionality, high performance, and widespread use of computer hardware, as well as the lowered cost of communication application interfaces, have created an environment in which such expensive equipment as disk storage devices and laser printers, scattered around a concentrated complex of buildings such as a university, is shared by many users. The emergence of LANs, which can achieve high-speed transmission of large quantities of data, has also resulted.

In general, a LAN uses coaxial cable or twisted pair as the transmission medium. It has a transmission speed below 10 Mbps and transmission distance that is limited to a radius of 3 km. Several transmission media have been developed as a result of recent technological advances, and the FDDI, which is a high-speed LAN that employs optical fiber as the transmission medium, has emerged on the scene.

The FDDI provides a transmission speed of 100 Mbps through optical fiber with the LAN technology as the basis, and it is widely used mainly as a backbone connection between LANs. In this section, the LAN topology and operation principle will first be reviewed, followed by a description of the FDDI.

5.2.1 LAN

The LAN's network topology can be categorized into ring, star, tree, and bus configurations, and currently the most widely used are the bus and the ring. The standards for these LAN protocols, such as *logical link control* (LLC), *carrier-sense multiple access with collision detection* (CSMA/CD), token bus, and token ring, were announced in 1985 by the IEEE 802 Committee, and were also adopted by ISO. LAN standards correspond to layers 1 and 2 of the OSI Reference Model, described in Section 5.1, and are configured as shown in Figure 5.11.

The 802.1 *high-level interface* (HLI) deals with issues relating to network architecture, internetworking, and network management for local networks. The 802.2 LLC is employed at the upper layers of MAC standards, and its objective is to provide a means of data exchange between users who use different MACs. The MAC protocol is a key function of the LAN standards and regulates procedures required for data transmission. It is treated in detail in IEEE 802.3, 802.4, and 802.5 standards.

Network topology can be categorized into bus configuration in CSMA/CD and token bus, and ring configuration in token ring and FDDI. The transmission control scheme can be categorized into CSMA/CD, which is a contention-based scheme, and into token bus, token ring, and FDDI, which are token control schemes.

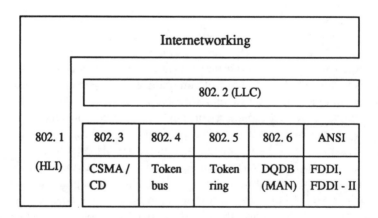

Figure 5.11 IEEE 802 standards and FDDI.

CSMA/CD Scheme

CSMA/CD is currently the most widely used scheme, and its most representative product is the Ethernet. In this CSMA/CD scheme, a station that wants to transmit can transmit a data frame if the medium is not being used by another station. The transmitted frame has a format as shown in Figure 5.12.

7 octets	1	2 or 6	2 or 6	2	<- - - - Length < 1600 - - - ->		CRC - 32
Preamble	SFD	DA	SA	LC	Information field	Pad	FCS

SFD : Start Frame Delimiter
DA   : Destination Address
SA   : Source Address
LC   : Length Count
FCS : Frame Check Sequence

Figure 5.12 802.3 CSMA/CD MAC frame format.

The media access algorithm of the CSMA/CD scheme is as follows:

Step 1: If the medium is "idle," then commence transmission; otherwise, go to Step 2.

Step 2: If the medium is "busy," then monitor the medium until "idle" is detected; if "idle" is detected, then commence transmission immediately.

Step 3: If collision is detected during transmission, then send a jamming signal that notifies all the stations of frame collision and discontinue transmission.

Step 4: Reattempt transmission sometime after jamming signal has been transmitted. (Go to Step 1)

After a given frame has collided with another frame, the source station that has transmitted the colliding frame must continue the transmission until the frame returns in order to discern whether the frame has been in a collision (see Figure 5.13). Consequently, the minimum MAC frame size is determined according to the maximum propagation delay of the medium.

Token Bus Scheme

The token bus scheme has a physical bus structure, but adopts a logical ring structure in transmitting frames between stations. In order to form a logical ring structure, each station possesses a predecessor parameter, which denotes the station that has sent the token to that particular station, and a successor parameter, which denotes the station that is to receive the token. Figure 5.14 is a representation of the token

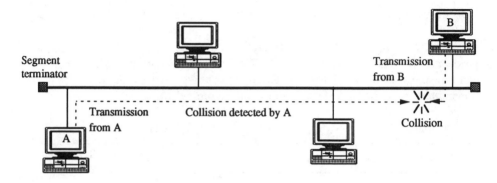

Figure 5.13 Frame collision detection.

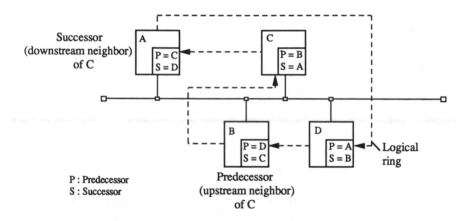

Figure 5.14 Token bus.

bus structure, and a logical ring is formed through the path A-D-B-C. When a station is newly registered or removed, the ring structure is reconstructed by altering the *next station* (NS) parameter contained inside the station contiguous to the station in question, as well as the *previous station* (PS) parameter of the next station.

For a station to transmit data, it has to acquire a token, and once the token has been obtained, it can transmit one or more data frames over a specified period of time. A station that has acquired the token hands over the right to transmit to the next station if there are no more data frames to be transmitted or if the *token holding time* (THT) that it has been assigned has expired. A station on the ring performs such functions as ring initialization, registration and removal of stations, recovery when the token gets lost or duplicated, and priority control.

In the token bus scheme, four priority classes are defined: 6, 4, 2, and 0. Each station can possess more than one priority class. At the time of ring initialization, each station is assigned a THT, which allows the station to send Class 6 frames, and *token rotation time* (TRT) values are specified, which are used in transmitting Class 4, 2, and 0 frames. Once a station acquires a token, it can transmit the highest priority frame (Class 6) during the preassigned THT interval, and in the case of low-priority frames (Class 4, 2, 0), the rotation time of the circulating token and the already designated TRTn (n = 0, 2, 4) value are compared. If the TRTn value is greater (i.e., if the token arrives sooner than the TRTn of the frame to be transmitted), the frame can be transmitted only during the time difference.

Token Ring Scheme

The token ring is the oldest ring control technique. IBM was the first to develop a product based on the token ring standard, and since then numerous companies have brought out compatible products. Also, the token ring scheme subsequently became the base frame of the FDDI standards, described in Section 5.2.2.

In a token ring structure, a station can transmit a data frame when it receives a token; I-bit of the *end delimiter* (ED) portion is set to 1 during transmission, and to 0 when the final frame is being transmitted. If all of the frames transmitted by a given station have completed their rotation around the ring and returned to the source station, the station releases the token so that another station can transmit data. Each station checks the *destination address* (DA) when it receives the frame transmitted by the previous station, and if DA is the same as its own, it copies the frame and alters the C-bit of the ED portion to 1, changes the E-bit to 1 if the frame's CRC code is in error, and transmits the frame to the next station. The station that had transmitted the frame verifies whether the returned frame had been correctly transmitted and whether any error had occurred, and then removes the frame from the ring. Such a data transmission procedure of the token ring scheme is depicted in Figure 5.15, and Figure 5.16 represents the format of the frame used.

The priority control scheme of the token ring is controlled using the AC field inside the token. The AC field's priority bits (PPP) and reserved bits (RRR) can be used to designate eight priority classes (see Figure 5.16 (c)). A token can have several priority classes, and a station is allowed to transmit if it has a frame with a higher priority than the token. Also, when a data frame passes by, a station possessing a high-priority frame can alter the RRR value of the AC field to its own priority value, thus reserving the right to transmit. After a station has completed the transmission of the data frame, it stores the RRR value (contained in the data frame) in the buffer, and hands over the token after replacing the token's PPP value with the data frame's RRR value. When the token rotates around the ring, if there are no stations with a priority higher than the PPP value of the token, the token arrives at

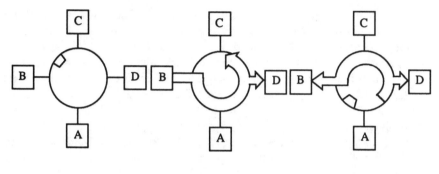

- Sender looks for token
- Changes token to frame
  and appends data

- Receiver copies
  data addressed
  to it

- Sender generates
  token upon receipt
  of data

Figure 5.15 Token ring operation.

the station that has made a reservation. After the transmission of high-priority data, the station that has accepted the token returns the token that has the same PPP value as when the token was received. The station that has transmitted by increasing the token's PPP value compares the priority value of the token (when it arrives) with the value stored in the buffer, and if the two values are the same, it assumes that there is no higher priority station and releases the token. In other words, the station that releases the token after increasing its priority has the responsibility of restoring the original priority of the token when it returns.

5.2.2 FDDI

The FDDI uses optical fiber as the transmission medium and is a LAN protocol based on the token ring access method of IEEE 802.5, providing a transmission speed of 100 Mbps. The FDDI was proposed by the X3T9.5 Working Group of the *American National Standards Institute* (ANSI) and is being applied in back-end local networks (which are used for connecting mainframe computers and large-capacity storage devices), high-speed office networks, and LAN backbone networks of the IEEE 802 party.

The FDDI has a dual ring structure and can link up to 500 stations within the radius of 100 km, with the distance between stations being limited to 2 km. Also, the FDDI-II, which is an advanced version of FDDI, is in the final stages of standardization. The FDDI-II can transmit real-time data such as voice and circuit-switched data traffic such as video data.

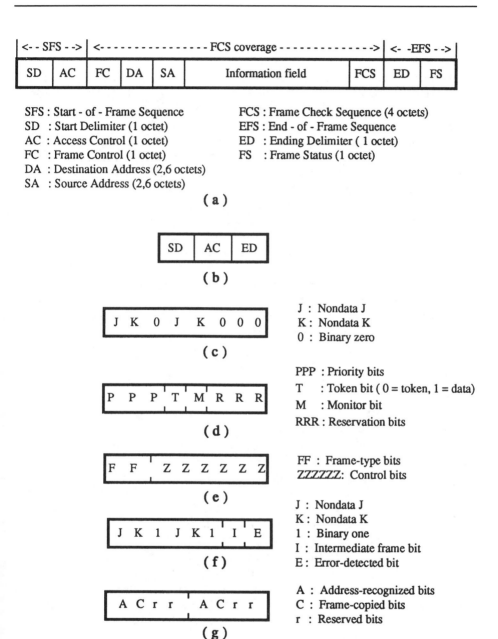

Figure 5.16 IEEE 802.5 token ring frame format: (a) frame format; (b) token format; (c) start delimiter (SD); (d) access control (AC); (e) frame control (FC); (f) end delimiter (ED); (g) frame status (FS).

FDDI Configuration

As shown in Figure 5.17, the FDDI ring is composed of a primary ring and a secondary ring that have opposite data transmission directions. In normal operation, data flows in the primary ring only, while the secondary ring remains in the idle state. A station in the ring is categorized into Class A and Class B, depending on how it is connected to the ring. These two types of stations are respectively named *dual-attachment station* (DAS) and *single-attachment station* (SAS) in Figure 5.17. Class A station is a station that is connected to both the primary ring and secondary ring and can change the configuration of the ring when a fault occurs in the link or station (see Figure 5.17 (b)). On the other hand, Class B station is connected only to the primary ring through a concentrator and cannot reconfigure the ring, even when a link fault occurs. The concentrator is a special form of Class A station and is a device that concentrates multiple Class B stations by connecting them to its lower part.

The FDDI has a layered architecture, as shown in Figure 5.18, and is composed of the following layers corresponding to the OSI layers 1 and 2: *physical medium dependent* (PMD), *physical* (PHY), LLC, MAC, and *station management* (SMT). The PMD layer regulates the characteristics of a fiber-optic medium, the connector for connecting each station to the medium, the wavelength to be used for transmission, the power requirement of the transmitter, and the method of optically bypassing nonoperation node. The PHY layer regulates the 125-MHz clock speed, clocking scheme, and control symbol, while the MAC layer regulates token passing, frame formation, addressing, error detection and recovery, and the bandwidth allocation method between nodes. Finally, the SMT layer provides such network management services as station insertion and removal, ring configuration, and error logging. In the FDDI standards, the protocol of the LLC layer is not separately prescribed; hence, the IEEE 802.2 protocol of Figure 5.11 can be used.

Each station above the FDDI ring can transmit information when it receives a token, and the information transported from the LLC layer to the MAC layer is transmitted by being loaded onto a variable-length frame that has the format shown in Figure 5.19.

In Figure 5.19(a), the field information of each frame is indicated through the use of twenty-four different symbols, with each symbol indicating four bits. Among the twenty-four symbols, sixteen are used as data symbols, three are used as a line status signal that is recognized at the physical layer, two are used as a control indicator, and the remaining three are used for the *start delimiter* (SD) and ED.

FDDI-MAC Layer

The MAC protocol of FDDI is analogous to the token ring of IEEE 802.5, but differs in token handling, priority, and management mechanism.

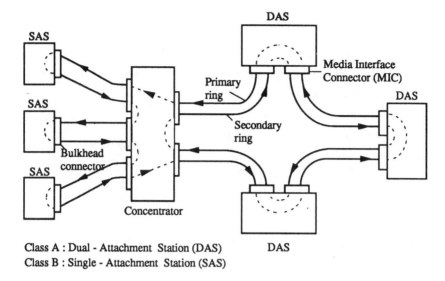

Class A : Dual - Attachment Station (DAS)
Class B : Single - Attachment Station (SAS)

(a)

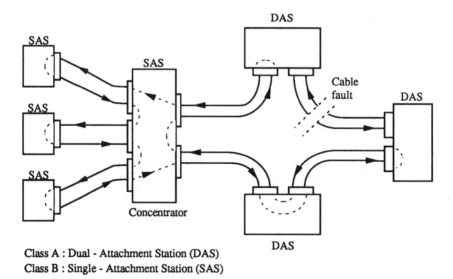

Class A : Dual - Attachment Station (DAS)
Class B : Single - Attachment Station (SAS)

(b)

Figure 5.17 FDDI ring configuration: (a) normal operation; (b) during a fault.

OSI layer

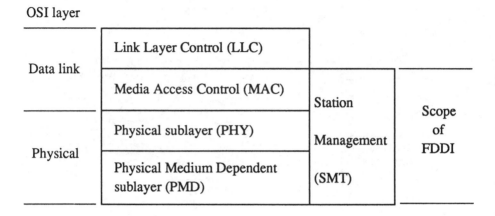

Figure 5.18 Four key standards of FDDI specification.

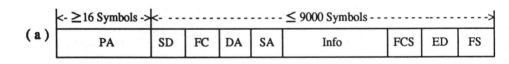

PA : Preamble   Info : Information
SD : Start Delimiter   FCS : Frame Check Sequence
FC : Frame Control   ED : End Delimiter
DA : Destination Address   FS : Frame Status
SA : Source Address

Figure 5.19 FDDI frame format: (a) FDDI information frame format; (b) FDDI token format.

A token is a frame with a special format, and a station with a token possesses the right to transmit data and can transmit a multiple number of frames during a designated time interval. Each station that is connected to the ring releases the token to the next station if there is no more data to transmit or after the designated data transmission time has elapsed. Also, each station repeats the frame transmitted from the previous station to the next station, and when the frame arrives at the destination station designated by the frame, the destination station obtains a copy of the frame. Here, the destination station establishes frame error detection status, address acknowledgment status, and frame duplication status in the status bit, and retransmits the frame to the next station. The station that has transmitted a frame must remove the frame after it has rotated around the ring and returned. This is called *stripping*. Whether the frame had been properly transmitted can be determined here by checking the frame's status information. But error recovery is handled by an upper layer.

In contrast to the token ring of IEEE 802.5, the token in the FDDI is released after a station has transmitted a frame, and hence frame transmission can continue even if the frames transmitted prior to the release of the token still exist in the ring. Thus, multiple frames transmitted from multiple stations can exist above the ring at specific periods of time. A diagram in Figure 5.20 illustrates the frame flow mechanism in the FDDI.

Physical Layer

The physical layer is composed of PHY and PMD, with PHY regulating upper layer protocols, while the PMD regulates hardware parts associated with optical fibers composing the FDDI link.

The FDDI node uses the optical wavelength of 1300 nm and uses multimode fiber with a core diameter of 50 μm, cladding diameter of 125 μm, and a bit error rate of 10^{-9}.

The PHY transmitter converts the four-bit symbols sent from the MAC into a five-bit code group and transmits it to the medium, and the PHY receiver examines the SD from the encoded data stream, separates the symbol boundaries, and delivers the decoded symbols to the MAC. Additional symbols such as QUIET, IDLE, and HALT are acknowledged at the PHY and are used in supplementing *single-mode fiber* (SMF) interface functions.

In token ring or Ethernet, the Manchester coding method is used in data line coding. In Manchester coding, two transition bauds are generated in marking one bit. In the FDDI, the 4b/5b coding method is used, which uses five bauds to indicate four bits (see Table 5.1). The 4b/5b coding method has the virtue of limiting run lengths and allowing small transition, thus enabling the transmission of more bits using the same bandwidth. Consequently, data transmission speed in the FDDI is around 100 Mbps, and the clock speed of each node can be as high as 125 MHz.

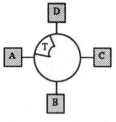

1) A waits for token to arrive.

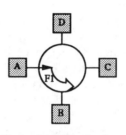

2) A seizes token, begins transmitting frame 1.

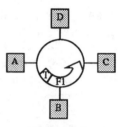

3) A adds token to the end of frame 1.

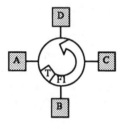

4) C copies frame 1, which is addressed to it.

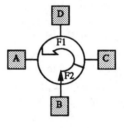

5) While C continues to copy, B seizes token from the ring and begins transmitting frame 2.

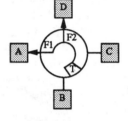

6) B emits token. D copies frame 2, which is addressed to it, and A removes frame 1 from the ring.

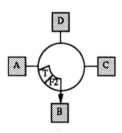

7) A removes frame 1 completely, but lets frame 2 and token pass. B removes frame 2.

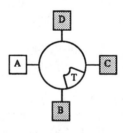

8) B removes frame 2 completely and lets token pass.

Figure 5.20 FDDI token operation.

Table 5.1
4b/5b Code

Symbol	Encoded Bits	Symbol	Encoded Bits
0	11110	C	11010
1	01001	D	11011
2	10100	E	11100
3	10101	F	11101
4	01010	Q (Quiet)	00000
5	01011	I (Idle)	11111
6	01110	H (Halt)	00100
7	01111	J (Start 1)	11000
8	10010	K (Start 2)	10001
9	10011	T (Terminate)	01101
A	10110	R (Reset)	10111
B	10111	S (Set)	11001

While in the token ring of IEEE 802.5 an active monitor exists for the entire ring, a distributed clock scheme is used in the FDDI. Also, a FIFO elastic buffer is employed when a station retransmits a bit in order to compensate for the difference between the input and output clock speeds that results from the jitter of the multi-mode fiber. The receiver employs such techniques as PLL in order to recover the clock of the previous station from the received data, while the transmitter uses a fixed local clock.

If the length of the preamble inside the frame is too short, symbols might get lost when the frame circulates around the ring, which can lead to the loss of the frame as well. Such a problem is solved through a smoothing buffer. A smoothing buffer inspects the length of the preamble between frames in order to maintain the length of 16 symbols.

SMT layer

SMT of the FDDI is a part of the FDDI management functions possessed by each station, and it enables the station to control a process that goes on at several different FDDI layers. That is, SMT regulates system management functions, including the control function required for the proper operation of an FDDI node in the ring. Other functions provided by SMT include link management, insertion and removal of a station, station initialization, configuration management, fault isolation and recovery, schedule policy, and statistical resources accumulation. Services defined in FDDI

SMT can be separated into three types: service access management employing SMT frame, the service for connecting PHY and MAC, and the service for reporting the MAC condition via *ring management* (RMT) and for resolving error conditions.

FDDI-II

In FDDI-II, the FDDI has been supplemented by the *hybrid ring control* (HRC) function, which dynamically divides the ring's 100-Mbps bandwidth into small time slots for the transmission of delay-sensitive isochronous data such as voice traffic, allowing each station to use the divided bandwidth (see Figure 5.21).

FDDI-II uses the PHY and PMD layers of the FDDI in their original form, and HRC exists between the MAC layer and the PHY layer. HRC carries out the

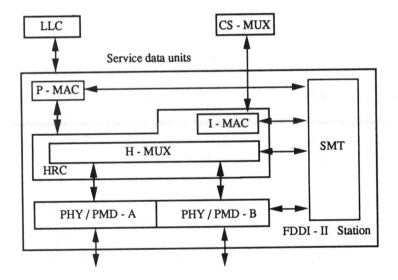

LLC   : Logical Link Control
CS-MUX : Circuit-Switched Multiplexer
P - MAC : Packet Medium Access Control
I - MAC   : Isochronous Medium Access Control
H - MUX : Hybrid Multiplexer
HRC   : Hybrid Ring Control
PHY   : Physical Layer
PMD   : Physical Medium Dependent
SMT   : Station Management

Figure 5.21 FDDI-II architecture.

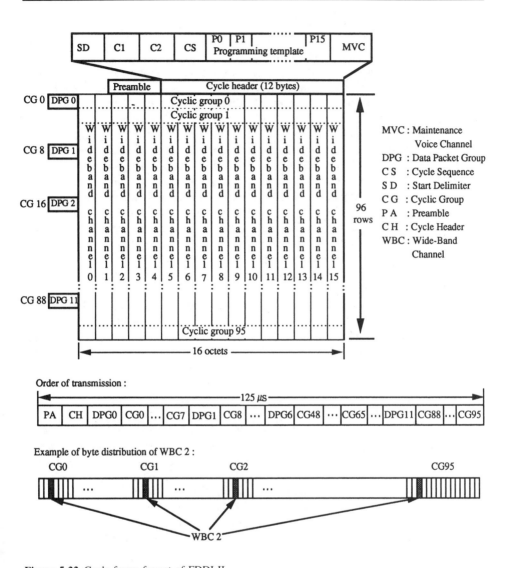

Figure 5.22 Cycle frame format of FDDI-II.

isochronous MAC (I-MAC) function, as well as the function of multiplexing *packet MAC* (P-MAC) data and I-MAC data.

An FDDI-II station operates either in basic mode or hybrid mode, depending on the presence of isochronous data. Basic mode operates as in the case of the FDDI. When user asks SMT for the transmission of isochronous data through appropriate signaling, SMT transits the ring to the hybrid mode.

When FDDI-II operates in hybrid mode, a specified station becomes a cycle master that administers isochronous transmission. The cycle master creates a cycle that transmits packets as well as data every 125 μs, and also assumes the role of assigning channels after receiving the band assignment request from another station. If transmission of isochronous data is required, each station is assigned the required time slot in advance and uses the slot to transmit data. The cycle created by HRC has the format shown in Figure 5.22. The ring's bandwidth is separated into *wide band channel* (WBC) units, and up to 16 WBCs can be allocated. Each WBC can transmit 6.144 Mbps, and once a station uses a WBC, hypothetically, WBC can be divided into 8-kbps units inside the station.

The preamble of the cycle frame is used in adjusting synchronization between stations, while cycle header's *cycle sequence* (CS) indicates a modulo 192 sequence counter for the cycle frame. The *maintenance voice channel* (MVC) provides a 64-kbps voice channel for maintenance. Programming templates from P0 to P15 indicate whether each WBC has been assigned to a packet or isochronous data. C1 and C2 are symbols for indicating formation of synchronization and cycle procedures.

FDDI Standardization

Although the standardization of the FDDI has already been completed, the development of optical-fiber technology has created a necessity for a new standardization of PMD, and one of the byproducts is the *single-mode fiber-PMD* (SMF-PMD), which is currently going through standardization. While the SMF-PMD basically has the same function as the PMD, single-mode optical fiber and laser diode transmitters are used in order to improve performance, making it possible to use 60 to 100 km of repeater spacing. In addition, standardization activities are in progress on *twisted Pair-PMD* (TP-PMD), *low-cost fiber-PMD* (LCF-PMD), and *SONET physical layer mapping-PMD* (SPM-PMD), which is intended for interworking with SONET. Currently, the standardization of FDDI-II is nearing completion.. Also, standardization of *FDDI follow-on LAN* (FFOL) has been in progress at ANSI X3T9.5 since 1990. FFOL is an advanced form of the FDDI that can achieve connection at a higher speed than the existing LANs, as well as link easily with the BISDN.

5.3 FRAME RELAY

With the increasing demand for high-speed data services, frame relay, which can provide higher performance than the traditional X.25 packet switching, has appeared as one of the LAN interconnection technologies. Frame relay technology is the next evolutionary step of X.25 technology and is designed to improve the efficiency of packet networks, as well as accommodate wide-area interconnection of LANs at the 1.544-Mbps rate.

X.25 packet standards were developed under the assumption that the transmission medium is error-prone, and to ensure end-to-end quality, error management is performed at every node through resource-intensive *high-level data link control* (HDLC) protocol. Accordingly, error detection and recovery functions are executed link by link, which becomes the leading cause of network delay, thus hindering the network from operating at higher speeds.

In frame relay, such error correction and flow control functions are handled at the end users' *customer premises equipment* (CPE) to enhance performance. As a consequence, bandwidth requirements can be lowered, which in turn curtails communications costs and reduces the number of items of packet handling equipment in the network.

In conclusion, frame relay is a connection-oriented technology that supports variable-length packets and can be viewed as the next logical step of the X.25, and, like the X.25, it regulates the interface between computer customers and networks (public or private).

In this section, we will examine trends in frame relay technologies and discuss frame relay protocol and standards.

5.3.1 Background

Frame relay is a technique for accessing wide-area networks and can be described in comparison with the general network topologies in existence. The general network operational mode can be categorized into connection-oriented mode, such as the X.25 packet-switched data network, and connectionless mode, such as the Internet protocol, which executes relaying in OSI network layers. An intermediate node in such a network topology possesses complete data link layer functions that are performed at each connection segment for frame delimiting, sequence control, error detection, error recovery, and flow control, and network layer functions for multiplexing, relaying, and routing. The network layer protocol cannot be implemented in very-high-throughput operations due to the requisite flow control processing and limitations in current hardware.

Frame relay realizes high-speed transmission and low delay by minimizing formats and procedures required in relaying through dynamic bandwidth allocation, and thus has the advantage of being able to process bursty traffic that could not be handled by existing networks.

Frame relay protocol supports data rates from 64 kbps to 2 Mbps, and its applications include (1) block interactive data application: applications that require low delay and high throughput such as high-resolution graphics (i.e., high-resolution videotex and CAD/CAM); (2) file transfer (very large file transfer): applications that require high throughput with short response time; 3) multiplexed low bit rate: applications that require the multiplexing capabilities of layer 2 protocol; (4) character-interactive traffic: applications that require short frame, low delay, and low throughput. However, frame relay is not suitable for voice or steady-flow traffic, which require real-time processing.

Frame relay is a multiplexed data networking service that supports connection between CPE and a node, and will be implemented in such products as the LAN bridge, router, and T1 multiplexer. Figure 5.23 indicates the position of frame relay among several categories of internetworking technologies. Some of the rival technologies of frame relay include T1 links, fractional T1, fractional T3, ISDN primary rate service, switched DS-1, and SMDS.

Fast-packet switches must be used in order to achieve the inherent benefits of frame relay. Fast-packet switches employ statistical multiplexing techniques in order to adapt a channel's entire bandwidth for transmission, and does not allocate bandwidth for users not requesting transmission.

While fast-packet switches can support non-frame relay traffic, they can also raise throughput between locations with large bursty traffic by utilizing statistical multiplexing techniques. Consequently, for users with bursty traffic it is more advantageous to use the frame relay and fast-packet technologies to upgrade T1 equipment that employs time-division multiplexing.

The current technology in high-speed communications is focused on frame relay and cell relay, which is the underlying technology of the BISDN. Accordingly, some vendors accommodate frame relay, and some are planning strategies for a migration to cell relay, while others are pursuing both technologies. Also, some view frame relay as being complementary to cell relay, while others view it as a competing technology. However, frame relay and cell relay were designed to accomplish different objectives and are evolving in two different directions.

Frame relay is a medium- to high-speed data interface for the private networks to be implemented in the next few years, and its standardization is in progress at the DS-1 rate. However, cell relay is a high- or very-high-speed switching system that supports not only data services but also voice and video services, and is being standardized at the SONET/SDH level that transmits with bit rates from 51 Mbps to 2.4 Gbps.

5.3.2 Frame Relay Protocol Architecture

Frame relay can be described in terms of the modeling techniques of the OSI Reference Model and OSI service convention. Hence, the *data link* (DL) layer in frame relay can be divided into the DL-core sublayer and the DL-control sublayer, as shown

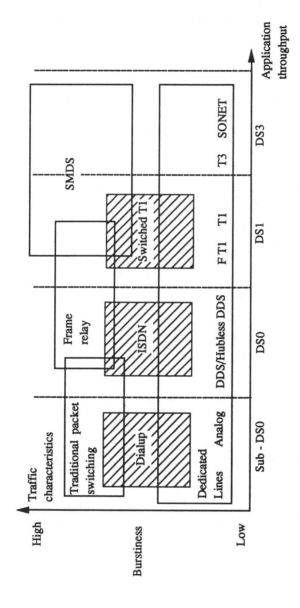

Figure 5.23 Frame relay in contrast.

in Figure 5.24. The DL-core sublayer is a functional group that makes up the core of HDLC and uses physical layer services to provide a DL-core service to the DL-control sublayer, while the DL-control sublayer uses a DL-core service to provide OSI data link layer services. Figure 5.24 depicts layering and sublayering in the frame relay protocol suite of the lower three layers.

The DL-core service provides connection-oriented, transparent transfer of data between service users, and service users do not have to be knowledgeable of protocol executed at the DL-core sublayer. Also, the DL-core service delimits DL-core SDUs from service users and transparently transmits the SDUs according to a specified sequence.

If such a layering concept is illustrated from the OSI Reference Model point of view, then the result is as shown in Figure 5.25. In the figure, routers, bridges, front-end processor, and control devices are defined as access devices, and the intelligent nodal processors located at a different end than the UNI are defined as network devices. The data link protocol operates between network access devices,

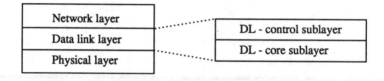

Figure 5.24 Layering and sublayering in frame relay protocol suite.

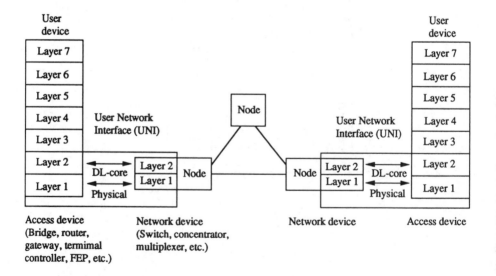

Figure 5.25 Frame relay protocol model.

and it is responsible for transporting data from one end of the network to another. Also, the data link control protocol operates between an access device (such as a router) and a network device (such as a nodal processor).

5.3.3 Frame Relay Protocol

The frame format in frame relay follows ANSI T1.6ca, and some of the data link layer core functions defined in ANSI T1.6ca include frame delimiting, alignment and transparency, addressing, and congestion control. In this section, we will first examine the frame format and then describe some of its main functions.

Frame Format

As shown in Figure 5.26, the frame format consists of flags, header, information, and *frame control segment* (FCS). Flag denotes the beginning and end of the frame and has the pattern "01111110." Header is composed of *data link connection identifier* (DLCI), *extended address* (EA), *forward explicit congestion notification* (FECN), *backward explicit congestion notification* (BECN), *discard eligibility* (DE), and *command and response* (C/R). The DLCI is employed as an addressing mechanism, and the EA bit is employed in address expansion. FECN/BECN and the DE bit are utilized for congestion control, while the C/R indication bit is transmitted transparently and used at the access device of the user rather than in the network. The FCS employs the CCITT 16-CRC and is used in inspecting the presence of errors in the frame.

Addressing

The DLCI of the frame header designates end-to-end *permanent virtual circuit* (PVC) access between data link layers and can employ a two- to four-byte address field format to designate a point-to-point or point-to-multipoint access point.

Ten bits of the DLCI are employed in the case of the two-byte header; hence, a total of 1024 DLCIs can be used. Among them, DLCI 0 is reserved for channel call-control signaling that defines the *signaling virtual channel* (SVC) function of CCITT Q.933/ANSI T1.6fr standard, and thus is not currently applied. Also, DLCI 1 to 15 and 1008 to 1022 are reserved for future improvements, while DLCI 1023 is used for the *local management interface* (LMI). Hence, 992 DLCIs from 16 to 1007 can be used. DLCI 1023 performs PVC link maintenance-related functions. In the case of a three-byte header, 16 addressing bits (65,536 DLCIs) are used, and 23 addressing bits (8,388,608) are used in the case of a four-byte header.

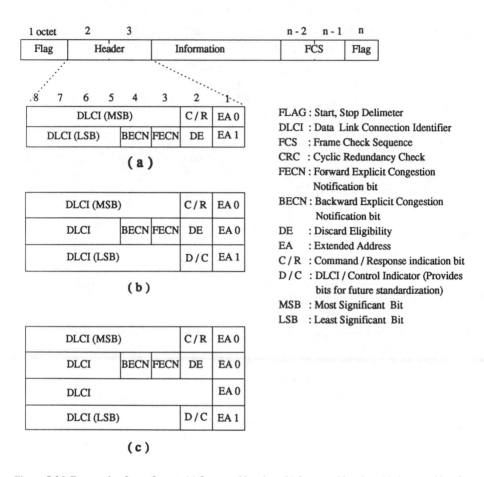

Figure 5.26 Frame relay frame format: (a) 2-octet addressing; (b) 3-octet addressing; (c) 4-octet addressing.

Information Field Length

While frame relay can accommodate variable information lengths, it is desirable to fix the frame size for efficient circuit utilization and reduction of error rate. Consequently, frame size is defined at the time of establishing the PVC or is determined at the time of establishing the call-connection. But in the absence of any special requirement, compatibility with ISDN *Link Access Procedure-D* (LAP-D) is taken into account to establish the maximum frame size at 262 bytes. In the draft standard, frame size up to 1600 bytes is recommended in order to support interlinking between IEEE 802.3 or Ethernets, and up to 4000 bytes for interlinking between token ring LANs or FDDIs.

Congestion Control

One of the special features of frame relay is that a band can be variably allocated depending on user demand (On Demand), and hypothetically the entire T1 band can be used by one user. However, traffic congestion can occur if several users simultaneously generate traffic, which results in frame loss. Therefore, congestion control has emerged as a crucial problem, and research using many different approaches is in progress to resolve it.

Currently, the T1.6ca standard recommends the use of a congestion control method that employs the FECN/BECN field. In case congestion occurs, the node that detects it sets the FECN bit to 1. When the receiving side sees that the FECN bit has been changed to 1, it perceives that congestion has occurred and sets the BECN bit to 1 when transmitting a frame. The source of congestion receives the frame with the altered FECN and BECN bits, acknowledges that the frame it has sent has instigated congestion, and adjusts its traffic accordingly, as depicted in Table 5.2.

Table 5.2
Case of Terminal A and Host B

Traffic	*No Congestion*		*Congestion A → B and B → A*	
	FECN	BECN	FECN	BECN
A → B	0	0	1	1
B → A	0	0	1	1
Traffic	*Congestion A → B No Congestion B → A*		*Congestion B → A No Congestion A → B*	
	FECN	BECN	FECN	BECN
A → B	1	0	0	1
B → A	0	1	1	0

Another congestion control method is congestion avoidance. In this method, the *committed information rate* (CIR) is fixed at the time of establishing the PVC, and when traffic occurs that exceeds the CIR value, the DE bit contained in the frame header is set to 1 before being transmitted. When congestion occurs, the node that detects it removes those frames first whose DE bit is 1.

While the capacity to allocate bandwidth on user demand can also be the main cause of congestion, the CIR value that is fixed below the total maximum trunk value can always be guaranteed to each user.

Error Checking

The FCS field, which is appended to the tail of the frame, is used for inspecting for the presence of an error occurrence. The FCS, generated at the access device of the transmitting side using CCITT 16-CRC, is checked at the access device of the receiving side, and any errored frame is removed. The function related to the retransmission of the removed frame is handled at an upper layer.

5.3.4 Trend in Frame Relay Standards

Frame relay service and interface standards were developed through the ANSI T1S1 Committee. The T1S1 Committee defines T1.606 as the service draft standard, and I.431, T1.6ca, and T1.6fr as the interface draft standards.

T1.606, which is the frame relay architectural standard, gives a description of the SVC and PVC and deals mainly with details on bandwidth allocation, identities of the virtual channel, quality of service, and network management commands for call setup and removal. T1.606 was approved by the ANSI in 1990, and is planned to become a part of CCITT standards in 1992.

CCITT I.233.1 recommends frame relay service as ISDN's frame mode bearer services and specifies services provided by virtual call and PVC. CCITT's frame relay transmission technique is defined as LAP-F (LAP to Frame mode bearer services) in Q.922, and the Q.933/Q.921 signaling protocol is used for data transmission path setup and release in virtual call.

Interface between the user and a network node is defined in CCITT I.431, T1.6ca, and T1.6fr. The T1S1 Committee prescribes the *primary rate access* (PRA) interface proposed in CCITT I.431 as the standard as a physical interface suitable for both the SVC and PVC. T1.6ca is the data transfer protocol draft standard to be used for SVC and PVC and defines a frame format for encapsulating packets between the network and the user. T1.6fr is a control protocol for call setup of SVC services, and the T1S1 Committee is standardizing an expanded version of Q.931, which is an ISDN call control protocol.

5.4 DQDB MAN

5.4.1 Background

As was explained in Section 5.2.1, the IEEE P802 Committee has so far standardized three classes of LANs: 802.3 CSMA/CD, 802.4 token bus, and 802.5 token ring. As shown in Figure 5.1, a LAN is used for interconnecting computers, terminals, and peripheral devices that are in close proximity on the premises of an office, a building, or a university campus.

As LANs gradually become more widely distributed, the necessity for inter-connecting the LANs that are scattered about locally has increased. Accordingly, the IEEE 802.6 Committee has been working on the MAN technology standardization since 1981 for provision of integrated services such as data, voice, and video in large metropolitan areas, and in December 1990 it approved the DQDB protocol as the IEEE 802.6 standard. DQDB was first proposed by Telecom Australia in 1986 under the name of *Queued Packet Synchronous Exchange* (QPSX), and was sub-sequently adopted and renamed by IEEE, who began to standardize it in 1987.

DQDB has a dual bus structure and features distributed queue that depends on the reservation scheme. Accordingly, DQDB accommodates data, voice, and video signals at high speeds, and can provide integrated services efficiently, without any waste in bandwidth. Broadly speaking, DQDB can provide three types of services: connectionless data services, connection-oriented data services, and isochronous ser-vices. As can be seen in Figure 5.27, the DQDB protocol corresponds to the physical

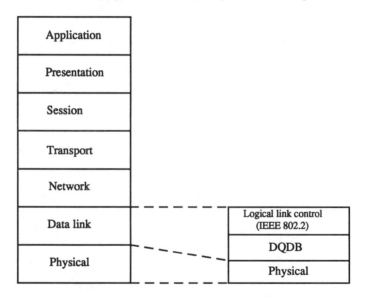

Figure 5.27 Correlation of DQDB protocol and OSI 7-layer architecture.

layer and data link layer among the seven OSI Reference Model layers described in Section 5.1. Since DQDB transmits data in 53-octet slot units, which is the same as in ATM transmission, it has the advantage of being the same cell relay trans-mission scheme in the BISDN.

5.4.2 DQDB Architecture

A DQDB network possesses a dual bus structure that consists of two unidirectional buses with opposite transmission directions. Such a bus is shared by multiple access nodes, as depicted in Figure 5.28, and, as shown in Figure 5.29, each node is linked to the transmitter module and receiver module, respectively, of the two unidirectional buses. Therefore, full-duplex mode communication is possible between the nodes. Also, the operations of the two buses are independent of one another with regards to data transmission; hence, a DQDB network has twice the capacity of a comparable system that employs only a single bus.

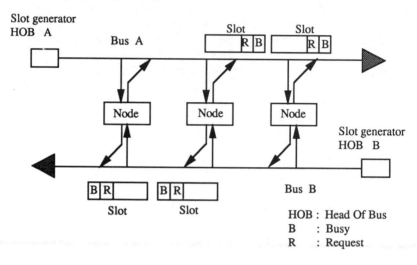

Figure 5.28 DQDB structure.

The first node of each bus performs the function of *head of bus* (HOB), which entails periodically producing empty slots or management information and releasing them into the bus. Other nodes transmit information by loading it onto the slots sent by the HOB. The bus terminates with the last node, and thus it is not necessary to erase data sent from the bus intentionally. DQDB is basically a bus structure, and hence it can be configured so that a malfunctioning node can be easily disconnected from the bus so as not to affect the operation of the overall network.

While DQDB has a dual-bus structure, it can be adapted into the looped bus topology shown in Figure 5.30. Here, DQDB has physically a ring shape, but has a bus structure logically.

A DQDB network with the looped bus topology provides reinforced fault tolerance. That is, if the bus becomes disconnected, as shown in Figure 5.31, the beginning and end points of the bus are joined together at the HOB node, and the two nodes adjacent to the broken point are made into the HOB so that the network can regain normal operation.

5.4.3 DQDB Access Control

In a DQDB network with a dual bus structure, the HOB node at the beginning of each bus sends 53-octet empty slots into the bus. A node that has data to transmit

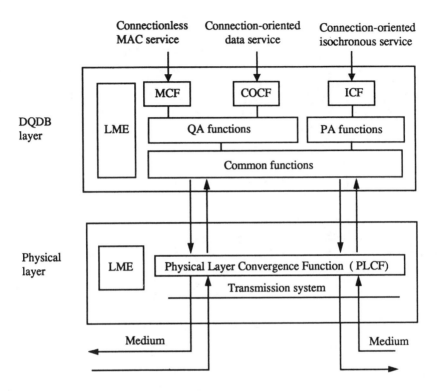

MCF : MAC Convergence Function
COCF : Connection-Oriented Covergence Function
ICF   : Isochronous Convergence Function
LME : Layer Management Entity

Figure 5.29 Functional structure of DQDB node.

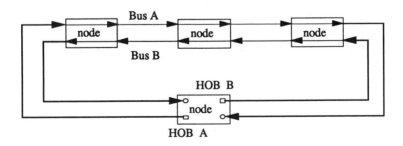

Figure 5.30 DQDB network of looped bus topology.

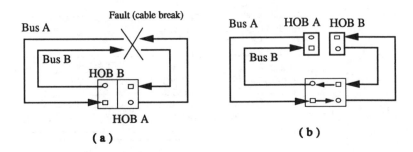

Figure 5.31 Fault tolerance of looped bus topology: (a) fault loop; (b) regained operation.

does so by loading such empty slots with its own information through the employment of the distributed queuing method. Slots are divided into *queue-arbitrated* (QA) slots for nonisochronous traffic, and *pre-arbitrated* (PA) slots for isochronous traffic. QA slots are used for either connectionless MAC services or connection-oriented data services. PA slots are used for isochronous services such as voice and video.

QA Access Control: Distributed Queue Access Protocol

DQDB network access through the QA slots is controlled according to the distributed queuing principle. The distributed queuing concept involves controlling the order of the nodes attempting to access the network in terms of the overall network, and a virtual *first-come first-served* (FCFS) queue exists for the entire network. That is, the request by a node to access the network gets in the distributed queue, and the network handles the access requests one by one from the head of the distributed queue. Controlling the distributed queue at each node to operate as if it were a single queue is the essence of the distributed queuing concept.

In the QA slot, a BUSY bit and a *request* (REQ) bit are placed in the *access control field* (ACF) in order to control the usage of each channel. The REQ bit of each QA slot actually consists of three bits in order to support three priority queues. Here, we discuss the basic distributed queuing method which controls the access at the same priority level, the distributed queuing method to set the priority depending on the connection-oriented or connectionless services, and bandwidth balancing, in that order.

Basic Distributed Queuing

The distributed queue control method of the QA slot at the single priority level is depicted in Figure 5.32. An internal node of the DQDB network possesses a *request* (RQ) counter corresponding to each bus, as well as a *countdown* (CD) counter. When

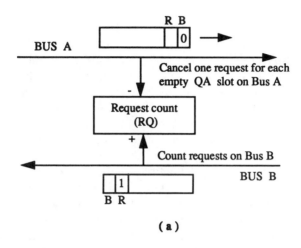

(a)

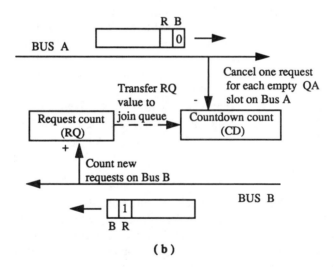

(b)

Figure 5.32 Distributed queuing protocol: (a) operation of request counter before joining distributed queue; (b) operation of request and countdown counter after joining distributed queue.

a node has data to send, it waits for a slot whose REQ bit is 0 among the slots that pass through the reverse direction bus, and when such a slot is found, its REQ bit is altered to 1 to notify an upper node of the request for transmission. The node without data to transmit increments the RQ counter if the REQ bit of the slot that is passing through the reverse direction bus is 1, and decrements the RQ counter if the BUSY bit of the slot transported to the forward direction bus is 0 (see Figure 5.32(a)). In this case, the value of the RQ counter belonging to a node indicates the number of slots waiting to be transmitted that have been placed in the queue by the nodes located in the downstream of the forward direction bus.

After setting the REQ bit to make notification of the request for transmission, the node with data to transmit copies the RQ counter value onto the CD counter and goes into the countdown state after setting the RQ counter value to 0 (See Figure 5.32(b)). The node in the countdown state increments the RQ counter if a slot whose REQ bit is 1 passes through the reverse direction bus, and decrements the CD counter if an empty slot with a 0 BUSY bit passes through the forward direction bus. Here, if the CD counter value becomes 0, data are transmitted by loading them onto the next arriving empty slot. In the countdown state, the CD counter value represents the total number of requests that had been queued by the downstream nodes on the forward bus before the moment in which the node queued the new request. The RQ counter keeps track of the accumulated number of requests that have been queued by the downstream nodes on the forward bus since the moment when the node queued the request. Therefore, transmitting data in an empty slot when the CD counter value becomes 0 is equivalent to operating the distributed queue as if it were a single queue. To transmit a slot, an empty slot with 0 BUSY bit is awaited after the CD counter value becomes 0, and the slot is transmitted after BUSY bit is converted to 1.

Priority Distributed Queuing

The distributed queuing protocol supports the assignment of priority to QA segment access. However, priority requests are not supported in the base standard; all connectionless data segments must be sent at the lowest priority. Future use of priorities for other services is under study. For upward compatibility, distributed queues for each level of priority are required in this implementation.

The operation of separate distributed queues for each level of priority is achieved by using a separate REQ bit at the access control field on the reverse bus for each level of priority, and separate RQ and CD counters for each priority level. The counters operate similarly to the single priority case, except that account must be taken of REQs at higher levels. That is, for an access unit which does not have a QA segment queued at a particular priority level, the counter operating at that level will count REQs at the same and higher priority levels. Thus, the RQ counter records all queued segments at equal and higher priorities.

If the access unit does have a QA segment queued at a particular priority level, then the RQ counter operating at that level will only count REQs at the same priority level. However, the operation of the CD counter at that priority level is slightly altered. The CD counter will, in addition to counting down the received empty slots, increment for REQs received at higher priority levels. This allows the higher priority segments to claim access ahead of already queued segments.

It should be noted that decrementing the RQ counters and CD counters at all priority levels occurs when an empty QA slot is received at the function within the node operating the distributed queue, not when it is sent by this function. This ensures that the correct counter values are maintained if the highest priority segment queued by the access unit gains access to the empty slots and the access unit marks the slot as busy.

The intent of the priority scheme is for the access performance of the highest priority traffic to be unaffected by lower priority traffic. Such a feature is very important in network signaling. However, it should be noted that priority should be decided depending on subnetwork distance, speed, and loading conditions.

The IEEE 802.6 standard specifies three levels of access priority. The definition of how these levels are used is a matter for the operator of the particular DQDB subnetwork, although it is likely that the highest level would be used for network management and signaling. The DQDB layer assumes that the user of the QA access requests the appropriate priority level for a particular segment transfer.

Bandwidth Balancing

If the speed of an electromagnetic wave is assumed to be infinite, then the DQDB queuing method processes data segments arriving at each node in the ideal FCFS manner. In reality, however, propagation delay exists which might cause the REQ bit transmitted by a lower node on a bus to be delivered to an upper node after a finite time delay, which allows the upper node, if it has data to send, to use the available empty slot first. This creates a problem of unfairness, which might become more severe with the increase in the network size and transmission speed. To resolve this problem, DQDB employs a bandwidth balancing counter for each of the buses. Each node increments the counter every time a slot is transmitted, and when the counter reaches the fixed bandwidth balancing modulus (BWB_MOD) value, its value returns to zero and the CD counter and RQ counter values increase by one. In this arrangement, a node that has transmitted BWB_MOD number of slots concedes one empty slot to a low-priority node. This has the effect of reducing unfairness to some extent.

Pre-arbitrated Access Control

PA slot access is typically used to provide for transfer of isochronous service octets. PA slots are distinguished from the QA slots as shown in Table 5.3 by a combination

Table 5.3
DQDB Slot States

BUSY Bit	SL_Type Bit	Slot State
0	0	Empty QA slot
0	1	Reserved
1	0	Active QA slot
1	1	PA slot

of the BUSY bit and the slot type (SL_type) bit of the access control field, which is the first octet of the slot's frame.

In contrast to QA slots, a PA slot can be shared by several nodes inside the DQDB network. In other words, the payload space inside a PA slot is composed of several octets, and the node sending isochronous data is allotted a place to load its data (among the PA slot's payload space) according to a DQDB layer management procedure. Each node uses VCI to identify its respective slots among the PA slots passing through the channel. In order to ensure provision of isochronous service, the HOB node of each bus must produce PA slots at regular intervals, as well as designate the VCI corresponding to the service provided in the PA slot's header.

5.4.4 DQDB Layer Architecture

As depicted in Figure 5.29, DQDB maintains functions for provision of three types of services: MAC services for the LLC layer, connection-oriented services, and isochronous services.

MAC Services for LLC Layer

In the DQDB layer, the header and trailer for transmission are appended to the *MAC service data units* (MSDU) delivered from the LLC layer to produce the *initial MAC protocol data units* (IMPDU). The IMPDU header section contains B/ETag for verifying the beginning and end points of IMPDU, IMPDU length information, address of the transmitter/receiver, and quality of service. An IMPDU is divided at the MCF block into segmentation units with the fixed size of 44 octets, and each segmentation unit is appended with two bytes, respectively, of header and trailer to form a 48-octet *derived MAC protocol unit* (DMPDU). Each DMPDU is transmitted through the payload space of QA slots and reassembled at the receiving node. Figure 5.33 depicts the process of creating an IMPDU as well as a DMPDU.

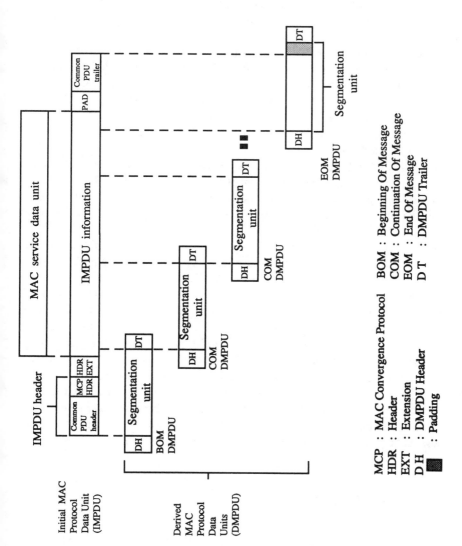

Figure 5.33 Generation of IMPDU and DMPDU.

The QA segment is divided into the QA segment header of four octets and the QA segment payload space, which contains the 48-octet DMPDU, as shown in Figure 5.34. The QA segment header includes the VCI to which the QA segment belongs; payload type, which denotes the characteristics of the data being transmitted; priority; and the *header check sequence* (HCS) for detecting bit errors within the QA segment.

The header section of the DMPDU segment payload contains the segment type, which denotes the location of the information of 44 octets transmitted by DMPDU within the IMPDU; sequence number, which indicates the order of a DMPDU within the IMPDU; and *message identifier* (MID), which is used in identifying the DMPDUs derived from a single IMPDU. The DMPDU trailer section contains the length of IMPDU information transmitted by the DMPDU and the payload CRC for detecting DMPDU transmission errors.

The production of a QA slot is complete with the addition of a 1-octet ACF to the 52-octet QA segment. The ACF consists of the BUSY, SL_type, and REQ bits mentioned earlier, as well as the *previous slot release* (PSR) bit, which is used for raising the utilization rate of DQDB. Figure 5.34 shows the overall format of the DQDB slot.

The operation at the receiving unit is as follows. Each node of DQDB node checks the VCI of every slot that passes through the bus, and in case a slot is found that corresponds to itself, it examines the DMPDU existing in the payload space of the slot. If the DMPDU indicates BOM, the destination address is examined; and if the DMPDU is intended for itself, it makes a copy of the data, memorizes the sequence number and message identifier, and goes on to accept the slots with that particular MID until the message terminates. After it has finished receiving the message, it removes the information of the MID corresponding to that message. This is due to the possibility that the transmitting unit might use the same MID for transmitting a different message. As described, a single message is transmitted through several slots; hence, the receiving unit can receive several messages concurrently.

The QA function block of Figure 5.29 transmits 48-octet nonisochronous connectionless MAC service and connection-oriented data segments.

Connection-Oriented Data Services

The *connection-oriented convergence function* (COCF) block is responsible for transmitting connection-oriented data, but the procedure associated with the maintenance or disassembly of data links is something that should be performed at an upper layer rather than at the DQDB layer. Like the MCF, the COCF exchanges data through the QA function block of Figure 5.29 via a data disassembly/assembly procedure.

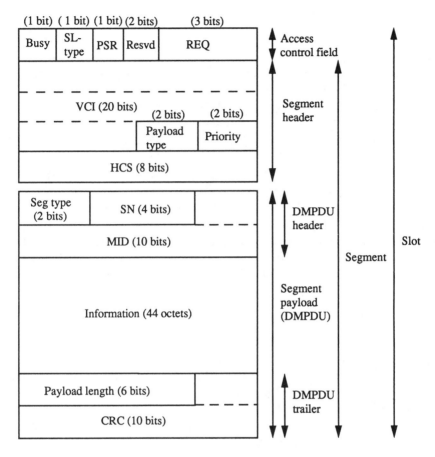

				(3 bits)
(1 bit)	(1 bit)	(1 bit)	(2 bits)	
Busy	SL-type	PSR	Resvd	REQ

VCI (20 bits)

	(2 bits)	(2 bits)
	Payload type	Priority

HCS (8 bits)

Access control field

Segment header

| Seg type (2 bits) | SN (4 bits) | |

MID (10 bits)

DMPDU header

Information (44 octets)

Segment payload (DMPDU)

Payload length (6 bits)

DMPDU trailer

CRC (10 bits)

Segment

Slot

S L   : Slot
REQ   : Request
HCS   : Header Check Sequence
MID   : Message Identifier
DMPDU : Derived MAC Protocol Data Unit

PSR : Previous Slot Release
VCI : Virtual Channel Identifier
S N : Sequence Number
CRC : Cyclic Redundancy Check

Figure 5.34 DQDB slot.

Isochronous Services

In order for a DQDB network to provide isochronous services, the *access unit* (AU) of each node must be inherently capable of controlling the access of PA slots, and the HOB of each bus must generate PA slots periodically.

In case the HOB is incapable of producing PA slots periodically, the PA function block of Figure 5.29 does not operate in actual isochronous mode. Therefore, the *isochronous convergence function* (ICF) block performs buffering in order to provide sufficient isochronous services.

Common Function and Layer Management

The common function block performs transmission of PA and QA slots through PA and QA function blocks, as well as the provision of DQDB layer management information octets. The DQDB *layer management entity* (LME) block performs header maintenance functions and functions for assigning a MID page to each node.

5.4.5 Physical Layer

As shown in Figure 5.29, the physical layer of a DQDB layer consists of a transmission system, a *physical layer convergence function* (PLCF) block, and a physical LME block. In the DQDB standard, the type of transmission system is not specified, and convergence procedures for the physical layers of ANSI DS-3 (44.736 Mbps), CCITT G.702 DS-3E (34.386 Mbps), DS-4E (139.264 Mbps), and G.707–9 SDH (155.520 Mbps) are currently being considered. Among them, the research is currently in progress on the convergence procedures for G.702 and SDH.

The PLCF block is provided so that the DQDB layer can perform its functions independently of the particular transmission system used, and it executes the function of converting the format of timing information, slot octets, and management information so that they can be delivered through the given transmission system. Consequently, each transmission system requires its own appropriate PLCF protocol. The LME block of the physical layer executes management-related functions, and hence performs such functions as fault detection of nodes and links and isolation of impaired nodes.

As a specific example of DQDB transmission systems, we consider the physical layer convergence procedure of the DS-3 transmission system. The DS-3 signal operates at the 44.736-Mbps speed and consists of 699 octets per 125-μs time period. One bit in 85 is used for DS-3 overhead functions providing a nominal information payload rate of 44.210 Mbps ($84/85 \times 44.736$ Mbps) and leaving approximately 690.78 octets available for use by the DS-3 *physical layer convergence procedure* (PLCP). As shown in Figure 5.35, the PLCF frame format consists of 12 rows by

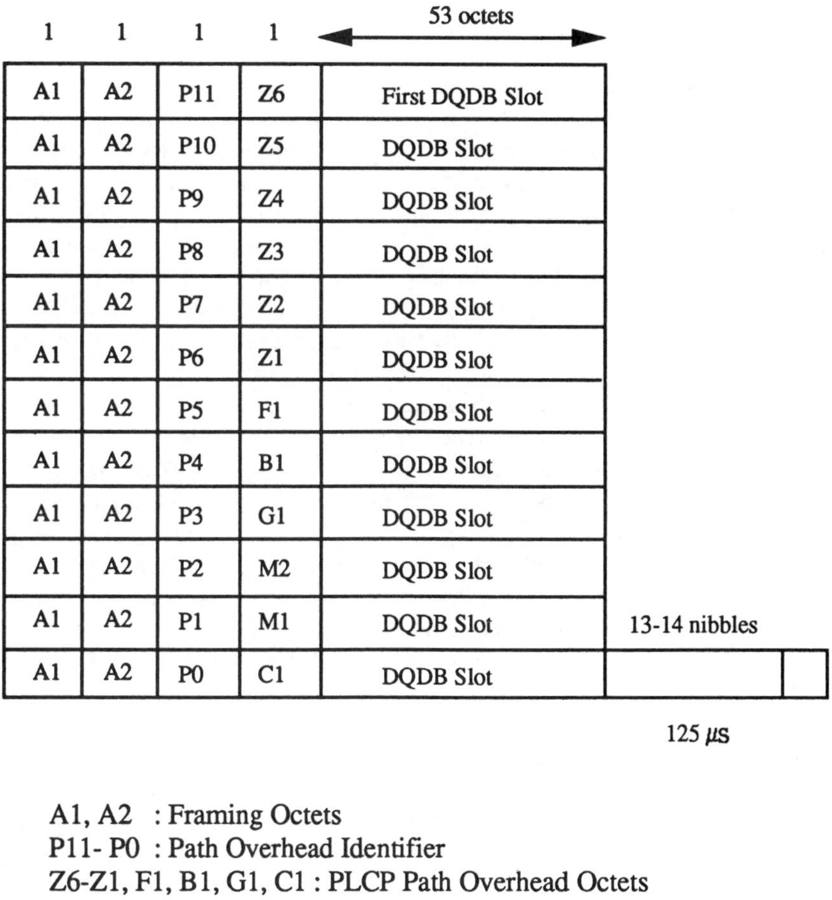

1	1	1	1	53 octets	
A1	A2	P11	Z6	First DQDB Slot	
A1	A2	P10	Z5	DQDB Slot	
A1	A2	P9	Z4	DQDB Slot	
A1	A2	P8	Z3	DQDB Slot	
A1	A2	P7	Z2	DQDB Slot	
A1	A2	P6	Z1	DQDB Slot	
A1	A2	P5	F1	DQDB Slot	
A1	A2	P4	B1	DQDB Slot	
A1	A2	P3	G1	DQDB Slot	
A1	A2	P2	M2	DQDB Slot	
A1	A2	P1	M1	DQDB Slot	13-14 nibbles
A1	A2	P0	C1	DQDB Slot	

125 μs

A1, A2 : Framing Octets
P11- P0 : Path Overhead Identifier
Z6-Z1, F1, B1, G1, C1 : PLCP Path Overhead Octets

Figure 5.35 DQDB physical layer convergence protocol frame of DS-3.

57 octets, with the last row containing a trailer of either 13 or 14 nibbles. The PLCP frame has a nominal duration of 125 μs, and each frame transmits 12 DQDB slots to the DQDB layer. The PLCP frame format is asynchronously mapped into the DS-3 information payload space using a nibble-stuffing technique. A nibble-stuffing opportunity occurs once every 375 μs to maintain a nominal frame repetition rate of 125 μs. Within the stuffing opportunity cycle, there are three PLCP frames. The first frame contains a trailer of 13 nibbles, the second frame contains a trailer of 14 nibbles, and the third frame contains either 13 or 14 nibbles, depending on whether a nibble stuffing has occurred. Figure 5.35 shows the PLCP frame format for the DS-3 signals.

5.5 SWITCHED MULTIMEGABIT DATA SERVICE

5.5.1 Background

The necessity for a high-speed data switching service has recently surfaced due to the appearance of LANs and high-performance computers, and such a demand is being felt most strongly in companies and on campuses. Some organizations are relying on such means as high-speed leased-line or private networks in order to meet the demand for high-speed data switching service. This demand will continue to increase, and unless there is a public high-speed data network that provides high-speed data transmission services, the cost for constructing separate leased-line and private networks will escalate tremendously. In case high-speed data services are provided by way of a switched public network, the economic gain from sharing transmission facilities will return directly to the users, and for this purpose public network operators must provide a private network level of speed and privacy.

SMDS is a connectionless packet switching (datagram) service standard that is designed to meet exactly these objectives. Intended to provide high-speed data communications in long-distance networks, it was standardized by Bellcore in 1989 as a MAN construction plan in order to accommodate high-speed data switching services inside the *local-area transport area* (LATA) of RBOCs. As stated earlier, in addition to the economic gains to be obtained due to the sharing of public networks that provide switching services, SMDS has the further advantage of allowing more efficient transmission as the number of subscribers increases and services diversify. The benefits of such economical usage of transmission links emerge more clearly when broadband services such as video communication are added; hence, SMDS can be interpreted as an initial service vehicle in the evolutionary process towards the BISDN.

5.5.2 SMDS Architecture

In order to satisfy the demand for high-speed data switching services, SMDS employs the network access and data switch technologies based on the rapidly developing MAN technology. Figure 5.36 shows the basic structure of an SMDS network. A subscriber terminal is connected to the *MAN switching system* (MSS) through a *subscriber network interface* (SNI). Inside an SMDS network, several MAN switching systems are interconnected through the *interswitching system interface* (ISSI).

The *SMDS interface protocol* (SIP) employs the IEEE 802.6 DQDB protocol, and the terminal based on the IEEE 802.6 protocol is connected through the SMDS network via an access DQDB, which is a DQDB-based subscriber network unit connection protocol. Here, the DS-3 level access network allows either a single or multiple terminals, but the DS-1 level access network allows the connection of single

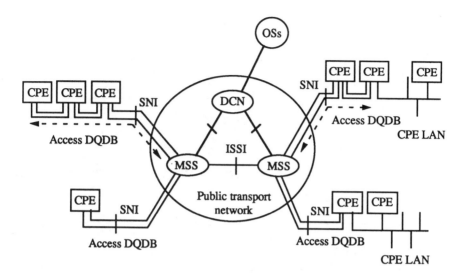

SNI : Subscriber Network Interface
MSS : MAN Switching System
ISSI : Inter-Switching System Interface
OSs : Operations Systems

DCN : Data Communications Network
CPE : Customer Premises Equipment
CPE LAN : CPE Local Area Network
DQDB: Distributed Queue Dual Bus

Figure 5.36 Network in support of SMDS.

terminals only. The DQDB subnetwork itself can operate in bus configuration or loop configuration. However, access DQDB must operate in the bus configuration.

5.5.3 SMDS Interface Protocol

The SIP is a connectionless data transmission protocol based on the MAC service protocol of the DQDB mentioned in Section 5.4. As shown in Figure 5.37, the SIP is composed of three levels. SIP level 3 produces L3-PDUs by adding a header and trailer to the SMDS service data units from an upper layer user. The header section contains the source/destination address, as well as information for verifying the loss of segments to be transmitted, and the trailer section contains such information as the length of the transmitted service data. SIP level 3 corresponds to the functions associated with IMPDU creation and reception (handling) among the MCFs of the DQDB protocol. SIP level 2 performs functions associated with cell-unit segmentation and reassembly of L3-PDUs, which correspond to the IMPDU segmentation/ reassembly and DMPDU creation functions of the DQDB protocol. Also, slot transmit/receive functions are also performed, such as the access control function for

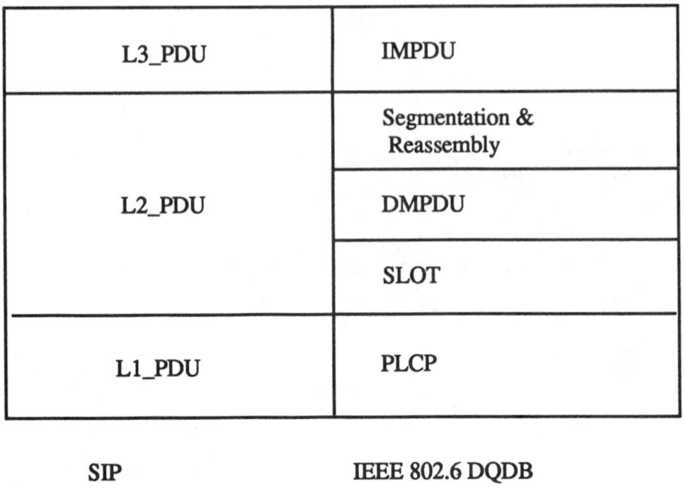

L3_PDU	IMPDU
L2_PDU	Segmentation & Reassembly
	DMPDU
	SLOT
L1_PDU	PLCP

SIP	**IEEE 802.6 DQDB**

Figure 5.37 Correlation of protocol layers between SIP and IEEE 802.6 DQDB.

cell-unit transmission, and these functions correspond to the QA function block of the DQDB protocol. SIP level 1 is a physical layer and corresponds to the PLCF of the DQDB protocol. Figure 5.37 illustrates the relationship between the SIP and the IEEE 802.6 DQDB protocol.

SMDS service data units are appended with a header and trailer to form the data units of the level 3 protocol (L3_PDU). L3_PDUs are subsequently divided into several segments, and a header and trailer are added to each of the segments to form the data units of the level 2 protocol (L2_PDU). Figure 5.38 depicts the conversion process of user information at each protocol level.

SIP Level 3 Protocol

L3_PDUs are formed with the addition of a header and trailer to 9188 octets or less of user data. Thus, SMDS can accommodate most LAN (Ethernet, token bus, token ring, X3T9 FDDI) packets. A detailed structure of L3-PDU is shown in Figure 5.39.

The B/Etag is used for indicating the beginning and end of the message in the header and trailer of L3_PDU, while the BAsize indicates the length from DA to Information. The DA and *source address* (SA) indicate the receiving and transmitting addresses of the message, respectively, and the *high-level protocol identifier* (HLPI) is used for aligning the SIP format with the DQDB protocol format. The *header extension length* (HEL) designates the length of *header extension* (HE) section, and the HE gets loaded with additional header information.

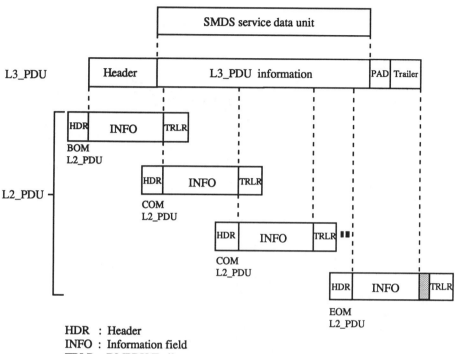

Figure 5.38 Mapping of SIP protocol data unit.

The address portion used in SMDS is composed of 4 bits of address type and 60 bits of the address itself. If the type is set to 1100, this implies that the DA is indicating 60 bits of individual addresses; if the type is 1110, then the DA indicates 60 bits of group addresses. The first 4 bits of the 60-bit address become 0001, the next 40 bits are occupied by the BCD code of 10 location addresses of SMDS, and the remaining 18 bits are filled with 1. The group address does not apply in the case of source address, and hence the source address type is always set to 1100.

SIP Level 2 Protocol

L2_PDU is formed by dividing an L3_PDU into 44-octet segments and adding a seven-octet header and a two-octet trailer to each of the segments. Figure 5.40 represents the structure of SMDS level 2 PDU, and it is similar to that of DQDB in Figure 5.34.

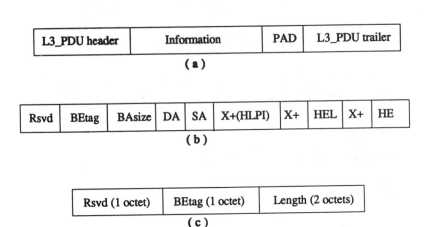

L3_PDU header	Information	PAD	L3_PDU trailer

(a)

Rsvd	BEtag	BAsize	DA	SA	X+(HLPI)	X+	HEL	X+	HE

(b)

Rsvd (1 octet)	BEtag (1 octet)	Length (2 octets)

(c)

D A   : Destination Address
S A   : Source Address
HEL   : Header Extension Length
H E   : Header Extension
Rsvd   : Reserved
BEtag : Beginning - End Tag
BAsize : Buffer Allocation Size
X+   : Carried across network unchanged
HLPI   : Higher Layer Protocol Identifier

Figure 5.39 L3_PDU structure: (a) L3_PDU; (b) L3_PDU header; (c) L3_PDU trailer.

Access control in Figure 5.40 provides a medium-access control function for transmitting data by way of slots delivered through a pair of buses. Here, the BUSY field indicates whether the slot is being used; it is set to 1 when L2_PDU contains information and to 0 if the slot is not used. REQ_3 to REQ_0 represent slot utilization requests, and in the distributed queuing method with four priority levels, they indicate slot request priorities. In the case of the L2_PDU of an MSS to the CPE, all REQ bits have the value of 0.

Value 11111111111111111111110000000100010 represents network control information in the case an L2_PDU contains information and 32 zero bits in the case of an empty L2_PDU.

The segment type indicates the location of the L3_PDU segment transmitted by L2_PDU and can have one of the following values: COM, EOM, BOM, and SSM, as in Figure 5.33 or Figure 5.38.

All L2_PDUs corresponding to the same L3_PDU have the same MID (message identifier). The MID is used in assembling several L2_PDUs into a single L3_PDU. The MID value for an L2_PDU that is not an SSM ranges between 4

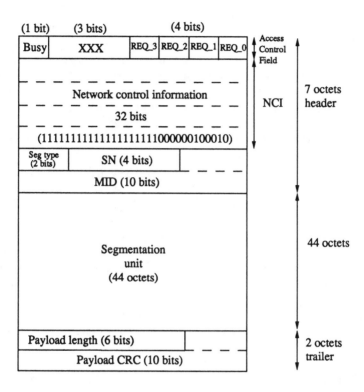

Figure 5.40 SIP L2_PDU.

and $(2^{14} - 1)$, and for an L2_PDU that is not being used or is an SSM, the MID has the value of 0. The MID is allocated according to the scheme defined in IEEE 802.6 standards.

The payload length designates the length of the portion occupied by actually transmitted information among the 44 octets of data field transmitted by L2_PDU. Payload CRC is a CRC-10 code used in transmission error detection for L2_PDU's information field.

SIP Level 1 Protocol

SIP level 1 is a physical layer protocol that operates between the subscriber terminal and the switched network at either 44.736 Mbps (DS-3) or 1.544 Mbps (DS-1) and is divided into the PLCP and the transmission system sublayer. The transmission system sublayer defines the method and characteristics of the connection with the transmission link. The PLCP assumes the role of mapping SIP level 1 control information and L2_PDUs in a format suitable for the transmission system sublayer.

The DS-3 frame is divided into seven 680-bit subframes, and each subframe is divided into eight 85-bit blocks. The first bit of each block is an overhead bit, and the remainder are used in information transmission. A total of 4760 bits (4704 information bits and 56 overhead bits) are transmitted at the 44.736-Mbps speed, and the transmission time of a single frame amounts to 106.4 μs. The DS-3 signal transmits 699 octets in 125 μs, but one of the 85 bits is an overhead bit; hence, the effective information transmission rate is 690.78 octets per 125 μs, which corresponds to 44.210 Mbps. This fact is the same as that in the DQDB physical layer already discussed in Section 5.4.5.

The frame format of the DS-3 PLCP of SMDS consisting of 12 L2_PDUs is obtained by substituting an L2_PDU in place of the DQDB slot of the DQDB frame format of Figure 5.35. The first three columns of the PCLP frame in Figure 5.35 are used for framing, and the fourth column represents the PLCP path overhead octet. The contents of each field in the DS-3 PLCP are as follows. A1 and A2 are framing octets used for slot identification and have the values 11110110 and 00101000, respectively. P11 to P0 are path overhead identifier octets, and they designate four columns of path overhead octets. Each octet consists of six bits of path overhead label, one reserved bit, and one parity bit. Z6 to Z1 are growth octets, and they have the default value of 0. F1 is a PLCP path user channel and is used for PLCP user communication between an MSS and a CPE. B1 is a bit-interleaved parity bit and is employed for PCLP path parity error detection. G1 is a PLCP path status octet, and it is used for monitoring PLCP status in both directions of the transmission path. M2 and M1 are SIP level 1's control information octets and are used for transporting control information. C1 functions as a cycle/stuff counter, and its value is incremented when nibble stuffing occurs every 375 μs.

5.5.4 SMDS Services

The SDMS is a high-speed packet switching service that possesses public or logical private network functions. Each data unit contains source/destination addresses and is transported to its destination together with user information. The addressing system is analogous to the telephone numbering system, and it employs a group address scheme to enable the transport of information to a multiple number of destinations.

SMDS possesses address screening functions. Destination address screening is the scheme in which data is transmitted only when its destination address is an approved network address. In source address screening, the data to be sent to the SNI is transmitted there only if it has an approved source address. By applying such address screening functions, an SMDS network can be used as a logical private network.

CPE can access an SMDS network via a DS-1 or DS-3 class transmission path, and a single CPE or multiple CPEs can exist at a single SNI. The important point here is that a single SNI should always be shared by way of a terminal belonging to one user only. This is essential for ensuring the privacy of subscriber information.

Since SMDS subscribers have several traffic requirements, SMDS provides several access classes. Each access class regulates a number of different transfer classes according to the allowed sustained information transfer and burstiness, and the traffic of each class is controlled by way of a credit manager algorithm. That is, the credit value is determined according to the specified class, and it gets lowered every time information is transmitted. The credit value increases periodically by a specified amount, but cannot exceed the maximum credit value. Therefore, the attributes of each class are represented by three parameters: credit increment value, credit increase period, and maximum credit value.

Five access classes are defined in the DS-3 path, while only one access class is defined in the DS-1 path. Such access classes are defined for the user-to-network direction of SNI, and the packets from the CPE to the network that exceed the access class are not transmitted. But in case a packet from the network to the CPE exceeds the access class, the packet is preserved in the network buffering and retransmitted when the credit is allowed.

SMDS specifies transmission delay objectives for high-speed data transmission in many different application areas. In the case of individually addressed L3_PDUs, the 95% of the transmission delay of the delivered L3_PDUs should be less than 20 ms in the case of the DS-3-based access path, while it should be less than 140 ms in the case of the DS-1-based access path.

In general, SMDS subscribers have already invested substantially on computers, hardware, and software for their own LANs; hence, in order for SMDS to be competitive, it must offer maximum additional advantages at the lowest possible cost.

The anticipated SMDS subscribers must be assumed to possess several corporate networks, including LANs, leased-line circuits, and X.25 packet networks, and in order to connect these various corporate networks as if they are operating as a single network, an internetworking protocol, situated between the host network and gateway (which connects the support networks), must operate above several different support network protocols.

Currently, the most widely used internetworking protocols are connectionless, and they rely on the overlay transport protocol in order to secure end-to-end reliability and control. Typical examples of such an internetworking/transmission protocol pair are DARPA TCP/IP, ISO 8073/ISO 8473, and Xerox, DEC. Figure 5.41 depicts the role of SMDS as a high-speed subnetwork between subscriber networks that employ the TCP/IP protocol. Figure 5.41(a) depicts the method of utilizing a router with the IP function to transmit, if needed, IP data from a LAN to a network that provides SMDS. In contrast, in Figure 5.41(b), a bridge rather than a router is used between the LAN and the SMDS subnetwork. The bridge does not participate directly in handling internetworking protocol, and it operates only at the subnetwork protocol layer.

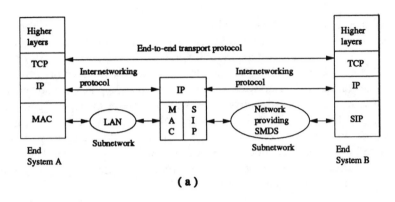

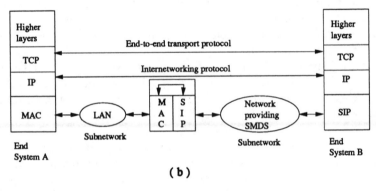

TCP : Transmission Control Protocol
MAC : Medium Access Control
IP   : Inter net Protocol
SIP   : SMDS Interface Protocol

Figure 5.41 Example scenario of the use of SMDS: (a) router functionality; (b) bridge functionality.

For SMDS to execute its role efficiently, compatibility with the protocols of the subscriber networks that it is linked with must be considered, and the access device between SMDS and the subscriber network must be simple so that subscribers can be connected to the network easily.

5.6 COMPARISON OF HIGH-SPEED DATA NETWORKS

Each of the high-speed data network protocols presented above has its own set of advantages and disadvantages from the standpoint of target users, provision range, speed, management, and performance. In this section, these protocols will be compared with one another from several viewpoints.

5.6.1 Characteristics Comparison

The general characteristics of each protocol are listed in Table 5.4. Frame relay represents services that were conceived in order to provide end-to-end high-speed transmission in narrowband ISDN. Its draft standards are recommended as CCITT Q.922 and Q.933 in 1992. The FDDI was developed by ANSI as a backbone network for interconnecting existing LANs. Since an actual system was implemented during its standardization process, and the field results were again reflected in the standardization, it has the advantage of having its final draft standards take into account such factors as network implementation, service provider's point of view, and user demand. FDDI-II was proposed in order to provide services that require real-time processing, such as voice and video. While the FDDI has strong private network characteristics, FDDI-II is extending its application area to public networks.

DQDB has been standardized by IEEE 802 Committee as a high-speed data communication network for connecting the LANs. The size and the format of cells used as the basic units of information transfer in DQDB were chosen to be the same as those of ATM cells in order to facilitate linking with ATM, and most of its draft standards have been completed. ATM, treated in depth in Chapter 4, was recommended by CCITT as the transmission scheme for the BISDN. Essential parts of the draft standards were completed by 1992, and the remaining unsettled issues and the entire draft standard are scheduled to be finalized by 1996. SMDS was proposed by Bellcore as a strategy for meeting the demands for broadband services by absorbing them into public networks before the BISDN becomes widely distributed. SMDS employs DQDB as an access protocol between the subscriber and the network. Also, it allows a diverse set of transmission modes, including DS-1, DS-3, SONET, and SDH. Therefore, SMDS is being considered in several countries as a stepping stone for the BISDN.

Table 5.5 lists the media access mechanism characteristics of each protocol. Taking into account possible applications at S or T reference points of the ISDN, frame relay utilizes the physical layer interface of I.430 and 431. Accordingly, in a point-to-multipoint connection, transmission is achieved in a competitive manner, whereas there are no such limitations in a point-to-point connection. The FDDI executes transmission control through the use of a token, while isochronous traffic of FDDI-II is transmitted by way of a bandwidth assignment scheme based on the preexchange of control information. In the DQDB scheme, information is transmitted through the reservation of idle slots using the REQ bit in the case of a QA service, and through preassigned slots in the case of a PA service. In ATM, control of transmission is achieved by placing the GFC field within each cell for the UNI.

Table 5.4
General Characteristics of Broadband Protocols

	Frame Relay	FDDI	FDDI-II	DQDB	SMDS	ATM
Standard organization	CCITT	ANSI	ANSI	IEEE	Bellcore	CCITT
Year of standard	1992	1987–1990	1990	1991	1990	1992
Targeted services	Data	Data	Data, voice	Data, voice, video	Data	Broad-band services
Main application	High-speed data comm.	LAN inter-connect.	LAN inter-connect.	LAN inter-connect.	High-speed data comm.	Broad-band comm. network
Transmission medium	Copper wire	Optical fiber	Optical fiber	Optical fiber	Copper, optical	Optical 4 fiber
Distance (range)	No limits	100 km	100 km	No limits	No limits	No limits
Transmission rates	1.544, 2.048 Mbps	100 Mbps	100 Mbps	150 Mbps	DS-1, DS-3 SONET	SDH
Network interwork	IEEE 802 LAN ISDN	IEEE 802 LAN ISDN	IEEE 802 LAN ISDN	IEEE 802 BISDN	IEEE 802 BISDN	BISDN
Operation	Public	Private network	Private network	Public network	Public network	Public network

Each protocol differs in addressing scheme as well. Frame relay basically recommends two octets of DLCI and also allows expansion to three or four octets. The FDDI and FDDI-II use 16 or 48 bits of actual addresses. DQDB uses 20 bits of VCI, and SMDS currently provides only connectionless services; it is thus recommended that the VCI field of the DQDB frame be set to all 1s. An SMDS address marks the boundary between the VCI fields of cells transferred from one network to another. In transmission between CPEs in a multiple-CPE connection such boundaries are not marked. At the UNI of the BISDN, 8 bits of VPI and 16 bits of VCI are defined, and 12 bits of VPI and 16 bits of VCI are defined at the NNI.

All the protocols employ CRC for detecting errors in the information being transmitted. Frame relay applies 16 bits of CRC, and the FDDI and FDDI-II apply 32 bits of CRC on the entire frame being transmitted. However, DQDB and ATM applies 8 bits of CRC just on the cell header to judge the validity of the cell at the

Table 5.5

Medium Access Characteristics of Broadband Protocols

	Frame Relay	FDDI	FDDI-II	DQDB	SDMS	ATM
Start of transmission	Contention	Token	Token or BW reserv.	Slot reserv. BW reserv.	Slot reserv.	Under study
Number of priorities	2	2	4	3	4	Under study
End of transmission	Frame unit	Time out	Time out/ BW release	Slot unit	Slot unit	Slot unit
Addressing	16-bit	16/48-bit	16/48 bit or preassigned	20-bit VCI or preassigned	Fixed (20 × 1)	8/12-bit VPI + 16 bit VCI
Error Check	16-bit CRC	32-bit CRC	32-bit CRC	8-bit HCS 10-bit CRC	8-bit HCS 10-bit CRC	8-bit HCS 10-bit CRC
Data removal	Not required	Source	Source	Not required	Not required	Under study

transit node. For verifying the end-to-end validity of a cell, 10 bits of CRC are applied to the DMPDUs in the case of DQDB, while in the case of ATM, an optional 32 bits of CRC are applied to the service data unit of AAL-3/4, and 10 bits of cell payload CRC are used for examining the SAR-PDU of the data service

While employing ATM to provide broadband services is the ultimate goal, key portions of the draft standard have not yet been completed and immediate demand for 155-Mbps or 622-Mbps class services is still minimal; hence, frame relay, the FDDI (FDDI-II), or SMDS (DQDB) should be considered as an interim broadband service vehicle. Since SMDS has no distance limitations in network construction, it has an advantage over the FDDI as a public network. Furthermore, SMDS can be implemented while accommodating current communications facilities, whereas the FDDI requires new installation of optical cables just for the regional FDDI. Also, the two differ significantly in that the transmission speed of SMDS is based on public network draft standards, whereas FDDI's 100 Mbps is not a public network standard, although transmission employing SDH is currently being studied. From this point of view, it can be seen that SMDS is oriented toward the public network and the FDDI in private network characteristics. Therefore, while SMDS provides optical connection between LANs, the FDDI is expected to be widely used as a backbone network on the premises of large buildings, research centers, or universities. Table 5.6 is a comparison of the respective characteristics of the FDDI and SMDS.

On the other hand, frame relay provides connection-oriented point-to-point services that are based on HDLC. Also, in contrast to DQDB or ATM protocol, frame

Table 5.6
Comparison of SMDS and FDDI

SMDS	FDDI
No distance limitations	Installation scale is limited
Number of stations not limited	Number of stations limited to 500
Accommodates physical layer standards	Incompatible with public network standards
Can use existing transmission equipment	Need to install new transmission equipment
Public network services	Private network services

relay uses variable-length frames, and is thus unable to handle isochronous traffic. Frame relay merely raises the bandwidth utilization efficiency of T1-class circuits; using a separate signaling protocol to achieve a single connection increases overhead and makes it difficult to apply frame relay at speeds higher than those of the T1 class. In contrast, SMDS appears to be capable of easily accommodating high-speed transmission speeds of DS-1, DS-3, and SDH. Table 5.7 gives a comparison of the characteristics of frame relay and SMDS.

Table 5.7
Comparison of SMDS and Frame Relay

SMDS	Frame Relay
DS-1 class or higher	DS-0 to DS-1
Compatible with growth of BISDN	Incompatible with BISDN (for ISDN)
Appropriate for high-speed transmission services	Appropriate for low-speed transmission services
Can provide point-to-multipoint services	Can provide point-to-point services only
Uses SMDS exclusive channels	Shares ISDN channels with others
Cell relay scheme	Frame unit transmission
Fixed packet size	Variable packet size
Only small number of commercialized products	Large number of commercialized products

5.6.2 Integration with BISDN

Future communication networks will be constructed with the BISDN as the center, and hence integrability with the BISDN must be considered in planning a construction of a broadband communications network for MAN-like public network services. That is, in order to realize the goal of providing connectionless data transmission services, as well as multimedia services of voice and video, and be able to interwork with the BISDN without deterioration in the quality of these services, interoperability with the BISDN must occur at the access protocol level.

Among the protocols reviewed above, frame relay employs variable size packets to transmit data and hence cannot be directly connected to an ATM layer of the BISDN that is based on cell-unit transmission. Instead, the service-specific convergence sublayer of AAL-3 can implement the frame relay protocol. The FDDI also uses an independent physical layer draft standard; the MAC layer also transmits variable-length packets in a unique format, and thus requires a mapping of the protocol for it to be linked to the BISDN. Since transmission in the BISDN is accomplished through fixed-size cell units, a procedure is required to segment the transmitted packets into cell units and reassemble them at the receiver. Such an alteration of protocol creates redundancies in some parts of the protocol functions and increases network overhead, thus deteriorating the efficiency of the overall network.

On the other hand, DQDB was designed while taking into account compatibility with the BISDN from the early stages of preparing the draft standard. DQDB recommends the use of SDH for the physical layer, and the cell format is also similar to that of ATM. The header and trailer of the DMPDU of the MAC layer are also identical to those of type 4 of the ATM adaption layer (AAL-4). Figure 5.42 illustrates the respective cell formats of SMDS, DQDB, and ATM. Since the SDMS also uses the connectionless service format of DQDB, it can be linked to the BISDN without difficulty.

5.7 EVOLUTION TOWARD BISDN

As we have discussed throughout this book, several different evolutionary scenarios toward the BISDN can be envisioned. One probable scenario for the BISDN from the high-speed data network's point of view calls for three steps. In the first step, the broadband services will be provided by MAN. In the second step, MAN will be interconnected by single ATM switches. In the final step, LANs, MANs, and ATM switches can be integrated into the BISDN. Further descriptions follow.

5.7.1 First Step

Local broadband communication services will be provided by LANs or enhanced PBXs. Larger organizations will require communications to support high-speed data

446

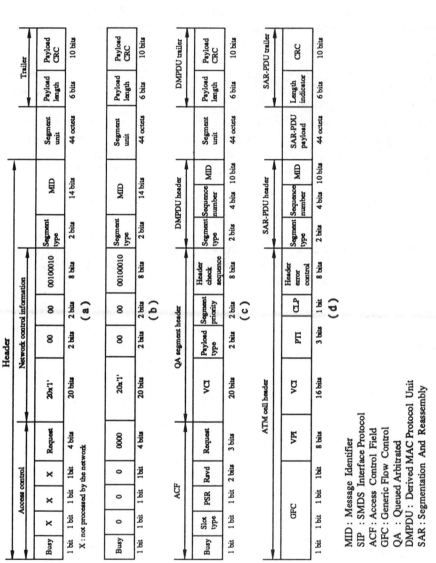

Figure 5.42 Comparisons of cell format among SMDS, DQDB, and ATM: (a) SMDS SIP_L2 (CPE → MSS); (b) SMDS SIP_L2 (MSS → CPE); (c) DQDB slot; (d) ATM cell (UNI).

service, and such demand will be satisfied by a high-speed FDDI LAN. Extension of the broadband service area will require high-speed backbone networks. The MAN can be the best approach prior to full BISDN using ATM cells. Since MAN is defined as an interconnection of high-speed subnetworks in a metropolitan area, each of these high-speed subnetworks could serve a variety of PBXs, voice/data workstations, mainframe hosts, and LANs. Various high-speed subnetworks could use the MAN as the metropolitan distributed backbone. This property, therefore, makes the MAN ideally suited to providing LAN interconnections as well as other data and digitized voice services.

Recently, there has been standardization activity to develop a public-network-compatible customer premises network based on the ATM protocol. The new customer premises network has three primary goals: to accommodate the large volumes of traffic generated by multimedia applications, to provide scalable throughput that is capable of growing both per-host bandwidth and aggregate bandwidth, and to facilitate seamless, end-to-end interworking of public and private networks. To meet these goals, ATM was selected as the core technology. The physical layer of the ATM LAN is structured by a block-coded layer, which is based on technologies developed for the fiber channel network, and by a SONET physical layer, which is based on technologies being deployed in the public wide-area network. Above the ATM layer, a very simple adaptation layer is supported which was designed to be efficient and easily integrated into existing higher layer protocols. Since the work on signaling in broadband standards bodies is incomplete, a PVC approach is supported initially. A *Simple Network Management Protocol* (SNMP) based *management information base* (MIB) is included to allow for the creation and deletion of PVCs. The addition of signaling protocols and additional adaptation layers is expected in future versions.

5.7.2 Second Step

ATM-compatible MANs will be interconnected by ATM switches, which can interconnect network adaptors between the LAN, MAN, and BISDN. Network adaptors perform the routing for the connectionless packets like a multiport router. As a result, associated ATM cells can be routed through the ATM network via corresponding virtual connections. Direct connection of LAN or MAN using the ATM switch is especially suitable for high-speed data exchange and high throughput rates, for example, between the LANs of one company at several locations, or between several MANs covering an industrial region.

The main drawback of this approach is that a mesh of connections must be created between all interconnecting units. This does, therefore, usually limit the number of LANs and MANs that can be accessed directly.

5.7.3 Final Step

LANs, MANs, and ATM switches will be interconnected into the BISDN network. In this step, the standard interface emerges at the MAN/BISDN interface and the implementation of MAN can provide transparent and highly reliable interconnection of LANs. From the BISDN point of view, the MAN reduces the load offered to the BISDN and acts as a traffic concentrator. From the MAN point of view, the BISDN offers fast MAN interconnection at high data rates. In the evolutionary transition from MAN to the BISDN, uniform hardware and software interface should be used to protect the capital already invested in MANs. In the longer term, the BISDN with the high-quality services will probably complement the use of MANs in the public sector. Figure 5.43 illustrates the BISDN network configuration with MANs and LANs.

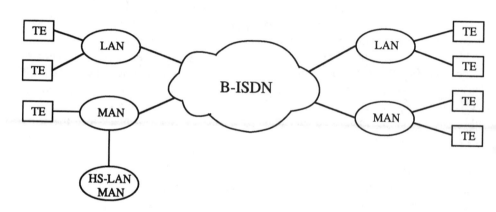

HS-LAN : High Speed LAN
T E   : Terminal Equipment

Figure 5.43 BISDN network configuration with MANs and WANs.

SELECT BIBLIOGRAPHY

Ali, M. J., "Frame Relay in Public Networks," *IEEE Commun. Mag.*, Vol. 30, No. 3, March 1992, pp. 72–80.

ANSI T1.6ca, "Core Aspects of Frame Protocol for Use With Frame Relay Bearer Service," (T1S1/90–214), 1990.

ANSI T1.606add, "Addendum to T1.606," (T1X1/90–175), 1990.

ANSI T1.606–1990, "Telecommunication-Frame Relay Bearer Service-Architectural Framework and Service Description," 1990.

ATM Forum, Network Compatible ATM for Local Network Applications, phase 1, version 1.0, April 1992.

Bellcore Technical Advisory, TA-TSY-000772, "Generic System Requirement in Support of SMDS," Issue 3, 1989.

Boudec, J. Y. L., "The Asynchronous Transfer Mode: A Tutorial," *Computer Networks and ISDN Systems*, Vol. 24, 1992, pp. 279–309.

Bracket, C. A., "Dense WDM Networks: Principle and Applications," *IEEE J. of Select. Areas on Commun.*, Vol. JSAC-8, No. 6, Aug. 1990.

Byrne, W. R., et al., "Evolution of Metropolitan Area Networks to Broadband ISDN," *IEEE Commun. Mag.*, Vol. 29, No. 1, Jan. 1991, pp. 69–82.

Carol, M., R. D. Giltin, "High Performance Optical Local and Metropolitan Area Networks: Enhancements of FDDI and 802.6 DQDB," *IEEE J. of Select. Areas on Commun.*, Vol. JSAC-8, Oct. 1990.

Cavanagh, J. P., "Applying the Frame Relay Interface to Private Networks," *IEEE Commun. Mag.*, March 1992.

CCITT Rec. I.233, "Frame Mode Bearer Services," 1992.

CCITT Rec. I.370, "Congestion Management for the ISDN Frame Relaying Bearer Service," 1991.

CCITT Rec. I.430, "ISDN Basic Rate User Network Interface Layer 1 Specification," 1988.

CCITT Rec. I.431, "ISDN Primary Rate User Network Interface Layer 1 Specification," 1988.

CCITT Rec. Q.921 (I.441), "ISDN User Network Interface Data Layer Specification," 1988.

CCITT Rec. Q.922, "ISDN Data Link Layer Specification for Frame Mode Bearer Services," 1992.

CCITT Rec. Q.933, "DSS1 Signaling Specification for Frame Mode Bearer Service," 1992.

Cheung, N. K., "The Infrastructure for Gigabit Computer Networks," *IEEE Commun. Mag.*, April 1992.

Clapp, G. H., "LAN Interconnection Across SMDS," *IEEE Network Mag.*, Vol. 5, No. 5, Sept. 1991, pp. 25–32.

Datapro Report, "Frame Relay Technology Issues & Trends," *Managing LANs, Datapro*, 1992.

Davidson, R. P., and N. J. Muller, *Interworking LANs: Operation, Design, and Management*, Artech House, 1992.

DEC, Northern Telecom, Stratacom, Cisco, "Frame Relay Specification With Extension Based on Proposed T1S1 Standards," Revision 1.0, 1990.

Eastern Research Corp., *Metropolitan Area Network: Networking's New Frontier 1990–1994*, 1990.

Fink, R. L., and F. E. Ross, "Following the Fiber Distributed Data Interface," *IEEE Commun. Mag.*, March 1992.

Halsall, F., *Data Communications, Computer Networks and Open System*, Addison-Wesley, 1992.

Handel, E., and M. N. Huber, *Integrated Broadband Networks: An Introduction to ATM-based Networks*, Addison-Wesley, 1991.

Hemrick, C. F., R. W. Klessig, and J. M. McRoberts, "Switched Multi-megabit Data Service and Early Availability via MAN Technology," *IEEE Commun. Mag.*, April 1988, pp. 9–14.

IEEE P802.6, "IEEE Standard: DQDB Subnetwork of a Metropolitan Area Network," 1991.

Imai, K., T. Honda, H. Kasahara, and T. Ito, "ATMR: RING Architecture for Broadband Networks," 1990.

Johnson, J. T., "Coping With Public Frame Relay: A Delicate Balance," *Data Communication*, Jan. 1992, pp. 31–38.

Johnson, J. T., "Frame Relay Products," *Data Communication*, May 1992.

Kasahara, H., K. Imai, N. Morita, and T. Ito, "Distributed ATM Ring-Based Switching Architecture for MAN and BISDN Access Networks," *Proceeding of Workshop on Broadband Communication*, IFIP Technical Committee 6, Jan. 1992, Estoril, Portugal.

Kung, H. T., "Gigabit Local Area Networks: A System Perspective," *IEEE Commun. Mag.*, April 1992.

Minoli, D., *Enterprise Networking: Fractional T1 to SONET, Frame Relay to BISDN*, Artech House, 1992.

Modiri, N., "The ISO Reference Model Entities," *IEEE Network Mag.*, Vol. 5, No. 4, July 1991, pp. 24–33.

Mollenaeur, J. F., "Networking for Greater Metropolitan Areas," *Data Communications*, Vol. 17, No. 2, Feb. 1988, pp. 155–178.

Mollenaeur, J. F., "Standards for Metropolitan Area Networks," *IEEE Commun. Mag.*, April 1988, pp. 15–19.

Mukherjee, B., "WDM-Based Local Lightwave Networks Part I: Single-Hop Systems," *IEEE Network Mag.*, May 1992.

Mukherjee, B., "WDM-Based Local Lightwave Networks Part II: Multihop Systems," *IEEE Network Mag.*, July 1992.

Muller, N. J., and R. P. Davidson, *LANs to WANs: Network Management in the 1990's*, Artech House, 1990.

Newman, R. M., Z. L. Budrikis, and J. L. Hullett, "The QPSX MAN," *IEEE Commun. Mag.*, April 1988, pp. 20–28.

Pehrson, B., P. Gunningberg, and S. Pink, "Distributed Multimedia Applications on Gigabit Networks," *IEEE Network Mag.*, Vol. 6, No. 1, Jan. 1992, pp. 26–35.

Rahnema, M., "Frame Relaying and the Fast Packet Switching Concepts and Issues," *IEEE Network Mag.*, Vol. 5, No. 4, July 1991, pp. 10–17.

Rannsom, M. N., and D. S. Spears, "Applications of Public Gigabit Networks," *IEEE Network Mag.*, Vol. 6, No. 2, March 1992, pp. 30–41.

Sequiun, H., "Optical Fiber Local Network for Distribution and Interactive Service," *Cable Television Engineering*, Vol. 14, No. 15, Dec. 1988. pp. 637–638.

Sher, P. J. S., et al., "Service Concept of the Switched Multi-megabit Data Service," *Proc. GLOBECOM '88*, 1988.

Takashima, S., "Network," *NTT R&D*, Vol. 38, No. 4, 1989, pp. 441–458.

Vetter, R. J., D. H. C. Du, and A. E. Kleitz, "Networking Supercomputing: High Performance Parallel Interface (HIPI)," *IEEE Network Mag.*, May 1992.

Chapter 6
Broadband Video Technology

Strengthened by rapidly developing optical communication, image processing, and VLSI technologies, the field of video communications has emerged into the limelight as an economically and technologically viable field. In fact, most services, excluding the high-quality video services, can already be provided in a limited way through the existing local data networks (i.e., LAN), public telephone networks (i.e., PSTN), as well as the narrowband integrated information networks (i.e., NISDN). Thus, it can be stated that the prerequisite to widespread residential deployment of the BISDN, which demands a comprehensive reorganization of existing networks, is the provision of high-quality video communications services.

From the standpoint of utilization format, the area of video services can be categorized into the distributive services (e.g., CATV, high-quality TV) which have distributed service characteristics, the video data services (e.g., videotex, video information retrieval, CD-ROM application) which have interactive service characteristics, the field of conversational bidirectional communication (video telephone/conferencing) which requires real-time transmission and switching, and the message services (e.g., store and forward services). In addition, there are multimedia services that provide various services such as video, voice, and data in a composite and integrated manner. There are challenging areas on the road towards an efficient dissemination of these various video communication applications. The most typical ones are the compression and efficient transmission of broadband video information, the communication procedures for simultaneous accommodation of multiple users, and the reliability and economic feasibility of various types of video terminals.

In its early stages, a video communication network was a separate network of the synchronous mode, independent of voice or data networks. However, due to the heavy cost of constructing several types of communication networks with the introduction of diverse sets of services, the concept of the asynchronous network emerged, which can provide integrated services of video, voice, and data through a single integrated network. However, the communication procedures and call connection of the asynchronous mode are a little more complex than those of the synchronous mode. Furthermore, the conversational video conferencing services must transmit various types of graphics and data that occur during the conference; hence, the associated communication and call connection procedures are much more complex compared to those of simple retrieval services such as a video database. Consequently, when an asynchronous conversational video service is to be provided, all these issues should be carefully considered in detail.

Section 6.1 will provide an overview of broadband video technology through a brief summary of the contents of this chapter. Section 6.2 will discuss narrowband video services available in the existing narrowband networks. Section 6.3 will examine image compression techniques, which have been steadily researched in the past few years and are currently being standardized and implemented. Section 6.4 will review video communication in high-speed packet networks, with an emphasis on the broadband ATM network, an area in which significant research effort is going on. Section 6.5 will discuss optical CATV technology, which employs the optical fiber subscriber network that will be the foundation for the upcoming construction of the BISDN. Lastly, Section 6.6 will provide descriptions of the development status and growth trends of HDTV, whose market potential is huge for home electronics, as well as for communications and other industrial applications.

6.1 OVERVIEW

Broadband video technology can be divided into coding technology for compressing tremendous amounts of video information, transmission technology for the efficient transmission of compressed video information, decoding technology for restoring compressed video information, and terminal technology, which integrates the first three. Usually, a broadband transmission medium is required for the transmission of a video signal; hence, video signal compression and restoration technologies are essential for the effective use of the transmission line. Video compression technology adopts various video/image coding techniques to eliminate redundant information from an image signal within the range that its characteristics do not change perceptibly. Image coding techniques can be classified into prediction coding, transform coding, vector quantization, subband coding, and entropy coding. Today, all of these coding techniques can be realized with the current VLSI technology. CCITT and ISO have adopted a coding technique that integrates prediction coding, transform coding, and entropy coding as the international standard.

For the economical provision of various information communication services with different characteristics, a communication network is required that can accommodate diverse forms of information media and at the same time maintain a unified access structure and transmission mode. From this viewpoint, it is difficult to provide a broad spectrum of video information communication services with the existing PSTN or the NISDN. An alternative approach is the BISDN based on ATM. In the

BISDN, the ATM transmission technique is adopted, which divides the information to be transported into ATM cells of a fixed size. The ATM transmission technique offers many advantages from several standpoints, since it can accommodate diverse types of services with a single type of network (see Chapter 4 for a detailed description of BISDN and ATM technology).

Terminal technology has a close relationship with the attributes of the services to be provided. For example, in services that have large-scale broadcasting characteristics, the video information compression stage is far more complex than the video information restoration stage, but in conversational services the compressor and the restorer must coexist inside the same device; hence, for an economical implementation, the two parts should have about the same degree of complexity. The worldwide development trend in terminals is to adopt common coding devices rather than using different decoders for different services.

6.2 NARROWBAND SERVICES

Video information possesses about 1000 times wider bandwidth than voice information; hence, the cost of transmitting a video signal is much higher than that for voice. Therefore, transmission bandwidth should be lowered through the use of sophisticated video signal processing algorithms such as *discrete cosine transform* (DCT), *difference pulse code modulation* (DPCM), *vector quantization* (VQ), *variable length coding* (VLC), and others. Also, since complex hardware is required for high-level video signal processing, the equipment required for video services is still extremely expensive. Consequently, service expansion has been difficult to achieve up till now. Nevertheless, video information services will become essential with the maturation of the information society, and accordingly, promising research activities are under way for reducing the prices of transmission and terminal equipment.

Figure 6.1 shows input and output device configurations of a typical video communication system. The input device is composed of a camera, which inputs images, the *analog-to-digital converter* (ADC), which converts an analog video signal from the camera into a digital signal, the grabber, which accepts the input images, the memory device, which temporarily stores the images, and the control unit for controlling all the components. The network access device plays the role of linking input/output devices to the network and is composed of the network interface device and the network termination device. The composition of the output device is similar to that of the input device, except that the camera, grabber, and ADC are replaced by the monitor, display unit, and *digital-to-analog converter* (DAC), respectively.

From the communication network point of view, video services can be classified according to the bandwidth, application format, and the service user requirements. In terms of transmission bandwidth, video services can be broadly categorized into the 64-kbps class of narrowband services and the broadband services that provide

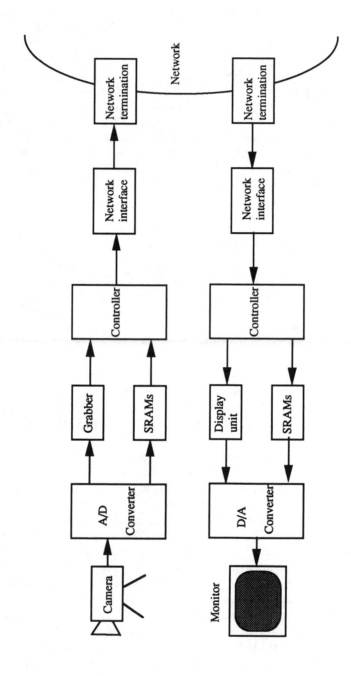

Figure 6.1 Video communication system.

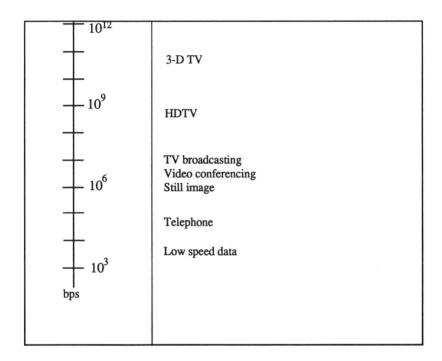

Figure 6.2 Service bandwidth.

video services with higher bandwidth than the 64-kbps bandwidth. Figure 6.2 illustrates bandwidths required for various types of services.

With respect to the application format, video services can be divided into distributive services with unidirectional service characteristics and the interactive services with bidirectional service characteristics. (A similar classification is provided in Chapter 4 for a general class of services, including the video/image services.) Distributive services can be separated into the simple distributive services, where user control is impossible, and the repetitive distributive services, where user control is possible. Simple distributive services are the type of service that provides continuous information to all of the subscribers who are connected to the network via a service provider. The subscriber merely accepts the services provided and cannot control or change the transferred information. Examples include TV broadcasting and simple, unidirectional CATV. Repetitive distributive services are the type where information is provided in a repetitive manner by first dividing it into specific information units; the user can select the required information on his or her own request. Examples of this type include the local community information services and the news and weather forecast services.

Interactive services can be classified into conversational services, message services, and retrieval services. Conversational services provide bidirectional conversational communication for real-time information transfer between users or between a user and a computer terminal, and the information flow can be bidirectionally symmetric or asymmetric. Examples of this type of service include video telephone, video conferencing, and bidirectional CATV. Message services provide communication between users through such means as store-and-forward, electronic mail, and message processing, and examples include picture processing, electronic mail service, and high-definition picture. Retrieval services provide information stored in the retrieval information center upon the user's request only. Some examples are film, bidirectional CATV, and video response system.

The characteristics of the services mentioned above range from one extreme to another—transmission channels from a few kilobits per second to over several hundred megabits per second, and the service period from a few seconds to several hours, depending on the service type. Therefore, it is difficult to accommodate all of the various services either by circuit switching alone or by packet switching alone. Some video services even demand real-time processing capability also. In order to resolve such problems, it is necessary to enhance service efficiency through the employment of ATM.

Table 6.1 summarizes the characteristics of some of the typical video communication systems in use today. Since optical CATV technology and HDTV will be treated in detail in Sections 6.5 and 6.6, the present section will focus on a brief examination of teletext, videotex, video conferencing, video telephony, and the video information retrieval system, in that order.

6.2.1 Teletext

Teletext uses the *vertical blanking intervals* (VBI) of the TV signal to broadcast text and graphic information such as news, weather forecasts, traffic information, market prices, and stock exchange situations at the same time as the TV video information. The subscriber can select the desired information and view it through the TV screen by pressing the appropriate keypad.

The user can view text and graphic information as they are overlayed on the regular program, or they can be viewed alone by turning off the TV video portion. That is, video information composed of texts and figures is superposed on the TV broadcast wave in the form of a digital data signal, which is converted by a decoder at the receiving side into the TV video signal and displayed by the TV receiver. Teletext, which is also called *multitext broadcasting*, was originally developed to provide captions for the hearing-impaired, but now it is widely used to complement regular programs. Up to now, three video information transmission modes (i.e., pattern mode, code mode, and hybrid mode) have been developed. Although teletext currently maintains an interlinked relationship with videotex systems, it is expected to develop into a new broadcast medium that is rich in variety, selectivity, promptness, and documentation.

Figure 6.3 depicts a configuration of teletext which can be broadly divided into transmitter and receiver. The transmitter multiplexes text signals coming from the text broadcasting editing unit of the broadcasting station into VBIs and transmits them through the TV transmitter. The receiver is composed of a decoder to restore the text signal that has been multiplexed into the existing TV and a display switching device that can switch between regular TV broadcasting and text broadcasting. The receiver also contains a selection keypad and a text signal processor.

6.2.2 Videotex

Videotex, provided in the conversational format through a telephone network, is a wired bidirectional video information system that provides various service information, which the user retrieves through a terminal from an information *database* (DB) composed of texts and graphics. This implies that the videotex requires complex system integration of DB management, video information processing, information transmission, system management, and information retrieval technologies. However, a user without professional knowledge of computers and communication can easily retrieve information from the enormous DB.

In order to provide information to users inexpensively at the proper moments, the videotex information provider or the system manager uses texts and graphics from many independent input sources to create and store new videotex graphics or renew old data.

The videotex system is composed of the user terminal, external computer, database service provider terminal, and communication network, and its basic configuration is given in Figure 6.4. The user terminal consists of the existing TV, decoder, and keypad. The information selected by the keypad is displayed on the TV after it is received from the DB through the network. The DB is where information provided by the information provider is stored, and it can be accessed by all users.

Tables 6.2 and 6.3, respectively, list service classifications and applications, and Table 6.4 compares teletext and videotex.

6.2.3 Video Conference System

The remote video conference system is a video communication system that breaks away from the conventional communication method, which was mainly voice- and data-oriented. By transferring video, graphic, voice, and data simultaneously to a remote place, it provides an environment that most closely resembles an actual conference situation, and it is often called video conference system. The employment

Table 6.1
Summary of Image Communication Systems

System	Characteristics	Transmission Channel	Bandwidth	Message	Terminal Components
Teletext	Distribution service Unlimited connection of multiple users	TV broadcasting channel		Character, figure, and graphic	Decoder TV
Videotex	Unbalanced bidirectional service Database at central node	PSTN	1200 ~ 2400 bps	Character, figure, and graphic	Decoder Monitor Key pad
Still videophone	Conversational service	PSTN	1200 ~ 9600 bps	Still image, voice	Codec Monitor Telephone Camera Modem
Video phone	Conversational service Multipoint connection Real-time communication	ISDN	$n \times 64$ kbps, $n = 1, \ldots, 31$	Moving image ($7.5 \sim 30$ frames/sec) Voice	Codec Monitor Telephone Camera Modem
Audio graphic	Conversational service Multipoint connection Real-time communication	PSTN ISDN	2.4 kbps	Voice and graphic	Telephone Input device for handwriting Monitor

System	Characteristics	Network	Bandwidth/Rate	Media	Terminal equipment
Video response system	Bidirectional communication; Still image or video on demand; Wide bandwidth	CATV network	About 4 MHz	Sound, still image and voice	TV; Key pad
Video teleconference system	Multipoint connection; Real-time service	$n \times 1.544$ Mbps	Leased line	Voice; Video; Document	Camera; Monitor; Microphone and speaker; Facsimile; Printer
CATV	Unbalanced bidirectional communication; Distribution service; Wide bandwidth	CATV network; BISDN	About 4 MHz	TV-quality video; Sound	TV with receiver; Key pad
High-definition TV	Distribution service; Wide bandwidth	CATV network; BISDN	About 20 MHz	High-quality video; Hi-fi stereo sound	HDTV receiver
Facsimile	Unidirectional communication	PSTN; ISDN	1200 bps; 64 kbps	Document	Facsimile device

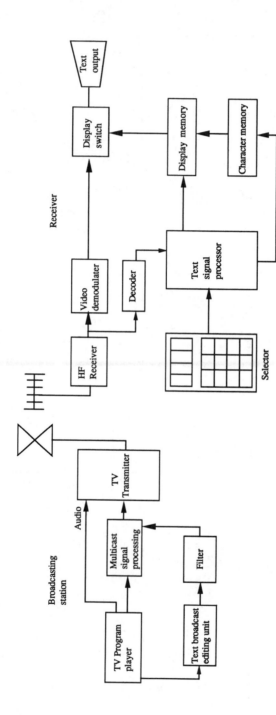

Figure 6.3 Teletext block diagram.

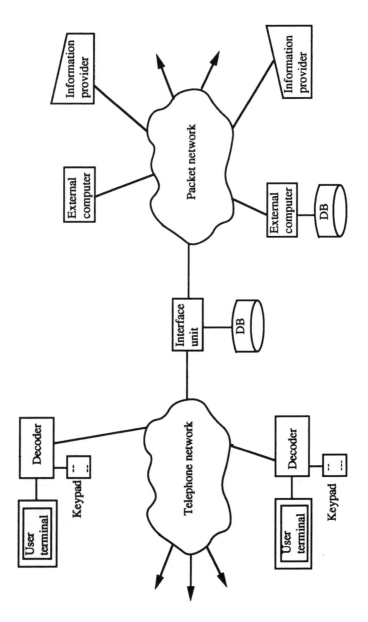

Figure 6.4 Schematics of videotex system.

Table 6.2
Classification of Videotex Service

Service	Characteristics
Public service vs. private service	System is classified based on the type of users
	Public service can be provided to anyone
	On the other hand, private service can be provided to specified person
Home service vs. business service	System is classified based on the type of service
	Home service contains household affairs; on the other hand, business service contains commercial affairs.
Response service vs. commercial service	Users select and receive service in response system
	Commercial trade (for example, ticket reservation and stock trade) is served in commercial service

Table 6.3
Application Area of Videotex

Application	Services
Information retrieval	Electronic publication, reference to book catalogue and database, local-area information, sightseeing information, traffic information, stock, trade, management, statistical information, immovables information, health, recreation, etc.
Commercial	Goods ordering, reservation, banking service, etc.
Message communication	Electronic mail, survey of public opinion, consumer prosecution, market reference
Others	Video game, private information storage, remote work, remote observation

Table 6.4
Comparison Between Teletext and Videotext

Contents	*Teletext*	*Videotext*	*Remarks*
Basic characteristics of media	One-way, simultaneous transmission	Bidirectional transmission	
	Simultaneous connection of multiple users	Limited simultaneous connection of multiple users	
	Comparatively small information storage	Storage for database	
Service type	Repetitive transmission, selective receipt	Referencing and conversational service	
Technical characteristics	Nationwide service	Local service	
	Fast transmission speed	Slow transmission speed	
	Easy interface between decoder and TV	Need the interface between decoder and TV	
	Poor channel condition	Comparatively good channel condition	
	Variable receiving condition	Restricted terminal specification	
Management	Manager and information provider are identical	Manager and information provider may not be identical	
Charge	No relations between information and charge	Charge per information	
Expenditure	Low development cost	High development cost	Videotex needs mass storage
Proper type of service	Nationwide general information	Local-area information	
	Program information	Special and individual information	
	Caption		
Characteristics of information	Quick report	Cyclopedic information	Videotex needs continuous accumulation
	Temporal information	Permanent information	

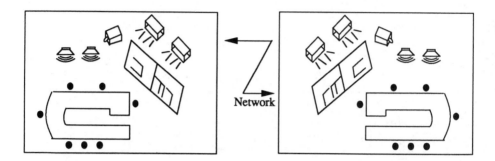

Figure 6.5 Basic concept of video conferencing system.

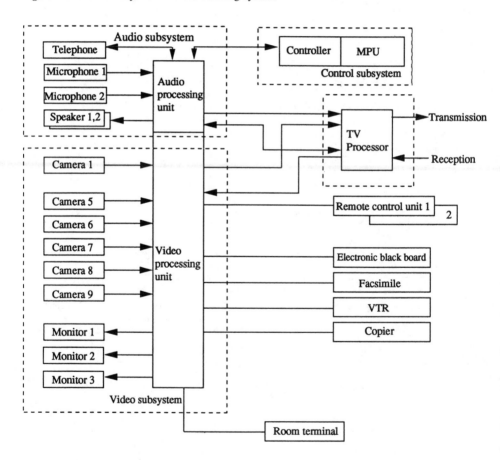

Figure 6.6 Block diagram of a video conferencing system.

of such a conference method takes away the lack of emotion in basic voice communication, enables effective adaptation to urgent situations that require fast decisions, and can maximize the efficiency of company activities by allowing prompt exchange of special information without expensive travel.

The basic concept of the video conference system is depicted in Figure 6.5. Unlike the VRS or the video phone, it not only transmits and processes voice information, but also applies various effects to video and voice in order to achieve the atmosphere of an actual conference room. The video conference system typically consists of an audio subsystem, TV processor, and auxiliary devices, as depicted in Figure 6.6.

The audio subsystem consists of a telephone, a microphone, speakers, and a sound signal processing unit, and it performs such functions as detection of camera motion signals by way of voice, echo cancellation, equalization, and mixing of several voices. The video subsystem consists of a camera, monitor, and video signal processing unit. The camera consists of a closeup camera, an overview camera, a multifunction camera, and a camera for documentation. the monitor consists of input video display and output video display, and the video processing unit consists of a video switching device and a camera control device.

The control subsystem performs control and OAM functions for the overall system and consists of a main control device and a *multiprocessor unit* (MPU). The TV processor is the most important part, and it compresses video, voice, and data signals and multiplexes and transmits them through the transmission line. It also possesses error correction and self-diagnosis capabilities. The auxiliary device is composed of the remote controller, electronic blackboard, facsimile, *video tape recorder* (VTR), and copier.

Table 6.5 lists video conference systems used in various countries.

6.2.4 Video Telephony

Video telephony can be divided into still-picture phone and video phone, depending on the user's request. The still-picture phone transmits pictures of the speaker every five to six seconds and can transfer information through the existing PSTN networks. The video phone can transfer not only voice but also the motion information of the speaker. It transfers information through an ISDN network where its information transfer speed is $n \times 64$ kbps. Since it must transfer motion information, it uses sophisticated data compression techniques, and point-to-point as well as multipoint communication is possible. Since video telephone is still expensive, it is not yet in popular use.

As shown in Figure 6.7, the video phone consists of a video/voice input/output device, video/audio codec, network interface part, and control device. The

Table 6.5
Video Conference System

Country	System	Organ	Number of Establishing Place	System Configuration				Charge (500 km basis)
				Capacity	Video Format	Display Format	Channel	
England	Confura vision	BT	8 cities	5 persons (public)	5-Mhz color	Parallel display on partitioned screen	Microwave reserved channel	$10/30 minutes
	Image communication service	BT	8 cities (50 terminals)	3 persons (home)	5-Mhz color	1 display on screen	Optical or coaxial cable (2 Mbps)	
U.S.	Picture phone meeting (~ 1981)	AT&T	12 cities	6 persons (public)	4-Mhz B/W	Voice cutting	Microwave reserved channel	$3.7/minute
	Picture phone meeting (1981 ~)	AT&T	14 cities	6 persons (home)	4-Mhz color	Voice cutting	Microwave reserved channel Satellite, terrestrial (3 Mbps T1)	$320/30 minutes
	TV conference	BL	2 cities	9 persons	4-Mhz color	Voice cutting	Microware	Usage in the private company
	CTS teleconference	Westinghouse	2 cities	6 persons	4-Mhz B/W	Voice cutting	CTS (satellite)	Usage in the private company
	CNS (Communication Network Service)	SBS	10 places	Integrated service (voice, data, facsimile, image)		SBS satellite (3 ~ 6 Mbps)		

Country	Service	Organization	Coverage	Capacity	Bandwidth	Feature	Transmission	Cost/Notes
Canada	TV conference	TCTS	7 cities	6 persons (public)	4-Mhz color BW	Parallel display on partitioned screen	Microware Reserved satellite channel	$90/first 30 minutes $40 for/5 minutes
Australia	CCTV conference	APO	2 cities	6 persons (public)	4-Mhz BW	Parallel display on partitioned screen	Microware Reserved satellite channel	A $12/hour
France	Video conference	CNET	4 cities	6 persons (public)	1-Mhz TV, phone	Voice cutting	TN 1 (2 Mbps)	F 1200/hours
Germany		Siemens AG	2 places (1 mile distance)	4 persons	1-Mhz BW	4 parallel display	Pair cable	Usage in the private company
Netherland		PTT Philips	5 cities	6 persons	1.3 Mhz TV, phone	Voice cutting	Microware Pair cable	Usage in the private company
Sweden	TV conference	Sweden PTT	6 cities	3 persons (public)	5-Mhz BW	1 display on screen	Optical cable Coaxial cable (T1)	Usage in the private company
Korea		POSCO	3 cities		4-Mhz color	1 display on screen	Optical cable Coaxial cable (T1)	
	Remote video conference	KT	4 places	6 persons (public)	4 Mhz color	Voice cutting		International and domestic commercial service

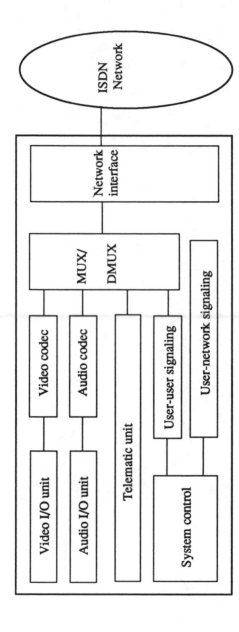

Figure 6.7 Block diagram of video phone system.

network interface performs such functions as a communication procedure with other video phones, interconnection with other services, multiuser conversation, frame generation, and encryption. Telematic equipment like the computer terminal, facsimile, and copying machine can also be linked to the video phone.

6.2.5 Video Response System

VRS is the system that allows the subscriber to use the keyboard to output video, still images, and information along with voice on the TV monitor at the desired moment. While CATV and videotex are in active development in many countries, examples of VRS are not yet widely known.

In Japan, NTT performed a demonstration experiment in 1986 and now provides VRS service under the title Super Captain, and in conjunction with INFAS, provides INN (INFAS and NTT Network) service to fashion companies.

VRS, shown in Figure 6.8, is analogous to CATV and videotex in the sense that it is serviced through wired networks, but it is different, since subscribers can select video information (videotape or video file) through a terminal at the time they desire it. It also differs from the pay-per-view service of simple unidirectional CATV. While videotex uses ordinary telephone line, VRS requires a broadband transmission

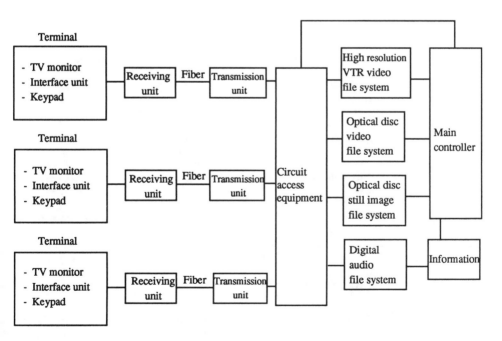

Figure 6.8 Block diagram of the video response system.

line that can transmit up to 4 MHz, which is 1000 times that of telephone. Since, in VRS, images of higher definition than videotex are sent together with voice, VRS can provide its own peculiar services that are different from videotex.

While CATV can transmit the same program to thousands of terminals linked to that particular channel, VRS provides the same information to only a few terminals. So it is appropriate for special services which require high-definition video.

VRS can provide three kinds of information: color video, still image, and voice. In actual service, video or still image is provided simultaneously with voice. Applications of VRS are those that require both video and voice and ranges from language education that needs to convey subtle facial expressions, to listening education and individual education at home. It can also be used for various information guide and retrieval purposes, product advertising, ordering, and home shopping. Table 6.6 summarizes various applications of VRS.

Table 6.6
Application Area of Video Response System

Area	Information	Application Contents
Official usage	Advertising and sales	PR and sales via monitor
	Designing and planning of merchandise	Detail design through motion picture New planning of merchandise
Referencing local area information	Public information	Administration information, news, event, understanding between the citizens and public offices
	Sightseeing information	Combining sightseeing resources and information Provide local sightseeing information
Private information	Video library	Referencing book database through accessing VRS system
	Research and teaching	Assistant materials for research and teaching

6.3 VIDEO COMPRESSION TECHNIQUES

The dramatic advances in signal processing and VLSI technologies in the past decade have brought about significant progress in the development of compression technology for video signals at various transmission speeds. So video coders which were regarded as technically impossible or economically unfeasible have emerged into practical use. Owing to such progress in video compression techniques, video communication services, together with existing voice communication, have become realizable. Most representative examples are HDTV, CATV, video telephony, video conference, and VRS. Since these video services require the transmission of tremendous quantities of information, for cost-effective transmission, video data must be compressed within the range that the effect of compression remains imperceptible.

Video information is provided to viewers in series of images or "frames," and the effect of movement is achieved through small, continuous changes in the frames. Since images are provided at the speed of about 30 frames/sec, continuous changes between frames appear as natural moving images to human eyes. Video pictures are composed of spatial and time domain information. Spatial domain information is provided in each frame, and time domain information is provided by images that change with time (i.e., by differences between frames). Since changes between neighboring frames are minute, objects appear to move smoothly.

In digital video systems, each frame is sampled in units of *pixels* or picture elements. Sample values for pixel luminance are quantized with eight bits per pixel in the case of *black and white* (BW) images. In the case of color images, each pixel maintains the associated color information; for instance, the three pieces of luminance information designated as *red, green, blue* (RGB) are quantized to eight bits. Video information composed in this way possesses tremendous amount of information; hence, for transmission or storage, the image compression (or coding) technique is required, which eliminates redundant information, mainly in spatial and time domains.

In general, redundancies in spatial domain are due to the small differences between neighboring pixels of a given frame, and those in the time domain are due to the minute differences in contiguous frames caused by the movement of an object. The method of eliminating redundancies in the spatial domain is called *intraframe coding*, which can be divided into DPCM, transform coding, and subband coding. On the other hand, time domain redundancies can be eliminated by the *interframe coding* method, which also includes the motion estimation/compensation method, which compensates for motion through estimation. In intraframe coding and interframe coding, run-length coding and variable length coding are additionally used, which exploit statistical characteristics of data to further compress data without any loss of important information. They will be discussed again in the following sections.

6.3.1 Intraframe Coding

Intraframe coding uses only the spatial information existing in each video frame. Since this type of coding does not use any temporal information, it can also be used for still-image coding, where real-time implementation does not matter. Intraframe coding of video signals can be realized rather simply and does not require memory that stores preframes or postframes. In general, the intraframe method can be categorized into three types: prediction coding, transform coding, and subband coding. Since each method has its own set of merits, a combination of two or more methods is often used. Each of three intraframe coding types will be discussed in order.

Prediction Coding

Prediction coding is one of the oldest image compression techniques and is based on the fact that prediction errors are very small when the present pixel is predicted from neighboring pixels. The DPCM technique encodes the quantized value of the difference between present pixel value and predicted value (prediction error). The use of a great number of neighboring pixels for prediction can decrease prediction error and raise performance. But as the merits of using a large number of pixels do not outweigh the accompanying complexity, the number of neighboring pixels used for prediction is generally not more than four. Figure 6.9 depicts the DPCM technique.

Image degradations in prediction coding are due to granular noise, slope overload, and edge business. Granular noise results when the quantization step size is

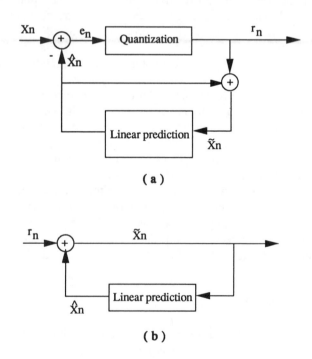

Figure 6.9 Block diagram of predictive coding: (a) encoder; (b) decoder.

too big, while slope overload results when quantization step size is too small. Granular noise and slope overload cause noise and degradations at boundaries of the restored image. Edge business results when an image signal is displayed continuously in time, since pixels at the boundary of the object are quantized differently in neighboring frames. Therefore, a technique that gives a good-quality image for still images does not necessarily provide good-quality image for moving images.

In order to alleviate these degradations, quantizers can be contrived to reflect human visual characteristics, a noise reduction filter can be applied, and different adaptive prediction and quantization schemes can be used according to image contents. For example, boundaries of objects can be treated differently from the flat parts. There has been much research based on this concept, but most of it is not very attractive, since hardware complexity increases too much compared to the corresponding improvement in the image quality. From the performance standpoint, the prediction coding scheme, though it can be easily implemented, is not as effective as transform coding in reducing redundant information. Transform coding has a better compression ratio than prediction coding.

Transform Coding

As a result of extensive research in the past 20 years, transform coding has been chosen as the world standard technique for still-image compression. The basic concept of transform coding is to obtain a high compression ratio by eliminating redundancies through orthogonal transforms.

Under the assumption that statistical characteristics of the image data do not change, the *Karhunen-Loeve transform* (KLT) is known to be the best transform from the standpoint of mean square error. But due to the fact that basis functions must be sent to the decoder because basis functions of KLT are data-dependent, and due to the difficulty of high-speed computation, it is impractical to employ KLT in real-time applications. Therefore, the fixed basis orthogonal transform, which can be easily implemented while maintaining a similar level of performance is widely used. An orthogonal transform that is the most similar to KLT is DCT, which manifests good performance even when no assumption has been made about the statistical characteristics of the image data. DCT performs transforms in real numbers and can thus employ fast computing algorithms already in existence. Moreover, since VLSI implemented products that operate in a wide range of transmission speeds are available, DCT is widely used for various image compression applications. The basic principle of DCT transform coding is depicted in Figure 6.10.

Input image is divided into blocks of $N \times N$ pixels in DCT, and block size is chosen by considering the requisite compression efficiency and picture quality. In general, the bigger the block size the greater the compression ratio is, since more pixels are used to reduce redundancies. But when block size is too large, the assumption that the statistical characteristics of the image data remain constant does

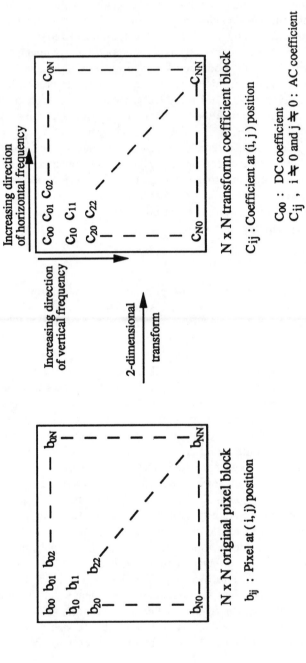

Figure 6.10 Illustration of block transform.

not hold, so various degradations occur, such as ringing in blocks, including abrupt boundaries or blocking effects at block boundaries. According to experimental results, the 8 × 8 block size is known to be the most desirable. After dividing an image into blocks, DCT is applied to each block.

The two-dimensional DCT and inverse DCT are defined as follows:

$$F(u, v) = \frac{1}{4} C(u)C(v) \sum_{i=0}^{N} \sum_{j=0}^{N} f(i, j) \cos\left(\frac{\pi u(2i + 1)}{16}\right) \cos\left(\frac{\pi v(2j + 1)}{16}\right) \quad (6.1)$$

$$f(i, j) = \frac{1}{4} \sum_{u=0}^{N} \sum_{v=0}^{N} c(u)c(v)F(u, v) \cos\left(\frac{\pi u(2i + 1)}{16}\right) \cos\left(\frac{\pi v(2j + 1)}{16}\right) \quad (6.2)$$

In the equations, $f(i, j)$ is the (i, j)th pixel of each block, and $F(u, v)$ is the transform coefficient corresponding to each frequency. Weighting factor $C(u)$ is $1/2$ when $u = 0$, and 1 otherwise. $F(0, 0)$, which designates the mean value of pixels of a specified block, is sometimes called the *DC* (or constant) *component*.

In this manner, the $f(i, j)$ are first transformed into $F(u, v)$ and then compressed through the coding steps shown in Figure 6.11. Transform coefficients $F(u, v)$ are quantized after thresholding to create as many 0 values as possible within the range that degradations in picture quality do not occur, since with more 0s there are more chances for a greater compression ratio. To guarantee continuity between mean values of different blocks, DC components are excluded from thresholding and the values are quantized by a finer step size. Lastly, coefficients arranged in two dimensions are rearranged into coefficients arranged in one dimension using zigzag scanning, and then run-length coding is applied to both nonzero coefficients and the zero-runs. Since long sequences of 0s occur when zigzag scanning is employed to change coefficients arranged in two dimensions to one dimension, the coding efficiency is improved correspondingly. Nonzero coefficients and zero-runs are coded using a variable-length code book designed on the basis of data statistics. As was mentioned previously,

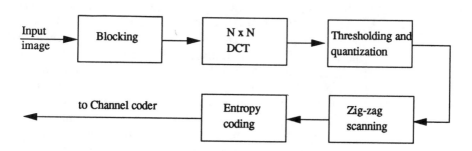

Figure 6.11 Block diagram of basic DCT transform coder.

image degradations due to the DCT coding scheme result from the ringing effects of blocks, including abrupt boundaries and traces of block boundaries in flat regions.

These visual degradations can be reduced using a DCT coefficient quantizer that is based on human visual characteristics. In this case, a larger quantizer step size is used for those DCT high-frequency coefficients that are not susceptible to human eyes, and a smaller step size for the low-frequency coefficients that are susceptible to human eyes.

The thresholding processing and quantization in the basic DCT coding algorithm can apply the same technique to all the blocks regardless of the contents of the image data, and fine thresholding and quantization step size are required for restoration of high-quality pictures. But then the requisite bit rate increases too much for complex images; hence, an adaptive coding scheme should be considered for a tradeoff between quality and bit rate.

Some of the DCT coding techniques categorize blocks into several characteristic models according to block characteristics and handle them according to the properties of each model.

As was described above, transform coding uses the orthogonal transform to reduce redundancies by eliminating data correlations, and its performance improves when there are fewer activities in a block. Using this fact, an adaptation method can be derived that divides image data into blocks of variable sizes according to the degree of data activities. That is, after dividing data into blocks of appropriate sizes, DCT coding can be applied to each block. Such an adaptive scheme divides highly active parts into very small blocks or low-activity parts into large blocks, and is thus suitable for the coding of text, drawings, and graphic images.

Subband Coding

Although the basic concept of subband coding is simple, progress in subband coding for image compression has only been achieved recently. Subband coding is composed of two major steps. The first step is the subband filtering step, which splits an image signal into its constituent frequency components, and the second step is the coding step, which compresses each frequency band according to its respective characteristics. The two subband coding steps will be separately discussed next.

Subband coding is accompanied by an analysis filter bank at the encoder and a synthesis filter bank at the decoder, respectively. The analysis filter bank splits the input into several different bands using a different sampling rate for each band. In contrast, the synthesis filter bank combines several band signals of different rates to synthesize the desired signal. Subband coding requires less processing time for each band, but requires many processors, say, one for each band. A simple example of one-dimensional subband coding system is shown in Figure 6.12.

After decomposing an image into several bands using the analysis filter bank, a different coding scheme can be applied to each band which is most appropriate

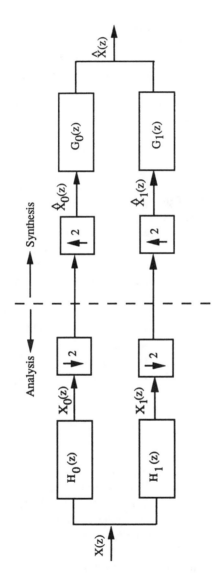

Figure 6.12 Block diagram for one-dimensional subband coding.

for the given band. Since data characteristics of each band vary widely and human visual sensitivity to degradation also varies from band to band, a better performance is obtained when each of the bands is processed according to its own set of characteristics.

The intraframe subband DCT coding scheme is currently widely used for subband coding, and it will be briefly described here.

As shown in Figure 6.13, each frame can be decomposed into four bands (LL, LH, HL, HH) by applying analysis filtering in the horizontal direction and then in the vertical direction.

The LL band includes most of the important data except the edges and boundaries; hence, it is necessary to minimize losses associated with coding of this particular band. Therefore, DCT coding is widely used for the coding of the LL band.

High-frequency bands (LH, HL, HH) mainly contain information about the edges of objects, backgrounds, and the boundaries, and pixel values are generally smaller than those of the LL band, so total information contained in these bands is in most cases smaller than that of the LL band. Also, human eyes are not sensitive to small changes in pixel values of the three high-frequency bands. Therefore, a simple nonuniform quantizer with a dead zone can be used which converts small pixel values to zero without any significantly perceptible degradations. A high compression ratio can be achieved by additionally applying run-length coding to nonzero values and zero-runs. Since the quantizer converts many of the pixel values in the dead zone into zeros, longer lengths of zero-runs are obtained.

Since sample rates decrease (e.g., to $1/4$ in the case of the four-subband coding mentioned above) after the band splitting, the subband coding technique is widely used for high-speed coding processing such as HDTV, which is difficult to perform before the band splitting procedure. Another effective application is packet image transmission, which exploits the fact that the importance of image information varies with each band (LL > HL, LH > HH). It will be discussed in detail in Section 6.4.

6.3.2 Interframe Coding

As was mentioned previously, numerous information redundancies exist between continuous image frames; hence, most information about the present frame can be determined from previous frames. For example, in most cases there is a great possibility that the same objects could occur among continuous frames, and if only the information related to motion is known, then data associated with the object can be coded logically in a single step. This concept also applies to backgrounds, and in order to achieve further compression of image information, such time axis redundancies should be eliminated as well. In general, the fast moving portion in a frame, even in TV programs or movies, is less than 5% of the frame; hence, motion estimation is the key to minimizing redundancies in time.

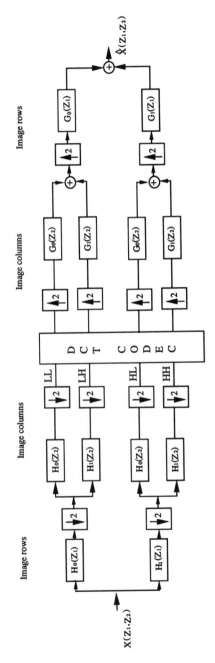

Figure 6.13 Block diagram for intraframe subband/DCT hybrid method.

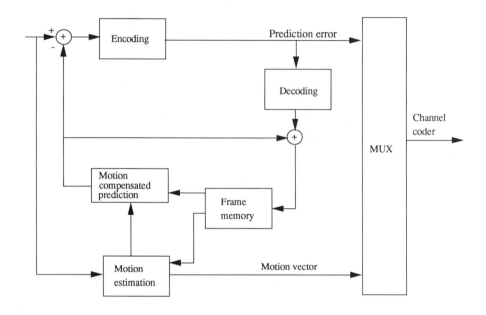

Figure 6.14 Interframe encoder for the motion compensation.

Figure 6.14 depicts the configuration of a general interframe coder. This basic configuration consists of two stages: the first for performing motion estimation and compensation, and the second for compression. The motion of an object is estimated by calculating relative displacement between the previous frame and its corresponding image data, generally in units of blocks. The difference between present data and motion-compensated past data is coded to be compressed. Motion compensation is used to effectively reduce time redundancies, and is quite similar to the prediction coding mentioned in Section 6.3.1, which predicts the present pixel from neighboring pixels of the given frame. We now discuss some of the most frequently used motion displacement estimation methods.

Motion Displacement Estimation

The motion displacement estimation method consists of the pel (which is another acronym for picture element) recursive algorithm, which estimates pel-to-pel motion recursively, the *block matching algorithm* (BMA), which estimates block-to-block motion, and the block recursive matching algorithm, which is a mixture of the first two. In general, extensive computation time is required for motion estimation, so block matching algorithm is widely used, since it is implementable in real time.

BMA estimates motion on a block basis. Since all pixels in a block are assumed to move in one direction in this algorithm, computation and the associated hardware are simple. The operation of BMA is as illustrated in Figure 6.15. Each frame is first divided into $N \times N$ size blocks, and motion displacement is estimated between the present frame and the previous frame. The reference for motion estimation can be normal mean square error or absolute difference error, and the block with the minimum error is picked for the decision of motion vector. The searching area of the previous frame is prespecified, so motion estimation is done on all the blocks within this searching area.

Since displacement estimation in BMA is simple, it has already been implemented on a real-time-processing VLSI chip and is actually in use for image coders. Recently, a VLSI architecture with adjustable block size and searching area has also been developed.

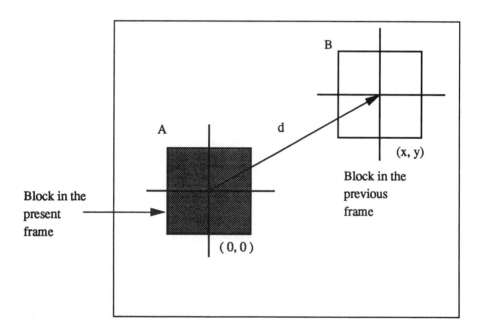

Figure 6.15 Illustration of motion vector estimation.

Compression Coding After Motion Displacement Estimation

The purpose of motion displacement estimation is to estimate present image data (or block) from previous or neighboring frames in order to reduce time redundancies. The most widely used technique is the motion compensation prediction coding scheme.

In this scheme, prediction error, which is the difference between the present block and the motion compensated block (from previous frame), is coded. Through precise prediction of the present block from the previous frame, it can reduce prediction error and thus raise compression ratio. This motion-compensated prediction coding scheme can be regarded as a method of the DPCM type that reduces time redundancies.

In general, the performance of the motion-compensated coding scheme relies on several factors. They are the maximum size of motion displacement (or the size of motion search area), the precision of the motion compensation method for estimating motion, and the adaptability of displacement estimation to variations in time and spatial resolution with different buffer control schemes.

The simplest scheme for coding prediction error between blocks estimated through the present block and motion estimation is the direct quantization method.

For interframe coding in general, most of the coding schemes described in 6.3.1 can be adapted for the interframe encoding of prediction errors. Among the schemes, DCT coding is the most popular, and Figure 6.16 shows the architecture of the motion-compensated DCT prediction coder, which is emerging as the international standard.[1]

To further improve performance, human visual characteristics can be incorporated into the encoder design. Performance can also be enhanced by employing the aforementioned adaptive coding schemes.

Motion-compensated prediction coding can be used in combination with subband coding. In this case, each frame is band-split first, then the motion-compensated prediction coding scheme is applied to each of the bands. This scheme is suitable for packet image coding provided by the ATM network described in Section 6.4.

6.3.3 Standardization Trends

Standardization of communication procedures, signal formats, and coding schemes is very important in order to exchange information precisely and effectively with anyone, at any time, and anywhere. TV, which has been the most popular mass medium up to now has not yet achieved worldwide standardization and has different signal formats (e.g., NTSC, PAL, and SECAM) in various regions around the world. HDTV, which is under development, is also experiencing hardship in international standardization; but it appears that worldwide standardization will be realized for video phone and video conference systems whose essence is bidirectional communication based on compatibility. In relation to this, trends in worldwide standardization of video compression techniques can be summarized as follows.

---

[1]Based on this interframe coding scheme, an international draft standard on video conferencing at 64 to 1920 kbps and on a storage medium with input/output speed below 1.5 Mbps is currently in progress, and motion compensation prediction coding that employs DCT at 45 Mbps is also being considered as the draft standard.

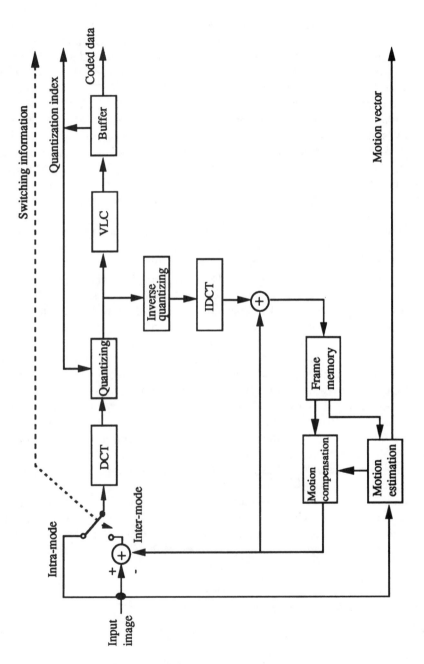

Figure 6.16 Motion-compensated hybrid DPCM/DCT interframe encoder.

The video compression technique consists of three steps: first, the preprocessing step, which preprocesses input signals from various video sources; second, the step for converting the image into *common intermediate format* (CIF); and third, the compression step. The compressed images are transmitted through digital transmission line and the receiver receives them and reconverts them into CIF and displays the reconstructed images after the postprocessing step. Figure 6.17 is a depiction of the three video processing steps for standardization.

The image signal source can be in various forms, such as video phone/conference, TV signals (NTSC, PAL, SECAM), HDTV signals (1050, 1125 scanning lines, etc.), VTR tape signal (VHS, S-VHS), video films, and so on. Also, format and the resolution of each signal source and the bandwidth required for transmission have different characteristics, even within the same application. In the past, there have been attempts to unify these sources with different characteristics into a single standard video source according to each application; but now standardization of image signals within the same application has been virtually given up because of sharp conflicts among companies and among countries. Instead, the trend is towards providing compatibility between different image sources by creating a common format according to several of the resolution requirements through a preprocessing procedure. The common format is a digital image format created from different signal sources through preprocessing and enables communication between different equipment. The common format has a hierarchical structure according to resolution, as shown in Figure 6.18. In countries where 525 scanning lines are used for TV (including the U.S.), the minimum common format is *quarter CIF* (QCIF) with 176 × 120 pixels, which is the image format of video phone. CIF, which is four times the size of QCIF, is used for multimedia services that employ video phone and video conference. As indicated in Table 6.7, CIF has been standardized by CCITT H.261 and the *source input format* (SIF) by ISO's *Moving Picture Expert Group* (MPEG) I. The CCIR 601 format (704 × 480) of MPEG II, which is currently a digital format for analog CATV and TV signals, is four times the size of SIF and will be employed for the digital transmission of TV signals, digital VTR, high-quality video phone/conference, and multimedia services.

Figure 6.19 shows system configurations of video phone and video conference systems recommended by CCITT for the narrowband ISDN. Among various devices in the system, the video codec is the main part for video signal processing, which employs interframe prediction with motion compensation, DCT, and variable-length

Figure 6.17 Three stages of image preprocessing for standardization.

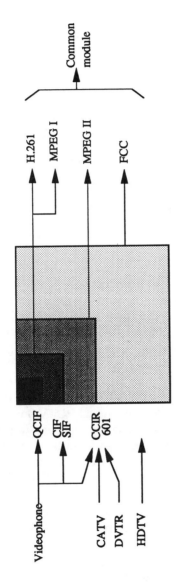

Figure 6.18 Hierarchical common intermediate format.

Table 6.7
Standardization of Image Data Compression

Organization		Application Area	Input Format (525 TV line)	Target Transmission Bit Rate	Remarks
CCITT	H.261	Video phone/ teleconference	QCIF (176 × 120) CIF (352 × 240)	$n \times 64$ kbps $n = 1, \ldots, 31$	Done
ISO/CCITT	JPEG	Still-image applications	Horizontal and vertical resolution $<2^{16}$	0.25–2.0 bit/ pixel	Done
ISO	MPEG I	Digital storage media	SIF (352 × 240) CCIR601	1–1.5 Mbps	
	MPEG II	Digital storage media	(704 × 480)	4 or 9 Mbps	~ 1992
FCC	Advanced TV	HDVT broadcasting	P(1280 × 720) (progressive) or I(1440 × 960) (interlace)	15–20 Mbps	Proposed

coding. This scheme is adopted by both ISO MPEG and CCITT Recommendation H.261. A block diagram for H.261 coder and decoder is shown in Figure 6.20.[2]

For HDTV, it is desirable to employ an all-digital scheme, which all HDTV signal processes composed of video, voice, and graphics in the digital domain and then transmits the TV signal through the existing 6-MHz analog transmission medium after a 16 *quadrature amplitude modulation* (QAM) or some such modulation processing. It will be quite a novel idea to employ almost the same video compression technique for both video phone and digital HDTV broadcasting. When the same video compression technique is executed by changing to a common format as described in Table 6.7, essential components of codecs can be maximally shared among different applications through a standardization of compression schemes. Then the mass production of video codec components becomes possible, which can decrease codec prices dramatically.

6.4 PACKET VIDEO TRANSMISSION

The recently developed packet network technology together with the advances in optical communication systems anticipate the realization of the BISDN, collectively

---

[2]Detailed description of the block diagram is omitted here, since one can easily extend the discussion in 6.3.2 to interpret its operation.

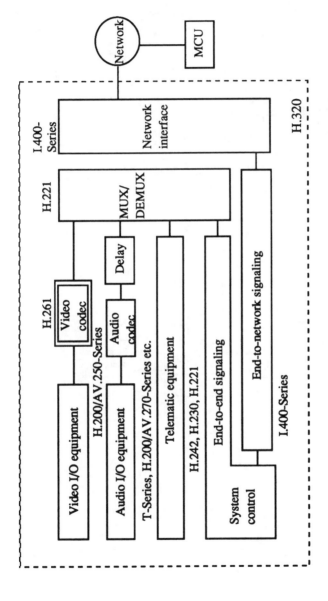

Figure 6.19 Functional block diagram of video terminal for narrowband ISDN application and related CCITT recommendations.

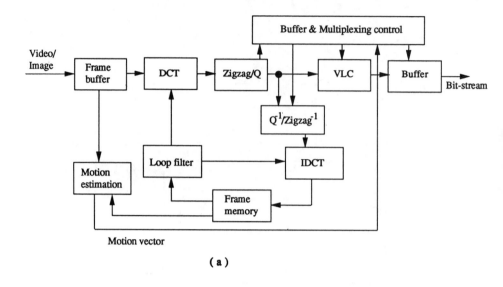

(a)

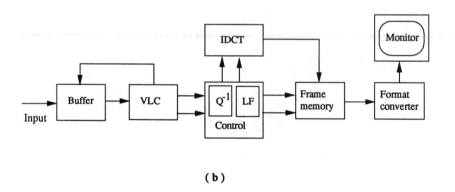

(b)

Figure 6.20 Block diagram of H.261 video codec: (a) video coder; (b) video decoder.

handling voice, data, and video information. The packet communication mode for video information such as videotex, video phone, and video conference is not only one of the key services for the realization of the BISDN, but also introduces numerous technological challenges.

Among the various video information switching modes, packet switching has a number of differences if compared with the conventional circuit switching mode. The most important difference is that, as shown in Figure 6.21, the packet switching mode allows VBR transmission whose bandwidth changes with time, while circuit switching transmits CBR according to the specified bandwidth.

As was described in Section 6.3, image information compressed by coding has a bandwidth that varies with time according to the amount of surplus information. Therefore, in order to transmit a compressed video signal through a circuit switching network, buffer memory is employed to adjust bandwidth. As shown in Figure 6.21, the device that indicates the state of buffer memory is connected to the encoder, and it adjusts the bandwidth transmitted from the buffer to the circuit switching network to the given CBR by preventing buffer overflow. It is achieved by reducing the quantity of the compressed image signal data by increasing the compression ratio when the buffer is in a state of overflow and by stuffing meaningless data or increasing the quantity of compressed image signal data by reducing the compression ratio when the buffer is in a state of underflow. Thus, using buffer memory has a drawback in that picture quality varies according to buffer state and in that it is difficult to exploit the given bandwidth effectively.

In contrast, the packet communication network allows VBRs, and hence no buffer is needed to maintain a constant bandwidth. Therefore, it has the virtue that the design of the encoder is simple and picture quality is constant with time. Furthermore, under the requirement of the same picture quality, statistical multiplexing of several video signals can result in far better utilization of bandwidth in packet networks than in circuit switching networks. Based solely on these results, packet transmission appears to be a highly proficient scheme that satisfies the need for both constant picture quality and efficient bandwidth usage.

If we go one step further and look at a network point of view, a more fundamental virtue of packet communications is that it can accommodate efficient integration of complex information like video, voice, data, image, and text through a single network, and that it can adapt easily to ever-changing consumer demands and service environments. Because of these reasons, ATM, which is a modification of packet communication, has been adopted as basic mode of transmission and switching for the BISDN. But it should be noted that packet transmission raises a new set of problems to be solved, including packet jitter and packet loss, which were not a problem in circuit switching networks.

In this section, various problems associated with the packet communication of video information will be discussed, as well as their solutions. Problems and requirements of video transmission in a packet network will be described in Section

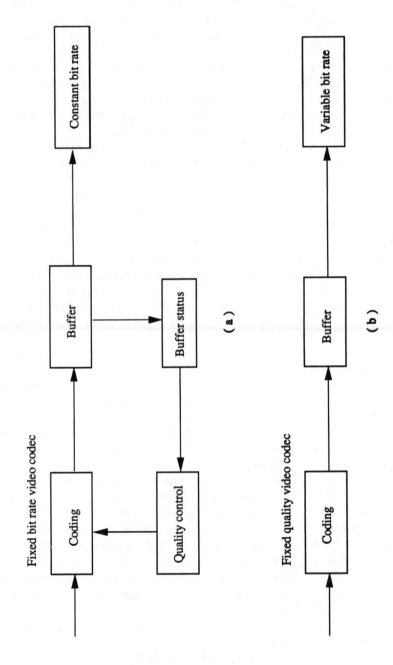

Figure 6.21 Fixed bit rate and fixed-quality video codecs: (a) for circuit switching; (b) for packet switching.

6.4.1, compensation of packet jitter and the clock synchronization method in VBR packet transmission in Section 6.4.2, problems due to packet loss and bit error and the respective correction methods in Section 6.4.3, and hierarchical video coding appropriate for packet networks in Section 6.4.4. Lastly, Section 6.4.5 will give a brief description of various possible transmission methods in a packet network.

6.4.1 Problems of Video Transmission in Packet Networks

We examine problems of video transmission in packet networks using Figure 6.22, assuming the packet length of 53 bytes (5 bytes for the header and 48 bytes for the user information space).[3] As shown in Figure 6.22, an analog video signal is changed into a digital signal and is compressed through video coding. Although it depends on the coding scheme used, the compressed video signal in most cases manifests a VBR flow whose bandwidth varies with time.

A compressed video signal is converted into packets with the addition of a header using a packetizer, a process that introduces delay. The amount of delay varies depending on the degree of change in the bandwidth of the compressed video signal, but if the average bandwidth of the compressed video signal is around 1 to 100 Mbps, the associated time delay is about 5 to 400 ms on average. As a reference point, coding in circuit switching networks introduces 10 to 100 ms of time delay at the buffer in changing a VBR signal to a CBR signal.

After the video packets have been formed, they arrive at the receiver terminal via a large number of packet multiplexers and packet switching networks. Here, packet jitter and packet loss can occur depending on the traffic condition of the network, and they must be compensated for at the receiving terminal.

Causes of packet loss in the network can be divided into two types. One is the packet loss due to limited buffer memories in packet switches and multiplexers, and another is the packet loss which occurs when packets do not arrive at the receiver terminal because of bit errors in the address of the header.

When packets arrive at the receiving terminal, it separates the misdelivered packets from the already arrived packets, compensates for the lost packets, and then stores them in the buffer memory. The buffer of the receiving terminal eliminates packet jitter; that is, it plays the role of adding compensating delay to varying delays of each packet in order to make the overall delay constant.

Afterwards, packets are read out from the buffer memory by the video decoder's clock, and additional packet losses could occur at this stage if the encoding clock of the transmitter is different from the decoding clock of the receiver. Therefore, a clock synchronization circuit is required at the receiving terminal to prevent additional packet losses.[4]

---

[3] In actual implementation of ATM video, 47 or less octets may be used for the user information space because 1 or more octets are used for the ATM adaptation layer.

[4] In ATM, synchronization may be implemented as an ATM adaptation layer function as well.

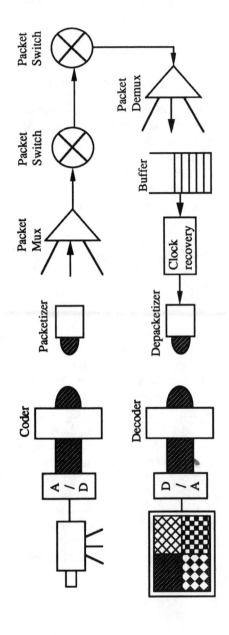

Figure 6.22 Visual communication in broadband packet network.

As has been discussed up to now, three main problems (i.e., time delay, packet jitter, and packet loss) have to be resolved for video transmission in a broadband packet network. Here, time delay in the packet networks is not anticipated to be much longer than the video transmission delay in the existing circuit switching networks, since no bandwidth adjustment buffer is needed other than the packetizing and depacketizing process. Consequently, packet jitter, the associated clock synchronization regeneration at the receiving terminal, and packet loss remain as the main problems of video transmission in packet networks. In other words, without effective compensation for these problems, the merits of packet video transmission (i.e., constant picture quality and efficient bandwidth usage) cannot be achieved. In order to maintain constant picture quality in a packet network, compressed video signal packets must arrive at the receiver terminal without any packet losses within a specified time. In order to achieve such a result, however, inefficient bandwidth (almost the maximum bandwidth of packet switching) must be allocated, as is the case in circuit switching networks. On the other hand, in order to achieve efficient bandwidth usage, packet loss and jitter due to packet multiplexing and the resultant delay are inevitable.

In Section 6.4.2, we will describe packet jitter compensation and receiver clock regeneration, which are the main problems of video transmission in broadband packet networks. In Section 6.4.3, we will consider the packet loss compensation methods, which offer a possible way to satisfy both of the two conflicting requirements mentioned above.

6.4.2 Packet Jitter Compensation and Clock Regeneration

Packet jitter refers to the fluctuations in intervals between packets caused by the variations in waiting time of packets at buffers of the packet multiplexers and switches according to the traffic condition of the network. In other words, packet jitter is attributable to the variable delay of each packet from transmitter to receiver.

If the time it takes for the ith packet to be formed, leave the transmitter, and arrive at the receiving terminal is defined as the waiting delay, $Dq(i)$, $i = 1, 2, \ldots$, then the delay that varies from packet to packet (i.e., packet jitter $J(i)$, $i = 1, 2, \ldots$) can be written as follows:

$$J(i) = \begin{cases} 0, & i = 1 \\ Dq(i) - Dq(i-1), & i = 2, 3, \ldots \end{cases} \tag{6.3}$$

This varying packet jitter changes to fixed delay D by adding compensation delay $Dr(i)$, $i = 1, 2, \ldots$, and in order to achieve perfect packet jitter compensation, the following relation must be satisfied:

$$Dq(i) + Dr(i) = D > \max_{j}\{J(j)\}, i = 1, 2, \ldots \tag{6.4}$$

Figure 6.23 illustrates packet jitter and compensated delay. In the figure, (a–c) represent image compression and packet generation, (d) delay at the receiver terminal, (e) delay compensation at receiver buffer until the packet is read out by the receiver clock, and (f) the degree of associated queuing delay, jitter, and compensation delay of each packet.

The general solution for preventing packet loss due to packet jitter is to delay the packet arriving first at the receiver's buffer as much as the maximum packet jitter, under the assumption that the receiver's clock is the same as the transmitter's clock.

In order to packetize video packets that have arrived, synchronization is required between the transmitting terminal and the receiving terminal. Therefore, the clock of the transmitting terminal must be regenerated at the receiving terminal. Since the clock cannot be sent separately, the receiver clock must be regenerated from the arriving packets. But since the arriving packets are not constant due to jitter and the occasional packet losses, the clock synchronization problem becomes complicated. For the clock regeneration, the receiver first checks for the presence of any packet losses and substitutes any lost packets with other packets stored in the buffer memory of the receiving terminal. Ample buffer memory is required to prevent extra packet losses and to accommodate the maximum jitter generated in the packet network as well. In the end, the transmitter clock must be regenerated from the packets that contain jitter, and therefore clock synchronization regeneration methods in VBR transmission are different from those in CBR transmission.

When the arriving packets have a CBR, the transmitter clock can be extracted using a digital PLL by observing the buffer state of the receiving terminal, even if packet jitter is present. However, if video packets are transmitted in VBR, clock information cannot be extracted directly from the buffer memory state, since it does not reflect the actual transmitter clock. Therefore, the clock information is generally included in the transmitted packets. Here, clock information should have a particular pattern that can be easily identified by the receiving terminal. For example, a particular clock pattern can be sent in every video scanning line period (63.6 μs). Although this clock information is inserted periodically at the transmitting side, the periodicity might become unclear as the packets arrive at the receiving terminal, due to packet jitter. Therefore, a clock generation method is required that can minimize jitter effects. Figure 6.24 shows a method that generates the transmitter's clock by detecting clock patterns from the received packets and connecting them to PLL. It calculates the number of clock patterns detected from the arrived packets over a fixed duration of time and compares it to the number of clock patterns generated by the receiver's clock during the same duration. The receiver's clock is then adjusted by lowpass-filtering the difference.

As an example, we consider the case when the difference between the transmitter clock and the receiver clock amounts to 10 ppm (10^{-5}). If jitter is not considered, in case one clock pattern is inserted in every video scanning period, one clock pattern difference appears in every 6.36 seconds, which is 100,000 times 63.6

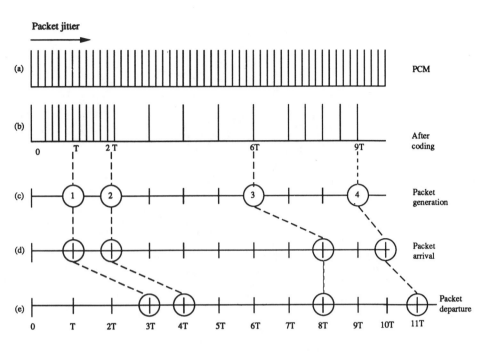

Figure 6.23 Illustration of packet jitter and delay compensation.

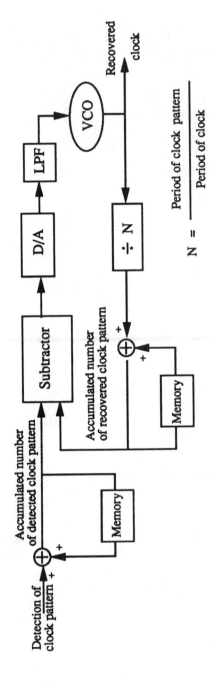

DPLL : Differential Phase Locked Loop

Figure 6.24 Clock synchronization recovery by DPLL.

μs. For the time unit that calculates the difference of the number of clock patterns, 1 minute is adequate. When this time unit becomes larger, the difference of the number of patterns approaches the difference in transmitter/receiver clocks excluding jitter effects. But if it becomes too long, the buffer may overflow or underflow, and hence the time unit should not be lengthened infinitely.

The method shown in Figure 6.24 is the time average method. Since mean jitter value approaches zero over a long period of time while the transmitter/receiver clock difference accumulates, the time average method uses this difference to control the receiver's clock and causes it to converge with the transmitter's clock. The memory in Figure 6.24 continues to add up the difference between clock patterns. Even though jitter effects remain in the receiver's clock for the first few periods (about 1 minute in this case), as time passes the memory plays the role of making it converge with the transmitter's clock.

6.4.3 Packet Loss Compensation

The extent of picture quality degradation of video information caused by packet losses or bit errors varies depending on the coding scheme used. In general, the bigger the compression ratio, the worse the picture degradation is. In the worst case, a single bit error or a single packet loss could cause loss of synchronization in the decoding stage, thus causing a severe picture degradation until synchronization is recovered.

Table 6.8 shows the mean time between bit errors and packet losses associated with network error and packet loss for various video transmission rates.

In the case of high-quality TV signal coded at around 155 Mbps, in order to guarantee more than 2 hours without error or packet loss, the bit error rate and packet loss rate should be 10^{-12} and 10^{-10}, respectively. But it is very difficult to meet this requirement at the network level. Therefore, in order to achieve such bit error and packet loss rates, an error compensation method must be considered at the transmitter/receiver terminal level. In general, subjective compensation methods are used that conceal picture degradation from human eyes using video signals near errored parts at the decoder of the receiving side. Also used is the method that regenerates packet losses and corrects bit errors by employing error correction coding.

In the case of a BISDN network, an error correction method is employed at the ATM cell level for correcting header errors separately. So we consider only the bit error and packet loss regeneration for the information portion, excluding the header.

Figure 6.25 is a block diagram of a system that simultaneously corrects bit errors and regenerates packet losses by employing the *Reed-Solomon* (RS) error correction coding scheme. The transmitter puts compressed video information and other information to be transmitted into the buffer and then takes them out in K-byte blocks and converts them into N-byte blocks by appending parity bytes through RS coding.

RS coding can regenerate up to $N - K$ deleted bytes among N bytes when there is no bit error. When bit errors exist, they can be corrected as well, but the capability

Table 6.8
Average Interval Due to Bit Error and Cell Loss

Average Bit Rate		64 kbps	256 kbps	1.5 Mbps	10 Mbps	45 Mbps	135 Mbps
Bit error	10^{-6}	16 seconds	3.9 seconds	0.7 seconds	0.1 seconds	22 ms	7.4 ms
rate	10^{-9}	4.3 hours	65 minutes	11 minutes	1.7 minutes	22 seconds	7.4 seconds
	10^{-12}	6 months	1.5 months	7.7 days	1.2 days	6.2 hours	2.1 hours
Cell loss	10^{-6}	1.7 hours	25 minutes	4.3 minutes	3.8 seconds	8.5 seconds	2.8 seconds
rate	10^{-8}	6.9 days	1.7 days	7.1 hours	1.1 hours	14 minutes	4.7 minutes
	10^{-10}	1.9 year	5.8 months	1 month	4.4 days	1 day	7.9 days

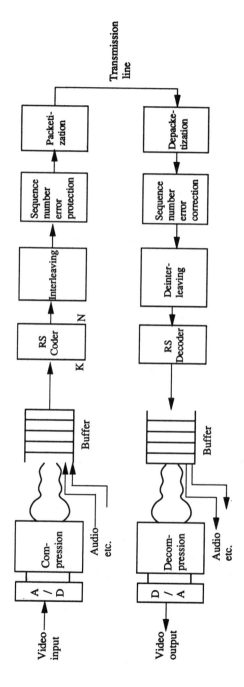

Figure 6.25 Reed-Solomon coding for packet loss recovery and error correction.

to regenerate deleted bytes decreases. This phenomenon can be mathematically expressed as

$$2e + E < N - K + 1 \tag{6.5}$$

where e designates the number of errored bytes caused by bit errors and E designates the number of deleted bytes. For example, in the case of RS coding with $N = 32$ and $K = 28$, with no error occurring in each byte, up to 4 deleted bytes among the 32 bytes can be regenerated, and with no deleted bytes, up to 2 byte errors can be corrected.

We now discuss how RS coding can be used to regenerate packet losses. Figure 6.26 depicts a packet loss regeneration method which appends block interleaving after performing RS coding ($N = 32$, $K = 28$).

The 32-byte (28 information bytes, 4 parity bytes) blocks coming via the RS coder are written sequentially in each row from left to right for 47 rows into the 48 × 32 block interleaving memory. The sequential numbers (s1, s2, ... , s32) for packet loss detection are written in the first row. Then, at the time of packet formation, the information capacity of each packet is formed by sequentially reading 48 bytes from top to bottom and column by column starting with the leftmost column. Packets are transmitted sequentially (p1, p2, ... , p32) after a 5-byte header is added to each. Transmitted packets arrive at the receiving terminal after experiencing bit errors and packet losses in the network. The receiving terminal first checks the sequential numbers (s1, s2,.., s32) in order to detect any lost packets, and stuffs deleted packets into the lost packet slots. Then the 48 bytes of information capacity of each packet are loaded onto the block interleaving memory of the receiving terminal from top to bottom in columns starting from the left, as depicted in Figure 6.26. After memory has been filled, the information is read in its original order from left to right in rows starting from the top, and deleted bytes and errored bytes are regenerated or corrected through the RS decoding process. When a packet gets lost in the network, this represents the deletion of one byte from each column through block interleaving memory; hence, the lost packet can be regenerated through the RS decoding procedure. In other words, block interleaving memory plays the role of changing the deleted-bytes regeneration function of RS coding into packet regeneration function.

The shortcoming of this regeneration method is that it has to send parity bytes needed for RS coding in addition to the actual information capacity. For this, 5% to 15% more bandwidth is required, in general.

Figure 6.27 shows the regeneration failure rate of bit errors and packet losses employing RS coding ($N = 32$, $K = 28$) under the given network bit error rate and

s1	s2	....	s27	s28	s29	s30	s31	s32
1	2		27	28	p1, 1	p1, 2	p1, 3	p1, 4
29	30		55	56	p2, 1	p2, 2	p2, 3	p2, 4
....								
1289	1290		1315	1316	p47, 1	p47, 2	p47, 3	p47, 4
s1	s2		s27	s28	s29	s30	s31	s32

L = 47, N = 32, K = 28, d = 5

s1, s2, .. : Sequence number to detect packet loss

pi, j : ith parity byte of jth data block

Figure 6.26 Block interleaving for packet loss recovery.

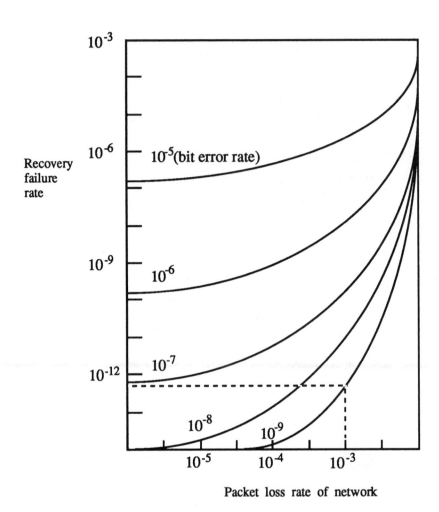

Figure 6.27 Improvement of packet recovery rate by Reed-Solomon coding.

packet loss rate specification. As was described above, it can be seen that the regeneration failure rate is reduced as the network bit error rate is lowered. We can observe that, in case network error rate is 10^{-6} (e.g., coaxial cable transmission system), in order to achieve the desired regeneration failure rate of around 10^{-10}, a network packet loss rate up to 10^{-6} is allowed, while for the network with a bit error rate of 10^{-9} (e.g., optical transmission system), the regeneration failure rate can be lower than 10^{-10}, even though the packet loss rate of the network becomes as high as 10^{-3}.

Whether to use the subjective compensation method or to use a regeneration method employing general error correction coding depends on the particular application.

6.4.4 Hierarchical Video Coding

A careful selection of video compression coding scheme is another way of minimizing picture quality degradation caused by packet losses in packet networks. First, hierarchical coding can be considered, whose most representative example is subband coding. In hierarchical coding, the video signal is decomposed into several parallel signals which are compressed separately. Here, each parallel signal has different hierarchical characteristics with a different priority. Among the various hierarchical coding schemes, the subband coding presented in Section 6.3.1 is one of the most versatile and widely applicable coding schemes in use.

The virtue of subband coding lies in the fact that the coding method for each band can be freely chosen, since the derivation procedure and compression procedure of each parallel signal are independent of those of other signals. Also, since the subband itself naturally converts video information into different hierarchical resolutions, in case terminals with different resolutions (e.g., NTSC, EDTV, HDTV) communicate with each other, just the required bandwidth can be used by adding and subtracting parallel signals. As was described in Section 6.3.1, the image signal is first split into different frequency bands via the filter bank, mainly into frequency bands of two-dimensional space. Here, the higher the frequency band, the lower the importance of each frequency band is for image regeneration.

Figures 6.28 and 6.29 depict a four-band rectangular subband and a three-band rhombic subband, respectively. We observe from the figure that as the number indicating each parallel signal increases, the importance of that band for regenerating the original image decreases. It should be noted that the overall information capacity of the subband parallel signal is the same as the original information capacity.

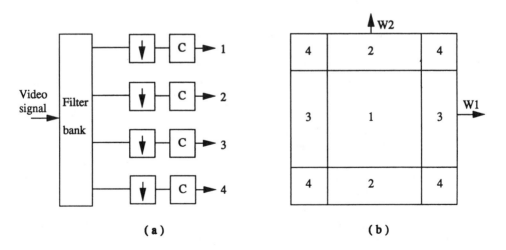

Figure 6.28 Two-dimensional four-channel square subband decomposition: (a) processing; (b) spectrum.

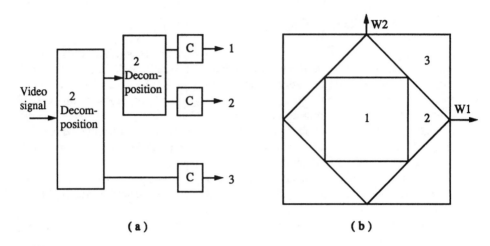

Figure 6.29 Two-dimensional three-channel rhombic subband decomposition: (a) processing; (b) spectrum.

Since the bandwidth allocated to individual parallel signals has decreased, the sampling rate of each parallel signal can be lowered in proportion to the reduced bandwidth. This is very important for high-speed circuit implementation, because a more complex coding method that could not be employed for the original high bit rate video signal can now be used for the new low-rate signal. For these reasons, subband coding is an effective coding scheme independent of network structure and is employed as an HDTV coding method.

In order to demonstrate how effective the subband coding is in packet networks, we consider the images shown in Figure 6.30. Figure 6.30(a) is the original image, and (b,c) are the reconstructed images. Figure 6.30(b) is the image reconstructed using only frequency bands 1 and 2 after the rectangular bandsplitting depicted in Figure 6.28, and (c) has been reconstructed from frequency bands 1 and 2 after the rhombic band splitting scheme of Figure 6.29.

Comparing (b,c) of Figure 6.30, it can be seen that since most image information is contained in the low-frequency bands, the difference in the degree of picture quality degradation is not as great as the difference in the bandwidths. In fact, rhombic band splitting is closer to the actual behavior of human eyes, but it requires more complex procedures in general.

Therefore, if different packets are formed for different frequency band signals, the influence on picture quality due to packet losses of high-frequency bands can be minimized. Low-frequency band packets still require minimal packet loss rate. But since the information capacity protected by band splitting is limited to low-frequency band packets, implementing of the error correction encoder circuit becomes easier.

As has been described so far, hierarchical coding which encompasses subband coding is an extremely effective coding method for video communication in packet

Figure 6.30 Images for illustration of band splitting: (a) original image; (b) reconstructed image using frequency bands 1 and 2 after rectangular band splitting (2D, separable QMF filter); (c) reconstructed image using frequency bands 1 and 2 after diagonal band splitting (2D, nonspecific QMF filter).

networks where packet losses are inevitable. Another major advantage of hierarchical coding is that it can be used for minimizing the overall information capacity to be processed by the network in multicast communication like video conference and CATV. Furthermore, the process of assembling various parts of different images into a single image is very simple in this multicast environment.

6.4.5 Video Transmission in Packet Networks

The following three methods can be considered for video transmission in packet networks. The first method is that in which the packet network guarantees maximum bandwidth for all video transmissions. This method minimizes picture degradation by guaranteeing very low packet loss frequency and packet jitter through a provisioning of connections, such as a circuit switching network inside the packet network. In this case, the design of terminals becomes very simple, but over-usage of bandwidth inside the network caused by guaranteeing maximum bandwidth becomes a major drawback.

The second is the method in which the transmission in the packet network and the design of switches are done simply, and in return packet losses and jitter are compensated for at the transmitting and receiving terminals. In this case, efficient use of bandwidth in the network could be an advantage, but the terminals become quite complex, since they must perform functions like error correction coding.

The third method is a compromise of the first two methods, assigning a priority ranking to each packet by employing hierarchical coding. That is, priority is given to low-frequency packets which have a visible effect on picture quality, and maximum bandwidth is guaranteed for this frequency band only. In this case, the contribution of packet losses in the high-frequency bands to picture quality degradation is minimized due to the advantages of hierarchical coding. Here, clock information patterns can be included in high-priority packets. While maximum bandwidth is guaranteed for packets corresponding to the low-frequency bands of high priority, empty bandwidth is used automatically by low-priority packets. But the synchronization of two kinds of packet stream with different priorities requires increased buffer memory capacity at the receiving terminal.[5]

6.5 OPTICAL CATV TECHNOLOGY

Up to the 1970s, the tree and branch type of coaxial CATV was the main trend of CATV architecture. As the demand for data services expanded and as the optical communication technology developed in the late 1970s, optical CATV emerged as the new CATV of the future.

---

[5]The actual suitability of this method requires further study.

Optical communication technology is the cornerstone for the realization of optical CATV. It is becoming practical to introduce optical fiber to homes, since price of fiber has continuously dropped through the past decade. Also, due to the low-loss and broadband characteristics of the optical fiber of today, it is possible to integrate telephone networks, data communication networks, and CATV networks into the BISDN. Optical CATV, especially, as one of broadband video services, is expected to play the role of catalyst to accelerate the growth of existing networks into a single integrated network. But establishing a separate optical CATV network just for optical CATV services is still uneconomical. Recently, in many countries, various forms of the FTTH subscriber network demonstration are actively in progress for telephone and data services in conjunction with CATV services (discussed in Chapter 2).

While optical CATV mainly employed analog techniques for video signal transmission previously, digital techniques have recently been proposed, and coherent transmission is also being introduced.

Digital transmission techniques applicable for optical CATV are SCM (which can utilize the existing microwave and digital technologies), WDM, and a mixture of these two.

6.5.1 Technologies for Optical CATV

For the construction of an optical CATV system, various types of technologies are required, such as distribution switch, optical cable and access, optical transmission, passive device, and optical amplification. In all of these technologies, except for the distribution switch technology, the optical subscriber component technology described in Chapter 2 can be directly applied. Hence, we only consider the distribution switch technology in this section.

In an optical CATV system, most traffic is unidirectional from the exchange center to the subscriber. So the configuration and control of the switching for an optical CATV network are somewhat different from those in a bidirectional switching network. What essentially is required for an optical CATV network are wide frequency band and high-speed operation. Switching technologies that can accommodate broadband services for the optical CATV systems are space-division switching, time-division switching, and packet switching.

Since space-division switching establishes paths between input and output in a lattice structure, switching and routing speeds are fast, and a means of controlling extra information flow is not needed for the established paths. Therefore, the independence of signal speed is its inherent strength and is thus suitable for high-speed broadband signal switching. Moreover, since its structure is simple, high-capacity switching networks can be constructed inexpensively. Therefore, space-division switching is efficient for the implementation of a single-transmission-speed optical

CATV switching network. However, it has the drawback that the network structure has to be split in order to accommodate various broadband services with different transmission speeds.

Time-division switching, in which switching is performed by dividing time axis occupied by a large number of subscribers into a particular order, has quite high input-output efficiency and therefore allows an economical construction of the switching network for large-scale subscribers. But for high-speed broadband switching, it must be supported by the development of ultra-high-speed and high-capacity memory device technology. Thus, time-division switching is more suitable for switching of low-speed broadband services.

In packet switching, information exchange is accomplished by the process in which each switching node can be occupied by packets of a multiple number of subscribers. Among various broadband switching techniques, ATM switching is the primary candidate for optical CATV switching. In ATM, control information to control paths for high-speed switching is also contained within the ATM cell. Therefore, high-speed switching can be accomplished by establishing a spatial circuit similar to the circuit switching network and then letting each ATM cell pass through the circuit according to its control information. While this is an advanced switching technique to be used for the BISDN, many technical problems have yet to be solved before it can be applied to optical CATV systems.

6.5.2 Worldwide Status of Optical CATV Technology Development

Optical communication technology, which has advanced at a tremendous rate during the past two decades, has also been applied in optical CATV transmission. It is widely used for rebroadcasting between central offices or between trunks for CATV transmission, and applications in subscriber networks, including CATV distribution networks, are actively in progress. We will review the worldwide development status of optical CATV technologies in this section.

The United States

In the U.S., unlike the situation in Europe and Japan, the telephone companies' efforts to take part in the CATV transmission enterprise by extending optical communication networks to subscribers have not been successful up to now. The two most dominant reasons are the FCC's restriction on telephone companies' participation in CATV and the widespread use of coaxial CATV service within the U.S. However, construction of optical CATV model networks for commercial businesses has been planned by the many telephone companies who believe that employing

optical fiber to subscriber lines would offer financial gain in the nineties and anticipate the lifting of the FCC restriction. Most companies plan to provide plain telephone service together with CATV service.

Bell South's Model. Bell South provides CATV service at Hunter's Creek through
digital transmission. This system has a double-star network structure whose head
ends provide 36 TV channels, where a single TV channel is digitized by a 45-Mbps
video codec, and each subscriber can receive 2 different channels. TV channel switching
is done in a *controlled environmental vault* (CEV), and single-mode optical fiber
and multimode optical fiber are employed for head end-to-CEV and CEV-to-subscriber,
respectively. Currently, 251 subscribers receive optical CATV services.

Raynet Model. Raynet developed a system with a star-bus structure that employs single-mode optical fiber to provide analog CATV and telephone services. This
system is a hybrid type, in which many (58) passive taps are connected in a cascade
to one optical fiber, and 28 subscribers can be connected to a tap through optical
cable or coaxial cable by installing an SIU. Thus, optical fibers and devices are
shared by a large number of subscribers, which can induce a drop in service prices.
Providing coaxial cables, which are already familiar to subscribers, is also an advantage. In all, 80 TV channels can be received, and telephone service is provided
independently of CATV by TDMA through optical fiber. This system is especially
appropriate for the economical introduction of optical CATV services under the existing coaxial cable CATV environment. Figure 6.31 shows a comparison of the star
network employing optical cable and the Raynet network.

Canada

Consotel, which is a research and development association of Canada, developed a
digital broadband switching distribution network employing optical fiber over the
period of two years and has been testing it at Rimouski, Quebec, since 1990. The
network is a switching network with a star structure, and telephone, data, videotex
and CATV services are possible. Especially by accommodating 48 CATV channels,
4 independent channels can be provided for each subscriber. In the model, single-
mode optical fiber is provided for each subscriber, and 1024 subscribers are accommodated per hub.

France

As examples of optical CATV or optical subscriber network research activities in
France, the Biarritz model network and video communication network can be mentioned. The Biarritz model network was developed in 1980 and has been in operation
since 1983. The video communication network supported by the French government

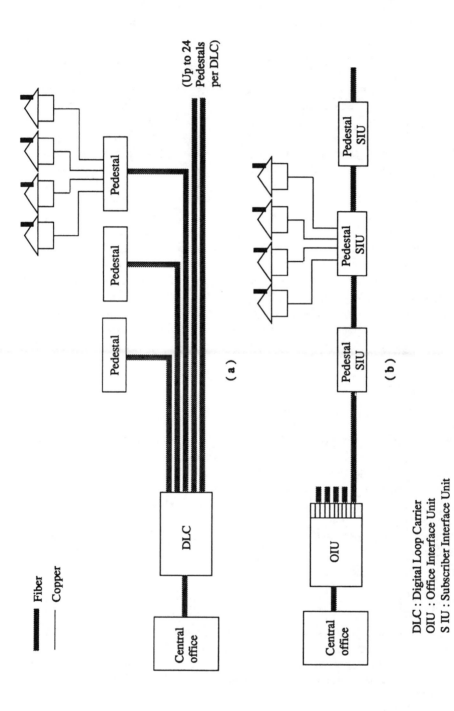

Figure 6.31 Fiber star network and Raynet fiber bus network: (a) fiber star network; (b) Raynet fiber bus network.

has been in construction since 1985, and its goal is the accommodation of about six million subscribers.

Biarritz Model Network. The Biarritz model network was designed to gain experience in subscriber network construction and insight into the performance and reliability characteristics of equipment and devices. It also aimed to test new services and to find out consumer response. The network has a switched star structure, and it provides bidirectional transmission by allocating two multimode optical fibers in all sections. It employs single-frequency optical devices and analog transmission because of the technical state at the time of conception. However, it is an advanced optical CATV network that provides not only simple TV distribution services but also video phone, telephone, and videotex services. Through successful test results of 1200 public subscribers and 300 business subscribers, the Biarritz model validated the applicability of optical fiber to subscriber networks.

Video Communication Network. In accordance with the nationwide video communication network construction plan of the French government, two companies, Velec-CGCT and Alcatel (ITT), developed a model video communication network and began implementing it in 1985. As was shown in Figure 2.15, the network has a double-star structure and adopts a scheme that links several DCs, each of which services about 1000 subscribers to a single operating center. In the first link of the trunk network, program transmission has a tree structure and data switching has a star structure, and all are constructed using optical fiber. The subscriber subsystem, especially, is designed to easily employ many types of interactive communication services. It services two channels of TV, FM audio, ISDN (144 kbps), and data (4.8 kbps).

England

Optical CATV research in England is centered around BT, and local CATV companies are commercializing the system developed by BT. The first research activity can be said to be the optical CATV model network operated by BTRL in 1982 for 18 subscribers at Milton Keyens in the suburb of London. This system employs optical fiber as far as the subscriber premises and has a star network structure. BT is also actively developing PON, which may evolve into the future BISDN.

CATV Network. This CATV system with a switched star network was conceived in March 1982, and its commercial services began in the Westminster region of London from the middle of 1985. In this system, optical cable is employed from head end to switching point, and coaxial cable is used for the subscribers. The switched star network is configured in a tree and ring structure suitable for distribution services, and a star structure suitable for circuit services. Services provided include two TV channels, seven FM channels, and pay-TV. In contrast, copper wire is employed for upward channel for TV channel selection.

PON. For places with uncertain broadband service demands for small business subscribers, BT proposed TPON, which employs only pure passive optical devices (WDM, coupler, etc.), as in Section 2.2.3, without employing the existing telephone systems. This network in the early stages accommodated only telephone services and leased data services in an attempt to lower service prices, and later accommodated broadband services as well. But since this network structure cannot accommodate all of the broadband services, BT eventually proposed the BPON system, similar to TPON, which provides video services such as TV by applying SCM. BT installed a model PON of star structure employing optical fiber at Bishops Strothford in 1990 as a test network employing passive optical devices. In this network, one single-mode optical fiber is connected per subscriber, who can select 2 channels out of 48 CATV channels with FM mode.

Korea

The *Socio-Welfare Advancement Network* (SWAN) system, which is under development by the *Electronics and Telecommunications Research Institute* (ETRI) of Korea, has a double-star structure that simultaneously provides NISDN services and CATV services. The feeder, distribution, and subscriber premises networks of the SWAN system are all composed of optical fiber, as depicted in Figure 6.32. It can accommodate up to 520,000 subscribers and up to eight local exchanges. Each local exchange accommodates up to 64 DCs, and one DC can accommodate up to 1024 subscribers. The bearer service (B of 2B + D) of NISDN, two NTSC TV channels, and one music broadcasting channel are transmitted as synchronous digital signals, and optical CATV services such as pay-channel and pay-per-view are provided. Development is currently in progress to evolve the SWAN system into a BISDN optical subscriber network that employs WDM devices, variable frequency laser diode, passive optical devices, and ATM techniques.

6.5.3 CATV Transmission

In optical CATV networks, WDM, TDM, or a mixture of the two has been employed as the transmission technique. Coherent optical communication technologies can also be applied together with WDM or TDM as new CATV transmission techniques (as described in Chapter 2). Since the TDM technique has been widespread and well understood, the present section will describe WDM and SCM.

Wavelength Division Multiplexing

In WDM, several optical sources with different wavelengths are used to modulate the corresponding input information, and the resulting lightwaves are combined and

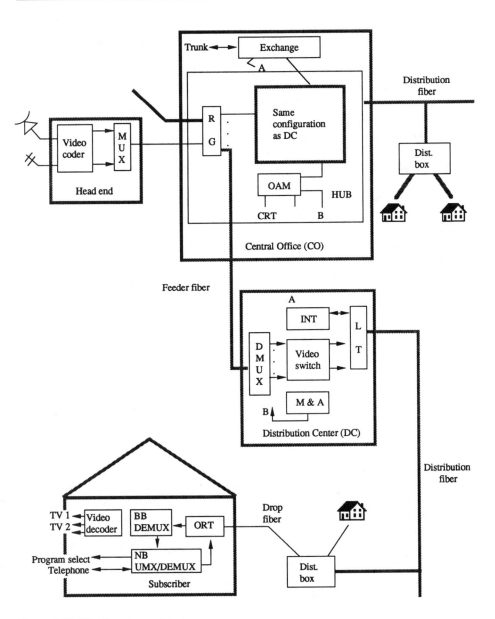

Figure 6.32 SWAN system architecture.

transported through a single optical fiber. The WDM demultiplexer decomposes the multiplexed lightwaves into individual wavelengths and then regenerates each piece of modulated information. WDM is a passive optical processor that can also perform wavelength multiplexing, and it is different from TDM or SCM in the sense that each of the WDM multiplexed channels is independent of other channels or of the format of the transmission data. Consequently, the performance of WDM is evaluated by a number of multiplexed channels, the bandwidth of light allocated for a single channel, interference between channels, and the insertion loss of WDM devices.

WDM was initially employed in extending the economical viability and transmission capacity of optical communication for interexchange carriers employing two to four different long or short waves. But as was illustrated with LambdaNet in Chapter 2, WDM now finds applications in optical subscriber loops, and multichannel WDM is employed for this purpose.

Figure 6.33(a) shows a video transmission architecture based on LambdaNet. As shown in the figure, LambdaNet multiplexes input video signals employing a star coupler and a *distributed feedback* (DFB) laser-diode source and sends the output signal to all the nodes so that the subscribers can view the desired TV channel. An electrical switch is located at each node, allowing channel selection according to the subscriber's request.

On the other hand, PPL was proposed for application in an actual optical subscriber network and has the structure shown in Figure 6.33(b). In PPL, two exclusive frequencies are allocated for each subscriber. At the *central office* (CO), wavelengths are sent to the remote terminal by way of wavelength multiplexing in order for the subscribers to share feeder cable by modulating downward signal by designated frequencies. At the remote terminal these frequencies are demultiplexed and transmitted to subscribers via distribution cable. Upward transmission is just the reverse of downward transmission.

In this PPL structure, the switching of electrical signals or an electrical power supply is not needed at the *remote node* (RN). Hence, an economical network that minimizes maintenance functions can be constructed. Furthermore, considering the wavelengths accommodated by the WDM device (i.e., the number of channels), the amount of distribution cables used can be cut down, since RNs including WDM can be installed close to subscribers. Also, since WDM, unlike the TDM, is independent of data structure, it can easily accommodate various service requirements. However, high-density WDM or the DFB laser diode with minute frequency adjustment capability is still expensive, and therefore it may take some time before it can be applied to actual subscribers.

Subcarrier Multiplexing

Recently, there have been attempts to employ microwave technology in optical communication. This is because the price of optical communication for simple video

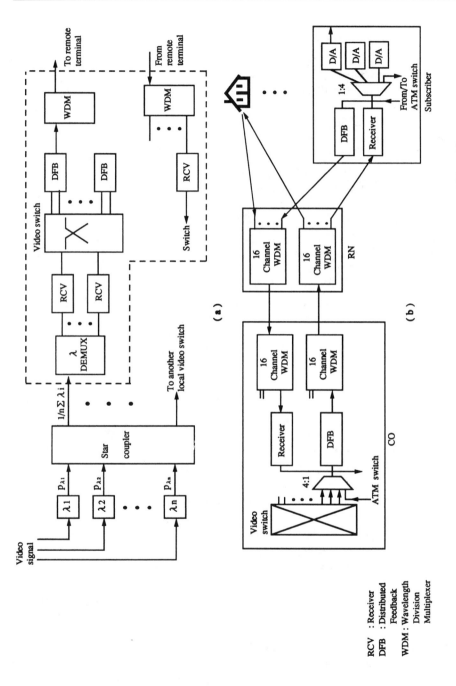

RCV : Receiver
DFB : Distributed
      Feedback
WDM : Wavelength
       Division
       Multiplexer

Figure 6.33 Video transmission architecture: (a) LambdaNet architecture for video transmission; (b) PPL architecture.

signal transmission is still far more expensive than that of existing coaxial cable transmission. That is, for the optical communication to be more economical than coaxial cable transmission, it must be able to provide not only telephone but also data and video signal simultaneously to subscribers. Therefore, as an effort to provide a low-cost broadband communication network, SCM, which employs existing stable and commercialized technology, has been attracting attention.

As shown in Figure 6.34, SCM modulates several channels of image signals into $f_1, f_2, \ldots f_n$ subcarrier *radio frequencies* (RF), which are frequency-multiplexed and sent through optical fiber after an amplitude modulation using a laser diode. The receiver performs O/E conversion and regenerates the desired signal employing a tuning circuit. The term *subcarrier* is derived from the fact that the RF is below a few GHz, while light frequency is about 200 THz.

In SCM, microwave band and baseband signals can be transmitted together, and analog and digital signals can also be transmitted simultaneously. Hence, its structure is simple and channel allocation can be easily done. It also has the advantage that the inexpensive FM video technology, which is employed as a subscriber receiver in satellite broadcasting, can be used. Therefore, 100-Mbps class baseband signals with these characteristics and 60 channels of FM video signal can be transmitted simultaneously.

6.5.4 Toward BISDN

As shown in Figure 6.35, CATV research in many countries is evolving from coaxial systems to optical systems. Services of subscriber network which have traditionally been unidirectional services used for TV channels are diversifying into bidirectional services and becoming broadband. Accordingly, network structure is also changing from the tree structure suitable for distribution services to the star structure suitable for telecommunication services. And the recent dramatic advances in optical communication technology, digital transmission technology, and semiconductor technology have enabled the introduction of the digital optical CATV system employing single-mode optical fiber. The economic problem is the only barrier to widespread applications.

Among the various video services of the BISDN, the one that is expected to spread widely in the 1990s is video service employing optical CATV network. In order to construct a BISDN based on the CATV network, bidirectional services should be provided in the CATV network, and 155-Mbps SDH transmission should be possible as well. In order to satisfy these requirements, the CATV network should be converted into an optical cable network first. Therefore, the key to early construction of the BISDN is the construction of the CATV optical subscriber network.

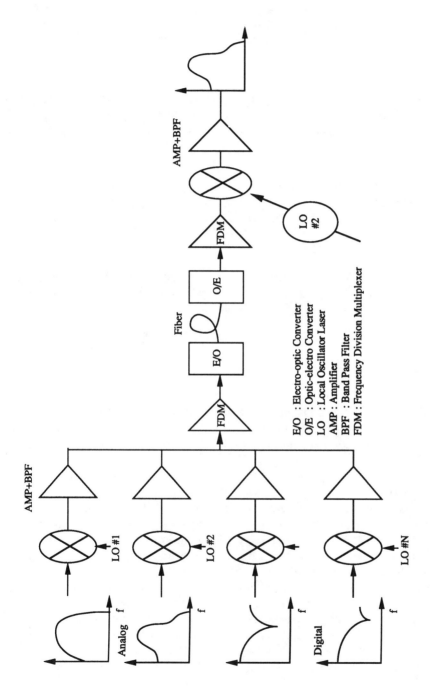

Figure 6.34 Description of SCM.

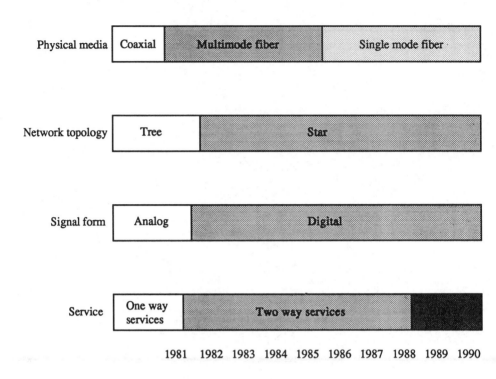

Figure 6.35 CATV evolution trend in research area.

In general, analog transmission of video signal is limited in its transmission distance by the signal-to-noise ratio. So in order to overcome any distance limitations, service integration should be considered by converting eventually to digital transmission.

If video signal is digitized, the transmission capacity of the existing TV video signal is about 100 Mbps and 6 to 20 Mbps when compressed employing video compression techniques. The transmission capacity of HDTV is anticipated to be around 1.2 Gbps if eight-bit PCM is applied, and 40 to 150 Mbps if compressed. If optical subscriber network technology is introduced to CATV network for transmission of such broadband signals, the accommodation of the future HDTV and BISDN will be easily achieved.

For the construction of an optical CATV network, the following two methods can be considered. First, the early-stage optical CATV network structure can be the double-star network, which takes into account economical distribution of TV signals. However, while the early-stage system can accommodate narrowband ISDN services, it is difficult to design it to provide the BISDN structure and services as well. Therefore, a way in which the existing CATV services can evolve into a BISDN network in the future should be considered. But such a scheme imposes heavy extra costs in requiring the alteration of CATV systems, and considering that CATV service is thoroughly different from telephone service, this scheme is expected to experience severe difficulties.

As an alternative, coherent optical transmission or WDM can be considered. Although in reality all information is provided through the same line in these methods, optical CATV network and the BISDN network become logically independent, so the two networks can coexist in this manner for a considerable period of time. In this scheme, specific wavelengths are assigned for upward and downward channels, respectively, for every subscriber who shares a given feeder network. For example, subscribers receive 622 Mbps, in which one 155-Mbps telecommunications channel and three 155-Mbps video channels can be accommodated. An optical CATV network employing such a WDM device has attractive qualities, as was mentioned in the previous section.

6.6 HIGH-DEFINITION TV

HDTV, which can be referred to as the next generation TV, was first conceived by NHK of Japan in 1968. Since then, Japan has been the leading runner in HDTV technology. Japan developed NHK-HDTV, or *Multiple Sub-Nyquist Sampling Encoding* (MUSE), in 1984, launched HDTV broadcasting satellite BS-2A in the same year, and performed experimental broadcasting of the opening and closing ceremonies of the Seoul Olympics in 1988. Also, in connection with the BS-3A launch in 1990 and the BS-3B launch in 1991, NHK has provided commercial services since 25 November 1990. Japan is continuing research to make smaller, lighter, and lower-priced HDTVs, and plans to have more than 800,000 HDTV receivers in circulation by 1999.

In Europe, the BBC proposed the *Compatible Multiplexed Analog Components* (C-MAC) in 1978, and England, France, and Germany each developed their own unique system until *High-Definition MAC* (HD-MAC) was adopted as the EC standard system. HD-MAC is currently being developed according to the EUREKA plan by 10 research teams (Philips, Thompson, BBC, etc.), and the Barcelona Olympic games were broadcast to 120 receiver stations via HD-MAC HDTV in August 1992.

The U.S., with Japan and Canada, initially agreed upon setting studio standards based on the NHK-HDTV system. But later, the U.S. began to develop HDTV under the concept of *advanced TV* (ATV), which is a more advanced version of the existing NTSC TV system. The U.S. is now developing a fully digital HDTV, which is different from the HD-MAC and MUSE adopting analog techniques. The fully digital system of the U.S. is more advanced in terms of signal processing and transmission. It is being developed not only under the concept of HDTV, but also from the viewpoint of furnishing integrated terminals for the various types of information services of a future society. In other words, it is being developed so that simultaneous transmission/reception not only of video and voice but also of various types of data and graphics is possible, and so that expansion of these functions can be done easily.

Meanwhile, the fully digital system of the U.S. has stimulated research in other countries, and digital coding and transmission systems, to supplement the existing analog systems, are actively being studied.

International specifications for the HDTV studio format, which is closely related to the transmission format, have been standardized by CCIR SG XI, but unilateral agreement has not been reached on several core parameters of the studio format, such as line frequency and field frequency.

In this section, we will review CCIR recommendations relating to HDTV, consider transmission techniques for HDTV, and introduce examples of HDTV systems, such as the fully digital system, MUSE, and HD-MAC. The section will close with some considerations on the prospects of HDTV.

6.6.1 CCIR Recommendations

Study for drafting recommendations on international specifications relating to HDTV is being carried out at CCIR.

Studio specifications must precede the establishment of international specifications on HDTV, and transmission specifications must be defined in accordance with them. The specification processes that are currently in progress at CCIR are for unifying international specifications on program development, and its activities up to now are as listed in Table 6.9. The contents of recommended HDTV basic parameters, subjective evaluation of image quality, and international exchange of programming are quoted from CCIR SG-XI recommendations of Rec.709, Rec.710, and Rec.714, respectively.

Basic Parameter Values for the HDTV Standard for the Studio (Rec.709)

Optoelectronic Conversion. Optoelectronic transfer characteristics before nonlinear precorrection are assumed to be linear; in the overall optoelectronic transfer characteristics at the source, the corresponding electrical signal is a function of the luminance of the image; chromaticity coordinates are chosen at R(0.640, 0.330), G(0.300, 0.600), and B(0.150, 0.060). The finalized values are expected at the interim meeting of the 1990–1994 study period.

Picture Characteristics. The aspect ratio is set to 16:9, sample per active line to 1920, the sampling lattice to be orthogonal; and the sample distribution and the number of active lines are interrelated and are still under study.

Picture Scanning Characteristics. The order of sample scanning is from left to right and from top to bottom; the interlattice ratio is currently 2:1, with the objective

Table 6.9
Standard Activities of CCIR for HDTV

Year	Activities
1972	Planning of HDTV study (NHK in Japan proposes informational studio specification)
1980	Drawing up the report about the present condition of HDTV
1986	Japan, U.S., and Canada propose the basic international standard (1125/60/2:1) but Europe opposes it.
1987	Europe (EC) proposes the HD-MAC system of EUREKA 95 project as the international standard
1989	Special meeting completes the frames of "basic parameters of HDTV for international exchange of HDTV program" and "conversion of HDTV program to film material"
1990	Proposes the concept of CIF and common data rate (CDR)
	24 items among 27 standardization items come to agreement
1991	Organize TG 11/3 for digital terrestrial broadcasting under leadership of U.S.
1992	About the studio format, correct and propose 709 related with 1125/60 2:1 system and 1250/50/2:1 system

of 1:1 (progressive scanning); and picture rate depends on a number of well-known factors.

Signal Format. Conceptual nonlinear precorrection of primary signals (gamma) is equal to 0.45; derivation of luminance signal (Y) is expressed as 0.2125R + 0.7154G + 0.0721B; derivation of color-difference signals (analog coding, B-Y/R-Y) is 0.6389 (B-Y) for PB and 0.6349 (R-Y) for PR; and derivation of color-difference signal (digital coding) are digitally scaled from the above values.

Analog Representation. Levels are specified in millivolts measured across a matched 75-ohm termination; nominal level (R, G, B, Y) is specified as Reference Black 0 and Reference White 350 mV; format of synchronizing signals is trilevel bipolar; timing reference is the center of the horizontal synchronization timing reference; and the synchronization level is 350 mV.

Digital Representation. Coded signals are R, G, B, or Y, C_1, C_2; sampling lattice (R, G, B, Y) is orthogonal; sampling lattice (C_1, C_2) consist of samples cosited with each other and with alternative luminance samples; sampling frequency (R, G, B, Y) is an integer multiple of 2.25 MHz; sampling frequency (C_1, C_2) is one-half of the luminance sampling frequency; the bit rate of the TV signal is 0.8 to 1.2 Gbps for current implementation, 2.0 to 3.0 Gbps for some future implementations.

Subjective Assessment Method for Image Quality (Rec.710)

The subjective assessment of image quality of high-definition television systems should be made with the following viewing conditions: ratio of viewing distance to picture height is 3; peak luminance on the screen is 150–250 cd/m^2; arrangement of observers is within 30 degrees horizontally from the center of the display (vertical limit is under study); display size is 1.4m (55 in).

International Exchange of Programs Electronically Produced by Means of High-Definition TV (Rec.714)

When programs produced in high-definition TV are exchanged between broadcasters, in order to preserve the best quality, they should be exchanged in video form, for example, live or video tape.

6.6.2 Transmission of HDTV

Transmission methods of HDTV can be classified according to analog bandwidth, digital bit rate, transmission medium, transmission system, and application. In terms of analog bandwidth, HDTV luminance together with chrominance has about 50 to 70 MHz of bandwidth. In contrast, the available existing channel, excluding optical cable, is about 6 to 12 MHz, and hence bandwidth reduction is inevitable. In terms of digital transmission rate, the HDTV signal has about a 1.2-Gbps data rate, while 15 to 25 Mbps can be utilized if terrestrial or satellite channels are employed, and 45 Mbps to several hundred Mbps if optical cable is employed. In terms of transmission medium, with terrestrial or satellite channels, bit error rate can be high due to instabilities in the atmosphere, while in transmission through an ATM network employing optical cable, cell loss and bit error have to be considered as well. In terms of transmission system, things to consider are complexity and system prices due to allocation of channels with wide bandwidths. Finally, from the standpoint of application, appropriate bandwidth allocation for transmission channels is required in distribution to general subscribers, program exchange between studios, and transmission of high-quality videos to small theaters. Table 6.10 summarizes the available bandwidth of each transmission medium. We now discuss briefly the transmission systems that are appropriate to the characteristics of each medium.

The representatives of analog transmission systems are MUSE of Japan and the HD-MAC system of Europe. Both were established for satellite broadcasting, and available bandwidth is 8 or 10 MHz, which implies that about 10:1 bandwidth reduction is necessary. In order to achieve this, we can take advantage of the fact that human eyes have low resolution for moving areas. Consequently, we can employ the scheme that subsamples in time axis for fixed parts of interframe coding, and subsamples in spatial direction for moving parts of intraframe coding (see Section 6.3). The final compressed signal expands about threefold in bandwidth when FM is modulated and the signal is transmitted to general subscribers through *direct broadcast by satellite* (DBS). Since bandwidth decreases to 6 MHz in the case of terrestrial

Table 6.10
Bandwidth of Transmission Media

Parameter	Terrestrial TV VHF/UHF	Satellite	Analog		Digital Optical Fiber
			Coaxial Cable	Optical Fiber	
Total bandwidth	VHF 34 + 42 MHz UHF 420 MHz	C and Ku band 500 MHz	Less than 1000 MHz	350 ~ 2200 MHz	560 ~ 2400 Mbps (single mode)
Bandwidth per channel	6 MHz (M, N) 7 MHz (B) 8 MHz (D, I, K, L)	Narrow RF 24, 27, 36 MHz Wide RF 54, 72 MHz	6 ~ 12 MHz	6 ~ 55 MHz	$n \times 155$ Mbps (SDH)

broadcasting, the number of lines or resolution to transmit should be reduced. Narrow-MUSE and MUSE-9 of NHK are typical examples. Since coaxial cable and optical fiber can allocate bandwidths rather liberally, the two media can transmit without significant picture degradations. But analog systems need converting to digital systems, since they are not compatible with the upcoming BISDN (or multimedia) and since picture quality degrades in case of retransmission.

The digital transmission system in conjunction with the development of digital source coding and the BISDN network is under active research. In the case of terrestrial broadcasting, the HDTV system of the U.S. transmits digitally coded data employing digital modulation in the existing 6-MHz band. For modulation, 2/4-VSB or 16/32-QAM are mainly used, and 20- to 25-Mbps digital data transmission is possible. But for reliable communication under bad conditions, 5- to 7-Mbps error correction code is required, and therefore the net video transmission rate is about 15 to 20 Mbps. In order to transmit a 1-Gbps HDTV signal using a 15- to 20-Mbps bit rate, 50:1 to 100:1 data compression is required through source coding. Therefore, the use of interframe DPCM, which employs motion-compensated prediction and transform coding, is inevitable. For error correction coding, RS coding, which is effective for burst error correction, is employed along with block interleaving. Also, in order to reduce interference with the existing TV signal in the final transmission stage, appropriate shaping of output spectrum is required. In the case of digital satellite transmission, 20- to 40-Mbps digital bandwidth allocation is possible if *quadrature phase shift keying* (QPSK) or 8-PSK modulation is employed.

If coaxial cable or optical cable is employed as the network transmission medium, a rather flexible transmission rate can be secured. Especially when the BISDN network is constructed based on the ATM, almost constant picture quality can be

Table 6.11
Table of Attributes, Characteristics, and Processes of Digital HDTV Terrestrial Broadcasting Systems

	Digicipher	DSC-HDTV	ADTV	ATVA-P
Lines per frame	1050	787/788	1050	787/788
Frames per second	29.97	59.94	29.97	59.94
Interlace	2:1	1:1	2:1	1:1
Horizontal scan rate	31.469 kHz	47.203 kHz	31.469 kHz	47.203 kHz
Aspect ratio	16:9	16:9	16:9	16:9
Active video pixels	1408H × 960V (luma) 350H × 480V (chroma)	1280H × 720V (luma) 640H × 360V (chroma)	1440H × 960V (luma) 720H × 480V (chroma)	1280H × 720V
Pixel aspect ratio	33:40	1:1	27:32	1:1
Bandwidth	21.5 MHz (luma) 5.4 MHz (chroma)	34 MHz (luma) 17 MHz (chroma)	27 MHz (Nyquist limit)	34 MHz (luma) 34 MHz (chroma)
Colorimetry	SMPTE 240M	SMPTE 240M	SMPTE 240M	SMPTE 240M
Video compression algorithm	Motion-compensated DCT coding	Motion-compensated transform coding (DCT & VQ)	Motion-compensated DCT coding (MPEG-based)	Motion-compensated transform/subband coding
Block size	8 × 8	8 × 8	8 × 8	8 × 8
Sampling frequency	53.65 MHz	75.3 MHz	54 MHz	75.3 MHz
Audio bandwidth	20 kHz	20 kHz	20 kHz	20 kHz

Audio sampling frequency	48 kHz	47.203 kHz	48 kHz	48 kHz
Dynamic range	85 dB	96 dB	96 dB	
Number of audio channels	4	4	4	4
Video data rate	12.59 Mbps (16QAM) 17.49 Mbps (32QAM)	Automatically varies from 8.6 to 17.1 Mbps	14.98 Mbps (can be shared with additional audio and/or data)	15.636 Mbits
Audio data rate	0.503 Mbps	0.5 Mbps	0.512 Mbps (nominal)	0.5 Mbps
Control data	126 kbps	40 kbps	40 kbps	126 kbps
Sync	N/A	292 to 544 kbps	N/A	N/A
Total data	19.51 Mbps (16QAM) 24.39 Mbps (32QAM)	11.1 to 21.0 Mbps	21.00 Mbps	19.43 Mbps
Error Correction overhead	6.17 Mbps	1.3 to 2.4 Mbps	23.6% (4.96 Mbps)	3.042 Mbps
3 dB modulation (terrestrial)	4.88 MHz	5.38 MHz	5.2 MHz	4.86 MHz
C/N threshold (terrestrial)	12.5 dB (16 QAM) 16.5 dB (32 QAM)	16 dB (4-level data) 10 dB (2-level data)	16 dB	19 dB
Channel equalization (ghost canceling)	−2 to +24 µs (multiple ghosts)	−2 to +24 µs (multiple ghosts)	16 µs (may be extended to 40 µs)	2 µs (complex multipath) 32 µs (single long multipath)
RF modulation (satellite)	QPSK	MSK	QPSK	
Bandwidth (satellite)	24 MHz/2 channels	20 MHz/channel	24 MHz/2 channels	
C/N threshold (satellite)	7.5 dB	8 dB	8 dB	

achieved through VBR transmission. In the early-stage BISDN, CBR services with around 45 Mbps considering the existing DS-3C transmission line were expected, but eventually VBR services with a 155-Mbps maximum rate of STM-1 will be mainly used. In addition, a 140- to 600-Mbps bit rate is expected for the transmission of studio-quality images, and for distribution to video theaters. At the source coder, interframe DPCM will be mainly used for 45-Mbps class signals and for those above 100-Mbps intraframe DCT/subband coding, or PCM can be used.

6.6.3 HDTV Coding Systems

Most HDTV systems have digital encoders, although some systems adopt an analog format for transmission purposes only. Fully digital American systems use digital source encoding and digital modulation (e.g., 16/32-QAM and 2/4-VSB). For transmission of the HDTV signal through the BISDN, digital encoding and direct transmission systems have been proposed with bit rates around 40 Mbps for home distribution, around 130 Mbps for high-quality distribution, and around 600 Mbps for studio quality transmission. In this section, we briefly examine the fully digital system of the U.S., the Japanese MUSE, and the European HD-MAC.

Fully Digital System

The four systems for terrestrial broadcasting in the U.S. have been submitted to the FCC as proposals for the U.S. HDTV standard. They are Digicipher HDTV of General Instrument, Digital Spectrum-Compatible HDTV (DSC-HDTV) of Zenith and AT&T, Advanced Digital Television (ADTV) of Advanced Television Research Consortium, and the ATVA progressive system of M.I.T. They all adopt fully digital techniques and use motion-compensated transform coding. All four systems allow easy conversion from/to existing NTSC TV, although technical details and parameters are slightly different in each case. The performance and features of a system are dependent on system design philosophy. For example, some proposed systems emphasize picture resolution, while others emphasize robust transmission. Under the constraint of fixed total data rate, data allocation is a trade-off issue. Table 6.11 (on the previous page) lists the attributes, characteristics, and principles of the systems.

For illustration purposes, the Digicipher system will be discussed briefly. Digicipher transmits a digitally encoded HDTV signal via terrestrial antenna with a 6-MHz bandwidth. For the modulation of the digital signal, 16- or 32-QAM is used. Figure 6.36 shows the encoder, the decoder, and the total system configuration of Digicipher.

Input video has the format of 1050 lines in luminance, 525 lines in chrominance, and 16:9 aspect ratio. The signal bandwidths are 21.5 MHz for luminance

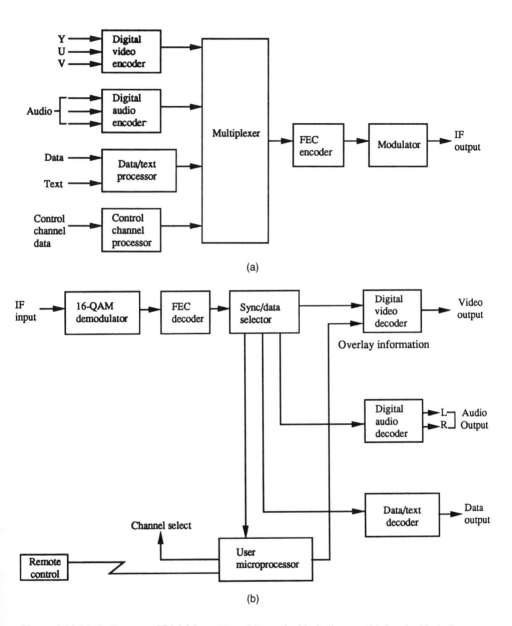

Figure 6.36 Block diagrams of Digicipher system: (a) encoder block diagram; (b) decoder block diagram.

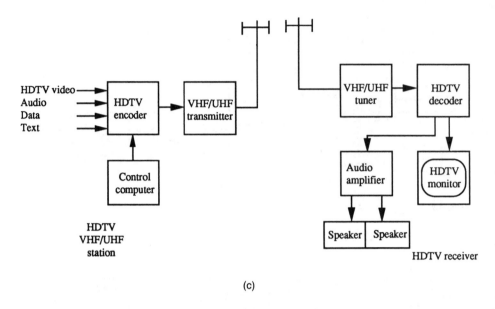

(c)

Figure 6.36 continued (c) overall system block diagram.

and 5.4 MHz for chrominance. After sampling with 53.65 MHz, the digital image has 960 lines per frame and 1408 pixels per line.

The interframe DPCM coder with BMA motion compensation and DCT is used for the compression of source image data. BMA is applied to every 32 × 16 block, called the *super block*. The prediction error after BMA is coded with 8 × 8 DCT. DCT coefficients are scaled with the quantization matrix and quantized with a given quantizer index, and then zigzag scanning and two-dimensional VLC of (zero run, quantized level) are applied (see Figure 6.20). The frame or field adaptive scheme is used for achieving high efficiency in the parts with large motion.

In interframe DPCM, the decoder must receive PCM-coded data corresponding to a single frame after channel selection. Digicipher periodically transmits PCM-coded data of each block. Its period is 11 frames per block, which is 0.37 second.

The source coder output has a variable rate because of VLC and the variation of input image statistics. The source coder buffer receives this variable-rate data and generates constant-rate data. For the prevention of buffer overflow or underflow, the coarseness of the DCT coefficient quantizer is controlled.

Bit rates for the video signal are 17.47 Mbps for 32-QAM and 12.59 Mbps for 16-QAM. Four-channel digital audio signals are compressed using the Dolby AC-II audio data compression algorithm. The total bit rate of four-channel audio is 503 kbps. The final bit rate of the source encoder with auxiliary data is 18.22 Mbps for 32-QAM and 13.34 Mbps for 16-QAM.

For reliable transmission, *forward error correction* (FEC) codes with 6.17 Mbps are added. The final transmission data rate is 24.39 Mbps for 32-QAM and 19.51 Mbps for 16-QAM.

MUSE System

The MUSE system is a bandwidth-reduced version of the NHK Hi-vision system for the DBS service. The wide bandwidth of the 1125-line NHK system cannot be handled by satellite transponders unless the signal bandwidth is compressed. The MUSE system reduces the total video bandwidth down to 8.15 MHz, suitable for DBS service. Figure 6.37 illustrates the MUSE encoder and decoder system.

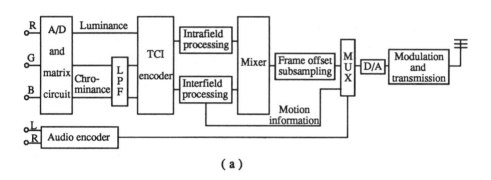

(a)

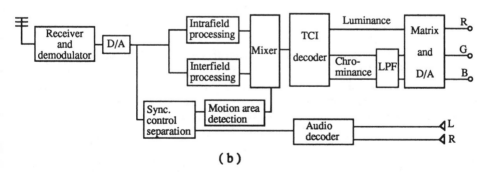

(b)

TCI : Time Compressed Integration

Figure 6.37 Block diagram of MUSE encoder and decoder: (a) encoding at the transmitter; (b) decoding at the receiver.

The 1125-line signal is initially sampled at 48.6 Mbps. After further processing, bandwidth reduction is applied to stationary parts and moving parts, respectively. The stationary parts are subsampled at one-third of the initial sampling rate after interfield filtering. Moving parts are controlled by two motion detectors (i.e., the boundary of moving area and direction of motion). After intrafield filtering controlled by the motion detectors, sub-Nyquist sampling at 16.2 MHz is applied. The resulting pulse train is converted to analog form with a base bandwidth of 8.1 MHz.

The subsampling at one-third of the initial sampling rate results in the successive transmission of signals representing every third pixel. Three adjacent pixels appear on three successive scans of the same line. Since the stationary pixels do not move during this three-field interval, they appear in the original positions. Thus, the stationary parts of the image have the full resolution of 1125-line systems.

The elements of the moving parts of the image do not appear in their original positions, so the resolution of the moving parts is reduced by about 50%. Since the human visual system has a lower sensitivity to the details of moving parts, the overall image quality is subjectively tolerable. However, camera panning reduces the whole resolution to 50% of the original 1125-line system.

NHK proposed a 6-MHz narrow-MUSE system to the FCC for terrestrial broadcasting. Narrow-MUSE manifests the intermediate quality of MUSE and existing TV, but it is not compatible with existing TV. The bandwidth compression scheme of narrow-MUSE is identical to that of the MUSE system. The only difference is the 1125 lines in MUSE versus the 750 lines in narrow-MUSE. The total bandwidth of narrow-MUSE with the stereo digital audio signal is reduced down to 6 MHz, which is the same as in the existing terrestrial broadcasting system. The vertical resolution is 750 lines/frame in still parts and 325 lines/frame in moving parts. Figure 6.38 shows adaptors of the encoder and decoder for the narrow-MUSE system.

HD-MAC System

HD-MAC has been developed on the basis of PAL, which is the TV system of Europe, and its video signal is 1250 lines, 50 field, and a 2:1 interlaced scanned signal. The input signal is band-compressed, and this compressed video signal together with the digital control signal is transmitted to the receiving side. Figure 6.39 shows the encoder and decoder of the HD-MAC system.

The digital control signal is composed of the decoding mode signal and various control signals, and it is transmitted by being inserted into vertical blanking intervals. The video signal is composed of band-compressed luminance and color signals, and it is regenerated at the receiver using the digital control signal.

In the HD-MAC system, the video signal is processed by being divided into areas of the stationary mode, slowly moving mode, and moving mode. The inter-

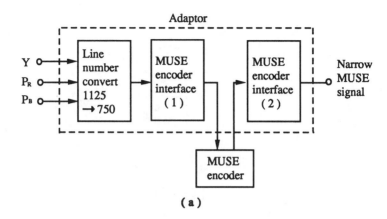

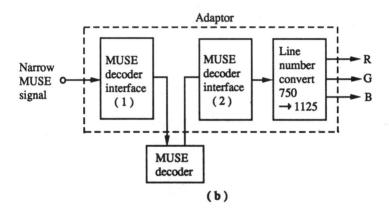

Figure 6.38 Encoder and decoder elements of narrow-MUSE: (a) narrow-MUSE encoder; (b) narrow-MUSE decoder.

frame motion of the stationary mode is in the range of 0 to 0.5 sample/40 ms, and the image is transmitted every 80 ms (field frequency of 12.5 Hz). The slowly moving area has interframe motion of above 0.5 to 12 samples/40 ms, and the image is transmitted every 40 ms. In the slowly moving mode, motion displacement is estimated in order to reduce redundancies.

The HD-MAC system has compatibility with existing TV that can be viewed through the MAC decoder, which is the European TV transmission standard employing existing DBS.

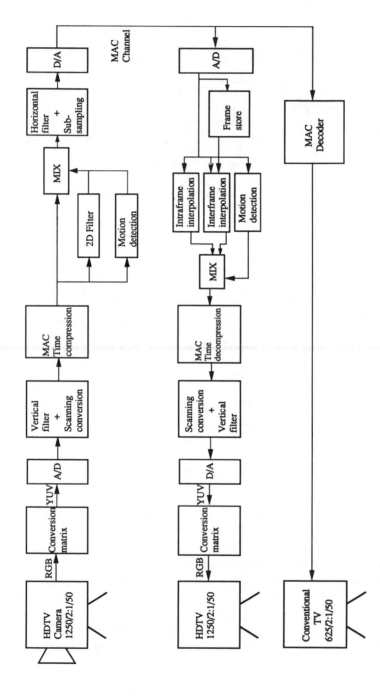

Figure 6.39 Block diagram of HD-MAC codec.

6.6.4 HDTV System for BISDN

With the visualization of broadband communication network, there is an increasing interest in the transmission of HDTV-class video. The digital coding, transmission, and switching of video will offer considerable advantages over conventional analog distribution in terms of image quality, control, and the variety of services that can be offered to the customer. In the network, digitally encoded TV signals are robust, since they are not susceptible to the gradual increase of distortion and noise that typically accumulates during the various stages of transmission, multiplexing, and switching of conventional, analog-encoded signals. Also, digital video signals are much easier to integrate with other digital services in terms of switching, multiplexing, and service provisioning, and they can be readily encrypted to provide security or access control. Digital coder/decoder can be designed to take advantage of VLSI circuits to realize the complex digital signal processing required to remove redundancies from the signal and thus reduce the bit rate. The coding and digital transmission of HDTV has also received considerable attention recently for the over-the-air broadcasting of HDTV in the U.S.

When the BISDN is employed for transmission, while VBR transmission is possible, cell loss could occur in some cases when traffic is concentrated. Especially when employing digital band compression, the error propagation is a big problem, and therefore a coding system that can cope with cell loss is required. Examples of such a system are a system that regenerates the cell by employing FEC code, a system employing layered coding, and an error concealment technique. In most cases, they are used in combination. Figure 6.40 shows an example of a VBR DPCM coder which employs these schemes.

Source coding varies depending on the transmission rate and transmission characteristics. In early-stage BISDN, CBR coding at about the 40- to 130-Mbps class appears to be mainly used, but eventually VBR coding of the STM-1 class will be used. The compression ratio of 155 Mbps is about 5:1 to 10:1, and the employed coding method is intraframe DCT or subband coding. In these systems, rather high picture quality can be maintained; influences due to cell loss are trivial, since they have intraframe coding structures, and their hardware is simple. But because of an expensive channel utilization payment due to a rather high rate, they will be mainly used for distribution services with high picture quality. The compression ratio of the 40-Mbps class coding scheme is about 20:1 to 30:1, and interframe DPCM which employs a mixture of BMA and DCT or subband coding is used. Since, in view of general users, no severe picture degradation occurs, and it has a rather low transmission rate, it is adequate for conversational transmission between users. On the other hand, its systems become complex and it has a severe error propagation drawback in that picture quality varies a lot according to the statistical characteristics of input video.

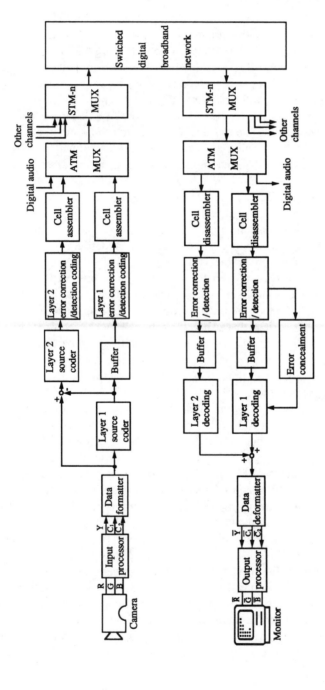

Figure 6.40 Example block diagram of VBR interframe DPCM coder with layer structure for the transmission of HDTV image sequence through BISDN.

The layered coding system which transmits with VBR has the advantage of being able to overcome these shortcomings and can provide constant picture quality. Layer 1 codes visually essential parts of video, such as low-frequency components of video, and transmits through a CBR (or VBR) channel with high reliability. Therefore, even though cell loss occurs in the data generated by layer 2, no significant visual degradation is effected. The layer 1 coder needs a buffer to create the CBR and can employ FEC coding to protect data. Layer 2 is directly connected to ATM MUX after being converted into cells without a buffer. In this process, layer 2 cells can be lost.

The cell assembler reads words from the buffer and maps them into a 48-octet ATM cell payload. FEC information can be located in the AAL overhead or the user layer. Synchronization and timing information are also inserted. The cell assembler informs the ATM circuit if the current cell contains high or low priority video data. The ATM circuit performs a reverse of these operations. The information type can be used to identify the different media information of the different components of a video or audio signal in a multimedia environment. Carrying information type at the AAL within a single virtual channel has the advantage that different media information or signal components will be received in the same order as they are transmitted. An alternative is to provide the same function at the ATM layer, where different information types corresponding to a multimedia call can be identified by using multiple virtual channel connections. This approach has more flexibility than the first, since the ATM network can readily access the information type. The disadvantage is that cell sequence integrity among multiple virtual channels is not guaranteed.

While ATM cells travel through the network, cell loss, misdelivery, bit error, and other things can happen. These are corrected during the error correction decoding stage, and uncorrected errors pass the detection step and then the error concealment step. Error concealment is the method that regenerates the lost video data without significant visual degradation by stuffing data of previous or surrounding images of the errored parts.

Nowadays, the research on employing the VBR coding scheme in a BISDN is actively being carried out, and it will be put into practical use when the BISDN is eventually constructed.

6.6.5 Development Trends of HDTV

The following development trends of HDTV can be considered: the field of over-the-air broadcasting, wired transmission employing the BISDN, the field of a multimedia terminal in conjunction with a computer, and their international standardization trends.

In the broadcasting field, Japan has started model broadcasting of the MUSE system employing the DBS system, and Europe will soon commence model broadcasting of the HD-MAC system. Both of these systems adopt analog transmission, but a digital system will be more cogent for future HDTV transmission. Major reasons are that a digital system whose performance is equal to analog systems can be constructed due to continuing development of digital data compression and transmission technologies and that development of the VLSI technology will lower the cost of these systems. Also, in terms of compatibility with future BISDN, optical CATV, and multimedia terminal, the future of digital systems is favorable. The present HDTV terrestrial broadcasting plan of the U.S. is testing a fully digital system employing the existing 6-MHz single VHF or UHF channel.

On the other hand, fully commercial broadcasting of HDTV will not be possible immediately after model broadcasting because home receivers are still expensive and the existing broadcasting systems and receivers cannot be upgraded in a short period of time. In most cases, HDTV systems in development have no compatibility with the existing TV, and for the next 10 to 20 years they will coexist with the existing TV under simulcasting.

The field of HDTV-wired transmission can be categorized into the CATV field and the transmission field employing the BISDN. CATV field is more favorable than digital transmission employing optical cable, and since bandwidth allocation is rather flexible, high-picture-quality HDTV service at 40 to 60 Mbps, which is higher than with terrestrial and satellite (broadcasting), can be provided. The network constructed for CATV could possibly evolve into a BISDN network in which mutual communication capability is possible. Characteristics of the BISDN network based on ATM are that it is capable of VBR transmission and that cell loss due to statistical multiplexing can occur. VBR transmission coding systems based on ATM that take these characteristics into account are undergoing active research, and they will be employed in the near future. On the other hand, in the broadcasting field, the encoder resides at the broadcasting station and the decoder at the receiver side, and therefore the complexity of the encoder does not matter much; but in conversational systems of the BISDN, both encoder and decoder have to exist inside the receiving terminal; therefore, reducing the complexity of encoder remains an important problem.

When the BISDN is constructed and when mutual conversational services of HDTV-class video can be provided, HDTV terminal will evolve from the simple TV of the present to a multimedia terminal combined with computers. The multimedia terminal can input/output, store, and communicate real-time video from video phone-class to HDTV-class voice, data, and graphics. In these cases, the terminal gets cheaper as the coding module of HDTV system has more in common with coding systems employed in the existing video telephone and digital VTR.

In relation to international standardization on HDTV, the standardization of the broadcasting field is being carried out by CCIR SG 11, and the standardization of long-distance transmission by the *Commission Mixte pour des Transmissions Tel-*

evisuelles et Sonones (CMTT). MPEG standardizes, in three stages, the motion picture coding method for digital storage media, and in MPEG III, the HDTV class will also be treated. On the other hand, in CCITT SG XV, the ATM video coding expert group is carrying out the standardization of transmission in the BISDN. Presently, it appears difficult to achieve a single standard for most of the important HDTV studio specifications, and each nation is attempting to put forth its own set of standards considering compatibility with its existing TV.

So far, the prospects of HDTV, which will become the most important video media, has been discussed. In the future, HDTV along with the BISDN will have a great influence on the whole telecommunications industry through its tremendous market and technological potential. When it is serviced in combination with the BISDN, HDTV will be established as an important part of human life and may become the hero of the future communication utopia.

SELECT BIBLIOGRAPHY

ARTC, "System Description of Advanced Digital Television," Feb. 1991.

Brotman, S. N., *Telephone Company and Cable Television Competition*, Artech House, 1990.

CCIR Rec. 601, "Encoding Parameters of Digital Television for Studios," 1982.

CCIR Rec. 656, "Interfaces for Digital Component Video Signals in 525-Line and 625-Line Television Systems," 1982.

CCIR Rec. 709, "Basic Parameter Values for the HDTV Standard for the Studio and for International Programme Exchange," 1990.

CCIR Rec. 710, "Subjective Assessment Methods for Image Quality in High-Definition Television," 1990.

CCIR Rec. 714, "International Exchange of Programme Electronically Produced by Means of High-Definition Television," 1990.

CCITT Rec. 242, "System for Establishing Communication Between Audiovisual Terminals Using Digital Channels up to 2 Mbps," 1990.

CCITT Rec. H.221, "Frame Structure for 64 to 1920 kbps Channel in Audiovisual Teleservices," 1990.

CCITT Rec. H.230, "Frame Synchronous Control and Indication Signals for Audiovisual Systems," 1990.

CCITT Rec. H.32x, "Audiovisual Communication Terminal for BISDN," 1992.

CCITT Rec. H.261, "Video Codec for Audiovisual Services at $p \times 64$ kbps," 1990.

CCITT Rec. H.320, "Narrowband Visual Telephone Systems and Terminal Equipment," 1990.

Datapro Reports on Telecom., "Video Conferencing Systems," Nov. 1990.

First International Workshop on Packet Video, Workshop Notes, New York, May 1987.

Fleisher, P. E., et al., "Digital Transport of HDTV on Optical Fiber," *IEEE Commun. Mag.*, Vol. 29, No. 8, Aug. 1991, pp. 36–41.

Fourth International Workshop on Packet Video, Workshop Notes, Aug. 1991, Kyoto, Japan.

Fox, J. R., "Cable Television Network Options in the U.K. for the 1990's," *IEEE J. of Lightwave Commun. Syst.*, Feb. 1990.

Haghiri, M. R., and F. W. P. Vreeswijk, "HDMAC Coding for MAC Compatible Broadcasting of HDTV Signals," *IEEE Trans. on Broad.*, Vol. 36, No. 4, Dec. 1990.

ISO-IEC/JTC1/CD 10918(JPEG), "Digital Compression and Coding of Continuous-Tone Still Images," 1991.

ISO-IEC/JTC1/CD 11172 (MPEG I), "Coding of Moving Pictures and Associated Audio for Digital Storage Media at up to About 1.5 Mbps," 1990.

ISO-IEC/JTC1/SC2/WG9N 36/CD 11154, "Progressive Bilevel Image Compression," Revision 4.1, 1992.

ISO-IEC/JTC1/SC29/WG11(MPEG II) "Coded Presentation of Picture and Audio Information," 1992.

ISO-IEC/JTC1/SC2/WG12(MHEG) Working Document S, Version 4, "Information Processing, Coded Representation of Multimedia and Hypermedia Information Objects."

ISO-IEC/JTC1/SC2/WG8, "Coded Representation of Picture and Audio Information," JPEG Draft, Jan. 1990.

Kang, M., and I. Lee, "Optical CATV Technology Development Direction," *J. of Korea Inst. of Telematics and Electronics*, Vol. 16, No. 16, Dec. 1989.

Karlsson, G., and M. Vetterli, "Subband Coding of Video for Packet Networks," *SPIE, Optical Eng.*, Vol. 27, July 1988.

Kishimoto, R., and I. Yamashita, "HDTV Communication Systems in Broadband Communication Networks," *IEEE Commun. Mag.*, Vol. 29, No. 8, Aug. 1991, pp. 28–35.

Lacert, C., et al., "The First Fully Digital Broadband Switched FTTH Pilot Trial," *Proc. of Broadband '90*.

Large, D., "Tapped Fiber vs. Fiber Reinforced Coaxial CATV Systems," *IEEE J. of Lightwave Tech.*, Feb. 1990.

Lee, S. H., and L. T. Wu, "Variable Rate Video Transport in Broadband Networks," *SPIE, Visual Comm. and Image Process*, Vol. 1001, 1988.

Legall, D. J., "MPEG: A Video Compression Standard for Multimedia Applications," *Com. of the ACM*, Vol. 34, No. 4, April 1991.

Leger, F. "The Prospect Optical Cable to the Home," *Cable Com. Mag.*, Jan. 1989.

Maglaris, B., D. Anastassiou, P. Sen, G. Karlsson, and J. D. Robbins, "Performance Models of Statistical Multiplexing in Packet Video Communications," *IEEE Trans. on Commun.*, Vol. 36, July 1988.

Netravali, A., and B. Haskell, *Digital Pictures—Representation and Compression*, New York: Plenum Press, 1988.

Ninomiya, Y., et al., "An HDTV Broadcasting System Using a Bandwidth Compression Technique-MUSE," *IEEE Trans. on Broad.*, Vol. 33, No. 4, Dec. 1987.

Paik, W., "Digicipher-All digital, Channel Compatible, HDTV Broadcast System," *IEEE Trans. on Broad.*, Vol. 36, No. 4, Dec. 1990.

Pangrac, D. M., "Application of optical Fiber Transmission Technology to Existing CATV Networks," *Cable Television Eng.*, Vol. 14, No. 6, June/Sept. 1989.

Second International Workshop on Packet Video, Workshop Notes, Sept. 1988, Torino, Italy.

Spears, D. R., "Broadband ISDN Switching Capabilities From a Services Perspective," *IEEE J. of Select. Areas in Commun.*, Vol. SAC-5, No. 8, Oct. 1987.

Third International Workshop of Packet Video, Workshop Notes, March 1990, Torino, Italy.

Verbiest, W., and L. Pinnoo, "A Variable Bit Rate Video Codec for Asynchronous Transfer Mode Networks," *IEEE J. of Select. Areas in Commun.*, Vol. 7, June 1989.

Yates, R. K., N. Mahe, and J. Masson, *Fiber Optics and CATV Business Strategy*, Artech House, 1990.

Zenith, AT&T, "Technical Description of Digital Spectrum Compatible HDTV," Feb. 1991.

Appendix A
Related Standards

Optical Communication

1. Bellcore TR-TSY-000303, "Integrated Digital Loop Carrier System Generic Requirements, Objectives, and Interface," 1990.
2. Bellcore TA-NWT-001209, "Generic Requirements for Fiber Optic Branching Components," 1991.
3. Bellcore TR-NWT-000909, "Generic Requirements and Objectives for Fiber-in-the-Loop Systems," 1991.
4. CCITT Rec.G.650, "Definition and Text Methods for the Relevant Parameters of Single Mode Fibers," (New, to be approved in 1993).
5. CCITT Rec. G.651, "Characteristics of a $50/125$-μm Multimode Graded Index Optical Fiber Cable," 1992 (Rev).
6. CCITT Rec. G.652, "Characteristics of a Single-Mode Optical Fiber Cable," 1992 (Rev).
7. CCITT Rec. G.653, "Characteristics of a Dispersion-Shifted Single-Mode Optical Fiber Cable," 1992 (Rev).
8. CCITT Rec. G.654, "Characteristics of a 1550-nm Wavelength Loss-Minimized Single-Mode Optical Fiber Cable," 1992 (Rev).

Synchronous Digital Transmission

1. CCITT Rec. G.703, "Physical/Electrical Characteristics of Hierarchical Digital Interfaces," 1991.
2. CCITT Rec. G.707, "Synchronous Digital Hierarchy Bit Rates," 1992 (Rev).
3. CCITT Rec. G.708, "Network Node Interface for the Synchronous Digital Hierarchy," 1992 (Rev).

4. CCITT Rec. G.709, "Synchronous Multiplexing Structure," 1992 (Rev).

5. CCITT Rec.G.744, "Synchronous Digital Hierarchy (SDH) Management Information Model," (New, to be approved in 1993).

6. CCITT Rec. G.781, "Multiplexing Equipment for the SDH," 1990.

7. CCITT Rec. G.782, "Types and General Characteristics of Synchronous Digital Hierarchy (SDH) Multiplexing Equipment," 1990.

8. CCITT Rec. G.783, "Characteristics of Synchronous Digital Hierarchy (SDH) Multiplexing Equipment Functional Blocks," 1990.

9. CCITT Rec. G.784, "Synchronous Digital Hierarchy (SDH) Management," 1990.

10. CCITT Rec. G.803, "Architecture of Transport Networks Based on the SDH," 1992.

11. CCITT Rec.G.825, "The Control of Jitter and Wander Within Digital Network, Which Are Based on the Synchronous Digital Hierarchy (SDH)," (New, to be approved in 1993).

12. CCITT Rec. G.831, "Performance and Management Capabilities of Transport Networks Based on the SDH," 1992.

13. CCITT Rec. G.957, "Optical Interfaces for Equipments and Relating to the Synchronous Digital Hierarchy," 1992 (Rev).

14. CCITT Rec. G.958, "Digital Line Systems Based on the Synchronous Digital Hierarchy for use on Optical Fiber Cables," 1990.

15. ANSI T1.105–1991, "Digital Hierarchy—Optical Interface Rates and Formats Specifications (SONET)," 1991.

16. ANSI T1.105a-1991, "Supplement to T1.105," 1991.

17. ANSI T1.105–1988, "American National Standard for Telecommunications—Digital Hierarchy—Optical Interface Rates and Formats Specification," 1988.

18. ANSI T1.106–1988, "American National Standard for Telecommunications—Digital Hierarchy—Optical Interface Specifications (single mode)," 1988.

19. ANSI, T1.117, "Digital Hierarchy—Optical Interface Specifications (SONET) (single mode-short reach)," 1991.

19. Bellcore, TR-NWT-000253, "Synchronous Optical Network (SONET) Transport Systems: Common Generic," Issue 2, 1991.

20. Bellcore, TA-NWT-001250, "Generic Requirements for Synchronous Optical Network (SONET) File Transfer," Issue 2, 1992.

21. Bellcore, TR-TSP-000496, "SONET Add/Drop Multiplex Equipment (SONET ADM) Generic Criteria," Issue 3, 1992.

22. Bellcore, SR-NWT-002224, "SONET Synchronization Planning Guidelines," Issue 1, 1992.

23. Bellcore, TR-TSY-000303, "Integrated Digital Loop Carrier System Generic Requirements, Objectives, and Interface," Issue 1, Revision 3, 1990.

24. Bellcore, TR-NWT-001230, "SONET Bidirectional Line Switched Ring Equipment Generic Criteria," Issue 2, 1992.

25. Bellcore, TR-TSY-00023, "Wideband and Broadband Digital Cross-Connect Generic Requirements and Objectives," Issue 2, 1989.

26. Bellcore, TN-NWT-001042, "Generic Requirements for Operations Interfaces Using OSI Tools: Synchronous Optical Network (SONET) Transport Information Model," Issue 1, 1992.

27. Bellcore, TA-NWT-001042, "Generic Requirements for Operations Interfaces Using OSI Tools: SONET Path Switched Ring Information Model," Issue 3, 1992.

28. Bellcore, SR-NWT-001756, "Automatic Protection Switching for SONET," Issue 1, 1990.

BISDN and ATM

1. CCITT Rec. I.113, "Vocabulary Terms for Broadband Aspects of ISDN," 1992 (Rev).

2. CCITT Rec. I.120, "Integrated Services Digital Network (ISDN)," 1992 (Rev).

3. CCITT Rec. I.121, "Broadband Aspects of ISDN," 1990.

4. CCITT Rec. I.140, "Attribute Technique for the Characterization of the Telecommunication Services Supported by an ISDN and Network Capability of an ISDN," 1992 (Rev).

5. CCITT Rec. I.150, "BISDN ATM Functional Characteristics," 1992 (Rev).

6. CCITT Rec. I.211, "BISDN Service Aspects," 1992 (Rev).

7. CCITT Rec. I.311, "BISDN General Network Aspects," 1992 (Rev).

8. CCITT Rec. I.321, "BISDN Protocol Reference Model and Its Application," 1990.

9. CCITT Rec. I.327, "BISDN Functional Architecture Aspects," 1992.

10. CCITT Rec. I.35B, "BISDN ATM Cell Transfer Performance," 1992 (Draft).

11. CCITT Rec. I.361, "BISDN ATM Layer Specification," 1992 (Rev).

12. CCITT Rec. I.362, "BISDN ATM Adaption Layer (AAL) Functional Description," 1992 (Rev).

13. CCITT Rec. I.363, "BISDN ATM Adaptation Layer (AAL) Specification," 1992 (Rev).

14. CCITT Rec. I.364, "Support of Broadband Connectionless Data Service on BISDN," 1992.

15. CCITT Rec. I.371, "Traffic Control and Congestion Control in BISDN," 1992.

16. CCITT Draft Rec. I.374, "Network Capability for the Support of Multimedia Services," 1992.

17. CCITT Rec. I.413, "BISDN User-Network Interface," 1992 (Rev).

18. CCITT Rec. I.432, "BISDN User-Network Interface—Physical Layer Specification," 1992 (New Draft).
19. CCITT Rec. I.610, "BISDN UNI Operations and Maintenance Principles," 1992 (Rev).
20. CCITT Rec. G.7xx, "ATM Cell Mapping into Plesiochronous Digital Hierarchy (PDH)," 1992 (Rev).
21. ATM Forum, "ATM User-Network Interface Specification," Version 2.0, 1992.
22. ATM Forum, "Network Compatible ATM for Local Network Applications," Phase 1, Version 1.0, 1992.

High-Speed Data Network

1. ANSI T1.606–1990, "Telecommunication-Frame Relay Bearer Service-Architectural Framework and Service Description," 1990.
2. ANSI T1.606add, "Addendum to T1.606," (T1X1/90–175), 1990.
3. ANSI T1.6ca, "Core Aspects of Frame Protocol for Use With Frame Relay Bearer Service," (T1S1/90–214), 1990.
4. CCITT Rec. I.122, "Framework for Providing Additional Packet Mode Bearer Service," 1991.
5. CCITT Rec. I.233, "Frame Mode Bearer Services," 1992.
6. CCITT Rec. I.370, "Congestion Management for the ISDN Frame Relaying Bearer Service," 1991.
7. CCITT Rec. I.430, "ISDN Basic Rate User Network Interface Layer 1 Specification," 1992 (Rev).
8. CCITT Rec. I.431, "ISDN Primary Rate User Network Interface Layer 1 Specification," 1992 (Rev).
9. CCITT Rec. Q.922, "ISDN Data Link Layer Specification for Frame Mode Bearer Services," 1992.
10. CCITT Rec. Q.921 (I.441), "ISDN User Network Interface Data Layer Specification," 1988.
11. CCITT Rec. Q.933, "DSS1 Signaling Specification for Frame Mode Bearer Service," 1992.
12. DEC, Northern Telecom, Stratacom, Cisco, "Frame Relay Specification With Extensions," Revision 1.0, 1990.
13. DEC, Northern Telecom, Stratacom, Cisco, "Frame Relay Specification With Extension Based on Proposed T1S1 Standards," Revision 1.0, 1990.
14. "IEEE Standard: DQDB Subnetwork of a Metropolitan Area Network," P802.6, 1991.
15. Bellcore Technical Advisory, TA-TSY-000772, "Generic System Requirement in Support of SMDS," Issue 3, 1989.

Broadband Video Technology

1. CCITT Rec. H.221, "Frame Structure for 64 to 1920 kbps Channel in Audiovisual Teleservices," 1990.
2. CCITT Rec. H.230, "Frame Synchronous Control and Indication Signals for Audiovisual Systems," 1990.
3. CCITT Rec. H.242, "System for Establishing Communication Between Audiovisual Terminals Using Digital Channels up to 2 Mbps," 1990.
4. CCITT Rec. H.261, "Video Codec for Audiovisual Services at p x 64 kbps," 1990.
5. CCITT Rec. H.320, "Narrowband Visual Telephone Systems and Terminal Equipment," 1990.
6. CCITT Rec. H.32x, "Audiovisual Communication Terminal for BISDN," 1992.
7. CCIR Rec. 601, "Encoding Parameters of Digital Television for Studios," 1982.
8. CCIR Rec. 656, "Interfaces for Digital Component Video Signals in 525-Line and 625-Line Television Systems," 1982.
9. CCIR Rec. 709, "Basic Parameter Values for the HDTV Standard for the Studio and for International Programme Exchange," 1990.
10. CCIR Rec. 710, "Subjective Assessment Methods for Image Quality in High-Definition Television," 1990.
11. CCIR Rec. 714, "International Exchange of Programme Electronically Produced by Means of High-Definition Television," 1990.
12. ISO-IEC/JTC1/CD 11172 (MPEG I), "Coding of Moving Pictures and Associated Audio for Digital Storage Media at up to About 1.5 Mbps," 1990.
13. ISO-IEC/JTC1/SC29/WG11 (MPEG II) "Coded Presentation of Picture and Audio Information," 1992.
14. ISO-IEC/JTC1/CD 10918 (JPEG), "Digital Compression and Coding of Continuous-Tone Still Images," 1991.
15. ISO-IEC/JTC1/SC2/WG9N 36/CD 11154," Progressive Bi-Level Image Compression," Revision 4.1, 1992.
16. ISO-IEC/JTC1/SC2/WG12 (MHEG) Working Document S, Version 4," Information Processing, Coded Representation of Multimedia and Hypermedia Information Objects."

Appendix B
List of Acronyms

AAL	ATM adaptation layer
AC	access control
ACF	access control field
ADC	analog-to-digital conversion
ADM	add-drop multiplexer
ADPCM	adaptive differential pulse code modulation
ADTV	advanced digital television
AIN	advanced intelligent network
AIS	alarm indication signal
AL	alignment
AM	asynchronous multiplexing
ANSI	American National Standards Institute
AP	access point
APD	avalanche photo diode
APS	automatic protection switching
ASK	amplitude shift keying
ATDM	asnchronous time-division multiplexing
ATM	asynchronous transfer mode
ATMR	ATM ring
AT&T	American Telephone and Telegraph
ATV	advanced TV
AU	access unit
AU	administrative unit
AUG	administrative unit group
B-NT	broadband network termination
B-TA	broadband terminal adaptor
B-TE	broadband terminal equipment
BA	building automation
BA	buffer allocation

BAS	building automation system
BBTG	broadband task group
BCC	basic connection components
BCN	backward congestion notification
Bellcore	Bell Communications Research
B/Etag	begin/end tag
BECN	backward explicit congestion notification
BER	bit error rate
BH	buried heterostructure
BIA	broadband integrated access
BIDS	broadband integrated distributed star
BIGFON	Breitbandiges Integriertes Glasfoser Fernmelde Ortsnetz Network
BIM	byte interleaved multiplexing
BIP	bit-interleaved parity
BISDN	broadband integrated services digital network
BISPBX	broadband integrated services private branch exchange
BMA	block matching algorithm
BOM	begin of message
BPON	broadband passive optical network
bps	bits per second
BSRF	basic synchronous reference frequency
BT	British Telecom
BTRL	British Telcom Research Laboratories
BW	black and white
BWB	bandwidth balancing
C	container
C-MAC	compatible multiplexed analog components
C.I.E.	Commission Internationale de L'Eclairage
CAC	connection admission control
CAD	computer-aided design
CAM	computer-aided manufacturing
CAS	channel-associated signaling
CATV	cable television or community antenna television
CBR	constant bit rate
CC	congestion control
CCIR	International Radiocommunications Consultative Committee
CCIS	common channel interoffice signaling
CCITT	Consultative Committee in International Telegraphy and Telephony
CCS	common channel signaling
CD	countdown
CDR	common data rate
CD-ROM	compact disk read only memory

CDV	cell delay variation
CE	connection element
CEPT	Conference Europeenne des Postes et Telecommunication
CEQ	customer equipment
CEV	controlled environmental vault
CIF	common intermediate format
CIR	cell insertion ratio
CIR	committed information rate
CL	connectionless
CLP	cell loss priority
CLR	cell loss ratio
CLSF	connectionless services function
CMOS	complementary metal oxide semiconductor
CMTT	Commission Mixte pour des Transmissions Televisuelles et sonones
CN	customer network
CNET	Centre National d'Etudes des Telecommunications
CNM	customer network management
CO	central office
CO	connection-oriented
CO-LAN	central office-local area network
COCF	connection-oriented convergence function
COM	continuation of message
COT	central office terminal
CP	call processor
CP	connection point
CPCS	common part convergence sublayer
CPE	customer premises equipment
CPI	common part indicator
CPN	customer premises network
C/R	command and response
CRC	cyclic redundancy check
CRF	connection related function
CS	convergence sublayer
CS	cycle sequence
CS-PDU	convergence sublayer protocol data unit
CSA	carrier serving area
CSDC	circuit-switched data capability
CSDN	circuit-switched digital network
CSI	convergence sublayer indication
CSMA/CD	carrier-sense multiple access with collision detection
CT	central terminal
DA	destination address

DARPA	defense advanced research projects agency
DAS	dual-attachment station
DAC	digital-to-analog conversion
DB	database
DBP	Deutsch Bundes Post
DBS	direct broadcast by satellite
DC	distribution center
DCC	data communication channels
DCS	digital cross-connect system
DCT	discrete cosine transform
DDS	digital data service
DE	discard eligibility
DFB	distributed feedback
DFB-LD	distributed feedback laser diode
DH	double heterostructure
DL	data link
DLC	digital loop carrier
DLCI	data link connection identifier
DMPDU	differential MAC protocol data unit
DPCM	differential pulse code modulation
DQ	distributed queue
DQDB	distributed queue dual bus
DQSM	distributed-queue state machine
DS-n	digital signal level n
DSS	distributed sample scrambler
DWDM	dense wavelength division multiplexing
DXC	digital cross-connect
EA	extended address
ECL	emitter-coupled logic
ECR	errored cell ratio
ED	end delimiter
EDFA	erbium-doped opitical fiber amplifier
EDTV	extended-definition television
EFCN	explicit forward congestion notification
E/O	electrical/optical
EOM	end of message
EQTV	extended-quality television
ESS	electronic switching system
ET	exchange termination
ETRI	Electronics and Telecommunications Research Institute
FA	factory automation
FAS	flexible access system

FAX	facsimile
FCFS	first-come first-served
FCN	forward congestion notification
FCS	frame control segment
FCS	fast circuit switching
FDDI	fiber distributed digital interface
FDM	frequency-division modulation
FDMA	frequency-division multiple access
FEBE	far end block error
FEC	forward error correction
FECN	forward explicit congestion notification
FERF	far end receive failure
FET	field-effect transistor
FFOL	FDDI follow-on lan
FIFO	first-in first-out
FITL	fiber in the loop
FLC	fiber loop carrier
FM	frequency modulation
FOA	first office application
FOH	fixed overhead
FPS	fast packet switching
FR	frame relay
FRP	fast reservation protocol
FSK	frequency shift keying
FSS	frame synchronous scrambler
FTTB	fiber to the building
FTTC	fiber to the curb
FTTH	fiber to the home
FTTO	fiber to the office
FTTZ	fiber to the zone
GaAs	gallium arsenide
GFC	generic flow control
GRIN	graded index
HBT	heterojunction bipolar transistor
HCS	header check sequence
HDLC	high-level data link control
HD-MAC	high-definition multiplexed analog components
HDTV	high-definition television
HE	header extension
HEC	head error control
HEL	header extension length
Hi-OVIS	highly optical visual information system

HLF	high-level functions
HLI	high-level interface
HLPI	high-level protocal identifier
HOB	head of bus
HOL	head of line
HPA	higher-order path adaptation
HPC	higher-order path connection
HPT	higher-order path termination
HRC	hybrid ring control
HSN	high-speed network
IBIS	interactive basic information systems
IBS	intelligent building system
IC	integrated circuit
ICF	isochronous convergence function
ICI	inter-exchange carrier interface
IDCT	inverse discrete cosine transform
IE	inter-exchange
IEEE	Institute of Electrical and Electronics Engineers
IF	intermediate frequency
IFU	interface unit
I-MAC	isochronous MAC
IMPDU	initial MAC protocol data unit
IN	intelligent network
INN	INFAS and NTT network
INS	information network system
IP	interworking protocol
IPRM	integrated protocol reference model
IRP	internal reference point
ISDN	integrated services digital network
ISLN	integrated services local network
ISM	interface subscriber module
ISO	International Standards Organization
ISSI	interswitching system interface
IT	information type
IWU	interworking unit
JFET	junction field effect transistor
JPEG	joint photographic experts group
KLT	Karhunen-Loeve transform
LAN	local area network
LAP	link access procedure
LATA	local access and transport area
LCF-PMD	low cost fiber-PMD

LD	laser diode
LE	local exchange
LED	light emitting diode
LEX	local exchange
LFC	local functional capability
LI	length indicator
LI	line interface
LLC	logical link control
LME	layer management entity
LMI	local management interface
LOC	loop optical control
LOF	loss of frame
LOP	loss of pointer
LOS	loss of signal
LPA	lower-order path adaptation
LPC	lower-order path connection
LPT	lower-order path termination
LS	local switch
LSI	large-scale integrated circuit
LT	line termination
LTE	lightwave transmission equipment
LUT	lookup table
LW	lightwave
MA	medium adaptor
MAC	medium access control
MAC	multiplexed analog components
MAN	metropolitan area network
MAP	manufacturing automation protocol
Mbps	megabits per second (Mbit/s)
MCF	MAC convergence function
MCF	message communication function
MESFET	metal semiconductor field-effect transistor
MHS	message handling service
MIB	management information base
MID	message identifier
MID	multiplexing identification
MIN	multistage interconnection network
MISFET	metal-insulator-semiconductor field effect transistor
MMF	multiplexer management function
MPDU	MAC protocol data unit
MPEG	moving picture expert group
MPU	multiprocessor unit

MQW	mutiple quantum well
MSDU	MAC service data unit
MSFC	multiservice flow control
MSOH	multiplex section overhead
MSP	multiplexer section protection
MSS	MAN switching system
MST	multiplexer section termination
MTG	multiplexer timing generator
MTPI	multiple timing physical interface
MTS	multiplexer timing source
MUSE	multiple sub-nyquist sampling encoding
MUX	multiplexer
MVC	maintenance voice channel
NDF	new data flag
NISDN	narrowband integrated services digital network
NJ	negative justification
NNI	network node interface
NOMC	network operator maintenance channel
NPC	network parameter control
NPI	null pointer indication
NS	next station
NT	network termination
NTM	network traffic management
NTSC	national television system committee
NTT	Nippon Telephone and Telegraph
OA	office automation
OAM	operation and maintenance
OAM&P	operation administration maintenance & provisioning
OC	operating center
OC-m	optical carrier level m
ODF	optical distribution frame
OEIC	optoelectronic integrated circuit
OIU	office interface unit
ONT	optical network termination
ONU	optical network unit
OS	operating system
OSI	open systems interconnection
OSIE	open systems interconnection environment
OSIP	open systems interconnection profile
OTDR	optical time domain reflectometer
PA	pre-arbitrated
PAD	padding

PAL	phase alteration by line
PBX	private branch exchange
PC	priority control
PCC	programmable cross-connect
PCI	protocol control information
PCM	pulse code modulation
PCN	personal communication network
PD	photo diode
PDH	plesiochronous digital hierarchy
PDU	protocol data unit
pel	picture element
PHY	physical layer protocol
PI	physical interface
PJ	positive justification
PLOAM	physical layer OAM
PLCF	physical layer convergence function
PLCP	physical layer convergence procedure (or protocol)
PLL	phase-locked loop
PM	physical medium
P-MAC	packet MAC
PMB	programmable multiplexer bank
PMD	physical medium dependent
POH	path overhead
PON	passive optical network
POS	point of sales
POTS	plain old telephone service
PPL	passive photonic loop
ppm	part per million
PRA	primary rate access
PRBS	pseudo-random binary sequence
PRM	protocol reference model
PS	previous station
PSDN	packet-switched data network
PSPDN	packet-switched public data network
PSTN	public switched telephone network
PSK	phase shift keying
PSM	protocol state machine
PT	path trace
PT	payload type
PTR	pointer
PTT	post, telephone, and telegraph
PVC	permanent virtual circuit

P/Z/N	positive/zero/negative
QA	queue arbitrated
QAM	quadrature amplitude modulation
QCIF	quarter common intermediate format
QOS	quality of service
QPSK	quadrature phase shift keying
QPSX	queued packet and synchronous exchange
RAI	remote alarm indication signal
RBOC	regional Bell operating company
REG	register
REQ	reqest
RES	reserved
RF	radio frequency
RG	regenerator
RGB	red green blue
RMN	remote multiplexer node
RMT	ring management
RN	remote node
RS	Reed-Solomon
RSOH	regenerator section overhead
RSP	regenerator section protection
PSR	previous slot release
RST	regenerator section termination
RT	remote terminal
RTS	residual time stamp
SA	section adaptation
SA	source address
SAP	service acces point
SAPI	service access point identifier
SAR	segmentation and reassembly
SAS	single-attachment station
SCM	subcarrier multiplexing
SD	start delimiter
SDH	synchronous digital hierarchy
SDU	service data unit
SECAM	sequential couleur avec memoire
SEMF	synchronous equipment management
SFET	synchronous frequency encoding technique
SG	study group
SIF	source input format
SIG	signaling processor
SIN	subscriber interface unit
SIP	SMDS interface unit
SIU	subscriber interface unit

SLC	subscriber loop carrier
SM	synchronous multiplexing
SMDS	switched multimegabit data service
SMF-PMD	single mode fiber-PMD
SMT	station management
S-MUX	synchronous multiplexer
SN	sequence number
SNA	systems network architecture
SNI	subscriber node interface
SNMP	simple network management protocol
SNP	sequence number protection
SOH	section overhead
SONET	synchronous optical network
SPAG	standards promotion and application group
SPC	stored program control
SPE	synchronous payload envelope
SPI	SDH physical interface
SPM-PMD	SONET physical layer mapping-PMD
SRG	shift register generator
SRTS	synchronous residual time stamp
SSCS	service specific convergence sublayer
SSM	single segment message
SSS	self synchronous scrambler
ST	segment type
STM-n	synchronous transport module level n
STP	signaling transfer point
STS-m	synchronous transport signal level m
SU	segment unit
SVC	signaling virtual channel
SW	switch
SWAN	sociocultural welfare advancement network
TA	telecommunication automation
TA	terminal adaptor
TC	transmission convergence
TCP	termination connection point
TCP/IP	transmission control protocol/internet protocol
TDM	time-division multiplexing
TDMA	time-division multiple access
TE	terminal equipment
TE	transit exchange
TEID	terminal equipment identification
THT	token holding time
TIE	time interval error
TMN	telecommunication management network

TOP	technical and office product system
TPE	transmission path endpoint
TP-PMD	twisted pair-PMD
TPON	telephony over passive optical network
TRT	token rotation time
TS	time stamp
TSI	time slot interchange
TTOSS	totally transparent optical subscriber system
TTRT	target token rotation timer
TU	tributary unit
TUG	tributary unit group
UHF	ultra-high frequency
UI	unit interval
UNI	user-network interface
UPC	usage parameter control
U-SDU	user service data unit
VBI	vertical blanking interval
VBR	variable bit rate
VC	virtual channel
VC	virtual container
VCC	virtual channel connection
VCCE	virtual channel connection endpoint
VCI	virtual channel identifier
VCO	voltage controlled oscillator
VCR	video cassette recorder
VHF	very high frequency
VLC	variable length coding
VLSI	very-large-scale integration
VP	virtual path
VPC	virtual path connection
VPCE	virtual path connection end point
VPI	virtual path identifier
VPT	virtual path terminator
VQ	vector quantization
VRS	video response system
VT	virtual tributary
VTR	videotape recorder
WAN	wide-area network
WBC	wideband channel
WDM	wavelength division multiplexing
WIM	word-interleaved multiplexing
WSP	wideband service point
XC	cross-connect

About the Authors

Byeong Gi Lee received B.S. and M.E. degrees in 1974 and 1978, respectively, from Seoul National University, Seoul, Korea, and Kyungpook National University, Taegu, Korea, both in electronics engineering; and a Ph.D. degree in 1982 from the University of California, Los Angeles, in electrical engineering. From 1974 to 1979 he was with the Department of Electronics Engineering of ROK Naval Academy, Chinhae, Korea, as an instructor and Naval Officer in active service. From 1982 to 1984 he worked for Granger Associates, Santa Clara, California, as a senior engineer doing research and development on applications of digital signal processing to digital transmission. During the period 1984 to 1986 he worked for AT&T Bell Laboratories, North Andover, Massachusetts, as a member of the technical staff participating in lightwave transmission system development, along with related standard work. Since September 1986, he has been with the Department of Electronics Engineering, at Seoul National University. In 1990 and 1991 he was chairman of the Telecommunications Society of KITE (Korean Institute of Telematics and Electronics). He is a coauthor of *Introduction to ISDN, Broadband Telecommunication Systems, Electronics Engineering Experiment Series* (5 volumes), and the editor of *HDTV Dictionary*, all in Korean. He holds four U.S. patents, with two more patents pending. Dr. Lee received the 1984 Myril B. Reed Best Paper Award and exceptional contribution awards from AT&T Bell Laboratories. He is a member of KITE, KICS, and ASK; a senior member of IEEE; and a member of Sigma Xi.

Minho Kang received a B.S. degree from Seoul National University, Seoul, Korea, an M.S. degree from the University of Missouri-Rolla, and a Ph.D. from the University of Texas at Austin in 1969, 1973, and 1977, respectively, all in electrical engineering. He worked for AT&T Bell Laboratories, Holmdel, New Jersey in the opto-electronics research area from 1977 to 1978, and then worked for the Electronics and Telecommunications Research Institute (ETRI), Daejon, Korea, in the optical communications and transmission systems development area until January 1990. He is presently the chief executive of the Research Center at Korea Telecom, the leading telephone network operator in Korea. He was a lecturer at Seoul National

University between 1979 and 1985 and served as the electronics research coordinator at the Korean Ministry of Science and Technology between 1985 and 1988. He is a coauthor of *Introduction to ISDN, Introduction to Electrical Communication Technology, Principles of Optical Fiber Communication Technology, Laser Applications,* and *Broadband Telecommunication Systems,* all in Korean. He received the National Order of Merit, Dongbaeg-Jang, and the Grand Prize of New Industrial Technology Management. Dr. Kang is a senior member of IEEE; a member of the Optical Society of America; a board member of KITE, KIEE, KICS, and KISS; and a member of Phi Kappa Phi and Eta Kappa Nu.

Jonghee Lee received a B.S. degree in electrical engineering from Seoul National University, Seoul, Korea in 1971, M.S. and Ph.D. degrees from the University of Pennsylvania, Philadelphia, Pennsylvania, in 1976 and 1980, respectively, both in system engineering. From 1980 to 1985 he was with AT&T Bell Laboratories and then with Bell Communications Research, where he was responsible for product planning and development in digital terminals and cross-connects. From 1985 to 1990 he worked for Daeyoung Electronics Co., where he was the executive managing director responsible for R&D in communication systems. In 1990 he founded Dongjin Datacom, an EDI software company, and in 1991 he founded MODACOM Co., a telecommunication consulting and system integration company. He is currently the president of MODACOM. He is a coauthor of *Broadband Telecommunication Systems,* which is in Korean. Dr. Lee is an editor of the KICS (*Korean Institute of Communication Sciences*); an advisory member of the KITE Telecommunication Society; and a member of IEEE.

Index

AAL. *See* ATM adaptation layer (AAL)
Absorption loss, 69
Access control (AC), 312
    DQDB, 420, 422–26
    pre-arbitrated, 422, 425–26
Access control field (ACF), 399, 401, 422
Access control reset (AC-Reset), 312
Access point (AP), 222
Access unit (AU), 430
AC-CTR-W. *See* AC-window counter
ACF. *See* Access control field
Acronyms, listing of, 545–57
Active region, 81
AC utility powering, 41–42
AC-window counter (AC-CTR-W), 312
Adaptation, 222
ADC. *See* Analog-to-digital converter
Add/drop multiplexer
    (ADM), 30, 188–90, 194, 225–26
Addressing
    in frame relay protocol, 415–16
    in signalling technology, 8
ADM. *See* Add/drop multiplexer (ADM)
Administrative unit (AU), 138
Administrative unit group (AUG), 115, 131–32, 138
    multiplexing, 141, 151–52
Administrative unit pointer (AU pointer), 112, 132,
    134–35, 138, 140–41
Admissible call connection, 348
Advanced digital television (ADTV), 524–26
Advanced Hi-OVIS, 55, 57
Advanced intelligent network (AIN), 26
Advanced TV, 519
Advance-investment strategy, 38
AIN. *See* Advanced intelligent network

Alarm indication signal (AIS), 170, 353
Alcatel, 96–98, 511
Aligning, 140
All-electronic switches, 8
AM. *See* Asynchronous multiplexing
American National Standards Institute
    (ANSI), 400, 418
Amplitude shift keying (ASK), 90
Analog mode, 23
Analog-to-digital converter (ADC), 453
ANSI. *See* American National Standards Institute
AP. *See* Access point
APD. *See* Avalanche photodiode
Application-oriented layers, 391
APS. *See* Automatic protection switching
ARPANET, 18, 392
ASK. *See* Amplitude shift keying
Assigned cells, 268
A-SW. *See* ATM switching system
Asynchronous digital transmission, 105–6
Asynchronous mapping, 153–54, 156, 159, 162
Asynchronous mode, 156
Asynchronous multiplexing (AM), 112–13, 228
Asynchronous time division multiplexing (ATDM)
    description, 31, 233, 241, 263–66
    information flow, 243
    versus TDM, 265–66
Asynchronous transfer mode (ATM)
    cell, 266–68
        in asynchronous transfer mode,
        241–43, 263–64
        cell-header field, 267
        classification, 267–68
        layer, 243
        mapping, 164, 167

The Artech House Telecommunications Library

Vinton G. Cerf, Series Editor

For further information on these and other Artech House titles, contact:

Artech House
685 Canton Street
Norwood, MA 01602
(617) 769-9750
Fax:(617) 762-9230
Telex: 951-659

Artech House
6 Buckingham Gate
London SW1E6JP England
+44(0)71 630-0166
+44(0)71 630-0166
Telex-951-659